VARIORUM COLLECTED STUDIES SERIES

# Historical Memory and Clerical Activity in Medieval Spain and Portugal

Peter Linehan

Peter Linehan

# Historical Memory and Clerical Activity in Medieval Spain and Portugal

**Published in the Variorum Collected Studies Series by**

Ashgate Publishing Limited
Wey Court East
Union Road
Farnham, Surrey
GU9 7PT
England

Ashgate Publishing Company
Suite 420
101 Cherry Street
Burlington, VT 05401–4405
USA

www.ashgate.com

ISBN 978–1–4094–5110–5

**British Library Cataloguing in Publication Data**
Linehan, Peter.
   Historical memory and clerical activity in medieval Spain and Portugal.
   – (Variorum collected studies series ; CS1011)
   1. Church history – Middle Ages, 600–1500. 2. Spain – Church history.
   3. Portugal – Church history. 4. Church and state – Spain – History – To 1500.
   5. Church and state – Portugal – History – To 1500.
   I. Title II. Series
   274.6'03–dc23

ISBN 978–1–4094–5110–5

**Library of Congress Control Number:** 2012932938

VARIORUM COLLECTED STUDIES SERIES CS1011

The paper used in this publication meets the minimum requirements of the American National Standard for Information Sciences – Permanence of Paper for Printed Library Materials, ANSI Z39.48–1984. ∞ ™

MIX
Paper from
responsible sources
FSC
www.fsc.org   FSC® C018575

Printed and bound in Great Britain by the
MPG Books Group, UK

# CONTENTS

This volume contains xxvi + 332 pages

# PREFACE

As stated in the Preface to *The Processes of Politics and the Rule of Law* (Variorum, 2002), my interests then were already shifting westwards from Spain, a process the consequences of which are about to be published by the Gulbenkian Foundation of Lisbon with the title *Portugalia Pontificia* (being a survey of the surviving materials for relations of the kingdom of Portugal and the Papacy between 1198 and the end of the Great Schism). But, as the remaining items in this volume indicate, my preoccupation with Portugal (represented here by item XV) has not necessitated neglect of matters Spanish.

Again, my warm thanks are due to John Smedley for his forbearance and encouragement. I wish also to thank Dr Margarita Torres and Dr Patrick Zutshi for allowing me to reuse work originally done in collegial collaboration with them.

PETER LINEHAN

*St John's College, Cambridge*
*6 May 2012*

# ACKNOWLEDGEMENTS

For permission to reprint the works included in this volume I wish to express my gratitude to Il Cigno Galileo Galilei Edizioni (Rome) for article I; *Cahiers de Linguistique Hispanique Médiévale* (Paris) for II and III; Fundación Sánchez-Albornoz (Ávila) for IV; M. Georges Martin and Paris-Sorbonne for V; Roma nel Rinascimento (Rome) for VI; Koninklijke Brill NV (Leiden) for VII; Prof. Manuel González Jiménez (Sevilla) for VIII; The Boydell Press (Woodbridge) for IX; *Historia. Instituciones. Documentos* (Sevilla) for X and XV; Seminario de Estudios Medievales y Renacentistas (Salamanca) for XI; Cátedra Alfonso X el Sabio (El Puerto de Santa María) for XII; Prof. Agostino Paravicini Bagliani and *Rivista di Storia della Chiesa in Italia* for XIII; and Oxford University Press for XIV and XVI.

Every effort has been made to trace all the copyright holders, but if any have been inadvertently overlooked the publishers will be pleased to make the necessary arrangement at the first opportunity.

## PUBLISHER'S NOTE

*The articles in this volume, as in all others in the Variorum Collected Studies Series, have not been given a new, continuous pagination. In order to avoid confusion, and to facilitate their use where these same studies have been referred to elsewhere, the original pagination has been maintained wherever possible. Articles V and VII have necessarily been reset with a new pagination.*

*Each article has been given a Roman number in order of appearance, as listed in the Contents. This number is repeated on each page and is quoted in the index entries.*

# By Way of Introduction:
# The Spanish Middle Ages and the
# Nineteenth Century

This is the text of a lecture delivered to the University of Liverpool Centre for Medieval Studies on 31 May 2005 as part of the series 'The Making of the Middle Ages, c. 1750–2000', lightly adapted and annotated for publication here. In retrospect, it can perhaps be seen as an introduction to the interests and some of the problems involved in the study of medieval Spanish history.

\*\*\*\*\*\*

Scanning the list of this distinguished series of lectures, I am struck by the fear that I am about to let the side down. I am also struck, and much affected, by the memory of my dear friend Richard Fletcher, who died a couple of months ago. Richard and I spent many happy hours together swapping stories about the sort of Spanish things I am going to be discussing and about the absurdity of it all. Forty years ago we went on archive-crawls together. There was a sort of understanding between us that one day we would produce a Bad Archives Guide, strictly not for publication. I miss Richard very much. But I am not going to dedicate this lecture to him, or anything like that. He would have thought that silly. I am just going to keep him in mind over the next hour.

\*\*\*\*\*

To the extent that they were not still alive and well, the Middle Ages had bequeathed to nineteenth-century Spain a heavy burden. Or rather, a heavily polluted one. For although some of the work of the false chroniclers of the early 1600s had been revealed for what it was, and although the seventeenth century had buried some of its own dead, there was still a huge quantity of infected material poisoning the historical environment. Take the case of the notorious lead books of Granada, for example. These, it will be remembered, began to be excavated in the year of the Armada, and were greeted as first-century works written in faultless first-century Castilian, as well (and this of course confirmed the miracle) as containing quotations from the Koran.[1] In 1682 Pope Innocent XI branded them as forgeries. Yet until his death in 1684 the bibliographer Nicolás Antonio, although author of the most comprehensive demolition of the false chronicles, persisted in maintaining the authenticity of all this holy debris.

And so it was that in the nineteenth century various of the chronicles exposed by Antonio as forgeries, those of Dextro, Maximo and Eutrando, were included by the Abbé Migne in vols 31 and 80 of his *Patrologia Latina* – despite the fact that all three, purportedly the work of a fifth-century Spaniard called Dextro and his sixth- and tenth-century continuators, and discovered in Germany in the library of Fulda, were in fact the work of the early seventeenth-century Toledan Jesuit, Jerónimo Román de la Higuera. About P. Jerónimo, the exact contemporary of Cervantes and El Greco, there are many things that might be said, some of them even complimentary, some of them needing first to be cleared by a competent psychoanalyst. Here I limit myself to just two: one, that he was especially interested in the church history of Toledo and familiar with all the disputes about the mission of St James to Spain and his burial at Compostela, and, in the words of Sir Thomas Kendrick's splendid account, that 'he knew the right answers to the questions being asked and thought that history, if it was worth studying at all, ought to give these answers clearly.'[2] In which conviction, P. Jerónimo had many successes to his deplorable credit. To this day St Hiereteo, a Greek of the apostolic period, is venerated as Segovia's first bishop. The second thing to be said about him is that he was a *confrère* of Juan de Mariana – to whom I shall return.

First though let me say something about that monument of the Spanish enlightenment, the Augustinian friar Enrique Flórez, and his *España Sagrada*, the diocese-by-diocese ecclesiastical history of Spain in which history is divided into ancient and modern at the year 711, in which respect it rather resembles the arrangements of the Oxford History school, with no formal Middle Ages at all. By the time of his death in 1773 Flórez had published or left ready for publication twenty-nine volumes of *España Sagrada*, full of material culled from the cathedral archives. A further thirteen were brought to fruition by Flórez's colleague, Manuel Risco, to whom King Carlos III entrusted the task of completing an undertaking calculated 'to dissipate the

---

[1]    See T.D. Kendrick, *St James in Spain* (London 1960), 145–7; J. Caro Baroja, *Las falsificaciones de la Historia (en relación con la de España)* (Barcelona, 1992), 115–40; A. Katie Harris, *From Muslim to Christian Granada. Inventing a city's past in early modern Spain* (Baltimore MD, 2007).

[2]    *Op. cit.*, 117; Caro Baroja, *Las falsificaciones*, 163–87, esp. p. 170 – albeit the starting point for investigation of the matter remains J. Godoy Alcántara, *Hist. crítica de los Falsos Cronicones* (Madrid, 1868; repr. 1981).

fables that false zeal had introduced into the narrative'. What the enlightened monarch had in mind was no doubt the equivalent of Ughelli's *Italia Sacra*, the *Gallia Christiana*, and the *Acta Sanctorum* of the Bollandists. But fables die hard in sunnier climes. Only in 1961 was the monarch's worthy objective realised.

How widespread that 'false zeal' was may be judged by the fact that until 1729, when the Bollandists declared themselves in favour of the authenticity of St James's Spanish mission, they had been condemned by the Spanish Inquisition for denying credit for the foundation of St Teresa's Order of Carmelites to the prophet Elijah. But, with sales of the Da Vinci Code topping the 25 million mark as I speak, we rationalist moderns can hardly afford to strike superior attitudes.

And, for that matter indeed how far may Carlos III's ambition to eliminate false zeal be said to have been fulfilled by Flórez & Co? How thorough in that cause was their scrutiny of the archives available to them? An answer to the question is provided by Flórez's own approach to the contentious issue of St James's alleged mission to Spain. It had been contentious since at least 1215 when, according to the story contained in a Toledo manuscript, Archbishop Rodrigo of Toledo had amazed the Fourth Lateran Council with a linguistically virtuoso lecture in which he asserted that St James had never come to Spain, though he generously admitted that as a child he had heard it said that not only had the Saint come but also that he had converted… one old woman. This was the so called 'Pars concilii Laterani'.

Now the 'Pars concilii Laterani', with its deconstruction of the entire basis of Compostela's place in the nation's history, had first been published by another Toledo apologist, in 1595. But was it authentic? Or was it a fabrication of the sixteenth century, or even of the thirteenth? In favour of its authenticity were both Gregorio Mayáns, in many ways the century's sharpest historico-critical mind, and Andrés Marcos Burriel, who from 1750 was engaged with his amanuenses in transcribing the contents of the Toledo archive for the government and who knew the contents of that archive better than anyone else. But as well as a critical mind, Mayáns possessed a timid temperament and confined himself to expressing his views in private correspondence rather than publishing them; while Burriel was a Jesuit, which in eighteenth-century Spain was sometimes a dangerous thing to be, and was also prevented from publishing because in 1756 a change of ministry in Madrid deprived him of both his protector and all his Toledo transcripts. With which, after all those days and nights of self-denying labour, his hugely ambitious scheme 'for the fomentation of letters', including his programme of synods, inscriptions and much else, came to nothing.[3]

For his part, Flórez, with the press at his disposal, was in no doubt but that the 'Pars concilii Laterani' was a fabrication. And the process whereby he reached that conclusion in the age of enlightenment is itself enlightening. For Flórez the story was not true because it could not be true. And it could not be true because it was impossible to imagine one of the pillars of the Spanish past, St James's Spanish mission, being impugned by one of its principal heroes, Archbishop Rodrigo of Toledo. For that reason alone, he wrote in volume 3 of *España Sagrada* in 1748, the story was therefore 'unworthy of all credence'. Indeed, it was so damaging to the reputation of the archbishop (he continued) that it was probably the work of foreigners, 'who pride themselves on their critical acumen'.

So there was no *need* for him to go to Toledo and inspect the manuscript of the 'Pars concilii Laterani' himself, and he didn't. Though if he had gone he would have found the 'Pars concilii Laterani' to be an indisputably thirteenth-century product. And, if he had gone, he would also have found there, if he had been interested in looking for it, incontestable evidence that D. Rodrigo had indeed been present at Rome in 1215: a fact denied by him and by other champions of Santiago de Compostela down to and including that great savant, Fidel Fita, at the beginning of the twentieth century: a fact the truth of which has since then been established beyond peradventure, as it might have been established by Flórez in 1748, if he had been willing to take the risk of discovering the truth.[4] But go to Toledo, he didn't. For Flórez there was no question of establishing that truth, in particular because the possibility of D. Rodrigo's having been mistaken about the story or, worse, of his having invented it himself was, by definition, out of the question. It was axiomatically the case that great national institutions such as D. Rodrigo did not make mistakes. Even less did they invent stories. Again, more recent study of D. Rodrigo's historical writings and of his attempt to establish the jurisdiction of the church of Toledo over the church of Valencia has indicated that, as a matter of fact, D. Rodrigo's primatial zeal rendered him more or less incapable of *not* indulging in wholesale invention of the past.[5]

---

[3]    '...habiendo trabajado todos estos años, día y noche con tesón, que ha traspasado largamente la raya de la prudencia'... his 'continuadas vigilias y fatigas': Antonio Valladares de Sotomayor, *Semanario Erudito* 17 (Madrid, 1789), 232–8 at p. 237.

[4]    Patrick Henriet, 'Political struggle and the legitimation of the Toledan primacy: the *Pars Lateranii Concilii*' (*sic*), in I. Alonso *et al.* (eds.), *Building Legitimacy. Political discourses and forms of legitimacy in medieval societies* (Leiden-Boston, 2004), 291–318, at p. 295: *q.v.* for exegesis of the whole matter.

[5]    Peter Linehan, *History and the Historians of Medieval Spain* (Oxford, 1993), 313–49.

I mention the incident of the 'Pars concilii Laterani' because it reveals the inadequacy of any sharp contrast drawn between a seventeenth century bedevilled by false chroniclers and an enlightened eighteenth century which, as to the latter, fails to distinguish between the likes of Mayáns and Burriel on the one hand and the authors of the *España Sagrada* on the other. For, when evidence for pious tradition was lacking, the authors of *España Sagrada* would always assume it. In the words of Flórez himself – they come from the high-minded essay to be found in his *Clave historial con que se abre la puerta a la historia eclesiastica y politica* (1749), with its ringing declaration: 'El Critico debe ser totalmente imparcial.' When 'reverend credulity' was in conflict with 'tenacity of criticism', 'reverend credulity' was always to be preferred.[6] Or, to put it another way, when 'reverend credulity' could not be positively proved to be mistaken, it was to be assumed that it enshrined a positive truth.

Now this was a working hypothesis regarding which, as Dr Patrick Henriet has recently indicated, there were problems. And particularly were there problems when those advancing it refused to look at the evidence, as Flórez refused to do in the Toledo case. Since, by definition, hard evidence for reverend credulity was usually lacking, the struggle was an unequal one. And all the more unequal was it when evidences of the wrong sort emerge – as when Flórez encountered in a manuscript of a work of the ninth-century Mozarab Leovigild, the *De habitu clericorum*, a passage which he adjudged 'contrary to the dignity both of Christian religion and the Spanish nation'. With the assistance of the king's confessor, Francisco de Rávago, he had such manuscripts of the work as he was able to identify sent to him and the offending passage torn out and consigned to the flames. And he did a thorough job, for no trace of the offending passage now remains. 'A sad page in our cultural history', Prof. Manuel Díaz describes the incident; 'and all the sadder inasmuch as it involved that adornment of the enlightenment and glory of Spain's historical knowledge, Padre Flórez.' 'Un triste página' indeed within 'una historia siniestra'.[7]

And there are other sad pages to be leafed through in the cultural history of the mid-eighteenth century, the high noon of the Spanish Enlightenment. It was, for example, in the year 1749 that the librarian of San Ildefonso de Alcalá sold off the medieval manuscripts to firework-makers for use as rocket wrappers in such profusion that for some time the bottom fell out of the rocket-

---

[6]    *Clave historial*, 36–44, at p. 43, cit. P. Henriet, '*La dignité de la religion chrétienne et de la nation Hispanique, ou Enrique Flórez et l'España Sagrada*', *Revue Mabillon* 12/73 (2001), 296–306, at n. 15.

[7]    G. Antolín, 'De habitu clericorum (siglo IX)', *BRAH*, 55 (1909), 102–20; M.C. Díaz y Díaz, *Códices visigóticos en la monarquía leonesa* (León, 1983), 277.

wrapper market.[8] There were indeed patches of silt in the streams of what, in his interesting work on the subject, Richard Herr has called 'the *channels* of the Enlightenment'.[9] *Les lumières* had their dark side.

Time presses, and I cannot afford to stay in the eighteenth century any longer. But it must already be clear that the implication that the years before the French Revolution were a period of enlightenment followed by one of inspissated gloom, was to a degree mistaken. Though that is not to say that the nineteenth century, with which I am chiefly concerned this afternoon, was entirely a period of sweetness and light either.

As it began indeed, the Spanish nineteenth century was not a period of sweetness and light at all. As it began and until well into its middle years, it was rather one of darkness visible, one within whose encircling gloom a sense was developing that Mariana simply would not do any more: that for an account of the history of the medieval centuries three hundred years there could be no depending on a work first published in the 1590s.

I cannot enter here into questions regarding Mariana and his History of Spain in his own lifetime, which was of course the period in which the False Chroniclers were in full cry. Nor do I refer to the issue of Mariana's connexions with the crown prince of those fabricators, Román de la Higuera – except to say that in his time Mariana was held to be a subversive. What with the opinions uttered by him in the *De rege* on the subject of tyrannicide – and his initial insistence in his *History* that, when Alfonso VIII died in 1214, his eldest daughter had been not Berenguela, from whom all the kings of Castile and then of Spain had descended, but Blanca (Blanche of Castile), which would have meant that the legitimate Spanish monarchy had ended on the scaffold with Louis XVI – in his time Mariana was widely regarded as dangerous and needing to be reined in.[10] It was for this reason that it was proposed to the Consejo de Estado in 1614 that the writing of history should be restricted to royal chroniclers.[11] But subversive though Mariana may have been in 1600,

---

[8]    I. Carini, *Gli archive e le biblioteche di Spagna in rapporto alla storia d'Italia in generale e di Sicilia in particolare*, I (Palermo, 1884), 70–71; Ian Robertson, *Richard Ford 1796–1858. Hispanophile, connoisseur and critic* (Wilby, 2004), 63.

[9]    *The Eighteenth-century Revolution in Spain*, chap. 6.

[10]    G. Cirot, *Mariana historien* (Bordeaux, 1905), 180–88. Cf. F.J. Hernández, 'La corte de Fernando III y la casa real de Francia. Documentación, crónicas y monumentos', in J.I. Ruiz de la Peña (ed.), *Fernando III y su tiempo* (Ávila, 2003), 103–55, at pp. 113–14, and works cit. in M. Shadis, *Berenguela of Castile (1180–1246) and Political Women in the High Middle Ages* (New York, 2009), 208 n. 38.

[11]    E. García Hernán (for whom Lucas of Tuy is the 'franciscanista…escritor palatino de Alfonso VI'(!), 'Construcción de las historias de España en los siglos XVII y XVIII', in R. García Cárcel (ed.), *La construcción de las historias de España* (Madrid, 2004), 139, 144.

by the 1830s it was a decaffeinated version of his History that continued to provide the only serviceable account of Spain's Middle Ages.

By the 1830s, as Spain emerged from its Napoleonic experience into the harsh glare of successive liberal governments, and despite the affection that educated ladies in the provinces were said to have for him, the consensus was growing that Mariana had to be replaced.[12] For Mariana was chock-full of fables and nonsense, and there was hardly a word of him that could be believed. Such at least was the opinion, such were the strictures, of the Englishman, Samuel Astley Dunham, whose *History of Spain and Portugal*, published in five volumes in 1832–3, sought to put the record straight.

Dunham was not a notable figure in his time. Indeed, in its obituary notice of him in July 1858 the *Athenaeum* commented: 'We fear the general public will only learn that he was lately alive amongst us on now hearing of his death.'[13] As a writer, he had showered his favours equally amongst the nations, with Histories of Poland to his credit before taking on Spain and Portugal, and thereafter four volumes on the History of Europe during the Middle Ages, three on the History of Denmark, Sweden and Norway, and another three on that of the Germanic Empire, all published, together with various miscellaneous historical works, before 1845: an output of heroic proportions which these days would have all the universities of the kingdom with an eye to their Research Assessment Exercises returns beating a path to his door. Instead, Dunham suffered the misfortunes of the debtor's prison, parish relief, and the workhouse – though it will doubtless have come as some consolation to him to have been elected to honorary membership of the Royal Spanish Academy and in 1844 to have had his History translated into Spanish.

So far as the Middle Ages went, Dunham's principal purpose seems to have been to expose the faults in Mariana, just as it was that of his translator, Antonio Alcalá Galiano, to defend Mariana's reputation, which made his job rather awkward. Alcalá Galiano was at pains to insist that it was for his 'style and diction' that Mariana was prized. These, he conceded, were not 'the gifts most highly prized by historians'. But 'amongst Spaniards', he suggested, 'they compensate for worse errors.'[14] Here was further confirmation that

---

[12]   Herr, *Eighteenth-century Revolution*, 340.

[13]   Cit. *Oxford DNB*, where also is found the opinion that 'his work [was] distinguished by original research and sound judgement.'

[14]   P. Cirujano Marín *et al.*, *Historiografía y nacionalismo español 1834–1868* (Madrid, 1985), 80.

Mariana would not do, and here it is that Modesto Lafuente's *Historia general de España*, published between 1850 and 1867, comes into the story. Though I had acquired them for a song, I had long come to regard Lafuente's 29-volume *Historia* as one of the less fortunate purchases of my optimistic book-buying youth. Occupying some three and a half feet of space, they had been gathering dust and looking down at me reproachfully from a top shelf for about forty years and in these increasingly straitened days I had been thinking of taking them round to Oxfam. But I'm glad I didn't do that now because, although it's too late for me to expect ever actually to *read* them, putting this lecture together has at last got me *glance* through the three twelfth- to fourteenth-century volumes (volumes V–VII), and in particular through volume V, which covers the long twelfth century from the reconquest of Toledo to the reconquest of Seville, 1085–1248. And this for two reasons: firstly to see what sources Lafuente used in compiling the work; and second, to gain some idea of the value that, like Mariana before him, Lafuente was to serve for the justly underrated medievalists who were his dependents. I mean, of course, his value for purposes of *plagiarism*.

In fact, Lafuente is not so very much unlike Mariana, who for the medieval period provides him with his template, except that he is longer, *much* longer. He ploughs on and on, doggedly waiting for inspiration to turn up. He is the historiographical equivalent of a Mahler symphony. As to his sources, in the 500 pages of his volume V he is largely dependent on Spanish secondary materials published over the previous two hundred years. Apart from something intriguingly described as the 'Latin chronicle of Toledo',[15] what little primary material he uses he takes from the autobiography of King James of Aragón, *España Sagrada*; and the editions of Rodrigo of Toledo and Lucas of Tuy, those of Lorenzana and Mariana respectively.[16] In his use of the Alfonsine chronicles and their derivatives he was no wiser in his generation than the children of light, though he can hardly be held to account for that. The only *archival* materials he cites are one item from Simancas, another from the 'archive of the University' (presumably the Universidad Central, Madrid) and an unspecified manuscript of the Academy of History from which he cites a couple of foral grants of Alfonso VII.[17] A larger number of references are to items in the Crown Archive of Barcelona, of which when Carlos IV had tried to visit it in 1802 the custodians hadn't been able to find the keys, but which under the direction of Próspero de Bofarull and his son and nephew since then

---

[15]    Lafuente, *Historia*, V. 114.
[16]    Ibid., 52, 103, 112, 183.
[17]    Ibid., 286, 458, 307.

had been being put in order.[18] Still, most of Lafuente's references had been provided by agents. Lafuente wasn't an archives man, as Flórez and Risco had been in the previous century. 'Laborious and wearing' was how he described archival work.[19]

So far as I can see, nowhere does Lafuente refer to Dunham and only once or twice does he notice Charles Romey's *Histoire*, which had been published in a Spanish translation in 1839. This is not surprising, however, for Romey, whose criticisms of Mariana had been even more extreme than the Englishman's, was French. And, as in the twelfth century, after their experience at the hands of Napoleon Bonaparte, patriotic Spaniards, like Nancy Mitford's Uncle Matthew, regarded all foreigners as fiends and the French as the very worst of them. For, as Richard Ford had recorded in his *Handbook* (where incidentally there is no mention of Dunham and precious little of Romey),[20] amongst other enormities the French had made a bonfire of Flórez's library and a stable of the church in which he was buried.[21] Accordingly, Lafuente takes Mariana to task, not once but twice, for what he calls the 'very grave error' of making Blanche of Castile Alfonso VIII's elder daughter, with all that that implied.[22] (On the other hand, he has no hesitation in describing Archbishop Rodrigo of Toledo's oration at the Fourth Lateran Council as a fact of history.)[23]

Light on footnotes, Lafuente was also light on his feet. With his fertile pen, he stood in that rhetorical tradition of Spanish scholarship which treated history in general and medieval history in particular as a branch of law. This was the case elsewhere too of course. At Oxford and Cambridge the liberation of academic history from the realm of *belles lettres* – and be it remembered that Lafuente's contemporary as Regius Professor of History at Cambridge was Charles Kingsley, author of that celebrated historical monograph, 'The Water Babies' – at Oxford and Cambridge that liberation had been *via* law and the lawyers' study of constitutional history.[24] But in Spain the subject was a

---

[18]    Ibid., 56, 58, 71, 73, 76, 79. Cf. [J. E. Martínez Ferrando], *Archivo de la Corona de Aragón. Guía abreviada* (Barcelona 1958), 13–15.

[19]    *Historia*, I, xxi–xxii. See also C. Pérez Bustamante, *Primer Centenario de la muerte de don Modesto Lafuente, discurso leído en la Junta solemne conmemorativa del 29 de enero de 1967*, 26.

[20]    *A Handbook for Travellers in Spain, and Readers at Home* ... [1845] (repr. Arundel, 1966), 203.

[21]    Ibid., 1185, citing *España Sagrada,* 43, p. ix.

[22]    *Historia general de España*, V. 181, 248.

[23]    Ibid., 359.

[24]    J.O. McLachlan, 'The origin and early development of the Cambridge Historical Tripos', *Cambridge Historical Jnl*, 9 (1947–9), 78–105, at pp. 81–2.

branch not so much of legal *theory* as of legal *practice*. Historical debate there not so much jurisprudential as forensic.

Whereas for Lafuente's contemporary Fernando Patxot y Ferrer – a historian possessed of such exquisite text-critical skill that he was able to date the death of the first Spaniards (Adam and Eve) to the years 3070 and 3060 BC respectively, and of such modesty that he chose to publish his revelations under a pseudonym – the historian was not 'a judge pronouncing sentence but rather a clerk of the court responsible for ensuring that the judge be fully apprised of the facts of the matter',[25] (and this was rather well put), Lafuente adopted a didactic posture. Don Modesto insisted on laying down the law from the bench and on stressing the lesson to be learnt from the Visigoths regarding the intrinsic merit of a unified nation, which meant of course the merits of a nation unified by religion. It was that that made the Spanish nation 'independent/ great/ and free'.

Lafuente was a member of the Spanish cortes. In 1844 he had served in the Progressive cause as a member of the constitutional commission. But his progressive politics did not prevent him from looking to the very early Middle Ages for reassurance. Progressive though he was, his choice of words in 1844 – 'independent/ great/ and free' – anticipates those of Menéndez Pelayo in 1894 and of General Franco in 1944.

Others involved in the mid nineteenth-century debate between monarchists and the third estate also found grist for their particular mills in certain periods of the Spanish Middle Ages. To point the moral or adorn a tale, the reign of Pedro 'the Just' (or 'the Cruel', depending on one's point of view) was regularly referred to.[26] This was in accordance with the conviction held by enlightened opinion on either side of 1789 that the 'ancient and venerable constitution of the country' had been best represented by the medieval Cortes and that the medieval Cortes had provided the form of government most in accordance with the general good of the nation.

In 1780 Jovellanos, the minister of Carlos III, had chosen the medieval Cortes as the subject of his discourse on the occasion of his reception into the Royal Academy of History.[27] Since 1738, when Felipe V had accorded it the royal warrant, the Academy of History had been increasingly preoccupied with the theme of the excellence of the medieval Cortes, and also with its corollaries: the tyranny of the Habsburgs, the outrages committed by the Inquisition, and

---

[25]    R. López-Vela, 'De Numancia a Zaragoza. La construcción del pasado nacional en las historias de España del ochocientos', in García Cárcel (ed.), *Construcción de las historias*, 200, 211–12.

[26]    Cirujano Marín *et al.*, *Historiografía*, 107–12.

[27]    Herr, *Eighteenth-century Revolution*, 341–2.

the criminal folly of the expulsion of the Jews and the Moriscos. In this account of the Spanish past, the revolt of the Comuneros in 1520–21 had marked the end of a golden age. It was not by chance that it was in 1808, the year in which Madrid rose against the French and Spanish patriots drove Joseph Bonaparte out of the country, that a new edition of the *Siete Partidas* of Alfonso X the Learned was published together with the accompanying Essay on the subject by the Director of the Academy, Francisco Martínez Marina.

Nor was there anything accidental about the coincidence of the closure of the Cortes of Cádiz in 1813 with the publication of the same author's much more sharply etched *Teoría de las Cortes*. That work was to provide nineteenth-century Spanish liberalism with both its agenda and its point of reference: the subtitle of the book proclaimed as much. Martínez Marina wrote about the medieval cortes, and the Visigothic councils, with an eye to the present – and indeed with a sovereign disregard for more or less everything that did not conduce to the present outcome. Martínez Marina was a corresponding member of the Whig Academy.[28]

Not that there was anything exceptional about that either. Writing about the English past in the 1870s, Bishop Stubbs was no less sharp-eyed in scanning the constitutional history of the fourteenth century for its significance for the nineteenth. Like Stubbs, Martínez Marina's ultimate inspiration was Tacitus, and boggy places in woods, and the raising of tribal leaders on shields, to the discomfiture of powdered favourites and the grotesque rulers perpetuated by Goya. But unlike Stubbs, Martínez Marina made the mistake of drinking deep at the spring of German Romanticism before the antidote (or emetic) of German scholarship was readily to hand in a Spanish translation. Though it wasn't only a question of the availability of translations. There is something else that distinguishes the Spanish from the English and other examples, and that is the intellectual poverty of the exercise and the distance at which it stood from the Great Historical Enterprises described by David Knowles, from the Bollandists and Maurists of previous centuries and from the scholarship soon to be deployed by the Monumentists in Germany and the editors of the Rolls Series in England.

There were reasons for this. For example, neither Martínez Marina nor Lafuente possessed an equivalent to Thomas Rymer's account of the English public records[29] – for the simple reason that the archives of the kings of

---

28 Peter Linehan, 'Ecclesiastics and the Cortes of Castile and León', *Las Cortes de Castilla y León en la Edad Media: Actas de la Primera Etapa del Congreso Científico sobre la Historia de las Cortes de Castilla y León, Burgos, 30.9–3.10.1986* (Valladolid, 1988), II. 113; Raymond Carr, *Spain 1808–1939* (Oxford, 1966), 92–7.

29 Cf. D.C. Douglas, *English Scholars 1660–1730*, 2nd edn (London, 1951), 222–34.

medieval Castile had not survived the Middle Ages. There wasn't, and there never had been, the equivalent of that material for them to work on. Nor was there the wealth of monastic chronicle material that the Rolls Series comprise. (This – according to another Lafuente: Vicente de la Fuente, who flourished, more or less, rather later in the century – because those who might otherwise have been *writing* chronicles had been occupied with the far more important business of *fighting* Moors.)[30]

Even so, there was no shortage of monastic *documentation* awaiting investigation in Madrid in 1850. Though the royal archives had gone for ever, by then all the documents appropriated from the kingdom's suppressed monasteries, providing ample opportunity for the 'laborious and wearing' exertions that Modesto Lafuente recoiled from, and no small number of manuscripts too, had been in the capital, at the Royal Academy of History, for some fourteen years.

The process of *desamortización*, that is, of disentailment of ecclesiastical property, had been begun by the Mendizábal ministry in 1836, and was continued during the First and Second Republics of 1873 and 1931–36 when the archives and libraries of the cathedrals were targetted and orders given for the transfer of all their holdings to the national capital. Naturally, the owners of these treasures did all they could to hold onto their own. And the consequences of their exertions are still emerging from the woodwork – literally. Quite recently a cupboard under the stairs in a private house in Astorga brought to light the medieval archive of the Franciscan house of Sahagún, and only the other day I learned of the discovery behind a false wall of another *fonds* belonging to a Praemonstratensian monastery in Catalonia. In the eighty years after 1836 early medieval manuscripts belonging to the incomparable library of S. Domingo de Silos, which the abbot of the day had taken care to ensure were nowhere listed, were periodically recovered from where they had been buried or from domestic chimneys and wells in the environs of the monastery.

But many were lost for ever. In the most pitiable of circumstances, of ignorance and villainy, in 1878 fifty-five Silos items were auctioned at Paris, with twenty of them disappearing into private collections all over Europe and the New World.[31] We are encouraged these days to think comparatively, and the account of these tragedies provided by Dom Martial Besse in 1897 has prompted me to do so and to observe that, by comparison with those members of the English aristocracy who contributed in one way or another to the

---

[30]   V. de la Fuente, *Hist. eclesiástica de España* (Madrid, 1873), IV. 200.

[31]   J. Martial Besse, 'Histoire d'un dépôt littéraire. L'abbaye de Silos', *Rev. Bénédictine*, 14 (1897), 210–25, 241–52, at pp. 223–4; W.M. Whitehill & J. Pérez de Urbel, 'Los manuscritos del real monasterio de S. Domingo de Silos', *BRAH*, 95 (1929), 521–601, at pp. 521–2.

advancement of the Rolls Series, those members of the Spanish aristocracy at least its *soi-disant* members) who come into Dom Martial's sorry story appear to have distinguished themselves by cheating the monks of their patrimony either for the enrichment of their own collections or for pecuniary profit.[32] Tales abound of early medieval chalices purchased by weight from gullible members of the community.

With all this trundling of medieval archives to and fro between their places of origin and provincial or national capitals, inevitably some items fell off the backs of chariots and later changed hands for the price of a meal. I have myself handled papal documents of the thirteenth century in the Archivo Histórico Nacional endorsed 'dos pesetas':[33] an endorsement presumably attributable to the flea market rather than to the papal chancery. On Christmas Eve 1966, as I wandered around the market outside Barcelona Cathedral I came upon an old woman tearing pages out of what looked like a late medieval choir book for sale as lampshades. When I asked her where the book had come from she made off. And in a cupboard in the archive of Seu de Urgell into which *pergamins* of every medieval century had been crammed, in the following spring I found… a revolver. 'República' it was grimly pronounced by the *guardia* who came to disable it – though he was surely wrong about this. The gun must have been enclosed by a nationalist soldier when the archive was returned to Urgell from Barcelona sometime after 1939.

But that small incident illustrates the sort of dangers archives and libraries are liable to suffer when they are carted around. In principle, the monastic collections were meant to remain in Madrid (or Barcelona) and the cathedral items eventually to return to their owners. In practice, there were many exceptions to the rule. Many of the most precious items belonging to the library and archive of Toledo Cathedral, appropriated in 1873, never went home, and are now in the Biblioteca Nacional and the Archivo Histórico Nacional respectively. Others never arrived anywhere. We have accounts of the mules heaving carts loaded with the precious spoils from the archive of the monastery of Guadalupe missing their footing as they toiled over the Montes de Toledo and plunging to their destruction. As well as of the unfortunate mules, there

---

[32]  For the role of 'un marquis plus ou moins authentique qui faisait à Madrid le commerce d'antiquités de comte à demi avec une femme qui ne savait ni lire ni écrire, très célèbre sous le nom de *tia Jesusa*' and the acquisitions of the Marqués de Cuba ('bien connu pour ses frequents achats chez les religieuses'), see Besse, 'Histoire', 222, 244.

[33]  E.g. AHN, Clero, carp. 3019/5 (an ex-chapter archive of Toledo item: a letter of Gregory IX, Feb. 1228) endorsed: 'Adquirido por compra a Manuel Rodríguez su precio de 2 ptas, Madrid, agosto de 1903'. Ironically perhaps, the letter conveyed a papal reproof to King Fernando III for presuming to make free with ecclesiastical revenues: Peter Linehan, *The Spanish Church and the Papacy in the Thirteenth Century* (Cambridge, 1971), 111.

is reason to suppose that that was also the end of the autograph of Rodrigo of Toledo's *Historia de rebus Hispanie*, which Dr Enrique Jerez has recently managed to trace as far as the Extremaduran monastery.[34]

I have lingered over the question of the *desamortización* in order to make the point that, if only by degrees, and if only with some grievous losses *en route*, in the years after 1836, potentially at least, Spanish students of the Middle Ages began to enjoy access to the sources of their subject to an extent to which they had not enjoyed them before, that is to say centralized in the capital (or capitals). Admittedly, Portugal had done it both first and better – with the initial process of centralization there being far more thoroughgoing, perhaps for the reason that the operation was in the hands of Alexandre Herculano who because he was engaged in writing his History of Portugal down to 1279 ensured that as much of the material as possible came to Lisbon – and had then not done it all, with, it is rumoured, bales of documents delivered in the 1840s still waiting to be unpacked.[35] It may be not by coincidence that the first peninsular work published in accordance with Germanic editorial standards were the *Consuetudines* and *Scriptores* volumes of *Portugaliae Monumenta Historica*, published in 1856.

To return to 1813 and Martínez Marina's *Teoría de las Cortes* for a moment. Of the twenty five documentary items of the period 1351–1499 published *in extenso*, ten derived from Burriel's copies, two from the Escorial, and the origins of nine more were unexplained.[36] In 1813, four out of twenty-five items from outside Madrid was not a bad tally. In 1850, however, the monastic archives came to the Academy of History, and in 1866 the Archivo Histórico Nacional was established – although another thirty years were to pass before it was moved from its squalid premises in the Academy's building to somewhere rather more suitable.[37]

And that ought to have been that. Though of course it took time for it to catch on, gradually the practice of consulting documents found favour. In the winter of 1830–31, shortly before the first spate of *desamortización*, Richard Ford had gained entry to the cathedral library of Toledo, a sanctum into

---

[34]    Enrique Jerez, 'La *Historia Gothica* del Toledano y la historiografía romance', *Cahiers de Linguistique et de Civilisation Hispaniques Médiévales* 26 (2003), 223–39, at p. 230.

[35]    See the preface to my *Portugalia Pontificia* (Lisbon, 2012), 12–13, 19–20.

[36]    Ed. Biblioteca de Autores Españoles, tom. 220 (Madrid, 1969), 79–175.

[37]    P. Ewald, 'Reise nach Spanien im Winter von 1878 auf 1879', *Neues Archiv der Gesellschaft für ältere deutsche Geschichtskunde*, 2nd ser. (1881), 217–398, at pp. 350, 397; L.G. de Valdeavellano, 'Vida y obra de D. Tomás Muñoz y Romero (1814–1867)', *BRAH*, 163 (1968), 89–142 at pp. 130–31; L.M. de la Cruz Herranz, 'La organización de los fondos del Archivo Histórico Nacional (1866–1989)', *Boletín de la Asociación Española de Archiveros, Bibliotecarios, Museólogos y Documentalistas*, 46 (1996), 63–94 at p. 68.

which, as he wrote fifteen years later, 'little indeed ever enters save the light and air of heaven.' In that same passage of the *Handbook* he described his exasperation at the presence of the 'hungry and siestose canon...yawning at his elbow' and chivvying him to buck up and finish.[38] The learned Englishman came from a country with the circumstances of whose medieval past he was as well acquainted as he was conscious of the consequences of its own *desamortización*. And he had an intelligence as sharp as his eye and his pen. But though he showed interest in Toledo's manuscripts, and provided some account of them,[39] of its collection of *documents*, the richest collection in the country, he had nothing to say.

Manuscript-mindedness was one thing. Curiosity about documents came later. Of antiquarian pottering about there had never been any shortage. But systematic work on the diplomatic collections recently transferred to the new Archivo Histórico Nacional appears only to have begun some twelve years after its opening. Earliest on the scene, of course, were the Germans, and first of all Paul Ewald. During the winter of 1878–79 Ewald covered an extraordinary amount of ground, inspecting manuscripts in the capital and in collections from Barcelona to Cádiz, travelling as no Spaniard other than Jaime Villanueva had travelled since the days of Flórez. But again it was these – manuscripts, codices – that Ewald confined his attention to, not documents. Documents, and above all (after Modesto Lafuente's modest incursions) the wonderful documentary riches of the Barcelona Crown Archive, which the Bofarulls had begun to uncover, would have to await the arrival of Heinrich Finke.

An example of the inveterate pre-archival mindset of these custodians of the Spanish past is provided by a letter sent to a friend by the university professor and biographer of Cervantes, Francisco Navarro Ledesma, in the spring of 1894. Writing from Toledo, Navarro Ledesma, whose *Lecciones de literatura general*, according to the website, 'are now little read', reported that 'We have had here an excellent lad who has only one defect, namely a mania for medieval Spanish chronicles. He appears to believe' – the professor continues – 'and he makes no bones about it, that such things can serve some useful purpose. What a tragedy it is that so a keen mind and so gifted an intelligence should spend themselves in such mousy matters'. The lad in question (though at twenty-five he was hardly still a lad) was Ramón Menéndez Pidal, whose dedication to those 'mousy matters' was soon almost single-handedly to place certain areas of Spanish medieval scholarship on equal terms with the learned Germans.[40]

---

[38]   *Handbook*, 1262; Robertson, *Richard Ford*, 62–3.

[39]   *Handbook, loc.cit.*

[40]   J. Pérez Villanueva, *Ramón Menéndez Pidal, su vida y su tiempo* (Madrid, 1991), 112.

Despite the creation of a corps of archivists and so on, since 1835 (it was observed)[41] just one cartulary had been published, and that without any learned apparatus. In 1894 there was still some way to go. It was a way whose pioneers had already trod a rocky path in favour of a more outward-looking prospectus for education in general and higher education in particular, and against all the odds, in the 'Institución Libre de Enseñanza'. Of the Institución's successor, the 'Junta para Ampliación de Estudios', Menéndez Pidal was to be a leading light. Two years earlier, however, two years before 1894, when Unamuno had been appointed to the chair of Greek at Salamanca, one of the electors had remarked: 'No one knows Greek. But we have given the job to the only man capable of learning it.'[42] And, not long after, when the Benedictine scholar and saviour of what was left of the Silos heritage, Dom Marius Férotin, visited the library of Toledo cathedral, Ford's yawning canon-archivist was still there, now enforcing a rule whereby no one was allowed to copy anything in full.[43] (Férotin's mistake, of course, was to be French.)

So, for all that the riches of the spoils from the monasteries and elsewhere beginning to be exploited and published in the Bulletin of the Academy of History by Fidel Fita, eventually the Academy's Perpetual Secretary and a matchless scholar richly deserving of a proper study,[44] as the nineteenth century ended there was still some way to go.

There was still some way to go. There still is. Of many of the various sections into which the loot of the *desamortización* was divided, there are still no published catalogues. While functionaries of the National Archive busy themselves with the study of the wholly fruitless study of the reclassification of its sections over the past 150 years, scholars wishing to discover the contents of the *Sección del Clero*, for example, into which the monastic material was eventually decanted, have to go to Madrid and, by leafing through the hand-lists, which contain dates and that's all, discover for themselves what there is there.

And this is splendid. It means that there is everything to be discovered. Research students chip away at bits of the edifice, producing *tesinas*, even full-grown theses from the rubble. Burriel's great projects remain to be fulfilled. True, the synods make progress, and in modern conditions their editor enjoys

---

[41]    Besse, 'Histoire', 252.

[42]    Pérez Villanueva, *Menéndez Pidal*, 111.

[43]    As reported in his *Le Liber Mozarabicus Sacramentorum et les manuscrits mozarabes* (Monumenta ecclesiae liturgica 6; Paris, 1912), 679–80; Linehan, 'History in a Changing World' (*Past and Present in Medieval Spain* [Aldershot, 1992]), 7–8.

[44]    See meanwhile J. M. Abascal Palazón, *Fidel Fita, 1835–1918: su legado documental en la Real Academia de la Historia* (Madrid, 1998).

access to materials which Burriel had no knowledge of. Yet, because no one in Spain has wanted to traipse round the provinces, work on the papal materials has hardly advanced since Paul Kehr downed tools in 1926. The truth of the matter is that the nineteenth century failed to do its work properly. By not centralising all ecclesiastical archives – or, as was the case in Portugal, almost all of them – the Spanish authorities of the period condemned later labourers in the vineyard to travel round the provinces and to knock at unavailing doors in pursuit of archivists who never turn up. And as I say, this is splendid. For which of us would wish not to have enjoyed the experiences those forays provided? Which of those of us who have been so regularly frustrated by them, would choose to have all the available materials of medieval history in a single place, and, in accordance with *1066 and All That*, to have the history of medieval Spain brought to a full stop – which, having tried your patience for so long, is what I must now do? But before doing so let me add just one further very late nineteenth-century particular.

In the year 1899 the editors of the newly founded *Bulletin Hispanique* at Bordeaux received from a Belgian scholar whose name was unknown to them a remarkable document recently encountered (it was reported) in an Antwerp manuscript: a hitherto unknown Spanish *fuero* granted by Alfonso I of Aragón in 1132. The editors of the *Bulletin*, and its secretary, the distinguished Hispanist, Georges Cirot, in particular, fell upon it with joy. Here was just the thing to put the *Bulletin* on the map, or even to edge it ahead of its rival and senior in the field, the *Revue Hispanique*, which the no less distinguished (but senior) Hispanist, Raymond Foulché-Delbosc, had launched five years earlier. So in 1900 the *Bulletin* proudly published the text of 'Le Fuero de Piedrafita', and sat back to await the plaudits of the international community of Hispanists.[45]

What instead it received was a liberal serving of egg on its face, in the form of a patronising account of its first two volumes by the editor of the rival *Revue*. How curious, Foulché-Delbosc reflected, that the *Bulletin*'s editor had failed to report that this charter was an *acrostic*-charter; even more so in view of the fact that the final letters of each of its clauses, when spelled out, read EMINENTISSIMUS CIROT. What was the 'very eminent Cirot' doing as a cipher in a charter of 1132?[46] The very eminent Cirot was astounded, played very pompous and never really recovered his dignity. Yet as well as the man who had gulled him into deceiving the Hispanic province of the republic of

---

[45]   E. M[érimée], *Bulletin Hispanique*, 2 (1900), 78–9.

[46]   R. Foulché-Delbosc, *Revue Hispanique*, 7 (1900), 521–8 at pp. 526–8; and 'Quelques mots à la «Revue hispanique »', *Bulletin Hispanique*, 3 (1901), 187–93 for Cirot's response to this 'laborieuse farce' (pp. 191–3). For the context see A. Niño Rodríguez, *Cultura y diplomacía: los hispanistas franceses y España de 1875 à 1931* (Madrid, 1988), 147–60.

letters, Cirot would surely have been even more astounded by the knowledge that to this day, more than a century later, the internet notice issued by the Piedrahita authorities continues to proclaim that *fuero* (in a 'versión española desde el latín medieval') as the authentic foundation charter of their small settlement in the province of Teruel.

# I

# A Papal Legation and its Aftermath. Cardinal John of Abbeville in Spain and Portugal, 1228-1229

Sometime in the first half of 1228 Gregory IX's legate came to Spain. Cardinal John of Abbeville spent barely a year and a half there, but he hit the place like a tornado and decades later fragments of the old order dislodged by him were still floating down to earth. In March 1295 when the archbishop of Tarragona, D. Rodrigo Tello, visited the diocese of Pamplona and denounced by name some scores of clerics convicted of concubinage and pluralism, in the matter of pluralism it was to the legate's constitution on the subject of almost seventy years earlier that he referred[1]. As late as the sixteenth century John of Abbeville's name was remembered within the Catalan province because even then certain of the constitutions of the council over which he had presided at Lleida in 1229 still remained in force there[2]. Any scholar with sufficient patience to trawl through the ecclesiastical archives of the peninsula and the registers of the popes between Gregory IX and Boniface VIII would discover not hundreds but thousands of thirteenth-century references to the legate of 1228-9. Just as, for Sherlock Holmes Irene Adler was *the* woman, so for thirteenth-century Spain John of Abbeville was *the* legate. Until the arrival of his immediate legatine successor all of ninety years later, the cardinal-bishop of Sabina remained the Spanish Church's distinctly uncomfortable benchmark.

As long ago as 1971 I constructed a provisional itinerary of John of Abbeville's legation and published it together with an account of his impact and influence for Spanish colleagues to anatomise and improve upon[3]. Because since

* My warm thanks are due to Mn. Miguel S. Gros Pujol (Arxiu Capitular de Vic), D. Antonio Chacón Gómez-Monedero (Archivo de la Catedral de Cuenca) and D. Ciriaco López de Silanes (Archivo de la Catedral de Santo Domingo de la Calzada) for photocopies of material, to Paul Freedman, André Gouron, Magnus Ryan and Patrick Zutshi for advice and information, and to the Humanities Research Board of the British Academy for the award of the Research Grant which enabled me to undertake research in the Portuguese archives during 1997-8.

[1] «Que est contra consuetudinem domini Johannis Sabinensis episcopi et contra ordinationem domini P. predecessoris nostri factam in ecclesia Pampilonensi»: Pamplona, Archivo General de Navarra, caj. 4, no.101 (reg. J. R. CASTRO, *Catálogo del Archivo General. Sección de Comptos. Documentos*, I, Pamplona 1952, no. 581). (For the archbishop's predecessor, D. Pere d'Albalat, and the Pamplona synod, see P. LINEHAN, *The Spanish Church and the Papacy in the Thirteenth Century*, Cambridge 1971, chap. 4 and p. 67 n. 2.) In Nov. 1290 Bishop Domingo of Lisbon was authorised to absolve those clergy of his diocese who had incurred the legate's penalties: E. LANGLOIS, ed., *Les Registres de Nicolas IV (1288-92)*, Paris 1886-1905, 3685.

[2] J. M. PONS GURI, *Constitucions conciliars Tarraconenses, Analecta Sacra Tarraconensia*, 47 (1974), p. 72.

[3] P. LINEHAN, *Spanish Church*, cit., pp. 20-34. For the extreme limits of his absence from the papal curia (still at Rome 22 Feb. 1228; *functus officio* by 3 Jan. 1230), see now A. PARAVICINI BAGLIANI,

I

then they have on the whole preferred to dine out on those meagre findings rather than continue the search for further information[4], I therefore take the opportunity now afforded by this celebration in honour of Ennio Cortese, and the occasion it provides to acknowledge both the magnitude of his contribution to the study of our subject and the beneficence of his genial influence, to return to old haunts, ultimately in order to present our honorand with something which I hope he may find of interest. Before that, however, there is some ground to be made up on.

As José Mattoso declared in his 1981 edition of Herculano's *História de Portugal*, John of Abbeville deserves a monograph[5]. Indeed so, though it is necessary to say that even in 1981 the available elements for that monograph were not quite as sparse as the Portuguese and superannuated Spanish authorities cited by Mattoso imply. And now there is more still that can be said. With its demand for ecclesiastical reform and its refrain that the Muslim occupation of Jerusalem was attributable to the collective sinfulness of Christian Europe, the future legate's crusading sermon, published by Penny J. Cole and dated by her to the years 1217-18, anticipated many of the themes developed by him a decade later, to the considerable consternation of the beneficed denizens of the peninsular Church[6]. Yet still we await an even half-way adequate account of the man.

What follows does not pretend to be that, or even a blueprint for such an undertaking. All it seeks to do is to present some further evidence relating to the legate's energetic progress around the peninsula, and to describe a single example of the immediate reaction which his relentless intervention elicited in those generally torpid parts.

As to the first of these, the evidence set out in Appendix I speaks for itself. It reveals that the legate covered a lot of ground. It can also be made to reveal the rate at which he did so. My best attempts to establish his work-rate suggest the following. Calculating the period of his legatine activity from 8 June 1228 (the date of the first certain sighting) until 30 September 1229 (when on the strength of other evidence he may be thought to have passed through Seu d'Urgell), and calculating, as best I have been able to do, the distance he covered during these 480 days as 6500 kilometres, I reckon that on average and day on day he completed about 13.5 kms. In fact the true daily haul must usually have been greater, since for considerable periods the legate was stationary (at ecclesiastical councils at Valladolid, Salamanca, Lleida and Tarazona, as well as at the cortes of Coimbra, for example). Moreover, whereas my calculations have been based on the assumption that he took the shortest route between one centre and another (and on even larger assumptions about the road-system at the time), his recorded presence at such places as Sotos and San Lorenzo de Parrilla implies that more

*Cardinali di curia e 'familiae' cardinalizie dal 1227 al 1254*, Padova 1972, i. 27, with the comment: «I registri e i documenti pontifici ci offrono poca documentazione su questa legazione.»

[4] See, for example, J. GONZÁLEZ, *Reinado y diplomas de Fernando III*, I, Córdoba 1980, pp. 215-16.

[5] *História de Portugal desde o começo da monarquia até o fim do reinado de Afonso III*, notas críticas de José MATTOSO, 1981, p. 547.

[6] *The Preaching of the Crusades to the Holy Land, 1095-1270*, Cambridge Mass. 1991, pp. 150-6, pp. 222-6. A copy of his sermons was in Boniface VIII's library in 1295: A. PELZER, *Addenda et emendanda ad Francisci Ehrle Historiae Bibliothecae Romanorum Pontificum tum Bonifatianae tum Avenionensis*, I, Vatican Library 1947, no. 405.

often than the record shows he may have been well off the beaten track. It is to be suspected therefore that a daily rate of progress of 13.5 kms is an underestimate. Sample readings confirm this suspicion. Between 6 and 17 August 1229, for example, he covered the distance between León and Lerma, some 280 kms, representing a daily rate in excess of 23 kms[7].

With his own couriers taking a day longer than this to cover a similar distance (and with no councils or cortes to delay them *en route*), this was an impressive rate of strike, especially for one who, as it was believed, had recently declined the patriarchate of Constantinople on health grounds[8]. No wonder therefore that the episcopal author of the so-called «Crónica latina de los reyes de Castilla» — the royal chancellor, Juan de Soria — describes him as «running through the province»[9]. True, the comparative study of legatine progresses is still is its infancy[10]. Even so, anyone who has traversed the peninsular archives, for example, as the legate did the peninsular churches over two Spanish summers and a winter, will appreciate the enormity of his achievement, the complexity of the logistical calculations involved, and, above all, the supreme importance of avoiding the need to double back. Of course, in at least one respect the thirteenth-century legate's situation was different from that of the twentieth-century *investigador* following his trail. For he was dealing not with archivists but with bishops, and they would have been awaiting his approach (and in some cases awaiting it with trepidation) rather than skulking behind the sacristan. Even so, sometimes it is evident, and sometimes it can reasonably be conjectured, that the legate *did* double back, and that he did so in order to ensure that the instructions which he had previously issued were being complied with[11]. Just as they were recovering from his investigation of their affairs, such vigour doubtless took the locals by surprise. It may even have caught them still in bed. If the evidence from Vic, to which I shall return, is anything to go by, it almost certainly did.

John of Abbeville travelled fast but he did not travel light. Amongst the seventeen original instruments of his of which I am aware it is possible to discern as many as five different Italian hands[12], and further evidence that he was well

---

[7] Equally impressive, because they included the Christmas period, were the almost 700 kms travelled between Porto and Coimbra *via* Lisbon in the course of just 37 days.

[8] Salamanca to Coimbra, 7-19 (not 18) February 1229: A. D. DE SOUSA COSTA, *Mestre Silvestre e Mestre Vicente, juristas da contenda entre D. Afonso II e suas irmãs*, Braga 1963, pp. 163-5; A. PARAVICINI BAGLIANI, cit., i. p. 26.

[9] «Currensque per prouinciam...»: ed. L. CHARLO BREA, Cádiz 1984, p. 77.

[10] For the earlier period there is S. WEISS, *Die Urkunden der päpstlichen Legaten von Leo IX. bis Coelestin III. (1049-1198), Forschungen zur Kaiser- und Papstgeschichte des Mittelalters. Beihefte zu J. F. Böhmer. Regesta Imperii*, 13; Cologne-Weimar-Vienna 1995.

[11] Consideration of his itinerary suggests that he may have visited Segovia, Avila, Sigüenza, Tarazona and Calatayud (for example) more than once.

[12] Avila, Lerma, Zuera: A[rchivo] C[atedral] Segovia, caj. 4, nos. 12-15 [a, b, c, d]; Carrión de los Condes: Logroño, Arch. de la Colegiada, doc. 18 [e]; place unstated: Astorga, Arch. Diocesano, carp. 2, no. 41[f]; Porto: Lisbon, A[rquivos] N[acionais/]T[orre do] T[ombo], C[olecção] E[special], Refoios de Limia, doc. 5 [g]; Seia: ANTT, CE, cx. 19 [h]; Celorico da Beira: ANTT, Mosteiro de Santa Cruz, Documentos particulares, mç. 16, doc. 39 [j]; Fuenteguinaldo:ANTT, Sé de Coimbra, mç. 42, doc. 1727 [k]; Ocaña: AC Toledo, Z.1.G.1.4a [l]; Sotos and San Lorenzo de la Parrilla: AC Cuenca, Institucional, caj. 3, nos. 63-65 [m, n, o]; León: Coimbra, Arq. da Universidade, Documentos de Guimarães, no. 16 [p]; Agreda: AC S. Domingo de la Calzada, leg. 22, no. 23 [q]; Gerona: AC Vic, cal. 37, vol. 6, no. 60 [r]. A palaeographical comparison

# I

provided with expert assistance is provided by the inclusion in certain of his letters of the distinctive formulae of the papal chancery[13]. Evidently, however, he also employed local scribes as they were needed, and both these and the members of his entourage wrote up his *acta* further down the road, after he had departed from the place to which they referred — at Coimbra for the church of Tojal, for example, at Ocaña for Toledo, at Martorell for Tarragona[14]. It may also be assumed that he maintained a register of his *acta* sufficiently detailed to enable him, when he reached Cuenca, to reproduce for that church the constitutions he had recently enacted for the church of Toledo regarding the capitular establishment there and related matters, and to do so almost to the letter[15].

Sometimes he had moved on a considerable distance before the letters in question were written up. Almost nine months elapsed before he was able to provide the church of Guimarães with its new constitutions[16], doubtless because during that period further representations had been made by that institution and its agents had been shuttling between northern Portugal and the cardinal way off in the east. Certainly there was much coming and going across the peninsula during 1228 and 1229. Thus, while he was somewhere between Lisbon and Coimbra a dispute was referred to his arbitration from as far away as Catalonia[17]. And all the time new instructions were reaching him from the pontiff, in some cases having taken time to locate him. On the last day of August 1228, for example, Gregory IX sent instructions regarding the see of Guarda where the dean of Lisbon and king's chancellor, Master Vicente (*alias* the canonist Vincentius Hispanus) had been elected bishop almost three years before but where he had not yet accepted election. The legate was to require him to do so within a month, and if he failed to comply was to order a fresh election there. The matter was urgent therefore. Yet the papal mandate had evidently not

---

suggests the following provisional identification: g, h: Hand 1; l, q: Hand 2; o: Hand 3; d, m: Hand 4; c: Hand 5. Similar characteristics have been observed in the letters of the cardinal-legates Guala Bicchieri in England (1216–18) and Conrad of Urach in France (1220–26): N. VINCENT, ed., *The Letters and Charters of Cardinal Guala Bicchieri, Papal Legate in England 1216–1218*; The Canterbury and York Society, vol. 83, Woodbridge 1996, pp. lxxxiv–lxxxv; F. NEININGER, *Konrad von Urach (†1226): Zähringer, Zisterzienser, Kardinallegat; Quellen und Forschungen aus dem Gebiet der Geschichte*, n.F. 17, Paderborn-Munich 1994, pp. 572-84. N. VINCENT, *The Letters*, cit., loc. cit., has located eight original letters relating to Cardinal Guala's English legation (out of a total of 37 the full text of which survives). Cf. C. R. CHENEY, *Cardinal John of Ferentino, papal legate in England in 1206, English Historical Review*, 76 (1961), pp. 654-60.

[13] E.g. «Si quis autem hoc attemptare presumpserit maledictionem dei omnipotentis et eterne dampnationis interitum necnon et indignationem beatorum Petri et Pauli apostolorum et sancte Romane ecclesie se nouerit incursurum»: ANTT, CE, Refoios de Limia, doc. 5; «Nulli ergo... Si quis autem...»: E. SAINZ RIPA, *Colección diplomática de las Colegiatas de Albelda y Logroño*, I. *924-1399*, Logroño 1981, no. 25; AC Cuenca, Institucional, caj. 3, nos. 63, 65; «Si quis autem...»: ANTT, Sé de Coimbra, mç. 42, doc. 1727; Coimbra, Arq. da Universidade, Documentos de Guimarães, no. 16. Cf. N. VINCENT, *The Letters*, cit., p. xciii.

[14] In one case (letter f) the instrument was dated according to the Spanish era as well as by the year of the incarnation. For details, see Appendix I.

[15] For the Toledo constitutions (Ocaña, 3 June 1229), see F. J. HERNÁNDEZ, *Los cartularios de Toledo*, Toledo 1985, no. 428. Those for Cuenca (San Lorenzo de la Parrilla, 22 June 1229), framed «secundum consuetudinem ecclesie Toletane quam imitari consueuistis», are at AC Cuenca, Institucional, caj. 3, no. 64 (*olim* cax. 5, leg. 20, no. 275).

[16] At León, 6 Aug. 1229.

[17] The case concerned Pere, sacrist of Barcelona, and others of that place, and B. Vincent, cantor of Tarragona: AC Barcelona, Diversarum B, no. 787 (9 Dec. 1228).

reached the cardinal either by January 1229 when he had the opportunity of addressing Master Vicente directly at the cortes of Coimbra, or thereafter when in all probability he visited Guarda itself. It was from Salamanca on 7 February, soon after he had left Portuguese territory and all of five months after the pope's mandate had been dispatched, that John forwarded the text of it to the reluctant prelate[18]. Meanwhile he received the guidance for which he had himself applied to the pope. For formidable though he was in the estimation of those upon whom he had descended, and charged as he was with both diplomatic and pastoral responsibilities, nevertheless in certain areas John of Abbeville evidently did not feel himself capable of proceeding without further instructions from headquarters. In view of recent scholarly discussion on the subject of the limits of legatine authority[19], his hesitations in this respect are of interest. Fortunately, however, they can be somewhat elucidated from the copies of material 'ex codice Barchinonensi apud Agustianos' made in the early nineteenth century by Jaime Villanueva, the indefatigable historian of the churches of the old Corona de Aragón. The evidence preserved by Villanueva is both curious and remarkable. Not only does it seem to suggest that just fifteen years after the Fourth Lateran Council a papal legate to Spain needed to be reassured before seeking to enforce even legislation which went back well before 1215[20]. It also raises the question

---

[18] A. D. DE SOUSA COSTA, *Mestre Silvestre*, cit., pp.163–6; J. H. DA CUNHA RIVARA, *Catálogo dos manuscritos da Biblioteca Pública Eborense*, III, Lisbon 1870, p. 73. See below, Appendix II.

[19] See R. C. FIGUEIRA, *The classification of medieval papal legates in the Liber Extra*, Archivum Historiae Pontificiae, 21 (1983), pp. 211-28; ID., *'Legatus apostolice sedis': the pope's 'alter ego' according to thirteenth-century canon law*, Studi Medievali, 3. ser., 27 (1986), 543-50; N. VINCENT, *The Letters*, cit., pp. xlvi-vii.

[20] On 28 February 1229 Gregory IX wrote to John of Abbeville as follows: «Ex parte tua fuit propositum coram nobis quod in civitatibus et villis majoribus legationis tuae non sunt parrochiae pro magna parte distinctae, sed quilibet quem et quanto tempore vult sibi eligit confessorem illum maxime qui de decimis vel primiciis vel aliis juribus parrochialibus plus sibi duxerit remittendum, vel qui aliqua familiaritate conjunctus ei fuerit, aut eius dissimulare peccata sive relinquere voluerit impunita (...) Multa quoque monasteria nigrorum monachorum quorum quaedam immediate ad apostolicam sedem pertinent collapsa sunt et destructa, quae non creduntur posse per nigros sed per albos monachos vel regulares vel seculares canonicos reparari, et de quibusdam non est spes aliqua quod resurgant nisi ad Cisterciensem ordinem convertantur...». Whereas the legate was surely aware what action was required to remedy the first of these problems and to control the evils to which it had led (including the public approval granted by a client clergy of liaisons — «contubernia tam a nobilibus quam ignobilibus» — contracted within the third or fourth degree), it was on both these matters as well as others that he had sought guidance: «super quibus *omnibus* apostolicum remedium implorasti.» «Super contuberniis vero prefatis statuta generalis concilii facias inviolabiliter observari», the pontiff ruled: [Madrid,] R[eal] A[cademia de la] H[istoria], MS. 9-24-5/4558, foll. 192ʳ-195ʳ. On 10 Sept. 1229 the legate forwarded the pontiff's directive to the archbishop of Tarragona and his suffragans. (It may be significant that in chap. 65 of the second [post-1230] part of the «Crónica latina de los reyes de Castilla» [above, n. 9] there is recurrent use of the word 'contubernium': a word nowhere employed in the earlier part [chaps. 1-59], despite the interest in the question of illicit unions of the author of that section, Juan de Soria. Whether or not Juan de Soria also penned the post-1230 part, he certainly claimed to have had conversations with the legate in 1228-9: L. CHARLO BREA, *¿Un segundo autor para la última parte de la "Crónica latina de los reyes de Castilla"?*: Actas I Congreso Nacional de Latín Medieval [León, 1-4 de diciembre de 1993], ed. M. PÉREZ GONZÁLEZ, León 1995, p. 253; Crónica latina, chap. 54 [p. 77]). For further papal communications to the legate see L. AUVRAY ed., *Les registres de Grégoire IX (1227-41)*, Paris 1890-1955, pp. 247, 266-8, 283.

# I

whether the Council of Valladolid, hitherto invariably ascribed to the year 1228, was not in fact held a year later[21]. There is one other point to be made about the legate as he continued on his punishing course. By contrast with Cardinal Guala's in England, John of Abbeville's retinue appears to have been limited in extent. His nameless scribes apart, only two of its members are known to us, one of these being his penitentiary, Raymond of Peñafort, who, according to Gérard de Frachet's contemporary account, was recruited by John during his Spanish legation and owed him his *entrée* to the papal curia[22]. The other was his cleric 'Master P.', to whom he subdelegated the thorny question concerning the clergy of Desojo in the diocese of Calahorra[23], and then wished upon the church of Cuenca[24]. As to

---

[21] No text of the Latin *acta* of the council has survived. All modern accounts of it derive from M. Risco's eighteenth-century transcript of the vernacular version in the archive of León cathedral (*España Sagrada*, XXXVI, Madrid 1787, pp. 213 ss.). But that version is of the fifteenth century. Moreover, its most recent editor — J. M. FERNÁNDEZ CATON, *Colección documental del Archivo de la Catedral de León (775-1230)*, VI, León 1991, no. 1955 — assigns it the date «era de mill e dozientos e LXIII annos», i.e. 1225, which is impossible. In these circumstances, all manner of palaeographical confusions in the vicinity of AD 1228/9 are imaginable, stretching over centuries. But in view of the date of the pope's response to the legate's queries regarding parochial arrangements (cited in the previous note) the language of the Valladolid decree on the subject (in its vernacular form: «*De clerico curatore preficiendo aliis*. Item, stablecemos que en las eglesias do son muchos clerigos el uno principalmiente aya la cura de las almas e los otros ayudenle en los seruicios de Dios, e el que ouiere la cura ayan *(sic)* offeriendas de las confessiones, ca derecho es quel que mays trabaia aya galardon mayor que el otro»: FERNÁNDEZ CATÓN, cit., loc. cit.), seems to justify a date later than the autumn of 1228 for the Valladolid Council. Although our knowledge of the king of Castile's movements is too imperfect to be of much assistance, it is to be noted that he was at Valladolid on 28 April and 20 June 1228 and again on 7 February 1229 (J. GONZÁLEZ, *Fernando III*, II, Córdoba 1983, nos. 234-5, 246). Since the legate's itinerary allows for the possibility that the council of the Castilian Church was held in mid-February 1229, immediately after that of the Leonese Church at Salamanca, it has been entered, with a question mark, in Appendix I.

Echoes of the Valladolid *acta* are audible in a papal letter of March 1235 incorporating the complaints of the archbishop of Toledo, D. Rodrigo, against the Master and brothers of the Order of Santiago, *inter alia* that «cum sint laici construunt auctoritate propria nouas ecclesias, altaria erigunt et clericos instituunt et destruunt in eisdem, furtiue utentes contra prohibitionem uenerabilis fratris nostri .. Sabinensis episcopi tunc apostolice sedis legati»: Madrid, Archivo Histórico Nacional, Sellos 90/6. Cf. FERNÁNDEZ CATÓN, cit., loc. cit: '*De iure patronatus*'.

[22] *Raymundiana seu Documenta quae pertinent ad S. Raymundi de Pennaforti vitam et scripta*, ed. F. BALME and C. PABAN, *Monumenta Ordinis Fratrum Praedicatorum Historica*, VI, 1, Rome-Stuttgart 1900, p. 2.

[23] «...Cum itaque ... coram dilecto clerico nostro magistro P. partibus auditore concesso questio esset aliquandiu agitata...»: SAINZ RIPA, cit., loc. cit.

[24] «Venerabili in Christo patri deo gratia episcopo . [*sic*] et dilectis filiis .. decano et capitulo Conchensi J. eiusdem permissione Sabinensis episcopus apostolice sedis legatus salutem in domino. Supplicastis nobis, uos pater episcope, ut donacionem medietatis prestimonii de Balancon in termino de Uclese quam ad opus refectorii capitulo uestro fecistis dignaremur confirmacionis nostre munimine roborare. Nos uero uestris supplicationibus inclinati eam presentis scripti patrocinio duximus confirmandum, ita uidelicet quod post uitam dilecti clerici nostri magistri . P. concanonici uestri cui capitulum de liberali gratia dictam medietatem in uita sua canonice concessit tenendam ad usum refectorii ipso iure in perpetuum reuertatur. Nulli ergo omnino hominum liceat hanc paginam nostre confirmationis infringere uel ei ausu temerario contraire. Si quis autem hoc attemptare presumpserit indignationem dei omnipotentis se nouerit incursurum. Dat. apud Sautiis [Sotos] .xvii. kal. julii»: AC Cuenca, Institucional, caj. 3, no. 63. «Cum venerabilis frater noster ... Sabinensis episcopus in societate suam dilectum filium magistrum . P. ecclesie Concensis canonicum habeat noscatur», on 14 April 1231 Gregory IX directed the archbishop of Toledo to

legatine abuses, the Spanish Church in general seems to have escaped remarkably lightly at the hands of the cardinal bishop of Sabina, with just one complaint known to have reached Rome[25].

\*\*\*

By the third week of September 1229, therefore, when he reached Vic, the legate had experienced to the full the moral extremes of which the peninsular Church was capable, and there, evidently, he discovered the same deficiencies that he had already encountered throughout the length and breadth of the peninsula. The chapter of Vic was an exclusive club of the socially privileged and more of an economic co-operative than an ecclesiastical community, with since 1176 a *numerus clausus* of forty canons designed to maintain profitability for the share-holders and the capitular revenues entrusted to twelve provosts appointed from within the chapter, each charged with the administration of its corporate lands and revenues for a month at a time and rewarded for his trouble by whatever surplus he was able to accumulate.

As Paul Freedman has shown, the twelfth-century canons of Vic had survived the storm of Gregorian reform pretty much unscathed[26]. And the same can be said of their post-Fourth Lateran Council successors. Indeed, in the years after 1215 the chapter of Vic became even more a gentleman's club than before. By 1229 the profit-sharing membership had dropped from forty to twenty-three, and one of the legate's measures on visiting the place was (as at Porto, for example)[27] to increase that number, in this case by the addition of seven in priestly orders: a measure which, in combination with other such radical departures as the elimination of laymen from the capitular pay-roll, consideration of the problem of non-resident or 'flying' canons («canonici qui etiam uolatiles nuncupantur», as they would be described seventeen years later)[28], and the insistence that in future all canons be of at least subdiaconal rank, only served to deepen existing divisions within the local church. Already in 1215, Innocent III had responded to a complaint from the bishop, Guillem de Tavertet, concerning the practice of a group within the chapter of frustrating discussion of items uncongenial to them — «rationabilibus dispositionibus contra Lateranensis statuta concilii» — by either not responding when summoned by the bell (as will be seen, deafness was rife in Vic) or alternatively, having come, by withdrawing, thus rendering the meeting non-quorate and anticipating the tactic of *retraimiento* which so effectively paralysed Spain's political processes in more recent times[29].

---

ensure that 'Master P.' should enjoy the income of his benefice «cum ea integritate (...) qua solent studentibus exhibere»: AC Toledo, X.1.E.2.8. Cf. N. VINCENT, *The Letters*, cit., pp. lxxxv-lxxxviii.

[25] From Bishop Martín Rodríguez of Zamora: *Reg. Greg. IX*, 1318.

[26] For the twelfth-century background, see P. H. FREEDMAN, *The Diocese of Vic. Tradition and regeneration in medieval Catalonia*, New Brunswick N.J. 1983, esp. pp. 48-67.

[27] Below, n. 71.

[28] Below, Appendix III.

[29] «Quia uero, ut asseris, quidam de canonicis tuis cum audiunt campanam pulsantem ad conuocationem capituli accedere dedignantur uel, si forsan accesserint, audito aliquo uerbo quod ipsis displiceat, statim recedunt et cum a te requirantur nolunt dare consilium aut suas exprimere uoluntates»: AC Vic, cal. 37, vol. 6, no. 54. For the other developments summarised in this and the next paragraph, see J.

On this occasion, the pope consoled the bishop with the doctrine of the *sanior pars*[30]. In northern Catalonia in 1216, however, and for the next thirty years, that old standby cut no ice, failing to do so precisely because, in the absence of agreement as to which group constituted which, there were no rules of engagement agreed between the *sanior pars* and the *pauciores*. Until 1246, therefore, when the old guard reasserted itself, with the legate's chapter of thirty reduced to twenty and the option of assigning capitular rents to laymen retained as a possibility *sine die* «if urgent necessity or evident advantage should so require», battle continued, with Guillem de Tavertet hounded out of office in 1233, after being charged with heresy in addition to the more familiar and less cerebral failings for which Spanish bishops were renowned[31].

These developments are not of concern to us here however. Nor was the case of Vic unique. The situation was much the same in Galicia, for example. «Rarely or never» could the canons of Orense be induced to have themselves ordained, the bishop of that place, the canonist Laurentius Hispanus, informed the pope in October 1232. Since the dean and capitular officials refused prebends to priests, but only ordained canons might celebrate at the high altar, the prelate therefore petitioned the pontiff to decree that henceforth six prebends in the church be reserved for those of priestly rank[32]. (Presumably John of Abbeville had missed Orense on his rounds.) In Girona also, next-door to Vic, over at least the last ninety years admission to the chapter had been restricted to those of noble birth, it was stated by one witness after another in 1239-40, and by definition the canons of Girona were deacons and not priests[33]. All that is unusual about Vic is that in this case we are for once able to observe the immediate reaction of these comfortable pensioners to the legate's uncompromising ordinances, and in particular to the novel proposition that receipt of income from their prebends should henceforth be dependent upon their attendance at services and performance of the liturgical office. For it was with that aspect of his recent visitation, and with this alone, that the canons were concerned in the record printed as Appendix II[34].

In Catalonia the legate had left it to the metropolitan, the archbishop of Tarragona, to tidy up after him and ensure that his orders were complied with, and evidence remains of the archbishop's activity in this connexion[35] (as, unsurprisingly, it does not in respect of the archbishop of Toledo in Castile:

---

L. DE MONCADA, *Episcopologio de Vich*, ed. J. COLLELL, Vich 1891, I, pp. 553-99; P. LINEHAN, *Spanish Church*, cit., pp. 42-4.

[30] «Quod a saniori parte capituli ordinatur nisi forte a paucioribus aliquid rationabile obiectum fuerit et ostensum»: loc. cit.

[31] See Appendix III; A. MUNDÓ, *La renúncia del bisbe de Vic, Guillem de Tavertet (1233) segons la correspondència de Bages i els registres vaticans, VII Congreso de Historia de la Corona de Aragón*, Barcelona 1962, IIII, pp. 77-95.

[32] *Reg. Greg. IX*, 916.

[33] AC Girona, *Causa del any 1240*. See P. LINEHAN, *Spanish Church*, cit., pp. 45-6.

[34] Item III of which indicates that it was copied after January 1231. The hand is contemporary.

[35] References to the legate's delegation to him of an appeal of the bishop of Girona and of his own instructions to the bishops of his province to observe the legatine decrees are to be found in AC Barcelona, *Liber Antiquitatum IV*, fol. 238ʳˢ⁻ᵇ; Tarragona, A[rxiu] H[istòric] A[rxidiocesà], Index del Indices (1679), fol. 2ʳ. See also below, n. 82, and R. GINEBRA I MOLINS ed., *El manual primer de l'Arxiu de la Curia Fumada de Vic (1230-1233)*; Acta Notariorum Cataloniae, 6, Barcelona 1998, no. 1703.

unsurprisingly, inasmuch as for the archbishop of Toledo, D. Rodrigo Jiménez de Rada, John of Abbeville was a bogeyman whose legation seemed to last twice as long as it actually did)[36]. So far as Vic was concerned, however, the archbishop of Tarragona was soon on the scene. On 21 October 1229 D. Sparago de la Barca was there, reiterating the text about the need for laws to be enforced which the legate had enunciated to him after the Council of Lleida[37], and insisting on compliance within the next fifteen days with the legate's instructions to the canons of Vic regarding attendance at divine office.

Presumably it was within those fifteen days that the canons presented their special pleading on the subject. Certainly it was another fifteeen days thereafter that the archbishop answered their queries one by one[38].

They speak volumes, do those queries. The legate had evidently taken the canons of Vic by surprise. Would a canon's uncorroborated assertion that he had been too ill to get up for matins suffice? it had been inquired. On the whole the archbishop was inclined to think that it would — though not if later that morning the canon in question was observed riding on horseback and appearing fit as a fiddle (and even less if this were to occur 'frequently'). As to those who alleged that they were too exhausted by manual labour to hear the bell summoning them to church he was unimpressed however. For the effect of making that excuse available to the spiritually feeble would be completely to undermine the legatine ordinance. Nor was he moved by the claim of the *fornicarius* that he had deserved to be excused (from attendance in choir presumably) because «what had happened had happened on account of sleep and was a natural thing». (Though it is not at all clear what *had* happened to the bastard[39], whatever it was it was something which the legate who at Coimbra and Toledo had been prepared to make due allowance for study, illness, bleeding and capitular business, had not allowed for)[40].

---

[36] «Vir bonus, sapiens, litteratus», D. Rodrigo described him in his History, «qui celebratis in singulis regnis conciliis, postquam monita salutis proposuit, ad sedem apostolicam est reuersus tribus annis legationis expletis»: *Roderici Ximenii de Rada Historia de rebus Hispanie siue Historia Gothica*, ed. J. FERNÁNDEZ VALVERDE; *Corpus Christianorum Continuatio Mediaeualis*, 72, Torhout 1987, p. 293. Cf. P. LINEHAN, *Spanish Church*, cit., pp.10-18, and chap. 3; L. K. PICK, *Rodrigo Jiménez de Rada and the Jews. Pragmatism and patronage in thirteenth-century Toledo*, Viator, 28 (1997), pp. 203-22.

[37] Appendix II [i]: «Parum est...». Cf. J. TEJADA Y RAMIRO, *Colección de cánones y de todos los concilios de la Iglesia de España y de América*, III, Madrid 1849, pp. 341-2.

[38] Appendix II [ii].

[39] Had he fallen asleep in choir and then had to leave in order to relieve himself? Or was the problem an incident of nocturnal pollution, the functional implications of which for clerical ministers had much exercised Gratian and the decretist commentators?: D.6 c. 1; J. A. BRUNDAGE, *Obscene and lascivious. Behavioral obscenity in canon law*: J. M. ZIOLKOWSKI ed., *Obscenity. Social control and artistic creation in the European Middle Ages*, Leiden 1998, pp. 252-8. If the latter, the canon of Vic whom the archbishop so singularly identified was perhaps unaware of the remedies prescribed at the time by the Englishman Thomas of Chobham, namely nettles and cold water: *Summa Confessorum*, ed. F. BROOMFIELD, Louvain-Paris 1968, p. 331.

[40] «...nisi studio uel infirmitate uel minutione fuerit excusatus uel ecclesie negociis de mandato capituli occupatus»: ANTT, Sé de Coimbra, 2ª Incorporação, mç. 42, doc. 1727. Cf. F. J. HERNÁNDEZ, *Cartularios de Toledo*, no. 428. For an account of the liturgical arrangements at Vic, written on the assumption that all was more or less well there, see J. MASNOU, *El mantiment del culte a la catedral deVic al segle XIII*, Miscel.lània Litúrgica Catalana, 8 (1997), pp. 163-77 — though that author does not refer to what is considered here.

# I

Evidently, the equestrian canons of Vic were now on their mettle. They had heard that at Barcelona the archbishop had not insisted that the canons be present in choir for matins of the Virgin. But the archbishop was on his mettle too, responding to them in this case that capitular custom at Barcelona was otherwise than at Vic. He was also ready to deal with the objection that the legate had exceeded his authority and that the sanctions of suspension and excommunication *latae sententiae* prescribed by him were unwarranted. Although this was a point on which the experts were in disagreement — «in hac parte quid iuris sit uarient sapientes» — he was not disposed to challenge the legate's contention that such sentences had been authorised by the General Council. It was, as he conceded, a moot point however, there being a «decretalis expressa» of Honorius III in existence to the contrary effect[41].

The reference to this decretal indicates that less than four years after its promulgation the archbishop of Tarragona had a copy of the *Compilatio quinta* to hand[42]. Whether either this or the various juristic maxims embedded in his response to the canons entitles him to be regarded as yet another of the forgotten jurists of thirteenth-century Spain is another matter however. True, allegedly he hailed from Montpellier (though that is not everything now, nor was it then). True also (though that was not everything either), on the occasion of his translation to the metropolitan see in 1214 he had been promoted as one «in quo quidem bona discretio et litteratura viget, cum sit in sacris scripturis et utroque jure sufficientissime eruditus»[43]. It is not necessary therefore to assume that he had acquired those maxims, and especially the Roman Law maxims, second-hand — from some such intermediary as Bernard of Pavia or Huguccio[44]. But in any case it is not that that is chiefly interesting about him. What is is that he went to

---

[41] Appendix II [ii.h]. The legate had not legislated at the Lleida council on the specific issue of unauthorised absence from choir — though the measures decreed against canons and other clergy of conventual churches appearing at choir and in the cloister «in habitu seculari» (c. 31; J. M. PONS GURI, *Constitucions*, cit., p. 90) were evidently relevant to the case of Vic. However, his rigorist approach seems rather to have stemmed from an identification of the legate's person with the pope's combined with a more extreme interpretation than Huguccio's of the effects of the canon relating to transgression of «apostolicae sedis precepta» (D. 19 c. 5): R. C. FIGUEIRA, *Legatus apostolice sedis*, cit., pp. 531-43; P. HUIZING, *The earliest development of excommunication latae sententiae, Studia Gratiana*, 3 (1955), pp. 289-91.

[42] Cf. 5 Comp. 3.1.3 (X--): «...Consuluistis tandem de clericis, qui chori silentium fugientes intendunt externis collocutionibus laicorum (...) si quid de talibus in eodem concilio noscitur institutum canon fuit latae sententiae uel ferendae; ad quod breuiter respondemus, quod penam illa constitutio non infligit...» (ed. E. FRIEDBERG, *Quinque compilationes antiquae nec non Collectio canonum Lipsiensis*, Leipzig 1882, p. 169). (Cf. P. HUIZING, cit., pp. 281-2: «Among the decretists after Huguccio one finds the term 'latae sententiae', but I have never come across the term 'ferendae sententiae'») The decretal (dated 1 Dec. 1216) had been occasioned by a series of questions raised by the dean and chapter of Compostela: P. PRESSUTTI, *Regesta Honorii pape III (1216-1227)*, Rome 1888-95, no. 132; D. MANSILLA, *La documentación pontificia de Honorio III (1216-1227)*, Rome 1965, no. 16. The decree of IV Lateran referred to was c. 17, *Dolentes*, with its graphic description of «minores clerici» and «praelati» who spent so much of their nights drinking («ut de aliis taccamus») that they remained incapable until lunchtime. While «ut de aliis taceamus» might well refer to the activities of the *fornicarius* of Vic, neither he nor the other canons were either *praelati* or (for the most part) *minores clerici*. Hence perhaps the substance of their objection to the legate's ruling.

[43] J. VILLANUEVA, *Viage literario a las iglesias de España*, XIX, Madrid 1851, p. 225. «Así apareció ante sus contemporáneos y así aparece también ante la historia», J. GOÑI GAZTAMBIDE remarks: *Historia de los obispos de Pamplona*, I. *Siglos IV-XIII*, Pamplona 1979, p. 541. Not before all historians however.

[44] A suggestion for which I am grateful to André Gouron.

the trouble at all of thus adorning his communication to the canons of Vic. He did so, presumably, because he thought he knew his correspondents and was confident that, because not all of them were red-necked riders to hounds, some of them at least would appreciate his learned allusions[45]. Not that any of this made him a committed reformer. Sparago de la Barca was a reformer abroad, in places like Vic for example. At home he dragged his heels[46]. As did the entire peninsula. According to popular tradition, some fifty or so years earlier a previous cardinal legate who had threatened to excommunicate the king of Portugal, Afonso Enriques, had barely escaped with his head on his shoulders. It had been the intervention of four of the king's knights that had saved him and their reasoning that if the king killed a cardinal Rome would adjudge him a heretic[47]. By 1229, however, it was not the legate that was at risk but rather the advancement of his initiatives at Rome as well as in Spain. On the one hand, in April 1231 Gregory IX, the pope who had sent the French cardinal to Spain to take a firm line with both pluralists and clerical anomalies of one sort or another, licensed the dean of Compostela (whose uncle happened to be a cardinal) to acquire additional benefices notwithstanding[48], having in the previous October authorised the dean's archbishop to dispense illegitimate and otherwise irregular clerics wholesale because unless he did so (he had been persuaded) there would be no clerical presence at all in the newly reconquered dioceses of Mérida and Badajoz[49]. On the other, instructions that had been sent while the legate had been in Spain had to be reissued thereafter evidently because no notice had yet been taken of them[50].

Already then, within months of his returning to Rome, the taut disciplinary fabric which John of Abbeville had drawn across the Spanish peninsula was beginning to fray at the edges if not to unravel altogether. Even so, as developments at Vic itself demonstrate, his labours had not been entirely without avail. Though there had never been any lack of interest in the learned law in the

---

[45] For civilian influence at Vic in the 1180s see P. H. FREEDMAN, *The Diocese of Vic*, cit., pp. 86-8.

[46] Although instructed by the legate (as at Vic) to increase the number of canons in his own cathedral church, he had failed to do so (his successor at Tarragona, Pere d'Albalat, reported to Innocent IV in 1248), «quamquam facultates ipsius ecclesie non sint aliquatenus diminute, propter quod [again as at Vic] predicta ecclesia ob defectum servitorum in spiritualibus non modicum patitur detrimentum»: AHA Tarragona, «Thesaurus», fol. 466; F. FITA, *Doce bulas inéditas...históricas de Tarragona, Boletín de la Real Academia de Historia*, 29 (1896), p. 110. Dissenting from my earlier characterization of him as a «political churchman», Goñi Gaztambide prefers to describe D. Sparago in post-Vatican II terms as «el obispo de la paz»: J. GOÑI GAZTAMBIDE, cit., I, pp. 541, 544. Cf. P. LINEHAN, *Spanish Church*, cit., pp. 35-6.

[47] «Oo Senhor, por Deus e por mercee, non matees o cardeal, ca dirã en Roma que sooes herege»: *Crónica Geral de Espanha de 1344*, ed. L. F. LINDLEY CINTRA, IV, Lisbon 1990, p. 228.

[48] *Reg. Greg. IX*, 604.

[49] «... non obstante defectu natalium si quem patiuntur geniti de solutis uel si forte suspensi ad ordines sunt promoti aut officium executi cum (...) earum ecclesie cultoribus nouis indigeant, nec inueniantur ex omni parte perfecti qui se periculis uelint obicere ad defensionem terre nouiter acquisite»: *Reg. Greg. IX*, 517.

[50] Thus the wording of the papal mandate of 11 October 1229 to the bishop of Palencia regarding the activities of Jews in his diocese is virtually identical to that of the previous 19 March, sent while the legate was in Spain: Archivio Segreto Vaticano, Reg. Vat. 14, foll. 140ᵛ-141ʳ, no. 70 (*Reg. Greg. IX*, 356); RAH, MS. 9.24-5/4558, foll. 194ᵛ-195ʳ.

# I

church in which Pere de Cardona had begun his career in the years after 1167[51], and although just weeks before the legate's arrival Bishop Guillem and the officials of the chapter had legislated to enable canons to study in Lombardy and France[52], it was not until the settlement of 1246 that the teaching of theology there was specifically provided for by the establishment of a *magisterscolarum* in accordance with *Quia nonnulli*, c. 11 of the Fourth Lateran Council[53]. True, Bishop Guillem's shelves contained theological as well as legal works[54]. Probably more typical, however, was the collection of Pere de Caderita, sacrist of Vic and Guillem's tormentor in chief[55]. As in neighbouring Girona, after 1229 the priests whom John of Abbeville had wished upon the chapter were regarded as an exotic luxury and any proposal to send them abroad to study was dismissed as an unnecessary extravagance. As the proctor of the chapter of Girona insisted, they could perfectly well make do with such instruction as was available to them locally[56]. He spoke of the chapter's new priests as though they were apprentice plumbers.

On the other hand, however, there is the testimony provided by the will of Pere de Pausa in December 1270. By 1270 Pere de Pausa must have been an old man, for he had been one of the priests introduced into the chapter of Vic by the legate more than forty years earlier. A member of that beleagured minority who not only had sought and secured papal confirmation of their status but had also gone to the trouble and expense of having it registered[57], he had witnessed the *memoriale* composed on his deathbed by the saintly and wholly unbusinesslike Bishop Bernat Calvó (a *memoriale*, be it noted rather than a will, «quia testamentum facere non possumus, nec debemus, cum simus monachus», and

---

[51] P. H. FREEDMAN, *The Diocese of Vic*, cit., p. 53; P. LINEHAN, *History and the Historians of Medieval Spain*, Oxford 1993, pp. 305-6

[52] «Volentes utilitati ac necessitati ecclesie prouidere ne propter defectum sciencie quorumdam canonicorum Vicensis capituli nostra ecclesia sustineat detrimentum, statuimus ut cuilibet canonicorum nostri capituli uolenti dare operam studio in Lombardia uel Francia sua cotidiana portio uictualium prebeatur a festo sancti Johannis junii primo ueniente usque ad triennium ac si personaliter in Vicensi ecclesia deseruiret...»: AC Vic, cal. 37, vol. 1, no. 13 (4 June 1229).

[53] «Item statuimus quod unius prebende seu canonie fructus tantum magistro in grammatica assignentur secundum constitutionem concilii generalis»: Appendix III.

[54] These were listed in the arbitration of the dispute over his possessions between Bernat Calvó, his successor, and the chapter on the one hand, and on the other the monastery of Sant Pere de Casserres where Guillem had ended his days, whereby the former were awarded his «psalterium glossatum et epistolas Pauli glossatas, libros Salamonis, Ysaiam et Matheum glossatos et omnes libros juris ciuilis cum rationibus cuiuslibet»: his entire library indeed,«exceptis Usaticis quos cum decretis, decretalibus et rationibus canonicis uniuersis» which the monks were to have, judgment being reserved regarding the fate of his *Historia scolastica*: AC Vic, cal. 37, vol. 8, no. 12 (3 July 1235).

[55] Who in his will of November 1239 bequeathed to a nephew «omnes raciones meas canonicas et ciuiles quas ego habeo ucteres et nouas et decretales meas nouas et ueteres»: AC Vic, *Libro de Testamentos 1*, fol. 13ʳ·ᵛ.

[56] «Item neget ex parte canonicorum quod aliqui de predictis sacerdotibus non debent ire ad scolas cum in ecclesia Gerundensi certos habeant magistros et cantus et grammatici et dialectice facultatis per quos possunt instrui circa intelligendas scripturas et officium ecclesiasticum ad quod sunt specialiter deputati»: AC Girona, *Causa del any 1240*, fol. 2ᵐ; P. LINEHAN, *Spanish Church*, cit., p. 46.

[57] Appendix II [iii].

which incidentally contained no mention of legal works)[58]. By contrast with the monk-bishop, Pere de Pausa did possess law books — the *Fuero Juzgo, Usatges, Decretum,* and copies of the *Decretals* and the *Institutes* both «veteres» and «novae». Indeed, his legal collection was altogether more impressive than his theological holding. Then there were the item intriguingly described as «quandam longam cartam quam dicitur Cronica in qua continentur Romani pontifices et imperatores» and «omnes meos libros fisice»[59]. Here, in short, was the library of a man whose intellectual development would seem to have taken him into all corners of the mid thirteenth-century's fast-developing academic world, and who to that extent may be judged a disappointment to the memory of the legate the principal themes of whose legation had been the inculcation of the study of theology and the discipline of regular councils and synods.

Not so however. That was not all. For while grinning and bearing the hail and fogs of the place which had entered into the calculations of the papal judges delegate in 1246, and working his way through his entitlement of bread and wine at lunch and dinner[60]. Pere de Pausa had added other items to his collection — items which he prized highly. «Illos sermones quod composuit Ihoannes de Abavilla, qui postea fuit cardinalis, et quamvis ille liber sit scriptus de villi littera tamen multa bona in hoc continentur», and the «librum constitutionum domini Sabinensis», which he bequeathed to the church of Vic «quod semper teneatur preparatus quando sinodus celebravitur»[61], suggest that John of Abbeville had not traversed those long, dusty roads entirely in vain.

---

[58] J. VILLANUEVA, cit., VII, Valencia 1821, pp. 252-8 (July 1243); E. JUNYENT, *Diplomatari de Sant Bernat Calvó abat de Santes Creus, bisbe de Vich*, Reus 1956.

[59] E. JUNYENT, *Un importante legado de libros en el siglo XIII, Hispania Sacra*, 2 (1949), pp. 425-9.

[60] Appendix III.

[61] E. JUNYENT, *Un importante legado de libros*, cit., p. 428.

# I

## APPENDIX I

Itinerary of Cardinal John of Abbeville, 1228-1229[62]

1228: [.........], Calahorra[63] - [.........], Burgos[64] - 8 June, San Pedro de Cardeña (dioc. Burgos)[65] - 16 July, Segovia - 20/21 July, Avila[66] - 8 August, San Pedro de Cardeña - [.........], ? Valladolid - 20 August, Carrión de los Condes (dioc. Palencia) - September, Astorga[67] - 29 September, La Pola de Gordón (León) - [.........], Oviedo - [.........], Lugo - 3 November, Santiago de Compostela[68] - [.........], Braga[69] - [.........],

---

[62] Where no evidence is cited here it is to be found in P. LINEHAN, *Spanish Church*, cit., pp. 22-6.

[63] *Contra* P. LINEHAN, *Spanish Church*, cit., p. 24 n.5, the legate's judgment dated 20 Aug. 1228 of the dispute between the bishop of Calahorra and the church of Albelda on the one hand and the clergy of Desojo on the other suggests rather than March/May 1229 as the likelier occasion of his visit to Calahorra. His non-participation in the agreement regarding the contentious translation of the see of Calahorra to La Calzada on 28 March 1228 may indicate that the legate had not reached the peninsula by that date. Cf. J. GONZÁLEZ TEXADA, *Historia de Santo Domingo de la Calzada*, Madrid 1702, pp. 203-4; C. LÓPEZ DE SILANES & E. SAINZ RIPA, *Colección documental calceatense. Archivo catedral (años 1125--1397)*, Logroño 1985, no. 12.

[64] The date of his presence at Burgos is unknown. If it was indeed his first port of call in Castile that was presumably because the court was in residence there. Unfortunately, however, the whereabouts of Fernando III between 28 April and 20 June, on both of which dates he was at Valladolid (above, n. 21), are unknown. In view of his position at court, however (J. GONZÁLEZ, I, pp. 504-7; above, n. 9), the testimony of the chronicler Juan de Soria — «Intrauit dictus legatus in Ispaniam circa festum Assumptionis» — may be regarded as authoritative, always allowing for the fact that by *Ispania* the chancellor meant Castile and by the Assumption he meant the Ascension, which in 1228 fell on 4 May.

[65] AC Burgos, vol. 73, fol. 30; ed. L. SERRANO, *D. Mauricio, obispo de Burgos y fundador de su catedral*, Madrid 1922, pp. 140-1.

[66] The instrument of 21 July is now publ. L.-M. VILLAR GARCÍA, *Documentación medieval de la catedral de Segovia (1115--1300)*, Salamanca 1990, no. 126. That of 20 July, however (AC Segovia, 4/13, *olim* no. 144) the author fails to mention.

[67] It would have been at about this time (rather than later, as proposed in P. LINEHAN, *Spanish Church*, cit., p. 22) that, together with Alfonso IX of León, the legate presided at the foundation of the monastery of S. María de Villabuena, O.Cist (dioc. Astorga) — if indeed he did so at all. The evidence is ambiguous: A. MANRIQUE, *Cisterciensium... Annalium*, IV, Lyons 1659, p. 433.

[68] Unaccountably, Armando Alberto Martins alleges that it was here that the legate initiated his legation: A. A. MARTINS, *O mosteiro de Santa Cruz de Coimbra. Séculos XII--XV. Historia e instituição*. Diss. Facultade de Letras da Universidade de Lisboa, 1996, p. 353.

[69] Conjectural, though it is inconceivable that the legate failed to visit Braga, in particular because the primatial see was vacant following the death of Archbishop Estevão Soares on 27 Aug. 1228. In accordance with the Lateran decree «Ne pro defectu» (X 1.6.41) the election of a successor had to be held within three months, and there is no suggestion in Gregory IX's letter of July 1229, in which he quashed their unanimous election of Master Silvestre Godinho but proceeded none the less to prefer him to the see, that the chapter had been at fault in that respect (their error having consisted in failing to record the particulars of their *scrutinium* «in scriptis» [X 1.6.42] and in securing the candidate's consent in advance): J. A. FERREIRA, *Fastos episcopães da igreja primacial de Braga*, I, Braga 1928, p. 405; A. D. DE SOUSA COSTA, *Mestre Silvestre*, cit., pp. 51-2. That at least was how the matter was formally reported. However, as reported in a *quaestio* of the canonist João de Deus, there was more to it than that: «Cavendum tamen ut hoc non fiat vocibus tumultuosis sine deliberatione eligendi et tractatui et collatione. Et tunc electio non valet, sicut contigit in electione Silvestri archiepiscopi Bracarensis...» (cit. I. da R. PEREIRA, *Silvestre Godinho, um canonista português*, Lumen, 26 [1962], p. 691). Since the legate was in the vicinity of Braga shortly after the abortive election it is reasonable to assume that he was involved in resolving the problem. Indeed quite possibly it was he who advised the chapter of the problem's existence. And indubitably he will have advised the pontiff on the merits of the chapter's choice, the distinguished glossator of both the

I

Guimarães[70] – 29 November, Porto[71] – [.........], Tojal (dioc. Lisbon)[72] – Alcobaça, O.Cist. (dioc. Lisbon)[73] 1229: 4/7 January, Coimbra[74] – 11 January, Seia (dioc. Guarda)[75] – 13 January, Celorico da Beira (dioc. Guarda)[76] – 23 January, Fuenteguinaldo (dioc. Ciudad Rodrigo)[77] – 5/7 February, Salamanca[78] – Valladolid? – 20 February, Talamanca (dioc. Toledo)[79] –16 March, Zaragoza – 29 March, Lleida[80] – 29 April,

*Compilationes antiquae* and the *Decreta*. Cf. S. KUTTNER, *Bernardus Compostellanus Antiquus, Traditio*, 1 (1943) [repr. S. KUTTNER, *Gratian and the Schools of Law 1140-1234*, London 1983], p. 310.

[70] From León on 8 Aug. [1229] the legate sent the prior and chapter of the collegiate church of Guimarães revised statutes. His letter begins: «Ex iniuncto nobis legationis officio ad uestram ecclesiam uisitacionis causa accedentes...»: Arq. Universidade de Coimbra, Documentos de Guimarães, no. 16.

[71] «apud Portum»: ANTT, CE, Refoios de Limia, doc. 5. (Here the legate increased the establishment of the cathedral church to the level of 24 canonries and six prebends: A. D. DE SOUSA COSTA, *Mestre Silvestre*, cit. pp. 208-9; *Censual do Cabido da Sé do Porto*, Porto 1924, pp. 12-13.)

[72] «Accedentes ad villam que Sanctus Julianus dicitur iuxta Ulysbonam, ex parte una et .. abbatem et conuentum Alcobatie ex alia cum multis laboribus et clamosam conquestionem populi eiusdem ville qui cum multis plangebant lachrymis quod nec habebant ecclesiam nec animarum suarum pastorem», the legate ordered a church to be constructed there: ANTT, S. V. DE F., Cx, 31, mç. 71, no. 9 (a 17th-century copy); CE (Bulas) cx. 19, dsn.

[73] It can only have been at this stage of his progress that the legate adjudicated the issue determined by him on 11 January 1229 (n. 75, below). The record reads: «Johannes dei gratia episcopus apostolice sedis legatus uniuuersis presentes litteras inspecturis salutem in domino. Cum inter magistrum et fratres militie Templi in Portugalia ex parte una et .. abbatem et conuentum Alcobatie ex alia cum multis laboribus et expensis et non sine graui scandalo diutius agitata fuisset contentio per plures litteras hinc inde obtentas super eo quod predicti abbas et conuentus Petrum Ioannis olim magistrum Templi receperant in monachum sine Templariorum licentia, quare Templarii eundem monachum sibi restitui postulabant pecuniam numerosam de qua eundem P. dicebant non redidisse rationem a predicto monasterio repetentes, tandem partes in nos compromiserunt et compromissum iuramento firmauerunt, renuntiantes omnibus litteris super hoc impetratis et impetrandis, ratum habiture quicquid super eadem causa pro bono pacis ordinare uellemus. Nos igitur negotii ueritate diligentius inquisita pro bono pacis iniuncximus abbati et monasterio Alcobatie ut decetero Templarios non reciperent in ordine suo nisi licentiam obtinuissent transeundi ad ordinem monachorum. Et quarumdam reliquiarum restitutione facta Templariis, eis iniuncximus ut quamcitius de possessionibus monachorum quas tenebant trecentos quadraginta aureos recepissent ipsas possessiones eisdem monachis redderent liberas et quietas, nec decetero super conuersione predicti monachi prefatum uexarent monasterium requirendo personam uel pecuniam repetendo. In cuius rei testimonium...».

[74] As note 72: «datis Colimbris». Herculano's error in bringing the legate to Coimbra in both Jan. 1228 and Jan. 1229, noted P. LINEHAN, *Spanish Church*, cit., p. 21, remains uncorrected in Mattoso's edition of that monumental work. The legate attended the Portuguese cortes at this time (above n. 18). He also presided over the first provincial chapter of the Portuguese regular canons at the church of Santa Cruz there: A. A. MARTINS, cit., pp. 356-63. The probable date of the meeting suggested however, March 1229, is impossible. For testimony as to his presence at Santa Cruz de Coimbra on 4 and 7 Jan. 1228 [=1229], see Thomas ab Incarnatione, *Historia ecclesiae Lusitanae*, IV, Coimbra 1763, p. 277.

[75] «apud Senis»: ANTT, CE, cx. 19. («Sena» was a border place *par excellence* and cited as such by VINCENTIUS HISPANUS in his commentary on X 2.19.13 ad v. limitatione: J. OCHOA SANZ, *Vincentius Hispanus canonista boloñes del siglo XIII*, Rome-Madrid 1960, pp. 80-1.)

[76] «apud Celoricum»: ANTT, Mosteiro de Santa Cruz de Coimbra, Documentos particulares, mç. 16, doc. 39; P. LINEHAN, *Spanish Church*, cit., p. 23 n. 5.

[77] «apud Fontem Guinaldum»: ANTT, Sé de Coimbra, 2ª Incorporação, mç. 42, doc. 1727.

[78] P. LINEHAN, *Spanish Church*, cit., p. 23, n. 6; A. D. DE SOUSA COSTA, *Mestre Silvestre*, cit., p. 163.

[79] «aput Talamancam»: ANTT, Colegiada de S. Maria de Alcaçova de Santarém, mç. 16, doc. 313 [cited in litigation post-May 1248].

[80] The visit to Tarragona, surmised in P. LINEHAN, *Spanish Church*, cit., p. 24 n. 5, is herewith disavowed.

Tarazona[81] – 1/2 May, Tudela (dioc. Tarazona) – [........] Huesca[82] – 20 May, Calatayud (dioc. Tarazona) – [........], Toledo[83] – 3 June, Ocaña (dioc. Toledo) – 14/15 June, Sotos (dioc. Cuenca)[84] – 22 June, San Lorenzo de la Parrilla (dioc. Cuenca) – 17 July, Sigüenza – 6 August, León – 17 August, Lerma (dioc. Burgos)[85] – 26 August, Agreda (dioc. Tarazona)[86] – 31 August, Zuera (dioc. Zaragoza)[87] – [........], Tarragona[88] – 10 September, Martorell (dioc. Barcelona)[89] – 11/19 September, Barcelona[90] – 20 September, Vic – 25/26 September, Girona – [........], Seu d'Urgell.

## APPENDIX II

[i] Vic, 21 October 1229. *On pain of suspension and thereafter excommunication, Archbishop Sparago of Tarragona requires members of the chapter of Vic to observe the decree of the papal legate, John of Abbeville, regarding attendance in choir.*

[ii] Tarragona, 21 November [1229]. *Archbishop Sparago of Tarragona responds to various queries raised by the bishop of Vic, D. Guillem de Tavertet, in respect of the legate's decree regarding attendance in choir.*

[iii] Rome, 7 January 1231. *Gregory IX confirms the legate's decree that seven of the canons of Vic be ordained priests.*

Vic, Arxiu Capitular, calaix 37, vol. 6, no. 45

[i] S. miseratione diuina Terrachonensis archiepiscopus dilectis filiis uniuersis prepositis et tenentibus locum ferialem ecclesie Vicensis salutem in domino. Parum est in ciuitate ius esse nisi qui illud tueatur existat et iura insurgere contra malos si desit iurium executor.[91] Ordinationis igitur Vicensis ecclesie facte a domino cardinali nobis executione commissa, uolentes eandem executioni inuiolabiliter mandari uobis presentium auctoritate precipiendo mandamus quatinus penam de cotidianis distribucionibus inflictam hiis qui prebendale beneficium percipere dignoscuntur, si matutinis non interfuerint[92] aut aliis diuinis officiis diurnis pariter et nocturnis, prout dinoscitur in instrumento ordinationis per seriem contineri, omni occasione remota infligatis eisdem ne propter negligentiam uestram aut remissionem pene sequatur diuini officii detrimentum. Alioquin quia ordinationem huius sub dissimulatione nec uolumus

[81] J. Tejada y Ramiro, cit., III, p. 348.

[82] The reason for attributing the legate's visit to Huesca to this stage of his puzzling progress through the north-east, rather than later, is that between 23 and 29 May the archbishop of Tarragona was in the diocese of Huesca evidently clearing up after him: A. Durán Gudiol, *García de Gudal, obispo de Huesca y Jaca (1201-36; † 1240), Hispania Sacra,* 12 (1959), pp. 297-8.

[83] «Accedentes ad ecclesiam uestram...»: F. J. Hernández, *Cartularios,* cit., no. 428.

[84] «apud Sotes»: AC Cuenca, Institucional, caj. 3, no. 65; «apud Sautiis»: ibid., caj. 3, no. 63.

[85] ed. (with numerous defects) L.-M. Villar García, cit., no. 127.

[86] «apud Aggredam» (*sic*): López de Silanes & E. Sainz Ripa, no. 14.

[87] L.-M. Villar García, cit., no. 128, misdated «(1230)... Nájera».

[88] «Venerabili in Christo patri dei gratia archiepiscopo et dilectis filiis preposito et capitulo Terraconesibus J. eiusdem permissione Sabinensis episcopus apostolice sedis legatus salutem in domino. Accedentes ad vestram ecclesiam visitationis causa et diligenter examinato statu ipsius ecclesie...»: AC Seo d'Urgell, cod. 2119, fol. 10ʳ⁻ᵛ: undated but assignable to this stage of the legation by means of the item cited in the following note.

[89] AHA Tarragona, «Index dels Indices», fol. 1ᵛ.

[90] RAH, MS. 9.24--5/4558, fol. 192ʳ⁻ᵛ.

[91] Cf. D.1.2.2 post originem: «Parum est enim ius in civitate esse nisi sint qui iura reddere possint».

[92] MS. interfuerit.

nec audemus[93], si in infligenda pena predicta extiteritis negligentes post .xv. dies a susceptione presentium ab officio noueritis uos suspensos. Si autem propria temeritate, quod non credimus, perseuerare uolueritis in delicto, cum crescente contumacia pena debeat augmentari post alios .xv. dies uos senciatis excommunicationis sententia innodatos. Dat. Vic. xii. kal. nouembris anno domini m.cc.xx.viiii.

[ii] S. miseratione diuina Terrachonensis archiepiscopus uenerabili fratri G. per eandem episcopo Vicensi salutem et dilectionem. Quod in dubiis nos consulere uoluistis gratum gerimus et acceptum et diligenciam uestram merito comendamus.

[a] In primis quesiuit a nobis fraternitas uestra utrum simplici uerbo canonici sit credendum qui dicit se infirmitatis uinculo prepeditum[94] et ideo matutinis non potuit interesse. Ad hoc duximus respondendum quod si presumpcio non sit contra eum quod causa malicie alleget, dum hoc dicat in fide et legalitate sua, poterit prepositus quod prebendam recipiat tolerare, maxime cum inter simplex uerbum et sacramentum parua differentia habeatur[95]. Si autem contra eum presumptio habeatur, ut quia in mane equitat tanquam sanus nec possit infirmitatis uestigia apparere, et maxime si frequenter pretendat huius excusationes, impedimentum huiusmodi asserat iuramento. Ne sepius ab eodem uitetur in uirtute prestiti iuramenti hoc dicat quociens in posterum se uoluerit excusare.

[b] De illis autem qui campanas se non audiuisse pretendunt ut prebendam percipiant manualem ita dicimus quod, cum in hiis qui publice fiunt aliquis non debeat pretendere ignoranciam[96], non possint propter huius excusationem friuolam se excusare quando cadant in penam in ordinatione domini legati constitutam, nisi adeo surdus fuerit quod ad sonitum campane non ualeat excitari. Nam si huius excusatio admitteretur illi qui debiles sunt in spiritualibus frequenter hoc allegarent, et sic ordinatio domini legati posset penitus eneruari.

[c] Nec mouet nos fornicarii allegatio quod[97] propter sompnum et quia naturalem rem passus fuit fuit merito excusatus.

[d] De illis autem qui matutinis beate Virginis nolunt interesse, cum de consuetudine ecclesie uestre in coro dicantur sicut ore canonice ita duximus respondendum, quia cum canonici uestri pro se inducant ecclesie consuetudines approbatas contra se debent eas similiter approbare. Alioquin procurator hanc inconstanciam recusaret[98], et ideo matutinis beate Virginis sicut aliis debent merito interesse, licet Barchinonensi duximus aliter respondendum quia ibi non in coro set seorsum per sacerdotes hore beate Virginis celebrantur, et quia deuocio canonicorum uestrorum in celebratione matutinarum beate Virginis per nos fuerit comendata, nobis auctoribus a bono proposito ipsos nolumus resilire.

[e] De illis autem qui ad ecclesiam ueniunt cum diuina officia celebrantur set corum non intrant, ita dicimus quod perinde est ac si non essent in ecclesia, cum ille qui latitat circa columpnas non uideatur coram presencia iudicis comparere[99], maxime cum ille qui non sit in coro non possit in celebratione fratrum honera supportare.

[f] De illis uero qui ad matutinas[100] ueniunt et postmodum sine causa se absentant, ita duximus respondendum quod, cum ille solus brauium accipiat qui perseuerauerit usque in

---

[93] Word missing (e.g. eneruare).

[94] Cf. Gratian, C. 13 q. 2 c.7.

[95] Cf. Gratian, C. 22 q. 5 c. 12.

[96] Cf. D.22.6.9.2: «Sed facti ignorantia ita demum cuique non nocet, si non ei summa negligentia obiciatur: quid enim si omnes in civitate sciant, quod ille solus ignorat?»; Gratian, C. 35 q. 1, c. 1 («pretendere ignorantian»).

[97] MS. qui.

[98] D.3.3.27.pr (Ulpian); MS. pretor.

[99] Cf. D.42.5.36.

[100] MS. om. ad.

# I

finem[101], nec uidetur esse nisi perseuerauerit, ac si non essent matutinis sunt perlectendi, nisi causa rationabili fuerint excusati.

[g] De illis autem qui propter negocia ecclesie sunt absentes, dum fraus non adhibeatur, ita dicimus quod eos credimus excusatos et sufficere generale mandatum, ne dum nimia subtilitate in huius articulo procedatur negocia ecclesie remaneant deserta.

[h] Super illo uero articulo utrum canonici sint suspensi uel excommunicati qui ordinationi domini legati obuiant sine causa, licet in hac parte quid iuris sit uarient sapientes, ab ore domini legati nos recolimus audiuisse quod non erat canon ferende sentencie set iam late, et ideo super isto articulo contra eius dictum nolumus temere diffinire, licet domini Honorii sit decretalis expressa quod huius sentencie pocius sunt cominationes quam canon sentencie promulgate.

[i] De monaco autem maiori ecclesie uestre et aliis clericis qui non sunt canonici set alias tenentur diuinis officiis interesse, licet ordinatio domini legati quoad uerba eos non tangat, cum de similibus ad similia sit procedendum,[102] potestis eo cohercere pena in ordinatione posita uel alia simili sicut uobis uidebitur expedire.

Dat. Terrachone .xi. kal. decembris.

[iii] Gregorius episcopus seruus seruorum Dei dilectis filiis J. Draper, P. de Pausa, P. de Campis, P. de Salent, R. de Capraria et B. de Mata presbiteris, canonicis Vicensibus, salutem et apostolicam benedictiònem. Cum a nobis petitur quod iustum est et honestum tam uigor equitatis quam ordo exigit rationis, ut id per sollicitudinem officii nostri ad debitum perducatur effectum. Significantibus uobis sane nobis innotuit quod uenerabilis frater noster Sabinensis episcopus tunc in partibus illis apostolice sedis legatus ad Vicensem ecclesiam causa uisitationis accedens eamque reperiens solito canonicorum numero diminutam, ipsam de personis ydoneis ordinauit, septenarium in eadem sacerdotum canonicorum numerum statuendo, prout in confectis super hoc ipsius legati litteris continetur. Nos igitur deuotis uestris supplicationibus inclinati, quod super hoc ab eodem legato factum est et in eisdem litteris continetur auctoritate apostolica confirmamus et presentis scripti patrocinio communimus. Nulli ergo omnino hominum liceat hanc paginam nostre confirmationis infringere uel ei ausu temerario contraire. Siquis autem hoc attemptare presumpserit[103] indignationem omnipotentis dei et beatorum Petri et Pauli apostolorum eius se nouerit incursurum. Dat. Lateranen .vii. id. januarii Pontificatus nostri anno quarto[104].

## APPENDIX III

Vic, 1 June 1246. *Master Mateu, archdeacon of Tierrantona (Lleida) and R. de Spelunca, canon of Lleida, prescribe statutes for the chapter of Vic.*

Vic, Arxiu Capitular, calaix 37, vol. 6, no. 44

[E]a que ad honorem dei in ecclesiis ordinantur scripture debent memorie commendari ne temeritate seu obliuione cuiuslibet perturbentur ac labentibus temporibus a memoria hominum dilabantur. Idcirco in nomine sancte et indiuidue trinitatis, patris et filii et spiritus sancti, uniuersis hec legentibus innotescat quod nos magister Matheus de Yllerda archidiaconus Tarrantone et R. de Spelunca canonicus

---

[101] Cf. I Cor. 9. 24.

[102] Cf. E. CORTESE, *La norma giuridica. Spunti teorici nel Diritto comune classico*, I, Milano 1962, pp. 302-3.

[103] MS. presumpsit.

[104] Orig. *apud* AC Vic, cal. 37, vol. 5, no. 17 = *Reg. Greg. IX*, 526.

Yllerdensis sub anno domini .M.CC.XLVI. quintodecimo kalendas aprilis [18 March 1246] recepimus domini Innocencii pape quarti litteras sub hac forma: Innocentius episcopus seruus seruorum dei dilectis filis B. Anagarii et magistro Matheo archidiaconis et R. de Spelunca canonico Ylerdensi salutem et apostolicam benedictionem. Dilecti filii .. electus et capitulum Vicensis ecclesie nobis humiliter supplicarunt quod, cum olim bone memorie .. Sabinensis episcopus tunc in partibus illis apostolice sedis legatus tricenarium canonicorum numerum statuerit in eadem et ad sustentationem ipsorum eiusdem ecclesie non superant facultates, statui in ipsa canonicorum numerum iuxta reddituum eius sufficientiam mandaremus, de uestra itaque circumspeccione plenam in domino fiduciam obtinentes discretioni uestre per apostolica scripta mandamus quatinus, facultatibus ecclesie prefate pensatis, numerum in ea statuere auctoritate nostra prout expedire videbitis procuretis, contradictores per censuram ecclesiasticam appellatione postposita compescendo. Quod si non omnes hiis exequendis potueritis interesse duo uestrum ea nichilominus exequantur. Dat. Lugduni .iiii. nonas augusti pontificatus nostri anno tercio [2 August 1245][105].

Harum auctoritate litterarum nos magister Matheus et R. de Spelunca superius nominati, tercio collega nostra scilicet B. Anagarii Ylerdensi archidiacono legitime excusato utpote in Romana curia existente, uenerabili patri episcopo et capitulo Vicensi ad instantiam eorundem certam diem duximus prefigendam ad quam personaliter accedentes circa executionem mandati apostolici tanquam filii obedientie curam adhibuimus uigilem et intentam. Nobis igitur ac uenerabili patri episcopo Vicensi et canonicis uniuersis qui debuerunt, uoluerunt et potuerunt comode interesse in Vicensi capitulo constitutis, de facultatibus ac redditibus eiusdem ecclesie uniuersis quesiuimus diligenter.

Inuenimus autem quod omnes redditus et prouentus ecclesie Vicensis ad comunem mensam spectantes per. xii. prepositos ibidem constitutos fideliter colliguntur. Preterea inuenimus ibi quamdam comunitatem que feriale uulgariter appellatur qua distribuitur inter canonicos et alios seruitores tam clericos quam laicos qui iuxta consuetudinem eiusdem ecclesie secundum magis et minus aliquam percipiunt portionem, et ex qua supletur prout[106] posibile est deffectus ne cotidianis distributionibus seu portionibus canonici seu alii seruitores ecclesie defraudentur. Tandem facta legitime computatione omnium receptorum et expensarum ab ipsis prepositis et ab illo qui fructus colligit ferialis quod sic se haberet rei ueritas, corporaliter prestito sacramento, inuenimus quod facultates seu prouentus eiusdem ecclesie non sufficiunt ad tercenarium canonicorum numerum quem uenerabilis pater .J. Sabinensis episcopus quondam apostolice sedis legatus statuit in eadem.

Idcirco habendo dominum pre occulis, pensatis eiusdem ecclesie facultatibus ab ipsis prepositis prestito sacramento prout superius est expressum,

quia sine mutilatione prebendarum vix possent decem et octo canonici sustentari simul cum aliis qui decem percipiunt portiones, presertim cum de cotidianis distributionibus siue portionibus ipsos oporteat hospitalitatem seruare, nuncios domini pape recipere et negocia omnia ecclesie pertractare, cum nichil comune habeant preter uictum cotidianum de quo expensas deducere ualeant supradictas;

considerantes insuper quod prouentus eiusdem ecclesie qui pro magna parte in pane et uino consistunt sepius grandine et nebula deuastantur;

attendentes etiam quod preter duas portiones quas dant domino episcopo et alias duas priori Destagno[107] duodecim dant alias continue portiones ultra numerum constitutum, presertim cum quosdam canonicos non residentes habeant qui etiam uolatiles nuncupantur propter quos eorum comunitas non modicum aggrauatur,

---

[105] Orig. *apud* AC Vic, cal. 37, vol. 5, no. 16.

[106] «prout» above line.

[107] The prior (otherwise the abbot) of S. María d'Estany, for whose singular connexion with the chapter of Vic see J. VILLANUEVA, cit., VI, Valencia 1821, p. 54.

auctoritate qua fungimur uicenarium canonicorum numerum duximus statuendum in eadem, ex quorum numero septem esse sacerdotes semper uolumus et mandamus iuxta constitutionem seu ordinationem domini Sabinensis, in contradictores et rebelles excommunicationis sententiam promulgantes.

Ad hec, quia in Vicensi ecclesia quedam minus prouide inuenimus ordinata, auctoritate qua fungimur ac de comuni consensu uenerabilis patris .B. episcopi et tocius capituli Vicensis sic duximus ordinanda.

Statuimus ergo quod prepositure que minus sufficientes dicuntur iuxta arbitrium episcopi et capituli ordinentur.

Item statuimus quod feriale tali persone comitatur que fideliter fructus colligat et expendat, reddatque compotum episcopo et capitulo annuatim donec aliter duxerint ordinandum.

De pane autem sic duximus ordinandum, quod quilibet canonicus maiorem panem in prandio et minorem in cena, explosa consuetudine de frustro panis, recipiat omni die. Item quilibet canonicus recipiat duas partes unius coponi[108] in prandio sine aqua et in cena terciam uini puri. Verum quia certis anni temporibus carnes recentes et salse nimis inordinate dabantur statuimus quod loco carnium secundum ordinationem episcopi et capituli denarii tribuantur.

Item quia de bonis ecclesie ministri altaris debent et clerici sustentari statuimus ne decetero laici ad portionem integram uel dimidiam aliquatenus admittantur. Item quia inuenimus quod tres laici quinque percipiunt in Vicensi ecclesia portiones districte precipimus et mandamus quod, illis sublatis de medio, loca illa aliis laicis nullatenus conferantur set portiones ille in usus capituli conuertantur, uel aliquibus clericis conferant prout episcopo et capitulo uisum fuerit expedire. Verumptamen si urgens necessitas uel euidens utilitas id exposcat concedendi aliquibus laicis portiones liberam eisdem tribuimus facultatem.

Item statuimus quod unius prebende seu canonie fructus tantum magistro in grammatica assignentur secundum constitutionem concilii generalis.

Postquam autem fructus seu prouentus Vicensis ecclesie adeo fuerint augmentati quod sine deffectu seu mutilacione prebendarum sufficere ualeant numero pretaxato auctoritate qua fungimur statuimus et mandamus quod quecumque largitione principum[109], oblatione fidelium uel aliis quibuscumque modis, iuste dante Deo Vicensis ecclesia poterit adipisci, in augmentum prebendarum seu portionum nullatenus conuertantur, set ex his canonicorum numerus prout possibile fuerit augmentetur uel fiat inde aliqua comunitas ex qua ualeant hospitalitatem tenere nuncios domini pape, metropolitanum ac alios procurare aliasque expensas facere pro comunibus ecclesie negociis exequendis. Item de canonicis non residentibus siue uolatilibus per quod ecclesia non modicum aggrauatur prout superius est expressum sic[110] duximus ordinandum, quod quater in anno tantum per octo dies si ibidem fuerint percipiant portionem. Quod est actum kalendis junii anno domini M.CC.XLsexto.

[*The autograph signatures of Bishop B(ernat de Muro) and twenty-three others, sixteen of them describing themselves as canons of Vic,[111] together with the certificates of «magister Matheus de Ylerda archidiaconus de Terranthone, iudex a summo pontifice in hoc negotio constitutus» and «R. de Speluncha canonicus Ylerdensis, iudex a domino papa delegatus».*]

---

[108] MS. coponis.

[109] MS. principium.

[110] MS. qsic. The part of the sentence «Item de canonicis... quod quarter» is written over an erasure. See below.

[111] Of the six ordained canons of 1231, all except J. Draper sign their names. Pere de Pausa signs in a fine hand, with the *signum* «Petrus firmat ita de pausa carmina dicta».

Ego Raimundus de Laurentio de mandato iudicum predictorum hoc scripsi cum litteris rasis et emendatis in penultima et ultima lineis ubi dicitur, Item de canonicis non residentibus siue uolatilibus per quos ecclesia non modicum aggrauatur prout superius est expressum sic duximus ordinandum, quod quater. et hoc SIGNUM feci.

# II

# Dates and doubts about don Lucas

The suddenness of the rehabilitation of D. Lucas *historiador* has been truly remarkable. The man presented by Fernández Conde as recently as 1985 in very much the same terms as those employed by Sánchez Alonso almost forty years earlier, as a writer imbued with « *una credulidad que más parece de hombre del campo que de un cortesano letrado* »[1], we now view in a new light – or think we can. We think we can see an altogether more sophisticated operator than Sánchez Alonso's country bumpkin. Over the last decade D. Lucas has received more attention than ever before. He is now taken seriously. And, above all, we are soon to have Dr Emma Falque's eagerly awaited edition of his *Chronicon mundi* [*CM*]. This will surely solve many puzzles and problems. For from my own limited experience of the matter, at crucial moments in his narrative there are highly significant textual variants to be found between three of the earliest manuscripts, the Salamanca codex on the one hand and those of León and Toledo on the other (MSS S, I and T respectively, as Dr Falque identifies them in her *stemma codicum*)[2].

Meanwhile, D. Lucas remains the enigmatic figure he always has been and, I very much suspect, will always remain. Certainly not credulous in any ordinary sense of the word, he is better described as calculating, part of his agenda in the writing of his chronicle having been that which in his *De altera vita* he ascribed to his contemporary, the heretic Arnaldus: the corruption of the received record and the introduction of error[3]. What he so roundly deplored in the case of theology he

1. F. J. FERNÁNDEZ CONDE, « El biógrafo contemporáneo de Santo Martino: Lucas de Tuy », in: *Isidoriana*, I. *Ponencias del I Congreso internacional sobre Santo Martino en el VIII centenario de su obra literaria (1185-1985)*, León, 1987, p. 309-10; B. SÁNCHEZ ALONSO, *Historia de la historiografía española*, I, Madrid, 1947, p. 126.
2. See below, p. 17.
3. « Quidam etiam haereticus nomine Arnaldus de confinibus Galliae venit in Hispaniam zizaniam erroris heretici seminando. Inter cetera pravitatis opera, erat studium sanctorum

freely indulged in himself in his treatment of the historical past. Here is a form of intellectual schizophrenia richly deserving of sympathetic psychoanalysis. In his historical work, when it suited him and suited the interests of St Isidore of Seville and León, Lucas treated what the past had bequeathed to the present more or less as his plaything, *zizaniam erroris seminando* to the confusion of the future[4]. And as to his own career, similar confusion reigns. Certainly, in what follows there are more doubts than dates, just as there are more dates with doubts attached to them than otherwise.

If some of what I have to say on this slippery subject may be thought convincing, and some of it regarded as new, the new things may not prove convincing, and most of the convincing things will be found not to be new. « Rem non nouam aggredimur ». For what can we say for sure about D. Lucas and the genesis of his Chronicle ? Let us begin with his own words in the prologue to that Chronicle in which he states that he had embarked upon the work at the behest of the queen Doña Berenguela – « praeceptis gloriosissimae Hispaniarum Reginae domine Berengariae ». And again : « Ipsa enim, cuius catholicis *praeceptis* non licet nec libet resistere, mihi Lucae indigno diacono, vt hoc perficerem, imperauit »[5].

Before considering the implications of this chronological notice, let me refer to two other chronological notices, both contained in the *De altera vita*. Here D. Lucas tells us two things. One, that he had been present at Rome and had been privileged to adore the crucifix held in the hands of Pope Gregory IX : « Hanc ergo crucis formam Romae in manibus gloriosi patris Gregorii papae noni cum multis millibus hominum videre et adorare merui : et in festo coenae Dominicae ab ipso Papa sanctissimo benedici »[6]. The other, that two of the miracle stories he recorded he had heard in sermons preached by D. Elias, the Minister General of the Franciscan Order : « quaedam quae narrante viro sanctissimo fratre Helia successore beatissimi patris Francisci didici litteris tradere dignum duxi »[7].

Now we know that these experiences of his must date from before early 1233 when he returned to León to do battle with the heretics there. Can we be more precise though ? I think we can. Or at least we can try. For example, it is unlikely that it was on *Jeudi saint* in the year

---

patrum Augustini, Hieronymi, Isidori & Bernardi opuscula minora corrumpere, subtrahendo vera, & adiiciendo falsa... » : *De altera vita* [=*DAV*], iii. 17, Ingolstadt 1612, p. 182.
4. Peter LINEHAN, *History and the Historians of Medieval Spain*, Oxford, 1993, chap. 11 *passim*.
5. *CM*, p. 3, 55-57.
6. *DAV*, ii. 10, p. 96.
7. *Ibid.*, iii. 14, 15, p. 178, 180.

1227 that Lucas witnessed Gregory IX exposing the crucifix at Rome, if only because it was not until three days after that that the pope was crowned: unlikely therefore, though not impossible. But the years 1229 and 1232 *are* impossible. At Easter 1229 Gregory IX was at Perugia, and at Easter 1232 he was at Rieti. This leaves as possible dates the years 1228, 1230, 1231 and 1233, in all of which the pontiff spent Easter at Rome. And of these four possibilities, *prima facie* 1233 appears the most probable because in the year 1233, and *only* in that year during Gregory IX's pontificate was D. Elias Minister General of the Franciscans.

But only *prima facie*, because, by his own account, by Easter 1233 Lucas had left Rome and was back at León[8]. We are therefore forced to the conclusion that it was in either 1228 or 1230 or 1231 that D. Lucas enjoyed his Roman Easter, and that when he heard Elias preaching, Elias did *not* in fact occupy the Ministership General of the Order (the office he had held between 1221 and 1227 and was to hold again between 1232 and 1239)[9]. And indeed, at any time between 1234 and 1239 (and these were the years during which he must have completed his text of the *De altera vita*) it would have been wholly natural for him to have referred to Elias as he was then, at the time of writing, rather than as he had not been at the time to which Lucas was referring, the unspecified date between the years 1227 and 1232.

So we are left with three possibilities: 1228, 1230 and 1231. As between these, we have no means of judging. But I am drawn to one or other of 1230 and 1231, though my reason for being so drawn is in fact not a reason at all but rather a conjecture. I just wonder whether D. Lucas may not have been recruited by the papal legate Cardinal Jean d'Abbeville on the occasion of the latter's visit to León in August 1229[10]. After all, we know that Jean d'Abbeville was a collector of talent. He it was who during his Spanish legation discovered Ramón de Peñafort and took him back with him to Rome in the autumn of 1229. We also know that he recruited others[11]. May it therefore not be that he recruited Lucas too? It would have made sense. For Lucas after all was something of a scholar. And not only something of a scholar. Also

8. *Ibid.*, iii. 9. *Cf.* Michael Lawrence HOLLAS, *Lucas of Tuy and Thirteenth Century León*, Ph.D. diss., Yale University, 1985, p. 33, n. 50, suggesting inconsistently that in 1234 Lucas was still at Rome.
9. R. B. BROOKE, *Early Franciscan Government. Elias to Bonaventure*, Cambridge, 1959, p. 112, 118, 161-167.
10. Peter LINEHAN, *The Spanish Church and the Papacy in the Thirteenth Century*, Cambridge, 1971, p. 25.
11. *Id.*, « A papal legation and its aftermath: Cardinal John of Abbeville in Spain and Portugal, 1228-1229 », in: *Studi E. Cortese* (in press).

something of a theological scholar; the continuator of the work of his patron, Santo Martino de León, and therefore committed to that branch of scholarship to which Jean d'Abbeville himself, the former Parisian theologian, was himself committed. I note in passing that Jean d'Abbeville is the *only* modern non-Spanish personality mentioned by D. Lucas in his Chronicle[12].

And while in the realm of speculation, let me suggest a further possibility: the possibility that the future bishop of Túy's origins were neither Leonese nor even Spanish. Doubtless, to suggest as much of the fervent Leonese patriot will appear perverse in the extreme. Yet does not that very fervour admit of the possibility? « The deacon doth protest too much, methinks ». Is there not something of the ardour of the *arriviste* about him, something of the commitment of the *converso*? Indeed, in that respect, does not his patriotism rather closely resemble that of another immigrant, the Toledan patriotism of his Navarrese contemporary, D. Rodrigo Jiménez de Rada?

Certainly, « Lucas » was an unusual name for a Leonese. With the assistance of Dr Fernández Catón's splendid edition of the documentation of León cathedral archive, it can be established, firstly, that in something over six hundred instruments belonging to the century prior to the year 1240 the name occurs just seven times[13], and further, that of those seven instances only one is relevant to the present enquiry: the Master Lucas who witnessed an agreement at León in March 1232. May he have been our man?[14] And if he was, had he come there from abroad, as one of those *sapientes a Galliis et Ytalia* whom, as his historiographical sparring-partner D. Rodrigo reports, Alfonso VIII of Castile had recruited to staff the *studium* at Palencia – whenever that was, whether before that monarch's Gascon campaign of 1205-6, as D. Rodrigo seems to indicate[15], or, as reported by Lucas, during the Palencian pontificate of D. Tello Tellez de Meneses, and therefore between 1208 (or even 1212) and Alfonso VIII's death in

12. *CM*, p. 114-116.
13. *Colección documental del Archivo de la catedral de León (775-1230)* [=*CDL*], V *(1109-1187)*, ed. J. M. FERNÁNDEZ CATÓN *et al.*, León, 1987, n°s 1614, 1758, 1873, 1884, 2026 (Domnus Lucas); 1946 (Lucas); 1992 (Magister Lucas). My warm thanks go to Dr Fernández Catón for providing me with these references in advance of the publication of the indices to the volumes covering these years. Apart from the case of the tenth-century « Luga » (198), all earlier references are to the Evangelist of that name. The earliest worthy of the name recorded in the cathedral is of the year 1288: M. Herrero Jiménez, *CDL. Obituarios medievales*, León, 1994, p. 360.
14. Frustratingly, a second mention of (the same?) Master Lucas (2101) cannot be dated more precisely than to 1227-1250.
15. *Historia de rebus Hispanie sive Historia Gothica* [=*DRH*], VII. 34, ed. J. FERNÁNDEZ VALVERDE, CCCM 72, 1987, p. 256.

1214 (which with the country in the state it was was the worst of times for such a lavish initiative)[16]. It is not my purpose here to become embroiled either in that contentious question, however, or in the larger issue in which (as of late has been the case) it is all too liable to become submerged, namely Palencia's pre-Alfonsine existence as an intellectual centre[17]. All I wish to do here is to observe that, if D. Lucas's origins were indeed extra-peninsular, then he would not have felt out of place in Palencia, where Italians had been prominent in the chapter since the late 1170s and D. Tello's immediate episcopal predecessor, Ardericus, had been Milanese[18]. Perhaps his own contemporary in the see of Coimbra, Master Tiburcius (†1246), a man with a name as un-Portuguese as Lucas's was un-Leonese, was from beyond the Pyrenees too[19]. Perhaps it was not to Palencia that he had come, but rather to Salamanca, as one of those outstanding theologians whom « salutary counsel » had persuaded Alfonso IX of León to bring to that place[20]. And in that case, whose had that « salutary counsel » been? In other words – always supposing that, like his victim, the theological hammer of the heretic Arnaldus also came de confinibus Galliae (or even from somewhere beyond) – was the basis of don Lucas's relationship with doña Berenguela a prior association with her father or with her sometime husband? Was it with Alfonso VIII of Castile or with Alfonso IX of León?

16. « Eo tempore rex Adefonsus evocavit magistros theologicos, & aliarum artium liberalium, & Palentiae scholas constituit procurante reverendissimo & nobilissimo viro Tellione eiusdem civitatis Episcopo »: CM, p. 109, 26-28. (D. Tello was still bishop-elect in July 1212: D. MANSILLA, La documentación pontificia hasta Inocencio III (965-1216), Rome, 1955, n° 485.)
17. For a critical review of recent debate on the matter arising from interest in the possibility that the Italian jurist Hugolino de Sesso taught there sometime after the mid-1180s, see A. IGLESIA FERREIROS, « Rex superiorem non recognoscens. Hugolino de Sesso y el Studium de Palencia », Initium, 3, 1998, p. 1-205, esp. p. 26ff. Cf. A. RUCQUOI, « La double vie de l'université de Palencia (c.1180-c.1250) », in: P. LINEHAN (ed.), Life, Law and Letters: Historical Studies in Honour of Antonio García y García, Rome, 1998 [Studia Gratiana, 29], p. 723-748.
18. Antonio GARCÍA Y GARCÍA, « El Studium Bononiense y la Península Ibérica », in : id., Iglesia, sociedad y derecho, i, Salamanca, 1985, p. 49; D. MAFFEI, « Fra Cremona, Montpellier e Palencia nel secolo XII. Ricerche su Ugolino da Sesso », Rivista Internazionale di Diritto Comune, 1, 1990, p. 18-19; Peter LINEHAN, History and the Historians, p. 309.
19. Cf. Peter LINEHAN, Spanish Church and the Papacy, p. 148, n. 4, where Portuguese origins are inferred from his presence amongst Portuguese churchmen at the papal curia in June 1229. Thus also Ingo FLEISCH, Kirche, Königtum und gelehrtes Recht im hochmittelalterlichen Portugal, M.A. diss., Otto-Friedrich-Universität Bamberg, 1998, p. 176-180. Whether or not he had started life as « Thibaut » and was of French extraction, Master Tiburcius was unquestionably closely associated with Palencia. Successively canon, archdeacon and treasurer of that church prior to his election to Coimbra in 1234, when he fell out with Sancho II of Portugal it was there that he took refuge: [Lisbon,] A[rquivos] N[acionais]/T[orre do] T[ombo], Sé de Coimbra, 1ª incorporação, cx. 26, rolo 4.
20. « Hic salutari consilio euocauit magistros peritissimos in sacris scripturis: & constituit scholas fieri Salmantiae »: CM, p. 113, 56-57.

And, either way, are such speculations given support by what
D. Lucas himself tells us, again in the *De altera vita*, that he had once visited Paris, and the monastery of St Denis in particular?[21] Now because
of its relevance to the claims of the church of Toledo to apostolic and
therefore primatial status, the mention of St Denis is especially interesting. It is not that aspect of Lucas's presence in Paris that interests us here
however. What interests us here is the question *when* he was there: whether as a student of theology relatively early in his career, and perhaps
before he had ever set foot in Spain, or later, after he had established a
base at León to return to, possibly in the course of the same grand tour
during which he set eyes on Gregory IX and Master Elias? For, if the
latter – if it was in the early 1230s that he was in Paris – then he would
surely sooner or later have been summoned to wait upon the queen-
mother, Blanche de Castille: also known as Doña Blanca de Castilla,
the sister of Doña Berenguela, on whose instructions (*praeceptis*) it was
that at about this time or slightly later he embarked upon the composition of his Chronicle.

At about this time or slightly later. But when? To attempt to answer
that question, let us return to those intriguing references to Doña Berenguela in the prologue to the *Chronicon mundi*. What are we to make of
them? What Julio Puyol made of them was this:

> Es casi seguro que don Lucas empezó a escribir el *Chronicon mundi* entre los
> años 1197 y 1204, siendo regular en el monasterio de san Isidoro de León,
> pues según declara en el *Prólogo*, emprendió su obra por orden de doña
> Berenguela, esposa de Alfonso IX, y el matrimonio de estos monarcas,
> contraído a fines de 1197, fue anulado en los comienzos de 1204. Doña
> Berenguela ya no vivió desde entonces habitualmente en León, sino en ciu-
> dades castellanas, y no es probable que diera aquella orden después de la
> proclamación de Fernando III [that is to say, of the proclamation of Fer-
> nando III as king of León in the year 1230], porque el mismo don Lucas
> dice que él era diácono cuando principió a escribir la Crónica, y, por tanto,
> no es tampoco verosímil que en 1230, fechas de la citada proclamación,
> tuviese tal grado eclesiástico el que seis años más tarde iba a ser nombrado
> obispo de Túy[22].

Now since it cannot have been concluded earlier than the year 1236,
the year in which its narrative ends with the reconquest of Córdoba, if
Puyol was correct in his view the *Chronicon mundi* must have been almost
forty years in the writing. Almost forty years. A long time to spend over
the writing of a single book – even in the case of an author who had
other works in progress on his table over the decades. Indeed, a *very* long

21. *DAV*, ii, 11, p. 103.
22. *Crónica de España por Lucas, obispo de Túy*, Madrid, 1926, p. V, n. 1.

time: about two-thirds of an individual's normal life-span in the early 13th century.

Is this credible? Plainly not. As to the starting point, it was pointed out by Dr Michael Hollas in 1985 that the description of Doña Berenguela as *Hispaniarum regina* indicates not the years 1197/1204, when that lady was so fully occupied bearing children for Alfonso IX of León, the man who was not her canonical husband, but rather a date after the year 1230 when one of those children, Fernando III, was king of both Castile and León, and when, not as queen but as queen mother, she really did deserve the title *Hispaniarum regina*[23]. And, as well as this, there is another correction to be made to Puyol's account of the matter: a rare lapse on the part of that fine scholar. This is the assumption that because D. Lucas describes himself in his prologue as *diaconus*, that prologue must have been written some time before 1236, the year in which, as Puyol mistakenly thought, D. Lucas became bishop of Túy (« *No es* [...] *verosímil que* [...] *tuviese tal grado eclesiástico el que seis años más tarde iba a ser nombrado obispo de Túy.* »). For in fact, not only was it not until 1239 that Lucas was « elected » bishop. It was also of course entirely normal for thirteenth-century Spanish bishops – and for thirteenth-century bishops elsewhere for that matter, including bishops of Rome – to remain deacons until the very day of their episcopal consecration. On the day of his election as pope Innocent III was not yet a priest.

So on those grounds alone Puyol's argument dissolves. And, in any case, it must have been *after* 1236 that D. Lucas composed the prologue to his chronicle, since surely that was not the first but rather the last part of it that he wrote. That is not to say of course that he may not have been at work on the *text* before 1230. That is certainly a possibility – and the need to accommodate his foreign travels as well as the composition of his hagiographical and theological works in these years, may even make it a necessity. Indeed, in view of D. Rodrigo's evident dependence on him, so too may the verdict of the editor of *DRH* that D. Rodrigo had completed a first draft of his work before the death of Alfonso IX of León in September 1229[24]. On the other hand, it has to be allowed

---

23. Peter LINEHAN, *History and the Historians*, p. 256-258; Michael L. HOLLAS, *Lucas of Túy*, p. 31-32.

24. FERNÁNDEZ VALVERDE, XVI-XVII. According to this hypothesis, and having regard to the routine nature of the limited number of instances noted by the editor in which his (pre-1229) MS. I (« *que sería el borrador* ») differs from the 1243 « *redacción definitiva* » (xvii-xviii), in 1229 D. Lucas's chronicle must have been substantially up-to-date. (There is, for example, no significant difference between the accounts in MS. I and manuscripts of Fernández Valverde's « *redacción definitiva* » of the, for D. Rodrigo, crucial issue of papal confirmation of Toledo's primacy in the reign of Chindasvinth [as opposed to D. Lucas's report that resolution of the question had been referred to *beneplacitum pontificum Hispanorum*] : *DRH* II. 21

that if what prompted Doña Berenguela to commission a work to celebrate León's historical identity was the threat to that identity presented by its union with Castille in the person of Fernando III, then the process of composition can hardly have begun until *after* the death of Fernando's father. In either case, however, all the indications are that that process must have begun twenty or even thirty years later than the date proposed by Puyol.

When did it end though? When did D. Lucas lay down his fertile pen? The fact that his narrative proper terminates with the reconquest of Córdoba in 1236 is certainly no indication that it was in that year that Lucas completed work on his Chronicle[25]. D. Lucas was not a journalist. If anything has been established over the last ten years or so it is that D. Lucas was not a journalist. He was a historian and, more than that, he was a historian with a mission, *un historien engagé* for whom the reconquest of Córdoba completed a cycle, closed a symbolic circle. No doubt, the reconquest of Seville would have completed it, and have closed it even more symbolically. And perhaps after 1236 D. Lucas hung on, waiting for the news that failed to arrive, the news that would have provided his narrative with a conclusion of perfect poetic justice: the news that Seville – St Isidore's Seville – had been restored to Christian control by a *Leonese* king.

As I say, it was the news that failed to arrive. So D. Lucas drew the line across his narrative in 1236. But *when* did he draw that line? Then, in 1236? Or later? On a practical level, of course, the *terminus ante quem* might be supposed to have been determined by his promotion to Túy and the separation, which that seems necessarily to have implied, from the books he needed for the perfection of his work. But again, we must not jump to conclusions. Instead, we must ask questions. And we must first observe that, in fact, the one thing did *not* necessarily imply the other. For if, as Enrique Flórez supposed and all later writers on the subject have supposed after him, it was indeed Doña Berenguela who secured his episcopal see for D. Lucas[26], then it would indeed have been

---

[ed. cit., p. 71] ; *CM*, p. 55, 3; Peter LINEHAN, *History and the Historians*, p. 378-80.) In view of D. Rodrigo's regular dependence on *CM* (in Fernández Valverdes own words, « [*el*] *telón de fondo en el que se van enmarcando las demás crónicas* » [xxxiii]), if that author's reasoning is correct then in 1229 D. Lucas's text must not only have been only up-to-date but also virtually in its final form. *Cf.* Peter LINEHAN, « On further thought: Lucas of Tuy, Rodrigo of Toledo and the Alfonsine histories », *Anuario de Estudios Medievales*, 27 (1), 1997, p. 428-429.

25. *Pace* Georges MARTIN, according to whom « *achève le* Chronicon Mundi » in this year : *Les Juges de Castille. Mentalités et discours historique dans l'Espagne médiévale*, Paris : Klincksieck, 1992, p. 201.

26. « Con esto debemos suponerla complacida de la elección para la Mitra » : *E[spaña] S[agrada]*, XXII, Madrid, 1767, p. 126.

remarkable if the queen who had commissioned the history of the kingdom of León could not equally have arranged for its author to have
books from S. Isidoro de León on long loan in order to enable him to
finish it.

But Doña Berenguela's responsibility for D. Lucas's advancement is
anyway no more than that: a supposition – and one which deserves to
be questioned on at least two grounds. First, if the queen mother was
indeed the principal promotor of his interests, is it not surprising that
Túy was the best she could do for him? And secondly, why the lengthy
wait for his election to be confirmed? Although bishop-elect of Túy by
December 1239, not until sometime between September 1240 and
March 1241 was D. Lucas acknowledged by Fernando III's chancery as
its bishop[27]. If indeed the queen-mother was promoting the matter, why
was this? And whether she was or not, what was the problem?

There might have been any number of explanations: a challenge
from within the chapter; complications involving the archbishop of
Braga whose suffragan the bishop of Túy was although his see was
situated in Leonese territory; the extreme difficulty of securing papal
confirmation at a time when the Emperor Frederick II was at the gates
of Rome and bishops *en route* for Pope Gregory IX's council were being
cast into imperial prisons. But, whatever the reason, not until April and
October 1242 is D. Lucas's presence in his episcopal city attested, by the
Túy charter cited by Hollas on the first occasion, and on the second by
another – lacking an episcopal seal unfortunately; and how much that
seal might have told us about him! – amongst the Braga *fonds* now in the
national archive at Lisbon[28].

And the evidence provided by the records of the Cistercian house of
Armenteira tells the same story. Time out of mind, bishops of Tuy had
been cited in the dating clauses of charters preserved in the Armenteira
archive. But between the last mention of D. Lucas's predecessor,

27. The charter in favour of the monastery of Oya, O. Cist., printed by Flórez (*ibid.*, p. 284-
285), now in [Madrid,] A[rchivo] H[istórico] N[acional], Clero, carp. 1799/19, is dated
« sub era .M.CC.LXX.VII. [AD 1239] mense decembris... electo Tudensi ». The previous
charter in the same *carpeta* (1799/18), however, penned by a different scribe, is dated « sub era
.M.CC.LXX.VII [...] episcopo in Tuda domino Luco [sic] ». Unreported by Flórez, and
misreported by F. Avila y La Cueva in his manuscript *Historia civil y eclesiástica de la ciudad de Tuy
y su obispado* (1852; Arquivo da Catedral de Tui. Facsimile edn, n.p., 1995), iii. 211, as well as
demonstrating the unfamiliarity of local scribes with the name « Lucas », this latter would
seem to imply that D. Lucas was consecrated sometime during the month of December
1239. For the royal chancery evidence, see Julio GONZÁLEZ, *Reinado y diplomas de Fernando
III*, iii, Córdoba, 1986, nᵒˢ 666, 672.
28. Michael L. HOLLAS, *Lucas of Tuy*, p. 39; ANTT, Mitra de Braga, maço 3, doc. 88
(« Actum est hoc Tude, in domibus episcopi per manus Petri Menendi publici notarii iamdicti
episcopi, sub era .M.CC.LXXX. [1242] quinto nonas obtubris [sic] »).

D. Esteban, in November 1236, and April 1242 when (as at Túy itself)
D. Lucas surfaces for the first time, bishops of Túy are notable by their
absence[29]. Instead, as late as April 1241, the archbishop of Compostela,
D. Juan Arias, is invoked[30].

Sparse though it is, therefore, the evidence is unanimous in indicating
that from 1239 until sometime between April 1241 and April 1242,
D. Lucas was not at Túy. He may have been at the court of Fernando
III – though we do not *know* that he was, as Hollas states, at least for the
reason adduced by Hollas, namely the inclusion of his name amongst
the *confirmantes* of royal privileges[31]. For that is no reason at all. In the
early 1240s all that such lists of *confirmantes* do is to establish the fact of
the individual's existence *somewhere* at the date in question[32].

And not only does he appear not to have been at Túy between 1239
and 1241/2. It has also to be questioned whether prior to 1242 he had
any formal connexion with the place at all. The regularly repeated
assertion that before his appointment as its bishop D. Lucas was *magister
scolarum* of Túy depends entirely on Flórez's reading of a single charter
– the afore-mentioned charter of sale to the Cistercian house of Oya,
dated 1239 *mense decembris* and witnessed presumably at that foundation
on the estuary of the Ria de Vigo to the north-west of his episcopal
city[33]. And Flórez's authority settled the matter. No one has looked at
that brief charter since 1767 when Flórez published it. No one has
noticed that Flórez's edition is flawed in nine places, one of which has
misled students of D. Lucas from that day to this, namely his transcription of the dating clause, which goes as follows:

> Rege nostro Fernando in Castella & in Legione regnante. Electo Tudensi L.
> Magistro Scholarum. Meuryno, J. Fernandi. Maiordomo, F. Johannis.

But this is not what the charter says. What it says is:

---

29. AHN, Clero, carp. 1754/1 (« S. Tuda [sic] episcopo, era [1274] .VI. id nouembris ») ;
1754/17 : a carta venditionis « era [1280]... mense aprilis » (Regnante regi .F. in castella et
in Legione. Episcopo domino Luca in tuda, tenente toronio domino .F. iohannis. maiordomo
suo maioris .F. menendi).
30. AHN, Clero, carp. 1754/15.
31. Michael L. HOLLAS, *Lucas of Tuy*, p. 39, dating this earliest supposed attendance at
court to Aug. 1242.
32. *Pace* Patrick HENRIET, « Hagiographie et politique à León au début du XIIIe siècle : les
chanoines réguliers de Saint-Isidore et la prise de Baeza », *Revue Mabillon*, n.s. 8 (= t. 69),
1997, p. 57-58 : « Il ne réside cependant que par intermittence [à Túy] et semble avoir suivi
régulièrement le roi Ferdinand III. Entre 1241 et 1249, en effet, il souscrit de nombreux
diplômes royaux à Cordoue, Tolède, Madrid, Burgos, Valladolid. Il est présent au siège de
Jaén (1245-1246) et lors de la prise de Séville (1248) ».
33. *ES*, XXII, p. 126, 284-285.

Rege nostro domino .F. in Castella et in Legione regnante, electo Tudensi .L. magistroscolarum. meiryno .J. Fernadi. maiordomo .F. iohannis[34].

As will be seen, by omitting the *punctum* before the abbreviation « L. », Flórez conflated two individuals – the unnamed bishop-elect and the *magister scolarum* « L. » – into the impossible diplomatic hybrid the « bishop-elect-and *magister scolarum*-L(ucas) ». It is from this evidence, and from this alone, that the belief that D. Lucas was *magister scolarum* of Túy before he was its bishop derives.

To return to the question of D. Lucas' whereabouts between 1239 and April 1242. If he was not at Túy, could he perhaps have been still at León and still at work on his Chronicle? The hypothesis is one against the epigraph to the prologue of his Chronicle would appear to provide a powerful argument. « Lvcae diaconi praefatio in Historiam seu Chronicam beati Isidori archiepiscopi Hispalensis », it reads, as printed by Mariana [*CM*, 1, 1]. Surely, it will be objected, after March 1241 (at the very latest)[35] *Bishop* Lucas would not have described himself as « deacon ». In fact, however, the apparently powerful argument is no argument at all. For the epigraph as printed by Mariana occurs in only one of the early manuscripts (BNM 10442 [=T] fol. 61r°) and the hand in which is written is clearly of the sixteenth century. None of the other early manuscripts refers to Lucas at all at this point[36]. And since the reference to himself later in his prologue [*CM*, 3, 57] refers to the time when at the queen's command he had embarked upon his labour (« … mihi Lucae indigno diacono, vt hoc perficerem, imperauit »), rather than to that at which he completed it, the hypothesis that he may still have been at work on it (and if still at work then in all likelihood still at León) as late as April 1242, remains intact.

And if he really was still at work on it there and then, an interesting possibility presents itself. For in April 1242 there was less than a year to elapse before the archbishop of Toledo, D. Rodrigo – the archbishop to whom D. Lucas paid such fulsome tribute – drew the line under *his* History and gave the *De rebus Hispanie* its colophon[37]. And the implications of the possibility are interesting too, if only because ever since the publication of Fernández Valverde's edition of the *De rebus Hispanie* in 1987 it has been apparent that D. Rodrigo's History was in large part based upon D. Lucas's Chronicle. Indeed, that much has been apparent ever since 1608 to anyone prepared to consult the existing editions of the

34. AHN, Clero, carp. 1799/19.
35. Above, n. 27.
36. For this information I am again obliged to Dr Falque.
37. *CM*, p. 113, 15; *DRH*, IX. 18, p. 301.

two works. It is not the lack of the then forthcoming edition of D. Rodrigo's History that was responsible for the remarkable claim advanced by Fernández Conde in 1985, that:

> Con relación a la prelación de Lucas de Túy y el toledano Jiménez de Rada, creo que es un estudio de historias paralelo; ambos utilizan fuentes comunes, en las que cada uno de ellos introduce tradiciones populares[38].

That anyone who has read the chronicles of D. Lucas and D. Rodrigo with any attention at all could ever have described them as parallel chronicles in this sense is a total mystery. And not only has it been abundantly clear at least since 1987 that D. Rodrigo's History was in large part *based upon* D. Lucas's Chronicle. More than that, it is now apparent that the one was based upon it *specifically in order to refute it*. I refer to Georges Martin's work on the subject and also to my own. It is that context that makes the possibility that D. Lucas may still have been at work in the spring of 1242 so particularly intriguing. In my *History and the Historians of Medieval Spain* I suggested that D. Rodrigo may first have become aware of the Chronicle of D. Lucas when his agent, the archpriest Mateo, visited S. Isidoro de León in 1239 in search of Visigothic evidences to be used in his litigation with the archbishop of Tarragona for jurisdiction over the church of Valencia[39]. What I failed to appreciate when I wrote that almost ten years ago, but what now seems to me a distinct possibility, is that when he visited S. Isidoro the archpriest Mateo found not just evidence of D. Lucas's Chronicle but also D. Lucas himself still at work on it[40].

And there is more to the matter than that. For we now have what then we did not have: the record of the *Ordinatio ecclesie Valentine* conveniently in print. We now know what it was that the archpriest Mateo brought back with him from S. Isidoro, certified as genuine by the abbot D. Martín and various of his canons. What he brought back with him was what you would expect, and what the Archbishop D. Rodrigo would have been especially interested in, and especially pleased with moreover, namely extracts from the bogus seventh-century *Hitación de Bamba* relating to the extent of the ecclesiastical provinces of Toledo

---

38. F. J. FERNÁNDEZ CONDE, « El biógrafo contemporáneo », p. 335. *Cf.* above, n. 24.

39. *Ut cit.*, p. 351.

40. Of course, according to what appear to be the inevitable implications of Fernández Valverde's codicological analysis (above, n. 24), D. Lucas had completed his labour all of ten years before. If that analysis is flawed, however, it might be surmised (there being no manuscript evidence in support) that in 1289 either D. Rodrigo was informed of D. Lucas's activity for the first time or that it was then revealed to him that the text that he had consulted (and perhaps borrowed from) at the earlier date had subsequently been revised to the church of Toledo's considerable detriment.

and Tarragona. For in the S. Isidoro text of the *Hitación* Valencia was assigned to Toledo: « Valentia teneat de Silva usque in Morvetrum, de mare usque Alpont... Isti inmediate subsunt archiepiscopo Toletano »[41]. And so it was assigned in D. Lucas's Chronicle: « Valentia teneat dc Sylua usque Muretum de mari usque Valerianum... Hae sunt sedes decem & nouem immediate subditae Archiepiscopo Toletano »[42]. So far so good, therefore – at least so far as the *Ordinatio ecclesie Valentine* was concerned.

And D. Rodrigo received many other certified copies of the *Hitación de Bamba*, from libraries from all over Spain, and all to the same effect. Yet despite the assistance it had provided in his litigation with Tarragona, in his History he made no mention of the *Hitación* at all. And why? On account – as I have suggested before – of the lethal qualification regarding Toledo's enjoyment of ecclesiastical primacy in at least one of the early MSS containing Lucas's version of it, to the effect that it should enjoy that primacy « for only so long as it pleases this holy [and wholly imaginary seventh-century] assembly », i.e. the Eleventh Council of Toledo allegedly – and (as D. Rodrigo feared) its thirteenth-century successors: « Toletum metropolis, regia sedes, inter ceteros Hispanie *quandiu huic sancto caetui placuerit* metropolitanos teneat primatiam »[43]. Thus in Salamanca, Universidad, MS. 2248 [= S] fol. 42v°a-b; and also in Mariana's edition (*CM*, 56, 48-9). Not in the S. Isidoro de León manuscript (MS. 20 [= I]), however. Here (fol. 62r°), the « lethal qualification » is absent – just as, interestingly, it is absent from T, fol. 120v°a: interestingly, because the Madrid manuscript is of the thirteenth century and was once in Toledo cathedral.

Once – but when? Until very recently, I was of the opinion that that ex-Toledo manuscript may be even more interesting still. Prior to a recent conversation I enjoyed with Dr Falque I was inclined to suspect that it was from this very manuscript of the *Chronicon mundi* that D. Rodrigo had compiled his History, my reason for doing so being the apparent resemblance of the marginal *sigla* in T to those in D. Rodrigo's copies of the *Historia scolastica* of Petrus Comestor and the Sermons of Stephen Langton now in the Biblioteca Pública de Soria (MSS 9, 10 respectively) and corresponding passages in the Escorial MS. (X.I.10) of his *Breviarium Historie Catholice*. I was encouraged in this supposition by

---

41. V. CASTELL MAIQUÉS (ed.), *Proceso sobre la ordenación de la iglesia valentina entre los arzobispos de Toledo, Rodrigo Jiménez de Rada, y de Tarragona, Pedro de Albalat (1238-1246)*, Valencia, 1995, i, p. 203-205.
42. *CM*, p. 56, 57-58... 57, 6-7. Mariana's text is evidently corrupt here. *Cf.* T, fol. 120v°a-b: *Valencia teneat de Alpont usque in Tarabellam.*
43. Peter LINEHAN, *History and the Historians*, p. 379.

the observable fact that in the case of T it is in particular alongside passages of the *Chronicon mundi* relating to the issue of ecclesiastical primacy that these *sigla* appear [44].
I have now to abandon that attractive hypothesis. I must do so on account of what I now know about the codicological status of the last two sentences of the *Chronicon* as printed by Mariana. These read as follows:

> O quam beatus iste Rex qui abstulit opprobrium Hispanorum, euertens solium barbarorum, & restituens Ecclesiae S. Iacobi campanas suas cum magno honore, quae multo tempore fuerant Cordubae, ob iniuriam & opprobrium nominis Christi. Acquisiuit etiam Rex Fernandus Turgellum, Sanctam crucem, Alhange, & quaedam alia castra (CM, 116, 35-41).

I had previously regarded the sentence beginning *Acquisiuit* as an artless scribal addition occuring in whichever manuscript of the *Chronicon* it was that Mariana had made use of, and in that manuscript alone. Referring as it does to events three years prior to the (for D. Lucas) supreme achievement of *beatus ille rex* in recovering Córdoba, after the symphonic finale of what precedes it (« ob iniuriam & opprobrium nominis Christi ») how otherwise could the jarring note struck by the trivial information that it imparts regarding the reconquest of Trujillo, etc., be regarded? Though it might altogether appropriately have been inserted at *CM*, 115, 32[45], for example, D. Lucas himself would never have appended so bathetic a notice to the up-beat finale of what I have above termed his narrative proper [46]. So I thought before my recent conversation with Dr Falque. And so I think still.

What I did now know before that conversation, however, but what I now know, is that it is not only in whatever manuscript of the *Chronicon mundi* that Mariana used that the *Acquisiuit* sentence occurs. It occurs in *all* the thirteenth-century manuscripts of the work that Dr Falque has consulted in the preparation of her edition, namely S, T, and I[47]. As

---

44. Peter LINEHAN, « Reflexiones sobre historiografía e historia en el siglo alfonsino », *Cahiers de linguistique hispanique médiévale*, 23, 2000, p. 106-108. Support for the conjecture is provided by the circumstance that the notice found in S to the effect that, « Romani Pontificis assensu », King Ervig decreed « vt nullus archiepiscopus Hispaniarum subderetur alicui primati nisi Romano » (*CM*, 69.6-7), is absent from both the León and the Toledo manuscripts.
45. For the reconquest of Trujillo, Alange and Santa Cruz in 1233-4, see Julio GONZÁLEZ, *Fernando III*, i, Córdoba, 1980, p. 318, 321.
46. *Cf.* the similar fate suffered by MS. *A* of *DRH*: FERNÁNDEZ VALVERDE, p. 301, *ap. ad* IX, 18.
47. In S, fol. 94rº, « Montor » (i.e. Montoro, reconquered in 1240/41: Julio GONZÁLEZ, *Fernando III*, i. p. 337) is inserted after « Alhange ». (Lacking as it does the final part of *CM*, B [Biblioteca de Catalunya, MS. 1003], also adjudged « s. XIII/XIV » by the learned editor, does not enter into the question. See Emma FALQUE, « Los testimonios manuscritos de Lucas de Tuy de la Biblioteca de Catalunya », *in*: I.-X. ADIEGO (ed.)., *Actes del XIII Simposi de la Secció catalana de la S.E.E.C., Tortosa, 15-18 d'abril de 1998*, Tortosa, 1999, p. 159-163.

Dr Falque will demonstrate in her forthcoming edition, all three derive from what she terms the *archetypon* of *CM*. That being so, and assuming (as I continue to assume) that its author would never have acquiesced in the undermining of the conclusion of his work we are inevitably driven to the conclusion that that *archetypon*, the parent of all the earliest surviving manuscripts of the *CM*, dates from after the death of D. Lucas in 1249. *Ergo* it cannot have been T, it must have been another copy of the work that D. Rodrigo used when compiling his History sometime before April 1243, a copy now lost along with so much else of his library[48]. (From all that has emerged of late regarding D. Lucas's possessive, not to say obsessive, personality, the alternative possibility that the *archetypon*, with its incongruous conclusion, was penned before April 1243 and without its author's knowledge, would appear to be extremely unlikely.) But there is more to it than that. For if the above reasoning is correct then we have to allow for the possibility that the text of *CM* in all the surviving earliest manuscripts is contaminated elsewhere also, with the result that when Dr Falque's edition is published what we will have will be not the text of the *Chronicon* as D. Lucas left it when he laid down his pen but a version of his work which was corrupt even before its text bifurcated in the manner indicated above[49]. And with that there will arise a further set of new questions to tax the ingenuity of the next generation of scholars and layers of fascinating problems for them to probe with their scalpels[50].

So even when we have Dr Falque's edition on our desks, doubts will remain, I suspect, and not only doubts about dates. In that spirit, allow me to throw one last brand onto the by now almost extinguished embers

48. T. ROJO ORCAJO, « La biblioteca del arzobispo don Rodrigo Jiménez de Rada y los manuscritos del monasterio de Santa María de Huerta », *Revista Eclesiástica*, 1, 1929, p. 196-219. Amongst other losses is that of D. Rodrigo's own annotated copy of his History which Ramón Menéndez Pidal believed he saw at Soria in 1894 : Peter LINEHAN, « Reflexiones », p. 107.
49. Above, p.212
50. Of which amongst the earliest needing to be addressed will be that of the true significance of the marginal *sigla* in T. If they do not date from D. Rodrigo's lifetime, and have nothing to do with the compilation of *DRH*, then to what context *do* they belong ? To Alfonso X's historical *atelier* of the next generation perhaps as they busied themselves with the *Estoria de España* ? Were they symbols employed by members of *el Rey Sabio's* team to indicate places where the text of *CM* had to be reconciled with that of *DRH* ? Is the existence of the three thirteenth-century MSS of *CM* to be similarly explained ? And if so, what of what appear to be the same *sigla* in D. Rodrigo's theological works ? Were these related to the preparation of the *General Estoria* ? Was D. Rodrigo's copy of the *Historia scolastica* borrowed by the king from S. María de Huerta just as in 1270 similar works were borrowed by him from Albelda and Nájera (*Memorial histórico español*, I, Madrid, 1851, p. 257-258) ? Or do the *sigla* in T and in the Soria MSS belong to a different context (or to different contexts) altogether ?

of scepticism. In view of the possibility (it is no more than that) that D. Lucas may still have been at work on his Chronicle as late as 1241-1242, *subtrahendo vera & adiiciendo falsa*, and for all the textual evidence that D. Rodrigo regularly acquired material from D. Lucas, can it still be so confidently assumed (I ask myself) that that is *always* the explanation of striking resemblances between their two accounts of Spain's past, and that *whenever* such resemblances are observable the only possible explanation is that it was to D. Lucas that D. Rodrigo was indebted?

Allow me, by way of conclusion and by means of a sort of parallel (or do I mean parable?), to illustrate the nature of the danger of that assumption. Imagine, 750 years from now, a scholar with Latin coming to this material for the first time – and that alone requires imagination: the prospect of a scholar with Latin coming to any material, even in *fifty* years' time. But, even so, imagine that scholar sooner or later discovering the works of Georges Martin and Peter Linehan, in both of which he finds some still quite interesting (not new any more but still quite interesting) ideas and suggestions about Lucas of Túy, Rodrigo of Toledo, and other things too. (And at this point you really do have to try hard. You have to imagine that 750 years from now there are still *libraries*.) He will mark, will that scholar, that Martin and Linehan published their books on the subject in the years 1992 and 1993. He will note the closeness of those dates. He will probably be able to establish that even in that far-off age communication between such distant centres as Paris and Cambridge was already possible; that there were horses, boats, even talk of telephones. And, above all, he will notice that, despite their ideological differences, the Frenchman and the Englishman shared a common interest in very *recherché* aspects of the remote Spanish past.

He will naturally assume therefore that in the years before 1992/1993 Martin and Linehan had been closely watching one another. He will scour the records for a late twentieth-century equivalent of Master Mateo travelling between Université Paris 13 and St John's College Cambridge, and between St John's College Cambridge and Université Paris 13. He will surely pay close attention to the role of Henriet in all this. He might even persuade himself that he has identified instances of plagiarism. What he may not appreciate, however, is the one aspect of the matter that actually counts for anything: namely that, although Martin and Linehan were both at work at the same time on the same material, neither was ever aware of what the other was up to.

I therefore live in hopes then that when that time comes and (assuming that academies there still be) the collective wisdom of the academy is concentrated on the question whether Linehan was influenced by Martin at this point or that, or Martin by Linehan at that point or this, the possibility of parallel development will not be entirely lost sight of, and that when all the circumstantial evidence to the contrary is presented there will be some contrary Abelard in the back row prepared to say aloud: « I doubt it »[51].

51. I am extremely grateful to Dr Emma Falque (Universidad de Sevilla), to Dr Maria João Branco (Universidade Aberta, Lisbon) and to Dr Alejandro Rodríguez de la Peña (Universidad Autónoma, Madrid), to Dr Falque for the supply of precious information, to Drs Branco and Rodríguez for supplying me with photocopies of material from the Lisbon and Madrid archives, and to all three for providing me with the benefit of their advice on an earlier draft of this paper.

# III

# Don Rodrigo and the government of the kingdom

Influenced no doubt by the celebrated description of him standing shoulder to shoulder with Alfonso VIII at the battle of Las Navas de Tolosa, don Rodrigo's admirers down the ages have concurred in treating him as more or less consubstantial with Fernando III and therefore as correspondingly immune from the judgement of historians[1]. As the mitred manifestation of the sainted ruler, the archbishop has accordingly

---

1. Thus E. ESTELLA ZALAYA regarding the shortcomings reported by his detractors, *inter alios* the Roman pontiff: «*Manchas tiene el sol y no deja de ser el astro rey, que fecunda e ilumina la tierra*» : *El fundador de la Catedral de Toledo : estudio histórico del pontificado de don Rodrigo Ximénez de Rada*, Toledo, 1926, p. 93.

been assumed to have occupied a central position in the government of the kingdom. I propose in what follows to question that assumption. I propose in particular to say something about the matter of the Castilian chancery and the transfer in 1230/31 of the office of chancellor of Castile which as archbishop of Toledo don Rodrigo enjoyed *ex officio*, from him to don Juan de Soria, abbot of Valladolid at the time. In his *History*, don Rodrigo says nothing of the matter. In his, don Julio González does have something to say about it. But I believe he wholly misunderstands the situation. What González says is this:

> *[Juan de Soria] no carecía de dotes ni dejaba de apreciarse en él su conocimiento de letras y de gentes. Algo de eso puede indicar que el arzobispo de Toledo, teniendo en su poder el privilegio real de 1 de julio de 1206 que le confería perpetuamente la real cancillería, no se opusiese al nombramiento de don Juan, si no fué él quien le recomendó para que el rey le colocase en tan importante puesto. Sin duda ambos eclesiásticos se conocían, al menos desde la época en que el arzobispo había ocupado la sede oxomense*[2].

According to González, therefore, not only did don Rodrigo not oppose the nomination of Juan de Soria for « *tan importante puesto* ». He may even have recommended his appointment to the king. Let us consider the plausibility of such a scenario.

Now of course the process under consideration, which involved the appropriation of not just one chancery but two, for the chancery of the kingdom of León was also involved – is related to the question which exercised Derek Lomax, and more recently has exercised both Roger Wright and Francisco Hernández, regarding the *language* of Fernando's chancery and the process of the transformation from Latin to the vernacular over this period[3]. But that, I suggest, is a consideration secondary to – and indeed to a degree dependent upon – the issue of *control* of those institutions. For what we see in 1231 is a masterful king taking control of the administration of the two kingdoms recently reunited in his person.

According to the formal record, so far as don Rodrigo was concerned the transfer of the Castilian chancery was done with his full acquiescence. When the matter was regularized on the first day of 1231[4], the set-

2. J. GONZÁLEZ, *Reinado y diplomas de Fernando III*, 3 vol., Córdoba, 1980-1986, t. 1, p. 506.

3. See D. W. LOMAX, « La lengua oficial de Castilla », in: *Actele celui de-al XII-lea congres internacional de lingvistica ·i filologie romanica*, t. 2, Bucaresti, 1971, p. 411-417; R. WRIGHT, « Latin and romance in the Castilian chancery (1180-1230) », *Bulletin of Hispanic studies* (Liverpool), 73, 1996, p. 115-128, p. 121-123; *id.*, *El tratado de Cabreros (1206): estudio sociofilológico de una reforma ortográfica* [*Papers of the medieval Hispanic research seminar*, 19], London: Queen Mary and Westfield College, 2000, p. 99-116; F. J. HERNÁNDEZ, « Sobre los orígenes del español escrito », *Voz y letra*, 10, 1999, p. 133-166, esp. p. 152-153.

4. « anno Incarnationis dominice MM.CC.XXX; era M.CC.LX.nona »: GONZÁLEZ, *Reinado*, nº 279.

tlement was represented as a private treaty voluntarily entered into by both parties, with Juan de Soria stating that he had received from the other « misericorditer » the « chancery of the lord king of Castile » which belonged to him, the archbishop, by right (« ad uos de iure spectantem ») ; that the concession was to the prejudice neither of the archbishop nor of his successors ; and that on don Juan's death or in the event of his appointment to « pontifical honour » outside (but not inside) the province of Toledo the chancery was then to revert to whoever was archbishop.

These formal assurances have been accepted at face-value by Julio González as well as by such other historians as have noticed the matter at all. No account seems to have been taken of the improbability of don Rodrigo, the resourceful defender of Toledo's primacy, willingly divesting himself of the highly symbolic office that in 1183 one of his predecessors had described as « his », and which in July 1206 Alfonso VIII had confirmed, acknowledging that the archbishop was free to dispose of it – « to concede it canonically » – as he wished[5]. That is, enjoying, in Roman law terms, not only *ususfructus* of the office but also *dominium* and *possessio*. And in July 1206 Alfonso VIII had sufficient Roman lawyers in his entourage to enable him to appreciate what all that meant[6].

And twenty-four years later, at Guadalajara on 12 April 1230, Fernando III confirmed that privilege of his « most famous grandfather » :

> ... Supradictum itaque priuilegium ego supradictus rex Ferrandus concedo, approbo, roboro et confirmo, instituens quod perpetuam obtineat firmitatem, ita tamen quod ex speciali gratia quam uos, domne R. archiepiscope, ad preces meas fecistis domno Iohanni, dilecto cancellario meo, abbati Vallisoleti, uos eam canonice concessistis, etiam in hoc casu quod, si eum ad pontificalem dignitatem in Toletana prouincia assumi contigerit, omnibus diebis uite sue plene et pacifice tenendam, nullum uobis uel successoribus uestris preiudicium generetur, immo altero istorum contingente, uidelicet, dicto cancellario uiam uniuerse carnis ingresso uel in alia prouincia ad pontificalem dignitatem assumpto, dicta cancellaria sicut superius continetur ad uos uel ad successores uestros libere redeat et quiete [...] Facta carta apud Guadalfaiaram, reg. exp., XII die aprilis, era M.CC.LX.octaua[7].

There are two points to be noticed here : (i) the fact that the chancery is being conveyed at Fernando's instigation (« ad preces meas ») ; and (ii) the date of the transaction. For that transaction does not *follow* the agreement to which it corresponds (the agreement dated 1 January 1231). It

5. F.J. HERNÁNDEZ, *Los cartularios de Toledo. Catálogo documental*, revised ed. [*CT*], Madrid, 1996, n° 204 ; A. MILLARES CARLO, « La cancillería real en León y Castilla hasta fines del reinado de Fernando III », *Anuario de historia del derecho español*, 3, 1926, p. 277. See Peter LINEHAN, *History and the historians of medieval Spain*, Oxford, 1993, chap. 10-12.

6. *Ibid.*, p. 305-307.

7. GONZÁLEZ, *Reinado*, n° 265.

*precedes* it, by as much as eight months. It precedes it, just as it anticipates the event that occasioned the need for it, namely the reunion of the kingdoms of Castile and León in the person of Fernando III on the death of his father Alfonso IX – for in April 1230 Alfonso IX still had five months of life left to him[8].

In short, here was the response to a practical need to unify the civil services of the two kingdoms in one safe pair of hands – to unify the kingdoms' chanceries, as well as the kingdoms themselves, in a single person. And the initiative was the king's. By an identical process, between January and September 1231 the archbishop of Compostela's possession of the Leonese chancery was also transferred to the abbot of Valladolid, with again the formal agreement between the contracting parties lagging months behind the king's ritual acknowledgement of the archbishop's rights in the matter[9].

Now at one level the bureaucratic revolution of 1230-31 may be seen as the first stage of that process of administrative unification which in the next reign Alfonso X's juridical reforms were to drive onto the rocks. « Quo uolunt reges uadunt leges » : the proverb quoted by don Rodrigo in his account of the abrogation of the Visigothic liturgy[10] had been turned on himself. «*Allá van leyes do quieren reyes*» – though by that token on the death of Juan de Soria in October 1246, don Rodrigo ought to have recovered the chancery, since that was what Fernando III had promised in his solemn privilege of April 1230 : that the chancery would revert to him or his successor «libere et quiete». But in 1246 that did not happen. Nor had it done so by the time of don Rodrigo's death in June 1247[11]. Instead, in due course the chancery passed to Pedro Martínez, who had been Juan de Soria's close associate in that department of state, and who in 1246 was moreover on his way to becoming bishop of Jaén[12]. And this is of interest.

It is of interest for the following reason. On 2 January 1231 (that is, on the very next day after his surrender of the chancery), don Rodrigo and the church of Toledo received from the king a significant grant of terri-

---

8. No particular significance is to be attached to the fact that it is in respect of the death of Alfonso IX that the second redaction of don Rodrigo's *History* differs most markedly from the first : RODERICI XIMENII DE RADA *Historia de rebus Hispanie sive Historia gothica* [*DRH*], J. FERNÁNDEZ VALVERDE (ed.), CCCM, 72, 1987, p. xvi-xvii.

9. MILLARES CARLO, « Cancillería », p. 287-288 ; GONZÁLEZ, *Reinado*, n° 299.

10. *DRH*, VI, 25.

11. When don Rodrigo confirmed new statutes for the chapter of Toledo in Jan. 1247, he did so simply as archbishop and primate : *CT*, n° 478.

12. Describing him as «domini regis notarius», in September 1246 Juan de Soria appointed Pedro Martínez one of the executors of will : L. SERRANO, « El canciller de Fernando III de Castilla », *Hispania*, 1(5), 1940-41, p. 3-40, p. 37.

tory in the *término* of Baeza in the eastern part of the kingdom of Jaén, and later that same month the towns and territories of Quesada and Toya in the same region (both letters being confirmed by Juan de Soria, «domini regis cancellarius», of course)[13]. In 1231 Baeza had been in Christian hands for five years and was under the command of Lope Díaz de Haro, *señor de Vizcaya*. Quesada was still in enemy hands and it was for don Rodrigo the warrior to make the king's grant a reality. This he did, at his own expense, that spring, as he reports in his *History*[14], giving rise to the creation of the *adelantamiento de Cazorla*.

But if, as seems possible, these royal grants were intended to compensate the church of Toledo for the archbishop's loss of the chancery – though, as Francisco Hernández demonstrates in these pages, grants to God, the Blessed Virgin and don Rodrigo were unlikely to benefit the *chapter* of Toledo[15] – again the archbishop seems to have been wounded by Juan de Soria where it really hurt, in his most sensitive parts, by having his metropolitan jurisdiction in the see of Jaén infringed be means of the annexation of its bishopric to the royal chancery and the conversion of its chapter into a twilight home for superannuated civil servants.

When in 1290 the archbishop of Seville attempted to deprive the archbishop of Toledo of the sees of Córdoba and Jaén, Sancho IV would intervene in Toledo's favour, saying that his grandfather don Fernando had «given» those sees to Toledo[16]. In fact, Toledo's effective authority over Jaén had been undermined long since. As the local members of the chapter complained in the famous letter they sent to archbishop Gonzalo Pérez in 1283-1284, «*el primer prelado que ouo el obispado de Jahen fue el obispo don Domingo et del a aca ffueron todos de Soria*»[17].

On Fernando III's reconquest of Jaén in 1246 there was a bishop in waiting in the person of don Domingo, bishop of Baeza since 1229/30, who was a Dominican friar and as such an altogether suitable prelate for that frontier place, one might have thought. But not so. For, as pope Innocent IV wrote in the first week of January 1246 – that is, during the siege of Jaén to which the see of Baeza was due to be transferred – «it had reached his [the pope's] ears» that don Domingo was a paralytic incapable of pastoral exertions. Accordingly, the pope provided him with the

---

13. GONZÁLEZ, *Reinado*, n° 281, 295 («Deo et beate Marie semper virgini, in cuius honore fundata est ecclesia, uobisque domno Roderico, Toletane sedis archiepiscopo, Hyspaniarum primati, et uestris successoribus in perpetuum»).
14. *DRH*, IX, 15.
15. See «La hora de don Rodrigo».
16. F. J. HERNÁNDEZ and Peter LINEHAN, *The Mozarabic Cardinal: the life and times of Gonzalo Pérez Gudiel*, Florence, 2003, p. 272.
17. Toledo, Archivo de la Catedral, X.1.D.2.1 (defectively, M. NIETO CUMPLIDO (ed.), *Orígenes del regionalismo andaluz*, Córdoba, 1979, p. 136-139).

assistance of the dean of Baeza as coadjutor in order to ensure that the pastoral needs of that « nouella plantatio » were suitably attended to. Three years later, however, the pope had to write again, having had it reported to him that, for all his paralysis, don Domingo remained sufficiently mobile to be leading « a detestable existence, displeasing in the sight of both God and men » and had made off with the books and ornaments of his church[18].

In other words, the bishop of Baeza who in January 1246 had been recommended by the pontiff to console himself in his affliction by reflecting on the example of Job was in fact living the life of Lazarus, and those earlier reports to Rome about his state of health had been grossly exaggerated.

And by whom can such exaggerated reports have been provided in late 1245 or early 1246, while the siege of Jaén was in progress, other than by Fernando III, which is to say by his chancellor Juan de Soria, that same Juan de Soria, who throughout the 1230s had been involved as papal judge delegate in adjudicating boundary disputes between don Rodrigo and bishop Domingo[19], and according to whose *History* don Domingo had been fit enough in 1236 to move « festinanter » to the assistance of the Christian uprising in Córdoba[20]? And for what purpose may the chancellor have intervened in the see of Jaén, other than to clear the way there for don Pedro Martínez, his own successor as Fernando's chancellor?

So maybe the historians are guilty of exaggeration too, of exaggerating don Rodrigo's importance in affairs of state, at least in the later years of the reign. Let us compare the situation of 1237 and 1246. In 1237 the chapter of León secured papal agreement to the translation of Juan de Soria from the see of Osma to the see of León[21]. But then Fernando III intervened and eight months later caused Gregory IX to change his mind. And why did the king wish the pope to change his mind? Ostensibly for two reasons. First, that the bishop was a « man of great counsel » and « useful and necessary to him and his kingdom », and secondly that the church of Osma could not sustain the loss of such a bishop[22]. But the second of these reasons was fatuous. Since don Juan was permanently at court anyway, what did it matter to the king where he had his see? What

18. Peter LINEHAN, « Don Juan de Soria: unas apostillas », *in: VIII congreso de estudios medievales*, Ávila, 2003.

19. M. DE XIMENA, *Catálogo de los obispos de las iglesias catedrales de la diócesi de Jaén y Annales eclesiasticos deste obispado*, Madrid, 1654, p. 130-141.

20. *Crónica latina de los reyes de Castilla*, L. CHARLO BREA (ed.), Cádiz, 1984, p. 77 (= *id.* (ed.), *Chronica hispana saeculi xiii*, CCCM, 73, 1997, p. 98).

21. L. AUVRAY *et al.* (ed.), *Les registres de Grégoire IX*, Paris, 1890-1955, n° 3591.

22. *Ibid.*, n° 3967.

did the king really care about the particular needs of the church of Osma ? They didn't trouble him in 1240 when don Juan was translated to the see of Burgos[23].

No, what that made don Juan's translation to León in 1237 problematic but his translation to Burgos in 1240 not so, was that clause of the compact between don Juan and don Rodrigo in 1231 according to which in the event of don Juan's appointment to « pontifical honour » outside the province of Toledo the Castilian chancery was to revert to the archbishop of Toledo. Because, since by no stretch of the imagination could the see of León be regarded as lying within the province of Toledo, in 1237 don Rodrigo would surely have objected to the chancellor's removal « in alia prouincia », and quite possibly did so object, whereas if three years later he was consulted by the king about don Juan's translation to Burgos he would not have objected to the see of Burgos being so regarded, if only for the reason that the *de facto* submission to themselves of a church which was *de jure* immediately subject to Rome was precisely what successive archbishops of Toledo had long been hankering after, don Rodrigo included[24].

If on the other hand don Rodrigo was *not* consulted by Fernando in 1240, the reason why not was that by that date he was no longer a force to be reckoned with. He was certainly no longer such in 1246 when, as stated, the chancery did not revert to him. Ten years earlier, even five years earlier, he would have put up a fight. It would appear that between early 1230 and late 1232 he may have used his best endeavours to delay or prevent Juan de Soria's initial promotion to the see of Osma[25]. By 1240, however, he was growing old ; old and perhaps ill. As early as 1225 he had been close to death, as he tells us himself[26]. Moreover, from 1244 until his death in 1247 he was an exile from his own cathedral city[27]. In the last three years of his life he appears to have been more planned against than planning.

It is difficult to establish how much earlier than that his powers may have been failing, not least because for all practical purposes his *History*,

---

23. *Ibid.*, n° 5079.

24. In 1218 he had acquired from the papal chancery a copy of a letter of Pascal II concerning the intervention of his predecessor, don Bernardo, in the affairs of the church of Burgos in the year 1115 : *CT*, n° 554.

25. LINEHAN, « Don Juan de Osma ».

26. « finis periculum vix euasit » : *DRH*, IX, 12.

27. HERNÁNDEZ and LINEHAN, *The Mozarabic Cardinal*, p. 44-45. See ESTELLA ZALAYA's account of these years, blaming Toledo's secular authorities for the archbishop's discomfiture while failing to acknowledge the cause of their hostility, namely don Rodrigo's packing of the chapter with alien appointees : *El fundador*, p. 183-184. For a prelate so sensitive to the symbolic, exclusion from the ancient capital was by any reckoning a sorry state to have come to.

as well as those of Juan de Soria and Lucas de Túy, ends at 1236. It is too often forgotten in the euphoric accounts of the Castilian 1240s that after 1236 the domestic chroniclers fall silent. For the last sixteen years of Fernando's reign we are as about as much in the dark as we are for the first sixteen of Alfonso VIII's. Or rather, it is from other sorts of sources that the account of these years with which we are familiar has been concocted[28].

That said, it may even be that it is to the year 1236 itself that the beginnings of don Rodrigo's political decline are to be traced, that it was then that the process of his political sidelining began, when Córdoba was reconquered and the king's chancellor Juan de Soria presided at the first high mass in the former mosque there while the archbishop (unfortunately for him) was at the papal court, as he was perhaps rather too often. In his *History* don Rodrigo would of course seek to save the situation by insisting that Juan de Soria was at Córdoba in his capacity as bishop of Osma, representing the archbishop and his primatial pretensions on that occasion[29]. More to the point is that this is the *only* place in that *History* in which don Rodrigo refers to himself as «primate», and that it is *only* at this point that he mentions Juan de Soria at all.

For of course the truth of the matter is that it was only *incidentally* in his capacity as the archbishop's suffragan that Juan de Soria was at Córdoba in 1243, that he was principally there as the king's chancellor, and that what he was really representing was the new deal that had been struck on 1 January 1231, the deal that had signalled the exclusion of don Rodrigo from the privileged position in the government of the kingdom that archbishops of Toledo had occupied over at least the previous century. We should not be altogether surprised therefore to find that when in the spring of 1237 Gregory IX sought to put pressure on Fernando to make peace with the king of Navarre, it was not to the archbishop of Toledo that he applied for assistance but to Juan de Soria and the queen mother doña Berenguela[30].

Now, that it was this pair, Juan de Soria and the queen mother doña Berenguela, who certainly down to 1236 were the principal political

---

28. For *contemporary* purposes the account of these years later incorporated into the Alfonsine *Estoria de España* leaves much to be desired. See C. L. CHAMBERLIN, «"Unless the pen writes as it should": the proto-cult of saint Fernando III in Seville in the thirteenth and fourteenth centuries», *in:* M. GONZÁLEZ JIMÉNEZ (ed.), *Sevilla 1248. Congreso internacional conmemorativo del 750 aniversario de la conquista de la ciudad de Sevilla por Fernando III, rey de Castilla y León. Sevilla, Real Alcázar, 23-27 de noviembre de 1998*, Madrid, 2000, p. 389-417, p. 402-405.

29. «Roderici Toletani primatis uices gerebat»: *DRH*, IX, 17.

30. Pamplona, Archivo general de Navarra, caj. 2, n° 40, 41; publ. in part L. CADIER, «Bulles originales du xiii° siècle conservées dans les Archives de Navarre», *Mélanges d'archéologie et d'histoire*, 7, 1887, n° xxiii, xxiv.

heavyweights of the reign, though occupying opposite poles in the political process of these years, is one implication of a powerful paper by
Francisco Hernández, still in press[31]. I shall not put my sickle to another
man's field, as don Rodrigo's canonist friends would have said, other than
to observe that a significant part of Hernández's case is founded on
resemblances observed by him between the chronicle ascribed to Juan de
Soria and book IX of don Rodrigo's *History*.

«*L'histoire est discours*», Georges Martin has reminded us[32], and we
must be grateful to him for that as for much else, even though etymolog-
ically investigation comes before narration – or if investigation is not to
your taste, then plagiarism. Prince of plagiarists, the archbishop copies
the chancellor in the time-honoured manner of Spanish historians down
the ages, pillaging whole sections of the other's work without acknowledgement and consulting his own genius only in order to score points off
his supplier of information. I have remarked already on the scantness of
the treatment he accords that supplier. Within the *longue durée* of Spanish
historiography, don Rodrigo elevated the black art to a level unsurpassed
until our own time.

Another implication of Hernández's paper is that in the contest
between Juan de Soria and doña Berenguela don Rodrigo seems usually
to have been aligned with the lady in the case, and it is not least in that
particular context, I suggest, that the events of 1230/31 are to be understood: as an instance of Fernando III's asserting himself in the government of his kingdom by liberating himself from the joint tutelage of his
mother and his archbishop[33].

Of course, that proposition is wholly at odds with what the chroniclers
appear to tell us about Fernando's exemplary filial devotion to doña
Berenguela. However, let us not forget what Lucas of Túy says about the
relationship of mother and son. What he says of the first king of his line

31. «La corte de Fernando III y la casa real de Francia. Documentos, crónicas, monumentos», in: *VIII congreso de estudios medievales*, Ávila, 2003.
32. G. MARTIN, *Les Juges de Castille. Mentalités et discours historique dans l'Espagne médiévale*,
Paris, 1992, p. 11.
33. Fernando's *démarche* is also to be viewed in a wider context however, namely the desire
of Western rulers generally at this period to liberate the offices of state from their hereditary
incumbents, as evidenced in the case of the French monarchy half a century earlier
( J. W. BALDWIN, *The government of Philip Augustus. Foundations of French royal power in the Middle
Ages*, Berkeley and Los Angeles, 1986, p. 32-33) and in that of Portugal in 1238 when, as in
Castile-León, the archbishop of Braga surrendered his possession of the royal chancery and
certain other rights enjoyed by him *ex officio* in exchange for an unfettered grant of churches
attached to the royal fisc «cum omnibus pertinentiis earumdem et cum omnibus iuribus que
[rex] ibi habebat uel de jure habere poterat ullo modo»: A. D. de SOUSA COSTA, *Mestre
Silvestre e Mestre Vicente, juristas da contenda entre don Afonso II e suas irmãs*, Braga, 1963, p. 378-380,
n. 486 (a reference which I owe to the kindness of Dr Maria João Branco).

not to be detected in adultery is that that «most prudent» lady exercised an iron discipline over her adult son «as though he were a little boy»[34]. What he does not remark upon is the willingness with which Fernando submitted to that discipline, the persistence of which is confirmed by don Rodrigo's approving report regarding Berenguela's provision of a second wife for Fernando in order to keep him on the straight and narrow, «lest the king's chastity should be soiled by alien commerce»[35].

Doña Berenguela's discipline closely approximated to that exercised by her equally formidable sister Blanche of Castile who was reluctant to let *her* son Louis IX even to go to bed with the lady who *was* his wife[36]. Mothers you have to make the best you can of however, and sometimes excuses for. Archbishops are a sometimes more easily dispensable sort of inheritance. Since it is currently fashionable to look for family traits inherited by doña Berenguela and her sister from their grandmother Eleanor of Aquitaine, it is perhaps worth remarking that Eleanor's youngest son, king John of England, also had an archbishop bequeathed to him, Hubert Walter of Canterbury, and that, according to some contemporaries, so much did the king resent Hubert's high-handedness and tendency to conduct his own foreign policy that on receiving news of the archbishop's death he made no pretence of his delight[37].

Moreover, if in 1230 Fernando III harboured sentiments at all similar to these, and *qua* chancellor Juan de Soria provided the means of enabling him to assert himself against both his mother and don Rodrigo, *qua* bishop of Osma he had reason of his own for resenting doña Berenguela and regretting the extent of her earlier influence over her son. That reason was the claim of the church of Osma to a piece of real estate even more impressive than the chancery, namely the *señorío* of the «castellum de Oxoma» itself, «cum uilla et cum omni iure», which Alfonso VIII had bequeathed to it in another gesture of compensation,

---

34. «ac si esset puer humillimus sub ferula magistrali»: LUCAS OF TÚY, *Chronicon mundi*, Emma FALQUE (ed.), CCCM, 74, 2003, p. 332.

35. «ne regis pudicicia alienis comerciis lederetur»: *DRH*, IX, 18. Perhaps that puritanism of the Fernandine court which, it has been alleged, excluded courtly poetry because courtly poetry was adulterous, was an ethos imposed as much by the king's mother as by the king. See C. ALVAR, «Poesía y política en la corte alfonsí», *Cuadernos hispanoamericanos*, n° 410, Aug. 1984, p. 5-20, p. 6-7.

36. Peter LINEHAN, «On further thought: Lucas of Tuy, Rodrigo of Toledo and the alfonsine histories», *Anuario de estudios medievales*, 27(1), 1997, p. 415-436, p. 421.

37. «rege admodum gaudente, quia de regis Francorum nimia familiaritate suspectus habebatur»: ROGER WENDOVER, *Flores historiarum*, H. G. HEWLETT (ed.), London: Rolls Ser., 1887, t. 2, p. 10. See Miriam SHADIS, «Piety, politics and power: the patronage of Leonor of England and her daughters Berenguela of León and Blanche of Castile», *in*: J. Hall McCASH (ed.), *The cultural patronage of medieval women*, Athens GA & London, 1996, p. 202-227.

this time to atone for an act of simony against that church committed in his name during his minority[38]. This extraordinary bequest is of interest to us for the further light it sheds on the previously neglected possibility that Alfonso VIII may have been intent on promoting Osma (where of course don Rodrigo was briefly bishop before his translation to Toledo) as a cultural centre as well as Palencia[39]. But it is also interesting on account of the furious reaction that it elicited from doña Berenguela. For whereas in February 1217 the child-king don Enrique (which is to say don Rodrigo) insisted on its implementation, after don Enrique's death that summer his successor don Fernando (which is to say doña Berenguela) resolutely refused to comply. No matter that Rome threatened the king and his mother with the direst of penalties. There was no Castilian churchman prepared to impose them. «You might have asked somebody else to do so», don Rodrigo replied lamely to the papal judge-delegate, the Aragonese bishop of Zaragoza[40].

No matter either that the bishop of Osma during these years was one of the principal jurists of the age. Bishop Melendo – a legal luminary enjoying one of the most lucrative of practices and a giant amongst papal chancery lawyers described at the time as «second to none in both laws» (though not the only Portuguese jurist of distinction whose presence at Osma and Soria in the first half of the reign of Fernando III further testifies to the intellectual vitality of those centres in which Juan de Soria began his career)[41] – Bishop Melendo was helpless.

38. Julio GONZÁLEZ, *El reino de Castilla en la época de Alfonso VIII*, 3 vol., Madrid, 1960, 3, p. 345-346. Regarding the deed for which the bequest was intended to make amends see Peter LINEHAN, «Royal influence and papal authority in the diocese of Osma: A note on "Quia requisistis" (JL 13728)», *Bulletin of medieval canon law*, n. s. 20, 1990, p. 31-41 [repr. Peter LINE-HAN, *The processes of politics and the rule of law. Studies on the Iberian kingdoms and papal Rome in the Middle Ages*, Aldershot, 2002]. The assertion of J. LOPERRÁEZ CORVALÁN, *Descripción histórica del obispado de Osma*, 3 vol., Madrid, 1788 [repr. Madrid, 1978], 1, p. 210, that it was actuated «teniendo presente los servicios que le habia hecho el obispo de Osma, don Mendo» is based on a misinterpretation of Enrique I's charter of Feb. 1217 (printed *ibid.*, t. 3, p. 50).

39. LINEHAN, «Don Juan de Soria».

40. *Ibid.*, t. 1, p. 213-218, 221-223; t. 3, p. 49-52, 56-59 and 61-63; Peter LINEHAN, *The Spanish Church and the papacy in the thirteenth century*, Cambridge, 1971, p. 10-11. It is of consider-able interest that at this very time archbishop Pedro Muñoz of Compostela was challenging don Rodrigo «super cancellaria vel capellania regis Castelle»: D. MANSILLA, *La docu-mentación pontificia de Honorio III (1216-1227)*, Rome, 1965, n° 132.

41. LOPERRÁEZ, 1, p. 208, is mistaken in stating Melendo's origins to have been Asturian rather than Portuguese. For both him and «Petrus Hispanus Portugalensis» (author of *Notabilia* on the «Compilatio Quarta», bishop of Oporto from 1235 and «vicario de Soria» in 1232), see LINEHAN, «Don Juan de Soria». The presence of Petrus Fernandi, «vicarius Soriensis», at Juan de Soria's deathbed suggests that that dignity was in the latter's gift: SER-RANO, «El canciller», p. 38.

He was ground into submission[42]. At the time of his death in 1225 Alfonso VIII's bequest remained a dead letter. And so it remained after Juan de Soria's accession to the see in 1232, by which time Fernando III was more master of his kingdom – or kingdoms. After all, what his grandfather had proposed for Osma – in modern parlance to surrender the State to the Church – was the very converse of the strategy developed by him after 1240 of having the State absorb the Church by placing his sons, the infantes Felipe and Sancho, in the major archbishoprics of the kingdom, with the ecclesiastical career of the first of these being evidently planned to follow precisely in the steps of Juan de Soria (the abbacy of Valladolid followed by the see of Osma) and entrusted to Juan's supervision[43]. Even so, it would not be altogether surprising if, as bishop of Osma himself, Juan de Soria harboured a measure of resentment against the woman who had been principally responsible for depriving his church of so rich a prize.

Yet there were compensations. As chancellor, Juan de Soria was the man to whom after 1240 the dynasty was entrusted. With him it was at Burgos, not with don Rodrigo at Toledo, that don Felipe resided. He it was, not the archbishop, who accompanied the two infantes to Paris and acted as their tutor in their French preparation for the role their father envisaged for them in resolving the problems that had for so long embittered the relationship of *regnum* and *sacerdotium* within the Western

---

42. Though not surrender, as stated disloyally by the historian of his church in his summary of the settlement of October 1223 the subject of which was the «decima reddituum regalium episcopatus Oxomensis»: «con lo qual se dió [don Melendo] por satisfecho ; y por lo mejorado que le pareció quedaba, cedió por su parte del pleyto y pretension del señorio de Osma, que fué el principal motivo de las discordias ; pero con la reserva de que no perdiera por ello la Dignidad Episcopal y su Iglesia el derecho »: LOPERRÁEZ, t. 1, p. 222. See the terms of the Latin text of which this is a summary: «cæterum quia inter dictos Regem, et Episcopum quæstio super Villam de Oxoma vertebatur, reservavit sibi quæstionem ipsam Episcopus Stephanus [sic; lege «supradictus», viz. Melendus], ut eam tractaret, prout sibi expedire videatur» (ibid., t. 3, p. 63).

43. HERNÁNDEZ and LINEHAN, The Mozarabic Cardinal, p. 54-55. When in March 1243 the thirteen-year-old don Felipe was elected secular abbot of Valladolid, the impresario of the process in whom the entire chapter vested its powers of election was one «Magister Nicolaus», described as «concanonicus» of the place and papal subdeacon, and identifiable as the archdeacon of Cuéllar (Segovia) of that name, witness of Juan de Soria's will in September 1246, and one of the two clerigos to whom were entrusted the rings, precious stones and rich cloths for disposal (in the dying bishop's words) «assi como ellos entendieren que yo avia voluntad de fazer». Doubtless it was he who had secured don Felipe's election in 1243 by persuading Innocent IV to oblige Fernando III on the understanding that the Infante had achieved the age of «fifteen or sixteen»: M. MAÑUECO VILLALOBOS and J. ZURITA NIETO, Documentos de la iglesia colegial de Santa María la Mayor (hoy Metropolitana) de Valladolid. Siglo XIII (1201-1280), doc. 41 (see SERRANO, «El canciller», p. 38-39; LINEHAN, Spanish Church and the papacy, p. 286); E. BERGER (ed.), Les registres d'Innocent IV, Paris, 1884-1921, n° 196 (printed A. QUINTANA PRIETO, La documentación pontificia de Inocencio IV (1243-1254), Rome, 1987, n° 16).

Church. And when he died at Palencia in October 1246, having shrewdly appointed don Rodrigo and doña Berenguela amongst his executors (shrewdly because he must have known that both of them were moribund too), that most elegant of resolutions appeared well on its way to realisation. True, in October 1246 the pontiff was still holding out against admitting the spectacularly under-age don Felipe to the see of Osma[44]. But on the capture of Seville two years later all pretence of principle was swept away. By then, with don Rodrigo dead too, nothing that Fernando III demanded could be denied him, and the same upward current wafted don Pedro Martínez into the see of Jaén[45] and secured the appointment of the beardless infante as procurator of the church of Seville, the church by whose ancient claims all that don Rodrigo had striven for on behalf of Toledo's primacy was placed at risk[46].

To conclude. For don Rodrigo the significance of the surrender of the Castilian chancery in 1230/31 may have been as real as it was symbolic; may indeed have been real *because* it was symbolic. And one final point. That description of him with which I began, standing shoulder to shoulder with Alfonso VIII in the rearguard at Las Navas, is don Rodrigo's own description[47]. In the chronicles of Lucas of Túy and Juan de Soria his virtuoso performance is not mentioned at all[48].

---

44. It must almost certainly have been before Juan de Soria's death that the chapter of Osma petitioned Innocent IV to allow them to have the Infante as their bishop. For the pontiff's refusal (Nov. 1246) of their postulation of him on grounds of age (canon law requiring a bishop to be thirty) and the need for him to complete his studies, see BERGER, *Les registres d'Innocent IV*, n° 2215 (printed QUINTANA PRIETO, *Documentación pontificia*, n° 334; better though also defective edition *apud* D. MANSILLA REOYO, *Iglesia castellano-leonesa y curia romana en los tiempos del rey san Fernando*, Madrid, 1945, p. 333-334).

45. The royal chancery was listing him as bishop of Jaén by mid-January 1249: C. DE AYALA MARTÍNEZ (coord.), *Libro de privilegios de la orden de San Juan de Jerusalén en Castilla y León (siglos xii-xv)*, Madrid, n. d., p. 518.

46. LINEHAN, *History and the historians*, chap. 11.

47. «in ultima acie»: *DRH*, VIII, 9.

48. *Chronicon mundi*, p. 329-330; *Crónica latina*, p. 61-62.

# IV

# DON JUAN DE SORIA: UNAS APOSTILLAS

Since it would be wrong, very wrong, for a mere *comunicante* to go on too long I propose to comment on just two of the many questions prompted by the wide-ranging and richly suggestive *ponencia* of Francisco Hernández, my debt in what follows to whose insights will be readily apparent.

The first is the issue to which he has drawn attention of signs of tension between the two episcopal chroniclers, el *Oxomense* — as perhaps we should now label Juan de Soria, the supposed author of at least the lion's share of the so-called 'Crónica latina de los reyes de Castilla'[1] — and el *Toledano*, and the associated matter of the latter's partiality for Fernando III's formidable parent, doña Berenguela, even at the expense of Fernando's own reputation. Just as it seems to have escaped the notice of students of the subject that D. Rodrigo's references in the prologue to his History to the king who had commissioned the work appear conventional almost to the point of perfunctoriness,[2] so too has it failed to be remarked by them that when on 1 April 1237 Pope Gregory IX was seeking to put pressure on Fernando to make peace with the king of Navarre so that Teobaldo I might depart on crusade, it was not to the archbishop of Toledo that the pontiff appealed but to Juan de Soria, royal chancellor and bishop of Osma, and to the queen mother.[3]

---

[1] *Pace* L. Charlo Brea, '¿Un segundo autor para la última parte de la Crónica latina de los reyes de Castilla?', in M. Pérez González (ed.), *Actas I Congreso Nacional de Latín Medieval (León, 1-4 de diciembre de 1993)*, León 1995, pp. 251-6.

[2] Compare the minimalism of his 'gloriosissime rex' and 'inclite rex' with Lucas of Tuy's affectionate reference to doña Berenguela ('praeceptis gloriosissimae Hispaniarum Reginae dominae Berengariae omni desiderio desiderantes fideliter satisfacere'): *Historia de rebus Hispaniae*, ed. J. Fernández Valverde, CCCM 72, Turnhout 1987, $7_{73,83}$; *Chronicon mundi*, ed. A. Schottus, *Hispania illustrata* IV, Frankfurt 1608, $3_{55-56}$. Especially in view of the exuberance of the remarks previously addressed to him in this context (Diego García, *Planeta*, ed. M. Alonso, Madrid 1943, esp. pp. 181, 207-8), it can hardly be supposed that the archbishop was unaware of what was called for on such occasions.

[3] 'secundum datam tibi a Deo prudentiam ad hoc moneas attentius et inducas' and 'ad hoc affectione materna moneas attentius et inducas' respectively: Pamplona, Archivo General de Navarra, caj. II, nos. 40, 41; publ. in part L. Cadier, 'Bulles originales du XIIIe siècle conservées dans les Archives de Navarre', *Mélanges d'Archéologie et d'Histoire*, 7 (1887), nn. XXIII, XXIV.

A mere four days thereafter, the pontiff approved the postulation of the canons of León for the translation of Juan de Soria.[4] But eight months later he changed his mind, relieving D. Juan of 'the need' to make the move, partly on the grounds that when the León delegation had come to Viterbo that spring D. Juan had not given his consent, partly because (as Fernando's agents at the papal curia had reported) the king objected to the proposal. He did so both because the church of Osma could not sustain the loss of its bishop and because that bishop was a 'man of great counsel' and 'useful and necessary to him and his kingdom'.[5]

Those ostensible reasons prompt the question why the whereabouts of D. Juan's see should have concerned the king at all. Since the 'useful and necessary' prelate's place was at the head of his chancery, why should it have mattered to him where he was nominally bishop? Can it really have been anxiety on Fernando's part for the welfare of the church of Osma? Was the king who within the previous year had acquiesced in the bequest by Juan de Soria's successor as abbot of Santander to the heirs of that clerical subject's body really so committed a student of the individual spiritual needs of his subjects, diocese by diocese?[6] Plainly not, or those needs must equally have caused him to resist the bid that the chapter of Burgos made for his chancellor just three years later. But this he did not do, and the bishop of Osma was duly translated to Burgos.[7] That then is the second question I have in mind, and I suspect that an answer to it may be provided by consideration of the circumstances surrounding the first.

My reason for suspecting that the two issues are connected, and my point of departure, is a detail concerning Gregory IX's privilege of 31 July 1234 in favour of Alfonso VIII's principal religious foundation, the royal convent of Las Huelgas de Burgos. It is not that there was anything remarkable about the terms of the privilege itself.[8] Nor would it be surprising if doña Berenguela had been active in petitioning for it — she who, in the words of the addition to the Alfonsine *Estoria de España*, 'seguie las buenas obras de su padre'.[9] True, as she confessed to the pontiff when she eventually did do so, she did not write to him often enough, though this was not because she was lacking in devotion for him. It was rather – as Eleanor of Aquitaine's grand-daughter and look-alike claimed, implausibly enough — 'on account of the modesty that was natural to her sex and of the reverence due to the Vicar of Jesus Christ'.[10] No, neither the privilege itself nor the likelihood of powerful royal lobbying behind the scenes

---

[4] L. Auvray *et al.*, *Les registres de Grégoire IX*, Paris 1890-1955, 3591.

[5] *Ibid.*, 3967.

[6] For Fernando's grant of property at Úbeda and Valdecanales 'vobis d. Santio abbati Santi Anderii clerico et scriptore meo vestraeque successioni', see J. Rodríguez Molina (coord.), *Colección documental del Archivo Municipal de Úbeda*, Granada 1990, no. 4.

[7] *Reg. Greg. IX*, 5079.

[8] J. M. Lizoain Garrido, *Documentación del monasterio de Las Huelgas de Burgos (1231-1262)*, Burgos 1985, no. 280.

[9] *Primera Crónica General de España*, ed. R. Menéndez Pidal, Madrid 1955, 735a$_{20}$. Dr Miriam Shadis (University of Ohio) has a monograph on doña Berenguela in preparation. See meanwhile her 'Berenguela of Castile's political motherhood: the management of sexuality, marriage, and succession', in J. C. Parsons and B. Wheeler (eds.), *Medieval Mothering*, New York and London 1996, 335-58.

[10] *Reg. Greg. IX*, 5165. Printed A. Quintana Prieto, 'Guillermo de Taillante, abad de Sahagún y cardenal de la iglesia romana', *Anthologica Annua*, 26-27 (1979-80), 74-5.

IV

at Rieti was remarkable. What was the identity of the man charged with steering the petition through the corridors of the papal chancery. For legible on the dorse of the instrument in the place reserved by that date for the proctor's name are the words 'Sacrista Oxomensis'.[11]

Despite the fact that over the previous twenty years he had played a not insignificant part in the affairs of the Spanish and Portuguese kingdoms, the said sacrist of Osma has never been fully taken account of by historians of this period of Castilian history. As *familiaris* and *nuncius* of Innocent III, 'frater Gundisalvus Hispanus' had made his peninsular début at Coimbra in December 1213 charged with both fiscal and more general responsibilities.[12] The outlines of his subsequent career until 1225, including his full name (Gundisalvus Garsie) and his membership of the Order of the Hospital, have been described elsewhere.[13] Here therefore we may limit ourselves to consideration of those aspects of his activity that are immediately relevant to the matter of his relationship with the archbishop D. Rodrigo and the chancellor D. Juan.

As to the former, it is recorded that sometime before January 1217 the archbishop made over to 'frater Gundisalvus' ('circa quem, vestris meritis precedentibus, speciali quadam affectione movemur') his part of the administration of the church of San Vicente del Monte,[14] and in May and June 1218 two further grants for life in gratitude for services rendered.[15] If it was D. Rodrigo's purpose by these concessions to purchase the other's further compliance and complaisance, however, that purpose singularly failed, for by November 1221 Gundisalvus (*familiaris* of Honorius III as he had been of his predecessor) had denounced the archbishop to Rome for his failure to enforce the legislation of the recent Lateran council regarding Jewish dress.[16]

---

[11] Monasterio de Las Huelgas de Burgos, 8/270 dorse. As is unfortunately all too often the case in collections of printed documents, although he provides the text of the papal privilege Lizoain Garrido fails to note its chancery endorsements and other diplomatic features.

[12] A. Herculano, *História de Portugal. Desde o começo da monarquia até o fim do reinado de Afonso III*, notas críticas de José Mattoso, Lisbon 1980, II. 237, 593; A. J. da Costa and M. A. F. Marques, *Bulário Português. Inocêncio III (1198-1216)*, Coimbra 1989, no. 199.

[13] Peter Linehan, *The Spanish Church and the Papacy in the Thirteenth Century*, Cambridge 1971, 18-19. (My description of him there as 'Master', adopted by J. González, *Reinado y diplomas de Fernando III*, I, Córdoba 1980, 217, was mistaken.) In August/September 1222 he was involved in the collection of the Aragonese *census*: P. Freedman, 'Two letters of Pope Honorius III on the collection of ecclesiastical revenues in Spain', *Römische Historische Mitteilungen* 32/33 (1990/1991), 37-40.

[14] P. Pressutti, *Regesta Honorii Papae III*, Rome 1895-95, 223 (printed D. Mansilla, *La documentación pontificia de Honorio III (1216-1227)*, Rome 1965, no. 24, reading 'movemus' for 'movemur').

[15] Of the *castrum* of Alamín and associated properties not far from San Vicente del Monte, and of all his 'tendas' in the Alcaná of Toledo and four pounds of meat daily from the archiepiscopal *almojarifazgo*, 'attendentes multa grata obsequia que dilectus frater et amicus noster frater G. Garsie familiaris domini pape nobis exhibuit et per nos ecclesie Toletane': F. J. Hernández, *Los Cartularios de Toledo*, Madrid 1985, nos. 373-4. His continuing possession of the *castrum* de Alamín is documented from the years 1226 and 1234: *ibid.*, no. 419; Toledo, Archivo de la Catedral, X.10.B.1.3 (ed. A. González Palencia, *Los mozárabes de Toledo en los siglos XII y XIII*. Vol. preliminar. Madrid 1926, 167).

[16] 'sicut a dilecto filio Gundisalvo fratre Hospitalis Hierosolymitani accepimus': Madrid, Archivo Histórico Nacional, Clero, carp. 3019/1 (ed. F. Fita, *Actas inéditas de siete concilios españoles celebrados desde el año 1282 hasta el de 1314*, Madrid 1881, 235-6, whence Mansilla, no. 381). The papal mandate is endorsed 'd[omi]no Tol[e]tan[o] sup[er] habitu iudeorum'. Had it been brought back to Castile by fr. Gundisalvus after discussion at the curia? If so, while there had he reported on the archbishop's activities more generally? Cf. Linehan, *Spanish Church*, 18.

Now, personally damaging though the archbishop's recent loss of credit at Rome may have been, during the years 1217-1221 he was suffering a loss that for his church and its prestige was more grievous still. For with the accession of Fernando III control of the Castilian chancery passed from the archbishop to the as yet unepiscopal D. Juan de Soria, abbot until mid-1219 of Santander and thereafter of Valladolid. And according to the record, the transfer was made with the archbishop's acquiescence. When the matter was regularized on the first day of 1231, the settlement was represented as a private treaty voluntarily entered into by both parties, with D. Juan stating that he had received from the other 'misericorditer' the 'chancery of the lord king of Castile' that belonged to him by right ('ad uos de iure spectantem'), that the concession was to the prejudice neither of the archbishop nor his successors, and that on his death or in the event of his appointment to 'pontifical honour' outside (but not inside) the province of Toledo the chancery was then to revert to the archbishop for the time being.[17]

And these assurances (which incidentally provide the explanation for Fernando III's veto on Juan de Soria's translation from Osma to León in 1237)[18] have been accepted at face-value by recent historians of the reign, with Julio González's suggestion that D. Rodrigo may even have recommended the abbot for the post exemplifying a tendency to gloss over the radical nature of the changes in progress strangely reminiscent of the anxiety of an earlier generation to make the vernacularizing Juan de Soria the son of that tenacious champion of Latin as the language of the Castilian chancery, Diego García author of *Planeta*.[19] No account seems to have been taken of the improbability of D. Rodrigo, the resourceful defender of Toledo's primacy, willingly divesting himself of the highly symbolic office that in 1183 one of his predecessors had described as 'his', and which in 1206 Alfonso VIII had acknowledged to be in the gift of another of them 'canonically to concede'.[20] Nor, apparently, has the significance of the date of Fernando III's approval of this latest 'canonical concession' been remarked upon. For the king's approval of the terms of what it suited the abbot to describe as a private agreement between himself and the archbishop, concerning as it were an unremarkable piece of real estate, did not follow that agreement in time. It anticipated it, by as much as eight months[21] - just as it anticipated the event that occasioned the need for it, namely the reunion of the kingdoms of Castile and León on the death of Alfonso IX of León. For in April 1230 Alfonso IX still had five months of life left to him.

---

[17] Printed, from a late copy identifiable as AHN, Clero 3019/8, by A. Millares Carlo, 'La cancillería real en León y Castilla hasta fines del reinado de Fernando III', *Anuario de Historia del Derecho Español*, 3 (1926), 286-7 (the original, unknown to the author, being found at AHN, Sellos 56/1).

[18] The agreement of 1231 had failed to anticipate the possibility that Juan de Soria would be courted by the canons of León, a diocese directly subject to Rome –as indeed was Burgos, the see to which he moved in 1240. But Burgos *was* Castile.

[19] González. *Fernando III*, I. 506. For the supposed relationship see Alonso, ed., *Planeta*, 75, repeating a suggestion of López Agurleta in the 18th century. This is not the place in which to attempt to deconstruct the altogether more remarkable genealogy and biography proposed by J. Hernando Pérez, *Hispano Diego García. Escritor y poeta medieval y el Libro de Alexandre*, Burgos 1992, 15-87. Cf. D. W. Lomax. 'La lengua oficial de Castilla', *Actele celui de-al XII-lea Congres International de Lingvistica ·i Filologie Romanica*, II, Bucarest 1971, 411-17; R. Wright, 'Latin and Romance in the Castilian chancery (1180-1230)', *Bulletin of Hispanic Studies* (Liverpool), 73 (1996), 121-8.

[20] Hernández, *Cartularios de Toledo*, no. 204; Millares Carlo, 277. Cf. Peter Linehan, *History and the Historians of Medieval Spain*, Oxford 1993, chaps 10-12.

[21] On 12 April 1230. Printed Millares Carlo, 284-5; González, *Fernando III*, no. 265.

IV

In short, there was a practical need as soon as possible to unify the civil services of the two kingdoms in one pair of safe hands, and the initiative was the king's. By an identical process, between January and September 1231 the archbishop of Compostela's possession of the Leonese chancery was also transferred to the abbot of Valladolid, with again the agreement between the contracting parties lagging months behind the king's formal acknowledgement of the archbishop's rights in the matter.[22]

The process of providing the Castilian chancellor with a Castilian see was already in train, an opening having been provided in the early months of 1230 by the (perhaps fortuitous) translation of Bishop Pedro Ramírez from the see of Osma to that of Pamplona in his native Navarre, the kingdom from which he had doubtless been brought at the instigation of the Navarrese archbishop of Toledo.[23] But to judge by the evidence of the lists of episcopal *confirmantes* to privileges issued by the chancery over which the abbot himself presided, the process was not straightforward. For although it was in mid-January 1230 that Pedro Ramírez figured in those lists as bishop of Osma for the last time, and although he had been duly installed in his new see by the July of that year,[24] not until mid-October 1232 did those records acknowledge that the abbot of Valladolid had succeeded him as bishop of Osma.[25] In the interim, all manner of chancery devices were employed to disguise the realities of a situation the complications of which remain as obscure to us as they must have been to the royal privilege-reading public at the time. Between mid-April 1230 and late February 1231 the see of Osma disappears from the record altogether, while the abbot of Valladolid continues to subscribe as 'domini regis cancellarius'.[26] Then, on 10 March 1231, in one privilege the church of Osma is described as vacant (apparently the first time that an untenanted church is thus described in products of the royal chancery) and there is no mention of the chancellor at all, and in another the novel (and unhelpful) formulation 'Ecclesia Oxomensis uacat conf[irmat]' is followed by the chancellor's confirmation.[27] Two days later, and until 1 May 1231, Osma is unequivocally vacant again and the chancellor is at his post, subscribing as abbot of Valladolid.[28] Then, on 10 May 1231, he appears for the first time as 'Oxomensis electus et domini regis cancellarius'. And so he remained, for a further sixteen months, sometimes listed with his episcopal colleagues, sometimes in the vicinity of the royal seal, symbolically uncertain until late September 1232 just where he did belong.[29]

For something like two and a half years, therefore, Juan of Soria's episcopal prospects had remained in doubt. It was not merely a case of the king's chancellor not being able to light upon a formula to describe a novel situation that happened to be *his own* situation. The length of the delays that elapsed before the chancellor was acknowledged as bishop-elect, and

---

[22] Millares Carlo, 287-8; González, *Fernando III*, no. 299.
[23] For whose 'Navarrization' of the church of Toledo in particular, see Francisco J. Hernández, and Peter Linehan, *The Mozarabic Cardinal. The Life and Times of Gonzalo Pérez Gudiel*, Florence 2003, chaps., 2, 5.
[24] González, *Fernando III*, no. 260; J. Goñi Gaztambide, *Historia de los obispos de Pamplona, siglos IV-XIII*, Pamplona 1979, I. 568.
[25] González, *Fernando III*, no. 487.
[26] *Ibid.*, nos. 265, 306.
[27] *Ibid.*, nos. 311, 312.
[28] *Ibid.*, nos. 313, 326.
[29] *Ibid.*, nos. 330, 352, 485.

between then and his consecration, indicates that the problems encountered were substantial rather than cosmetic. But why were they substantial? Conscientious objections raised by the chapter of Osma would hardly have sufficed to frustrate a king capable of the 'enormities' that, just two years after the departure of the legate John of Abbeville, Fernando III was reported currently to be committing against the church and clergy of Calahorra – although, for that very reason, the pontiff may very well have chosen to make such objections a pretext for delaying confirmation of D. Juan's election until his master mended his ways, withdrew his directive requiring the ecclesiastical goods of deceased clergy to pass to their offspring, and ceased to obstruct enforcement of the Lateran legislation regarding the Jews.[30] But apart from the absence of any evidence in support of it either in the papal registers or elsewhere, that conjecture fails to account for the further delay of almost a year and a half between the chancery record's earliest description of the chancellor as bishop-elect in May 1231 and his eventual consecration. Could the reason for that have been reluctance on the part of the consecrating metropolitan, the archbishop of Toledo, to do the honours?[31]

Be that as it may, it is hardly necessary to labour the point that would certainly not have escaped D. Rodrigo's attention, that Fernando III's accession to the throne of León had transformed the power-political profile of the entire peninsula. Rationalization of the royal civil service was only one aspect of this transformation. And the archbishops of Toledo and Compostela were only one casualty of the process. There are clear signs that, with the reconquest of Seville in prospect, the king had his eyes on the two archbishoprics themselves and by the mid-1240s he was grooming his sons, the Infantes Felipe and Sancho, to succeed

---

[30] These and other outrages were specified in Gregory IX's letter of 4 April 1231: *Reg. Greg. IX*, 594 (printed in part A. D. de Sousa Costa, *Mestre Silvestre e Mestre Vicente, juristas da contenda entre D. Afonso II e suas irmãs*, Braga 1963, 146-7, n. 264). Occasioned at least in part by Fernando III's strategic objections to the transfer of the see of Calahorra to Santo Domingo de la Calzada, they nevertheless continued until Bishop Juan Pérez's death at the papal curia in 1237: Linehan, *Spanish Church*, 26; P. Díaz Bodegas, 'Aproximación a la figura de D. Aznar López de Cadreita, obispo de Calahorra y La Calzada (1238-1263)', *Anthologica Annua*, 39 (1992), 39-42; A. Rodríguez López, *La consolidación territorial de la monarquía feudal castellana. Expansión y fronteras durante el reinado de Fernando III*, Madrid 1994, 209-18. (In May 1233 the pontiff again rebuked the king on the Jewish question 'cum in concilio fuerit Toletano statutum et in generali nichilominus innovatum ne judei publicis officiis proponantur': *Reg. Greg. IX*, 1427 [by the 'Toledan Council' he presumably meant c. 65 of IV Toledo *anno* 633].)

It is not apparent that these aspects of Fernando III's activities were either carefully considered or considered at all in the course of consideration of his cause for canonization between 1627 and 1671. For the king's modern apologists they certainly constitute an embarrassment. Thus, sixty years ago L. F. de Retana held Diego López de Haro responsible for the enormities reported, castigating 'autores poco reverentes y menos escrupulosos en anacronismos históricos [who] fustigan en esta ocasión la memoria de San Fernando', as to the king's alleged instructions regarding the bequest of ecclesiastical goods offering the suggestion, redolent of any *curia eclesiástica* of the 1940s, that the clergy in question were perhaps laymen in disguise, and concluding that 'Sin que la crítica aclare estos puntos, no se puede acusar a San Fernando de injusto con la Iglesia, y menos cuando le vemos por otra parte enriquecerla con grandes donadíos, y favorecer por mil modos la expansión de las Ordenes religiosas': *San Fernando III y su época*, Madrid 1941, 176, 173 (emphasis mine). In fact, these matters had been 'clarified' in 1234, when Diego López de Haro declared that all his actions had been undertaken on Fernando's instructions and Fernando had confirmed as much: M. Lecuona, 'Los sucesos calceatenses de 1224-1234', *Scriptorium Victoriense*, 1 (1954), 138.

[31] The absence of any record of D. Juan's oath of obedience to his metropolitan is inconclusive. The earliest (undated) such oath of a bishop of Osma of which evidence survives (that of 'P. ordinandus' to D. Rodrigo: AC Toledo, X.2.C.1.1.a) may as well refer to D. Juan's successor Pedro de Peñafiel as to his predecessor Pedro Rodríguez.

to them: a manoeuvre reminiscent of tenth-century Catalonia and one scarcely paralleled in Church-State relations in the post-Hildebrandine West.[32] Fernando III's more limited agenda of eliminating vested institutional interests, however, was not without contemporary parallel. Although the kingdom of León was not the duchy of Normandy, the case of post-Las Navas Castile invites comparison with that of post-Bouvines France- and not only because in both places Alfonso VIII's formidable daughters enjoyed a degree of influence that at times appeared destined to overwhelm their respective royal sons entirely,[33] but also for the reason that in Castile there was no Paris, no capital city.

As to the crucial years 1230-31 in particular, perhaps some allowance needs also to be made if not for another French parallel then at least for the influence of another recent French actor on the peninsular scene. For as Fernando III set about disposing of vested ecclesiastical interests in the conduct of national affairs, only a matter of months had elapsed since the departure of John of Abbeville, the papal legate of 1228-29 whose reforming vigour as, in the chancellor's telling phrase, he 'ran through the province',[34] is common enough knowledge. But it is not only for his subjection of the torpid system he encountered in Castile and León (as D. Rodrigo, still shuddering, remembered years later) as well as in Aragón and Portugal to a series of electric shocks that he deserves to be remembered.[35] He may also have given Gonzalo de Berceo a nudge in the right direction.[36] And since it was Valladolid that hosted his council for the Castilian Church, and since *el Oxomense*, then abbot of Valladolid, had it from his own very own mouth that reconquest strategy was 'the most powerful reason why the pope had sent him to Spain',[37] is it too much to suggest that the legate had thoughts on related subjects to share with the king too?

Whether or not he shared them, however, John of Abbeville at least serves the purpose of taking us back to fr. Gonzalo, the Hospitaller upon whose by then intimate knowledge of the terrain he must surely have depended during his peninsular progress.

---

[32] Hernández and Linehan, *The Mozarabic Cardinal*, chaps 2-3.

[33] Cf. the observation of J. E. Ruiz-Domènec, 'Les souvenirs croisés de Blanche de Castille', *Cahiers de Civilisation Médiévale*, 42 [1999], 51: 'La crise du système de parenté féodale n'est pas une idée fantaisiste. Elle se produit dans la même société qui a vu réaffirmer l'autorité royale après les batailles de Novas [*sic*] de Tolosa (1212), Muret (1213), Bouvines (1214) et Lincoln (1217). Ces quatre batailles définissent la géographie politique européenne'; W. C. Jordan, *Louis IX and the Challenge of the Crusade*, Princeton N. J. 1979, 35-6; J. W. Baldwin, *The Government of Philip Augustus. Foundations of French Royal Power in the Middle Ages*, Berkeley and Los Angeles 1986, 32-3; Peter Linehan, 'On further thought: Lucas of Tuy, Rodrigo of Toledo and the Alfonsine Histories', *Anuario de Estudios Medievales*, 27/1 (1997) 421-2.

[34] *Crónica latina de los reyes de Castilla*, ed. L. Charlo Brea, Cádiz 1984, 77 (republ., ed. Charlo Brea, *Chronica Hispana saeculi XIII*, C[orpus] C[hristianorum] C[ontinuatio] M[ediaeualis], LXXIII, Turnhout 1997, § 54, p. 98).

[35] Linehan, *Spanish Church*, 21-6 (on which the account in González, *Fernando III*, I. 215-16, is directly based, without acknowledgement, in accordance with bad practice on which I will further particularize in a forthcoming  analysis of plagiarism by Spanish historians of this period). Further details in Linehan, 'A papal legation and its aftermath: Cardinal John of Abbeville in Spain and Portugal, 1228-1229', in I. Birocchi *et al.*, *A Ennio Cortese*, Rome 2001, II. 236-56. Cf. *De rebus Hispanie*, 293.

[36] R. Menéndez Pidal, *Documentos lingüísticos de España*, Madrid 1919, 87. Cf. P. M. Cátedra, 'Nota introductoria' to *Gonzalo de Berceo. Obra completa*, ed. B. Dutton *et al.*, Madrid 1992, 937-9.

[37] *Crónica latina*, 77 [ed. CCCM, § 54, p. 98]: 'sicut idem nobis retulit uiua uoce'.

We last took account of fr. Gonzalo in November 1221, and really there is not much more to be said about him after that. In the following August he finds him at Tarazona again collecting the papal *census*, though this sighting is of interest only inasmuch as by then he was describing himself as sacrist of Osma.[38] So his formal association with that church – which had done well to recruit him in that capacity, rather as some Oxbridge colleges like to recruit retired senior civil servants (though as heads of house as a rule, because heads of house are largely decorative, rather than bursars) - dated from the time of the episcopate of D. Melendus and preceded by at least nine years that of Juan de Soria.[39] Not that Rome was yet aware of his circumstances, prohibited as his membership of a cathedral chapter was by the statutes of his Order. When writing either to or about him, Honorius III described fr. Gonzalo simply as his nuncio or *familiaris*.[40] Not until March 1231 did the superannuated papal tax-collector whose fiscal activities had been combined with others of a more vigorous nature seek the regularization of a situation that had been in existence for an entire decade.[41] Sensing that his days were drawing to a close and, before taking the wings of a dove, wishing to spend his twilight years ('residuum vite tue desideras terminare') at Osma in the enjoyment of his not inconsiderable profits of office ('attendens…quod…possessiones fructuosas et non modicas quas acquisisti labore tuo…vita tua poteras retinere'), he travelled to the papal curia to secure approval of an arrangement that the authorities of his Order had previously countenanced, and

---

[38] 'Notum sit… quod ego frater G. familiaris et nuncius domini pape in regnis Yspanie et sacrista Oxomensis' receives from prior of Tudela 'duos aureos pro .x. annis transactis cum teneretur singulis annis dare ecclesie romane pro censu duos solidos': AC Tudela, caj. 5, let. P, no. 1, summarized by F. Fuentes, *Catálogo de los archivos eclesiásticos de Tudela*, Tudela 1944, n. 206 as referring to an unnamed 'nuncio apostólico en España y tesorero de la iglesia de Osma'. Cf. P. Fabre and L. Duchesne (eds.), *Le Liber censuum de l'Église romaine*, I, Rome 1905, 216.

[39] Melendus was bishop-elect by 5 April 1210, had been consecrated by 28 February 1211, and continued in office until at least 26 May 1225: J. González, *El reino de Castilla en la época de Alfonso VIII*, Madrid 1960, nos. 865, 876; idem, *Fernando III*, no. 205.

[40] Thus, Aug.-Sept. 1222 (Freedman, above n. 13); Sept. 1222, regarding financial activities of late Bishop Guillermo of Pamplona (*Reg. Hon. III*, 4413: printed Mansilla, no. 413); October 1224, regarding recent discussions in Portugal with Master Vicente dean of Lisbon, the canonist Vincentius Hispanus (*Reg. Hon. III*, 5136: printed Costa, *Mestre Silvestre*, 136 n. 245).

[41] *Reg. Greg. IX*, 564 (printed J. Delaville le Roulx, *Cartulaire général de l'Ordre des Hospitaliers de S. Jean de Jérusalem*, II, Paris 1896, 416-17). In April 1226 he had represented his Order 'apud Fontem Almella' (near Toledo?) in an exchange of properties with the chancellor D. Juan (in his capacity as abbot of Valladolid) - an exchange witnessed by Fernando III, his queen Beatriz of Swabia, and the ubiquitous doña Berenguela: M. Mañueco Villalobos and J. Zurita Nieto, *Documentos de la iglesia colegial de S. María la Mayor (hoy metropolitana) de Valladolid. Siglo XIII (1201-1280)*, Valladolid 1920, 110-11 (and ill. 5; his seal). He described himself on this occasion as 'fr. Gundisalvus dictus Garsie, familiaris domini pape, sacrista Oxomense, comendator de Castrello de Ferruz', identified by Zurita Nieto as Castronuevo de Esgueva. Altogether more plausible, however, is Francisco Hernández's suggestion, for which I am extremely grateful, of a location in the archdeaconry of Alarcón (dioc. Cuenca). In June 1224 Fernando III had entrusted to the French military order of Selva Mayor the *castrum* of Alcalá de Júcar, together with a number of other properties in the area including 'cortigium in Atalaia de Ferrus': González, *Fernando III*, no. 197. Cf. D. W. Lomax, 'Las dependencias hispánicas de Santa María de la Selva Mayor', *Homenaje a José María Lacarra*, 'Príncipe de Viana', anejo 3, Pamplona 1986, II. 500. His presence so close to the strategically crucial frontier with the kingdom of Valencia is of course of particular interest. At Brihuega in July 1228, 'frater G. familiaris pape et sacrista Oxomensis' had witnessed an agreement between Archbishop Rodrigo and the representative of the Order of the Hospital, his name being listed not with those of his *confrères* but as one of the *capitulares* of Toledo: Hernández, *Cartularios de Toledo*, no. 423.

which Gregory IX (whose *familaris* he also was) now granted, having regard to the fact that he had had himself promoted to the order of deacon.[42] Even so, the retirement of the 'fragile vessel' who had been the repository of so many of the confidences of Castilian politics over the previous twenty years was not uninterrupted. As has already been said, in July 1234 he was at the papal curia again,[43] and within two years of that he was dead.

We do not know whether it was in 1235 or in 1236 that his life ended, because although the note that we have of the fact of his demise gives the day and the month it fails to mention the year. The note is what appears to be a draft of a letter whereby the chancellor sought to appoint 'J. Gutterii' as his successor in the *sacristanía* of Osma – and the insertion of the clause 'et si non possumus commendamus' suggests that it is indeed a draft rather than a copy of that letter.[44] His uncertainty regarding the extent of his authority in the matter says something about Juan of Soria's understanding of the affairs of his own church. So also do the terms in which he recommended his candidate, as someone who would serve that church well in matters both temporal and spiritual, in that order. The flyleaf of the chapter's copy of St Isidore on the Pentateuch[45] is an unusual place for a bishop to draft letters, moreover, particularly perhaps for a bishop supposedly in charge of the kingdom's chancery routines. On the other hand, apart from the fact that this is not the only known case of the chapter of Osma's library books being used for such purposes in these years,[46] we know both that D. Juan was no intellectual slouch, being a patron of other authors as well as one himself,[47] and that at least by the end of D. Juan's century that library contained a collection of wonderful richness (all too little accessible though it is today).[48]

---

[42] The preamble of the pontiff's 'special grace' appears peculiarly appropriate to the case of an exhausted bureaucrat-cum-warrior: 'Fragilis vas tui corporis esse considerans, sciensque imbecillitatem tuam, qui confractus es multis laboribus, et, cum in etate processeris viribus non modicum destitutum, timore super te venientibus ac tremore, in amaritudine annos tuos recogitare cepisti, et pennas sicut columbe appetere, ut advoles in solitudinem et quiescas, vacando ibi Deo in spiritus libertate et tua nihilominus peccata deflendo': It does not occur elsewhere in the papal registers of the period.

[43] Above, p. 388.

[44] Burgo de Osma, Biblioteca del Cabildo, MS. 89, fo. 1r, dated 'Toleti vii. die aprilis' (see Appendix I). Although the royal court is not known to have been at Toledo in any April in these years other than 1235, D. Juan's revelation that he was about to depart to join the royal army may equally suggest the year 1236 and the siege of Córdoba, for the details of which historians depend so largely on 'his' *Crónica*. Cf. González, *Fernando III*, i. 321, 327. In his will of Sept. 1246 'Johan Gutterrez' was the first-listed of D. Juan's 'clerigos e los de Criazon, a qui yo devo fazer algo'. A man of the same name had been in the entourage of Rodrigo of Toledo at the Fourth Lateran Council, at which D. Juan had also been present: L. Serrano, 'El canciller de Fernando III de Castilla', *Hispania*, 1/5 [1940-41], 38; J. F. Rivera Recio, 'Personajes hispanos asistentes en 1215 al IV Concilio de Letrán', *Hispania Sacra*, 4 [1951], 337; *Crónica latina*, 46 ['… uidi ego in concilio Lateranense conuocato sub Innocencio tercio': ed. CCCM, § 30, p. 72].

[45] Described T. Rojo Orcajo, 'Catálogo descriptivo de los códices que se conservan en la S. I. Catedral de Burgo de Osma', *Boletín de la Real Academia de la Historia*, 95 (1929), 178-9.

[46] Cf. P. Linehan, 'The Spanish Church revisited: the episcopal gravamina of 1279', in B. Tierney and P. Linehan (eds.), *Authority and Power. Studies on Medieval Law and Government presented to Walter Ullmann on his Seventieth Birthday*, Cambridge 1980, 138, n. 46.

[47] For his patronage of the translator Hermannus Alemannus at Toledo, see W. F. Boggess, 'Hermannus Alemannus's rhetorical translations', *Viator*, 2 (1971), 249.

[48] M. C. Díaz y Díaz, 'Notas de bibliotecas de Castilla en el siglo XIII', *Livre et lecture en Espagne sous l'Ancien Régime. Colloque de la Casa de Velázquez*, Paris 1981, 10-11. Cf. S. Guijarro, 'Libraries and books used by cathedral clergy in Castile during the thirteenth century', *Hispanic Research Journal*, 2 (2001), 191-210.

Furthermore, D. Juan's predecessor but two, during whose pontificate fr. Gonzalo had been preferred to the *sacristanía*, was Master Melendus, the Portuguese jurist who, according to the Englishman Thomas of Marlborough, 'was regarded as second to none in both laws at the time.'[49] That was in 1205 when he was engaged to act as the Roman proctor of the abbey of Evesham. Five years later he was bishop of Osma, and five years after that he was again at Rome attending the Fourth Lateran Council with as one member of his household fr. Gonzalo's predecessor as sacrist, Master Vicente, who was probably Portuguese,[50] and as another Pedro Salvadores, who certainly was. What makes the latter's association with Melendus particularly interesting is the fact that, as well as being a distinguished canonist too (as 'Petrus Hispanus Portugalensis' and author of *Notabilia* on the 'Compilatio quarta'), he also was to establish links with the churches of both Calahorra and Osma, figuring in August 1232 as treasurer of the one and 'vicario de Soria' in the other, benefices which he would continue to enjoy after his promotion to the see of Porto three years later.[51]

With his Portuguese origins and Bolognese credentials, Melendus of Osma may therefore be regarded as representative of another aspect of that extra-peninsular dimension of Fernando III's reign on which Dr Hernández sheds such penetrating light – though in Melendus's case the immediate context must have been the reign of Alfonso VIII and that ruler's celebrated programme for the recruitment of academic talent from abroad to provide faculty for the nascent *studium* at Palencia[52] – a process in which the chronicler Lucas of Tuy may have been

---

[49] Above, n. 39; *Chronicon Abbatiae de Evesham, ad annum 1418*, ed. W. Dunn Macray; Rolls Ser., London 1863, 153: 'nulli mortali simul in utroque jure tunc temporis habebatur secundus'. For Melendus' Santa Cruz de Coimbra origins, see Ingo Fleisch's excellent Magisterarbeit Dissertation, 'Kirche, Königtum und gelehrtes Recht im hochmittelalterlichen Portugal', Otto-Friedrich-Universität Bamberg 1998, 106-30. Cf. G. Fransen, 'Les gloses de Melendus et l'apparat d'Alain l'Anglais sur le Décret de Gratien', *Cahiers de Fanjeaux* 29; L'Église et le droit dans le Midi (XIIIe-XIVe s.), Toulouse 1994, 21-35.

[50] For 'magister Vincentius Oxomensis [prior?]' in the *familia* of Bishop Melendus at IV Lateran, see Rivera, 'Personajes hispanos', 337, whose reading 'prior' of a word truncated in the Toledo manuscript follows that of F. Fita ('Santiago de Galicia. Nuevas impugnaciones y nueva defensa', *Razón y Fe*, 2 [1902], 43). He must have been the *sacrist* of Osma of that name (not to be confused with the canonist Vincentius Hispanus) who was appointed to serve as judge-delegate in Portugal in May 1216. See A. D. de Sousa Costa, 'Presenza di Alessandro di Hales e di Vincentius Hispanus al I Concilio di Lione', *Antonianum*, 59 (1984), 187.

[51] I. Rodríguez de Lama, *Colección diplomática medieval de la Rioja*, IV. *Documentos siglo XIII*, Logroño 1989, 101 (cit. Fleisch, 140). When in December 1237 he was involved in litigation with Sancho II of Portugal his adversary's proctor would allege 'quod retinebat ecclesiam Sancte Montis Maioris [S. Maria de Montemor-o-Velho, dioc. Coimbra], thesaurariam Calagurritanam et vicariam perpetuam Sauriensem contra constitutionem et prohibitionem legati' (i.e. John of Abbeville): Porto, Arquivo Distrital, Mitra, Pergaminhos, Caixa 1867, doc. 7. (Although in May 1235 Gregory IX had permitted him to retain these benefices 'ad beneplacitum', that licence had not determined the question of his earlier possession of them in plurality: Archivio Segreto Vaticano, Reg. Vat. 18, fo. 32v, ep. 92 [*Reg. Greg. IX*, 2601]). It was also claimed against him in 1237 that he was excommunicated 'maiori excommunione ideo quia Bononie percussit Johannem Martini Denton clericum qui nunc est canonicus Bracharensis et quod hoc fuit XX. anni sunt elapsi. Respondit episcopus quod non percussit Johannem Martini Denton clericum, et si percussit ignorabat ipsum clericum esse, et paratus est iurare hoc': a biographical detail to be added to those assembled by I. da R. Pereira, 'O canonista Petrus Hispanus Portugalensis', *Arquivos de História da Cultura Portuguesa*, 2/4 (1968), 3-18.

[52] On which much-visited though far from exhausted subject, see D. Maffei, 'Fra Cremona, Montpellier e Palencia nel secolo XII. Ricerche su Ugolino da Sesso', *Rivista Internazionale di Diritto Comune*, 1 (1990), 9-30 Linehan, *History and the Historians*, 308-9; A. Iglesia Ferreirós, 'Rex superiorem non recognoscens. Hugolino de Sesso y el studium de Palencia', *Initium*, 3 (1998), 1-205.

yet another late chrysanthemum.[53] And, *en route* for Osma, Melendus had been at Palencia too.[54] Why indeed in the year 1210, other than on account of irresistible terms offered by its king, should a distinguished Portuguese jurist at the height of his powers and enjoying an international clientele have chosen to bury himself in the heart of rural Castile?

But whether or not Melendus had been invited into Castile on Alfonso VIII's initiative, he must soon have regretted having made the move. For in 1214 Alfonso VIII died, having ten years earlier bequeathed to the church of Osma the *señorío* of its cathedral city, in atonement for an injustice that had been done to that church in his name during his minority in the cause (curiously enough) of the defence of Calahorra,[55] a bequest that provoked the furious opposition of – who but doña Berenguela? Whilst the queen-mother's son, the saintly scourge of the see of Calahorra, turned a deaf ear to the incessant tirades of papal judges-delegate, and the bishop of Zaragoza, safe and sound across a political frontier wrung his hands and wondered aloud what was to become of justice if bishops were forever to remain in dread of princes, the contest scarred the remainder of Melendus' pontificate. Symbolically perhaps with regard to Alfonso VIII's academic initiative, it was not to the church of Osma but to that of Braga that in 1225 Bishop Melendus bequeathed his library.[56]

Moreover, throughout the twenty-one year period between then and the death of the chancellor D. Juan it was not with Osma that the staff of the nascent royal chancery were particularly associated, but rather, as Millares Carlo noticed as long ago as 1926, with Soria.[57] And Soria was not Osma, much as its attempt to secure con-cathedral status in 1267 shows that it aspired to be. Although that initiative failed therefore, on the discovery that Clement IV's mandate had been obtained by subreption (in particular on account of its failure to reveal the extent of Osma opposition to the proposal), the claim that had been made on behalf of the place by Alfonso X *inter alios*, the claim that the 'castrum de Soria' was distinguished by its production of *alumni* both clerical and lay 'by whom not only the royal court but also parts of Spain both near and far were honoured'[58], nevertheless deserves consideration. For by contrast with other allegations advanced on that occasion – its pretence of being 'fecundum in populis', for example[59] - that part of Soria's claim to fame was not wholly without

---

[53] See Peter Linehan, 'Fechas y sospechas sobre Lucas de Tuy', *Anuario de Estudios Medievales*, 32 (2002), XXX.

[54] For his sale to D. Tello bishop-elect of Palencia in July 1211 of 'domos quas habemus in Palencia', see T. Abajo Martín, *Documentación de la catedral de Palencia (1035-1247)*, Palencia 1986, no. 128.

[55] González, *Alfonso VIII*, no. 769 (III. 345-6). Cf. Peter Linehan, 'Royal influence and papal authority in the diocese of Osma: a note on 'Quia requisistis' (JL 13728)', *Bulletin of Medieval Canon Law*, n.s. 20 (1990) [reprinted Linehan, *The Processes of Politics and the Rule of Law. Studies in the Iberian kingdoms and papal Rome in the Middle Ages*, Aldershot 2002], 33-43.

[56] J. Loperráez Corvalán, *Descripción histórica del obispado de Osma con el catálogo de sus prelados*, I, Madrid 1788 [repr. Madrid 1978], I. 213-23, III. 49-63; Linehan, *Spanish Church*, 10-11. For the will of Archbishop Estêvão Soares of Braga (Aug. 1228) ordering the sale of legal texts and the purchase of 'libri ecclesiastici (...) qui semper serviant in coro bracarensi ad instar libros quod episcopus obsomensis [*sic*] bone memorie reliquit ecclesie bracarensi', see I. da R. Pereira, 'Livros de direito na Idade Média', *Lusitania Sacra*, 7 (1964-6), 15.

[57] Millares Carlo, 289-90; González, *Fernando III*, I. 511.

[58] '...tales producit alumnos tam clericos quam laicos per quos non solum regalis curia verum etiam tam propinque quam remote partes Yspanie honorantur': Loperráez, III. 200-02.

[59] Regarding which see the data assembled just three years later and analysed by E. Jimeno, 'La población de Soria y su término en 1270', *Boletín de la Real Academia de la Historia*, 142 (1958), 207-74, 365-494.

substance. And the letter regarding *los sorianos* written by the locals within the chapter of Jaén in 1283, a letter celebrated in a different context, provides ample confirmation of it, albeit from a very different standpoint.

On Fernando III's reconquest of Jaén in 1246 there was a bishop in waiting in the person of D. Domingo, bishop of Baeza since 1232 and, as a Dominican friar an altogether suitable prelate for that frontier place, it might be thought. But not so. For, as Pope Innocent IV wrote in the first week of January 1246, 'it had reached his ears' that D. Domingo was a paralytic incapable of pastoral exertions. Accordingly, the pontiff provided him with the assistance of the dean of Baeza as co-adjutor in order to ensure that the pastoral needs of that 'nouella plantatio' were properly provided for.[60] Three years later, however, the pope had to write again, having had it reported to him that D. Domingo remained sufficiently mobile to be leading 'a detestable existence, displeasing in the sight of both God and men' and to have made off with the books and ornaments of his church.[61] Otherwise stated, the bishop of Baeza to whom Innocent had recommended the example of Job to ease his disappointment had since been leading the life of Lazarus. So, reprehensible although such a life-style doubtless was, it would appear that what had been earlier reported to Rome about the bishop's state of health had been factually incorrect. And by whom can such reports have been provided in late 1245 or early 1246, while the siege of Jaén was in progress and Fernando III was still harbouring schemes to put his sons into the sees of Toledo and Seville in due course, other than Fernando himself and his chancellor Juan de Soria, then in the last year of his life, according to whose History ten years earlier D. Domingo and his retinue had hastened to the assistance of the Christian uprising in Córdoba *festinanter*?[62] And for what purpose other than to clear the way for D. Pedro Martínez, Juan de Soria's successor as Fernando's chancellor?[63]

Be that as it may, according to the complainants in 1283, 'el primer prelado que ouo el obispado de Jahén fue el Obispo don Domingo et del aca ffucron todos de Ssoria.' And the rest of the story is sufficiently familiar. Jaén's second bishop had been Pedro Martínez, and its third D. Pascual, the man favoured by Alfonso X for appointment to the see of Toledo at the very time that both of them were pressing for Soria's advancement.[64] Thus, by 1267 Soria

---

[60] Archivio Segreto Vaticano, Reg. Vat. 21, fo. 257r-v, ep. 312. Although calendared in É. Berger, *Les registres d'Innocent IV*, Paris 1884-1921, 1664-1666, the pontiff's letter to the bishop and associated correspondence are not printed there, and unaccountably they are missing from A. Quintana Prieto, *La documentación pontificia de Innocencio IV (1243-1254)*, Rome 1987. Despite being alerted to the Vatican evidence by C. Eubel's note (*Hierarchia Catholica medii aevi*, I, Münster-in-W., 1913, 130) — whence the fragment published by D. Mansilla, *Iglesia castellano-leonesa y curia romana en los tiempos del rey San Fernando*, Madrid 1945, 184 n. 176, omitting the information that D. Domingo was to be reinstated if he recovered from his paralysis – and by Linehan, *Spanish Church*, 234, historians of the church of Jaén over the last century have neglected the substance of the information that is now printed below as Appendix II (a-e). Cf. J. Rodríguez Molina, *El obispado de Baeza-Jaén (siglos XIII-XVI). Organización y economía diocesanas*, Jaén 1986, 34. As Berger noted in 1884, it is remarkable that, according to the record of the Vatican Register, the clergy and people of the city and diocese appear to have been informed of D. Domingo's retirement in advance of the bishop himself.

[61] Appendix III.

[62] *Crónica latina*, 95 [ed. CCCM, § 71, p. 113].

[63] Who by February 1249 was bishop-elect of Jaén, though D. Domingo was still alive and kicking: below, n. 76.

[64] M. Nieto Cumplido, *Orígenes del regionalismo andaluz*, Córdoba 1979, 136-7; E. Jordan, *Les registres de Clément IV*, Paris 1893-1945, 1036; Rodríguez Molina, *El obispado de Baeza-Jaén*, 35-6. The ascendancy of the

was a principal seminary of Castile's civil service, the location of its *École normale supérieure*. And, as the locals complained in 1283, well before then those civil servants of Soria who were clerics had long enjoyed the church of Jaén as a retirement home.

In 1237, this process was already well undersay, it is suggested, a process that paralleled the part played in the reconquest and settlement of the area by other contingents of Sorians as well as by Lope Ruiz de Haro, the son of Fernando III's zealous agent in the diocese of Calahorra.[65] Castile's irruption into Andalucia necessitated changes in every department of society, not least in the operations of the civil service. So far, the consequences of those changes have hardly been appreciated by students of the period, for all that the insights of Hernández and Wright regarding the infiltration of the vernacular,[66] and those of the former in these very pages on the subject of the significantly different accounts of the events of the reign of Fernando III provided by the chancellor who had ceased to be, even nominally, and the chancellor by whom he had been supplanted, are beginning to redirect our quest for understanding of these years away from the now exhausted historiographical *cañadas* of the past.

There are many questions about those consequences that cry out for reconsideration and for liberation, not only from the old shibboleths that provided a cover for piety but also from the new that are allowed to pass for scholarship. Why, for example, was it that Soria came to enjoy its privileged position? Why not Palencia? When will someone competent to do so revisit the question of the idealised relationship of king and archbishop as presented in the prologue to the *De rebus Hispanie*, the work in which the only mention made of Juan de Soria emphasises his subjection to Toledo?[67] — which in view of the generous use he was making of the other's History at the time, as Hernández demonstrates here, was strangely uncollegial of him.

If it is to get under the skin of its subject, the new history of the reign of Fernando III will have to make allowance for the fast-developing state of things. Within the limited confines of the present *comunicación*, for example, and with regard to Juan de Soria, it will need to attempt to explain why it was that whereas Gregory IX was so reluctant to oblige the king regarding the Osma election in 1231, six years later it was a different story altogether. Why? Because of the king's recent victories in Andalucia? Because of Roman apprehension that unless the pope obliged him on this occasion the king of Castile might ease off? The suggestion is not altogether absurd. After all, both Gregory and, more fatally, his successor were prepared to make over to Fernando the financial seed-corn of the Castilian churches.[68]

---

Soria-Jaén axis at the end of Fernando III's reign is further attested by the transfer on papal instructions of all the benefices that D. Pascual had enjoyed before his election 'in diocesi Oxomensi' (and in particular in Soria) to his brother, Bartolomé: *Reg. Inn. IV*, 4901 (printed, with misleading lemma, Quintana Prieto, *Documentación pontificia*, no. 683). It was a particular grievance of the *naturales* in 1283 that 'el algo de las rentas et los beneffiçios de la eglesia et del obispado daualo [D. Pascual] a los suyos et a los de su tierra, posponiendo los naturales del obispado et non les dando nenguna cosa si non quando mas non podie': Nieto Cumplido, *loc. cit.*

[65] G. Argote de Molina, *Nobleza de Andalucía*, Jaén 1957, 166, 172, 440.

[66] See in particular F. J. Hernández, 'Sobre los orígenes del español escrito', *Voz y letra*, 10 (1999), esp. pp. 152-3; Roger Wright, *El Tratado de Cabreros (1206): estudio sociofilológico de una reforma ortográfica*; Papers of the Medieval Hispanic Research Seminar 19, Queen Mary and Westfield College London 2000, 99-116.

[67] Ed. cit., 299.

[68] Linehan, *Spanish Church*, chap. 6.

Albeit feebly, Gregory IX had resisted Fernando's unbridled opposition to the proposal to disturb the integrity of the see of Calahorra. Thirty years later, however, when Alfonso X was thought to favour a rearrangement of the same sort at the expense of the see of Osma, Clement IV readily acquiesced. Things did not stand still. Force ruled. In his long-running dispute with doña Berenguela for possession of the city of Osma it was no help to Bishop Melendus that he was rated second to none amongst jurists in both laws. Nor were similar qualifications of any assistance to his pupil Pedro Salvadores, sometime treasurer of Calahorra and vicar of Soria, in the bitter dispute in which, when bishop of Porto, he found himself engaged with the local Franciscans.[69] The law had its limitations and life had its hazards. Single-minded women were one of them, mendicant-inclined pontiffs another.

Since his promotion to the episcopate just fifteen years before, therefore, by the time that Juan of Soria, that 'man of great counsel and useful and necessary both to Fernando III and to his kingdom' died on 1 October 1246,[70] having shrewdly appointed doña Berenguela and the archbishop, both of them moribund, among his executors, everything had changed.

But, like doña Berenguela herself and the archbishop too perhaps, I have gone on too long after all.

### Appendix

I *Toledo, 7 April [?1235/1236].  Juan de Soria, bishop of Osma and chancellor of Fernando III, informs the prior and chapter of Osma of the death of the sacrist of Osma, fr. Gonzalo García.  Being about to join the royal army and expecting to be engaged there for some time, he appoints his cleric J. Gutiérrez to the vacant* sacristanía *- or if he is not empowered to do so recommends him to the prior and chapter for appointment.*

Burgo de Osma, Biblioteca del Cabildo, MS. 89, fo. 1r

J. dei gratia Oxomensis episcopus domini regis cancellarius dilectis in Christo filiis priori et capitulo Oxomensibus salutem et benedictionem. Noueritis quod frater Gundissaluus olim sacrista noster uiam est uniuerse carnis ingressus. Verum quia ad exercitum quantum possumus properamus et de protrahenda ibidem mora uehementer presumimus, ne medio tempore in officio sacristanie defectum aliquem ecclesie paciatur in hoc dubio, uiam elegimus tuciorem et quantum in nobis fuit si possumus sacristaniam dilecto clerico nostro J. Gutterii con-tulimus, et si non possumus commendamus[71], uiro discreto[72], prouido et honesto per quem speramus multa prouenire ecclesie tam in temporalibus quam in spiritualibus profutura. Quo-circa mandamus, monemus et rogamus quatinus cum ad uos accesserit eum bene et caritatiue recipiatis, honorem et gratiam ei in quibus poteritis impensuri. Dat. Toleti vii. die Aprilis.

---

[69] J. A. Ferreira, *Memórias arqueólogico-históricas da cidade de Porto. Fastos episcopais e políticos*, Braga 1923, i. 218-23.
[70] Serrano, 'El canciller', 24.
[71] et si non possumus commendamus, *interlin.*
[72] et *del.*

II (a) *Lyons, 6 January 1246. Innocent IV to the bishop of Baeza [fr. Domingo OP] who is afflicted by paralytic illness, appointing the dean of Baeza his coadjutor.*

Archivio Segreto Vaticano, Reg. Vat. 21, fo. 257r-v, ep. 312

Episcopo Beatiensi. Sicut nostris est auribus[73] relatum, adeo morbo paralytico es grauatus ut menbrorum tuorum destitutus officio tibimet grauis et Beatiensi ecclesie ad exequendum pastorale officium inutilis es[74] effectus, nos igitur infirmitati tue paterno compatientes affectu et tuum uolentes alleuiari laborem, dilectum filium decanum Beatiensem, de cuius circumspectione ac industria plenam in domino fiduciam obtinemus, tibi coadiutorem in spiritualibus et temporalibus duximus deputandum. Ideoque fraternitatem tuam monemus et hortamur attente mandantes quatinus uirtutem in infirmitate perficiens, et eandem infirmitatem exemplo beati Job sustinens patienter, curam eiusdem ecclesie una cum ipso decano sic utiliter geras, non que tua sunt sed que Jhesu Christi querendo, quod ad utilitatem ipsi ecclesie tibique cedat ad cumulum meritorum. Dat. Lugduni, viii. id. januarii anno tertio.

II (b) *Lyons, 6 January 1246. Innocent IV* mutatis mutandis *to the dean of Baeza.*

Archivio Segreto Vaticano, Reg. Vat. 21, fo. 257v, ep. 313

Decano Beatiensi. Sicut nostris auribus est relatum, venerabilis frater noster episcopus Beatiensis adeo morbo paralytico etc. usque *effectus*. Ne igitur ipsa ecclesia que tamquam nouella plantatio spiritualibus et temporalibus indiget incrementis sub inutilis sponsi nomine, licet sponsum uideatur habere, incomoda uidue diutius patiatur, te de cuius circumspectione ac industria plenam in domino fiduciam obtinemus eidem episcopo coadiutorem duximus deputandum, discretioni tue per apostolica scripta mandantes quatinus ipsius ecclesie curam tam in spiritualibus quam in temporalibus sic geras sollicite ac prudenter quod dignam deo exinde possis reddere rationem, nosque diligentie tue studium possimus in domino merito commendare. Si uero dictus episcopus, faciente illo qui percurat et medetur sanitati pristine ad plenum fuerit restitutus, ab huius cura uolumus te cessare. Dat. ut in proxima.

II (c) *Lyons, 6 January 1246. Innocent IV* mutatis mutandis *to the chapter of Baeza.*

Archivio Segreto Vaticano, Reg. Vat. 21, fo. 257v, ep. 314

Capitulo Beatiensi. Sicut nostris auribus est relatum, ut in proxima usque *diutius patiatur*. Decanum Beatiensem de cuius circumspectione ac industria etc. ut in proxima usque *deputandum*, nostris sibi dantes litteris in mandatis ut ipsius ecclesie curam etc. usque *restitutus*, ab huius cura decanum cessare uolumus memoratum. Ideoque uniuersitati uestre per apostolica scripta firmiter precepto mandamus quatinus eidem decano in premissis plene ac

---

[73] It should be of interest to historians of the papal chancery, and to students of the process of registration in particular, that one dash appears above 'est' and two above 'auribus' to indicate the need for transposition of the words, as was indeed effected in 2(b) and (c).

[74] *rectius* sis.

efficaciter intendatis. Alioquin sententiam quam ipse propter hoc rite tulerit in rebelles etc. usque *obseruari*. Dat. Lugduni, viii id. januarii anno tertio.

II (d,e) *Lyons, 21 December 1245.* Innocent IV mutatis mutandis *to the clergy of the city and diocese of Baeza, and to the people dean of Baeza of the city and diocese of Baeza.*

Archivio Segreto Vaticano, Reg. Vat. 21, fo. 257v, s.n.

In eodem modo clero ciuitatis et diocesis Beatiensis.

In eodem modo populo ciuitatis et diocesis Beatiensis usque *efficaciter intendatis*, ita quod uestra deuotio possit exinde merito commendari.[75] Dat. Lugduni, xii kal. januarii anno tertio.

III *Undated, but* post *15 January 1249.*[76] *Informed of the abusive behaviour of Bishop Domingo of Baeza, [Innocent IV] deprives the bishop of the (annual?) pension of fifty aurei previously awarded to him, and orders him to be secluded in a house of his Order outside the diocese of Jaén and to restore to the church of Jaén the books and ornaments detained by him.*

The so-called Formulary of Marinus of Eboli, *apud* Toulouse, Bibliothèque Municipale, MS. 473, fo. 92r, collated with Arles, Bibliothèque Municipale, MS. 60, fo. 76r.[77]

Quod quondam episcopus priuetur provisione sibi facta quominus[78] abutitur.

De benignitate sedis apostolice processisse percepimus quod, cum frater Dominicus de ordine predicatorum episcopus Beaciensis[79] cessisset oneri pontificalis[80] officii non honori, fuit ei quoad uiueret[81] de bonis Giennensis[82] ecclesie quingentorum aureorum prouisio assignata, quam deducens nequiter in abusum, ducit uitam detestabilem[83] et in conspectu dei ac hominum displicentem, multis mirantibus quod cum sit imbecillis et debilis et impotens ad executionem officii pastoralis, tamen super hiis fortitudinem habere dinoscitur per quem saluti ac fame

---

[75] MS. commendarit

[76] By which date the Castilian chancery listed Pedro Martínez as bishop of Jaén (although a month later he was listed as bishop-elect): C. de Ayala Martínez (coord.), *Libro de privilegios de la Orden de San Juan de Jerusalén en Castilla y León (siglos XII-XV)*, Madrid n.d., no. 308 (p. 518); González, *Fernando III*, no. 775. In September 1248 D. Domingo had still been acting as bishop, assisted by his co-adjutor: Rodríguez Molina, *El obispado de Baeza-Jaén*, 34.

[77] For copies of the letter on which the text printed here is based – T. and A. respectively — I am indebted to Dr. Martin Bertram (Deutsches Historisches Institut in Rom). Cf. F. Schillmann, *Die Formularsammlung des Marinus von Eboli*, I. *Entstehung und Inhalt*, Rome 1929, no. 461; M. Bertram, 'Zwei neue Handschriften der Briefsammlung des Pseudo-Marinus von Eboli', in K. Borchardt and E. Bünz (eds.), *Forschungen zur Reichs-, Papst- und Landesgeschichte. Peter Herde zum 65. Geburtstag von Freunden, Schülern und Kollegen dargebracht*, Stuttgart 1998, 457-75, esp. p. 461.

[78] T. qua minis; A. quo nimis

[79] A. Beannensis

[80] T. pontificatus

[81] T. quo aduiueret, A. quo adiuueret

[82] A. Gennensis

[83] A. detastabilem

ipsius multipliciter derogatur.[84] Quia uero super hoc debet taliter prouideri quod dicto episcopo salus inde proueniat, et occasione sui fama dicti ordinis non ledatur, mandamus quatinus, si quod de premissa uita ipsius episcopi proponitur[85] ueritate fulcitur, eum transire ad aliquam domum dicti ordinis extra diocesim Giennensem ac ibi uiuere sub obseruantia regulari necnon quod libros et ornamenta spectantia de iure ad Giennensem quondam Beaciensem ecclesiam que habere dicitur dilecto filio... electo Giennensi sine obiectu difficultatis assignet, monitione premissa, cessante appellationis obstaculo, auctoritate nostra compellas, et a soluendis sibi predictis aureis absoluas ecclesiam memoratam.

---

[84] **A.** derogantur
[85] *om.* **T.**

# V

## Juan de Soria: the Chancellor as Chronicler

It was the man who made known the only surviving manuscript of the anonymous Latin Chronicle [*CLI*][1] who first commented on the textual parallels of that work with Archbishop Rodrigo of Toledo's *De rebus Hispanie* [*DRH*], albeit, as parallels go, these may be said not to amount to much. The two chroniclers' accounts of the two great battles of their lifetime, for example, those of Alarcos and Las Navas de Tolosa, could hardly have been more different.[2] It is not so much in verbal similarities as in the sequence in which events are described that a resemblance between the two works is observable.[3] But one coincidence, remarked on by neither Cirot nor Julio González but by our absent colleague Francisco Hernández, clinches the matter and establishes the nature of their relationship. This is not something that they have in common in that from both it is missing. It is the absence of any account of the years 1220–23 as well as the manner in which each resumes his narrative after the lacuna: sufficient proof that here at least the archbishop was following our man.[4]

So D. Rodrigo made use of the Latin Chronicle, just as elsewhere in his work he made use of the chronicle of Lucas of Tuy. Now we medievalists

---

[1]   Georges CIROT, 'Chronique latine des rois de Castile (1236)', *Bulletin hispanique*, 14, 1912, pp. 30–46; 109–18; 244–74; 353–74 ; 15, 1913, 18–37; 17–87; 268–83; 411–27. Although in many respects Cirot's edition and commentary have never been bettered, for convenience I will cite the CCCM edition by L. CHARLO BREA (1997). I wish to thank members of the colloquium for helping me to change my mind about various of the issues discussed below, also Professors James Brundage, Richard Kinkade and Roger Wright for their comments on an earlier draft.

[2]   *CLI*, capp. 12–13; 22–4; *DRH* (ed. J. FERNÁNDEZ VALVERDE, CCCM, 1987), VII.29; IX.5–11. *Cf.* CIROT's characterisation of D. Rodrigo's of the earlier battle ('phraséologie ampoulée') by contrast with that of *CLI*: *Bulletin hispanique*, 14, p. 259n.

[3]   As for example in their descriptions of the rebellion of Gonzalo Pérez de Molina in 1223, analysed by F. J. HERNÁNDEZ, 'La corte de Fernando III y la casa real de Francia. Documentos, crónicas, monumentos', in: *Fernando III y su tiempo (1201–1252), VIII Congreso de Estudios Medievales*, León, 2003, pp. 103–55, p. 116. See also the unsystematic list of instances given by J. GONZÁLEZ, 'La crónica latina de los reyes de Castilla', in *Homenaje a don Agustín Millares Carló*, Gran Canaria, 1975, t. 2, pp. 55–70, p. 65.

[4]   *CLI*, 41: 5 ('Anno iterum postea revoluto'); *DRH*, IX.11: 13 ('Anno postea iterum revoluto'); HERNÁNDEZ, 'La corte de Fernando III...', pp. 111–12.

are broad-minded. We have to be: we regularly forgive plagiarism (provided it was done long ago, not recently).[5] But the deliberate suppression of items of information, or of an entire source of information, that is another thing. Is it thinkable that D. Rodrigo was responsible for the fact that, but for the chance survival of the unique copy published by Cirot, and its modern descendent, the Latin Chronicle would be unknown to us? That is to say, was the almost complete disappearance of the work accidental? Or was it deliberate? To put it another way, ought we even to be thinking in terms of an act of *depuración*, of elimination of the competitor who had eclipsed him? And in that case was that disappearance due either to D. Rodrigo himself, in his capacity as executor of the author's will in 1246,[6] or of a loyal Toledan claque later active and intent on promoting the former archbishop's account of modern times?[7]

As we all remember, that account of modern times had been written at the behest of Fernando III. We remember this because the prologue to the *De rebus Hispanie* tells us as much ; just as the prologue to Lucas of Tuy tells us that the *Chronicon mundi* was written on the instructions of doña Berenguela. By comparison, the Latin chronicle appears to have had no influential friends or protectors – though we are also told that it was the influence of the same doña Berenguela that secured Juan de Soria his promotion as chancellor in 1217.[8] Lacking even a prologue, the chronicle begins its account 'in medias res'. It enters shyly and anonymously into the confident and unforgiving world of thirteenth-century Spanish historiography.

That anonymity is in many ways the chronicle's most interesting feature. At any rate, it provides us with a starting point. Consider the possibilities. There are two. One is that once it had a prologue which identified its author, but that this somehow got detached from the body of the work. Here we must consider the relevance of the chronicle of the unnamed bishop of Burgos mentioned by Zurita.[9] Julio González considered it 'probable' that

---

[5]     Though I am reluctant to accept the descriptions of *CLI* as written '*lo suficientemente tarde para comentar y parafrasear el* Chronicon *del Tudense*' (cf. note 53 below), and *DRH* as '*no* [...] *mucho más que una paráfrasis y comentario, a veces discrepante, de la* Crónica *del Canciller*': *ibid.*, pp. 106n, 112.

[6]     L. SERRANO, 'El canciller de Fernando III de Castilla', *Hispania*, 1, 1941, pp. 3–40, p. 37. (By the author I mean Juan de Osma, a.k.a. Juan de Soria.)

[7]     Whether the disappearance of manuscripts of the Romance Jofré de Loaisa was engineered in order to assist the hypothetical deception I am not in a position to say.

[8]     SERRANO, 'El canciller...', pp. 4–5; A. BALLESTEROS, 'Don Juan el canciller', *Correo erudito*, 1,1940, pp. 145–51, p. 151; J. GONZÁLEZ, *Reinado y diplomas de Fernando III*, t. 1, Córdoba, 1980, p. 504.

[9]     J. ZURITA, *Anales de la Corona de Aragón*, Zaragoza, 1561–1580, III.3.

this was our bishop and our chronicle[10]– which, if correct, would date the work to 1240–46. But, of course, it is not correct. Either González did not read, or he failed to understand, Cirot's demonstration that the information about Aragonese affairs related by Zurita from the 'general history of Castile' of that bishop of Burgos was supplied not by our chronicler but by one of his episcopal successors.[11]

The other possibility is that it did *not* have a prologue And if it did not, then why not? Was it because it was never intended as a chronicle at all? Or rather, because in the mind of the compiler it had not yet reached that stage of development? Remember: though prologues are the first things the reader reads, they are normally the last thing the writer writes.

As has often been noted, the Latin chronicle is unusually outward-looking, with information about foreign affairs provided at points throughout the text – but not always, indeed not often, at relevant points. These are notices which cannot be said to belong where they have come to rest, where it looks as if they have simply been left in expectation of a decision regarding their final destination. So could it be that what we have is a form of draft annals, as Dr Hernández has suggested[12] an accretion of chancery annals prepared by a succession of, as it were, 'annalists on duty'?[13] In fact, ought we to be speaking of 'a' compiler at all? Despite evidence of stylistic consistency (the use throughout the work of the adverb 'intrinsecus', for example),[14] ought we not rather to be speaking of 'compilers' in the plural, amongst whom there was uncertainty whether entries were to be dated by the Spanish or the Christian era?[15] (To these hypothetical 'compilers' I shall return) And of

---

[10]   GONZÁLEZ, 'La crónica latina…', p. 69.

[11]   *Anales*, III.2 [*ad an.* 1228]: '*Hallo en las crónicas que compuso en latín un obispo de Burgos, que trasladó la historia general de Castilla y fue en tiempo del rey don Alonso el décimo, que la principal causa porque Zeit Abuzeit fue echado del reino…*'. Regardless of what Zurita may have meant by '*y fue en tiempo del rey don Alonso el décimo*', in our chronicle the king of Valencia is identified not by name but only as 'rex […] calidus et astutus' (c. 54). For Zurita's alternative identifications of this bishop of Burgos as Gonzalo Pérez 'Gudiel' (†1299) and Gonzalo de Hinojosa (†1327), see CIROT, 'Cronique latine…', *Bulletin Hispanique*, 15,1913, pp. 272–4.

[12]   HERNÁNDEZ, 'La corte de Fernando III…', p. 111, n. 28.

[13]   Herewith just one of the reasons for rejecting González's suggestion that rather than borrowing one from another, *CLI* and *DRH* may both have used a common source ('*una anotación común*'): 'La crónica latina…', pp. 64–5. For in that case, where more appropriately might that source have been preserved than … in the royal chancery?

[14]   *CLI*, 4: 4; 12: 18; 19: 24; 38.13. The word occurs just twice in *CM*: 4.67.8; 4.88.3.

[15]   The former system is employed in chapp. 28–51, 64 and 68–9, the latter in chapp. 52–9, 65 and 67.

chronicles in the sense of the 'chronicles' mentioned by Guillermo Pérez de la Calzada, his 'Rithmi de Iulia Romula seu Ispalensi Urbe', into which new material might be 'added' or 'written'?[16] Consider the end of chap. 62 and chap. 63 in its entirety, concerning the year 1231–32:

> **62** [visit to Galicia and Asturias] … alios secum duxit Burgis.
> **63** Confluxit ad eandem ciuitatem maxima hominum multitudo populorum et nobilium tam de Castella quam de Gallecia et aliis partibus regni, ubi logam(!) protaxit moram rex, expediendo negocia multiformia cum consilio bonorum uirorum.

To me (but not to all) this looks suspiciously like an uncompleted annal.[17]

Reference to a chancery context brings us to an aspect of the matter which I have discussed elsewhere so will not repeat here, namely the probable extent of D. Rodrigo's resentment at the loss of prestige implied by the transfer of the Castilian chancery to Juan de Soria in 1231. Previous writers, sustained perhaps by the unspoken conviction that the bishops of a canonised king could never have been in discord with one another, have gone so far as to suggest that the transfer was made on the archbishop's own recommendation[18] (It has even been suggested that the pair were cousins).[19] In fact, the case was probably the opposite. The loss of the royal chancery represented a huge shrinkage of Toledo's prestige at the very moment at which its archbishop was planning its apotheosis in both script and stone.[20] The case did not go by default. Confirmation of Juan de Soria's episcopal promotion to the see of Osma was delayed by a year and a half or more, and by whom if not by his Toledo metropolitan?[21] And almost a century later the issue of Toledo's claim on the chancery was still alive. Out of concern for the state of the original

---

[16]   R. CARANDE HERRERO (ed.), CCCM 73 (1997), prol. lin. 11 ('in cronicis annotari'); lin. 170 ('scripta sunt <in> cronicis').

[17]   *Cf.* the contribution of Inés Fernández-Ordóñez to the present volume.

[18]   Peter LINEHAN, 'Don Rodrigo and the government of the kingdom', *Cahiers de linguistique et de civilisation hispaniques médiévales*, 26, 2003, pp. 87–99. *Cf.* J. GONZÁLEZ, *Fernando III...*, t. I. p. 506. For the same blithe assumption about D. Rodrigo's attitude to D. Juan's appointment in 1217, see L. SERRANO, 'El canciller...', p. 6.

[19]   Thus Roger WRIGHT, *Late Latin and Early Romance in Spain and Carolingian France*, Liverpool, 1982, p. 257. If so, blood was evidently thinner than water.

[20]   Peter LINEHAN, *History and the historians of Medieval Spain*, Oxford, 1993, pp. 350–412.

[21]   Id., 'D. Juan de Soria: unas apostillas', in: *Fernando III y su tiempo (1201–1252)*, pp. 377–93; p. 381.

of the chancellor's 1231 undertaking to surrender the chancellorship to the archbishop if he died or if he were promoted to a see outside the province of Toledo, in August 1329 the treasurer of the Toledo would seek to secure an authenticated copy of the instrument.[22]

On this occasion I wish to make just two observations and one suggestion. The first observation is this. In January 1218 (that is within three months of D. Juan's first appearance as royal chancellor) D. Rodrigo was seeking compensation for his loss of the royal chancery and thereby of the opportunity to influence expressions of the royal will, by securing two privileges from the papal chancery, one confirming the church of Toledo's primacy over the metropolis and province of Seville, the other granting it possession of the church of 'Zucketa' (*hispanice* 'Zuqueca'), which the archbishop had persuaded the pontiff was identical with the Visigothic see of Oreto;[23] then, in 1231, in the very month of the transfer of Toledo's hereditary chancellorship to D. Juan, D. Rodrigo had these privileges confirmed by Gregory IX.[24] It is difficult to believe that these coincidences were wholly fortuitous.

The second refers to the chancery of the kingdom of León which its traditional incumbent, the archbishop of Compostela, was also made to surrender to the abbot of Valladolid in 1231. Interest here attaches to the fact that in November 1216 Honorius III had sought to persuade Alfonso IX to bestow that office upon Juan Gaitán, papal subdeacon, *magister scolarum* of León, and nephew of Cardinal Pelayo Gaitán.[25] Notice two things: first, that none of those concerned pretended for a moment that the *cancelleria* of the kingdom of León was a purely decorative office. Far from it, the *cancelleria* of the kingdom of León (and of the kingdom of Castile too for that matter) was a licence to print money.[26] Secondly, that the pontiff's request bordered on

---

[22] '[…] *la qual mostrada el dicho thesorero dixo quela dicha carta era meester de mostrar en muchos logares et por periglos que podrian acaesçer en terminos e en otros logares*': [Madrid,] A[rchivo] H[istorico] N[acional], Clero, carp. 3019/8.

[23] D. MANSILLA, *La documentación pontificia de Honorio III (1216–1227)*, Rome, 1965, n° 153, 144.

[24] A[rchivo de la] C[atedral de] Toledo, X.7.A.3.6, X.1.A.1.3a ['Zucheta'] (4, 8 Apr. 1231; printed S. DOMÍNGUEZ SÁNCHEZ, *Documentos de Gregorio IX (1227–1241) referentes a España*, León, 2004, n° 176, 179 ['Çucheta' in Archivio Segreto Vaticano, Reg. Vat. 15, fol. 77r°]. For further implications of this 'little essay in creative antiquarianism', see P. LINEHAN, *History and the historians…*, pp. 340–44.

[25] D. MANSILLA, *La documentación pontificia…*, n° 10.

[26] It was seen as a suitably 'juicy' return for the benefits of the cardinal's influence at Rome, 'qui tibi et regno tuo esse potest multipliciter fructuosus'. The pope's letter continues: 'Preces nostras sic efficaciter impleturus affectui de affectu non subtrahens, et effectui

the limits of permissible interference in affairs of state, and that in November 1216, when it was made, Alfonso IX was in a peculiarly vulnerable position since another eighteen months were to pass before the pope was to declare his bastard son, the king of Castile, fit to rule the kingdom of León.[27]

The suggestion is simply this: that the almost complete disappearance of what we call the Latin chronicle may have provided the archbishop with further compensation for the loss of that office.

The chancellor had replaced the archbishop as the intimate of princes. The spectacle of him celebrating the first mass in the purified mosque of reconquered Córdoba in 1236 may well have seemed to endanger that primatial jurisdiction regarding whose defence D. Rodrigo had been so exercised just five years earlier, and all the more so after 1243 by which time Fernando III was poised to deliver the Castilian Church into the hands of two of his sons and the chancellor was the bishop of an exempt see beyond the other's jurisdiction.[28] The chancellor's will recalls the man who had accompanied the infantes to Paris and Murcia.[29]

His is the voice of the courtier, the insider who can record such intimate details as Queen Leonor climbing into bed with her dead son and trying to resuscitate him (20: 10–13) or letters from the king of Aragón concerning the capture of Mallorca (55: 24). But it is also the voice of government, with his remarks on the profitlessness of Gascony (c. 17: 41–3) representing, as it were, the considered opinion of the Ministry of Foreign Affairs. With his unusual emphasis on extra-peninsular events and their complexities, he was the first Castilian chronicler of international range. In his cosmopolitanism he provides the perfect foil for those doughty champions of Christendom,

---

adiciens per affectum, quod et nos precibus tuis ex hoc specialius grata teneamur vicissitudine respondere'. *Cf.* the same play on the words *effectus-affectus* (and in this case *affectio*) in the begging letter on behalf of another of the cardinal's nephews ('P. latorem presencium') contained in the formulary of Thomas of Capua (datable from its context to 1218–21 and perhaps meant for the bishop of Salamanca) in S.F. HAHN, *Collectio monvmentorvm* […] *Antiqvitates, geographiam, historiam omnem, ac nobiliores ivris partes havd mediocriter illustrantivm*, Brvnsvigae, t. 1, 1724, pp. 383–4; Peter LINEHAN, *The Spanish Church and the Papacy in the thirteenth century*, Cambridge, 1971, pp. 291–2.

    [27]  MANSILLA, *La documentación pontificia…*, n° 179; LINEHAN, *History and the historians…*, pp. 258–9.

    [28]  CLI, chap. 73–4. D. Rodrigo was at pains to insist that the chancellor had done the honours 'Roderici Toletani primatis uices [gerente]' (*DRH*, IX.17: 8): apparently the only occasion in his chronicle on which he described himself as primate. See F.J. HERNÁNDEZ & P. LINEHAN, *The Mozarabic Cardinal. The life and times of Gonzalo Pérez Gudiel*, Florence, 2004, pp. 30–32.

    [29]  SERRANO, 'El canciller…', pp. 39–40.

Alfonso VIII, Fernando III and…Cardinal Pelayo Gaitán, leader of the ill-fated Fifth Crusade.[30] D. Juan had his cultural formation in the Burgos of Bishop Mauricio while Alfonso VIII was scouring France and Italy for staff for his new university of Palencia, and maintaining Gerard of Cremona in his translation work at Toledo: a tradition which, by his support there of Hermannus Alemannus, D. Juan himself would continue in the 1240s.[31] His attitude with regard to Islam and the Islamic foe is more nuanced than Juan Gil has suggested.[32]

He had been in Rome at least twice (30: 63, 67). Was it on his travels abroad that he had learnt the practice of royal annals, with the material for each year collected separately – and therefore that much more liable to be lost (as in Castile indeed it was) – and written up over a period of years, with assistants in the chancery involved in the process, but not 'for publication' as they stood. The unpacked reference to Gratian in c. 1, recently identified by Prof. James Brundage in a footnote to O'Callaghan's translation, provides an indication of this.[33] As do the playful reference 'discordiam discordantium ad concordiam reuocauit' in c. 35: 9 apropos of Fernando III's acclamation as

---

[30]   *CLI*, cap. 58–9, where the author reveals (59: 6–7) that the cardinal had previously been bishop-elect of León: a fact confirmed by Thomas of Capua (HAHN, *Collectio, loc. cit.*) though it has passed unnoticed by most modern historians of the Spanish Church. See D. MANSILLA, 'El cardenal hispano Pelayo Gaitán', *Anthologica Annua*, 1, 1953, pp. 11–66, pp. 12–14; LINEHAN, *The Spanish Church and the Papacy…*, p. 279 n. 3. 'Domnus Pelagius' is first recorded as bishop-elect of León in April 1207 and Feb. 1208 but has disappeared by Jan. 1209 (J.M. FERNÁNDEZ CATÓN, *Colección documental del archivo de la catedral de León (775–1230)*, VI *(1188–1230)*, León, 1991, p. 18, n° 1793, 1800, 1806). He had been cardinal-deacon of S.Lucia since 1205 and was promoted cardinal-bishop of Albano in 1213: C. EUBEL, *Hierarchia catholica medii et recentioris aevi*, vol. 1, Munich, 1913, p. 3.

[31]   LINEHAN, *History and the Historians…*, pp. 308–9; 'libri [geomancie] quem [sic] magister Gerardus de Cremona [† 1187], magnus medicus in phisica, transtulit de arabico in latinum, habens expensas a rege Castelle': ms. Chantilly 322, fol. 45v° (cit. C. BURNETT, 'Filosofía natural, secretos y magia', in L. GARCÍA BALLESTER (ed.), *Historia de la ciencia y de la técnica en la Corona de Castilla*, t. 1, *Edad Media*, Salamanca, 2002, pp. 95–144, p. 128 n. 144); W.F. BOGGESS, 'Hermannus Alemannus's rhetorical translations', *Viator*, 2, 1971, pp. 227–50, p. 248 (identifying the chancellor as 'Juan Domingues de Medina'), p. 249.

[32]   E.g. in his description of Ibn-Tūmart as 'uir sapiens et discretus licet infidelis' (6: 14). *Cf.* GIL, 'La historiografía': *La cultura del románico, siglos XI al XIII. Letras, religiosidad, artes, ciencia y vida*, F. LÓPEZ ESTRADA (ed.) [*Historia de España Menéndez Pidal*, XI], Madrid, 1995, p. 86: '*no hay piedad para los infieles* […] *La religión islámica y sus ritos provocan náusea: las mezquitas han de ser limpiadas de la inmundicia* (spurcicia) *agarena antes de ser consagradas al culto cristiano*'. There was nothing particularly significant about his use of the term *spurcicia*, which at this time was routine usage in the papal chancery for all things Muslim.

[33]   J. O'CALLAGHAN, *The Latin Chronicle of the kings of Castile*, Tempe, AR., 2002, p. 3.

king of Castile, and the description of the king of Aragón, Ramiro the Monk, in c. 4: 56 as 'tamquam inutilis regni regimini'. Here were the coded allusions for the *cognoscenti* amounting almost to a series of internal memoranda.[34]

Coming after him, D. Rodrigo either sacrificed such foreign material to his by 1243 increasingly eccentric arrangement of both peninsular and other matters (for example, and in defiance of all chronological considerations, displacing Peter of Aragón to Book VI, chap. 4, and the affairs of the Latin Empire to Book VII, chap. 24) or felt no need to incorporate it at all, as in the case of the Albigensian Crusade, the Fourth Lateran Council (though, like D. Juan, he had been there), and Italian developments. Did D. Rodrigo find it easier to distribute non-Castilian material in this way, or to ignore it altogether, because it had not been assigned a place in the abandoned Latin chronicle's narrative?

The 'annalist on duty' hypothesis might be thought to account for the fact that more than half of all the classical allusions that the text contains occur in just five of its 75 chapters (concerning the years 1195–1211).[35] The same explanation, namely that the 'annalist on duty' had simply failed in that duty, might account for the complete absence of any record for the years 1220–23. But it also raises other problems, in the words of scripture making 'the last state worse than the first'. For example, in the years before 1217 Juan de Soria was not yet chancellor, so when did he begin writing *or superintending the writing* of the Chronicle? Did he inherit a going concern? Or, from 1217, did he project back to the beginning of the reign of Alfonso VIII, 'borrowing' the first eight thin chapters from somewhere, evidently not Lucas? Why, when the chancellor continued in office until his death in 1246, does the Chronicle end in 1236? Why was it that D. Rodrigo appears not to have made use of the *CLI* after 1224? For that matter, how did D. Rodrigo gain access to the chancellor's account at all? Above all, how is the work's concluding pentameter to be explained? 'Hoc opus explui tempore, credo, breui' (75: 5). What is the work that is being completed in short order here? Dr Charlo Brea has discerned changes in the texture of the Chronicle from chap. 60 onwards. But whether he is right or wrong about that, the problems concerning *CLI* go far further.

---

[34]  Acquaintance with at least the jargon of civil law is evident at chap. 2: 11–12 and 65: 4.

[35]  *CLI*, 2: 6 and 11–12 (Lucan); 13: 28 (Prudentius); 14: 5 (Virgil); 15: 1–2 (Seneca); 17: 1–2 (Ovid); 17: 34 (Virgil); 17: 41 (Horace); 18: 15–16 (Horace); 18: 30–31 (Virgil); 23: 43–4 (Claudian); 40: 23=44: 26 (Horace); 74: 24 (Virgil). I have been assisted in the task of identification by O'Callaghan's translation, though not all his suggestions have I accepted. Biblical references provide a less useful index. They abound throughout the work, though as many as 30 of its 75 chapters lack them.

Allow me to approach these problems from two directions, first the contextual and then the textual.

During the troubled period at the beginning of Fernando's reign as king of Castile, after Berenguela had abdicated to him her rights of succession, it was alleged that in fact she had had nothing to abdicate because it was not she but her sister Blanca (Blanche of Castile) who was Alfonso VIII's eldest surviving daughter. So Fernando's domestic enemies stated in letters probably of 1224 in which they offered the Castilian crown to Blanche's son, the future Louis IX. This, they claimed, was what on his deathbed Alfonso VIII had decreed should happen in the event of his son Enrique dying without issue. It was, one of them stated, the king's 'last will'. That claim – which was to enjoy a measure of credence in interested circles, and particularly interested French circles, for centuries to come down to Bodin and beyond – depended entirely on the credibility of the story that Berenguela was junior to Blanche.[36] But that story had already been discredited, and it was the Latin Chronicle that had discredited it.

There in chap. 33 we read that Alfonso VIII's wishes regarding the succession to Berenguela as his eldest surviving daughter had been proved ('declarabatur') by a certain charter sealed with his lead seal at the curia celebrated at Carrión, 'que reperta fuit in armario Burgensis ecclesie'. Now from its place in the narrative we seem to be meant to understand that this discovery was made in 1217 (the year in which Juan de Soria began to function as chancellor) and there is evidence in the same chapter that the account was written up before 1230 (33: 18–20). It was from here that D. Rodrigo got his version of the story.[37] But by the time D. Rodrigo's 'opusculum' left his hands in March 1243, that Burgos item was probably in the royal chancery, transferred there by Juan de Soria who had known Burgos since his youth[38] and been bishop of the place since 1240. And no doubt that is why it is no longer in the Burgos archive along with the associated documentation

---

[36]   F.J. HERNÁNDEZ, 'La corte de Fernando III…', pp. 110–18, 141–3; A. RODRÍGUEZ LÓPEZ, '*Quod alienus regnet et heredes expellatur*. L'offre du trône de Castille au roi Louis VIII de France', *Le Moyen Âge*, 105 ,1999, pp. 109–28, pp. 113–15; Peter LINEHAN, 'The accession of Alfonso X (1252) and the origins of the war of the Spanish succession' [repr. LINEHAN, *Past and present in Medieval Spain*, Aldershot, 1992], pp. 59–79, esp. pp. 71–3. (Berenguela had been born in 1171, Blanca in 1188.)

[37]   J. GONZÁLEZ, *Fernando III*, t. 2, n° 4; *DRH*, IX.5: 10–13: adding that the whole kingdom had twice done homage to her before the birth of Enrique.

[38]   SERRANO, 'El canciller…', p. 5.

# V

concerning Berenguela's aborted marriage to Conrad of Hohenstaufen (which would have served the purpose equally well).[39] Another example of the chancellor's international confidence was his relationship with the cardinal bishop of Sabina, John of Abbeville. It was with the chancellor rather than with the archbishop that in 1228–29 the papal legate was in contact and at Valladolid where the chancellor was abbot that he held his council for the churches of Castile and León (chap. 54). Moreover, as is shown by an inscription on a papal letter of April 1231 (*again* at the very time of the transfer to D. Juan of the archbishop's chancellorship) he certainly kept in touch with Castilian affairs thereafter.[40] The chancellor's insistence on canonical marriage and his altogether sounder record on the subject of illicit liaisons, frequently remarked upon, may have had something to do with that.[41]

This consideration leads me from the contextual to the textual. The use, no fewer than four times in a single chapter, chapter 65, of the word 'contubernium' to describe these liaisons was one of the reasons adduced by Charlo Brea in support of his conjectural second author of chapters 60 to 75 of the Latin chronicle.[42] 'Contubernium' can serve as something of a bench-mark here since, for all its author's repugnance to such relationships, never before – not even in describing the clerical 'sedition' that the legatine measures caused – had he made use of that pejorative description.[43] Nor had the word been employed in the relevant decrees of the Fourth Lateran

---

[39] 'Si rex A. sine filio masculo superstite obierit, succedat illi regno filia sua B. et uir eius Conradus cum ea': AC Burgos, vol. 17, fol. 434: printed J.M. GARRIDO GARRIDO, *Documentación de la catedral de Burgos (1184–1222)*, Burgos, n.d., n° 277, failing to note that the instrument is a chirograph. See photograph in P. RASSOW, *Der Prinzgemahl: ein Pactum matrimoniale aus dem Jahre 1188* (Quellen und Studien zur Verfassungsgeschichte des Deutschen Reiches in Mittelalter und Neuzeit, Bd VIII. Heft 1; Weimar, 1950), *ad fin.*

[40] AHN, Órdenes Militares. Calatrava, carp. 442, n° 6: mandate to absolve brothers of Calatrava for minor violence against clergy: inscription of papal chancery: 'd[omi]n[u] s Sabin[ensis] fi[eri] et sc[ri]bi p[re]cepit' (text S. DOMÍNGUEZ SÁNCHEZ, *Documentos de Gregorio IX...*, n° 186, Apr. 1231). For Spaniards in the cardinal's Roman household, see Peter LINEHAN, 'A papal legation and its aftermath: Cardinal John of Abbeville in Spain and Portugal, 1228–1229', in: I. BIROCCHI *et al.* (ed.), *A Ennio Cortese*, Rome, 2001, t. 2, pp. 236–56, p. 241. Also in April 1231 (regarding which see above, note 24) the maintenance of one of them, Master P., was wished upon the church of Cuenca: AC Toledo, X.1.E.2.8.

[41] LINEHAN, *History and the Historians...*, p. 254, n. 32.

[42] '¿Un segundo autor para la última parte de la *Crónica latina de los reyes de Castilla*?', in: M. PÉREZ GONZÁLEZ (ed.), *Actas I Congreso Nacional de Latín Medieval (León, 1–4 de diciembre de 1993)*, León, 1995, pp. 251–6, p. 253.

[43] *Cf. CLI*, 10: 18–20; 11: 9; 14: 23; 14: 23–5. *Cf. ibid.*, 54: 16–18.

Council.[44] Nor when Lucas of Tuy had used it had he done so in other than a neutral or even a favourable sense.[45]

So what was it that had changed between the composition of chapter 14 of the Latin chronicle and chapter 65 to justify the usage of the word *contubernium* in contrast to (lawful) *connubium*? What had changed was that in 1229 that was the word used by John of Abbeville to describe such relationships.[46] After that (or rather, after chapter 65 of the Latin chronicle) even D. Rodrigo got the message – but only as regards foreigners: Aragonese husbands and Portuguese wives.[47] In the case of Alfonso IX of León and doña Berenguela of Castile, although he concedes that the pair were 'consanguinitatis linea [...] iuncti',[48] nowhere does the archbishop describe their union in terms so demeaning – understandably perhaps since, after all, these delinquents were the parents of his king. Nor does he find space anywhere to mention that this particular *contubernium* was eventually dismantled.[49]

The relationship between the offspring of that liaison and doña Berenguela, already close, was further strengthened at Burgos in 1219 by the latter's role in ungirding her newly knighted son, with all that that implied.[50] One generation on, the Latin chronicle recorded Fernando III returning to his mother and his wife from his exploits: to his mother and his wife, *in that order*[51] and on one occasion *just* to his mother.[52] With a possessive mother reluctant to surrender her hold on her son, these must have been difficult times for the chancellor, whose emphasis seems to confirm, in diplomatic terms, what Lucas of Tuy declared openly: namely that, even as an adult, Fernando remained subject to his mother's *ferula*, 'as though he were a little boy'.[53] A similar remark about

---

[44]  *Ibid.*, 50–52 (X 2.20.47; 4.4.8).

[45]  C[hronicon] M[undi], E. FALQUE (ed.), CCCM 74.1 (2003), prol. 2.54; 3.5.43; 4.46.25.

[46]  LINEHAN, 'A papal legation...', p. 240.

[47]  *DRH*, VII.1: 10; VII.5: 47; IX.2: 29.

[48]  *Ibid.*, VII.31: 7–8.

[49]  LINEHAN, *History and the Historians...*, pp. 255–8.

[50]  *DRH*, IX.10.37. For the spiritual effects of ungirding, akin to those of godparenthood, see Peter LINEHAN, 'Alfonso XI of Castile and the arm of Santiago (with a Note on the pope's foot)', in: A. GARCÍA Y GARCÍA & P. WEIMAR (eds), *Miscellanea Domenico Maffei dicata*, Frankfurt, 1995 [repr. LINEHAN, *The processes of politics*], pp. 121–46, pp. 130–32.

[51]  *CLI*, 47: 20; 67: 22.

[52]  *Ibid.*, 50: 36.

[53]  *CM*, 4.93.11 (p. 332); Peter LINEHAN, 'On further thought: Lucas of Tuy, Rodrigo of Toledo and the Alfonsine histories', *Anuario de Estudios Medievales*, 27, 1998, pp. 415–36 [repr. LINEHAN, *The processes of politics and the rule of law. Studies on the Iberian kingdoms and papal Rome in the Middle Ages*, Aldershot, 2002], at pp. 420–21. (I take this opportunity of acknowledging the

Berenguela – the 'queen of Toledo', as the papal chancery curiously addressed her[54]– was made by the Mantuan poet Sordello da Goito. In his plaint in memory of Blacatz d'Alms, Sordello imagines Europe's rulers feasting off the heart of the deceased patron of troubadours in order to acquire the qualities they lacked themselves. In this scenario the king of Castile requires two helpings because he is the ruler of two kingdoms. 'But if he does dine twice', the poet observes, 'he will have to do so secretly because if his mother finds out she will beat him with her stick'.[55]

Which brings us back to court and to differences of opinion there regarding the role of doña Berenguela, the queen mother and to these differences as they are reflected in the chronicles of the two prelates, the archbishop and the chancellor. Here is one, arguably the key event of Fernando III's reign: the resumption of the reconquest in 1224. Whose idea was that? According to D. Rodrigo it was the queen-mother's; it was to doña Berenguela that credit was due; this is recorded in a bare four lines of text.[56] The chancellor though, while recording the king's acknowledgement of his debt to his mother ('to whom after God I owe everything I possess') devotes a complete chapter to his address to the nobility. In the chancellor's account then it is not the queen-mother, it is the youthful king (I mean, the Holy Spirit speaking through him) 'ex insperato, humiliter et devote tanquam filius obediencie' (43: 6–7) who is made responsible for the Great Leap Forward –though, even now, only after the queen-mother has seized the opportunity of providing her son with a toe-curlingly embarrassing object lesson in constitutional punctiliousness.[57]

If these indications are significant, the conclusion must be that, although at the start of Fernando's reign, D. Juan was closely allied to the queen-mother

---

persuasive demonstration provided by Enrique JÉREZ, 'El Tudense en su siglo: Transmisión y recepción del *Chronicon mundi* en el Doscientos', in: Francisco BAUTISTA (ed.), *El relato historiográfico: textos y tradiciones en la España medieval*, Papers of the Medieval Hispanic Research Seminar, 48 (London: Department of hispanic studies, Queen Mary, University of London, 2006), pp. 19–57, pp. 32–4, that '*la versión más acabada que conocemos del* Chronicon mundi *hay que fecharla antes de finales de noviembre de 1238'.*)

[54]     DOMÍNGUEZ SÁNCHEZ, *Documentos de Gregorio IX...*, n° 418.

[55]     'Planher vuelh En Blacatz en aquest leugier so', M. BONI (ed.), *Sordello, Le poesie*, Bologna, 1954, pp. 158–65. For an acute appreciation of the queen-mother as represented by the three chroniclers, see G. MARTIN, 'Régner sans régner : Bérengère de Castille (1214–1246) au miroir de l'historiographie de son temps', *e-Spania*, 1 (2006).

[56]     *DRH*, IX.12: 14–17: remarked on by F.J. HERNÁNDEZ, 'La corte...', p. 116, n. 50.

[57]     'Nobilis regina [...] breuibus filium allocuta est: '[...] Astant uassalli uestri, curia interest, ipsi consulant nobis sicut tenentur et consilium eorum sequimini in hoc facto': *CLI*, 44: 1–7.

to whom he owed his advancement, by the middle of it he, like her son, was striving to liberate himself from her continuing interference in affairs of state. Though until 1224 the lady who for D. Rodrigo was invariably 'nobilis' also merited the same encomium and others from the chancellor,[58] after the resumption of the *reconquista* only once do we hear her praised, and then in the same breath as her 'prudent' daughter-in-law.[59] Other issues also existed, specific to Osma, which must have strained its bishop's relationship with the queen-mother.[60] Be that as it may, when in 1236 the king received the call to hasten to Córdoba he made it clear that nothing she might say would stop him. In D. Rodrigo's account, by contrast, it is she who, although not physically present, is the brains behind the whole operation of restoring to *Hispania* the ancient dignity shamefully squandered of old, with her son little more than her agent.[61] But when, in April 1237, Gregory IX wrote to Castile in order to encourage Fernando III to make peace with the king of Navarre, it was not to the queen-mother and the archbishop that he did so but to the queen-mother and the chancellor.[62] Sordello's contemptuous squib, therefore, which is datable to that same year or to early 1237, was founded on reality, as was his matching swipe at the expense of that other mother's boy, the king of France, Louis IX, who, the poet claimed, like the king of Castile also lacked for appetite.[63]

But that brings us back to the old claim that Castile belonged to France, which is far too delicate a matter for an Englishman in Paris to enter into.

---

[58] *DRH*, IX.1: 12; 2: 6 ('prudens'); 10: 27; 11: 18; 12: 5,14; 14: 11; 15: 12; 17: 36; *CLI*, 41: 8 ('clarissima'); 35: 15; 42: 11 ('tanquam prudens'); 44: 1, 1, 19.

[59] *Ibid.*, 66: 23.

[60] Namely Alfonso VIII's bequest to the church of Osma of the lordship of the city (in 1204), which after 1214 both Berenguela and Fernando III strenuously and effectively opposed, resisting or ignoring all papal sanctions: LINEHAN, 'D. Juan de Soria...', p. 387.

[61] 'matrem, que tunc erat apud Legionem, de longe salutauit per nuncium, qui nunciaret ei fideliter ea que acciderant et firmum propositum filii, quod nulla ratione poterat inmutari': *ibid.*, 70: 22–5. *Cf. DRH*, IX.17.30–35: 'Stabilita incolis et bellatoribus ciuitate rex Fernandus Toletum ad reginam nobilem est reuersus, que pari uictoria iocundata utpote que consilio et subsidio, licet absens, omnia procurarat, gracias cum lacrimis egit Deo, quod antiqua dignitas, ignauia principum liturata, sui sollercia et studio filii fuit Hispanie restituta'.

[62] L. CADIER, 'Bulles originales du XIIIe siècle conservées dans les Archives de Navarre', *Mélanges d'Archéologie et d'Histoire*, 7, 1887, pp. 268–338, n° 23–4; LINEHAN, 'D. Juan de Soria...', p. 377.

[63] Since his meal would encourage him to recover Castile, lost by his own stupidity, though only if his mother allowed him to eat (since he did nothing without her permission): M. BONI, *Sordello*, p. 160; R. MENÉNDEZ PIDAL, *Poesía juglaresca y orígenes de las literaturas románicas*, 6th ed., Madrid, 1957, pp. 141–2. For Sordello's exile in Spain and France, see M. BONI, pp. 47–8.

# V

So instead, and by way of conclusion, let me return to Juan de Soria himself. As Julio González noticed, only three individuals in the Latin chronicle are allowed the luxury of an epithet: the chronicler himself (*qua* chancellor), the papal legate, of whom I have spoken, and Martín López de Pisuerga (1192–1208), D. Rodrigo's predecessor as archbishop of Toledo, upon whom the chronicler lavishes words of unparalleled warmth.[64]

Before his election to Toledo, Martín López had been archdeacon of Palencia.[65] This brings him into the mainstream of intellectual, and in particular of canonical, activity which I have discussed elsewhere and which, in the early decades of the thirteenth century, as well as Palencia, involved Osma, Soria, Calahorra and Zamora. There would therefore have been no shortage of compilers, or annalists, in that burgeoning *École normale supérieure*, the seminary out of which the personnel of the Castilian chancery was to emerge, under the control of its first professional chancellor.[66]

There are all sorts of other things I might have spoken about but haven't – one of them the language question, the (to me futile) question why the chancellor's charters were in the vernacular while the Latin chronicle was in Latin. I say futile because from the mechanical treatment of historical questions you get mechanical answers: in this case, the conclusion, both futile *and* mechanical, that it must have been the chancellor Diego Garcia, the author of *Planeta*, or possibly his son, who was the author of our chronicle, as well as of much else.[67]

We may wonder what more there is to be said about these chroniclers – Lucas of Tuy, the Latin chronicler, and Rodrigo of Toledo – who in the last ten or twenty years have received more attention than in the previous seven hundred. Ought they not now to be left alone to acquire a sort of historiographical patina, a sort of bottle age? 'Whereof we cannot speak', it was once said, not altogether unreasonably, 'thereof must we be silent'. But

---

[64]   'uirum discretum, benignum et largum, qui adeo ab omnibus diligebatur quod pater omnium putaretur' (12: 9–11).

[65]   J.F. RIVERA, *La iglesia de Toledo en el siglo XII*, t. 1, Rome, 1966, pp. 202–3.

[66]   LINEHAN, 'D. Juan de Soria…'; pp. 388–9; *id.*, 'The case of the impugned chirograph, and the juristic culture of early thirteenth-century Zamora', in: M. ASCHERI *et al.* (eds), *Manoscritti, editoria e biblioteche tra medioevo ed età moderna. Studi offerti a Domenico Maffei*, Rome, 2006, pp. 461–513; *id.*, *Spanish Church and the Papacy…*, p. 66; I. FLEISCH, *Sacerdotium – Regnum – Studium. Der westiberische Raum und die europäische Universitätskultur im Hochmittelalter. Prosopographische und rechtsgeschichtliche Studien*, Berlin, 2006, pp. 292–8.

[67]   J. HERNANDO PÉREZ, *Hispano Diego García, escritor y poeta medieval, y el Libro de Alexandre*, Burgos, 1992. For a refreshingly sane review of the evidence, see R. WRIGHT, *El tratado de Cabreros (1206): estudio sociofilológico de una reforma ortográfica*, London, 2000, pp. 99–122.

it wasn't a historian who said it. If that were the historian's code there would be no history. As one of the twentieth century's most acute medievalists once observed, 'history would be a duller subject than it is if historians limited themselves to questions which admit of answers on the evidence available'.[68] Still, questions do deserve answers and, by the same token, answers demand questions. Indeed, it is almost the only reason historians have for communicating at all.

---

[68] Beryl SMALLEY, 'Ecclesiastical attitudes to novelty c.1100–c.1250', in: D. BAKER (ed.), *Church, society and politics* (*Studies in Church history*, 12; Cambridge, 1975), pp. 113–31, p. 129.

# VI

## The Case of the Impugned Chirograph, and the Juristic Culture of early Thirteenth-century Zamora*

The scene is one with which all those who have been privileged to observe Maffei at work in his library will be familiar. But on this occasion the *savant* at his desk whose figure I wish to conjure up is not Domenico. The luminary poring over his law books is the archdeacon of Zamora, don Ysidoro, an early thirteenth-century juristic practitioner of whom not even the sage of Siena will have heard and whose judgment in the interesting case of 'S.' and others *versus* 'G. presbiter Sancti Leonardi' is printed as

---

\* Abbreviations employed:
AC: Archivo de la catedral *or* del cabildo
ACZ: AC Zamora
ADB: Arquivo Distrital de Braga
ADP: Arquivo Distrital de Porto
AHN: Archivo Histórico Nacional, Madrid
AHPZ: Archivo Histórico Provincial de Zamora
ASV: Archivio Segreto Vaticano
BNM: Biblioteca Nacional, Madrid
*Bul. Port.*: A. JESUS DA COSTA & M. A. FERNANDES MARQUES, *Bulário Português. Inocêncio III (1198-1216)*, Coimbra 1989.
*Bul. Brac.*: M. DA A. JÁCOME DE VASCONCELOS & A. DE SOUSA ARAÚJO, *Bulário Bracarense. Sumários de diplomas pontifícios dos séculos XI a XIX*, Braga 1986.
*Bull. Santiago*: A. F. AGUADO DE CORDOVA, A. A. ALEMAN ET ROSALES, J. LOPEZ AGURLETA, *Bullarium equestris ordinis S. Iacobi de Spatha*, Madrid, Joannis de Ariztia, 1719.
CCCM: Corpus Christianorum Continuatio Mediaevalis
CDL: Various authors, *Colección documental del Archivo de la Catedral de León (775-1230)*, 7 vols; vol. VIII *(1230-1269)*, León 1987-2002; 1993.
COSTA: A. D. DE SOUSA COSTA, *Mestre Silvestre e Mestre Vicente, juristas da contenda entre D. Afonso II e suas irmãs*, Braga 1963.
*DhI*: D. MANSILLA *La documentación pontificia hasta Inocencio III (965-1216)*, Rome 1955.
DSG: S. DOMÍNGUEZ SÁNCHEZ, *Documentos de Gregorio IX (1227-1241) referentes a España*, León 2004.
DSL: S. DOMÍNGUEZ SÁNCHEZ, *Documentos pontificios referentes a la diócesis de León (siglos XI-XIII)*, León 2003.
Fr.: Æ. FRIEDBERG, *Corpus iuris canonici*, 2 vols, Leipzig 1879-81.
IANTT: Instituto dos Arquivos Nacionais Torre do Tombo, Lisbon

462

Appendix I to this too brief tribute to *mi queridísimo amigo y compañero de tantos años*[1].
What makes the dispute between 'G. presbiter Sancti Leonardi' (for convenience let us call him Fr. García) and 'S.' and others interesting is not so much the substance of the matter at issue as the time and place at which it was debated, and the sophisticated not to say sophistical manner in which that debate was conducted. For the issue itself was unremarkable: the objection of six *populatores* of the parish of S. Leonardo, situated to the southeast of Zamora's city walls[2], to an attempt by Fr. García, the rector of its then (but alas no more) handsome church, to anticipate payments of his

LERA: J. C. DE LERA MAÍLLO, *Catálogo de los documentos medievales de la Catedral de Zamora*, Zamora 1999.
MANSILLA: D. MANSILLA, *La documentación pontificia de Honorio III (1216-1227)*, Rome 1965.
OO. MM.: AHN, Ordenes Militares
POTTHAST: A. POTTHAST, *Regesta pontificum Romanorum*, 2 vols, Berlin 1874-1875.
QP: A. QUINTANA PRIETO, *La documentación pontificia de Inocencio IV (1243-1254)*, Rome 1987.
*Reg. Greg. IX: Les registres de Grégoire IX*, ed. L. AUVRAY *et al.*, 4 vols, Paris 1890-1955.
*Reg. Hon. III: Regesta Honorii Papae III....*, ed. P. PRESSUTTI, 2 vols, Rome 1885, 1895.
*Reg. Inn. IV: Les registres d'Innocent IV*, ed. E. BERGER, 4 vols, Paris 1884-1921.
*TB*: ACZ, *Tumbo Blanco*
*TN*: ACZ, *Tumbo Negro*
[1] ACZ, 16/II/18 (LERA, 355). The parchment is in bad condition, with parts of lines 5-11 and 41-86 illegible on account of damp stains. But for the kindness of Sr. José Carlos de Lera Maíllo in locking me in a dark cupboard for some hours together with the document and a lamp, what follows could not have been written. I am further obliged to Sr. Lera, *archivero ejemplario*, for his generosity in allowing me to consult his transcripts of other ACZ documents of the period. For assistance in the interpretation of the text, warm thanks are due to Professors J. A. Brundage, J. A. Crook and M. D. Reeve, and Drs M. J. Ryan and P. N. R. Zutshi.
[2] See A. REPRESA, *Genésis y evolución urbana de la Zamora medieval*, «Hispania», 32 (1972), pp. 535-536, map opp. p. 530. Systematically despoiled over the last century, Fr. García's once splendid and splendidly decorated church is now in ruins and partially given over to use as a coal-store. See M. GÓMEZ-MORENO, *Catálogo monumental de España: Provincia de Zamora (1903-1905)*, Madrid 1927, I, pp. 154-155; and, for more recent accounts, G. RAMOS DE CASTRO, *El arte románico en la provincia de Zamora*, Zamora 1977, pp. 180-184, and (with a scalding denunciation of the custodians of the 'patrimonio cultural'), M. A. GARCÍA GUINEA & J. M. PÉREZ GONZÁLEZ (eds), *Enciclopedia del Románico en Castilla y León. Zamora*, Aguilar de Campo 2002, pp. 525-528.

scheduled salary (*pensio*)[3]. What makes it interesting is the fact that the rector had brought the case to law at all We might rather have expected those *populatores* to have settled the matter by direct action one Saturday night well out of sight of the archdeacon and of everyone else. As Bishop Gonzalo of Segovia had only recently learnt to his cost at Sepúlveda some way to the east, when settling their differences frontiersmen, frontier clergy included, tended to prefer direct action to the niceties of legal process[4]. Yet, as the present case shows, there were also those amongst them no less imbued than their rulers with the Justinianian precept, 'Imperatoriam maiestatem non solum armis decoratam, sed etiam legibus oportet esse armatam'.

The case had a pre-history without futher knowledge of the particulars of which only limited sense can be made of our text. All that we can infer regarding the content of the *libellus* presented by the advocate for the Six is what is revealed in his opponent's opening *allegatio*: that after an agreement acceptable to both the rector and the majority of his parishioners had been arrived at and 'per instrumentum a dompno .G. approbatum' (A6), the Six had then concocted a different. spurious settlement and had it recorded by chirograph ('per alfabetum')[5]. And in the making of that chirograph, it is to be understood from his advocate's pleadings, Fr. García had been in no way involved. For it was not only the part of it presented by the Six that he rejected (A1). *Both* parts were defective, he insisted. Since each was written in a different hand, 'it would appear that both had been in the other party's possession and that at various times the other party had written in them whatever it chose to write' (A2).

Although the text of Fr. García's *libellus* containing full particulars has not been preserved, from his advocate's *allegatio* it is therefore evident that the essence of it was that, after heads of agreement acceptable to the rector had been established, the scribe charged with engrossing the text of the settlement for delivery to both parties was suborned by the Six, resulting in variant texts of it attributable to different hands.

In the event, Fr. García failed to persuade the judge that anything of the sort had occurred, and the archdeacon don Ysidoro found both halves of the chirograph to be valid, the only doubtful ('esitabile') element of their text being a matter of interpretation concerning the residence requirement of parishioners of the parish of S. Leonardo (lines 82-85). Before that conclusion had been reached, however, the parties had engaged in a series of exchanges in the course of which they provided a wealth of revealing infor-

---

[3] For use of the word in this sense, see Gratian, C.10 q. 2 c. 2 §6; C. 12 q. 2 c.25.
[4] P. LINEHAN, *Segovia: a "frontier" diocese in the thirteenth century*, «English Historical Review», 96 (1981), pp. 484-485.
[5] Lines 3, 21, 82.

mation relating to the juristic culture of the city of Zamora in the year 1223.

Nor are the exchanges of the parties regarding the impugned chirograph itself devoid of interest. In addition to the other objections he raised, Fr. García's advocate complained that the instrument – and now, be it noted, he is speaking of only *one* instrument – was just about as defective as instruments came, 'corruptum, viciatum et deturpatum', full of false Latinity from start to finish, written in a variety of hands, and chock-full of interlinear corrections. He had already indicated the flawed character of the instrument exhibited by his adversaries, 'utpote nec manu publica confectum nec sigillo autentico roboratum' (A1). Was it conceivable, he now asked (revealing by the question something of that instrument's ostensible character), that anything of the sort could have been authenticated by a bishop or archdeacon, by those, that is, 'to whom the care and custody of ecclesiastical things are entrusted' (A11)?

In support of Fr. García's objection as to the instrument's lack of credibility his counsel had been able to adduce 'Scripta vero', Alexander III's crisp ruling regarding the need for an instrument to have been drafted by a public official and corroborated by an authentic seal (line 4). However, the requirement in that decretal had been qualified. Only if the witnesses to the act were dead ('si testes inscripti decesserint') did it apply, and counsel for the Six spotted and was quick to invoke the qualification. For in this case the witnesses to the act *could* be produced. Moreover, the requirement in respect of a public official was not absolute. The custom 'in these parts', the west of the kingdom of León, was that *all* chirographs drafted by a notary were held to be valid, especially when there were witnesses to vouch for them. And not only was 'custom the best interpreter of laws'. Trumping Alexander III's decretal, the decree of the Fourth Lateran Council could also be prayed in aid, 'where it is said that if the judge cannot find a public official then one or two suitable men will serve.' 'And amongst us there is no such public official to be found', counsel for the Six continued[6], before piling on a whole host of authorities from *both* laws that it had not occurred to Fr. García's advocate to recruit (B1) and countering his adversary's palaeographical objections regarding 'diversity of hands' with a se-

---

[6] A point to which he returns in his *quadriplicatio*: 'Sed hic in terra ista, prout dictum est, non sunt publice persone, et ideo adhibere possum ad scripturam aliquam faciendam duos vel tres scriptores diversis temporibus et non nocebit dum modo quod scriptum fuit in carta testibus probare possim' (D2). The earliest evidence I am aware of of such an official active 'in these parts' concerns D. Silvestre, notary public 'por auctoridad del papa' and canon of Husillos (Palencia), and dates from the years 1271-76: *TB*, ff 134v-5v, ACZ, 13/59c, 9/2, 9/14, 8/28b (Lera, 813, 849C, 861B, 769B, 423E).

ries of animadversions on the subject of the variable propensities of pens and ink and the possible effects on a scribe of a good lunch, (B2) on the last part of which the opposition did not deign to be drawn[7].

Now that counsel for the Six had brought Roman Law into play his opposite number needed to sharpen up his act, which he did, with the consequence that further consideration of the diplomatic aspects of the matter descended into an exchange of exegeses on the subject of the nature of the relationship of custom and law[8], and reference by counsel for the Six to a decretal to which his opponent appears to have thought it unnecessary to respond on the sufficient grounds that its subject matter was Scottish[9].

For present purposes enough has been said to indicate the extent of the professionalism exhibited by the advocates involved in the dispute. Here I shall not pursue their analysis of the other themes into discussion of which the argument now followed. Others may wish to trace the course of their exchanges regarding matters as diverse as the operation of the law of prescription, the evidential value of negative propositions, contemporary attitudes regarding the alienation of ecclesiastical property, and much else besides. Historians of the Spanish frontier too may find material here that bears on the question of the psychology of its rugged inhabitants. And all of them may be moved to speculate as to what ensued after 25 March 1223 when our narrative concludes with the disappointed Fr. García 'petens apostolos', that is, seeking and being granted leave to appeal to the bishop.

Instead I shall venture a little way into the world that these advocates inhabited, a world which seems to have been neglected by historians, though to historians of law in particular it ought to be of interest if only on account of the identity of the two bishops who between them ruled the see of Zamora for a period which spanned the greater part of the most eventful half-century in the legal history of Western Europe. Martín Arias (1193-1217) and Martín Rodríguez (1217-1238), Bishops Martín I and Martín II respectively, were both canonists of note[10]. It was under their aegis that the

---

[7] 'Ad hoc quod dicit quod diversitas manuum in instrumentis non nocet, respondemus quod nocet cum secundum confessionem suam unus scriptor fuerit in utroque instrumento et in eisdem locis littera diversificetur ita quod alia manu facta videtur, et ideo sus[pecta est carta]...' C2.

[8] As to which see A. GOURON, *Coutume contre loi chez les premiers glossateurs*, in A. GOURON & A. RIGAUDIÈRE (eds), *Renaissance du pouvoir legislatif et genèse de l'état*, Montpellier 1988, pp. 117-130, esp. p. 119.

[9] App. I, C1, n. 127.

[10] For the former's glosses to Gratian's Decretum, see S. KUTTNER, *Repertorium der Kanonistik (1140-1234): Prodromus corporis glossarum*, Vatican City 1937 (Studi e Testi, 71), pp. 11, 53; for the latter's to 'Compilatio I' and his *Notabilia* to 'Com-

competent advocates who appeared in the case of Fr. García operated, the advocates who not only had the classic schoolroom texts – Gratian, the First and Third Compilations, and the texts of Roman Law – at their fingertips but who also were able to confront their forensic opponents with the recent commentaries of Laurentius Hispanus and Vincentius Hispanus (commentaries of which modern scholarship is still in search)[11].

Indeed, for all the technical expertise of the conduct of Fr. García's case, the record of its hearing conveys only an indistinct impression of the importance of the church of Zamora as a juristic centre in, before and after the year 1223. In order to gain an idea of the scale of that activity some statistics are required. These are provided in Appendix II and show that in the forty-five years that elapsed between June 1209 (a date the significance of which will be explained shortly) and the death of Pope Innocent IV in December 1254, on no fewer than 262 occasions successive bishops of Zamora and members of the chapter of that church either received papal mandates to act as judges delegate or were appointed as executors in respect of at least 133 causes of action.

I say 'at least' because, although I have taken into account some 1600 original papal letters of these years conserved in Spanish and Portuguese archives, as well as the relevant entries in the Vatican Registers, there are surely many more that have either not survived or have escaped my attention. However, it is unlikely that additional data would necessitate significant revision of the conclusions regarding the pattern of recruitment from within Zamora's cathedral establishment and the limited number of recipients amongst whom those 262 commissions were distributed that the evidence presented here suggest – though a more precise calculation of how limited that number was is hampered by the almost invariable practice of the papal chancery of identifying the addressees of mandates by office rather than by name, and the infuriating anonymity of the documentary record in the Zamora archives[12]. For example, at no point during the peri-

---

pilatio IV', ID., *Bernardus Compostellanus Antiquus*, «Traditio», 1 (1943), p. 335; A. GARCÍA Y GARCÍA, *La canonística ibérica medieval posterior al Decreto de Graciano*, in *Repertorio de las Ciencias Eclesiásticas en España*, I, Salamanca 1967, p. 412.

[11] 'Et ita intelligitur decretalis inducta in extra i. de in integrum resti. Requisiuit, a magistro Laurentio et Vincetio. Dicunt enim...': D6. Cf. A. GARCÍA Y GARCÍA, *Laurentius Hispanus. Datos biográficos y estudio crítico de sus obras*, Rome-Madrid 1956, pp. 73-74; J. OCHOA SANZ, *Vincentius Hispanus. Canonista boloñes del siglo XIII*, Rome-Madrid 1956, p. 119 (with references to the only known manuscript of Vincentius' *Apparatus* to *Compilatio I*, destroyed in Leipzig during the Second World War).

[12] Wherein all too often the instruments best supplied with witness lists are undated.

od that interests us are we able to put names to the *magistri scolarum* and only rarely to the treasurers of the place. With these exceptions, however, by dint of a laborious trawl through the documentation of the chapter it has proved possible to identify most of those *zamoranos* upon whom the burden of judicial responsibility fell, with five individuals in particular being kept regularly occupied: Bishops Martín I and Martín II with 23 and 34 commissions (nos. 1-25, 28-94), the dean D. Juan Juánez with 12 (nos. 103-132), and the chanters D. Egas and D. García de Uliolo[13] with 12 and 17 (nos. 2-45, 46-120), and a sixth kept busier than all the rest.

That sixth was Master Florencio, who between 1209, when he first features in the capitular record, and 1237, the year of his death, must indeed have been one of the busiest men in the entire peninsula. As 'archdeacon of the city' and then as dean, he loomed larger in the affairs of the church of Zamora than anyone else[14]. His impact there was exceptional. But so too was the fact that by contrast with his colleagues, the chanter D. Egas and Pedro Mona(n)zino[15], and with the man who replaced him as 'archdeacon

---

[13] Egas had been present in the chapter since at least Feb. 1182 (*TN*, f. 324r-5r: Lera, 126) but only after the arrival of Bishop Martin I in 1193 did he advance to the office of chanter (first sighting May 1195: ACZ 12/2: Lera 163). Between February and August 1221 he was succeeded by García who, notwithstanding the will he made in 1230, was still active in Nov. 1237: App. II, nos. 45, 46; CDL, 1922; *TN*, fo. 88v-90r (Lera, 431); below, n. 38.

[14] He remained archdeacon until at least Sept. 1217: ACZ, 17/37 (Lera, 308). Although his earliest appearance as dean in the capitular record is of February 1219, already in the previous June he was describing himself as 'decanus olim archidiaconus': ACZ, 1/15 (Lera, 317); AHN. *OO. MM. San Marcos de León*, carp. 377/9 – and the likelihood is that he had succeeded to that office by the beginning of 1218 since (i) of his decanal predecessor Master Juan nothing further is heard after June 1217, when he made his will (*TN*, ff. 88r-v: Lera, 305), and (ii) it is inconceivable that the well-connected impetrator of the mandate of January 1218 (App. II, no. 30) would have entrusted the preservation of his personal interests to an unknown quantity.

[15] Numerous instruments in ACZ show 'Mona[n]zino' to have been a corrupt Latinized form of the patronymic 'Munionis' (Span. 'Moniz', or 'Muniz'), a linguistic refinement evidently unfamiliar to the scribes of the papal chancery (cf. App. II, no. 27). Petrus (or Pedro) Moniz first appears as witness to capitular *acta* in July 1181. By Feb. 1182 he occupied fifth place in a list of 29 or 30 witnesses, perhaps indicating that he was already a senior figure in the chapter: *TN*, ff. 76v-78r, 34r-35r (Lera, 121, 126). In March 1212 a 'Petrus Monazinus presbyter' is recorded, and in June 1217 'P. Monzino capellanus' was remembered in the will of the dean don Juan: *TB*, ff. 103r-v, *TN*, ff. 88r-v (Lera, 279, 305). Though there would seem to have been at least two men of this name at large in the church of Zamora during these years, the *capellanus* and the canon were in fact one and the same per-

of the city', D. Ysidoro[16], it was not there that he had served his appren-
ticeship. Like the Athenian Pallas from the head of Zeus, he had sprung into the chapter of Zamora fully clad. In February 1209, on the occasion of
his earliest recorded appearance in that body, he was already archdeacon 'of
the city'[17]. So we may wonder where he had come from. Could he possibly
have been one of those 'sapientes' reportedly recruited 'a Galliis et Ytalia'
to provide faculty for Alfonso VIII of Castile's new *studium* at Palencia[18]?
Despite our honorand's pioneering study[19]. we still know all too little about
the origins of and the process of recruitment to that *studium*. And of the origins of the contemporary process of recruitment to the Salamanca *studium*
in Alfonso IX's kingdom of León we know even less.

Partly on the grounds that Lucas was not a Leonese name, I have previously suggested that Lucas 'of Tuy' as he is remembered, the Leonese

son (AHN, OO. MM., S. Marcos de León, carp. 377/9; T. MINGUELLA Y ARNEDO,
*Hist. de la diócesis de Sigüenza y de sus obispos*, I, Madrid 1910, p. 542), and by
September 1225 Rome was aware that that person was its treasurer: *Reg. Hon. III*,
5652 (MANSILLA, 573). By Aug. 1230 he had disappeared from the scene: ACZ,
18/2 (LERA, 427).

[16] A witness list of Sept. 1210 mentions both 'D. Ysidorus portionarius, clericus episcopi' and 'Ysidorus clericus domni Munionis Moniz' (the archdeacon of
Toro), and by Feb. 1219 there was a canon of this name: ACZ, 17/35; AHPZ, 1/15
(LERA, 263, 317). He was in office as archdeacon by August 1221 and was still
alive in June 1238: ACZ, 36/4, 12/7 (LERA, 342, 491). What appears to be an in-
terpolation in a capitular constitution dating from the pontificate of Martín II
(Martín Rodríguez), confirming the archidiaconal prerogative to present to vacant
churches, seems to imply a rift between Ysidoro and the bishop on the subject:
'Non negamus tamen quod valde (?) sed raro, scilicet bis vel ter presentaciones
clericorum ad ecclesias vacantes inchoatas per archidiaconum Ysidorum domnus
Martinus Roderici, olim episcopus, expedivit. Non tamen credimus hoc invito
archidiacono factum fuisse sed de voluntate dicti archidiaconi processisse. Et si, eo
invito, episcopus prefatus illud fecisset, fieret ecclesie et dicto archidiacono iniuria
contra antiquas consuetudines quas predecessores sui ecclesie et archidiaconi qui
fuerunt pro tempore observaverunt' (ACZ, 10bis/4 [*Liber constitutionum*], f.
103ra).The curious style 'Domnus Ysidorus de Xuramio archidiaconus', as printed
by J. RODRÍGUEZ FERNÁNDEZ, *Los Fueros locales de la provincia de Zamora*, Salamanca 1990, p. 348, derives from an egregious misreading of '...archidiaconus
*domnus Ysidorus, et in Tauro archidiaconus* magister Iohannes' (ACZ, 14/25:
LERA, 456).

[17] ACZ, 13/14 (LERA, 247).

[18] RODERICI XIMENII DE RADA *Historia de rebus Hispanie sive Historia Gothica*, VII.34, ed. J. FERNÁNDEZ VALVERDE, CCCM 72, Turnhout 1987, p. 256.

[19] D. MAFFEI, *Fra Cremona, Montpellier e Palencia nel secolo XII. Ricerche
su Ugolino da Sesso*, «Rivista Internazionale di Diritto Comune», 1 (1990), pp.
9-30.

chronicler of the age *par excellence*, may not have been of Leonese origin at all[20]. Since Florencio was not a common Leonese name either, may not a similar suspicion also attach to the dean of Zamora[21]? May not Master Florencio have been yet another of those recruits from abroad, a successor to the various Italians whose presence is attested in the chapter of Palencia in the decades before Palencia was promoted to the status of Castile's *studium*? May he not have been attracted by the prospectus for the parallel establishment at Salamanca[22], only then to be head-hunted by the seriously overburdened bishop of Zamora[23]? If so, it would not be the earliest example of such an initiative on the part of the canonist prelate[24].

Be that as it may, the newcomer to Zamora was soon altogether part of the place. Indeed, by 1213 so well was he ensconced there that Martín I prevailed upon the chapter to grant him use of the residence into which he had moved, rent-free and for life, with the further proviso that after his death his successors as archdeacons of the city should be entitled to occupy it at a charge of five maravedis *per annum* payable on the anniversary of the man who had put the place into good order at his own expense[25]. In due course there would be further compensations: a regular income from his thriving

---

[20] P. LINEHAN, *Fechas y sospechas sobre Lucas de Tuy*, «Anuario de Estudios Medievales», 32 (2002), pp. 22-24.

[21] CDL, VII (*Apéndices e índices*), 166, *s.v.* Florencio. The name, and variants thereof, occur just six times in Sahagún documentation of the years 1186-1213: J. A. FERNÁNDEZ FLÓREZ, *Colección diplomática del monasterio de Sahagún (857-1300)*, IV, V, León 1991, 1994, nos. 1426, 1464, 1471, 1507, 1526, 1590.

[22] A. GARCÍA Y GARCÍA, *Iglesia, sociedad y derecho*, I, Salamanca 1985, p. 49. As to Alfonso IX's foundation we have only the enigmatic notice provided by Lucas of Tuy: 'Hic salutari consilio euocauit magistros peritissimos in Sacra Scriptura et constituit scolas fieri Salamantice' (*Chronicon Mundi*, IV.96, ed. E. FALQUE, CCCM 74, Turnhout 2003, p. 335). Although the chronicler provides no clue regarding the date of the king's initiative, probably because he had no idea of it himself, historians of the institution have known better. See H. RASHDALL, ed. F. M. POWICKE & A. B. EMDEN, *The Universities of Europe in the Middle Ages*, Oxford 1936, II, pp. 75-76.

[23] Between 1198 and 1209 Martín I had been the recipient of all but one of the 31 recorded papal commissions addressed to Zamora judges: *DhI*, 131, 134, 139, 156, 172, 173, 176, 177, 202a, 203, 213, 251, 254, 282, 284, 293, 298, 299, 304, 305, 326, 333, 335, 337, 354, 366, 408; CDL, 1738; *Bul. Port.*, 102, 114, 137. The dean of Zamora, Master Juan, was involved in eight of these cases, responsibility for some of which would automatically have devolved upon Florencio on his succession to that office.

[24] See above, n. 13.

[25] '...quia predictas domos suis laboribus et expensis pro maiori parte construxit et reparavit': *TN*, f. 66v (LERA, 285).

legal practice, presumably[26], not to mention the intellectual stimulation provided by his dealings with the likes of the canonists Melendo of Osma and Laurentius Hispanus and the royal chancellor Juan de Soria[27]. But already, after just four years, Master Florencio was very much at home at Zamora. Whether or not he was also very often in residence there is another matter. For during the last twenty-eight years of his life Master Florencio was involved in as many as two-thirds of cases remitted to Zamora judges, with his tally of 67 out of 100 far exceeding that of the most active of his English contemporaries, Richard de Mores[28]. And although in the case of most of these disputes the parties came to Zamora to wait upon Master Florencio[29]. thereby contributing to the juristic reputation of the place of course, not a few of them required the dean to travel far afield within Zamora's extensive catchment area, as when he was appointed to determine diocesan boundary disputes between the sees of Guarda and Coimbra in 1213 (no. 21)[30], and of Ávila and Plasencia between 1217 and 1223 (nos. 28, 57), or in 1233-4 to establish the limits of the diocese of Baeza in recently reconquered Andalusia (nos. 84, 92), or to attend to the affairs of the church of León in 1225 (no. 64) and the monastery of Sahagún in 1226 and 1234 (nos. 65, 88). Although defendants were afforded a measure of protection from being hauled before tribunals more than two days distant from their dioceses, judges were not similarly safeguarded, and the trek from Zamora to Baeza and back would have occupied the dean for something more like two whole weeks[31].

And when such expeditions took a judge out of the kingdom of León

[26] For the customary though prohibited ten per cent charge on the suit ('decima litis'), see X 3.1.10; J. E. SAYERS, *Papal Judges Delegate in the Province of Canterbury 1198-1254. A study in ecclesiastical jurisdiction and administration*, Oxford 1971, p. 135.

[27] App. II, nos. 26, 37, 52, 84, 92.

[28] Canon of Merton and prior of Dunstable, for whom see SAYERS, *Papal Judges Delegate* cit., pp. 114-116, 296-301.

[29] E.g., below, n. 166.

[30] 'Prefati vero episcopus et archidiaconus Çamorenses suis nobis litteris intimarunt quod, cum ipsi, eorum coniudice [*scil*. Bishop Martinho of Porto] legitime suam absentiam excusante, partibus ad suam presentiam convocatis, examinassent causam huiusmodi diligenter, ad ipsius Colimbriensis instantiam postulantis ut personaliter ad loca, super quibus questio vertebatur, accederent ac promittentis se solum sufficientes expensas ipsis iudicibus in eundo et redeundo ac limitando daturum...': COSTA, p. 324 n. 440.

[31] IV Lateran, can. 39, decree *Nonnulli gratia*: X 1.3.28. In 1199, Coria in Leonese Extremadura, to which the Compostela party had caused a hearing of its dispute with Braga over the church of Zamora to be transferred, was said to be ten

and across political frontiers, as well as distracting him from with his other responsibilities[32] they might even prove physically hazardous. For apart from the fact that for Leonese churchmen prior to the union of the two kingdoms in 1230 Castile remained a foreign country, Portugal was always a problem. It was not just that, in common with their disputatious brethren throughout Christendom, Portuguese prelates insisted that judges personally inspect landmarks and river-courses as well as muniments, all at the inspectors' financial as well as personal risk[33]. Also there was the perennial problem of Portugal's kings. With Zamora so conveniently situated just across the border with that kingdom, it was on Master Florencio and his juristic colleagues that Rome regularly relied for delivery of her ultimata to those most unpredictable of monarchs on behalf of ecclesiastics subject to their arbitrary rule (nos. 9-10, 66-68, 78-79, 86, 95). And whereas in May 1227 the three judges charged with intervening on the bishop of Porto's behalf – Bishop Martín II, Master Florencio and the chanter D. García – were authorised to engage religious or other persons for the purpose, six years later they were specifically instructed to confront Sancho II in person[34].

First they had to find him though. And that was not easy, for, as their replacements discovered on reaching the city of Porto in the winter of 1237-8, Sancho II was rather good at avoiding meetings that promised to prove uncomfortable.[35] In addition to which, according to the bishop of Porto, Pedro Salvador, writing in March 1238, the very month in which Gregory IX responded to their report on the elusive monarch, the kingdom of Portugal was no place for the likes of the dean of Zamora. For D. Pedro, himself a distinguished canonist, spoke of a land in which brigands ruled, monasteries had been converted into barracks and brothels, and the butchering of babies and

---

days distant from Braga: *DhI*, 199 (p. 223); R. A. FLETCHER, *The Episcopate in the Kingdom of León in the Twelfth Century*, Oxford 1978, p. 201.

[32] Cf. the letter of Bishop Martín Arias to his co-delegates Master Mauricio archdeacon of Toledo and Master Miguel canon of Segovia in a number of cases requiring his presence in the diocese of Burgos (undated but attributable to 1210; see App. II, nos. 4-8): '... ad presens multis causis impediti quia rex Legionensis uocat nos ad curiam quam in continenti est celebraturus apud Legionem et statim iturus [*sic*] ad colloquium regis Castelle nullomodo possumus interesse' (ACZ, 11/II/8: LERA, 270). The meeting of the Leonese cortes here alluded to is otherwise undocumented.

[33] Though judges were allowed food expenses, there is no mention in the relevant decretal (X 3.1.10) of travel costs.

[34] App. II, nos. 66, 68 ('per aliquos religiosos aut alios quos ad hoc videritis aptiores'), 86 ('ad regem prefatum personaliter accedentes').

[35] '...cum idem rex nollet, licet sciret vos esse in eadem civitate, in qua personaliter existebat, aliquatenus vos videre' (App. II, no. 98).

the violation of young girls were every-day occurrences[36].

By that date the even grimmer reaper had dispensed Master Florencio from further exposure to such perils[37] – though as the chanter D. García and his colleagues, the new dean D. Gil, and the treasurer, had demonstrated by the assurance with which at their session in the cloister of Zamora cathedral in the previous November they parried the arguments from both laws advanced by Sancho II's proctor, the juristic renown associated with the late dean had not died with him[38]. But it did not long survive Bishop Martín II's translation to the see of León twelve months later, in November 1238[39]. Of the corps of canonists of which the group who had witnessed an ordinance issued by that prelate in May 1234 may be regarded as representative[40], of only one – Pedro Pedrez, promoted archdeacon of Toro – is anything certain heard after mid-1239. And thereafter the number of commissions to Zamora judges falls off sharply (nos. 103-124).

None the less, in terms of the volume of business delegated to Zamora judges, during the previous thirty years the chapter of Zamora had probably been the most active centre of canonistic activity within the entire peninsula. It had certainly out-performed Salamanca as (in the words of the decree of I Lyons) a 'large and well-known place' to which the hearing of legal causes was to be reserved because it was there that 'many men learned in the law' were to be found[41]. So it is not unreasonable to enquire why it was that it was Salamanca rather than Zamora that Alfonso IX had chosen as the lo-

---

[36] L. CACEGA & L. DE SOUSA, *Primeira parte da Historia de S. Domingos, particular do reino e conquistas de Portugal* (1623), pp. 151-152: cit. COSTA, p. 405, n. 516. Cf. P. LINEHAN, *Juan de Soria: unas apostillas*, in *Fernando III y su tiempo (1201-1252): VIII Congreso de Estudios Medievales*, León 2003, p. 386.

[37] Its date, the year 1237, is the only detail we possess of his lost will: LERA, 489.

[38] ADP, *Mitra da Sé do Porto*, Pergaminhos, caixa 1867, doc. no. 7.

[39] *Reg. Greg. IX*, 4594.

[40] 'Florencius decanus, G. cantor, Ysidorus archidiaconus, I. thesaurarius, P. Petri canonicus, dompnus Parens canonicus Zamorensis': ACZ 21/2 (LERA, 468); printed J.-L. MARTÍN, *Documentos zamoranos. I. Documentos del Archivo Catedralicio de Zamora, primera parte (1128-1261)*, Salamanca 1982, p. 115.

[41] According to the criteria applied in Appendix II just eleven cases occur: (i) 3 Aug. 1209. Bp (Gonzalo Fernández), F. and V. archds, to implement judgment of Zamora judges in dispute of S. Cruz de Coimbra and certain clerics of that house. *Inter dilectos filios*: DhI, 408; (ii) 24 July 1224. Master Pascual, canon, third judge in Viseu-Idanha dispute. *Cum in causa*: *Reg. Hon. III*, 5079 (MANSILLA, 513); (iii) 27 March 1230. Bp (Martín Fernández), dean, for bishop of Zamora in dispute with clergy of Toro. *Sua nobis venerabili*: ACZ, 11/I/8 (LERA 426); (iv) 6 May 1234. Bp (Martín Fernández), Toledo/Compostela primacy issue. *Cum super causa*: *Reg.*

cation of his kingdom's university, and that in April 1243 Fernando III had followed suit by confirming 'aquellas costumbres et aquellos fueros que ouieron las escolares en Salamanca en tiempo de myo padre quando establesçio hy las escuelas'[42]. Whereas universities in England developed organically, and did so where they did largely because Oxford and Cambridge were the places within the politically important area of the kingdom where juristic activity was concentrated[43], in the kingdom of León different considerations operated. There, as in the case of Frederick II's foundation at Naples in 1224 and Alfonso VIII's at Palencia before that, it was the monarch who determined the matter *de haut en bas*[44]. And in this process Zamora failed to find favour.

But why? Evidently not for lack of either academic infrastructure or academic alternatives, even beyond the limits of the realm. In the will he made in 1230 the chanter García de Uliolo readily acknowledged his indebtedness to the church of Zamora for all the advantages he had enjoyed since boyhood 'both in the schools and elsewhere' – and by elsewhere he probably meant Palencia[45]. Nor on account of a marked preference on the part of Fernando III for the other place, the city on the Tormes. In terms of

---

*Greg. IX*, 1907 (=AC Toledo, X.8.C.1.1); (v) 31 Aug. 1235. Bp (Martín Fernández), with Zamora judges, against king of Portugal: App. II, no. 95; (vi) 14 Jan. 1236. Repetition of (iv). *Venerabilis frater noster*: AHN Cod. 987B, fo. 111v; (vii) 8 Feb. 1236. Chanter, with Zamora judges, for prior and chapter of Guimarães. App. II, no. 96; (viii) 7 May 1236. Repetition of (iv). *Cum super causa*: Reg. Greg. IX, 3148 (AC Toledo, X.8.C.1.2); (ix) 26 Jan. 1238. Bp (Martín Fernández), dean and treasurer, for Master and brothers of Ord. Alcántara against *concejo* of Talavera regarding castle of Cogolludo. *Dilecti filii magister*: I. J. DE ORTEGA ET COTES *et al.*, *Bullarium ordinis militiae de Alcantara, olim S. Juliani del Pereiro*, Madrid, Antonii Marin, 1759, pp. 45-46; (x) 23 Feb. 1239. Repetition of (iv). *Significante venerabili*: AC Toledo, X.2.E.1.2; (xi) 21 Dec. 1239. Bp (Martín Fernández) and chanter, conservators for bishop of Lisbon. *Cum sicut accepimus*: Reg. Greg. IX, 5009. Cf. I Lyons, c. 2 ('Praesenti').

[42] J. GONZÁLEZ, *Reinado y diplomas de Fernando III*, Córdoba 1980-1986, III, no. 709. The nature of the relationship between Alfonso IX's foundation for theologians (above, n. 21) and his son's, in which the study of theology was not provided for, remains obscure. See RASHDALL, *Universities* cit., II, pp. 80-81.

[43] R. W. SOUTHERN, *From Schools to University*, in J. I. CATTO (ed.), *The History of the University of Oxford*, I, *The Early Oxford Schools*, Oxford 1984, pp. 12-17; J. A. BRUNDAGE, *The Cambridge faculty of canon law and the ecclesiastical courts of Ely*, in P. ZUTSHI (ed.), *Medieval Cambridge. Essays on the pre-Reformation University*, Woodbridge 1993, pp. 23-25.

[44] Thus RASHDALL, *Universities* cit., II, pp. 22, 75-77.

[45] 'Cum (...) a puericia mea de bonis ecclesie alitus et nutritus ab eadem, non meis meritis set sola sua gratia multa in scolis et alibi receperim beneficia': *TN*, ff.

474

the number of days spent by his court at Salamanca and at Zamora since 1230 there is virtually nothing to choose between the two[46]. May there have been uneasiness then apropos what the late Richard Fletcher described as 'the Zamora imbroglio', the twelfth-century contest for metropolitan authority over the place between the churches of Compostela and Braga across the Portuguese frontier? Had anxiety been created regarding the possibility of that murky question being reopened at some future date and, just as the primacy dispute between Toledo and Compostela threatened to do as it rumbled on, invoked as a coded assertion of some sort of Portuguese hegemony over Zamora[47]? Or was it for a different reason altogether, albeit a related one, namely Zamora's failure to satisfy one of the principal criteria for the establishment of *studia generalia*, as later defined by Fernando's son, Alfonso X, in the second of his *Siete Partidas*? Was it the lack of security of the place on account of its frontier situation? Was it, paradoxically, the corollary of the very circumstance that had contributed to the enhancement of its juristic reputation over the previous three decades that was responsible for Zamora's failure to develop as Spain's Cambridge – or even its Oxford[48]?

It can hardly have been because of the chapter of Zamora's infiltration by outsiders, for in that respect the church of Salamanca was no less grievously affected[49]. Even so, according to Bishop Martín II's complaint to

88v-89r (LERA, 431). For evidence of Zamora students at Palencia in the 1220s, see A. M. BARRERO GARCÍA, *Un formulario de cancilleria episcopal castellano leonés del siglo XIII*, «Anuario de Historia del Derecho Español», 46 (1976), pp. 671-711, especially letters 36-37, in which Bishop M. of Zamora orders the return of scholars from Palencia to their parishes for the Christmas season, and the scholars ask to be allowed to remain at the schools.

[46] 20 and 15 respectively according to the admittedly imperfect data supplied by GONZÁLEZ, *Reinado de Fernando III* cit., vols II, III. The itinerary of Alfonso IX between 1188 and 1230 records 33 visits by the royal court to Salamanca, and 30 to Zamora: ID., *Alfonso IX*, Madrid 1944, pp. 749-827.

[47] The most recent papal pronouncement on the Zamora issue, by Innocent III in 1199, had stopped short of disallowing Braga's claims *de jure*: MANSILLA, 199. Innocent 'did not confirm the rights of Compostela over Zamora; but neither did he deny them': FLETCHER, *Episcopate* cit., p. 202. Further particulars in O. HAGENEDER, W. MALECZEK & A. A. STRNAD, *Die Register Innocenz' III.*, II, 2. *Pontifikatsjahr, 1199/1200. Texte*, Rome-Vienna 1979, no. 97 (105). See also below, n. 174; P. LINEHAN, *History and the Historians of Medieval Spain*, Oxford 1993, pp. 334-349.

[48] Cf. II Partida, 31.2: 'Et por ende mandamos que los maestros, et escolares, et sus mensageros et todas sus cosas sean seguros et atreguardos en veniendo a los estudios, et en estando en ellos et en yendose para sus tierras...' (ed. Real Academia de la Historia, Madrid 1807, II. 340-1).

Rome in May 1233, Zamora's situation in this respect was indeed dire. At the instigation of the papal legate Cardinal John of Abbeville and of the Spanish cardinals Pelayo Gaitán and Gil Torres in particular, the bishop reported, over the previous seventeen years no fewer than thirteen capitular benefices had been awarded by papal provision to outsiders, in consequence of which there had been none available for deserving local men who had spent all their lives in the service of the institution[50]. Now if such was indeed the case (and the complaint was repeated in the following year, in even sharper terms)[51], then here was the complement of the benefits that had accrued to the place on account of the access of the likes of Master Florencio with their friends in high places[52], If such was the case, the successors of García de Uliolo, that scholarship boy of the previous generation, were being driven to seek advancement elsewhere.

And during the episcopal vacancy that followed Martín II's translation to León matters deteriorated further, since for most of the quinquennium prior to Fernando III's confirmation of Salamanca's status as a *studium generale*, the crucial quinquennium during which the bishop of Zamora might have been lobbying on Zamora's behalf in that connexion, it was unclear whether Zamora had a bishop at all. For although D. Pedro had been in some sense elected soon after his predecessor's departure, on account (possibly) of some diplomatic stone-walling by Fernando III and (certainly) of the twenty-two month vacancy in the papal office after August 1241, so far as the papal curia was concerned as late as July 1243 he was still 'bishop elect'[53]. And by then three months had already elapsed since Fernando III had issued his charter in favour of the schools of Salamanca.

We would give much to know more than we do about Fernando III's

[49] P. LINEHAN, *El cardenal zamorano D. Gil Torres y la sociedad zamorana de su época*, in *2° Congreso de Historia de Zamora*, Nov. 2003 (in press *apud* Zamora: Instituto de Estudios Zamoranos «Florián de Ocampo» (C.S.I.C.)/Diputación de Zamora).

[50] 'auctoritate etiam venerabilis fratris nostri .. Sabinensis episcopi tunc in partibus illis legationis fungentis officio, necnon et ad preces bone memorie episcopi Albanensis et dilecti filii nostri Egidii Sanctorum Cosme et Damiani diaconi cardinalis...': *Reg. Greg. IX*, 1318.

[51] *Ibid.*, 2009.

[52] In 1267 the dean of León, Master Johán, recalled the provision of Reliegos (dioc. León), valued at eighty gold *maravedís*, 'por auctoridat del bispo de Sabina que fura legado de Rroma en Espanna' [Cardinal John of Abbeville in 1228-9] 'a mestre Florenz, que estuencia yera dean de Zamora, e por so companero el chantre desse lugar' (viz. D. García): CDL, 2268. Cf. P. LINEHAN, *A papal legation and its aftermath: Cardinal John of Abbeville in Spain and Portugal, 1228-1229*, in I. BIROCCHI *et al.* (eds.), *A Ennio Cortese*, Rome 2001, II, pp. 236-56.

[53] IANTT, *Sé de Coimbra*, 2a incorporação. mç. 42, doc. 1733 (*Sua nobis* [11

relationship with the bishops of Salamanca over the period of Martín I and Martín II's custody of the see of Zamora, and especially during the crucial years 1229 to 1245, the pontificate of Martín Fernández, to whom, according to Julio González, 'se atribuye la construcción del primer edificio que ha tenido la Universidad [de Salamanca][54]. According to González, Martín Fernández was the second member of an episcopal dynasty, following his brother Gonzalo Fernández and followed in turn by his nephew Pedro Pérez, who, having ascended through Alfonso IX's chancery from the rank of notary to that of chancellor between 1202 and 1230, in his capacity as *magister scolarum* of Salamanca devoted himself thereafter to the affairs of the nascent university and ruled the see from 1247 until 1263[55].

In fact, González's account of the succession of the see in the posses-

July 1243]). The situation in the see of Zamora between 1238 and 1243 is at best obscure, the evidence of the lists of *confirmantes* to the royal privileges printed by GONZÁLEZ, *Reinado de Fernando III* cit., being vitiated by the inclusion of items of dubious authenticity. Thus on 18 Oct. 1239 D. Pedro is recorded as both 'episcopus' (no. 651) and 'electus' (nos. 652-4), and on 25 Nov. 1239 in an Úbeda copy 'Martínus episcopus' resurfaces (no. 656; J. RODRÍGUEZ MOLINA, *Colección documental del Archivo Municipal de Úbeda. I. (Siglo XIII)*, Granada 1990, no. 5), while 'Petrus electus' is authenticated by the chancery (GONZÁLEZ, no. 657). The conflict between 'Petrus episcopus' on 22 Dec. 1239 (no. 663) and 'Petrus electus' on 9 July 1240 (no. 664), however, is more difficult to resolve since, although no. 664 derives from a cartulary, the miscopying of 'episcopus' as 'electus' is less likely than the reverse error. On this evidence, the earliest recorded date of Pedro I as bishop is 17 Sept. 1240 (no. 666). At Zamora itself, the record of the capitular constitutions of the church (ACZ, 10bis/4) seems to point to a questioning of D. Pedro's authority sometime in the autumn of 1239, for whereas new constitutions were approved 'a domno P. dei gratia Zamorensi electo et confirmato [but by whom confirmed?] et a capitulo Zamorensi' (ff. 94vb-95va) on 1 July 1239, in mid-November 1239 and again in mid-April 1240 further new constitutions were sanctioned 'a capitulo' alone (ff. 100va, 100vb). There D. Pedro was still *electus* in April 1242 (ACZ, 18/2: LERA, 516). His deathbed recollection of the visit he paid the king at Burgos 'post confirmationem obtentam (...) ut decens erat' (ACZ 13/46 [LERA, 602], cit. P. LINEHAN, *The Spanish Church and the Papacy in the Thirteenth Century*, Cambridge 1971, p. 114, n. 6) fails to assist in defining the period between election and confirmation. Since there is no sign of a disputed election having occurred at Zamora on the occasion of Martín II's translation to León (*ante* Nov. 1238; *Reg. Greg. IX*, 4594), the reason for the delay is not apparent, though it is to be noted that only recently Fernando III had had his way with the pope in obstructing the filling of the same León vacancy by the translation of his chancellor: LINEHAN, *Juan de Soria*, pp. 377-378. For the wider diplomatic perspective, ID., *El cardenal zamorano*.

[54] *Alfonso IX*, p. 460.
[55] *Ibid.*, 483, 486-91.

sion of a single family is demonstrably wrong[56], just as his assumption that any thirteenth-century churchman could have remained active for as much as sixty years defies belief[57], Nor, within the smooth episcopal succession imagined by him, is allowance made for the short-lived interloper Pelayo, translated thither in 1227 from the Palestinian see of Lydda[58].

There is an alternative continuum observable, however. By the time that control of the kingdom of León passed to Fernando III in 1230, the tradition of colonisation of the chapter of Salamanca by members of the church of Compostela was long established, and indeed oppressive to the locals of both the diocese and the city, to judge by the complaints they addressed to successive pontiffs[59]. This was the tradition in accordance with which Archbishop Bernardo had recently put the bishop of Lydda into the see after the chapter had failed to settle the matter themselves[60]. Nor would D. Pelayo's prospects have been damaged by his Galician associations, for Fernando III was notoriously partial to Galicians[61]. And above all there was the reputation enjoyed by the church of Compostela for good written Latinity, competence in which was essential to the personnel of the royal chancery[62]. In the calculations of the kings of León, Compostela and its Salamanca dependency constituted a species of default position.

---

[56] As was observed by V. BELTRÁN DE HEREDIA, *Cartulario de la Universidad de Salamanca (1218-1600)*, I, Salamanca 1970, p. 71, the 'M. Fernandi archidiaconus', mentioned as the brother of Bishop Gonzalo Fernández in June 1220, was still active as archdeacon in October 1236, six years into the pontificate of *Bishop Martín Fernández*. Cf. J. L. MARTÍN MARTÍN ET AL., *Documentos de los archivos catedralicio y diocesano de Salamanca (siglos XII-XIII)*, Salamanca 1977, pp. 146, 183, 193. But which of these was the 'M. Fernandi', canon of Salamanca, whose silence Bishop Gonzalo allegedly purchased with an archdeaconry of the church in 1218/1219 in return for his silence after the bishop had been charged with a whole range of crimes (MANSILLA, 252)? His *brother*?

[57] The 'Petrus Petri canonicus [of Salamanca]', recorded as 'nepos' of Bishop Gonzalo Fernández in June 1220 cannot have been the same man as the archdeacon of Salamanca of that name reported as 'tenen[s] cancellariam' in January 1217: GONZÁLEZ, *Alfonso IX*, no. 342 (p. 451). Cf. BELTRÁN DE HEREDIA's conflation of the two and the difficulty resulting: *Cartulario* cit., I, pp. 70, 74.

[58] *Reg. Greg. IX*, 101; LINEHAN, *Spanish Church* cit., p. 19.

[59] BELTRÁN DE HEREDIA, *Cartulario* cit., I, pp. 59-68.

[60] '...cum (...) canonicis eiusdem ecclesiae ad eligendum nequentibus concordare in unum eligendi potestas fuerit ad prefatum archiepiscopum devoluta': ASV, Reg. Vat. 14, f. 15v, no. 101 (*Reg. Greg. IX*, 101).

[61] In 1223 Honorius III had restored to the bishop *in partibus* 'redditus quos hactenus in Auriensi ecclesia dinosceris habuisse': *Reg. Hon. III*, 4197 (MANSILLA, 430). Cf. BELTRÁN DE HEREDIA, *Cartulario* cit., I, p. 73.

[62] R. WRIGHT, *A Sociophilological Study of Late Latin*, Turnhout 2002, p. 259.

The fact that in January 1217 Pedro Pérez, archdeacon of Salamanca at the time but Compostellan by origin, was in control of the chancery may shed some light on the issue of the decline of Zamora beneath the peninsular horizon. For in 1217, and over the following two or three decades, the chanceries of the kingdoms of León and Castile were engaged in the process of replacing Latin with forms of the vernacular as their language of ordinary business. And though this was of course a process directed from above, the rulers and their ministers were not acting in a void. They were responding to the needs of ordinary Leonese and Castilians, ecclesiastics as well as laymen, and the increasing Latinlessness of the age which the Zamora material itself illustrates, with one of Fr. García's objections to the impugned chirograph, it will be recalled, being that it was 'full of false Latinity from start to finish'[63]. More significant than its substance, however, is the fact that Fr. García's objection failed to persuade the judge of the case. In the view of the archdeacon Ysidoro, linguistic imperfections in a Latin document did not necessarily imply its inauthenticity. It is also deserving of note that although the proceedings of the archdeacon's court were recorded in Latin, as befitted an ecclesiastical tribunal, the record itself reveals that part at least of the instrument to which Fr. García objected was written in Spanish, the only particular requiring elucidation by the learned judge being the meaning of the clause 'que sean felegreses todos aquelos que i moraren'[64]. That was in 1223.

In the following year, this time as judge-delegate of a dispute with which he had been occupied earlier, D. Ysidoro was involved in another case which turned on the question of Latin literacy. Diego Rodríguez and his wife had impetrated letters against the abbot of Arbás in the papal chancery. But the letters were flawed. In addition to failing to identify the wife by name, they lapsed into the plural where the singular was required, and on the strength of these defects the abbot had succeeded in frustrating the tribunal's proceedings[65]. However, Honorius III dismissed the abbot's objections as abuse of procedure, set aside the scribal lapses, and instructed the judges to proceed with their investigation of the plaintiffs' complaint[66]. So even the supreme pontiff was willing to shrug off third-form

---

[63] Above, p. 464.

[64] App. I, §E.

[65] App. II, no. 59: 'quia nomen uxoris predicti militis non erat in litteris ipsis expressum, et quia erat in latinitate peccatum iniuriandi uerbo pluraliter posito, ubi poni singulariter debuisset...'

[66] '... Nos ergo litteras ipsas, quas ueras esse comperimus, licet in predicto uerbo fuerit uicio scriptoris erratum uobis sub bulla nostra remittentes inclusas, discretioni uestre (...) mandamus quatinus non obstantibus occasionibus supradictis in negotio ipso iuxta earundem continentiam litterarum ratione preuia procedatis': *ibid.*

solecisms committed in the language of the Universal Church[67]. In 1223-1224 Zamora and the kingdom of León were at a linguistic crossroads, with the expertise displayed by the abbot of Arbas the exception rather than the rule. The autograph witness-list to a settlement agreed between M., archdeacon of Toro (this must be Munio Muniz) and the perennially problematic clergy of that place reveals the state of affairs in the second city of the diocese of Zamora in the years 1216-1219. First to sign was the archpriest Martinus, who got proceedings off to a shaky start with 'confirmo anc conposicionem'. Following him came the rector (or somesuch) of S. Lorenzo (the parchment is damaged at this point) with 'han composicionem', and his colleague of S. Trinidad with 'hanc composicianem'. At number four, the rector of S. Juan steadies the boat with a confident 'hanc composicionem', and thereafter each of the remaining eighteen faithfully follows his lead, evidently (and in some cases evidently painfully) copying what the man before had written. It does not take much imagination to visualise the faces of some of those eighteen as one after another of they concentrated on the task of making their mark[68].

At a linguistic crossroads then, or rather at a linguistic T-junction, the various implications of which have been intensively as well as fruitfully studied of late[69]. But a T-junction which with the reunion of the kingdoms of León and Castile in 1230, in the person of Fernando III, was converted into the site for a super-highway, a super-highway designed to obliterate every feature of the existing landscape, organisational as well as linguistic. For concomitant with the dislodging of the language previously used by the separate national chanceries was the dislodging of the respective chancellors *ex officio* of the two kingdoms, the archbishops of Toledo and Com-

---

[67] Ironically, the text of the correcting mandate, as edited, is also full of howlers, diplomatic as well as grammatical: 'Cumque super hoc ad bone memorie cantorem Zamorensem et uos fil*ii* archidiacon*i*, et *te* fil*ii* Ysidore, tunc canonic*o* Zemorens*i*, commissionis litteras a sede apostolica impetrarunt...'. I have not been able to establish when it was between November 1224 and sometime in 1991 that these errors were introduced into the text.

[68] ACZ, 36/6 (LERA, 386, ascribing it the date [1216-1224]. The date suggested here is ascertainable from internal evidence. Cf. below, n. 160).

[69] See D. LOMAX, *La lengua oficial de Castilla*, in *Actele celui de-al XII-lea Congres Internaţional de Lingvistica şi Filologie Romanica*, t. 2, Bucarest 1971, pp. 411-417; R. WRIGHT, *Latin and Romance in the Castilian chancery (1180-1230)*, «Bulletin of Hispanic Studies» (Liverpool), 73 (1996), 121-3; ID., *El Tratado de Cabreros (1206): estudio sociofilológico de una reforma ortográfica*, London 2000 (Papers of the Medieval Hispanic Research Seminar 19), pp. 99-116; F. J. HERNÁNDEZ, *Sobre los orígenes del español escrito*, «Voz y letra», 10 (1999), pp. 133-166. esp. pp. 152-153.

postela, and their replacement by a single chancellor of the now single kingdom in the person of Juan de Soria, bishop successively of Osma and Burgos[70]. In 1218 Archbishop Pedro Muñoz of Compostela had been thought to have designs on the 'cancellaria vel capellania Regis Castelle'[71]. By 1230 times had moved on. 'Allá van leyes do quieren reyes.' Laws went where kings would have them go. So did lawyers, chanceries and *studia*.

With Juan de Soria we return to the Zamora-Salamanca issue, though here admittedly we are on thin ice since, so far as I am aware, there is no evidence bearing on Juan de Soria's preference regarding the whereabouts of the Leonese *studium generale*. Speculation regarding the question has to proceed by analogy, therefore, analogy with what is beginning to emerge regarding the development of Soria, within Bishop Juan's diocese of Osma, as some sort of alternative for the Castilian *studium generale* at Palencia. In the event, when Palencia perished Soria did not replace it, at least not in that role. What instead it did was develop as a seminary for civil servants[72]. By analogy again, may it not have been the case that it was that civil service tradition that recommended Salamanca to both Fernando III and his chancellor?

A further question remains. Master Florencio and his contemporaries had lived through a period during which not only had the language of government changed, so also had the reference points of the canon law which they had proved so adept both at administering and also, in the case of two of Zamora's bishops, at elucidating (though to nothing like the extent of their colleagues from Compostela and Galicia)[73], until, at a stroke, the publication of the Gregorian decretals in 1234 rendered redundant the compilations on which they and the parties in the case of 'S.' and others *versus*

---

[70] For these developments, see LINEHAN, *Juan de Soria* cit.; ID., *Don Rodrigo and the government of the kingdom*, «Cahiers de Linguistique et de Civilisation Hispaniques Médiévales», 26 (2003), pp. 87-99.

[71] MANSILLA, no. 132.

[72] LINEHAN, *Juan de Soria* cit., pp. 388-389.

[73] See A. GARCÍA Y GARCÍA, *Canonistas gallegos medievales*, «Compostellanum», 16 (1971), pp. 114-116; ID. & I. VÁZQUEZ JANEIRO, *La biblioteca del arzobispo de Santiago de Compostela, Bernardo II (†1240)*, «Antonianum», 61 (1986), pp. 547-548, 561-563; M. BERTRAM, Gallecia unde duxi originem. *Johannes Hispanus Compostellanus (de Petesella) und seine Dekretalensumme (ca.1235/36)*, in P. LINEHAN, ed., *Law, Life and Letters: Historical Studies in Honour of Antonio García y García [Studia Gratiana, 28]*, Rome 1998, pp. 89-119. For the Galician origins of the earlier of Zamora's two bishops Martín, the protégé of Archbishop Pedro Suárez de Deza of Compostela, see A. LÓPEZ FERREIRO, *Historia de la santa iglesia de Santiago de Compostela*, V, Santiago de Compostela 1902, pp. 40-41, 117-118.

Fr. García had depended. Long accustomed to serving more than one master and to operating more than one system of law, they now faced the prospect of doing so in more than one language. Here were two worlds turned upside down simultaneously.

So what became of them? What became of the successors of Master Florencio and his colleagues? For, as the evidence of Appendix II shows, the recruitment of members of the Zamora chapter as papal judges delegate does rather sharply tail off after 1243. Plaintiffs who had previously opted for Zamora judges, according to the to our eyes bizarre system whereby plaintiffs were allowed that liberty, now looked elsewhere[74]. Where then did the next generation of Zamora's jurists go?

The answer to that question must in large part have depended on the age of the individual. To such youngsters as could afford it, or for whom the chapter was willing to make allowance – and, if circumstances remained as Bishop Martín II had described them in 1233, of these there will have been few[75] – Salamanca, just sixty kilometres to the south, must have beckoned, and it would seem doubtful whether as many of them did as García de Uliolo had done forty years before, and received their higher education at home. Here was a principal difference between Zamora in the 1200s and in the 1240s. And when D. Suero Pérez arrived there as its new bishop in 1255, bringing with him 'many good books' of both law and theology, he discovered a cultural desert – or so he would later imply[76].

Now it is indeed the case that neither in the will of García de Uliolo nor in that of any other canon or dignitary of the place during these years, although we find livestock, cooking utensils, the contents of their *bodegas*, and on one occasion a 'gilded bed' listed, do we find any mention of spe-

---

[74] The collegiate church of Guimarães to dignitaries of the churches of Guarda, Porto and Salamanca, for example: IANTT, *Colegiada de Guimarães*, docs. eclesiásticos, mç. 1, docs. 39, 41; mç. 2, doc. 10. Cf. App. II, nos. 70-75, 96, 101-2, 106-7. For the procedure see SAYERS, *Papal Judges Delegate* cit., pp. 54-58, 109-112, and, from the year 1282, the letter of Archbishop John Peckham of Canterbury to his Roman proctors identifying as 'boni', 'meliores' and 'optimi' the judges proposed by him for appointment in cases in which he had an interest: *Registrum epistolarum fratris Johannis Peckham, archiepiscopi Cantuariensis*, ed. C. MARTIN, I, Rolls Ser., London 1882, p. 280. None of the original mandates inspected here shows signs of having been contradicted in the *audientia publica*. For present purposes however the absence of information on that score is immaterial.

[75] Above, n. 50.

[76] P. LINEHAN, *The economics of episcopal politics: the cautionary tale of Bishop Suero Pérez of Zamora*, in ID., *The Processes of Politics and the Rule of Law. Studies on the Iberian kingdoms and papal Rome in the Middle Ages*, Aldershot 2002, pp. 4, 36-37.

482

cific books – or indeed of books at all[77]. Moreover, even in the late 1280s the very few works of canon law listed in the inventory of the treasury of the church were all a century out-of-date[78], with not so much as a single copy of Gratian or the Gregorian Decretals or any civil law text specified, not even one of Tancred's procedural treatise, his *Ordo justiciarius*, which must have been within arm's reach of the archdeacon D. Ysidoro in 1223[79]. However, neither at this nor at any other date can the argument from bibliographical silence be allowed to count. For one thing, it is possible that more recent items were not listed in the treasurer's inventory because at the time it was made they were on loan to members of the chapter, as was the case in the chapter of Toledo some ten years earlier[80]. And for another, not only is it evident that the dean D. Juan (†1217) was at least a competent jurist. It is also on record that in 1281 his successor in office, Pedro Juanes, had passed on to his nephew copies of both those indispensable authorities[81]. It would further appear that, whereas individual canons and dignitaries were in the habit of bequeathing works of theology to the capitular library[82], they had other means, which their wills do not reveal, of disposing of the legal items on their shelves[83].

[77] *Ibid.*, 18. To the references provided there, the evidence of the will of the dean D. Juan (June 1217) may now be added: 'Ecclesie Sancti Spiritus relinquo mulam mozellam et ruciam ad extrahendam aquam de noris et lectum meum cum apparatu suo et duo parva breviaria et maiorem sarraginem ferream et maiorem caldariam et ollam cupream' (*TN*, f. 88v: Lera, 305). Cf. the global description, 'omnes libros meos', in the will of Bishop Martín I (June 1223): López Ferreiro, *Hist. Santiago de Compostela* cit., V, app. XII, p. 36.

[78] Namely, copies of 'Compilatio I', a second partial copy of the same work, the 'Collection in 74 Titles', the *Summa Decreti* of Johannes Faventinus (*c*.1171), and two unidentified works of Ivo of Chartres: M. Guadalupe, *El tesoro del cabildo zamorano: aproximación a una biblioteca del siglo XIII*, «Studia Historica. Historia Medieval», 1/2 (1983), 169-70, 175.

[79] F. C. Bergman (ed.), *Pillii, Tancredi, Gratiae libri de iudiciorum ordine*, Göttingen, Vandenhoeck & Ruprecht, 1842, esp. pp. 142-146.

[80] F. Hernández & P. Linehan, *The Mozarabic Cardinal. The life and times of Gonzalo Pérez Gudiel*, Florence 2004, pp. 123 n. 59, 167-168.

[81] App. II, nos. 1-22; *TB*, f. 160r (Lera, 931)

[82] Guadalupe, *El tesoro* cit., p. 174, nos. 5-7.

[83] Though in the case of the will of the canon Parens (Apr. 1242) one procedure was alluded to: 'Quamdam donationem fatio predictis pueris, secundum quod continetur in quadam cedula, sigillo meo et capituli sigillata, que sic incipit: "Ego Parens, canonicus Zamorensis et cetera." (...) De mobilibus vero meis dispono per testamentum, secundum quod continetur in alia cedula, sigillo domini electi et capituli Zamorensis et meo communita. Omnia alia que specialiter a me legata non sunt vel donata, sint in dispositione predictorum executorum, ut inde faciant secun-

But what above all is evident from the constitutions of the chapter is that the cultural condition of Zamora in the 1240s was considerably healthier than was alleged by Bishop Suero Pérez, an invincible curmudgeon who, in order to emphasise the magnitude of his contribution to the welfare of the place, towards the end of his life chose to paint in the darkest of colours the situation of the see at the time of his arrival there[84]. For from these we learn that in April 1240 the chapter agreed to allow those of its members who had been duly licensed by the chapter to study to do so on full stipend for up to five years[85]: generous provision in a land which at the time was seriously strapped for cash.

It is to be noted that the bishop, or bishop-elect, of the day was not party to this concession. The body that approved this measure was headless[86]. But it was not wholly reckless. It was well aware of the problems that might ensue, as the two qualifications to its constitution indicated. These were as follows. Anyone at the schools who wished to visit the papal curia was permitted to do so, but only for a period of two months maximum, including travel there and back. If he stayed there longer, unless on account of illness, his stipend from the chapter would be deducted *pro rata*[87].

These provisions may help to explain where many of those previously thriving jurists went after the death of Master Florencio in 1237 and the departure of Bishop Martín II for León in November 1238[88]. They had gone to Rome, and they had gone there, taking with them the juristic expertise that until the late 1230s had evidently been so effectively exercised within

---

dum quod viderint expedire, quia ipsis communicavi aliqua secreta mea': ACZ, 18/5 (LERA, 516).

[84] LINEHAN, *The economics* cit., pp. 22-26.

[85] 'Item, statutum est a capitulo ut quando aliquis de personis, canonicis vel portionariis iverint ad scolas, petita licentia et obtenta, habeat portiones suas per quinquennium, a die recessus sui quinquennio computato': ACZ, 10/4, f. 101ra.

[86] See above, n. 53.

[87] 'Et si existens in scola curiam visitaverit, liceat ei ibi manere per duos menses, si voluerit, computato in his duobus mensibus tempore eundi et redeundi et in curia existendi. Et si maiorem ibi traxerit moram, nisi infirmitate detentus, quanto tempore plus ibi permanserit tanto sibi portio subtrahatur': ACZ, 10/4, f. 101ra.

[88] Although it may have been fortuitous it was none the less significant that in the same month as he approved the translation of Martín Rodríguez, thereby depriving Zamora of its canonist bishop, Gregory IX approved the election of Juan Arias as archbishop of Compostela in succession to Bernardo II (nephew of the canonist Bernardus Compostellanus Antiquus), having previously declined to admit the postulation of the canonist bishop of Orense, Laurentius Hispanus, 'eo quod multi in eadem ecclesia reperiebantur idonei': *Reg. Greg. IX*, 4177, 4588.

the kingdom of León as well as to both east and west, because whereas in Zamora in 1240 there was no securely constituted bishop competent to advance their careers, in Rome there was a Zamoran cardinal with twenty-six years of curial experience behind him and another fourteen still to come.

I have attempted elsewhere to provide some account of the career and activities of Gil Torres, cardinal deacon of SS. Cosmas and Damian, and his role in the development of the system of papal provisions at the expense of the ordinary collators about which Bishop Martín II had complained in 1233, identifying the cardinal as one of three prelates responsible for damaging the prospects of promotion for local men[89]. Not that the problem was peculiar to Zamora. It was widespread throughout the peninsula as well as further afield. The church of Salamanca was suffering too – though in this case it was the archbishop of Compostela who was responsible for their plight and Cardinal Gil Torres who provided solace, if only briefly[90]. And already by 1233 Zamora's locals, together with many other peninsular hopefuls, were repairing the damage by travelling to the papal curia and attaching themselves to the Zamoran cardinal's household. The lengthy episcopal vacancy after 1238 merely increased the flow of traffic. So did novel restrictive practices both before and after that date[91].

The notable reduction in the number of commissions to Zamora judges was just one consequence of this development, reflecting the fact that plaintiffs were hardly likely to nominate as judges men who could not investigate their grievance because they were resident in Italy or Lyons – as for example the chanter Master Gil was in 1254[92]. Likewise, the absence of

---

[89] LINEHAN, *El cardenal zamorano* cit.; above, n. 50.

[90] By the cardinal's constitutions for the chapter (April 1245), provided suitable candidates were available, and with the single qualification 'nisi pensatis ecclesie utilitate et necessitate propter litteralis scientie eminentiam et morum prerogativam aliunde alii assumantur', appointment to prebends, canonries and dignities was restricted to residents of the diocese or members of the chapter: D. MANSILLA, *Iglesia castellano-leonesa y curia romana en los tiempos del rey San Fernando*, Madrid 1945, pp. 323-324.

[91] Thus in 1236 Martín II infringed the rights of the chapter with whom he shared collation by securing a papal grant of exclusive provision to the next three vacant canonries (*Reg. Greg. IX*, 3258), and ten years later Innocent IV nullified a statute introduced by Pedro I and the chapter requiring unanimity in the conferment of benefices, declaring it objectionable since as well as infringing the rights of the 'maior et sanior pars', and incidentally their own statute of July 1239, it sometimes had the effect of excluding 'viros litteratos et providos': *Reg. Inn. IV*, 2003 (ed., MANSILLA, *Iglesia* cit., p. 218; QP, 289, with notable errors in both cases); ACZ, 10/4, f. 95rb-va.

[92] Below, n. 186.

commissions known to have been addressed to the archdeacon of the city
after Ysidoro's last appearance in January 1233 (App. II, no. 82), may be
attributable in large part to the incumbent of that dignity by 1245 being the
abbot of Husillos, Master Esteban, Gil Torres' *nepos*-in-chief, and a plural-
ist *par excellence* himself who in the final years of the cardinal's long career installed himself at the papal curia and seems to have acted as benefice-
broker in his uncle's name[93].

Of course this is not to suggest that the juristic expertise had been entirely squandered. After all, the likes of the abbot of Husillos[94] needed to
know their way at least around the canon law relating to the provision of
benefices – and, being the professional he was, sure enough Master Esteban possessed his own copy of the Gregorian decretals[95]. Nor in Zamora itself were other copies of that work allowed to gather dust. During the last
decade of Cardinal Gil's life, while the abbot of Husillos was feathering his
own nest and those of others at Lyons and in Italy, by the banks of the
Duero the dean Juan Juánez soldiered on[96]. Indeed, there is clear evidence
that the reputation of Zamora judges had not faded altogether. In March
1254, the archbishop of Braga, D. João Egas, complained to Innocent IV regarding certain infringements of his jurisdiction in the parishes of his city

---

[93] *TN*, f. 135v (LERA 532); LINEHAN, *El cardenal zamorano* cit., n. 54, with the
suggestion that he may also have appropriated the cardinal's seal in the final stages
of the latter's life.

[94] The secular abbacy of Husillos in the diocese of Palencia, which served as a
training-ground for fast-track royal bureaucrats, may also have siphoned off some
ambitious *zamoranos* in these years, especially through the influence of Bishop
Suero Pérez, formerly notary for León. See LINEHAN, *The economics* cit., p. 14; P.
LINEHAN and M. TORRES SEVILLA, *A misattributed tomb and its implications: Cardinal Ordoño Álvarez and his friends and relations*, «Rivista di Storia della Chiesa
in Italia», 57 (2003), p. 57. It is of interest that on 18 May 1255 the archdeacon of
Coimbra, G. Facundi, to whom the chanter of Zamora, Master Gil, had subdelegated his responsibilities as *receptor* of evidence in the Braga-Porto case (App. II, no.
131), wrote from Husillos to the chanters of Lisbon and Lamego, his *co-receptores*,
excusing himself from attendance at the hearing to be held at the monastery of Vi-
larinho on 1 June, 'propter urgentissima negotia ecclesie Fussellensis que coram
domino rege Castelle vertuntur': ADB, *Gav. dos Arcebispos*, 29.

[95] Which he bequeathed to the *magister scolarum* of Zamora, Pedro Beneítez
(Bishop Pedro II of Zamora after 1286 and his *nepos* as well as *nepos* of Cardinal
Gil Torres): P. LINEHAN, *The Ladies of Zamora*, Manchester 1997, p. 86; *Reg. Inn.
IV*, 5564, 5805; J. C. DE LERA MAÍLLO, *El testamento del obispo de Zamora Pedro
II, año 1302. Edición diplomática*, in *Homenaje a Antonio Matilla Tascón*, Zamora
2002, p. 358.

[96] App. II, nos. 106-132.

and diocese and the case was remitted to judges delegate at Santarém and Lisbon. However, since Portuguese judges were evidently thought unlikely to prove effective, the archbishop's Roman proctor secured substitutes, Zamora judges. 'Innouetur sub iudicibus Zamorensibus', the chancery clerk annotated the original mandate[97]. As had been the case between 1209 and the mid-1230s, in King Afonso III's Portugal *any* Zamora judges were preferable to those liable to be subject to local pressures. It mattered not that those judges were now more likely to have received their professional training at Salamanca, or Bologna[98].

Even so, from a Zamoran perspective times had changed since D. Ysidoro had given judgment in the case of Fr. García *versus* 'S.' and others. And on that occasion, be it remembered, D. Ysidoro had been sitting not as a papal judge-delegate but in his own court in his own archidiaconal capacity. The 1223 case serves to remind us of the weight of the judicial burden borne by those 'to whom the care and custody of ecclesiastical things were entrusted'[99]. And throughout a period so pregnant with consequences not only for canon law but also for the Spanish language, that activity continued to occupy the successors in title of D. Ysidoro and Master Florencio. The pity is that, as a rule, the particulars of its exercise, and the examples it might provide of the operation of the law as the point at which life and logic met, as F. W. Maitland somewhere described the reality of it all, as a rule remain hidden from view.

---

[97] ADB, *Gav. das Religiões*, Mosteiros e Seminário, 58.

[98] Cf. A. PÉREZ MARTÍN, whose study – *Estudiantes zamoranos en Bolonia*, «Studia Zamorensia», 2 (1981), pp. 23-66 – commences in the 1260s.

[99] Below, n. 108. Of interest in this connexion is the survival in ACZ of a number of witnesses' depositions, all apparently of the 1220s: LERA, 394-400. While none of these refers to questions considered here, the very fact of the preservation of material of such ephemeral interest may be regarded as significant, nothing of the sort having been preserved there from earlier or later periods. By contrast, only one of the papal mandates listed in App. II (no. 34) survives.

APPENDIX I

Zamora, March 1223

*Allegationes* of 'G.', *presbiter* of S. Leonardo regarding a payment he claims to be due to him, and of 'S.' and others, *populatores* of the place, contesting the claim, presented to D. Ysidoro archdeacon of Zamora , and the archdeacon's judgment on the matter.

[— — — — — —]: words cancelled
[*conjectural readings*]
<letter/s or word/s supplied>

Notum sit omnibus tam presentibus quam futuris, quod cum G. presbiter Sancti Leonardi [— — — -] ex una parte et s. et p. et d. et g. et m. et i., populatores ex altera coram nobis .Y. Zemorensi archidia-/²chono constituti essent, ex parte populatorum querimonia deposita est in hunc modum, quod .g. presbiter supradictus iniuriabatur eisdem, petendo pensionem infra tempus quod statutum erat in carta/³ per alfabetum divisa et de voluntate parcium confecta.

Ad quam querelam ex parte .G. presbiteri [— — — —] sic responsum est:

**A1** Quod instrumentum a parte adversa exibitum non valet quia non est au-/⁴tenticum utpote nec manu publica confectum nec sigillo autentico roboratum, ut extra i. de fide instru. c. ii.[100]

**A2** Item diversa manu scriptum est et in utroque instrumento in eodem loco diversificat littera,/⁵ unde patet quod utrumque penes adversarios erat et in utroque diversis temporibus quicquid volebant scribebant.

**A3** Item in instrumentis continetur quod illi pacto interfuerunt omnes parrochiani Sancti Leonardi et consen-/⁶serunt, quod falsum est. Et si dicitur quod maior pars interfuit ponamus illud sine preiudicio nostre cause, tamen alia spreta fuit et non vocata. Unde quod factum esset non valeret ut consimiliter dicitur de electione, extra iii./⁷ de electione. Quod sicut[101].

**A4** Item ponimus sine preiudicio nostre cause quod tenor illorum instrumentorum probari possit per testes, ut dicunt adversarii. Dicimus quod neque instrumenta neque tenor eorum de iure/⁸ tenere potest quia ibi fit alienatio rei ecclesiastice inconsulto episcopo, quod prohibetur xii. q. II. Abbatibus[102].

**A5** Item secundum tenorem illorum instrumentorum lederetur ecclesia sancti Leonardi enormiter cum in instrumentis dicitur quod/⁹ vendant vel dent cui voluerint, et si hoc fieret et darentur religiosis possessiones ille vel albergarie ibi fierent a qualibet sorte non haberet in anno nisi XVI denarios, cum etiam si ibi domus non esset /¹⁰ fundus sine edificiis in dupplo vel amplius redderet et ita cum ec-

---

[100] 'Scripta uero': I Comp. 2.15.2 (=X 2.22.2).
[101] 3 Comp. 1.6.13 (=X 1.6.28 ).
[102] Gratian, C.12 q. 2 c. 41.

clesia per illud pactum enormiter lederetur iure minoris in integrum deberet restitui, ut extra iii. de <in> integrum resti. Auditis[103].

**A6** Item/[11] maior pars illorum quibus isti adversarii successerunt peciit et
voluit regi per instrumentum a dompno .g. approbatum. Unde modo isti contra-
venire non possunt quia aliud ius accipere non potuerunt/[12] nisi illud quod anteces-
sores eorum eis tradiderunt.

**A7** Item pono sine preiudicio nostri quod aliquando dompnus .g. receperit
illos XVI denarios secundum quod continetur in instrumentis. Tamen dicimus quod
non nocet quia non recepit tanto/[13] tempore quod alii possent prescribere, et delictum eius non redundaret in dampnum ecclesie. Immo dicimus quod nunquam recepit.

**A8** Item dicimus instrumentum hoc eo quod alienationem continet non
valere, extra i. de rebus ecclesie./[14] Nullius [sic][104], cum clericorum subscriptio non
appareat in eo. Et si hoc fit ubi necessitatem habet ecclesia multo fortius ubi non
urgetur, x. q. ii. Huiusmodi.[105]

**A9** Item si episcopi conmutatio vel vendicio rei ecclesiastice vel donatio ir-
rita esse cen-/[15]setur sine conniventia et subscriptione et tractatu et consensu tocius
cleri multo fortius simplicis clerici, xii. q. ii. Sine exceptione[106].

**A10** Item licet cuilibet ecclesiastice persone contradicere et cum fructibus
alie-/[16]nata repetere, xii. q. ii. Non liceat[107], quod ius licere non sineret si penam ex
alia parte infligeret.

**A11** Item dicit lex quod instrumentum debet esse non viciatum, non corruptum, non in aliqua sui parte deturpatum, sed/[17] quod istud sit corruptum, viciatum
et deturpatum patet. Nam a principio usque ad finem plenum est falsa latinitate, diversis manibus confinctum, interlinearibus remendatum, ex quibus apparet quod
nec de con-/[18]scientia episcopi vel archidiaconi fuerit fabricatum, quibus conmissa
est cura et sollicitudo rerum ecclesiasticarum.[108]

Ex parte vero populatorum ad allegationes adversarorium sic respondetur.

**B1** Dicunt enim ipsi quod/[19] cum instrumentum productum a parte populatorum sigillum autenticum non habeat nec per manum publicam confectum fuerit
ei standum non esse. Et ad hoc inducunt extra i. de fide instru. c.ii.[109] Sed consuetudo que est opti-/[20]ma legum interpres, ut extra iii. de verborum sig. c. ult.[110], illi
decretali et omnibus iuribus que locuntur de hac materia silentium imponit. Nam de
consuetudine est in partibus istis ut instrumenta per manum /[21] unquam confecta

---

[103] 3 Comp. 1.24.2 (=X 1.41.3).
[104] I Comp. 3.11.4 (=X 3.13.5). *Recte* 'Nulli'.
[105] Gratian, C.10 q. 2 d. p. c.3.
[106] Gratian, C. 2 q. 2 c. 52.
[107] Gratian, C. 2 q. 2 c. 20.
[108] Cf. 4 Comp. 1.11.1: 'Sane consuluit nos tuae fraternitatis devotio, quid ad
officium archidiaconi debeat pertinere, et in quibus per ipsum cura episcopalis sol-
licitudinis debeat relevari' (=X 1.23.7).
[109] Above, n. 100.
[110] 3 Comp. 5.23.10, 'Abbate' ad v. *Eadem* (=X 5.40.25).

dum modo sint per alfabetum divisa, et maxime cum hoc idem testibus probari potest, debeant valere. Et ad hoc bene facit constitutio domni Innocencii, Quoniam contra falsam. Ibi enim dicitur quod si iu-/[22]dex non poterit habere publicam personam adhibeat alios duos viros[111], et apud nos talis publica persona non habetur. Et quod consuetudo loci seruanda sit probatur, extra iii. de fide instru. c. ult.[112] Et obtime facit/[23] ad hoc decretalis in extra iii. de arbitris c.i[113], et etiam contra legem obtinet in loco suo in extra iii. de consue. Ex litteris[114], et in extra primis de testamentis. Ad hec[115], et .C. de emancipa. l.i.[116]

**B2**  Ad hoc quod di-/[24]citur quod diversa manu scriptum est, respondemus quod illud non nocet quia ex multis causis potest accidere, vel propter incaustum vel propter incisionem penne vel etiam quia ante prandium scripsit partem et post prandium aliam vel/[25] una die partem et alia die aliam. Item scriptor qui scripsit vivit a quo veritas sciri poterit.

**B3**  Ad hoc quod dicitur quod instrumentis continetur quod illi pacto interfuerunt omnes parrochiani Sancti Leonardi <et> consen-/[26]serunt, et ipsi adversarii dicunt falsum esse quia pars fuit spreta et non vocata, hoc probare debent quoniam illi qui dicit et non ei qui negat incumbit probatio, ut ff. de probatione, l. Ab ea parte[117],

**B4**  Ad hoc quod/[27] dicunt quod etiam si probari possit per testes tenor instrumentorum quod neque instrumenta neque tenor valeret cum ibi alienatio facta fuerit rei ecclesiastice, respondemus quod ibi alienatio proprie sumpto voca-/[28]bulo facta intelligitur ubi aliquis a dominio removetur alicuius rei quia hoc proprie est alienare, de meo alienum facere. Sed hic ecclesia dominium penes se retinet cum a populatoribus annuum censum percipiat./[29]

**B5**  Item dicunt quod ecclesia Sancti Leonardi ex populatione ista leditur cum populatores vendere possint domos et donare. Sed falsum est quia vendere possunt cum honere sibi imposito.

**B5a**  Item ecclesia restituenda non est cum non le-/[30]datur adhuc quia restitutio non datur nisi lesis, ut in ff. in titulo generali de restitutione in inte. fere per totum[118], et in .C. eodem titulo[119]. Et bene scitis quod ecclesia comparatur minori in extra i. de in/[31] integrum resti. c. uno[120]. Et restitutio non datur minori nisi ledatur enormiter. Et non datur nisi intra quadriennium, ut probatur in .C. de in integrum

---

[111] IV Lat. c. 38: 'iudex semper adhibeat aut publicam, si potest habere, personam, aut duos viros idoneos, qui fideliter uniuersa iudicii acta conscribant...'

[112] 3 Comp. 2.13.4, 'Cum dilectus' (X 2.22.9).

[113] 3 Comp. 1.25.1, 'Dilecti filii', ad v. *Quamvis*: '...iuxta constitutionem approbatam, quae pro lege servatur' (=X 1.43.4).

[114] 3 Comp. 1.3.1 (=X 1.4.2).

[115] I Comp. 3.22. 7: 'licet consuetudo illa non sit consona rationi' (=X 3.5.13).

[116] C. 8.48(49).1

[117] Dig. 22.3.5 (Paulus).

[118] Dig. 4.1.

[119] Perhaps C. 2.21(22).

[120] I Comp. I.32, c. un., 'Requisivit' (=X 1 41 1).

resti. l. ult. et C. de sacrosanctis ecclesiis. Ut inter di-/[32]vinum[121], ergo nec ecclesie concedenda est. Et quod ecclesia non ledatur patet, quia unde non consuevit aliquid habere utilitatis, videlicet quia locus ille sine aliqua utilitate erat, modo habet inde XVI denarios a quolibet/[33] populatore et decimas et oblationes ab eisdem.

**B6** Item dicunt ipsi quod maior [MS. maiors] pars illorum quibus isti adversarii successerunt peciit et voluit regi per instrumentum approbatum a dompno .G., quod falsum est. Et /[34] ponamus etiam sine preiudicio nostro quod verum esset, tamen illis qui nunquam consenserunt et a quibus predictus .G. recepit supradictum censum preiudicare non potuit cum in re communi potior sit conditio prohibentis,/[35] ut ff. communi dividundo, l. Sabinus[122].

**B7** Item ipsi dicunt quod si aliquando dominus .g. recepit illos XVI denarios secundum quod continetur instrumentis, tamen non preiudicatur ei vel ecclesie, quia non recepit tanto tempore quod alii prescribere pos-/[36]sent. Nec etiam nos intendimus probare prescriptionem, cum ipsi confiteantur se censum debere ecclesie annuatim.

**B8** Item dicunt quod delictum eius non debet redundare in dampnum ecclesie. Nec etiam nos volumus sed convertatur in capud/[37] illius qui contra formam instrumentorum venit.

Item istis responsionibus ex adversa parte sic respondetur.

**C1** Ad hoc quod dicit adversa pars quod secundum consuetudinem talia instrumenta valent quia consuetudo est obtima/[38] legum interpres, respondemus quod fallitur quia nulla consuetudo vel constitutio proibet quin ea que in detrimentum ecclesie aguntur, et maxime a laicis, infirmentur, ut expresse habetur extra iii. de constitutioni-/[39]bus. Que in ecclesiarum et ecclesiasticorum virorum preiudicium attemptantur firmitatem sortiri non debent sed ad ecclesiarum in dempnitatem [*sic*] debent potius infirmari[123]. Et habemus quod consuetudo non vincit leg-/[40]em aut rationem, ut xi. di. Consuetudinis[124]. Constitutio Quoniam contra falsam loquitur de actis in iudicio[125]. Cum dilectus filius loquitur de instrumentis regis Scotie[126]. Alia de arbitris loquitur de arbitrio regi-/[41]ne roborato consilio et presencia episcoporum[127], quod non tangit causam nostram. Ex litteris[128] et Ad hec[129] non locuntur contra legem et in eis attenditur favor [MS. favorum] episcoporum et clericorum.

**C2** Ad hoc quod dicit quod diversitas manuum/[42] in instrumentis non nocet, respondemus quod nocet cum secundum confessionem suam unus scriptor fuerit in utroque instrumento et in eisdem locis littera diversificetur ita quod alia manu fac-

---

[121] C. 2.21(22).9; C. 1.2.23 (neither of which refers to the quadriennial limitation, however, for which see C. 2.50.5; C. 2.52.7pr.).

[122] Dig. 10.3.28.

[123] 3 Comp. 1.1.2 (=X 1.2.7).

[124] Gratian, D.11 c. 4.

[125] Above, n. 111.

[126] Above, n. 112.

[127] Above, n. 113.

[128] Above, n. 114.

[129] Above, n. 115.

ta videtur, et ideo sus[*pecta est carta*,]/[43] ut extra iii. de fide instrumentorum. c. i.[130] in illo uersu Instrumentum paulum ultra medium decretalis[131].

**C3**    Ad hoc quod dicit quod nobis dicentibus non interfuisse incumbit probare, respondemus quod non est verum quia negativam /[44] non tenemur probare, sed ei incumbit probare qui dicit dictam parrochiam pacto consensisse.

**C4**    Ad hoc quod dicit quod ibi non est alienatio cum annua pensio ecclesie solvatur, respondemus quod non valet quod dicit cum de rebus da-/[45]tis in infiteosim pensio solvatur et tamen alienatio dicitur, et quod pensio solvi debeat, habetur x. q. II. Hoc ius porrectum[132]. Et quod alienatio sit habetur, extra i. de rebus ecclesie non alienandis. c. i.[133] /[46]

**C5**    Ad hoc quod dicit quod non leditur ecclesia dicimus quod iam lesa est quia in quibusdam domibus non moratur aliquis, in aliis tales a quibus fere nichil perciperit ecclesia, immo cum ibi sint XXX domus in populatione/[47] tamen non inhabitantur nisi VIIII a propriis dominis, et si etiam nunc non lederetur sed posset in posterum ledi, tamen consulendum et providendum esset ne postea lederetur.

**C5a**    Ad hoc quod dicit quod non potest petere [*ecclesia*]/[48] in integrum restitucionem ultra quadriennium, respondemus quod ecclesia semper debet illesa servari, ut extra i. in de indempnitate et in integrum restititione ecclesie. Requisivit[134]. Extra i. de rebus ecclesiasticis alienandis [*vel non.*]/[49] *Ad v.*] Sub modico[135].

**C6**    Ad hoc quod dicit quod in re communi potior est conditio proibentis dicimus quod non habet hic locum, immo ubi aliqua congregatio est quod maior pars illius congregationis [*mandat*],/[50] et quod isti contradicere non possint patet cum publice propositum fuerit in ecclesia quod omnes convenirent ad divisionem instrumenti approbati a dompno .G. die statuta, et convenientibus illis/[51] qui voluerint omnibus placuit regi per illud instrumentum et extunc denarios pensionis secundum illud instrumentum solverunt.

**C7**    Ad hoc quod ipsi petunt cum instantia dicimus quod principale non [*extinguitur*]/[52] propter [*eius*] accessorium[136]. Item par in parem potestatem non habet, extra iii. de electione. Innotuit[137]. Item antecessor successorem ad penam obligare non potest, ut extra i. de precariis. c. [*unicum*][138]/[53]

**cf. B1**    Ad hoc quod dicit pars adversa consuetudinem in partibus istis

---

[130] 3 Comp. 2.13.1, 'Inter dilectos' (=X 2.22.6).

[131] Ibid: 'Instrumentum quoque sententiae multis modis inveniebatur suspectum, tum quia in ipso quaedam apperebant liturae, tum quia subscriptio notarii videbatur manus alterius fuisse, quam subscriptio instrumenti...' (Fr. 2.348).

[132] Gratian, C.10, q. 2 c. 2, ad v. *Qui rem*.

[133] I Comp 3.11.1, 'Non licet' (=X 3.13.1).

[134] Above, n. 120. The title 'in de indempnitate et in integrum restititione ecclesie' seems to be unfamiliar in MSS of 'Compilatio Prima'.

[135] I Comp. 3.11.8, De possessionibus. Cf. X 1.41.1, 'Requisivit'.

[136] Cf. Dig. 33.8.1-2: 'Nam quae accessionum locum optinent, exstinguuntur, cum principales res peremptae fuerint.'

[137] 3 Comp. 1.6.5, ad v. *Quamvis* (=X 1.6.20).

[138] I Comp. 3.12.2 (= X 3.14.2).

esse ut instrumenta per manum cuiuscumque confecta dum modo sint per alfabetum divisa [*valeant*], verum est cum dividuntur inter partes que possunt consen-
/⁵⁴tire vel dissentire ita quod utraque pars habeat cartam conformem alteri carte in
stilo et in divisione. Nam si ita plane intelligitur valere iam quilibet [MS. quibusli-
bet] posset conficere instrumentum et dividere in domo/⁵⁵ propria in dampnum alterius confectionem huius nescientis. Unde si aliter intelligit consuetudinem dico
non esse consuetudinem. Item ad constitutionem Innocentii, scilicet Quoniam contra falsam¹³⁹, quam scilicet contra nos allegavit,/⁵⁶ secundum quod ipse adversarius
subiunxit hoc modo, scilicet apud nos non est talis publica persona. Preterea constitutio loquitur de iudice et de actis in iudicio.ᶦⁱᶜ ᵛᵉʳᵒ ⁿᵉᶜ ᶠᵘⁱᵗ ⁱᵘᵈᵉˣ ⁿᵉᶜ ᵃᶜᵗᵘᵐ ⁱᵘᵈⁱᶜⁱˢ.

**cf. B2** Item ad hoc quod dicitur quod scriptor vivit a quo sciri veritas
potest,/⁵⁷ [*dico*] non esse credendum ei cum non sit publica manus nec uni testi
standum esse quamvis dicat.

**cf. B4** Item quod dicit quod illa sola alienatio rei ecclesiastice prohibetur in qua quis a dominio removetur dico falsum esse/⁵⁸ <cum> decretalis dicat
Verbum alienationis continere conditionem, donationem, permutationem et emphiteosim perpetuum contractum et ab huiusmodi alienationibus abstinendum¹⁴⁰.

**cf. B5** Item quod dicit ecclesiam non esse lesam nos dicimus [*eccle-
/⁵⁹siam*] ad maiorem lesionem nisi iudex subveniat paratam esse. Et si necesse fuerit probabimus suo loco.

**cf. B5a** Item quod dicit ecclesiam non posse petere restitutionem nisi intra quadriennium et si ita sit non intelligitur/⁶⁰ quadriennium post XXV annos .C.
de titulo in [MS. iñ] integrum testi. per totum et l. ii¹⁴¹, licet forte posset dici a parte
nostra ecclesiam Sancti Leonardi in casu isto a iure non concesso non [*indigere
resti-/⁶¹tutione*] cum contractus qui proponitur non tenuerit ipso iure, .C. Si adver-
sus donationem. l. ii.¹⁴² Et quod non possent omnes alienare in casu non concesso,
dicit lex .c. de sacrosanctis ecclesiis. Iubemus¹⁴³./⁶²

Ex parte populatorum,

**D1a** ad capitulum Consuetudinis, .xi. di.¹⁴⁴ sic respondemus, quod ibi loquitur de speciali consuetudine que non preiudicat legi generali verum est nisi in
loco suo quia in loco suo [*bene*] pre-/⁶³iudicat legi, ut probatur in .C. Que sit longa
consuetudo, l. i et l. iii.¹⁴⁵

**D1b** Ad decretalem autem in extra iii. Que in ecclesiarum etc.¹⁴⁶, sic respondemus quod ibi laici fecerant constitutionem suam in damnum/⁶⁴ ecclesie, et ideo
non valuit constitutio illa. Sed in casu nostro quicquid factum fuit factum fuit ad
utilitatem ecclesie prout patet.

---

¹³⁹ Above, n. 111.
¹⁴⁰ Above, n. 104, ad. v. *Alienationis*.
¹⁴¹ C. 2.21(22).2.
¹⁴² C. 2.29(30).2.
¹⁴³ C. 1.2.14 pr.
¹⁴⁴ Above, n. 124.
¹⁴⁵ C. 8.52(53).1;3. But these assert that 'longa consuetudo' *does* prevail.
Citation needed is C. 8.52.2.
¹⁴⁶ Above, n. 123.

494

**D2**   Ad illam decretalem de fide instru. c. i. quam ipsi inducunt pro se[147], videlicet quod /[65] diversitas manus in scriptura debeat nobis nocere, multis de causis ibi factum fuit, videlicet quia ille qui scripserat erat publica persona, et multe alie presumptiones faciebant contra instrumentum, ut patet in/[66] littera decretali. Sed hic in terra ista, prout dictum est, non sunt publice persone, et ideo adhibere possum ad scripturam aliquam faciendam duos vel tres scriptores diversis temporibus et non nocebit dum modo quod scrip-/[67]tum fuit in carta testibus probare possim.

**D3**   Ad hoc quod ipsi dicunt quod negativam non tenentur probare nec nos dicimus quod probent negativam sed affirmativam quia dicunt se spretos fuisse./[68]

**D4**   Ad hoc quod dicunt quod si res ecclesie datur in emphiteosim et solvatur inde pensio tamen dicit decretalis[148] alienationem esse, respondemus quod non tangit casum nostrum quia locus ille non fuit datus in/[69] emphiteosim sed ad populandum, et ideo cessat lex et decretalis inducta.

**D5**   Ad hoc quod dicunt quod ecclesia lesa est iam quia in quibusdam domibus non moratur aliquis, et in aliis morantur tales a quibus /[70] ecclesia fere nichil percipit, et sunt ibi etiam XXX domus in populatione illa et non inhabitantur nisi VIII[149] a propriis dominis, respondemus quod hoc non preiudicat nobis quia in carta continetur quod quicumque ibi inhabita-/[71]verit pensionem supradictam et decimas et oblationes solvere teneatur, et poterit esse quod dicior domino inhabitabit ibi vel pauperior, quia non facit iniuriam alicui qui iure suo utitur.

**D6**   Ad hoc quod/[72]dicunt quod ecclesia semper debet servari illesa, respondemus quod semper debet servari illesa in tempore statuto et semper debemus esse in ecclesia, id est oris constitutis. Et ita intelligitur decretalis inducta in extra i. de in integrum/[73]resti. Requisiuit[150], a magistro Laurentio et Vincetio [*sic*]. D7/cf. A5, A7 Dicunt enim quod ecclesia utitur iure minoris iam facti maioris ita quod intra quadriennium possit petere in integrum restitutionem a tempore lesionis/[74] et non ultra, ut probatur in .C. de quadriennii prescriptione[151], et in .C. de sacrosanctis ecclesiis. Ut inter divinum[152]. Et utrum lesa sit vel non lesa hoc relinquimus arbitrio iudicantis, quia unde non consue-/[75]vit ecclesia habere aliquid utilitatis modo habet .XVI. denarios et decimas et oblationes a cohabitantibus ibidem omni anno. Ad decretalem autem in extra i. de rebus ecclesie alienandis. De possessionibus laicis./[76] Sub modico etc.[153], respondemus quod non loquitur in casu nostro nam ibi loquitur de possessione fertili vel utili ecclesie de qua consuevit percipere emolumentum, quia si datur possessio talis sub modico cen-/[77]su et si ecclesia ledatur restituenda est, de loco autem nostro modo populato non consuevit aliquid habere.

---

[147] Above, n. 130.

[148] Above, nn. 132-133.

[149] Cf. line 47: VIIII.

[150] Above, nn. 120, 134.

[151] C.7.37.1.

[152] C.1.2.23.

[153] Above, n. 135: 'Requisivit a nobis tua fraternitas, quid addendum sit de possessionibus laicis sub modico censu concessis?'

**D8a/cf. C6**  Ad hoc quod dicunt quod isti modo contradicere non possunt quia omnes vocati fuerant ad ecclesiam/[78] ad divisionem instrumenti approbati a dompno .G. die statuta, respondemus quod nec venire nec vocari debuerunt quia illi tantum vocandi sunt quos causa tangit, et res inter alios acta aliis non preiudica-/[79]t.

**D8b**  Ad hoc quod dicunt quod omnibus placuit regi per illud instrumentum novum et extunc denarios pensionis secundum illud instrumentum persoluerant, respondemus quod non placuit omnibus nec displicuit quia non interfuerunt, nec/[80] [ — —] divisio instrumenti secundi, de solutione denariorum pensionis, respondemus quod ad instanciam et ad preces parrochianorum [et] gratis et quia instabat necessitas ecclesie ante tempus statutum/[81] [persolverunt] coacti vi alicuius instrumenti.

**E.**  Nos vero perspectis et auditis hincinde rationibus et allegationibus et responsionibus et habito prudentum virorum consilio sentenciando pronunti-/[82]amus instrumenta per alfabetum divisa valere nisi in illo articulo ubi dicitur "que sean felegreses todos aquelos que i moraren", quod verbum nobis et aliis esitabile visum/[83]fuit. Quod etiam verbum sic interpretati sumus quod quicumque emerit domos illas ibi moretur, vel faciat ibidem aliquem morari qui predictam solvat pensionem, et sit parrochianus/[84] Sancti Leonardi. Condempnavimus etiam .G. presbiterum sepe fatum in expensis .XI[cim]. morabitinorum declaratis et iuratis et a nobis taxatis. Lecta fuit ista sententia sub Era/[85] [1261] in mense martii, sequenti die post festum Sancti Benedicti [22 March]. A qua sentencia .g. presbiter supradictus in die Annunciationis Sancte Marie [25 March] petens apostolos ad episcopum/[86] appellavit. Nos etiam illius appellationi<nis> differentes acta in iudicio sibi dedimus, ei transmissa prefigentes VI feria post transitum Sancti Ysidori [10 April].

ACZ, 16/II/18 (LERA, 355)

VI

APPENDIX II

*Zamoranos* as judges delegate and executors
June 1209 to November 1254[154]

(1) 9 June 1209. **Bp (Martín I)**, **(Juan) dean**, **F(lorencio) archd**.: mandate to
determine complaint of Abp (Martinho Pires) of Braga regarding refusal of abt of
Vimieiro, OSB (dioc. Braga) and priors of Rates, OSB (dioc. Porto) and Costa.
OSA (dioc. Braga) to pay procurations and other dues. *Oblata nobis venerabilis*:
*Bul. Port.*, 137.

(1a) 25 Nov. 1209. **Bp (Martín I)**, **(Juan) dean**, **F(lorencio) archd**.: mandate at request of bp of Ávila to compel citizens of that city to desist from molest-
ing clergy and bringing them before secular tribunals. *Venerabilis frater noster*:
AHN Clero, carp. 19/12 (A. BARRIOS GARCÍA, *Documentación medieval de la catedral de Ávila*, Salamanca 1981, no. 46).

(2) 11 April 1210. **Bp (Martín I)**, **(Egas) chanter**, prior of Moreruela,
O.Cist. (Zamora dioc.): mandate impetrated by Bp (Gonzalo Fernández) of Sala-
manca to execute settlement of dispute between churches of Salamanca and Ciudad
Rodrigo *ex una parte* and abp of Compostela *ex altera*. *Venerabilis frater noster*[155].

(3) 24 April 1210. **Bp (Martín I)**, Bp (Rodrigo Álvarez) of León: mandate
to execute settlement between Bp (García) of Burgos and mon. of Oña, OSB (dioc.
Burgos). *Suscitata super diversis*: *DhI*, 425.

---

[154] Use has been made of published papal registers (and where necessary of the
originals in ASV), POTTHAST, other printed texts as indicated, and relevant items
from amongst original letters preserved in Spanish and Portuguese archives which
I have had occasion to inspect, as follow: for the pontificates of Innocent III beginning in 1209, 71 items; of Honorius III, 301; of Gregory IX, 444; of Innocent IV,
776. The listing therefore is not exhaustive. No such listing can be. While reflecting
that the chanceries of these popes could not have done as well, I shall nevertheless
be grateful for information regarding items I have missed.

Mandates requiring action within the church of Zamora itself, e.g. mandates
for provision, have been excluded from consideration.

Where double references are provided it is usually because the later reference
raises questions about the correctness of the earlier.

Identification of dignitaries by name is based on evidence from ACZ. In some
cases further references are provided in the footnotes.

Names shown in **heavy type** are those of bishops and members of the chapter
of Zamora. It is to be noted that the diocese of Zamora boasted two archdeacons:
the archdeacon of Zamora, described as 'archidiaconus Zamorensis' or 'archidiaconus civitatis', and the archdeacon of Toro ('archidiaconus Taurensis').

[155] MARTÍN MARTÍN ET AL., *Documentos de Salamanca* cit., p. 126.

(4)    24 April 1210. **Bp (Martín I)**, Master Mauricio archd. of Toledo, Master Miguel can. of Segovia: mandate to hear witnesses of mon. of Oña in dispute with Bp (García) of Burgos. *Suscitata super diversis*: *DhI*, 426.

(5)    28 April 1210. **Bp (Martín I)**, Master Mauricio archd. of Toledo, Master Miguel can. of Segovia: mandate to adjudicate dispute between Bp (García) of Burgos and clergy of secular abbacy of Castrojériz. *Cum in causa*: *DhI*, 427.

(6)    28 April 1210. **Bp (Martín I)**, Master Mauricio archd. of Toledo, Master Miguel can. of Segovia: mandate to execute settlement between Bp (García) of Burgos and certain clerics of mon. of S. Juan de Ortega, OSA (dioc. Burgos). *Burgensi capitulo dudum*: *DhI*, 428.

(7)    30 April 1210. **Bp (Martín I)**, Master Mauricio archd. of Toledo, Master Miguel can. of Segovia: mandate to recover expenses due from mon. of Oña to Bp (García) of Burgos in respect of (3). *Cum super quatuor*: *DhI*, 429.

(8)    7 May 1210. **Bp (Martín I)**, Master Mauricio archd. of Toledo, Master Miguel can. of Segovia: mandate impetrated by mon. of Oña to collect further evidence regarding dispute with Bp (García) of Burgos. *Cum Lupus procurator*: *DhI*, 431.

(9)    13 May 1210. **Bp (Martín I), Master Flo(rencio) archd.**, abt of Moreruela: mandate to investigate allegations of Bp (Martinho Rodrigues) of Porto regarding conspiracy against him by members of his church in league with Sancho I of Portugal. *Grave gerimus et*: *DhI*, 435.

(10)    *ante* 13 May 1210. **Bp Martín (I)**, Master P. dean of León, J(uan) dean has negotiated settlement between Sancho I of Portugal and Bp (Martinho Rodrigues) of Porto. In *Iustis petentium desideriis*: *DhI*, 437.

(11)    13 May 1210. **Bp (Martín I), Master Florencio archd.**, abt of Moreruela: mandate requiring Sancho I of Portugal to make restitution to Bp (Martinho Rodrigues) of Porto. *Graves oppressiones et*: *DhI*, 436.

(12)    26 Oct. 1210. Bp (Rodrigo Álvarez) of León, Bp (Juan) of Oviedo, **Bp (Martín I)**, Bp (Pedro Andrés) of Astorga, *et al.*: mandate to act as conservators of interests of mon. of Sandoval, O.Cist. (dioc. León). *Non absque dolore*: DSL, 134.

(13)    26 Oct. 1210. Bp (Rodrigo Álvarez) of León, Bp (Juan) of Oviedo, **Bp (Martín I)**, Bp (Pedro Andrés) of Astorga, *et al.*: mandate to act as conservators of tithe interests of mon. of Sandoval. *Audivimus et audientes*: DSL, 135.

(14)    28 Oct. 1210. **Bp (Martín I), (Egas) chanter**, abt of Moreruela: mandate to confirm election of chanter of ch. of Salamanca. *Dilecto filio nostro*: *DhI*, 440.

(15)    26 Jan. 1211. **Bp (Martín I), (Juan) dean, Master F(lorencio) archd.**: mandate to determine complaint of Bp (Pedro) of Coimbra regarding appropriation

of churches in Leiria by canons of S. Cruz de Coimbra, OSA. *Significavit nobis venerabilis*: *Bul. Port.*, 150.

(16) 22 Feb. 1211. Abp (Rodrigo) of Toledo, Bp (Pedro) of Coimbra. **Bp (Martín I)**: mandate to prevent 'aliquid regum Hispanie' from impeding proposal of Infante Fernando of Castile to take the fight to Spain's Muslim enemy. *Significavit nobis dilectus*: *DhI*, 446.

(17) 27 May 1211. Abp (Pedro Muñoz) of Compostela, Abp (Pedro Mendes) of Braga, **Bp (Martín I)**: mandate to ensure observance of will of Sancho I of Portugal. *Is qui tangit*: *DhI*, 454.

(18) 7 Oct. 1211. Abp (Pedro Muñoz) of Compostela, **Bp (Martín I)**, Bp (Pedro Andrés) of Astorga: further mandate in respect of (17). *Ad petitionem olim*: *DhI*, 458.

(19) 12 Nov. 1211 [Zamora]. **Bp (Martín I), Master F(lorencio) archd.**, 'judices a domino papa delegati', pronounce canonical sentences against citizens of Porto for their contumacy in contesting Bp (Martinho Rodrigues)'s temporal lordship of the city. *Bul. Port.*, 172.

(20) 23 Apr. 1212. Abp (Pedro Muñoz) of Compostela, **Bp (Martín I)**, Bp (Pedro Andrés) of Astorga: mandate to defend interests of Teresa and Sancha, daughters of Sancho I *quondam* kg of Portugal. *Ad petitionem olim*: IANTT, Most. de Lorvão, mç. 1, no. 8.

(21) 24 Feb. 1213. **Bp (Martín I)**, Bp (Martinho Rodrigues) of Porto, **Master Florencio archd.**: mandate to determine diocesan limits of sees of Guarda and Coimbra. *Venerabilis frater noster*: *DhI*, 499 (= IANTT, Sé Coimbra, 2ª incorporação, mç. 40, no. 1694).

(21a) Zamora, 9 June 1214. **Bp (Martín I), J(uan) dean, F(lorencio) archd.** 'convenientia' dictated by them as judges delegate in dispute of between bp and chap. of Ávila and parish clergy of city concerning payment of *tercias* and other dues. AHN Clero, carp. 19/13 (Barrios García, *Documentación de Ávila* cit., no. 50).

(22) 6 Feb. 1216. **Bp (Martín I), (Juan) dean, (Florencio) archd.**: mandate requiring Alfonso IX of León to restore certain castles to Ord. Santiago. *Quanto amplius dilecti*: AHN, OO. MM., Santiago, Uclés, carp. 4.ii/1 (*DhI*, 542, defective edn derived from *Bull. Santiago*).

(23) March/July 1216. **F(lorencio) archd.**, F. archd. of Astorga: mandate to adjudicate dispute between Abp (Estevão Soares) of Braga and ch. of Guimarães. *Sacrosancta Romana ecclesia*: *DhI*, 560; *Reg. Hon. III*, 987 (Mansilla, 127).

(24) *ante* 1 May 1216. Master of Temple and Prior of Hospital in Toledo province, **(Egas) chanter, (Florencio) archd.**: mandate to collect crusading tenth in province of Toledo. In *Cum felicis recordationis*: *Reg. Hon. III*, 337 (Mansilla, 35).

HONORIUS III

(25)  23 October 1216 [Benavente]. **Bp (Martín I), (Florencio) archd., (Munio Muniz) archd.** of Toro, judges delegate, negotiate settlement of dispute between Abp (Estevão Soares) and chap. of Braga *ex una parte* and prior and ch. of Guimarães *ex altera*. *Bul. Port.*, 226 (cf. no. 23).

(26)  20 Dec. 1216. Bp (Rodrigo Álvarez) of León, Bp (Melendo) of Osma, **F(lorencio) archd.**[156]: mandate to adjudicate Toledo-Ávila dispute. *Venerabili fratre nostro*: AC Toledo, I.4.N.1.12.

(27)  4 May 1217. **F(lorencio). archd., (Egas) chanter, 'P. dicto Monaco' canon.**[157]: mandate to determine complaint of conv. of S. Marcos, Ord. Santiago (dioc. León) against *concejo* of Villafrechós and others of that dioc. *Dilecti filii prior*: In AHN, OO. MM., S. Marcos de León, carp. 377/9 (DSL, 159).

(28)  9 June 1217. **Bp (Martín II), (Juan) dean, (Egas) chanter**: mandate to determine complaint of bp of Ávila against bp of Plasencia regarding ch. of Béjar and other churches. *Venerabilis frater noster:* AC Ávila, d.s.n.[158]

(29)  4 Aug. 1217. **F(lorencio) archd., (Egas) chanter, *magister scolarum*[159]**: mandate to determine complaint of Ord. Santiago against abt of Nogales, O.Cist (dioc. Zamora) and others of Astorga dioc. *Dilecti filii magister*: MANSILLA, 75.

(30)  9 Jan. 1218. **(Florencio) dean, *magister scolarum*, 'P(etro) Monanzino' canon**: mandate to execute award of León benefice to chaplain of Cardinal Pelayo Gaitán. *Benignitatem apostolice sedis*: *Reg. Hon. III*, 984 (MANSILLA, 125).

---

[156] 'dilecto filio F. archidiacono Çamorensi'. RV 9, fo. 29v has 'Oxomensi' in error, whence MANSILLA, 19.

[157] See above, n. 15.

[158] C. M. AJO GONZÁLEZ Y SAINZ DE ZÚÑIGA, *Inventario general de los archivos de la diócesis de Ávila*, Ávila 1962, p. 101, no. 8 (misdated). Printed BARRIOS GARCÍA, *Documentación de Ávila* cit., no. 53.

[159] In April 1216 the *magister scolarum* was 'Johannes', and in his will of June 1217 the dean don Juan referred to the *magister scolarum* as his 'nepos': *TN*, ff. 139r, 88r (LERA, 299, 305), but whether these two were the same man is uncertain. The next *magister scolarum* encountered in the record is 'Petrus' (July 1225; ACZ, 17/40 [LERA, 392]), presumably the same man as the *magister scolarum* of that name, 'Magister Petrus', 'nepos' of Cardinal Gil Torres, who in June 1236 was permitted to enjoy the dignity of the secular abbacy of S. Quirce (Burgos), which had a cure of souls attached to it and appears to have been in the cardinal's gift. Subsequently, 'casu fortuito', Petrus lost the papal letters permitting the pluralism. In September 1238 this lapse was forgiven, on the strangely severe condition that he pay to the church of Zamora the income he had meanwhile received from Burgos, though with an allowance to retain, should he so desire, both situations thereafter:

(31)  12 Jan. 1218. Archd. of Sigüenza, **archd. of Toro**[160], Master Aparicio can. of Burgos: mandate to determine claim of Abp (Rodrigo) of Toledo against Abp (Pedro Muñoz) of Compostela to metropolitan jurisdiction over ch. of Plasencia. *Venerabilis frater noster*: Reg. Hon. III, 996 (MANSILLA, 133).

(32)  5 July 1218. **Bp (Martín II), (Florencio) dean, (Egas) chanter**: mandate to determine claim to tithes of S. Juan de Camba (dioc. Astorga) of Juan Meléndez and other clerics in dispute with Velasco cleric.[161]

(33)  5 July 1218. **Bp (Martín II), (Florencio) dean, (Egas) chanter**: mandate to determine claim to property at Benavente (dioc. Oviedo) of clergy of Astorga in dispute with clergy of Oviedo. LINEHAN, *Adiciones*, no. 13.

(34)  13 July 1218. **(Florencio) dean, *magister scolarum*, archd. of Toro**:[162] mandate requiring dean of Coimbra to comply with injunction granted to D. 'canonicus crucesignatus' of Coimbra. *Cum olim de*: ACZ, 1/7[163] (*Reg. Hon. III*, 1526: MANSILLA, 180).

(35)  24 Apr. 1219. **Y(sidoro) archd.**: mandate to determine complaint of parishioners of S. María de Villafáfila in dispute with abt and conv. of Eslonza, OSB (dioc. León). *Sua nobis parrochiani*: DSL, 169.

(36)  19 Sept. 1219. **(Florencio) dean** (and others unspecified): mandate impetrated by Bp (Gonzalo Fernández) of Salamanca to execute canonical sentences against clergy of Medina. In *Clerus et populus*: Reg. Hon. III, 2656 (MANSILLA, 312).

(37)  16 Nov. 1219. **(Florencio) dean, (Juan) archd. of Toro, (Egas) chanter**: mandate to confirm or annul sentence of excommunication against prior of S. Sepulcro 'in Hyspania' in dispute with bp of Orense (Laurentius Hispanus). *Prior Dominici Sepulchri*: Reg. Hon. III, 2259 (MANSILLA, 248).

*Reg. Greg. IX*, 3212, 4525 (DSGr, 569, 790). There is no sign of the presence of Master Petrus either in Burgos or Zamora during these years. By July 1244, he had been replaced as abbot of S. Quirce by Juan de Medina (L. SERRANO, *El ayo de Alfonso "el Sabio"*, «Boletín de la R. Academia Española», 7 [1920], p. 600 n. 3). (This was not the Juan de Medina who in 1248 would become archbishop of Toledo: HERNÁNDEZ & LINEHAN, *The Mozarabic Cardinal* cit., p. 42 n. 67.)

[160] Either Munio Muniz (last sighted Sept. 1217: ACZ, 17/37 [LERA, 308]) or Juan, who had acquired the dignity by Feb. 1219 (ACZ, 1/15 [LERA, 317]).

[161] P. LINEHAN, *La documentación pontificia de Honorio III (1216-1227): unas adiciones a la Regesta de D. Demetrio Mansilla*, «Anthologica Annua», 16 (1968), pp. 385-408, no. 12.

[162] See no. 31.

[163] Misassigned by LERA (1039) to Honorius IV (†Apr. 1287) and July 1289. Cf. LERA, 315, from MANSILLA, 180.

(38) 26 June 1220. Archd. M. of León, **F(lorencio) dean, (Egas) chanter**: mandate to determine complaint of Ord. Santiago in dispute with Ord. Hospital regarding ch. and castle of Castrotorafe (dioc. Zamora). *Dilecti filii magíster*: AHN, OO. MM., Santiago, Uclés, carp. 88/11 (MANSILLA, 295, defective edn derived from *Bull. Santiago*).

(39) 27 June 1220. **Bp (Martín II)**, Bp (Rodrigo Álvarez) of León: mandate to determine complaint of Ord. Santiago in dispute with Ord. Temple *et al.* regarding possessions in dioc. Astorga and Zamora. *Dilecti filii magister*: MANSILLA, 296.

(40) 1 July 1220. **Bp (Martín II)**, Bp (Rodrigo Álvarez) of León: mandate to determine complaint of Master and brothers of Santiago that Templars of kgdom of León have dispossessed them of convent of *Alcaniz* (Alcañices de Aliste). *Dilecti filii magister*: AHN, OO. MM., Santiago, Uclés, carp. 58/3 (MANSILLA, 297, defective end derived from *Bull. Santiago*; DSL, 180).

(41) 10 July 1220. **Bp (Martín II), (Florencio) dean**: mandate to determine complaint of dean of Coimbra that he has been defamed by D. canon of Coimbra. *Ad nostram audientiam*: *Reg. Hon. III*, 2544 (MANSILLA, 303). Cf. no. 34.

(42) 4 Nov. 1220. **Bp (Martín II)**, Bp (Rodrigo Álvarez) of León, abt of Moreruela: mandate to admonish Alfonso IX of León in person. *Ad audientiam nostram*: POTTHAST, 6386.

(43) 26 Nov. 1220. **Bp (Martín II), (Florencio) dean, (Egas) chanter**: mandate to determine complaint of Bp (Pedro Andrés) of Astorga in dispute with clergy of S. Andrés and S. Nicolás de Benavente regarding ch. of S. María Renueva. *Venerabilis frater noster*[164].

(44) 9 Jan. 1221. **Bp (Martín II), (Florencio) dean**, abt of La Espina, O.Cist. (dioc. Palencia): mandate to determine complaints of Bp (Pedro Andrés) of Astorga in dispute with Ord. Temple and churches of his diocese. LINEHAN, *Adiciones*, no. 38.

(45) 1 Feb. 1221. **Bp (Martín II), (Florencio) dean, (Egas) chanter**: mandate to act as conservators of interests of abt and convent of Aguiar, O.Cist. (dioc. Lamego). *Non absque dolore*: IANTT, S. Maria de Aguiar, mç. 7, no. 14.

(46) 16 Aug. 1221 [Zamora]. 'Ex delegatione apostolica', **Bp Martín II, G(arcía)**[165] **chanter, Y(sidore) archd.** record acknowledgement by clergy of ch. of S. Pedro de Castronuevo (dioc. Zamora) that their church is the property of the mon. of Sant'Angelo di Orsara (dioc. Troya, Puglia): ACZ 36/4 (LERA 342).

---

[164] G. CAVERO DOMÍNGUEZ, C. ÁLVAREZ ÁLVAREZ & J. A. MARTÍN FUERTES, *Colección documental del Archivo Diocesano de Astorga*, León 2001, no. 43.
[165] MARTÍN, *Documentos zamoranos* cit., no. 89, inexplicably extending 'G.' as Gil.

502

(47) 18 July 1223. **Bp (Martín II), (Florencio) dean, (Juan) arch. of Toro**: mandate to determine complaint of Master of Santiago that Masters of Calatrava and Alcántara had appropriated property at Monasteruelo. *Dilecti filii magister*: AHN, OO. MM., Santiago, Uclés, carp 222/6 (MANSILLA, 451).

(48) 19 July [1223]. **Bp (Martín II), (Florencio) dean, (Juan) arch. of Toro**: mandate to determine complaint of prior of S. Marcos de León that chamberlain of S. Zoilo de Carrión, OSB (dioc. León) had appropriated the share of tithes of Villamuriel de Campos due to S. Marcos. *Insinuante priori Sancti*: AHN, OO. MM., San Marcos de León, carp. 377/12 (MANSILLA, 452; DSL, 192).

(49) 21 July 1223. Abt and prior of Peleas, O.Cist. (dioc. Zamora), **(Florencio) dean**: mandate to determine complaint of Master of Ord. Santiago that Templars of kgdom of León had appropriated mon. of S. Félix de Eremo (dioc. Orense). *Dilecti filii magister*: MANSILLA, 457.

(50) 21 July 1223. Abt and prior of Peleas, **(Florencio) dean**: mandate to determine complaint of Master of Ord. Santiago that Templars of kgdom of León had appropriated certain houses and property of the Order. *Dilecti filii magister*: AHN, OO., MM., Santiago, Uclés, carp. 332/5 (MANSILLA, 458).

(51) 27 July 1223. **Bp (Martín II), (Florencio) dean, (Ysidoro) archd.**: mandate to determine complaint of Master of Ord. Santiago that Hospitallers of kgdom of León had appropriated certain houses and property of the Order. *Dilecti filii magister*: AHN, OO., MM., Santiago, Uclés, carp.179/4 (DSL, 195).

(52) 2 Aug. 1223. **Bp (Martín II), (Florencio) dean, 'Petro Monazino' canon**: mandate to determine complaint of Bp (Melendo) of Osma regarding certain parishes allegedly detained by Bp (Lope Pérez) of Sigüenza. *Ex parte venerabilis*: MANSILLA, 460[166].

(53) 21 Aug. 1223. **Bp (Martín II), (Florencio) dean, treasurer**:[167] mandate to determine complaint of Master of Santiago regarding detention of certain possessions in dioc. of Palencia, León and Zamora. *Dilecti filii magister*: AHN, OO. MM., Santiago, Uclés, carp. 4.ii/2 (MANSILLA, 466, partial edn derived from *Bull. Santiago*).

(54) 26 Aug. 1223. **(Ysidoro) archd., (Juan) archd. of Toro, (García) chanter**: mandate to determine complaint of Master of Santiago that abt and convent of Castañeda, OSB (dioc. Astorga) have buried body of fr. Facundus of their Order appropriating his goods. *Dilecti filii magister*: AHN, OO. MM., Santiago, Uclés, carp. 65/8 (MANSILLA, 470, defective end derived from *Bull. Santiago*); DSL, 205.

---

[166] On 18 March 1224 the parties were summoned to attend at Zamora on 7 July following: AC Sigüenza, documentos pontificios 13 (MINGUELLA, *Hist. de la diócesis de Sigüenza* cit., I, p. 543).
[167] In March 1224 the treasurer was one 'G': ACZ, 13/19 (LERA, 374).

(55) 27 Aug. 1223. **Bp (Martín II), (Florencio) dean, (Ysidoro) archd.**: mandate to determine complaint of Master of Santiago that Hospitallers of kgdom of León have appropriated certain houses and possessions. *Dilecti filii magister*: MANSILLA, 471.

(56) 28 Aug. 1223. **Bp (Martín II), (Florencio) dean, treasurer**: mandate to determine complaint of Master of Santiago that Templars of kgdom of León have appropriated certain houses and possessions. *Dilecti filii magister*: MANSILLA, 241.

(57) 20 Nov. 1223. **Bp (Martín II), (Florencio) dean, (García) chanter**: mandate correcting failure of letters of 9 June 1217 (no. 28) to record chap. of Ávila as party to dispute with ch. of Plasencia over Béjar etc. *Venerabilis frater* noster: AC Ávila, d.s.n.[168]

(58) *ante* 27 May 1224. **Treasurer, (Pedro) *magister scolarum*, 'Egidius' canon**[169] had been commissioned to investigate state of ch. of León. In *Cum dilectis filiis: Reg. Hon. III*, 5017 (MANSILLA, 504).

(59) 22 Nov. 1224. **(García) chanter, Ysidoro archd., Master J(uan) archd. of Toro**: mandate correcting scribal errors in earlier letters for Diego Rodríguez *miles* and wife (Elvira Martínez) in dispute with abt of Arbas, O.Cist. (dioc. Oviedo). *D. Roderici miles*: CDL, 1922.[170]

(60) 23 Dec. 1224. **(Florencio) dean, treasurer, 'P. Petri' canon**: mandate to overrule exceptions previously admitted by executors of provision of 'D. presbiter' in favour of Bp (Gonzalo Fernández) and chap. of Salamanca. *Dilecto filio Gregorio: Reg. Hon. III*, 5237 (MANSILLA, 530).

(61) 11 March 1225. **Abt of Sandoval, (Florencio) dean**: mandate to restore to mon. of Sahagún full possession of certain churches long the subject of litigation. *Olim a venerabili: Reg. Hon. III*, 5378 (MANSILLA, 545).

(62) 26 May 1225. **Bp (Martín II)**, Bp (Tello Téllez) of Palencia, dean of Palencia: mandate to investigate application of Bp (Pedro Andrés) of Astorga to resign his see. *Venerabilis frater noster: Reg. Hon. III*, 5512 (MANSILLA, 558).

---

[168] AJO, *Inventario de Ávila*, 101, no. 9 (misdated). Printed BARRIOS GARCÍA, *Documentación de Ávila* cit., no. 57.

[169] The activity of this trio is impossible to date. In the surviving *acta* in ACZ 'Egidius canonicus' appears just once, in Sept. 1222: *TN*, f. 111v (LERA, 350).

[170] The information here provided to the effect that the previous mandate had been addressed 'ad bone memorie cantorem Zamorensem [i.e. Egas] et vos filii archidiaconi et te filii Ysidore, *tunc canonico Zemorensi*', establishes that it had been issued between Feb. 1219 and Aug. 1221 (above, n. 16). See also CDL, 1533: a record relating to this same issue, unfortunately undated, the edition of which gives the initial of the chanter as 'S.', evidently an error for either 'E.' or 'G.'

504

(63)  6 June 1225. **Bp (Martín II)**, Martín Alfonso archd. of León, treasurer of León: mandate to investigate and, if appropriate, ratify division of rents between bp and chap. of Astorga. *Cum venerabilis frater*: DSL, 223.

(64)  13 June 1225. **(Florencio) dean**: mandate impetrated by chap. of León regarding injuries attributable to episcopal negligence and requiring Bp (Rodrigo Álvarez) to repair defects alleged, failing which the addressees have pontifical authority to provide adequate remedy. *Cum episcopus ex*: *Reg. Hon. III*, 5534 (MANSILLA, 563).

(65)  7 Jan. 1226. Abt of La Espina, dean of Astorga, **(Florencio) dean**: mandate to enforce reform of mon. of Sahagún as specified by abt of Moreruela and colleagues. *Dilecti filii J.*: *Reg. Hon. III*, 5772 (MANSILLA, 594).

(66)  18 Jan. 1227. Bp (Martín II), (Florencio) dean, (García) chanter: mandate to provide for Bp (Martinho Rodrigues) of Porto if exiled on account of dispute with Sancho II of Portugal and to proceed against the latter in accordance with previous mandates. *Cum causam que*: *Reg. Hon. III*, 6187 (MANSILLA, 623).

(67)  18 Jan. 1227. **Bp (Martín II), (Florencio) dean, (García) chanter**: mandate to proceed against Sancho II of Portugal on account of persecution of Bp (Martinho Rodrigues) of Porto. *Carissimus in Christo*: *Reg. Hon. III*, 6188 (MANSILLA, 624).

GREGORY IX

(68)  5 May 1227. **Bp (Martín II), (Florencio) dean, (García) chanter**: mandate reiterating no. 66. *Cum causam que*: *Reg. Greg. IX*, 71 (COSTA, n. 271; DSGr, 12).

(69)  7 Feb. 1228. **Bp (Martín II), (Florencio) dean, (García) chanter**: mandate to determine complaint of Bp (Pelayo) of Salamanca in dispute with bp of Coria regarding possessions at Montemayor (dioc. Salamanca). *Ex parte venerabilis*: MARTÍN MARTÍN *et al.*, *Docs Salamanca*, 176; DSGr, 44.

(70)  18 June 1228. **(Florencio) dean, (García) chanter, treasurer**: mandate to determine complaint of prior and chap. of Guimarães that rector and clergy of chapel of Santiago, Guimarães (dioc. Braga) are receiving parishioners of Guimarães *ad divina* and otherwise prejudicing their rights. *Conquesti sunt nobis*: IANTT, Colegiada de Guimarães, docs. eclesiásticos, mç. 1, doc. 10 (DSGr, 63).

(71)  21 June 1228. **(Florencio) dean, (García) chanter, treasurer**: mandate to determine complaint of chap. of Guimarães that their prior has acted in breach of the *divisio mense* agreed between them. *Conquesti sunt nobis*: IANTT, Colegiada de Guimarães, docs. eclesiásticos, mç. 1, doc. 11 (DSGr, 64).

(72)  19 Oct. 1230. **(Florencio) dean, (J.) treasurer,**[171] '**Mag. Helie' canon**:

mandate to determine complaint of G., J., N. and other canons of Guimarães that
P., prior of that church, has unlawfully conferred canonry and prebend on P., son of
S. *quondam* canon. *Exposita nobis G.*: IANTT, Colegiada de Guimarães, docs.
eclesiásticos, mç. 1, doc. 16 (DSGr, 151).

(73) 13 Jan. 1231. **(Florencio) dean, (J.) treasurer, Parens canon**: mandate
to determine complaint of chap. of Guimarães that their parishioners, R., P., D. and
others, attend divine office at other churches. *Conquerentibus dilectis filiis*: IANTT,
Colegiada de Guimarães, docs. eclesiásticos, mç. 1, doc. 17 (DSGr, 163).

(74) 13 Jan. 1231. **(Florencio) dean, (Master Juan) archd. of Toro, (J.)
treasurer**: *Sua nobis*. In letters of subdelegation (Zamora, 'mense madio altera die
post festum Victoris et Corone', 1233) regarding complaint of G., V., P., J., G., N.,
and other canons and prebendaries of Guimarães that their prior has infringed the
patronal rights they share with him to ch. of S. Tomé *de Caldelis* (Caldelas) and
chapel of S. Paio: IANTT, Colegiada de Guimarães, docs. eclesiásticos, mç. 1, doc.
20 (DSGr, 164).

(75) 29 Apr. 1231. **(Florencio) dean, (Master Juan) archd. of Toro, (J.)
treasurer**: mandate to determine complaint of chap. of Guimarães that rector and
clergy of ch. of Santiago (dioc. Braga) refuse obedience and admit to divine service
parishioners of Guimarães and its dependency, the chapel of S. Paio. *Dilecti filii
capitulum*: IANTT, Colegiada de Guimarães, docs. eclesiásticos, mç. 1, doc. 18
(DSGr, 187).

(76) 31 July 1231. **Bp (Martín II)**: mandate impetrated by Abp (Silvestre
Godinho) of Braga to investigate circumstances of bequests of his predecessor
(Abp Estêvão Soares) and to protect D. Silvestre from the consequences of those
bequests. *Ex officii nostri*: COSTA, n. 468; DSGr, 198.

(77) 7 Oct. 1231. **Bp (Martín II)**, abt of Peleas, abt of Tarouca, O.Cist. (dioc.
Lamego): mandate to compel Sancho II of Portugal to restore to Bp (Paio) of Lisbon *decime regalium reddituum* of his diocese and other revenues appropriated by
him and Afonso II, in accordance with instructions of the latter's will. *Venerabilis
frater noster*: *Reg. Greg. IX*, 732 (COSTA, n. 296j; DSGr, 202).

(78) 11 Nov. 1231. Abt of Tarouca, **(Florencio) dean**: mandate to induce
Sancho II of Portugal to release vacant churches of dioc. of Lisbon to Bp (Paio).
*Venerabilis frater noster*: ADB, Gav. das Noticias Várias, 31; IANTT, Bulas, mç.
35, no. 10 (COSTA, n. 299; DSGr, 204).

(79) 15 Dec. 1231. **Bp (Martín II), (Florencio) dean, (J.) treasurer**: mandate impetrated by Infanta Teresa of Portugal to act as conservators of settlement
between her and her sisters S(ancha) and B(ranca) *ex una parte* and Sancho II *ex*

---

[171] 'J.' was treasurer by Aug. 1230: ACZ, 18/2 (LERA, 427).

506

*altera. Cum ex iniuncte*: IANTT, Mosteiro de Lorvão, docs. eclesiásticos, mç. 1, doc. 23.

(80)  12 Oct. 1232. **Bp (Martín II), (Florencio) dean, (Pedro)** *magister scolarum*: mandate, good for three years, to act as conservators of three named *nepotes* of Cardinal Pelayo Gaitán in enjoyment of the deaneries of Compostela, León and Salamanca. *Movet nos et*: *Reg. Greg. IX*, 918 (DSGr, 228).

(81)  19 December 1232. **(Florencio) dean, (Ysidoro) archd., (J.) treasurer**: mandate to determine complaint of Master of Santiago that María Peréz has appropriated the castle of Gozón, the property of the Order. *Sua nobis magister*: AHN, OO. MM., Santiago, Uclés, carp. 261/6 DSGr, 247 (from *Bull Santiago*).

(82)  13 Jan. 1233. **(Florencio) dean, (Ysidoro) archd.**: mandate to determine complaint of Master of Santiago in dispute with Hospitallers of kgdom of León regarding possession of *ville* of *Tribilio* (Trebejo) and *Rubea* (Rubio) and other possessions. *Dilecti filii magister*: AHN, OO. MM., Santiago, Uclés, carp. 331/7 DSGr, 251(from *Bull Santiago*).

(83)  20 Jan. 1233. **(Florencio) dean, archd. of Toro**:[172] mandate to determine complaint of Master of Santiago in dispute with Templars of kgdom of León regarding possession of *villa* of *Alcaniz* (Alcañices de Aliste).[173] *Dilecti filii magister*: AHN, OO. MM., Santiago, Uclés, carp. 58/4 (DSGr, 253: partial edn derived from *Bull. Santiago*).

(84)  24 Jan. 1233. Bp (Juan de Soria) of Osma, **(Florencio) dean**, sacrist of Palencia: mandate to determine boundaries of dioc. of Baeza: *Venerabilis frater noster*: *Reg. Greg. IX*, 1065 (DSGr, 254).

(85)  26 Feb. 1233. Bp (Martín II): mandate impetrated by certain brothers of Order of Santiago complaining at intention of their Master to cede castle of Castrotorafe to Fernando III of Castile. *Quanto carissimus in*: (DSGr, 268).

(86)  26 May 1233. **Bp (Martín II)**, (Florencio) dean, (García) chanter: mandate in continuation of no. 67 to impose interdict on Sancho II of Portugal if he remain contumacious. *Si quam graviter*: *Reg. Greg. IX*, 1328 (COSTA, n. 321; DSGr, 290).

(87)  10 June 1233. **Bp (Martín II), (Florencio) dean, (García) chanter**: mandate reiterating no. 68. *Cum causam que*: *Reg. Greg. IX*, 1404 (COSTA, n. 322; DSGr, 297).

**(87a)**  19 April 1234. **Bp (Martín II), (Florencio) dean, (García) chanter**:

---

[172] In ACZ the latest record of the archdeacon of Toro Master Juan is of Nov. 1232: ACZ, 14/25 (LERA, 456).
[173] Cf. no. 40.

mandate impetrated by Bp (Martinho Rodrigues) of Porto requiring payment of diocesan procurations. *Significante venerabili fratre*: COSTA, n. 331; DSGr, 345.

(88) 13 May 1234. Bp (Mauricio) of Burgos, Master Arnaldo bp-el. of León, **(Florencio) dean**: mandate to determine complaint of abt of Sahagún against apostolic visitors of his monastery. *Dilectus filius abbas*: *Reg. Greg. IX*, 1908 (DSGr, 352).

(89) 27 June 1234. **(Florencio) dean, (J.) treasurer, (Pedro)** *magister scolarum*: mandate to determine complaints of Master and brothers of Ord. Santiago in dispute with abt and mon. of Moreruela and others regarding alleged usurpation of property in dioc. of Zamora, Salamanca and Astorga. *Conquerentibus dilectis filiis*: DSGr, 368.

(90) 29 June 1234. **(Florencio) dean, (J.) treasurer**, dean of León: mandate to determine complaints of Master and brothers of Ord. Santiago in dispute with Hospitallers and others regarding alleged usurpations of property in dioc. of Zamora, Astorga and León. *Dilecto filii magister*: DSGr, 373.

(91) 3 July 1234. **Bp (Martín II)**: mandate to relax canonical sentences imposed on Ord. Santiago in Castrotorafe case. *Presentium tibi auctoritate*: *Reg. Greg. IX*, 1994 (DSGr, 374). (Cf. no. 85.)

(92) 20 July 1234. Bp (Juan Pérez) of Calahorra, Bp (Juan de Soria) of Osma, **F(lorencio) dean**: new mandate to collect evidence regarding delimitation of dioc. of Baeza. *Cum Beaciensis ecclesie*: *Reg. Greg. IX*, 2022 (AC Toledo, X.2.P.1.6): DSGr, 384. (Cf. nos. 84, 94a)

(93) 27 July 1234. **(Florencio) dean, (García) chanter, (Pedro)** *magister scolarum*: mandate to determine complaints of Master and brothers of Ord. Santiago in dispute with Bp (Nuño) of Astorga regarding usurpations of property. *Ex parte dilectorum*: AHN, OO. MM., Santiago, Uclés, carp. 58/22 (DSGr, 387: partial edn derived from *Bull. Santiago*).

(94) 25 Oct. 1234. **Bp (Martín II), (Florencio) dean, (J.) treasurer**: mandate to determine complaints of Abp (Silvestre Godinho) of Braga in dispute with Ord. Temple regarding alleged usurpations of diocesan property. *Ex parte venerabilis*: *Reg. Greg. IX*, 2154 (COSTA, n. 474; DSGr, 407).

(94a) 25 Feb. 1235. Bp (Juan Pérez) of Calahorra, dean of Palencia, **(Florencio) dean**: mandate subsituting dean of Palencia for bp of Osma in investigation regarding delimitation of dioc. of Baeza. *Ex parte venerabilis*: AC Toledo, X.2.P.1.4a (ed. J. F. RIVERA, *Notas y documentos para el episcopologio de la sede de Baeza-Jaén durante los siglos XIII y XIV*, «Boletín del Instituto de Estudios Giennenses», 1974, p. 54).

(95) 31 Aug. 1235. Bp (Martín Fernández) of Salamanca, **(Florencio) dean**,

(**Pedro**) *magister scolarum*: mandate requiring Sancho II of Portugal to desist from persecution of clerical estate on pain of excommunication and interdict. *Licet quantum cum*: Reg. Greg. *IX*, 2753 (COSTA, n. 514; DSGr, 499).

(96)  8 Feb. 1236. (**Florencio**) **dean**, (**J.**) **treasurer**, chanter of Salamanca: mandate to determine complaint of prior and chap. of Guimarães that chap. of Braga harasses them over quantity of corn and wine 'que vota vulgariter appellantur', mortuary payments and other matters. *Dilecti filii prior*: IANTT, Colegiada de Guimarães, docs. eclesiásticos, mç. 1, doc. 21 (DSGr, 529).

(97)  *ante* 1237. (**Florencio**) **dean**, archd. Martín of León, archd. J. of Palencia: renewed mandate, impetrated by Abp (Rodrigo) of Toledo, regarding dispute with ch. of Compostela over ch. of Plasencia. *Significante venerabili fratre*: AC Toledo, X.2.E.1.2.[174] -

(98)  1237x30 March 1238.[175] (**Gil**) **dean**, (**García**) **chanter**, (**J.**) **treasurer**: mandate to rebuke in person Sancho II of Portugal on account of continuing harassment of Bp (Pedro Salvador) of Porto. In *Exposita nobis venerabilis* (no. 99).

(**98a**) 5 April 1237. **Bp (Martín II)** instructed to receive oath of fealty to Roman Church from Juan de Soria on admission of postulation to see of León. In *Gaudemus in Domino*: Reg. Greg. *IX*, 3591 (DSGr, 653).

(99)  30 March 1238. (**Gil**) **dean**, (**García**) **chanter**, (**J.**) **treasurer**: mandate to collect evidence in Portugal relating to no. 98 from 'testes senes et valetudinarios et alios de quorum morte vel absentia diuturna timetur'. *Exposita nobis venerabilis*: Reg. Greg. *IX*, 4243 (COSTA, n. 518; DSGr, 748).

(100) 30 March 1238. (**Gil**) **dean**, (**García**) **chanter**, (**J.**) **treasurer**: mandate to investigate and rule on frustratory exception alleged by Sancho II of Portugal that Bp (Pedro Salvador) of Porto is and his predecessor (D. Martinho Rodrigues) had been excommunicate. *Ex parte venerabilis*: Reg. Greg, *IX*. 4244 (COSTA, n. 519; DSGr, 749).

---

[174] This mandate, dated 23 Feb. 1239, records that the first two of the judges named were now dead and is endorsed by Fortunius, the archbishop of Toledo's proctor: 'Ista causa accelerationem requirit et periculum tocius cause est in mora quia multi testes mortui sunt et timendum est de morte aliorum.' The enquiry had been in train since Dec. 1213 when one of the two earliest commissioners had been Martin Rodriguez archd. of León (later Bishop Martín II of Zamora): *DhI*, 511.

[175] The terms of the date of this mandate is provided by the information it contains to the effect that at the time of its issue the chanter of Zamora was ill and therefore unable to attend to it and by the absence of any suggestion that the dean to which both mandates were addressed were not one and the same person (i.e. don Gil).

(101) 26 July 1239. **Archd. of Toro, Parens canon, J. Petri canon**: mandate to determine complaint of rector of ch. of *S. Martinus de Vila Cova* (S. Martinho de Villa Cova da Lixa; dioc. Porto) that chap. of Braga and others of city and dioc. of Braga harass them over payment of *vota. Conquestus est nobis*: IANTT, Colegiada de Guimarães, docs. eclesiásticos, mç. 1, doc. 22 (DSGr, 860).

(102) 31 July 1239. **Archd. of Toro, treasurer,** *magister scolarum*: mandate to determine complaint of prior and chap. of Guimarães that Abp (Silvestre Godinho) and chap. of Braga refuse to abide by terms of *amicabilis compositio* between D. *quondam* prior and Estevão Soares *quondam* abp, negotiated by **F(lorencio) archd. of Zamora** and F. archd. of Astorga and confirmed by Honorius III (above, nos. 23, 25). *Sua nobis prior*: IANTT, Colegiada de Guimarães, docs. eclesiásticos, mç. 1, doc. 23 (DSGr, 790).

(103) 1 April 1240. **Bp-elect (Pedro), dean,**[176] **archd. of Toro.**[177] *Dilecti filii abbas.*[178]

(104) 24 March 1241. Bp of Plasencia, **treasurer,**[179] *magister scolarum*: mandate to mediate, failing which to refer to the Apostolic See, dispute of bp of Coria and Master and brothers of Alcántara (Ord. Calatrava) regarding seizure by the latter of churches of Mascoras, Alcántara and Portezalo and other infringements of episcopal rights: *Venerabilis frater noster*: *Reg. Greg. IX*, 5954 (DSGr, 984).

## INNOCENT IV

(105) 11 July 1243. **Bp-elect (Pedro)**, abt of Peleas: mandate to oblige Sancho II of Portugal to surrender bequest of his father (Afonso II) to ch. of Coimbra. *Sua nobis dilectus*: IANTT, Sé de Coimbra, 2a incorporação, mç. 42, doc. 1733.

(106) 2 June 1245. **(Juan Juánez) dean, (Pedro Pedrez) archd. of Toro,** He(lias) *magister scolarum*:[180] mandate to determine complaint of prior and chap.

---

[176] Sometime between August 1239 and March 1244 don Gil was succeeded as dean by don Juan (Juánez): ACZ, 17/32bis (LERA, 526); SOUSA COSTA, 413.
[177] By June 1241 the archdeacon of Toro was Pedro Pedrez: ACZ, 16/II/50 (LERA, 513).
[178] G. BATTELLI, *Schedario Baumgarten. Descrizione diplomatica di bolle e brevi originali da Innocenzo III a Pio IX*. Riproduzione anastatica con introduzione e indici a cura di G. BATTELLI, 2 vols, Vatican City 1965-1966, no. 1294 (AHN, Zamora, S. Sofía, 1E).
[179] The succession of the treasurership of Zamora from 'J.' to Master Gil occurred sometime between March 1238 and June 1251: ACZ, TB, f. 134v (LERA, 557).
[180] Helias occupied the office of *magister scolarum* in succession to Master Pedro (above, n. 159) from an uncertaion date until at least 17 June 1252 (A. QUINTANA PRIETO, *Tumbo Viejo de San Pedro de Montes*, León 1971, p. 536) and by 11

of Guimarães that Stephanus Johannis can. of Braga and other clergy of Braga dioc. withhold annual *census* due in respect of ch. of S. Martinho da Villanova (?de Famalição), and harm them otherwise. *Dilecti filii prior*: IANTT, Colegiada de Guimarães, docs. eclesiásticos, mç. 1, doc. 27[181].

(107) 2 June 1245. (**Juan Juánez**) **dean**, (**Pedro Pedrez**) **archd. of Toro, He(lias)** *magister scolarum*: mandate to determine complaint of prior and chap. of Guimarães that Petrus Petri, Johannes Egee and other laymen of Braga dioc. infringe their rights regarding ch. of Santiago do Subradelo. *Dilecti filii prior*: IANTT, Colegiada de Guimarães, docs. eclesiásticos, mç. 1, doc. 28[182].

(108) 12 Aug. 1245. (**Juan Juánez**) **dean, treasurer**: repeats no. 79. *Cum ex iniuncte*: IANTT, Mosteiro de Lorvão, docs. eclesiásticos, mç. 1, doc. 31.

(109) 25 Sept. 1245. (**Juan Juánez**)[183] **dean**: mandate to act as conservator of interests of mon. of Castañeda. *Etsi quibuslibet*: AHN, Clero, carp. 3566/9.

(110) 6 March 1247. (**Juan Juánez**) **dean**: mandate to determine complaints of Master and brothers of Ord. Santiago in dispute with prior and brothers of S. Cristóbal (Ord. Sepulchre) and others of dioc.of Salamanca, Zamora and León regarding alleged usurpations of property. *Dilecti filii magister*: DSL, 320.

(111) 16 June 1248. (**Juan Juánez**) **dean, (Helias)** *magister scolarum*: conservators for abt and mon. of S. Pedro de Montes (OSB, dioc. León) in enjoyment of patronal rights to ch. of Corporales. *Sua nobis dilecti*: *Reg. Inn. IV*, 3961 (QP, 529).

(112) 16 June 1248. (**Juan Juánez**) **dean, (Helias)** *magister scolarum*: conservators for abt and mon. of S. Pedro de Montes in enjoyment of patronal rights to ch. of Santo Tomás (dioc. Astorga). *Sua nobis dilecti*: *Reg. Inn. IV*, 3962 (QP, 530).

(113) 16 June 1248. (**Juan Juánez**) **dean, (Helias)** *magister scolarum*: conservators for abt and mon. of S. Pedro de Montes in enjoyment of patronal rights to ch. of S. María de Cesuris (dioc. Astorga) under threat from Rodrigo Alfonso brother of Fernando III of Castile. *Sua nobis dilecti*: *Reg. Inn. IV*, 3963 (QP, 531).

(114) 3 July 1248. (**Juan Juánez**) **dean, (Helias)** *magister scolarum*: conservators for abt and mon. of S. Pedro de Montes in enjoyment of patronal rights to ch. of Capilla de Domiz (dioc. Astorga). *Sua nobis abbas*: QP, 535.

August of that year had been succeeded by Pedro Beneítez (*ibid.*, 545, 547).

[181] *Littere citatorie* (Zamora, 12 Dec. 1245), whence the names supplied.

[182] *Littere citatorie* (Zamora, 16 Apr. [1246]), whence the names supplied.

[183] Name supplied by ASV, *Collectoriae* 397, f. 126v (ed. P. LINEHAN, *La iglesia de León a mediados del s. XIII*, in *León y su historia. Miscelánea histórica III* [León 1975], p. 60; DOMÍNGUEZ SÁNCHEZ, 415 [p. 482]).

(115) 25 July 1250. **Bp (Pedro I)**, bp of Astorga, bp of Salamanca: conservators of jurisdictional exemption of ch. of Cartagena. *Novella plantatio Cartaginensi*: BNM MS. 13075 (A. de Morales, 'Compulsa de los privilegios, bullas y otros instrumentos sacados del archivo de la S. I. de Cartagena, 1751), ff. 96v-97r; *Reg. Inn. IV*, 4783 (QP, —).

(116) 20 Dec. 1251. **Bp (Pedro I)**: mandate to determine complaint of bp and chapter of Coimbra in dispute with Master and brothers of Temple in Portugal regarding terms of *compositio* prejudicial to the former in respect of episcopal rights over churches 'de Polumbari, de Ega at de Redina' (Coimbra dioc.). *Sua nobis venerabilis*: ANTT, Sé de Coimbra, 1a incorporação, documentos eclesiásticos, mç. 2, no. 87.

(117) 1 Feb. 1252. **Bp (Pedro I)**: mandate to relax canonical sentences that canons of S. María de Trianos (OSA, dioc. León) may have incurred in relation to deposition of abbot and to proceed to new abbatial election. *Johannem quondam abbatem*: *Reg. Inn. IV*, 5668 (QP, 737).

(118) 3 March 1252. **(Juan Juánez) dean**: mandate to determine complaint of abp of Braga that abt of Lomar and other heads of houses and rectors of his diocese refuse payment of procurations. *Venerabilis frater noster*: *Bul. Brac.*, 114.

(119) 3 March 1252. **(Juan Juánez) dean**: mandate to determine complaint of abp of Braga that rectors of S. Maria de Idães and other churches of his diocese refuse payment of procurations. *Venerabilis frater noster*: ADB, Gav. das Propiedades e Rendas da Mitra, 28.

(120) 6 March 1252. **(Pedro Pedrez) archd. of Toro**: executor of provision in city or dioc. of Ciudad Rodrigo for Jacobus archd. of Coria 'in Galisteo'. *Cum proventus archidiaconatus*: *Reg. Inn. IV*, 5806 (QP, 754).

(121) 5 July 1252. **G(arcía Peláez) chanter**[184]: mandate to act as conservator for Andrés, *alumnus et familiaris* of Card. Gil Torres in possession of office of prior of S. Maria de la Vega *extra muros*, OSA (Salamanca). *Obtentu dilecti filii*: *Reg. Inn. IV*, 5882 (QP, 775).

(122) 4 Oct. 1252. Bp (Pedro Gallego) of Cartagena, **Bp (Pedro I)**: commission to grant faculty to religious nominated by Alfonso X of Castile to absolve from sentences of excommunication clerics and laymen assisting him either in person or by proxy in his campaign against the Saracens of Africa. *Carissimus in Christo*: *Reg. Inn. IV*, 6029 (QP, 807, misdated).

---

[184] García Peláez had been chanter since at least April 1247: ACZ, 31/II/1 (LERA, 536).

(123) 4 Oct. 1252. Bp (Pedo Gallego) of Cartagena, **Bp (Pedro I)**: commission to grant faculty to religious or secular clergy nominated by Alfonso X of Castile to appropriate to his war chest monies acquired by usury if those entitled to remuneration cannot be identified. *Carissimus in Christo*: *Reg. Inn. IV*, 6030 (QP, 808, misdated).

(124) *ante* 8 Nov. 1252. **(Juan Juánez) dean**: executor of provision in city or dioc. of Astorga for Master Esteban abt of Husillos (dioc. Palencia). In *Significavit nobis dilectus*: *Reg. Inn. IV*, 6696 (QP, 814).

(125) 28 July 1253. **(Juan Juánez) dean**: mandate to hear and determine complaint of Abp (João Egas) of Braga that the rectors of ch. of *Villaficta* and others, 51 of them specified, refuse payment of 'catedraticum vel synodaticum'. *Sua nobis venerabilis*: ADB, Gav. de Concílios e Sínodos, 4.

(126) 11 May 1254. **(Juan Juánez) dean**: mandate on petition of Abp (João Egas) of Braga to proceed against noble and other patrons of churches in dioc. and province deserving of deprivation for laying violent hands on rectors and clergy in accordance with provisions of General Council[185]. *Sua nobis venerabilis*: ADB, Gav. 1ª das Igrejas, 2.

(127) 20 Feb. 1254. Chanter of Lisbon, **(Master Gil)**[186] **chanter**, chanter of Lamego: mandate, at behest of Cardinal Ottobono of S. Adriano, to collect and transmit evidence of witnesses relating to claim of Bp (Vicente Mendes) of Porto against Abp (João Egas) of Braga regarding ch. of S. Cruz de Ribadouro and others (dioc. Porto). *In causa que*: ADP, Cabido da Sé do Porto, Pergaminhos, doc. 1672/f.50.

(128) 25 June 1254. Archd. of Sabugal (dioc. Ciudad Rodrigo), **(Master Gil) chanter**, chanter of Lisbon: mandate, at behest of Cardinal Ottobono of S. Adriano, to collect and transmit evidence of witnesses relating to cases of violation of canonical sentences alleged by Abp (João Egas) of Braga and Bp (Vicente Mendes) of Porto. *In causis que*: ADB, Gav. dos Arcebispos, 86[187].

(129) 9 Aug. 1254. **(Juan Juánez) dean**, **(Master Gil) chanter**: mandate to implement instructions of Gregory IX regarding dispute of Kg (Afonso III) of

---

[185] II Lateran (1139) can. 15, 'Si quis suadente' (Gratian, C.17 q.4 c.29).

[186] Master Gil was chanter by 26 Sept. 1253, and also vicar of Bishop Rodrigo of Palencia, though his usefulness in the latter capacity must have been limited since the *littere citatorie* issued by him and his *co-receptores* in respect of no. 131 on 12 Sept. 1254, just sixteen days after the issue of the mandate, suggests that he was at the papal curia at the time. AC Palencia, 8-15-7; AD Braga, Gav. dos Arcebispos, 27.

[187] A defective rescript with same *incipit* and addressees, dated 17 June 1254 and endorsed 'Ista est cassata' three times, is at ADB, Gav. dos Arcebispos, 23.

Portugal and Bp (Vicente Mendes) of Porto and provide for the latter in the event of his incurring exile on that account. *Cum sicut asseritur*: *Reg. Inn. IV*, 7943 (QP, 1009). Cf. nos. 86, 87.

(130) 12 Aug. 1254. Bp (Pedro Pérez) of Salamanca, **(Juan Juánez) dean**, *magister scolarum*: mandate regarding same issue as no. 128. *Cum prout asseritur*: *Reg. Inn. IV*, 7945 (QP, 1012).

(131) 27 Aug. 1254. Chanter of Lisbon, **(Master Gil) chanter**, chanter of Lamego: mandate impetrated by Abp (João Egas) of Braga to interrogate 'testes senes et valetudinarios' and receive evidence concerning ch. of S. Cruz de Ribadouro and others (dioc. Porto) alleged by Bp (Vicente Mendes) of Porto to belong to his jurisdiction. *In causa que*: ADB, Gav. dos Arcebispos, 28.

(132) 1 Sept. 1254. **(Juan Juánez) dean**: mandate on petition of Abp (João Egas) of Braga to declare null powers claimed by Kg (Afonso III) of Portugal to proceed against ecclesiastics. *Per nostras litteras*: *Bul. Brac.*, 61[188].

(133) [1243 1254]. **dean, treasurer**: executors of provision of León dignity, other than archdeaconry of Triacastella, in favour of Melendo Pérez, archd. of Astorga. ASV, *Collectoriae* 397, f. 117v (ed. LINEHAN, *La iglesia de León a mediados del s. XIII* cit., p. 53; DSL, 415).

---

[188] Where it is misassigned to Innocent III and the year 1209.

# VII

# *Columpna Firmissima*:
# D. Gil Torres, the Cardinal of Zamora*

In November 1254 D. Gil Torres, the cardinal of Zamora, died somewhere in Italy, perhaps at Naples where Pope Innocent IV was at the time – or perhaps not, since, even if not almost a centenarian by then, as one contemporary was to allege,[1] after thirty-eight years in the service of the papacy the cardinal was almost certainly in no condition to be carted round with an itinerant court.

The reports that we have of his demise come not from a Zamoran source. They come from the *Obituarios* of the cathedral church of Burgos and Toledo.[2] Nor does Zamora, where Richard Fletcher and the present writer both cut their archival teeth, have any street or square named after one of its most notable sons, who at the time of his death was the second most senior cardinal. Over time that neglect, or indifference, which the pope who raised him to the purple commented on more than once, has allowed the Zamoran cardinal to be claimed by other places. According to Luciano Serrano, as well as 'doctor en derecho' D. Gil was *burgalés* and 'originario de Bureva'. But for this assertion the learned abbot of Silos offered no proof, and his misreporting of another Torres as 'sobrino del abad de Valladolid' hardly encourages confidence.[3] In any case, the *apellido* Torres was scarcely

---

* A revised version of my contribution to *Cross, Crescent and Conversion: studies on medieval Spain and Christendom in memory of Richard Fletcher*, ed. Simon Barton & Peter Linehan (Leiden: Brill, 2008), 241–61, itself the revision of a paper read in Spanish at the 2° Congreso de Historia de Zamora in November 2003. My warm thanks are due to Sr. José Carlos de Lera Maíllo, archivist of Zamora cathedral, for all manner of kindnesses.

1    See below, n. 84.

2    Reporting the date as 11 November: L. Serrano, *El obispado de Burgos, y Castilla primitiva desde el siglo V al XIII*, III (Madrid, 1936), 391. The Toledo *Obituario* says 5 November (for 'Egidius cardinalis, huius ecclesie canonicus'): Toledo, Biblioteca Capitular, MS. 42–30, fo. 133v. But the Toledo *Obituario* is unreliable, with the obits of various fourteenth-century cardinals (for example) wrongly given.

3    L. Serrano, *D. Mauricio, obispo de Burgos y fundador de su catedral*, (Madrid, 1922), 70 and n. 1. The source cited – M. Mañueco Villalobos and J. Zurita Nieto, *Documentos de la iglesia collegial de Santa María la Mayor (hoy Metropolitana) de Valladolid. siglo XIII (1201–1280)* (Valladolid, 1920), 150 – refers to Johan de Torres as '*merino* del Abbat'.

less common in thirteenth-century Burgos than the *nombre* Egidius. The most that can be said for sure about D. Gil's connexion with Burgos is that at the time of his promotion in 1216 he was an archdeacon of that church, a dignity he had acquired sometime between March 1209 and November 1210.[4]

Despite the gift of tithes made to the Portuguese bishops by their king, Afonso II, in 1218 'pro amore magistri Egidii cardinalis', his Portuguese credentials are equally supposititious. Like those of the Leonese Cardinal Ordoño Álvarez sixty years later, they are to be attributed to the assumptions of the cultural colonists of seventeenth-century Portugal.[5]

The reasons for regarding D. Gil as *zamorano* are twofold. First there is the fact that whereas his bequests to the church of Burgos were for anniversaries for himself,[6] those at Zamora were also for his nearest and dearest, his parents and his sister, though at modest cost in comparison with his expenditure on the daily commemoration of himself there.[7] And although, by contrast with his senior Leonese colleague, Cardinal Pelayo Gaitán, he did not possess sufficient local property for the purpose,[8] suggesting that by the date of these endowments his material links with Zamora were tenuous, the terms in which, on successive occasions, Honorius III rebuked the *zamoranos* for

---

[4]    J.M. Garrido Garrido, *Documentación de la catedral de Burgos (1184–1222)* (Burgos, 1983), nos. 410, 430; E. Berger (ed.), *Les Registres d'Innocent IV* [hereafter *Reg. Inn. IV*] (Paris, 1884–1921), 4436.

[5]    A.D. de Sousa Costa, *Mestre Silvestre e Mestre Vicente, juristas da contenda entre D. Afonso II e suas irmãs* (Braga, 1963), 67, 69; idem, 'Cultura medieval portuguesa. Português, o Cardeal Gil?', *Itinerarium*, i (1955), 296–306 at pp. 303–6; Peter Linehan and Margarita Torres Sevilla, 'A misattributed tomb and its consequences. Cardinal Ordoño Álvarez and his friends and relations' [here, item XIII], 55–6.

[6]    E. Flórez, *España Sagrada*, XXVI (Madrid, 1771), 323–5; Serrano, *Obispado de Burgos*, III. 391.

[7]    For this, and the testimony of Juan Gil de Zamora OFM, see Peter Linehan, *The Spanish Church and the Papacy in the Thirteenth Century* (Cambridge, 1971), 277; Zamora, Archivo de la Catedral [hereafter ACZ], 12/1; ACZ, Tumbo Negro [hereafter TN], fo. 131r–v (José Carlos de Lera, *Catálogo de los documentos medievales de la catedral de Zamora* (Zamora, 1999) [hereafter Lera], 370, 373): eighteen *aurei* as against six hundred. Details have not survived of the original endowment of the anniversary on 4 May recorded in the 16th-century Zamora *Obituario* (ACZ, MS. 211, fo. 21v; Lera, 2332): 'Yten aniversario por el cardenal don Guillen [*sic*] cient maravedís con missa cantada al altar mayor. Yaze en Roma. CVI maravedís.'

[8]    'Possessionem aliquam ydoneam usque ad sexcentos aureos alfonsinos ad arbitrium venerabilis patris Zamorensis episcopi qui nunc est volumus comparari': ACZ, TN, fo. 131v. Cf. the houses in León assigned to the same purpose by Cardinal Pelayo in 1230: J.M. Fernández Catón, *C[olección] d[ocumental del] A[rchivo de la] C[atedral de] L[eón] (775–1230)*, VI *(1188–1230)* (León, 1991), 1966. Pelayo's bequest was made at the end of his life. D. Gil's is undated. Lera's proposal of the year 1223 requires reconsideration.

their reluctance to oblige him by accommodating his clients, cannot be ignored. If only the chapter of Zamora had reflected on the benefits that their association with the cardinal would bring them – the pontiff reflected in May 1218, in words which D. Gil himself may have supplied – rather than ignoring papal mandates on behalf of such people for promotion in their church they would be falling over themselves to anticipate his wishes.[9] Honorius's register contains two further letters, framed in almost identical terms, on behalf of one or other of the cardinal's clients.[10] And of such clients, many of them the cardinal's *nepotes* and *consanguinei* for whom he secured papal support, there was to be no end over the coming decades. To one of them in particular, his *nepos dilectissimus* Master Esteban de Husillos, I shall return.

From information contained in the papal registers it might even be possible to reconstruct his family tree.[11] What is certain is that that family tree included two bishops of Zamora, both named Pedro, who occupied the see between 1239–1243 and 1255[12] and 1286 and 1302 respectively. The second of these (Pedro Benítez before his promotion), was the *nepos* not only of Cardinal Gil and Esteban de Husillos (whose copy of the Gregorian decretals he disposed of in his will) but also of Bishop Pedro I,[13] while the fact that the latter ('Petrus Bonus': Peter the Good) was yet another of the cardinal's *nepotes* is confirmed by some English evidence to which we shall return.[14]

So the cardinal was a member – perhaps a founding member – of one of those episcopal dynasties with which the kingdom of Castile-León was well supplied during his century. One thinks in particular of the see of Burgos and of that of Cuenca, four if not five of whose thirteenth-century bishops were

---

[9]    P. Pressutti, *Regesta Honorii Papae III* [hereafter *Reg. Hon III*] (Rome, 1885–95), 1277 (ed. D. Mansilla, *La documentación pontificia de Honorio III (1216–1227)* [hereafter MDH] (Rome, 1965), 169). Cf. the letter in the formulary of Thomas of Capua (datable from its context to 1218–21 on behalf of 'P.', a nephew of Cardinal Pelayo, urging the church of León 'quatinus quem ad patruum geritis in nepote monstretis affectum': S.F. Hahn, *Collectio monvmentorvm, vetervm et recentivm…* (2 vols; Brunswick, 1724–26), I. 383–4; Linehan, *Spanish Church*, 291–2.

[10]   *Reg. Hon III*, 2405, 4878 (MDH, 277, 498).

[11]   Francisco 'nepos', son of Teresa, herself allegedly the cardinal's 'nepta'; Rodrigo Domínguez, 'consanguineus'; Johannes son of Rodericus Tomás, 'consanguineus'; Sancho Alfonso, 'nepos', all dating from the years 1252–54: *Reg. Inn. IV*, 5808, 6696, 6870, 7710.

[12]   Concerning the reasons for Pedro I's differing status in the estimation of papal and royal courts during these five years, see Peter Linehan, 'An impugned chirograph and the juristic culture of early thirteenth-century Zamora' [here, item VI], 475–6.

[13]   Idem, *The Ladies of Zamora* (Manchester, 1996), 86; *Reg. Inn. IV*, 5564, 5805; J.C. de Lera Maíllo, 'El testamento del obispo de Zamora Pedro II, año 1302. Edición diplomática', *Homenaje a Antonio Matilla Tascón* (Zamora, 2002), 355–60.

[14]   ACZ, 31/II/1 (Lera, 536), April 1247); Linehan, *Spanish Church*, 294n.; below, n. 78.

4                          *D. Gil Torres, the Cardinal of Zamora*

members of a single family.[15] Indeed, one may even think of Zamora itself where for more than forty years during the twelfth century the see had been governed by Bishops Esteban and Guillermo who, as well as probably being French, were also certainly uncle and nephew,[16] and where in the thirteenth D. Suero Pérez, who was elected in February 1255, just three months after the cardinal's death, would accordingly have been regarded by the cardinal's connexion as an intruder.[17] In 1216, however, the date of Cardinal Gil's elevation, Zamora had a pastor whose origins were Galician, namely Martín Arias, Bishop Martín I.[18] And at the date of Cardinal Gil's elevation in 1216 Bishop Martín's pontificate was in the process of drawing to an untidy close.

With these considerations in mind, let us return to the papal letter of May 1218, for it may have more to tell us than first appears. In it Honorius III states that he had already required the chapter of Zamora to confer the deanery upon the cardinal's brother. But they had failed to oblige. He now instructs the new bishop – Martín Rodríguez (Martín II) to award him the archdeaconry that was vacant.[19] But the cardinal's brother was no more successful on this occasion than on the last. Under Martín II, who had come to Zamora from León and who returned there as bishop in 1238,[20] there was no archdeacon of Zamora with a name beginning with 'P'.[21]

---

[15]   F.J. Hernández and P. Linehan, *The Mozarabic Cardinal. The life and times of Gonzalo Pérez Gudie*, (Florence, 2004), 19, 42 and references there.

[16]   Witness the testimony of 'Rodericus presbiter et canonicus Bracarensis' (*ante* 1193) concerning Bishop Esteban's tearful deathbed repentance in 1175 for having failed in his obedience to the archbishop of Braga: 'et dixit [Rodericus] quod ille episcopus tunc dixit cuidam suo sobrino qui nunc est episcopus Zamorensis: "Et tibi dico quod si forte Deus dederit tibi episcopatum Zamorensem ut Bracarensi ecclesie debeas obedire." Predicto episcopo mortuo, electus fuit ille sobrinus eius…': Lisboa, Instituto dos Arquivos Nacionais Torre do Tombo [hereafter IAN/TT], Colecção Especial, Mitra de Braga, cx. 1, no. 2. I owe this information to the kindness of Richard Fletcher. Cf. Peter Feige, 'Die Anfänge des portugiesischen Königtums und seiner Landeskirche', *Spanische Forschungen der Görresgesellschaft*, I. Reihe: *Gesammelte Aufsätze zur Kulturgeschichte Spaniens*, xxix (1978), 318–23, 383–5.

[17]   Peter Linehan, 'The economics of episcopal politics: the cautionary tale of Bishop Suero Pérez of Zamora', *The Processes of Politics and the Rule of Law. Studies on the Iberian kingdoms and papal Rome in the Middle Ages* (Aldershot, 2002), item V, 6–9.

[18]   R.A. Fletcher, *The Episcopate in the Kingdom of León in the Twelfth Century* (Oxford, 1978), 44.

[19]   *Reg.Hon.III*, 1277 (above, n. 9).

[20]   L. Auvray (ed.), *Les Registres de Grégoire IX* [hereafter *Reg. Greg. IX*] (Paris, 1890–1955), 4594: S. Domínguez Sánchez (ed.), *Documentos de Gregorio IX (1227–1241) referentes a España* (León, 2004), 803.

[21]   The earliest appearance in the record of Pedro Pérez, archdeacon of Toro, is in June 1241: ACZ, 16/II/50 (Lera, 513).

Of course, one might regard such flagrant contempt of papal instructions as just another example of that overweening peninsular self-confidence that historians have observed in action in the years after the battle of Las Navas de Tolosa, particularly in the writings of the canonist Vincentius Hispanus. It was at this very time, indeed, in glossing a decretal of Alexander III – addressed as it happened to a bishop of Zamora (D. Guillermo) who had defied the summons of a papal legate, and then lied to him, as well as having himself consecrated while excommunicate – that Vincentius asked rhetorically: 'Why did the pope not depose him? Why did he tolerate such behaviour and dispense him', and came up with the answer: 'Because he was a Spaniard!'[22]

But in the present case the concerted defiance of bishop and chapter may be symptomatic of something more specific, namely schism within the chapter of Zamora itself in the transition from the rule of Bishop Martín I to Martín II between 1217 and 1219. In the final months of Innocent III's pontificate Martín I had requested and had been granted permission to resign the see. Then he changed his mind – or had it changed for him by forces within the chapter, other members of which later reported to Honorius III that in consequence the church was 'tam in temporalibus quam in spiritualibus multipliciter (…) collapsa', with the result that in June 1217 the pope positively required him to withdraw.[23] Yet although the royal chancery was already describing Martín II as bishop-elect by that date, in the capitular record it was not until May 1220 that he figured as bishop.[24] Indeed throughout those three years of obscurity between the two bishops Martín the capitular record is strangely silent, and during it the chapter's senior personnel had all been replaced,[25] with none of those who had profited in the process being a client or relation of the pope's principal advisor on all matters Zamoran, namely the cardinal of Zamora himself.

One thing most of these new men shared was a juristic training because, partly no doubt on account of the expertise of the two bishops Martín,

---

[22]  'Gratia yspanorum dicamus specialis, uel est maxima dispensatio': cit. J. Ochoa Sanz, *Vincentius Hispanus, canonista boloñes del siglo XIII* (Rome–Madrid, 1960), 15, 21, 123. Cf. Peter Linehan, *History and the Historians of Medieval Spain* (Oxford, 1993), 296–7, 637.

[23]  *Reg. Hon. III*, 629 (MDH, 64). Innocent III's permission must have been granted later than 6 Feb. 1216: D. Mansilla, *La documentación pontificia hasta Inocencio III* (Rome, 1955), 542.

[24]  J. González, *Alfonso IX* (Madrid, 1944), II. 483, no. 369; ACZ, TN, fo. 96r (Lera, 330).

[25]  Dean Juan made his will in June 1217 (ACZ, TN, fo. 88r–v: Lera, 305) and between Sept. 1217 and Feb. 1219 was replaced in that office by Florencio, archdeacon of Zamora (ACZ, 17/37, Archivo Histórico Provincial de Zamora, pergaminos, 1/15: Lera, 308, 317). In the same period Master Juan replaced Munio Muñiz as archdeacon of Toro, and by Aug. 1221 the archdeaconry of the city had passed to D. Isidoro (ACZ, 36/4: Lera, 342).

6                     *D. Gil Torres, the Cardinal of Zamora*

early thirteenth-century Zamora was one of the peninsula's principal juristic centres.[26] Juristic expertise though was less the cause of this distinction than a symptom of Zamora's situation on the frontier with Portugal. At a time when successive kings of Portugal were so regularly at odds with Rome on account of their reportedly beastly treatment of their bishops, Zamora was the safest centre from which to attempt to exercise canonical control, as well as providing a haven for Portuguese bishops in exile.[27] This was a development that had been facilitated by Innocent III's acquiescence in the detachment of the see of Zamora from the metropolitan authority of the church of Braga, a subject on which Richard Fletcher wrote such persuasive pages.[28]

For this and no doubt other reasons, in the first three decades of the thirteenth century Zamora was arguably the principal centre of juristic activity in the Spanish peninsula, with its chief practitioner the archdeacon, later dean, D. Florencio.[29] From this milieu Cardinal Gil emerged. *Dominus Egidius* in December 1206; by March 1209 he had acquired the title *Magister*.[30] At this date the title *Magister* did not necessarily imply attendance either at Bologna or indeed at any other legal academy.[31] There were other possibilities, one of which of course was Palencia. However, there were also others, Coimbra, Calahorra and Osma for example, to the last of which the celebrated Portuguese canonist Master Melendus came from Rome in 1210 as bishop of the place. Although the Master Melendus who was alongside our Master Egidius at Burgos in March 1209 was almost certainly not the

---

[26]     For the former's glosses to the Decretum, see S. Kuttner, *Repertorium der Kanonistik (1140–1234): Prodromus corporis glossarum*, Studi e Testi, 71 (Vatican City, 1937), 11, 53; for the latter's to 'Compilatio I' and his *Notabilia* to 'Compilatio IV', idem, 'Bernardus Compostellanus Antiquus', *Traditio*, i (1943), 277–340 at 335; A. García y García, 'La canonística ibérica medieval posterior al Decreto de Graciano', *Repertorio de las Ciencias Eclesiásticas en España*, i (Salamanca, 1967), 412.

[27]     As evidenced by the depositions of witnesses arraigned at a hearing in 1252 of the dispute between the bishop and chapter of Coimbra and Santa Cruz de Coimbra relating to these years: 'Interrogatus in quo loco fuit tempore exilii episcopus, respondit quod Zamore et in curia Romana'; 'Interrogatus super alio articulo qui sic incipit "Item quod episcopus fuit exul etc.", dixit quod nescit, audiuit tamen quod multo tempore fuit in curia et Zamore et non erat ausus uenire ad regnum propter regem et de hoc erat publica fama': IAN/TT, Cabido da Sé de Coimbra, 1ª incorporação. docs. particulares, cx. 26, rolo 4, membranas 8, 12.

[28]     Mansilla, *Inocencio III*, 199; Fletcher, *Episcopate*, 195–203.

[29]     See Linehan, 'An impugned chirograph', 467–71.

[30]     Garrido, *Documentación de Burgos*, nos. 392, 410.

[31]     O. Weijers, *Terminologie des universités au XIIIe siècle* (Rome, 1987), 133–42.

episcopal Melendus,[32] it can be demonstrated that the episcopal Melendus had been at Palencia at or shortly before that date. Moreover, Zamora lies on the road from Coimbra, from whose Augustinian church of Santa Cruz Melendus seems to have emerged, towards Osma, where he ended his days.[33]

It is possible that the future cardinal's *cursus studiorum* paralleled that of Melendus.[34] Moreover, since the Roman reputation of Gil Torres was such as to merit advancement within the first six months of Honorius III's pontificate (though not, be it noted, to be included in Innocent III's promotion of cardinals in the previous year), a possible explanation for his absence from the Burgos record after November 1210 (and perhaps the most likely) is that he was at Rome on capitular business,[35] that he remained there for the Fourth Lateran Council in November 1215, and that it was then that he caught somebody's eye.[36]

Once installed in Honorius III's curia, Gil Torres adopted a low profile. Sometime in the year after April 1217 he was listed by a Roman agent of Philip Augustus as one of the cardinals 'who are attached to (*qui diligunt*) King Frederick (i.e. the young Hohenstaufen emperor-elect) and the lord king of France (i.e. the ageing Philip Augustus)'.[37] But there was nothing surprising

---

[32]  Garrido, *Doumentación de Burgos*, 410–11. Cf. no. 471: 'domnus Melendus decanus' (April 1214).

[33]  Peter Linehan, 'D. Juan de Soria: *unas apostillas*' [here, item IV], 386–7; Ingo Fleisch, *Sacerdotium – Regnum – Studium. Der westiberische Raum und die europäische Universitätskultur im Hochmittelalter* (Berlin, 2006), 120–27.

[34]  Ibid., 238–9.

[35]  As capitular or episcopal proctor in relation to litigation against the collegiate church of Castrogeriz and the abbey of Oña, as surmised by Serrano, *D. Mauricio*, 70–71; Garrido, *Documentación de Burgos*, 430.

[36]  Although, admittedly, documentary confirmation of his attendance is lacking, we may regard Bishop Melendus, who *was* present (J. F. Rivera, 'Personajes hispanos asistentes en 1215 al IV Concilio de Letrán', *Hispania Sacra*, iv (1951), 335–55 at 343) as at least as likely to have advanced his career as the Leonese Cardinal Pelayo and the Portuguese Hospitaller 'frater Gundisalvus Hispanus' who have been credited with doing so: Serrano, loc. cit., whence A. Blanco Díez, 'Los arcedianos y abades del cabildo catedral de Burgos', *Boletín de la Real Academia de la Historia*, cxxx (1952), 267–98 at 273–5. Be it noted that fr. Gundisalvus, papal factotum in the Spanish kingdoms and Portugal since at least 1213, was to be appointed sacrist of Osma during Melendus' pontificate, despite his membership of the Order of the Hospital: Linehan, 'Juan de Osma', 384–5; Fleisch, *Sacerdotium*, 239. However, the dedication by João de Deus of his 'Notabilia cum Summis super titulis Decretalium' to Gil Torres and João's description of himself as the cardinal's 'humilis clericus' (Costa, 'Cultura medieval portuguesa', 299–300) are neutral witnesses as to Gil's relationship with Melendus.

[37]  R. Davidsohn, *Philipp II. August von Frankreich und Ingeborg* (Stuttgart, 1888), 318, 320.

VII

about that. In 1217, after all, as well as there being an Infanta of Castile (Doña Blanca: Blanche of Castile) installed at Paris as queen-consort in waiting, there was also the same lady's nephew in the process of ascending the throne of Castile (as King Fernando III) and awaiting delivery of his Hohenstaufen bride. The English diplomatic records of the following decade refer to the cardinal occasionally, but only *very* occasionally.[38] Unlike his senior Spanish colleague, Cardinal Pelayo, and his junior, Cardinal Guillermo the former abbot of Sahagún, Gil Torres did not become involved in diplomatic missions abroad.[39] Rather, he remained at the curia, active as an auditor of disputes, sometimes in combination with Cardinal Pelayo, until the latter's death in 1230. But it would be too wearying to repeat here the details of these that are recoverable from the Vatican registers and elsewhere.[40] Suffice it to say that although, by contrast with both both Melendo of Osma and Cardinal Pelayo,[41] Cardinal Gil enjoys no reputation as a glossator, and that descriptions of him as 'prestigioso canonista' and 'jurista de gran reputación en la curia pontificia'[42] appear excessive, he was nevertheless well served by that expertise in procedural law which would be exemplified in the following generation by the Zamoran author of the *Summa aurea de ordine iudiciario*, Fernando Martínez.[43]

---

[38]   P. Chaplais (ed.), *Diplomatic Documents Preserved in the Public Record Office*, I, *1101–1272* (London, 1964), nos. 153, 184. For further details see W. Maleczek, *Papst und Kardinalskolleg von 1191 bis 1216* (Vienna, 1984), 144, 265.

[39]   Cf. J.M. Powell, *Anatomy of a Crusade, 1213–1221* (Philadephia, 1986); A. Quintana Prieto, 'Guillermo de Taillante, abad de Sahagún y cardenal de la iglesia romana', *Anthologica Annua*, xxvi–vii (1979–80), 11–83.

[40]   For these see Linehan, *Spanish Church*, 280–85. See now M.J. Branco, 'Portuguese ecclesiastics and Portuguese affairs near the Spanish cardinals in the Roman curia (1213–1254), *Carreiras eclesiásticas no Ocidente cristão (séc. XII–XIV)* (Lisbon 2007), 79–100.

[41]   Cf. S. Kuttner, *Gratian and the Schools of Law* (London, 1983), *ad indicem*; G. Fransen, 'Les gloses de Melendus et l'apparat d'Alain l'Anglais sur le Décret de Gratien', *Cahiers de Fanjeaux*, xxix; L'Église et le droit dans le Midi (XIIIe–XIVe s.) (Toulouse, 1994), 21–35.

[42]   Cit. Linehan, *Spanish Church*, 277; Serrano, *D. Mauricio*, 71.

[43]   A. Pérez Martín, 'Estudiantes zamoranos en Bolonia', *Studia Zamorensia*, ii (1981), 23–66 at 34–7; idem, 'El Ordo iudiciarius "Ad summam noticiam" y sus derivados', *Historia. Instituciones. Documentos*, viii (1981), 195–266 at 254ff; ix (1982), 327–423 at 354ff. Further revelations may be expected from investigation of the connexion of this man with the jurist Ferrandus Zamorensis whose *siglum* is found attached to various *additiones* and *summulae* in the Liber Extra MS. Pistoia, Comunale Forteguerriana A.65: information kindly supplied by Dr Martin Bertram. Cf. G. Murano *et al.*, *I manoscritti medievali della provincia di Pistoia* (Florence, 1998), 95–7. In the papal chancery Bern[ardus] Zamorensis was active as both scribe and proctor in the mid-1270s: Linehan, *Spanish Church*, 295n.

Despite the best efforts at the time of the chapters of both Tarragona and Toledo to recruit him as their archbishop and the assurances of various historians since, most recently the author of a work on the diocese of Ciudad Rodrigo who remembers him as 'el cardenal Gil Robles' (*que es otra cosa*), Cardinal Gil never returned to Spain.[44] The belief that he did so arises from a confusion between the functions of delegate and legate ('delegado' and 'legado'). Accordingly, the description of him as 'Visitador Apostólico' of Burgos in 1252[45] is without foundation.

Instead Spain came to him. It came to him, at the papal curia, in the form of contingents of prelates and *capitulares* anxious to negotiate under his chairmanship there the division between bishop and chapter of their *mensae communes* and the assignment of particular rents to particular members of the chapter. These constitutions, starting with those for Salamanca in April 1245, had the practical purpose of placing the cathedral and other churches of the kingdom of Castile on a sounder economic footing and of minimising occasions of strife within their governing bodies. Curiously, no such constitutions were adopted at Zamora itself at this time.[46] Can that have been because the bishop of Zamora, Bishop Pedro 'the Good' (the cardinal's nephew, it will be remembered) may not have been overly anxious to surrender to the chapter certain prerogatives, prerogatives of the sort which the cardinal was insisting that other Castilian and Leonese bishops must surrender?

The economic and social objectives of D. Gil's constitutions were described by Mansilla in 1945 and discussed again in 1971.[47] A further purpose might now be suggested, namely that they were part of a concerted response on the part of the papacy to Fernando III's attempt in these years to effect a revolution from above by governing the Castilian Church through the agency

---

[44]     J.J. Sánchez-Oro Rosa, *Orígenes de la iglesia en la diócesis de Ciudad Rodrigo. Episcopado, monasterios y órdenes militares (1161–1264)* (Ciudad Rodrigo, 1997), 194.

[45]     Blanco Díez, 'Los arcedianos', 274. V. Beltran de Heredia, *Cartulario de la Universidad de Salamanca (1218–1600)*, I (Salamanca, 1970), 61, 71, is similarly mistaken.

[46]     *Pace* J. Sánchez Herrero, *Las diocesis del Reino de León. Siglos XIV y XV* (León, 1978), 98 ('También hacia 1240 elaboró [Gil Torres] unas constituciones para la catedral de Zamora'), what the source cited ('ACZ, *Liber Constitutionum*') actually states is that it was not until 1266 was even a preliminary division of the *mensa communis* was achieved: ACZ, 10/4, fos. 96rb–97vb. The assignment of particular *praestimonia* to particular *personatus*, dignities and others, in the manner of the procedures adopted by Cardinal Gil, must therefore have come later, at a date unspecified in the *Liber Constitutionum*, fos. 105vb–108rb. See further Linehan, 'Economics of episcopal politics', 10.

[47]     D. Mansilla, *Iglesia castellano-leonesa y curia romana en los tiempos del rey San Fernando* (Madrid, 1945), 195ff; Linehan, *Spanish Church*, 269–75.

of infantes: a royal strategy without parallel in post-Hildebrandine Europe, and for earlier generations of Spanish historians unthinkable behaviour in 'un rey santo', but one which had been facilitated by the virtual elimination of D. Rodrigo Jiménez de Rada as a political force after 1230.[48] Hence, incidentally, the chapter of Toledo's desire to secure D. Gil as their archbishop in 1247, an ambition in which they were disappointed. All that they secured of him (*via* Archbishop Sancho of Castile) was the silver enamelled bowl 'con reliquias' 'que fue del cardenal don Gil' listed in the inventory of the sacristy of that church in 1277.[49]

Now that item had been repatriated by D. Sancho (the Infante-archbishop of Toledo, son of Fernando III) in respect of debts of his predecessors, D. Rodrigo and D. Juan de Medina, for which don Gil had gone surety,[50] or it was a bequest – which in the absence of any such endowment at Toledo must be adjudged unlikely.[51] But not more than that, because although by 1311 the papal library at Avignon possessed a copy of the cardinal's will bound into a handsome paper cartulary,[52] the text of it has not survived. All we know about it is that it charged Cardinal Giovanni Orsini (the future Pope Nicholas III) and D. Gil's *nepos* Pedro Benítez (the future Bishop Pedro II of Zamora) with the task of collecting debts owed to him.[53] On his death in November 1254, the cardinal to whom had been entrusted the last wishes of others – Cardinal Pelayo[54] and the exiled Archbishop Silvestre Godinho of Braga (yet another glossator)[55] – left no mark of his own.

---

[48]     Hernández and Linehan, *Mozarabic Cardinal*, 54–9; P. Linehan, 'D. Rodrigo and the government of the kingdom' [here, item 3].

[49]     A[rchivo de la] C[atedral] Toledo, X.12.B.1.1. For the date 1277 (rather than 1281, as proposed by R. Gonzálvez Ruiz, *Hombres y libros de Toledo* (Madrid, 1997), 709), see Hernández and Linehan, *Mozarabic Cardinal*, 168.

[50]     AC Toledo, O.4.L.1.18; Hernández and Linehan, *Mozarabic Cardinal*, 167.

[51]     Above, n. 2.

[52]     F. Ehrle (ed.), *Historia Bibliothecae Romanorum Pontificum tum Bonifatianae tum Avenionensis ennarata* (Rome, 1890), 82, no. 485.

[53]     Linehan, *Spanish Church*, 217n. (now printed, J. M. Ruiz Asencio, *CdACL*, VI *(775– 1230), VIII (1230–1269)* (León, 1993), 2276); A. Paravicini Bagliani, *I testamenti dei cardinali del Duecento* (Rome, 1980), 14.

[54]     Fernández Catón, *CdACL*, VI, nos. 1966–7 (Jan. 1230).

[55]     Who at Città di Castello in July 1244 appointed him his sole executor ('confido tantum de domino meo Egidio cardinali...'): I. da Rosa Pereira, 'Silvestre Godinho, um canonista português', *Lumen*, xxvi (1962), 691–8 at 693–5; Kuttner, *Gratian and the Schools of Law*, VII, 310 & R. Note also the will of Archbishop João Egas of Braga (?Oct. 1255) recording his bequest to the Roman house of Santa Anastasia (O.Cist.) of the *hereditas* 'de S. Marina de Oleiros

But, as said, Spain came to him, and came to him in droves. His curial household hummed with Spanish visitors and Spanish proctors. His own mark on the dorse of papal letters testifies to the personal interest he took in the affairs of all the peninsular kingdoms. All this has already been described and although, if space permitted, more might be said about it; and more lists of names made *ad infinitum*,[56] here attention may be more usefully addressed to two different issues, namely signs of change both in the cardinal's Zamora during his years at the papal curia, and in the cardinal himself in the later years of his residence there.

As to the first, it is to be noted that soon after the death of D. Florencio (sometime before November 1237),[57] the frenetic activity of Zamora's jurists seems to have abated. So where had all the Zamoran jurists gone? To Salamanca? Presumably. To Bologna? Evidently.[58] To royal service at Husillos? An interesting possibility.[59] Or to the papal curia and the household of Cardinal Gil? Certainly, if D. Florencio, who survived until half way through the cardinal's public career, was representative of the Zamora from which Gil Torres emerged, it is the cardinal's own nephew, Master Esteban the abbot of Husillos, who may be regarded as epitomizing the latter part of it. One of the mega-pluralists of his generation, with a portfolio extending from Prague to Palencia, in August 1252 Master Esteban was provided by Innocent IV to one of Zamora's two archdeaconries (of which in fact he had already been in possession for at least seven years).[60]

But well before 1252 pluralism on this scale had created disaffection and tension in Zamora. For whereas, in his will of 1230 the precentor of Zamora,

---

quam comparavi de morabetinis quos mihi dedit Egidius cardinalsi de argento quod sibi dimisit [Silvester]': Braga, Arquivo Distrital, Liber de testamentis , no. 19.

[56] See meanwhile Peter Linehan, 'Proctors representing Spanish interests at the papal court, 1216–1303', *Archivum Historiae Pontificiae*, xvii (1979) [repr. Linehan, *Past and Present in Medieval Spain* (Aldershot, 1992)], nos. 485a–c, 523–4 (for bishop and chapter of Palencia, Apr. 1247, 'Sanctorum Cosme et Damiani'; for bishop and chapter of Burgos, May 1252, 'dominus Egidius cardinalis'); also for bishop of Lisbon, Nov. 1231, 'd[omi]n[u]s Egidius [Hugonīs (?)]: IAN/TT, Cx. Bulas, mç. 35 no. 10. Usually of course the donkey work was done by others, many of them the cardinal's chaplains: Linehan, *Spanish Church*, 280–86.

[57] Porto, Arquivo Distrital, Mitra da Sé do Porto, pergaminhos, caixa 1867, n. 7.

[58] Pérez Martín, 'Estudiantes zamoranos', 31–3.

[59] Amongst the many other benefices Master Esteban had acquired since 1229 was the secular abbacy of Husillos, which he had added to his portfolio by November 1251.

[60] Linehan, *Spanish Church*, 294–5; ACZ, TN, fo. 135v (Lera, 532); *Reg. Inn. IV*, 5912. Stephanus Geraldi, the canon who appears in the capitular record in 1217 and 1220 (ACZ, 17/37, 31/I/2: Lera, 308, 337), is not seen there again.

Garsias de Uliolo, had acknowledged that all the advantages he had enjoyed since his boyhood, 'in scolis' and elsewhere, he owed to the church of Zamora,[61] in May 1233, Bishop Martín Rodríguez complained to Gregory IX that over the previous seventeen years, at the instance of Cardinal Gil *inter alios*, thirteen of Zamora's benefices had been awarded by papal provision to outsiders, with the result that there had been none to spare for local men who had had spent their entire lives in the service of the church. And the pope acknowledged the justice of the bishop's complaint, conceding that favours shown to individuals 'were injurious if they redounded to the disadvantage of the many.'[62]

Now here was a startling statement of principle, and one to which historians of the period have not given sufficient attention. For sentiments such as these were wholly subversive of the practice and system of papal provisions upon which the operation of the thirteenth-century Church at large depended. At issue was the very morality of that practice and system. What the papal *obiter* implied was the need for fairness and moderation, for 'moderation in applying the rules of positive law, and in softening the rigours of the law according to the circumstances in unusual cases' – to quote a contemporary translator of Aristotle's Nichomachean Ethics on the Aristotelian concept of épieíkeia, a concept corrresponding to what Catholic theologians used to describe as an 'outward sign of inward grace', the inward grace in this case manifesting itself (and again I quote) in 'thoughtfulness, modesty and love of self-knowledge', in short what we would call a spirit of equity.[63]

As the bishop's complaints of 1233 make clear, in Zamora the argument for selflessness cut no ice. There, as elsewhere, the situation continued unchanged, because the mind of the pope and the hand of the papal chancery were not effectively co-ordinated. Since there was no reason in canon law why provisions to benefices in the diocese of Zamora should have affected the cathedral church of Zamora at all,[64] if they did it can only have been because

---

[61]    'Cum (…) ego Garsias, cantor Zamorensis ecclesie, a puericia mea de bonis ecclesie alitus et nutritus ab eadem, non meis meritis set sola sua gratia multa in scolis et alibi receperim beneficia...': ACZ, TN, fos. 88v–89r (Lera, 431).

[62]    'Quam injuriosa est gratia que fit uni si in grauamen uideatur plurium redundare': *Reg. Greg. IX*, 1318.

[63]    R. W. Southern, *Robert Grosseteste. The growth of an English mind in medieval Europe*, 2nd edn (Oxford, 1992), 289.

[64]    Although not enshrined in canon law until the end of the century (VI 3.4.4), according to Bonaguida de Arezzo (his 'Consuetudines curiae Romanae') the rule was already observed in the papal curia of his day 'quod generale mandatum pape super provisione alicuius de aliqua canonia in aliqua civitate vel diocesi non extendatur ad ecclesiam cathedralem' (cit. G.

someone at headquarters with an interest in the matter was making them do so. And that someone can only have been the Zamoran cardinal. In 1234, and again in 1236, the pontiff was again alerted to the dire consequences for laity as well as clergy of the disruption of the local clerical economy.[65] What made them so dire were the unemployment and its effects. In the overpopulated Europe of the 1230s that was the case everywhere. But nowhere more so than in a community whose temper was anyway volatile, as the social history of twelfth-century Zamora attests,[66] and where it was not just unemployment that was the problem, but also – given the evidence of high-grade juristic expertise in the vicinity – *graduate* unemployment. If consequences so far-reaching could follow – or be thought to have followed – upon the ownership of a dead fish, what was the response to invasion of the career structure by aliens and absentees likely to be?

Violence remained endemic. Not long after his promotion as cardinal, Gil Torres had to intervene on behalf of one of his clerics (another Gil), charged with having caused the death of 'a certain scholar' who reportedly had attacked him.[67] By 1249 such emotions feeding the development of a clerical proletariat, with 'los clérigos del choro que non an racion' the recipients of two bequests from the layman D. Mateo, and two years later with 'la confraría de los clérigos' similarly favoured in the will of the precentor García Peláez.[68] (Also present at the deathbed of D. Mateo were representatives of another element in Zamoran society whose presence tended to disturb the delicate ecology of thirteenth-century society. These were the mendicant orders, in the case of Zamora the Dominican Order in particular, which by 1230 at the latest had begun to impact on Zamoran society.)[69]

---

Barraclough, 'The English royal chancery and the papal chancery in the reign of Henry III', *Mitteilungen des Instituts für österreichische Geschichtsforschung*, lxii [1954], 365–78 at p. 376 n. 16).

[65]    *Reg. Greg. IX*, 2009, 3258 (Aug. 1236); Domínguez Sánchez, *Documentos de Gregorio IX*, 379. 579.

[66]    E. Fernandez-Xesta y Vázquez, '"El motín de la trucha" y sus consecuencias sobre don Ponce Giraldo de Cabrera', *Primer Congreso de la Historia de Zamora* (Zamora, 1991), III, 261–83.

[67]    *Reg. Hon. III*, 1367 (DM, 170), May 1218.

[68]    ACZ, 18/15, 18/12a (Lera, 550, 563).

[69]    'A los predicadores el so lecho con una cocedra e con tres xumazos. (...) E esta manda lexa en mano del chantre, presentibus predicatoribus duobus et multis aliis': Lera, 550; Linehan, *Ladies of Zamora*, 1–11. The Order's rising stock is indicated by the level of bequests during these years: four maravedís (Pedro Pérez, 'hermano de Vimani': ACZ, 18/2, Aug. 1230); five maravedís (Martín Martínez, canon: ACZ, 18/6, July 1236); ten maravedís (García Peláez: ACZ, 18/12ª, 1251): Lera, 427, 476, 563.

In the view of some historians, it was not only D. Mateo who was moribund in 1249. So also was the medieval Church itself. In which case, one of those responsible for its condition was D. Gil Torres. For he it was who had been instrumental in dismantling the stringent disciplinary programme imposed by the papal legate John of Abbeville.[70] True, he was viewed otherwise at the time, as the case-sensitive medic who rejected a universal panacea and instead responded to the needs of the individual patient.[71] Not for nothing perhaps were his cardinalatial titulars Saints Cosmas and Damian, the patron saints' of doctors. It was by shifting responsibility for the aforementioned scholar's death to the medic who had attended him that the cardinal secured the acquittal of the cleric of his who had struck the fatal blow.[72]

As to the Church at large, however, and to the church of Zamora in particular, it was the likes of *el sobrinísimo*, Master Esteban, who struck that blow. As archdeacon of Zamora, he should have been there, keeping an eye on the place, functioning as the bishop's eye indeed, which was precisely how the role of archdeacons was defined.[73] On all the evidence so far, therefore, Gil Torres emerges in stark contrast to Innocent III, the pope who had stipulated that a cleric who had petitioned him for provision at Zamora be subjected to rigorous examination, the pope who had not promoted him cardinal.[74]

And so D. Gil would deserve to be remembered, were it not for some discrepant English evidence concerning his relationship with the Englishman who, first amongst all of the churchmen of his time, set his face against the abuses that Master Esteban characterised: that is, Robert Grossesteste, the bishop of Lincoln famous for lecturing Innocent IV and the cardinals in person and by letter on their misconduct of the government of the Church in general and the evils of pluralism in particular, and the author *inter alia* of the gloss on the concept of *épieíkeia*, reported by Walter Burley († *c*.1344), to which I referred earlier:

> Notandum est hic secundum Linconiensem quod hoc nomen epichia multas habet significationes. Nam uno modo significat studiositatem

---

[70] Linehan, *Spanish Church*, 20–34; idem, 'A papal legation and its aftermath: Cardinal John of Abbeville in Spain and Portugal, 1228–1229' (here, item I).

[71] J.L. Villanueva, *Viage literario a las iglesias de España*, V (Madrid, 1806), 286; Linehan, *Spanish Church*, 279n.

[72] '…qui non tam propter acerbitatem vulneris quam imperitiam medici, ut creditur, expiravit': *Reg. Hon. III*, 1367.

[73] The address of *Reg. Inn. IV*, 5806 (5 March 1252) establishes that Esteban was archdeacon of the city.

[74] Mansilla, *Inocencio III*, 134.

i. virtuositatem et decentiam et moderationem et modestiam et amorem cognitionis sui ipsius qualis sit in virtute ex prudentium et cognoscentium ipsum iudicio. Alio modo significat virtutem cognoscitivam moderaminis legum: qualiter scilicet leges positivae de his quae ut frequentius et in pluribus contingunt non sunt obervandae in aliquibus casibus quae contingunt raro et paucioribus, sed moderandus est earum rigor secundum circumstantias rarius accidentes cuius rei exempla satis inferius patebunt. Haec Linconiensis.[75]

Cardinal Gil was not one of the cardinals present at the confrontation of 1250.[76] But he had been in contact with Grosseteste since at least 1229–32 when he had written to him on behalf of his nephew Petrus Bonus (the future Bishop Pedro I),[77] a letter to which the then archdeacon of Leicester might well have replied, as he had replied tongue-in-cheek to another cardinal regarding an Italian providee, that this son of the south was unlikely to flourish in sodden Lincolnshire.[78] Moreover, in 1245 the two men met at Cluny.[79] Then, in 1253, Grosseteste refused to obey a papal mandate of provision on behalf of one of the pope's own nephews, denouncing the system of provisions as encompassing the 'most manifest destruction' of the Church, and delivering a

---

[75] Publ. M. Grabmann, *Forschungen über die lateinischen Aristotelesübersetzungen d. xiii. Jhdts.*; Beiträge zur Gesch. der Philosophie des Mittelalters, xvii, 5–6 (Münster.i.W., 1916), 252.

[76] S. Gieben, 'Robert Grosseteste at the papal curia, Lyons 1250. Edition of the documents', *Collectanea Franciscana*, xli (1971), 340–93 at p. 350. Cf. J. Goering, 'Robert Grosseteste at the papal curia': Jacqueline Brown and William P. Stoneman, eds, *A Distinct Voice. Medieval Studies in Honor of Leonard E. Boyle, O.P.* (Notre Dame, Ind.), 1997, 253–76 at p. 257 n. 22.

[77] 'Quando fui archidiaconus Leicestrensis, pro speciali et amicissimo mihi in Christo magistro P. bono nepote vestro, in archidiaconatu praedicto beneficiato, mihi subscripsistis familiarius' (Grosseteste to Gil Torres, ?1236, referring to the years 1229–32): H.R. Luard (ed.), *Roberti Grosseteste episcopi quondam Lincolniensis Epistolae*, Rolls Ser. (London, 1861), 127–8.

[78] 'A wise gardener in a cold region will know that he should choose plants from that region, for although they are not equal in quality to the luxuriant plants of warmer climes, they will at least bear fruit': cit. L.E. Boyle, 'Robert Grosseteste and the pastoral care', *Medieval and Renaissance Studies*, viii (1979), 3-51 at 17-18. There was also the language question. Cf. the high-minded refusal of another English prelate to award a benefice to an Italian client of the future Boniface VIII, 'quoniam, ut nobis dicitur, non solum linguae Anglicanae inscius est, verum etiam satis literaliter loqui nescit': C.T. Martin (ed.), *Registrum epistolarum Fratris Johannis Peckham, archiepiscopi Cantuarensis*, Rolls Ser. (London, 1882-5), I. 351 (May 1282).

[79] Reported in the Cluny Chronicle, cit. Hernández and Linehan, *Mozarabic Cardinal*, 43, and referring to Grosseteste as 'episcopus Lingonensis'.

lecture to Innocent IV of all pontiffs on the meaning of 'plenitudo potestatis'. Grosseteste's finest letter, the English chronicler Matthew Paris called it.[80] And Paris had more to report. When the letter was read out, the pontiff was incandescent, and threatened terrible reprisals against the man he was later to describe (again according to Matthew Paris) as one of his two greatest enemies. But the cardinals restrained him. The bishop of Lincoln was renowned both for his sanctity and for his learning, they reminded him. Moreover, 'what the bishop said was true.' 'Thus spoke lord Egidius the Spanish cardinal', Paris reported, 'and others whose own consciences were touched.'[81] Had he known the language, Paris might have described the intervention of don Gil and his colleagues as a plea for *épieíkeia.*.

It was Paris who reported that Cardinal Gil was 'almost a centenarian' when he died in 1254,[82] as to which he is scarcely to be believed. (For Matthew Paris, most elderly gentlemen were 'almost centenarians', Pope Gregory IX, for example, who was probably only in his seventies when he died in 1241). But Paris also described the Zamoran cardinal as incorruptible and as a unique pillar of truth and justice at the Roman court: 'columna veritatis et justitiae', and that was a judgement confirmed by Innocent IV himself. When refusing to countenance his election to Toledo seven years earlier, Innocent had described him the 'columpna firmissima' on which the stability of both the Roman Church and the Church at large depended.[83] Coming from a pope such an encomium was almost a cliché of course. But coming from the English chronicler for whom on the whole the only good cardinal was a dead cardinal, it was remarkable. And all the more remarkable was it in view of his career as a trafficker in benefices, culminating in the activities of the *sobrinísimo* in the very last year of both his life and that of the pontiff whom his successor, according to Paris, described as 'venditor ecclesiarum'.[84]

Hence the paradox, an explanation for which eludes me. For Paris, as it is now acknowledged, was on the whole rather well informed on the

---

[80] 'Breviter autem recolligens dico, quod Apostolicae sedis sanctitas non potest nisi quæ in ædificationem sunt, et non in destructionem, hæc enim est potestatis plenitudo, omnia posse in ædificationem. Hæ autem quæ vocant provisiones; non sunt in ædificationem sed in manifestissimam destructionem; non igitur eas potest beata sedes Apostolica [acceptare]': *Epp. Grosseteste*, 437; Southern, *Grosseteste*, 290-1.

[81] '..."Ut enim vera fateamur, vera sunt quæ dicit. (...)". Hæc dixerunt dominus Ægidius Hispanus cardinalis et alii, quos propria tangebat conscientia': *Chronica Majora*, ed. H.R. Luard, Rolls Ser., V (London, 1880), V. 393; *ibid.*, 460.

[82] Ibid., 529 (cit. Linehan, *Spanish Church*, 278n.); IV (London, 1887), 162.

[83] *Reg. Inn. IV*, 3654.

[84] *Chron. Majora*, V, 492.

Roman matters he reported.[85] Can it have been that it was *only* in his dealings with Grosseteste that the cardinal exhibited the characteristics so admired by the English chronicler? There is some reason for suspecting as much.[86] Alternatively, or additionally, may it be that after all he really *was* very old when he died, that in his final years he had lost not only the plot but also control of his stylistically interesting seal[87] and that Maestre Esteban and others were operating in his name whilst the cardinal himself was afflicted with Alzheimers and in a Roman old people's home, though enjoying remissions frequent enough to enable him to attend the occasional consistory and, as a venerable, and therefore indulged member of the college of cardinals, occasionally to speak out there, as he is reported to have done in favour of Grosseteste (for example).

Though none of them is decisive, there are various reasons for entertaining such suspicions. There is the fact that don Gil had ceased to subscribe papal privileges as early as July 1246.[88] Then there is the notable acceleration after 1252 of provisions in favour of persons allegedly related to him, and, if so, also of course related to Master Esteban and Bishop Pedro I. Now in theory, petitions for such provisions were subject to close scrutiny at the curia, being publicly read out no fewer than three times. That close observer of the curial scene, Bonaguida de Arezzo, described the process as analogous to a process that Romans really were concerned be have done properly, namely the process of baking bread. For many hands were involved, as well as fire, water and cool

---

[85]  Southern, *Grosseteste*, 6–13, 291–2. Cf. J. McEvoy, *Robert Grosseteste* (Oxford, 2000), 64–6.

[86]  His reported inability to determine the dispute between the papal subdeacon John of Vercelli and the archdeacon of Buckingham (dioc. Lincoln) in January 1236 was subsequently ascribed to his absence from the curia. But if so, where was he? *Reg. Greg. IX*, 2948, 4836–9; *Reg. Inn. IV*, 568.

[87]  For the following description of which I am indebted to Professor Julian Gardner: 'Vesica showing two standing nimbed male figures on architectural plinth supported by foliate(?) capital within frame moulding. The left beardless figure approaches from the left with right hand raised. He holds a round object (?jar) in left hand. Frontal bearded figure on right turns head towards left towards companion. He raises his right hand in blessing. Holds a book(?) in left hand. The drapery style of the figures is timidly gothic, but there is not enough evidence to say where from. It could be Spanish or French. If you compare sculpture *c*.1250, say Burgos or Reims, it precedes anything like this in Rome by about a generation. But so much metalwork is lost one can't be certain.' Damaged impressions are preserved in Cuéllar, Archivo parroquial, no. 11t (Lyons, 25 Jan. 1250), and AC Burgos, vol. 7.i, fo. 370 (Perugia, 1 July 1252).

[88]  A. Paravicini Bagliani, *Cardinali di curia e 'familiae' cardinalizie dal 1227 al 1254* (Padua, 1972), 424–5.

before, like good loaves, petitions could be declared 'done'.[89] Such was the theory. But it was a theory to which all too often curial practice in the last years of the pontificate of Innocent IV failed to conform. Take, for example, the case of the papal letter of March 1252 addressed to Bishop Pedro of Zamora in favour of his *nepos* Francisco, described as 'son of Teresa, niece (or so you say: *ut asseris*) of Cardinal Gil.'[90]

*Ut asseris.* Now this hardly sounds like good baking practice, this failure to check that it was wheat not sand that the supplier's sack contained. Furthermore, there was the allegation made by Bishop Pedro Pérez of Salamanca early in the pontificate of Alexander IV, that after the cardinal's death his seal-matrix had been appropriated by interested parties 'in those parts' and used to fabricate letters which purported to 'interpret' and thereby extend to other churches of the city and diocese of Salamanca the restrictions on the appointment of aliens contained in the cardinal's constitutions for the cathedral chapter: an allegation which, because in the following March it was found to be proven,[91] inevitably implicates Master Esteban de Husillos. There

---

[89] 'Et nota, quod omnes litterae beneficiales sunt legendae coram domino papa. Leguntur primo in petitione, secundo in nota, tertio in littera grossa, at aliter transire non sinuntur, et per multas manus transeunt, et quasi per ignem et aquam currunt ad refrigerium, et ad magnam maturitatem decoquuntur': *Summa introductoria super officio advocationis in foro ecclesie*, ed. A. Wunderlich, *Anecdota quae processum civilem spectant* (Göttingen, 1841), 332.

[90] 'nato Tarasie, nepte, ut asseris, dilecti filii E. Sanctorum Cosme et Damiani diaconi cardinalis': *Reg. Inn. IV*, 5808. And the bad old ways continued into the next pontificate. In October 1257, three years after the death of don Gil, Egidius Guillelmi received a dispensation to enjoy the church of S. Frontón, Zamora 'cum cura animarum' in plurality with his prebends in the chapters of Zamora and Palencia, on account of his alleged relationship with the cardinal 'cuius nepos esse diceris': C. Bourel de la Roncière *et al.* (eds.), *Les Registres d'Alexandre IV* (Paris, 1895–99), 2298.

[91] '(…) Super hoc [the 'interested parties'] litteras cardinalis eiusdem post ipsius obitum in illis partibus, ostenderunt', D. Pedro reported, continuing: 'Verum quia in partibus istis, pro eo quod sigillum prefati cardinalis, non fractum post ipsius obitum, apud quosdam remansisse dicitur, huiusmodi littere admodum sunt suspecte': *ibid.*, 747 (Aug. 1255). The finding of the judges delegate to whom the matter was referred (or rather, of one of them together with the canon of León to whom the others had remitted their authority) is found appended to the transcript of Alexander IV's mandate in A[rchivio] S[egreto] V[aticano], Reg. Vat. 46, fo. 129r. In the failure of the 'pars concilii, canonicorum et portionariorum' to appear at the hearing, and for that reason alone, '(…) quia nobis per ipsam ordinationem cum vero filo et vera bulla nobis exhibitam ac alias plene constitit de premissis, habito peritorum consilio prefatas ordinationem et interpretationem auctoritate apostolica denunciamus secundum mandatum apostolicum non tenere ac reverendum patrem episcopum et capitulum Salamantinum, clerum et populum civitatis et diocesis Salamantini ad earum observationem iuxta mandatum apostolicum non teneri' (E. Langlois (ed.), *Les registres de Nicolas IV* (Paris, 1887–93), 6365): a judgment that appeared to

is also the deletion from the papal register itself (a remarkable enough event in any circumstances) of two letters of provision, both of mid-August 1252 and both in favour of Master Esteban de Husillos, and their replacement by other letters hedged round by even more *non obstante* clauses.[92] And finally there is that plethora of *non obstante* clauses itself.

For it was the profligate use of such clauses in papal letters of provision that was bringing the entire system of papal provisions into disrepute. As Leonard Boyle observed years ago, it was the 'supercumulation' of such clauses, clauses which negatived existing papal privileges without so much as acknowledging their existence, that had been fomenting the 'cataclysm' of vices by which mid thirteenth-century Church and society were beset.[93]

But then, just three weeks after receiving Grosseteste's final damaging indictment of his government of the Universal Church, Pope Innocent acknowledged the justice of the Englishman's criticisms. The pontiff's encyclical letter of October 1253, *Postquam regimini*, acknowledged that in the matter of papal provisions mistakes had been made. Serious mistakes. There had been dishonesty amongst petitioners and in the procedures. On occasion he himself had been prevailed upon to authorize provisions against his better judgement. In future, bishops and chapters and other patrons were to 'tear up' papal letters purporting to appoint foreigners to benefices in their gift.[94]

---

nullify not only the attempted 'interpretatio' but also Cardinal Gil's 'ordinatio' for the chapter, the earliest of his sets of constitutions, which Innocent IV had confirmed in May 1245: *Reg. Inn. IV*, 1262. This doubtless was why in 1291 the bishop of Salamanca (D. Pedro Fechor) was moved to seek copies of the documentation from the papal chancery. The influential comma before the word 'ostenderunt', supplied by Bourel de la Roncière to the text of the letter cited in the first sentence of this note, may be thought to imply that, as well as visiting Spain as cardinal (as some have imagined), Gil Torres had died 'in illis partibus', viz. in or near Salamanca. In fact, as the evidence of ASV, Reg. Vat. 24, fo. 90v makes clear, all that had happened 'in illis partibus' was that the 'interested parties' had published ('ostenderunt') their (spurious) letters there.

[92]   Archivio Segreto Vaticano, Reg. Vat. 22, fos. 202r–v, 203r (*Reg. Inn. IV*, 5913, 5919; cf. *ibid.*, 5951, 5992, printed A. Quintana Prieto, *La documentación pontificia de Inocencio IV (1243–1254)* (Rome, 1987), nos. 788, 785, 788, 790 respectively, where the editor complicates the task of comparison by substituting for the chancery's 'eidem' forms of address of his own devising.

[93]   Boyle, 'Grosseteste', 30–31, citing *Epp. Grosseteste*, no. 128 (p. 434). Cf. B. Tierney, 'Grosseteste and the theory of papal sovereignty', *Journal of Ecclesiastical History*, vi (1955), 1–17 at p. 15.

[94]   '...licitumque sit vobis universis, & singulis, tanquam nostris, in hâc parte, ministris, nostras seu legatorum nostrorum lacerare litteras, siquæ, statuto ipsi contrariæ, vobis, aut alicui vestrûm, fuerint presentatæ': T. Rymer, *Fœdera... fideliter exscripta.* [1727] (London, 1816), I.i.294 (A. Potthast, *Regesta pontificum Romanorum*, (Berlin, 1874–75), 15162).

*Postquam regimini*, which was issued on the pope's own motion ('proprio motu') was not only 'quite unusual' but also, as Boyle rightly remarks, 'dramatic'.[95] But in his conjecture that, as well as having been prompted by Grossesteste's latest outburst, the encyclical may have been directed exclusively at the English Church, he was mistaken.[96] In Castile, for example, the churches of Palencia and Segovia both secured copies.[97] The church of Zamora, however, did not – or, if it did, there is no sign of it in the cathedral archive now. And if it did not, perhaps that was because what *Postquam regimini* referred to was *foreign* providees. And, thanks to don Gil, all or most of Zamora's providees over the previous thirty years had been local men, the cardinal's own friends and relations. If the Zamoran cardinal had saved his native church from anything during that period, it was from the intrusion of *foreigners*, whether from Palermo or from Palencia.

Almost all we can know about don Gil Torres comes from the papal registers, and this may well give us a skewed view of him. After all, how would Grosseteste appear if that was all we had to judge him by? We have to remember that we know next to nothing about the cardinal's intellectual preparation. We have no correspondence between him and the Spanish rulers of his day. Yet correspondence there must have been, and in abundance, between them and the man who wrote so 'gracefully' to the bishop of Lincoln. What would we not give for sight of just part of it? Regarding the cardinal's role in the complex matter of Fernando III's relations with the papal curia, for example? Or the reasons for the lengthy delay in confirming Pedro I's episcopal election? And, above all, as contributing to a better understanding of the Cardinal of Zamora and providing him with the third dimension that, alas, he still lacks?

---

[95]   Boyle, 'Grosseteste', 34–5.

[96]   Ibid., 35–6, influenced perhaps by the fact that Potthast's principal sources for *Postquam regimini* were Matthew Paris and the (also English) Burton annalist. However, in stating that 'scholars in general have not paid [it] much attention' (p. 34), the author is absolutely correct. In his study of Grosseteste, for example, Southern does not so much as mention it.

[97]   AC Palencia, 2/1/59; AC Segovia, caj. 5, no. 12 (*aliter* Bulas, no. 9) (ed. respectively, and in both cases with numerous misreadings, Quintana Prieto, *Inocencio IV*, 928; L.-M. Villar García, *Documentación medieval de la catedral de Segovia (1115–1300)* (Salamanca, 1990), no. 154). The church of Santiago acquired a copy at one remove: AC Santiago de Compostela, leg. no. 13, 'Tumbillo de privilegios, concordias, constituciones', fos. 112r–113v.

# VIII

## LA CONQUISTA DE SEVILLA
## Y LOS HISTORIADORES [1]

No voy hablar sobre la reconquista de Sevilla en absoluto. Sobre lo que voy a hablar bien podría llamarse su «prehistoriografía» o historiografía previa en las obras de Lucas de Tuy y Rodrigo de Toledo (ninguna de las cuales alcanzó a historiar el año 1248, por supuesto). En primer lugar, hablaré del enfrentamiento ideológico que ambas obras presentan y cómo resolvieron las diferencias entre ellas los compiladores de la *Estoria de España* alfonsí. Se trata de algo que he expuesto *ad nauseam* en otra parte, por lo que trataré de no repetirme [2]. También tengo algunas nuevas ideas que compartir con ustedes, aunque todavía no estoy muy seguro de algunas de ellas.

Respecto a mi primer objetivo, sigo siendo de la opinión de que Lucas de Tuy y Rodrigo de Toledo estuvieron envueltos en una contienda por el control del presente y del futuro que se reflejó en sus peculiares y parciales reconstrucciones del pasado remoto.

Mientras trabajaba en la faceta eclesiástica de esta contienda, la que hoy nos ocupa, Georges Martin estaba investigando independientemente otra de sus dimensiones, en concreto, los relatos conflictivos de Lucas y de Rodrigo sobre los orígenes de Castilla, que publicó en su estudio magistral *Les Juges de Castille*. Al estudiar las diferencias en los relatos de la elección de los jueces de Castilla, Martin identifica (si simplificamos sus conclusiones) un don Lucas monárquico y un don Rodrigo aristocrático. Martin pone de manifiesto las libertades que los dos se tomaron con respecto al relato histórico que ambos conocieron para subordinarlo a sus fines ideológicos respectivos. Lucas el leonés manipula el orden de los sucesos con el fin de convertir la elección de los jueces en un acto de rebelión de la nobleza [3]. Rodrigo el castellano (castellano de adopción en realidad) reorganiza la narración de acuer-

---

[1] Quiero dar muy cordiales gracias a Inés Fernández-Ordóñez por haber discutido conmigo varios detalles de este trabajo y por su valerosa lucha con la traducción del mismo.
[2] *History and the Historians of Medieval Spain* (Oxford 1993), 350-412; «On further thought: Lucas of Toledo, Rodrigo of Toledo and the Alfonsine histories», *Anuario de Estudios Medievales*, 27/1 (1997), 415-36, esp. 425-32.
[3] *Les Juges de Castille. Mentalités et discours historique dans l'Espagne médiévale* (Paris 1992), 219, 233, n. 31; y en el mismo sentido LINEHAN, *History and the Historians*, 369, 371, 384, 405.

do con una visión alternativa de la sociedad en que la relación correcta entre el rey y la nobleza no es la hostilidad, sino la coexistencia[4].

Si tuviera una hora o dos, trataría de demostrarles a ustedes procesos similares en la forma en que los dos historiadores trataron el III Concilio de Toledo. Deben considerarse afortunados de que nuestro anfitrión posea un puño de hierro. Así que todo lo que diré sobre el III Concilio de Toledo es que mientras el Tudense presenta esa asamblea como un acontecimiento majestuoso y monárquico completamente dominado por Recaredo, en cambio, según el Toledano, se trataría de una reunión presidida por un monarca constitucional nada menos: «pontificibus et palacii primioribus, clero et milicia aprobantibus cum populo universo»[5]. En el año 589 tendríamos la primerísima reunión de las cortes en realidad[6].

El III Concilio de Toledo nos devuelve a la sección del pasado peninsular por cuyo control se enfrentaban Lucas y Rodrigo en los años inmediatamente anteriores a la reconquista —o incorporación— de Sevilla. El contexto nos lo ofrece el enfrentamiento por la primacía eclesiástica en el siglo VII (el siglo de san Isidoro) y las implicaciones seglares que el resultado de esa contienda tuvo en época de Fernando III. Para los contendientes la cuestión de la primacía no era menos fundamental que el relato de los jueces. Es más, existen muchos paralelismos fascinantes entre los dos casos. Los dos se relacionan con un mito fundacional y ambos se ocupan de la cuestión del ejercicio de la soberanía.

Para entender los orígenes inmediatos de la contienda historiográfica sobre la primacía necesitamos remontarnos a una otra incorporación, la incorporación de León a Castilla en 1230.

El *Chronicon mundi* de Lucas de Tuy ha sido descrito como una «crónica de la reconciliación, incluso de la unión» de esos dos reinos[7]. Ese juicio me parece discutible —como también me lo parece la conclusión del reciente editor de *De rebus Hispanie*. Es verdad que «es la crónica del Obispo de Tuy la que a partir de este momento [mediados del siglo VIII] va a servir de eje de la narración en el que se van engarzando las demás». También es cierto que «el Tudense es el telón de fondo en el que se van enmarcando las demás crónicas»[8]. Pero no se sigue de esto que existiese entre los dos historiadores una «estrecha amistad», o que (en sus palabras) «quizás sea ésta la causa de que el Toledano enmascare en lo posible los pasajes que recoge de él»[9].

Por mi parte sospecho que Rodrigo no sigue a Lucas con la sonrisa culpable que es la nota característica de todos los plagiadores, incluso de los plagiadores toledanos, sino más bien con una expresión profundamente preocupada, y con buenos motivos. Rodrigo camina armado de un detector de metales porque Lucas había sembrado minas a lo largo y a lo ancho de la historia del pasado, y en particular, en la historia de la sede de la primacía en el siglo VII.

---

[4] MARTIN, 270-95.

[5] *De rebus Hispanie*, ii. 15: «eidem concilio religiossisimus princeps deuotus aduenit gestaque concilii subscriptione firmauit abdicans, pontificibus...uniuerso, perfidiam...» (ed. J. FERNÁNDEZ VALVERDE, *Corpus Christianorum Continuatio Mediaevalis* 72/1 (Turnhout 1987), 62$_{14-15}$). Cf. *Chronicon Mundi*, ed. A. SCHOTTUS, *Hispania Illustrata*, IV (Frankfurt a.M., 1608), 50$_{14-16}$: «Cui concilio idem religiossisimus princeps interfuit, gestaque eius praesentia sua & subscriptione firmauit, abdicans cum omnibus suis perfidiam...»

[6] P. LINEHAN, «Impacto del III Concilio de Toledo en las relaciones Iglesia-Estado durante el Medioevo», *Concilio III de Toledo. XIV Centenario. 589-1989* (Toledo 1991), 433.

[7] M. RECUERO ASTRAY, «La conciencia histórica», L. SUÁREZ FERNÁNDEZ *et al.* (ed.), *León en torno a las Cortes de 1188*, (s.l., s.f.), 108.

[8] FERNÁNDEZ VALVERDE, xxxi, xxxiii.

[9] Ibid., xxxiii.

Por tanto, lo que tenemos que buscar no son las ocasiones en que Rodrigo sigue a Lucas, sino más bien aquéllas en que *no* le sigue.

Lucas tuvo dos principales fidelidades: León (tanto la ciudad como el reino) y, por extensión, San Isidoro, cuyos huesos estaban enterrados allí y cuyos milagros había recopilado previamente.

En cuanto a la primacía, la pregunta que esperaba respuesta era la siguiente. Según Lucas, en el III Concilio de Toledo Leandro de Sevilla había sido primado y, después de él, había continuado en el cargo su hermano Isidoro durante cuarenta años.[10] Así que ¿cómo era posible que, según el propio Lucas admitía, después de Isidoro hubiera disfrutado de la primacía San Ildefonso de Toledo? ¿Cómo podía dar cuenta Lucas de esta *translatio primacie* a mediados del siglo VII?

Bien, pudo hacerlo gracias a una crónica ficticia que atribuyó al mismo San Ildefonso, y en ello fue muy astuto, ya que Ildefonso era el Isidoro de Toledo.[11] Según esta pseudofuente, Theodisclus (o Theodistus) el griego, un villano que había adoptado el Islam, sucedió en Sevilla a Isidoro, con lo cual el rey Chindasvinto invitó a los obispos hispánicos a decidir por votación si la primacía debía permanecer en Sevilla o pasar a Toledo. Y los obispos eligieron Toledo.

Todo ello constituía por supuesto un anatema para don Rodrigo, para el que Toledo siempre había disfrutado de la primacía. Pero lo peor estaba por venir. Treinta años más tarde, afirmaba Lucas, el rey Wamba dispuso en su Hitación que Toledo continuaría disfrutando de ese honor sólo «mientras ello complaciese a esta sagrada asamblea» (*quandiu huic sancto coetui placuerit*). Y en la misma ocasión, de nuevo según Lucas, se describía a Sevilla como *hactenus prima*[12].

Para la iglesia de Toledo, las implicaciones de todo esto eran potencialmente catastróficas. Aquí se daba una «Donación de Chindasvinto» equivalente en sus consecuencias para Toledo a lo que representó la Donación de Constantino para los emperadores occidentales. Toledo quedaba en un estado de libertad condicional permanente, con su primacía sujeta a la transferencia en el momento en que le pareciese conveniente a «esta sagrada asamblea».

No resulta nada claro qué podría ser el equivalente en el siglo XIII a la «sagrada asamblea» de rey y obispos en tiempos de Wamba. Pero lo mejor que Rodrigo podría haber esperado era una asamblea mixta, semejante a su propia versión democrática del III Concilio de Toledo, por ejemplo, más bien que la de Lucas. El paralelismo que ofrecía la *translatio imperii* papal era desalentador. Si la primacía había sido transferida una vez, entonces podría serlo de nuevo, pero en otra dirección. Es más, era en este tiempo, al principio de la década de 1240, mientras Rodrigo estaba escribiendo su Historia (o cuando su equipo de investigadores la escribía para él) cuando la curia romana comenzó a explotar a fondo la Donación

---

[10] *Chronicon mundi*, 50$_{19}$, 52$_{41}$.

[11] «que personne n'á pu identifier»: MARTÍN, *Les Juges*, 205. De hecho es un personaje ficticio, como ya señaló Juan Bautista Pérez hace cuatrocientos años: J. VILLANUEVA, *Viage literario a las iglesias de Espana*, iii (Madrid, 1804), 322-6. Pero la «Crónica de Ildefonso» continuó viviendo. Ni siquiera Nicolás Antonio se dio cuenta de las objeciones de Pérez. Y es que la «Crónica» había echado raíces desde muy pronto. Según Juan GIL DE ZAMORA, contemporáneo de Alfonso X con fama de crítico, «Sanctus Illefonsus descripsit tempora Gothorum...usque ad octavum decimum [annum] Recensuyndi»: *De preconiis Hispanie*, ed. M. DE CASTRO Y DE CASTRO (Madrid 1955), 181. Sin embargo, el sabio franciscano no pudo citar al cronista.

[12] LINEHAN, *History and the Historians*, 376-9.

de Constantino como un arma contra el emperador[13]. Y entretanto, más cerca, en casa, la restauración del arzobispado de Sevilla era inminente. Para el arzobispo de Toledo la perspectiva era alarmante.

Así que don Rodrigo, que acababa de estar envuelto en una contienda judicial con Tarragona a causa de Valencia, se vio empujado ahora a una batalla historiográfica con Lucas debido a su condición de cónsul honorario de Sevilla.

Aunque para su arzobispo Toledo siempre había disfrutado de la primacía, sin embargo Lucas lo había puesto en serias dificultades al haber escrito antes y haber podido elegir el campo de batalla. Como Rodrigo desconocía qué otras armas secretas podía tener Lucas, se vio forzado a incluir la crónica fantasma de San Ildefonso entre sus fuentes (engañando así a la posteridad hasta Nicolás Antonio e incluso más allá). Es éste un error que también cometen los plagiarios de hoy en día. Rodrigo incluso menciona al ficticio Teodisclus, aunque para perjudicar a Sevilla, claro está, pero no percibe la dificultad que representaba adoptar el Islam en la Sevilla de 640[14]. Lucas se había puesto en ridículo por su incompetencia en cronología[15], pero sabía poner trampas al docto don Rodrigo.

Por otra parte, Rodrigo manipula sus materiales libremente. Al igual que Lucas, cambia fechas para adaptarlas a sus propósitos. Por ejemplo, anticipa el decreto conciliar *Cum longe lateque*, un texto clave a favor de las pretensiones de Toledo por la primacía, del año 681 a 675, del XII Concilio de Toledo, al que pertenecía, al XI. De esta manera podía neutralizar la versión que Lucas daba de la Hitación de Wamba[16]. Y es más, evita mencionar por completo este acontecimiento a pesar de que muy recientemente lo había empleado en su litigio sobre Valencia[17]. Parafraseando a Clausewitz, podemos decir que la historiografía no era para Rodrigo sino otra manera de continuar el litigio.

Llegados a este punto, debo subrayar por qué tenían lugar estas batallas sobre el pasado remoto al principio de la década de 1240: tenían lugar porque Sevilla estaba a punto de reconquistarse.

---

[13] Para el punto de partida de esta contienda, la letra de Gregorio IX a Federico II en octubre de 1236, véase D. MAFFEI, *La Donazione di Costantino nei giuristi medievali* (Milano, 1969), 76-8: «Gregorio IX utilizza, pertanto, decisamente il Constitutum. A lui si deve, fra altro, il pieno collegamento tra Constitutum e Translatio imperii».

[14] *De rebus Hispanie*, prologo, $6_{65}$-$7_{72}$: «Ea que ex libris beatorum Ysidori et Ildefonsi ... compilaui.» J. GÓMEZ PÉREZ asume que al mencionar a «Ildefonso» Rodrigo se estaba refiriendo a *Julián* de Toledo: «Manuscritos del Toledano», *Rev. de Archivos, Bibliotecas y Museos*, 60 (1954), 196. Pero al afirmar que Ildefonso había historiado el período comprendido entre el año quinto de Suinthila y el decimoctavo de Recesvinto (*De rebus Hispanie*, ii. 22), Rodrigo no puede estarse refiriendo a ninguna obra conocida de Julián ni al *De uiris illustribus* de Ildefonso. Parece más bien que Rodrigo cita a Ildefonso por precaución, simplemente porque Lucas lo había citado: *De rebus Hispanie*, ii. 21: $71_{10\text{-}1]}$. Cf. J. B. PÉREZ, cit. VILLANUEVA, *Viage literario*, iii. 325: «Ait Theodistum archiep. successise Isidoro in ecclesia Hispalensi. At tale nomen non legitur in catalogo archiepiscoporum Hispalensium veteris libri gotthici S. Aemiliani. Item in conciliis Toletanis usque ad XVII. subscribunt varii episcopi Hispalenses; nusquam tale nomen. Item nemo veterum talis historiae meminit... Ait dignitatem primaciae translatam ab Hispalensi ad Toletanam propter Theodistum. Primo non constat usquam de primacia Hispalensi. Secundo, tempore gothorum nusquam nomen primatis nisi pro metropolitano, ut in concilio sub Gundemaro; neque de contentione primaciae usquam loquuntur auctores eius temporis.»

[15] F. RICO, «Aristoteles Hispanus: en torno a Gil de Zamora, Petrarca y Juan de Mena», *Italia medioevale e umanistica*, 10 (1967), 143-4.

[16] LINEHAN, *History and the Historians*, 61, 366, 381-3.

[17] Ibid., 341, 381; L. VÁZQUEZ DE PARGA, *La división de Wamba* (Madrid 1943), 46.

Pero en 1248 don Lucas callaba y don Rodrigo había muerto. El futuro historiográfico reside en la *Estoria* alfonsí. Nosotros lo sabemos, pero es importante no olvidar que ellos no lo sabían. Dicho esto, don Rodrigo no consiguió ganar ninguna de sus batallas. En la medida en que los compiladores de la *Estoria* alfonsí fueron jueces del tribunal de última instancia de la historiografía hispánica, sus decisiones no fueron tan regularmente favorables al arzobispo de Toledo como suele suponerse[18]. Tanto en el III Concilio de Toledo como en el asunto de la *translatio primacie* prevaleció la versión de Lucas. Aunque Rodrigo era un estratega hábil, en materia de táctica Lucas tuvo la ventaja.

Ahora que estos dos casos (el III Concilio de Toledo y la *translatio primacie*) no son quizás tan sorprendentes, especialmente si ustedes consideran que algunos jueces tienen su precio y que también lo tienen todos los historiadores. Y puesto que esta parte de la *Estoria* alfonsí alcanzó su forma final durante un período del reinado del Rey Sabio cuando la causa de la monarquía, si no la del nacionalismo sevillano, estaba en ascenso.

«E pues que los arzobispos et los obispos ouieron fechas sus posturas et sus establescimientos, oyo [el rey] tod aquello que pusieran, et touolo por bien et pagosse ende et confirmolo», afirma la *Estoria* sobre Recaredo en 589[19]. Ese hito de la historia hispánica, descrito por algunos como el «bautismo» del pueblo español, se presenta en la primera historia nacional española como una confirmación rutinaria de un informe emitido por un comité episcopal. «Et touolo por bien...» El lenguaje es el lenguaje de la cancilleria real, empleando las *formulae* habituales que pueden encontrarse en 1001 cartas reales relativas a tierras, molinos y hornos[20].

Quizá no deberíamos sorprendernos de descubrir este lenguaje propio del gobierno en una historia nacional. Al fin y al cabo, la historia nacional era entonces, como lo es hoy, una ramificación de las tareas de gobierno. Esto no es lo que debe preocupar a los historiadores de hoy. Lo que debe preocupar a los historiadores de hoy es si pueden penetrar esa imponente fachada gubernamental, y en ese caso, si pueden encontrar el camino que conduce al departamento historiográfico de los reyes castellanos del siglo XIII (que por supuesto estaba siempre al otro lado del pasillo, en el cuarto de enfrente de la cancillería).

Por ello resulta sorprendente encontrar en esa parte de la *Estoria* que todavía se estaba elaborando en el reinado de Sancho IV paréntesis gratuitos que bien podrían haber sido introducidos por el mismo Lucas. Limitándome al relato de 1248 ofrecido por la *Estoria*, hay que destacar, por ejemplo, la descripción de Sevilla como el «capitolo del coronamiento real del Andalozia»[21], y la prominencia dada a la fiesta del traslado de «sant Esidro de Leon, arzobispo [*sic*] que fue de Seuilla» que cae en el 22 de diciembre, el día que Fernando III entró en Sevilla (descrita como «capital de todo ese sennorio del Andalozia») en lugar de en el día de S. Clemente, 23 de noviembre, el día en que se rindió la ciudad[22].

Sin embargo, aquí existe un problema textual, ya que no podemos estar seguros de que esta parte de *la Estoria*, llamada por Diego Catalán *Crónica particular de San Fernando*, fuera efectivamente compuesta en tiempos de Alfonso X. El primer testimonio que nos permite asegurar la composición de esta crónica es *la Crónica abreviada* de don Juan Manuel,

---

[18] LINEHAN, *History and the Historians*, 383-4; «On further thought», 424, 427-32.
[19] *Primera Crónica General de España*, c. 476, ed. R. MENÉNDEZ PIDAL (Madrid, 1955), 264b$_{10-15}$.
[20] For the *Estoria*'s account of the *translatio primacie* (ibid., c. 504, 278b$_5$-279a$_4$) see LINEHAN, «On further thought», 432.
[21] *Primera Crónica General*, c. 1075, 748b$_{49}$.
[22] Ibid., cc. 1125, 1129, 767b$_{10}$, 769b$_{21}$.

texto compuesto entre 1321 y 1325.[23] Por ello, puede conjeturarse con cierta seguridad que este relato de los hechos de 1248 no tuvo su origen en el reinado de Alfonso X. Pero tampoco pudo surgir en el de Sancho IV[24] cuando tanto la cancillería real como la historia regia estaban firmemente controlados por el más patriótico y despiadado toledano que había estado en la corte desde la muerte de don Rodrigo en 1247: un hombre para el que, al igual que para don Rodrigo, era impensable cualquier otro lugar que no fuera Toledo como el «capitolo del coronamiento real». Georges Martin incluso llega a hablar de una «versión toledana de la *Estoria de España*»[25]. Quizá esto sea ir demasiado lejos, pero antes de hablar de mi «patriótico y despiadado toledano», permitidme decir algo sobre lo que podría ser llamado «el concepto de Andalucía en el siglo XIII».

Hace años Maravall llamó la atención sobre el surgimiento al principio del siglo XIII de la forma romance *andaluz* para describir el área de España todavía bajo control musulmán en esas fechas.[26] Pero ignoro que nadie haya considerado la cuestión relacionada con la que se enfrentaron los historiadores latinos de esos años: esta es, cómo describir esa área. Para Lucas de Tuy carecía de nombre. Era simplemente *terra Maurorum*[27]. Sin embargo, existía un nombre, el nombre que usó un estricto contemporáneo de Lucas, el autor anónimo de la llamada *Crónica latina de los reyes de Castilla*, para describir *cismarina terra Maurorum: a saber, Handalucia*. Y ese autor incluso insinuó una etimología, *via* sus habitantes (*Handaluces*) «de los que algunos creen que son vándalos»[28].

Pero no todos estaban preparados para aceptar la etimología Vandalia/Andalucía, Rodrigo de Toledo entre ellos. En su *Hunnorum, Vandalorum [etc]...Historia*, Rodrigo la rechaza: *Andalucia, corrupto vocabulo, vulgariter appellamus*, objetó[29]. *Corrupto vocabulo*, dice, y con razón[30]. Y del mismo modo, en su *De rebus Hispanie*, lo que el autor anónimo de la historia latina había descrito como «Handalucia», Rodrigo insiste en llamarlo «Vandalia», o bien *Vandalia Hispanorum* o *cismarina Vandalia*[31].

¿Qué está pasando aquí? ¿O mejor, qué *no* está pasando? ¿Por qué se resiste el arzobispo de Toledo a aceptar el latinismo «[H]andalucia» entre la nómina de palabras latinas cuando, como hemos visto, su contemporáneo el anónimo autor de la *Crónica latina* no tiene ningún inconveniente en admitirlo? Y aunque anónimo, podemos saber con bastante seguridad quién fue: el obispo Juan de Osma y Burgos, colega episcopal de Rodrigo[32]. También sabemos que en otras ocasiones don Rodrigo no fue tan puntilloso en cuestiones etimológicas. Sus *mixti arabes* son notorios[33]. Además, estaba dispuesto a admitir nuevos to-

---

[23] D. CATALÁN, «Don Juan Manuel ante el modelo alfonsí: el testimonio de la *Crónica Abreviada*», *La Estoria de España de Alfonso X. Creación y evolución* (Madrid, 1992), 224-5.

[24] *Pace* las consideraciones *con*textuales aducidas por A. IGLESIA FERREIRAS, «Alfonso X, su labor legislativa y los historiadores», *Historia. Instituciones. Documentos*, 9 (1982), 20-41.

[25] En su estudio en prensa «L'escarboucle de Saint-Denis, le roi de France et l'empereur des Espagnes», *Saint-Denis et la royauté, en l'honneur de Bernard Guenée*.

[26] J. A. MARAVALL, *El concepto de España en la Edad Media*, 2ª ed. (Madrid, 1964), 228-9.

[27] *Chronicon mundi*, $114_{2, 5, 25, 56}$. Cf. «fines maurorum» ($115_{38}$); «frontaria maurorum» ($115_{59}$).

[28] «Sic enim uocatur cismarina terra Maurorum, unde et populi Handaluces uocantur, quod quidem credunt Vandalos esse»: *Crónica latina de los reyes de Castilla* [c. 53], ed. L. CHARLO BREA (Cádiz, 1984), 75.

[29] Ed. F. DE LORENZANA, *Patrum Toletanorum quotquot extant Opera*, III (Madrid, 1793; reimpr. Valencia, 1968), 234b.

[30] J. VALLVÉ BERMEJO, «El nombre de al-Andalus», *Al-Qantara*, 4 (1983) 301-55.

[31] *De rebus Hispanie*, vii. 25 (ed. cit., $247_8$); ix. 13 ($294_{20, 32}$).

[32] D. W. LOMAX, «The authorship of the *Chronique latine des rois de Castille*», *Bulletin of Hispanic Studies*, 40 (1963) 205-11.

[33] *De rebus Hispanie*, iii. 22 ($107_{60}$).

pónimos en su repertorio de latín. Escribiendo sobre los siglos IX y X, habla de *Bardulia quae nunc Castella dicitur*[34]. Y a partir de entonces, siempre habla de *Castella* y no vuelve a insistir en llamarla Bardulia.

Entonces, ¿por qué este puntillismo etimológico en el caso de *Vandalia*, especialmente en un momento en que el movimiento vernáculo iba tomando cada vez más fuerza? Hay tres puntos que no debemos olvidar: 1) que en esos mismos años el mismo obispo de Osma y de Burgos estaban a la cabeza de ese movimiento en la mismísima cancillería real[35]; 2) que don Rodrigo parece no haber compartido el entusiasmo vernacular de su colega en el episcopado[36], y 3) que, según observa Martin sobre los compiladores de la *Estoria* alfonsí (que no tuvieron inconveniente en traducir la «Vandalia» de Rodrigo como «Andalucía» de vez en cuando), el corazón del actividad del arzobispo late movido por lo que Martin llama «une intention de propos»[37].

Teniendo esto en cuenta, sugiero que la insistencia de Rodrigo en la *cismarina Vandalia* no se explica por preocupación alguna con la otra «Vandalia»: la «Vandalia ultramarina» (aquellas partes del norte de África que un siglo más tarde Álvaro Pelayo recordara a Alfonso XI que constituían su propiedad *iure hereditario*, como heredero de los reyes visigóticos)[38], sino por otra más cerca de casa, en el mismo Toledo. Me inclina a pensar así el hecho de que menos de cincuenta años después de la muerte de don Rodrigo «Vandalia» reaparece, y de nuevo en un contexto toledano.

Durante esos casi cincuenta años la contienda entre Toledo y Sevilla parece haberse apagado. Durante ese tiempo ninguna de las dos iglesias había tenido un arzobispo tan interesado por la historia. Toledo o había estado ocupada por infantes o no había tenido arzobispo. Mientras tanto, Sevilla había estado gobernada por Remondo de Losana, al que (según dice literalmente la *Crónica particular de Fernando III*) Fernando III había «dado el arzobispado», y quien, pese a los intentos posteriores de presentarlo como un escritor de renombre, en realidad no fue más que un siervo, enormemente solícito y decididamente leal, de Alfonso el Sabio.[39]

La corte de Alfonso residió más tiempo en Sevilla que en Toledo, por lo que no es un disparate conjeturar que la *Estoria de España* fuese compilada principalmente en Sevilla. Y como queda dicho, fue la versión del Tudense sobre los dos incidentes cruciales de la historia visigótica, antes mencionados, la preferida por los compiladores de la *Estoria* (y no di-

---

[34] Ibid., iv. 13 (132$_5$), v. 1 (148$_{13}$).

[35] J. GONZÁLEZ, *Reinado y diplomas de Fernando III*, I (Córdoba, 1980), 504-9; R. WRIGHT, «Latin and Romance in the Castilian chancery (1180-1230)», *Bulletin of Hispanic Studies*, 73 (Liverpool, 1996), 121-2 —aunque el obispo escribió su *historia* en latín.

[36] Ibid., 124-6.

[37] *Les Juges*, 377. Cf. *Primera Crónica General*, c. 1037, 721b$_{34, 42}$.

[38] Cit. LINEHAN, *History and the Historians*, 563.

[39] *Primera Crónica General*, c. 1129, 769b$_{48}$; cf. abajo, n. 56. En lo que respecta a la extravagante afirmación de que Remondo de Losana fue un miembro de la orden dominicana y (¿tal vez para equipararle a don Rodrigo?) que habría estudiado en Bolonia y con Alberto Magno en París, véase J. BENEYTO PÉREZ, *Los orígenes de la ciencia política en España* (Madrid, 1949), 357, donde además se le atribuye la autoría del *Libro de los Doze Sabios*. Ninguna de estas suposiciones son demostrables, ni tan siquiera creíbles. Además, aunque rechazó la atribución de la autoría, en 1975 J. K. WALSH dio nuevo crédito al error de que Remondo fue responsable de la *ordo* del Escorial (MS. III.&.3), que en realidad fue creada por orden de Alfonso XI en 1332 *(El Libro de los Doze Sabios o Tractado de la Nobleza y Lealtad [ca. 1237]* [Madrid, 1975], 31). J. M. NIETO SORIA juzga esta teoría «no del todo descabellada»: *Fundamentos ideológicos del poder real en Castilla (siglos XIII-XVI)* (Madrid, 1988), 63. Véase LINEHAN, *History and the Historians*, 439 n. 85, donde se da cuenta de la confusión de la que forma parte esta tradición.

gamos en el relato de los jueces de Castilla)[40]. Y eso que el texto de la «versión regia» de la *Estoria* que cubría el período visigótico había sido redactado en una época previa, antes de que Alfonso llegara a estar tan vinculado a Sevilla. Resultaría, por tanto, instructivo comprobar cómo fueron tratados el III Concilio de Toledo y la *translatio primacie* en la reelaboración de la *Estoria de España* que estaba en marcha en el mismísimo final de su reinado, y, por tanto, en Sevilla: la llamada *Versión crítica* de la obra, datable entre octubre de 1282 y abril de 1284[41].

Ahora bien, la *Versión crítica* fue el resultado de una atmósfera de traición y engaño en la corte de un rey obsesionado por el tema de la deslealtad. Es justamente por eso que ha podido ser datada. Al poner al día la lista de casos de «traycion» enumerados por la primera redacción de la *Estoria* en el relato de la pérdida de España en 711, la *Versión crítica* culmina su puesta al día con la rebelión del Infante Sancho.[42] Dada la luz que podrían arrojar sobre la envenenada atmósfera que se respiraba en los últimos meses del rey Sabio, creo que no es inconveniente que me refiera aquí a dos testimonios de esta época, uno de ellos conocido, pero de forma incompleta, el otro nunca ha sido tenido en cuenta, que yo sepa.

El primero es el privilegio del rey que garantiza a su hija ilegítima, doña Beatriz, reina de Portugal y la más leal de sus descendientes, el *regno de Niebla*. Aunque este documento ha sido publicado antes, y más recientemente por Manuel González Jiménez, había aparecido en una transcripción defectuosa e incompleta realizada por el cronista portugués del siglo XVII António Brandão.[43] Así, las evocadoras palabras del preámbulo se han perdido: *Por que segund dize el sabio la amistad uerdadera mas complidamientre se prueua en la coyta que en otra sazon, e aquel es verdadero amigo que ama en todo tiempo ...* Lo que sigue da testimonio de la desintegración de la autoridad del viejo rey. ¿Cuándo, desde los días de Alfonso VII (por no ir más atrás) se había descrito el rey de Castilla a sí mismo como *regnant* en lugar de «rey de Castilla, León» etc.? Aquí tenemos a un rey —un rey cuyas ambiciones imperiales no habían conocido límites— que empieza a parecerse peligrosamente a esos reyes peninsulares caracterizados por Maravall como reyes «no ... de un reino, sino de un espacio»[44]. Y no de «un espacio» en el sentido que otorgan a la palabra esos modernos medievalistas que hallan su inspiración en la última moda de París, sino en el sentido de que en el tiempo transcurrido entre el comienzo del privilegio concedido a su hija y su final Baeza y Badajoz se habían añadido a sus territorios. Desintegración de verdad.

En marzo de 1283 (mientras los compiladores de la *Versión crítica* estaban metidos en faena) el pasado se había perdido de vista y el futuro aparecía oscuro: *Et despues que finare que finque este Regno de Niebla con los logares e con los terminos sobredichos a aquel*

---

[40] MARTÍN, *Les Juges*, 354.

[41] I. FERNÁNDEZ ORDÓÑEZ, *Versión crítica de la Estoria de España* (Madrid, 1993). Véase el texto de la «Hitación de Wamba» de esta *Versión*, con su descripción del «arçobispado de Seuilla, que fue la primera se de las Españas»: ibid., 280.

[42] Ibid., 54-5, 222-4. Nótese también la referencia a Vellido Adolfo, el asesino de Sancho II en 1072. En abril de 1284 el procurador de Alfonso X en la curia papal denunciaba al deán de Sevilla, Ferrán Pérez, *inter alia* como descendiente del regicida («cum...sit proditor et de genere proditorum, descendens de genere Bellid Adolfe qui dominum suum dominum Sancium quondam regem Legionis prodiit et interfecit»): P. LINEHAN, *The Spanish Church and the Papacy in the Thirteenth Century* (Cambridge, 1971), 231.

[43] Lisboa, Arquivos Nacionais da Torre do Tombo, Mosteiro de Santa Maria de Aguiar, maño 1, doc. 16: Appendix I. Cf. M. GONZÁLEZ JIMÉNEZ, *Diplomatario andaluz de Alfonso X* (Sevilla, 1991), nº 508. Brandão dice que su transcripción fue hecha a partir de los registros de la cancillería de Afonso III —curiosamente, dado que Afonso había muerto en 1279. En cualquier caso, no pudo estar basada en el original, que edito aquí, ya que éste no se incorporó al archivo de Lisboa hasta el siglo XIX.

[44] *Concepto*, 359.

*que nos heredaremos en el Regno de Seuilla e mandaremos que sea Rey*. Pero ¿quién podría ser *aquel*? El segundo documento (que en realidad son tres, incluidos en el Apéndice II) parece que tiene que ver con esa pregunta.

Se trata de tres cartas papales, ninguna de ellas registrada o conservada de otra manera, incluidas en el formulario atribuido a Marinus de Eboli, vicecanciller de la curia papal entre 1244 y 1252, pero que de hecho es una compilación continuada hasta bien entrado el siglo XIV[45]. De estas tres cartas, sólo la segunda y la tercera afectan directamente al final del reinado de Alfonso X. La primera, en cambio, no está totalmente desconectada con ese escenario.

Como es usual en los formularios de ese período, se han suprimido la mayor parte de los rasgos que identifican a las personas implicadas, ya que las cartas fueron incluidas en la colección por el modelo compositivo que representaban, sin interesarse por las circunstancias concretas a que aludían. Lo mismo sucede con la identidad del destinatario. Así, no es necesario que asumamos que el «regi Castelle» en [i] y «eidem» en [ii] son el mismo rey de Castilla. Hay que entender, asimismo, que los nombres propios no interesaban. En el caso de [i] sólo existen, sin embargo, dos identificaciones posibles para el irreverente rey que había tolerado discordia entre su propia madre y sus propios hijos[46]: Fernando III y Sancho IV. Y de los dos, el segundo es más que improbable ya que cuando Sancho murió en abril de 1295 el nieto mayor de su madre, doña Yolanda, todavía tenía solamente nueve años. En cambio, cuando murió la madre de Fernando III en noviembre de 1246, el futuro Alfonso X tenía ya veinticinco y varios de sus hermanos eran también adultos[47], aunque no puedo detenerme aquí para tratar de la posible causa de este distanciamiento, hasta hoy insospechado, entre el santo *incorporador* de Sevilla y doña Berenguela, esa señora tan formidable que, según Lucas de Tuy, continuaba ejerciendo una disciplina férrea sobre su hijo incluso cuando éste ocupaba las máximas dignidades del reino, «como si fuera un niño pequeño»[48].

---

[45] Enumeradas en F. SCHILLMANN, *Die Formularsammlung des Marinus von Eboli. I. Entstehung und Inhalt* (Roma, 1929). Cf. M. BERTRAM, «Zwei neue Handschriften der Briefsammlung des Pseudo-Marinus von Eboli»: K. BORCHARDT & E. BÜNZ (eds.), *Forschungen zur Reichs-, Papst- und Landesgeschichte: Peter Herde zum 65. Geburtstag von Freunden, Schölern und Kollegen dargebracht* (Stuttgart 1998), 457-75, esp. 457-9, 469-70.

[46] «Miramur non modicum respersi stupore quod sicut nostris auribus est relatum carissimam in Christo filiam nostram illustrem reginam Castelle matrem tuam non reuerearis reuerencia filiali dum eam permittis tractari a tuis filiis inhoneste, quod non decet matrem, filium ac nepotes.»

[47] R. DEL ARCO, *Sepulcros de la casa real de Castilla* (Madrid 1954), 210-27; GONZÁLEZ, *Fernando III*, i. 96-101.

[48] «Etenim ita obediebat prudentissime Berengarie regine matri sue quamuis esset regni culmine sublimatus, ac si esset puer humillimus sub ferula magistrali»: *Chronicon mundi*, 112₃₇-₃₈. Sugiero que son dos los posibles contextos para estas diferencias entre madre e hijo: 1) el asunto del segundo matrimonio de Fernando III después de la muerte de Beatriz de Suabia en marzo de 1235, y 2) el intento del rey de asegurar la herencia alemana de Beatriz para su hijo el Infante Fadrique, herencia que, según en diciembre de 1239 recordaba a Gregorio IX, había reclamado al emperador Federico II «sepe et sepius» (publ. A. QUINTANA PRIETO, «Guillermo de Taillante, abad de Sahagún y cardenal de la iglesia romana», *Anthologica Annua*, 26-7 [1979-80], 73-4). En lo que respecta al primero de los asuntos, cf. el relato de don Rodrigo según el cual doña Berenguela fue la responsable de arreglar el segundo matrimonio con Juana de Ponthieu «ne regis pudicicia alienis comerciis lederetur»: *De rebus Hispanie*, ix.18 (ed. cit., 300₂); véase también GONZÁLEZ, *Fernando III*, I. 114-15; R. P. KINKADE, «A royal scandal and the rebellion of 1255»: F. M. TOSCANO (ed.), *Homage to Bruno Damiani from his Loving Students and Various Friends. A Festschrift* (Lanham-New York-London, 1996), 187-8. Por lo que respecta al segundo, es de interés la carta de doña Berenguela a Gregorio IX en diciembre de 1239 (una carta fechada justo el día siguiente después de la carta de Fernando antes mencionada y que la reina confió al mismo mensajero del rey, el abad de Sahagún), porque aparte de

# VIII

De forma similar, no es posible concebir otro contexto para las cartas [ii] y [iii] que los primeros meses del año 1284. Ningún otro rey de Castilla del siglo XIII, salvo Alfonso X, estuvo peleado con su hijo en esos términos; ningún otro infante salvo el Infante Sancho mereció ser denunciado por el pontífice como «rebelde»[49]. (Aunque en la víspera de la reconquista de Sevilla el entonces Infante Alfonso había desobedecido a Fernando III por causa de la guerra civil portuguesa, no parece que su contienda hubiese alcanzado tales extremos)[50]. Así que las cartas ofrecen más pruebas de la reconciliación con el Infante Sancho, reconciliación sobre la que hay que destacar que faltan pruebas irrebatibles del lado castellano aparte del testimonio tardío de la Crónica del reinado[51]. Más que eso, en vista de sus últimos intentos de comprar la regularización de su matrimonio, resulta tranquilizante saber que el infante había estado tentando al papa con sobornos (exenia)[52]. La naturaleza humana no cambia, se mire por donde se mire.

---

intentar justificar que su escasa correspondencia con el pontífice no era debida a una falta de devoción hacia su persona sino a «verecundiam quam contrax it sexus femineus a natura» (!), por lo demás su misiva está enteramente desprovista de contenido. Pero, ¿cuál era la naturaleza de las instrucciones secretas que encomendó al abad y que prefirió no reflejar por escrito ("quedam que litteris commendare nolui")?: Quintana Prieto, 74-5. Cf. P. LINEHAN, «Some observations on Castilian scholars and the Italian schools in the age of Frederick II»: A. ROMANO (ed.), ... *Colendo iusticiam et iura condendo. Federico II legislatore del regno di Sicilia nell'Europa del Duecento*. Atti del Convegno Internazionale di Studi. Messina-Reggio Calabria 20-24 gennaio 1995; (Rome, 1997), 521-2.

[49] Schillmann trata de fecharlas en los años 1274-80, pero sin fundamento. No hubo tal rebelión filial en esos años. El problema que tuvo Alfonso X entonces era con sus *hermanos*.

[50] GONZÁLEZ, *Fernando III*, i. 273-5; A. QUINTANA PRIETO, *La documentación pontificia de Inocencio IV (1243-1254)* (Roma, 1987), nos. 400, 478.

[51] Una copia de la carta de Alfonso X a Martin IV, en la que le informa de su acuerdo con el infante, encontró la forma de llegar a los archivos reales ingleses y fue publicada por T. Rymer a principios del s. XVIII: *Foedera, Litter, Conventiones et cujuscunque generis Acta Publica*, I (London, 1816), ii. 640. La carta (a la que las dos misivas descritas aquí indudablemente constituyeron la respuesta pontificia) está fechada en Sevilla el 23 de marzo de 1284 y sellada con «sigillo nostro parvo aureo». En contra de lo que afirma A. J. LÓPEZ GUTIÉRREZ, «Sevilla, Alfonso X y el «sigillum aureum»», *Archivo Hispalense*, 2ª época, 72 (1989), 315, el empleo del sello áureo no estaba reservado al emperador y al papa por entonces, ni su uso por parte de Alfonso X se limitaba a los documentos emitidos desde Sevilla y Toledo. Para un instrumento alfonsí con sello de oro fechado en Burgos el 1 de noviembre de 1254, véase RYMER, I.i. 310. Cf. H. BRESSLAU, *Handbuch der Urkundenlehre für Deutschland und Italien*, 2ª ed., ii, (Leipzig, 1931), 567. ¿Pero era auténtica la carta alfonsí? Dado que hasta ahora su existencia sólo era conocida por el *inspeximus* emitido por Sancho IV en el octubre de 1284 (Rymer, I.ii. 649), había parecido sospechosa: así F. J. HERNÁNDEZ, «Alfonso X in Andalucia», *Historia. Instituciones. Documentos*, 22 (1995), 298-300. Además, no se halla hoy en el Public Record Office. En efecto, aunque transcrito en el «Liber B» de la tesorería inglesa *c*.1300, de donde sacó Rymer su copia, ya faltaba cuando se inventarió el contenido de la tesorería en 1322 y 1323: G. P. CUTTINO, *The Gascon Calendar of 1322*; Camden 3rd ser., 70 (1949), 8-9, 80-81, 86-7, 111; F. PALGRAVE, *The Antient Kalendars and Inventories of the Treasury of His Majesty's Exchequer*, i (London, 1836), 153. Me sugiere el Dr. Pierre Chaplais, a quien agradezco por su muy amable asesoramiento, la posibilidad de que la carta castellana se hubiese perdido entretanto bien en el departamento del «Exchequer» o bien en el de la «Wardrobe». De todos modos, puesto que Alfonso murió el 4 de abril, las cartas del papa debieron de haber llegado demasiado tarde o nunca fueron enviadas. Cf. J. F. O'CALLAGHAN, *The Learned King. The Reign of Alfonso X de Castilla* (Philadelphia, 1993), 267-9; trad. M. GONZÁLEZ JIMÉNEZ, *El Rey Sabio. El reinado de Alfonso X de Castilla* (Sevilla, 1996), 318-20.

[52] Véase A. MARCOS POUS, «Los dos matrimonios de Sancho IV de Castilla», *Escuela Española de Arqueología e Historia en Roma. Cuadernos de trabajo*, 8 (1956), 7-108; P. LINEHAN, *The Ladies of Zamora* (Manchester, 1997), 124-8.

Pero en abril de 1284 el viejo rey murió y un nuevo rey le sucedió, un rey que no se sintió muy atraído por el lugar que había demostrado hasta el final lealtad a su padre[53]. Sancho IV prefirió Toledo. Y cuando en 1284, después de nueve años de vacancia y ausencia, Toledo tuvo de nuevo arzobispo, el puesto fue ocupado por don Gonzalo Pérez, llamado Gudiel, quien muy pronto disfrutó con Sancho IV de la misma relación privilegiada que Remondo de Losana había mantenido con Alfonso X. Francisco Hernández y yo estamos a punto de publicar —o liberar— un amplio estudio sobre su carrera. Anteriormente le hemos dedicado algunas páginas, y he tratado de demostrar que esa relación privilegiada con el rey le permitió influir en la compilación de las últimas secciones de la *Estoria de España* a favor de Toledo[54]. El motivo que me lleva a mencionarlo hoy es que durante su estancia como arzobispo de Toledo, entre 1284 y 1295, se reavivaron las hostilidades entre Toledo y Sevilla. Y no sólo las hostilidades rutinarias de la cruz alzada. Había más.

Primeramente, a la muerte de Remondo de Losana en 1289, Roma impuso a Sevilla un arzobispo que era *persona non grata* para Sancho IV. Se trata de García Gutiérrez, un antiguo partidario de Alfonso que había regresado del exilio gracias a lo pactado en el tratado de Lyon[55]. Pronto volvió al ataque, exigiendo de Roma en 1290 la jurisdicción sobre las sedes toledanas de Córdoba y Jaén. Por ese motivo el profesor Gonzálvez, el último de los historiadores de Toledo, lo desprecia, lo que resulta muy patriótico de su parte, mientras que el profesor Nieto Soria le atribuye la responsabilidad de lo que llama la reciente «concesión» papal a Sevilla del estatus de iglesia metropolitana, lo que es evidentemente erróneo. Sevilla había disfrutado de rango metropolitano desde 1259, aunque, quizá para crear problemas a Alfonso X, Remondo de Losana no había explotado las posibilidades que tal estatus le proporcionaba[56]. En 1290, en cambio, el arzobispo que ocupaba el cargo en Sevilla no fue tan considerado con su rey[57].

Ignoramos sobre qué bases fundamentaba don García Gutiérrez su reclamación a Toledo de las dos sedes andaluzas. En la Hitación de Wamba de nuevo, tal vez, más bien que en el nacionalismo andaluz[58]. Pero cualesquiera que fuesen, Sancho IV no iba a tomarlas en consideración. Su abuelo, Fernando III, había «dado las dos sedes a Toledo y así eran las cosas. No iba a permitir que la integridad metropolitana de Toledo resultase dañada. Cualquier

[53] «...a la capital andaluza no parecía tenerle gran afición don Sancho, y sólo le vemos allí requerido por las circunstancias»: M. GAIBROIS DE BALLESTEROS, *Historia del reinado de Sancho IV de Castilla*, i (Madrid, 1922), 46.

[54] LINEHAN, «The Toledo forgeries c.1150-c.1300»: *Fülschungen im Mittelalter*, I (MGH Schriften, 33/1; Hannover 1988), 663-71; reimpr. LINEHAN, *Past and Present in Medieval Spain* (Aldershot, 1992); *History and the Historians*, 477-81; LINEHAN and F. J. HERNÁNDEZ, «Animadverto: a recently discovered *consilium* concerning the sanctity of King Louis IX», *Revue Mabillon*, n.s. 5 [t. 66; 1994], 83-105; HERNÁNDEZ, «La fundación del Estudio de Alcalá de Henares», *En la España Medieval*, 18 (1995), 61-83.

[55] *Les registres de Nicolas IV*, ed. E. LANGLOIS (Paris, 1887-1893), no. 493; G. DAUMET, *Mémoire sur les relations de la France et de Castille de 1255 a 1320* (Paris, 1913), 185.

[56] En cuanto a su gestión esencialmente quietista véase M. FERNÁNDEZ GÓMEZ, «La defensa de la primacía de la iglesia de Sevilla en el siglo XIII», *Archivo Hispalense*, 73[224] (1990), 38-44.

[57] «Hombre de tan escaso relieve como de breve pontificado»: R. GONZÁLVEZ, *Hombres y libros de Toledo (1086-1300)* (Madrid, 1997), 368. Cf. J. M. NIETO SORIA, *Sancho IV 1284-1295* (Palencia, 1994), 219, quien sigue la sugerencia de M. GONZÁLEZ JIMÉNEZ & I. MONTES ROMERO-CAMACHO sobre la acción del arzobispo fue incitada por haber recibido recientemente el pallio («Reconquista y restauración eclesiástica en la Espana medieval. El modelo andaluz»: *IX Centenário da dedicaçao da Sa de Braga. Congresso Internacional. Actas* [Braga, 1990], 76). D. Remondo había disfrutado del «usus pallii» desde 1259: D. ORTIZ DE ZÚÑIGA, *Annales eclesiásticos y seculares de Sevilla* (Madrid, 1677), 87-8.

[58] Cf. M. NIETO CUMPLIDO, *Origenes del regionalismo andaluz,* 2ª ed. (Córdoba, 1979), 95, 144-5, fechando mal el comienzo del asunto en enero de 1290 en vez de 1291.

ataque a Toledo sería interpretado como un ataque a sí mismo»[59]. Esto sucedió en 1290, como es bien sabido.

Lo que no es en cambio tan conocido es que seis meses después «Vandalia» reaparece en Toledo. En esa fecha, mayo de 1291, Gudiel era «chanceller del Rey de Castiella e en Leon e en el Andaluzia», y así se le describe en el protocolo romance de la ordenanza capitular toledana a que me refiero. Pero en la suscripción latina de la misma, sin embargo, Gudiel es «in... Wandalia cancellarius»[60]. Hay todavía otro caso de este empleo en febrero de 1294.[61] Es posible que haya otros casos más en la documentación toledana que nos hayan pasado inadvertidos. Pero el simple hecho de que existan quizá constituya por sí solo una noticia. Ambos aparecen en un contexto privado, en documentos internos del arzobispo en su condición de arzobispo más bien que en su condición de canciller real. ¿Cómo hubiera traducido Gudiel «Andalucía» en documentos *latinos* elaborados en la cancillería real?[62] No conozco ningún documento de esa clase. Ojalá lo conociera.

Concluyo, por tanto, con una nota de incertidumbre. Pero no me disculpo por ello. No se puede saber todo.

APÉNDICE I

**1283, marzo, 4. Sevilla**

*Alfonso X concede a su hija natural, doña Beatriz reina de Portugal, «el Regno de Niebla con [sus] logares».*

A Arquivos Nacionais da Torre do Tombo (Lisboa), Mosteiro de Santa María de Aguiar, março 1, doc. 16.

Por que segund dize el sabio la amistad uerdadera mas complidamientre se prueua en la coyta que en otra sazon, e aquel es verdadero amigo que ama en todo tiempo, por ende Sepan quantos este priuilegio uieren e oyeren como nos Rey don ALFONSO por la gracia de dios Regnant en Castiella en Leon en Toledo en Gallizia en Seuilla en Cordoua en Murcia en Jahen e enel Algarue, Catando el grand amor e verdadero que fallamos en nuestra fija la mucho onrrada donna Beatriz por essa misma gracia Reyna de Portugal e del Algarue e la lealdat que siempre mostro contra nos, et de como nos fue obediente e mandada en todas cosas como bona fija e leal deue seer a padre, e sennaladamientre por que ala sazon que los otros nuestros fijos e la mayor parte delos omnes de nuestra tierra se aliaron contra nos por cosas queles dixieron e les fizieron entender como no eran, El qual leuantamiento fue contra dios e contra derecho e contra razon e contra ffuero e contra sennor natural, e veyendo ella esto e conosçiendo lo que ellos desconoscieron del, amparo fijos e heredamientos e todas las otras cosas que auie e ueno padecer aquello que nos padeçiemos pora beuir e morir conusco, e como quier

[59] Archivo Capitular de Toledo, X.1.C.2.1; Nieto Cumplido, 154.

[60] «Nos supradictus .G. dei gratia Toletane sedis archiepiscopus Ispaniarum primas ac domini Regis in Castella et Legione et Wandalia cancellarius confirmamus et propria manu subscribimus»: Archivo Capitular de Toledo, I.6.B.1.2.

[61] Ibid., X.8.C.1.4: «Vandalie cancellarius».

[62] Hay que destacar que en su carta latina a los genoveses de mayo de 1251 Fernando III evita el problema, refiriendo exclusivamente a «Hyspalis» y a los «Hispalenses»: GONZÁLVEZ, *Fernando III*, iii (1986), nº. 823.

que ella mereçiesse todo el bien que nos fazerle pudiessemos, pero por que luego tan complidamientre no lo podemos fazer como nos querriemos daquello que nos finco e tenemos en
nuestro poder, Damosle por heredat despues de nuestros dias pora en toda su uida la villa de
Niebla con toda su Regnado, que es Gibraleon, Huelua, Saltes, Aymonte, Alffaiar de Penna e
Alffaiar daLate, e con todos los otros logares que son sos terminos e fueron antiguamientre, en
tal manera que lo no pueda dar ni uender ni camiar ni empennar ni enagenar a Eglesia ni a Orden ni a omne de Religion ni a otro omne que sea de ffuera de nuestro sennorio ni a otro nin-
guno, mas que aya ella ende las rentas e los derechos pora seruirse dello en toda su uida. Et
despues que finare que finque este Regno de Niebla con los logares e con los terminos sobredichos a aquel que nos heredaremos enel Regno de Seuilla e mandamos que sea Rey.

Onde rogamos e mandamos al Conceio de Niebla e alos otros Conceios de sus terminos e coniuramoslos por el debdo de naturaleza que an conusco e por la lealdat que siempre
fizieron e nos deuen fazer que recuda ellos e sean tenudos de fazer recudir bien e complidamientre despues de nuestros dias con las Rentas e con los derechos que son en sos logares a nuestra fija la Reyna sobredicha o aquella mandare en toda su uida. E que ella o aque-
las que touieren por ella Niebla e Gibraleon e Huelua e Aymonte e Alfaiar de Penna e
Alffaiar daLate e todas las otras logares de so termino, que fagan ende guerra e paz a
aquel que heredare el Regno de Seuilla segund sobredicho es.

E otrossi mandamos a aquel que heredare el regno de Seuilla e fuere y Rey por nuestro
mandado que aguarde a nuestra fija la Reyna sobredicha todas estas cosas de suso dichas en
este Priuilegio en toda su uida. E si alguno esto quisiesse embargar o yr en alguna cosa contra ella, si fuere de nuestro linaje que aya la maldiçion de dios e de aquellos onde nos venimos, e la nuestra, e sea por ende traydor assi como que trahe castiello e mata sennor, e no se
pueda saluar desta trayçion por ninguna manera. E demas sea dannado con Judas en los inf-
fiernos. E ella que se pueda deffender de aquellos que contra este Priuilegio quisieren yr.

E si los del Conceio de Niebla e delos otros Conceios de sus terminos no deffendiessen
e no manparassen a nuestra fija la Reyna sobredicha de que quier que fuesse contra ella o
contra este nuestro Priuilegio pora quebrantarlo o pora minguarlo en alguna cosa, o ellos no
quisiessen cunplir esto segund sobredicho es, que ayan esta misma pena de trayçion que de
suso es dicha, e la yra de dios e la nuestra e de aquellos que regnaren despues de nos por
nuestro mandado.

E pedimos merçed al Papa que lo otorgue segund que sobredicho es e lo confirme por
so privilegio.

E rogamos al rey de Ffrancia que lo otorgue e lo confirme por so privilegio otrossi.

E por que todo esto sea firme e estable nos Rey don ALFONSO sobredicho, Regnant
en Castiella en Leon en Toledo en Gallizia en Sevilla en Cordova en Murcia en Jahen en Ba-
eña en Badaioz e en el Algarue mandamos fazer este Priuilegio e confirmamos lo.

Ffecho en Sevilla yueues quatro dias andados del mes de Março en Era de mill e trezientos e Veynt e un anno.

*[Confirmantes en cinco columas así]*:

    I.  El Inffante don Jaymes cf.
       Don ffrey Aymar Electo de Auila
       La Eglesia de Plazencia Vaga

    II.  Don Johan Alffonso de Haro
       Don Gutier Suarez de Meneses

Don Garçi Gutierrez
Alffonso Ffernandez sobrino del Rey e su Mayordomo
Alffonso Perez de Guzman
Pero Suarez
Tel Gutierrez Justiçia de casa del Rey
Garçi Ioffre copero mayor del Rey
Pero Royz de Villiegas Repostero mayor del Rey
Lope Alffonso portero mayor del Rey en el Regno de Castiella
Diaz Alffonso Thesorero del Rey

III. Don Remondo Arçobispo de Seuilla cf. *Abajo la rueda conteniendo los epígrafes: (i) central:* SIGNO DEL REY DON ALFONSO; *(ii) periferal:* SENNOR:DE CAS-TIELLA:DE LEON:DE TOLEDO:DE GALIZIA:DE SEVILLA:DE CORDO-VA:DE MURCIA:DE JAEN E DEL ALGARVE. *Al fondo:* Pelay Perez Abat de Va-lladolit e Chanceler del Rey en Castiella e en Leon

IV. La Eglesia de Santiago Vaga
Don Ffredolo obispo de Ouiedo
La Eglesia de Salamanca Vaga
La Eglesia de Orens Vaga
La Eglesia de Lugo Vaga
La Eglesia de Mendonedo Vaga
Don Suero obispo de Cadiz

V. Don Martin gil
Suero Perez de Baruosa
Don Garçi Fferrandez Maestre dela Orden de Alcantara
Don Johan Fferrandez Maestre dela Orden del Temple
Garçi Fferrandez de Senabria portero mayor del Rey en el Regno de Leon.

*al fondo a la izquierda:* Pelay Perez
*al centro:* Yo Millan Perez de Aellon lo fiz escriuir por mandado del Rey en treynta e un anno que el Rey sobredicho regno.
*debajo del col. IV, todo muy borrado:* [?Roy][suarez...][?scripsit].
*Restos de seda; falta el sello.*

APÉNDICE II

Arles, Bibl. Municipale, MS. 60, fo. 110ᵛ *

De maioritate et obediencia
[i]   Regi Castelle. Humani generis primeuitas introduxit, publice honestatis iusticia suggerente, ut maiores natu reuerencia a posteris haberentur ac prioritate nature repellerent

---

\* Colacionado con Archivo Segreto Vaticano, Arm. XXXI.72, fo. 140ʳ y Toulouse, Bibl. Municipale, MS. 473, fo. 139ʳ⁻ᵛ. Estoy en deuda con el prof. Dr. Martin Bertram (Deutsches Historisches Institut in Rom) que tuvo la gentileza de facilitarme copias de los folios pertinentes de los MSS. de Arles y de Toulouse.

a bonorum successione post ipsos ab eodem stipite uenientes. Cum autem hoc ab homine traditum periculum pene non importans obseruetur utencium[1] moribus approbatum, quanto magis quod ex ore prolatum est altissimi asserentis `Honora patrem tuum et matrem tuam ut sis longeuus super terram»[2] obseruari debet, per quod satisfit diuino mandato et vite longeuitas promeretur, et contrarium faciens incurrit opposita eorumdem. Miramur non modicum respersi stupore quod sicut nostris auribus est relatum carissimam in Christo filiam nostram illustrem[3] reginam Castelle matrem tuam non reuerearis[4] reuerencia filiali, dum eam permittis[5] tractari a tuis filiis inhoneste, quod non decet matrem, filium ac nepotes. Ut igitur rex regum super dies tuos annos adiciat regnumque tuum in eternum committet, serenitatem regiam monemus et hortamur per apostolica tibi scripta mandantes quatenus predictam matrem tuam honorans reuerencia filiali facias eidem a predictis filiis honorem similem exhiberi ita quod preter humane laudis titulum aggregari iustorum consortio merearis ac dicta mater de senecta in senium iam prouecta a sua[6] posteritate se gaudeat honorari. Nosque prouide tibi circa celsitudinem regiam dignis in domino laudibus commendemus.

[ii]  Eidem. Congratulatio super eo quod filius regis rediit[7] ad obedientiam patris etc.[8] Laudem et gloriam eterno regi referimus quod tu nostris precibus et monitis acquiescens cum filio tuo ad desideratam nobis et aliis concordiam deuenisti, per diuersa laudabilia[9] signa declarans quod sacrosanctam romanam ecclesiam affectu sincero diligis et eam desideras honore proficere ac uotiua tranquillitate gaudere. Super hoc autem tibi quas in domino possumus gratias referentes, celsitudini tue attente rogandam duximus et monendam tibi in remissionem peccaminum quatinus pro reuerencia diuini nominis in illo semper proposito perseueres[10] quod uerbo et opere honorem ecclesie memorate promoueas et eius persecutoribus[11] cum oportunum fuerit te potenter ac[12] patenter opponas ita quod apostolica sedes tibi et tuis heredibus pro tam claris meritis nunc et inposterum teneatur ad fauoris premia specialis. Ceterum tua serenitas pro constanti teneat quod grauiter cordi nostro displicuit predictum filium tuum tibi olim fuisse oppositum ac rebellem, quod[13] nullum omnino sibi fauorem in hac parte prestitimus uel procurauimus exhiberi, sed ad nostre pocius turbationis iudicium exenia[14] recipere noluimus[15] que ipse nobis obtulit per nuncium specialem, illam in hac parte considerationem habentes quod ipse perciperet nullum exenium[16] ex parte sua posset[17] uobis prouenire gracius quam quod ipse tibi haberetur obediens et deuotus.

---

[1] Vat: pene periculum non importans obseruetur utencium ; Toulouse: pene non importans periculum obseruetur utencium.
[2] Exod. 20.12.
[3] Vat: Albam ; Toulouse: *om.* illustrem.
[4] Vat, Toulouse: ueneraris.
[5] Vat: promittis.
[6] Vat: poterate [*del.*] posteritate.
[7] Vat: redit.
[8] Toulouse *om.* rubric.
[9] Vat: laudabilia diuersa.
[10] Toulouse: proseueres.
[11] Vat; Toulouse: prosecutoribus.
[12] Vat: *om.* potenter ac.
[13] Vat; Toulouse: et quod.
[14] Vat: encennia.
[15] Arles: nolumus.
[16] Vat: encennium.
[17] Vat; Toulouse: posse; Arles: ex parte [nostra *del.*] sua posset.

**[iii]**   Filio regis. [18] Multa super eo prouenit cordi nostro leticia quod uirtutum domino inspirante te ad karissimi in Christo filii etc. patris tui [19] reuerenciam reduxisti et conformis eius beneplacito inueneris, cessante discordia que in conditoris omnium redundans offensam, tibi et eidem regi uertebatur in dispendium et producebat aliis multiplex detrimentum. Cum itaque, fili karissime, tibi magna claritas nominis uotiua longitudo dierum possit ex eo potissime prouenire quod paternis beneplacitis secundum deum semper obediens habearis, serenitati tue affectuose rogandam duximus et monendam in remissionem quatinus, nullis iniquis suggestionibus inclinans auditum, ipsius patris tui benedictionem et gratiam per exhibitionem assiduam reuerencie filialis studeas promereri et firmus in concordia reformata persistas, ita quod status tue magnitudinis optatis deo propicio perficere ualeat incrementis et nullis possit iacturis affici, que sepe per discordiam solent taliter exoriri ut ad statum pristinum vix possit haberi resumptio infra multum temporis, multis [20] hinc inde consurgentibus detrimentis. De hoc autem deuotionis studio circa patrem apud nos tibi proueniet quod circa personam tuam interne [21] beniuolencie affectum augebimus, liceat alias inter filios principum orbis terre te karissimum habeamus. Ceterum de honorabili exenio [22] oblato nobis per tuum nuncium specialem referentes tue celsitudini actiones uberes graciarum, licet illud non duximus admittendum, scire te uolumus quod ex parte tua nichil potuit uel posset hodie nobis gracius prouenire quam quod predicto patri tuo te constituas gratum in omnibus, sed hiis precipue que deo possint et ecclesie complacere.

---

[18] Vat: Filio regis filio regis super eodem.
[19] Arles: tue.
[20] Vat: *om.* multis.
[21] Vat: tue [*del.*] interne.
[22] Vat: encennio.

# The King's Touch and the Dean's Ministrations: Aspects of Sacral Monarchy

As was agreed at the Royaumont meeting five years ago, it is towards the periphery that students of medieval royalty and its mystique ought now to be turning their attention.[1] But that is a large undertaking, and time and space set their own limits. Here, therefore, attention will be focused on the Iberian sector of that periphery – though not (I hope) on account of that blinkered 'tendency to treat Iberia as a world unto itself' recently identified by Cambridge's principal historian of medieval Sicily.[2]

Another way of coping with the challenge of the periphery, of course, would be to take issue with the concept of peripherality itself, as Adeline Rucquoi has done in an illuminating paper published in Mexico[3] – which really *is* peripheral. The very concept of Iberian peripherality might well be regarded as both *passé* and dated – and therefore doubly unsuitable for the present occasion. Nevertheless the concept retains its usefulness. For whether or not *passé* and dated, it is also venerable.

Just how venerable it is is demonstrated by the work entitled a 'Breif abstract of the question of precedencie between England and Spaine . . .', 'collated' in the year 1600 by the English antiquarian Sir Robert Cotton 'at the commandment of her Majesty Queen Elizabeth'. The extent of Cotton's enquiry was impressive. Because in 1600 Bishop Stubbs had not yet been invented, it might be supposed that in demonstrating England's 'Precedencie' over Spain Cotton would have set his own agenda, and that in

---

[1] A. Boureau and C.-S. Ingerflom, eds, *La Royauté sacrée dans le monde chrétien* (Paris, 1992), p. 5. As to what follows I am grateful for advice and information to Alain Boureau, George Garnett and Ingrid Lundegårdh.

[2] D. Abulafia, *A Mediterranean Emporium. The Catalan Kingdom of Majorca* (Cambridge, 1994), p. xvi.

[3] 'De los reyes que no son taumaturgos: los fundamentos de la realeza en España', in *Relaciones* 13 (1992), pp. 55–100.

beginning in the first century AD with Joseph of Arimathea he was beginning where he himself chose to begin. But this was not so.

According to Cotton, it was a point in England's favour that in 1600 the queen of England was already in the forty-second year of her reign, whereas Philip III of Spain was 'yet in the Infancy of his Kingdome' – though this he 'would not have alledged,' he states, 'but that the *Spanish* Ambassador at *Basil* objected in this respect the minority of *Henry* the sixth.'[4] This takes us back. It was the issues that had been raised at the Council of Basle in 1435 that set Cotton's agenda in 1600.

In fact the controversy had been brewing even earlier. In 1422 Martin V's Easter Mass had been shamefully disturbed by the bishops of Cuenca and Chichester pushing and shoving for the better seat in St Peter's.[5] For Cotton, however, it was at the Council of Basle that the great set-to had begun, and the Castilian and English delegations had embarked in earnest upon a trial of strength disguised as rational debate. In order to determine which contingent should sit where the contestants presented all manner of more or less relevant argument. For example, England's need to import wine and oil was a clear indication of English inferiority, the bishop of Burgos claimed.[6]

Mentioning oil was a mistake. It enabled the Spanish prelates' adversary – his brother of London, Robert Fitzhugh – to observe that for all their oil, the Castilians failed to anoint their kings: a very palpable hit in 1435, but one the significance of which has escaped the attention of historians in more recent times.[7]

Whereas (Fitzhugh stated) ever since the time of Pope Leo V (*sic*) the kings of England had been anointed,[8] the kings of Castile enjoyed no such privilege or, if they did, they had received it later. In comparison with consecrated kings they were as mere clerics to anointed bishops. Those

---

[4] *Cottoni Posthuma*, ed. J. Howell, 2nd edn (London, 1672), pp. 86–7. Cf. 'Proposicion que el muy reverendo padre e senor don Alfonso de Cartagena, obispo de Burgos, fiso contra los ingleses . . . sobre la preheminencia que el Rey nuestro Senor ha sobre el Rey de Inglaterra', ed. M. Penna, *Prosistas castellanos del siglo XV*, i, Biblioteca de Autores Españoles, 116 (Madrid, 1959), p. 221.

[5] 'Omni Deo et nostra reverentia postposita', the pontiff complained to the king of Castile, Juan II: V. Beltrán de Heredia, 'La embajada de Castilla en el Concilio de Basilea y su discusión con los ingleses acerca de la precedencia', *Hispania Sacra* 10 (1957), p. 29.

[6] Penna, 'Proposicion', pp. 227–8.

[7] See M. Bloch, *Les Rois thaumaturges. Étude sur le caractère surnaturel attribué à la puissance royale particulièrement en France et en Angleterre* (Strassburg, 1924).

[8] For King Alfred's legendary anointing by Leo IV in 853, see Janet L. Nelson, 'The Problem of King Alfred's Royal Anointing', *Journal of Ecclesiastical History* (henceforth *JEH*), 8 (1967), pp. 145–63 repr. Nelson, *Politics and Ritual in Early Modern Europe* (London, 1986), pp. 309–27.

*The King's Touch and the Dean's Ministrations*

whose enjoyment of the privilege was more venerable deserved the better place at sessions of general councils.[9] And more. Because they were consecrated on their heads (and not, as other kings were, on their shoulders or elsewhere), the kings of France and England had the power to cure the sick by the imposition of hands and the use of cramp rings blessed on Good Friday – the sick of every description, be it noted. This the English believed and English experience had proved.[10] And yet more. According to the ceremonial protocol of the councils which had assembled since the beginning of the Great Schism (which was as far back as the bishop's precedents extended), the king of England came second only to the king of France, enjoying precedence not only over the king of Castile but also over the ruler of Sicily, who in turn enjoyed precedence over the Castilian,[11] all in accordance with the precept that 'if I excel over him who excels over you, all the more do I excel over you'.[12] (It was smart of Fitzhugh to confront the Castilians with the very argument that the Spanish canonist Vincentius

[9] 'Ex qua sacra unccione prefati regis, ex qua merito Christianissimus dici potest, antiquissime facta de ipso videlicet Rome per Leonem papam quintum; que sacra unccio nec data regi Castelle nec concessa legitur et, si concessa legatur, tamen diu post. Et sicut precedens consecracio epicopi facit illum aliis anteferri, quia nec ante bene potest dici episcopus, sed solum clericus dicitur et confirmatus, sicut jura volunt, ita et in regibus dicendum necessarium, ut illum plenum et sacrum sceptrum atque solium regale sacratum tenere senciatur, qui est sacra unccione unctus et qui prior unctus, prior in sede sit et loco aliis non unctis vel expost unctis juste et merito debeat anteferri', *England und das Basler Konzil*, ed. A. Zellfelder (Berlin, 1913), p. 286. See also A. N. E. D. Schofield, 'The Second English Delegation to the Council of Basel', *JEH* 17 (1966), pp. 51–2.

[10] 'Ex modo unccionis et loco persone, cui unccio sacra applicatur. Nam reges Francie et Anglie in eorum capitibus unguuntur, ceteri vero in scapulis aut aliis membris, ex quo modo unguendi et loco persone secundum Hostiensem archidiaconum et doctores major dignitas et excellencia subinfertur, quia ad instar David et Saulis, quos sic Samuel canone attestante perunxit, et eo major, quo dicte unccionis virtute, ut firmiter in Anglia tenetur et creditur, experimento probatur, quod eciam caduco morbo infecti et aliis nonnullis languoribus laborantes manus regie imposicione cum certis in die parasceves consecratis anulis liberantur ad instar virtutis unccionis regis Francie, que infirmos, ut refert Johannes Andree in notula super VI°, sanos reddit', in Zellfelder, *England*, p. 287 (where 'Hostiensem archidiaconum' should read 'Hostiensem, Archidiaconum', and 'notula super VI°' 'Novella super VI°'). It is to be observed that the bishop made no claim that it was Joseph of Arimathea who had introduced the use of cramp rings to England. See Bloch, *Les Rois thaumaturges*, p. 161.

[11] 'Compertum est in omnibus conciliis nostra etate celebratis dictum regem Anglie non solum locum anteriorem regis Castelle plene possedisse, sed regis ipsum regem Castelle videlicet Cecilie justa seriem et ordinem ipsum dicti ceremonialis libri ipsum precedentis in concilio Pisano, Constanciensi, Papiensi et Senensi, quibus locum illi omnino illis et omnibus regibus excepto Francie rege anteriorem rex Anglie tamquam verus et ligitimus dominus dicti juris et prelacionis et ut talis habitus tentus et continuo reputatus possedit, prout juste possidet et possidere intendit', Zellfelder, *England*, p. 288.

[12] 'Si precello precellentem te, multo forcius precello te', *ibid.*, p. 288.

had employed almost 200 years earlier to demonstrate Spain's superiority over the Empire.)[13]

Such was the polemical tradition which Cotton inherited in 1600, a tradition sharpened by religious controversy. Inasmuch as it derived from a practice thought to have been instituted by a Roman pope, for a loyal subject of a Protestant queen the whole sacral nexus was of course not without awkwardness.[14] But more awkward still was the absence of a credible claim to membership of the sacral international. This was the difficulty under which Cotton's Spanish contemporary, Diego de Valdés, laboured.

Valdés' *De dignitate regum regnorumque Hispaniae* was published in 1602, two years after Cotton's 'Breif abstract'[15] – though if its author was aware of Cotton's work he refrained from attempting anything resembling a point-by-point refutation. Anyway, it was the French that he had in his sights, and the French conviction that they enjoyed a monopoly of the *ius unctionis*, with the kings of Jerusalem and Sicily ('and even England') having somehow secured admission to that exclusive club, membership of which entitled the king of France to read the epistle just as the emperor was to read the gospel when the pope said Mass.[16] Not so, according to

---

[13] 'Si uinco uincentem te uinco te' (on the grounds that while France may have had the better of the Germans the Spaniards had had the better of Charlemagne): Peter Linehan, *History and the Historians of Medieval Spain* (Oxford, 1993), pp. 296–7.

[14] In 1597 another loyal subject, the Queen's chaplain, William Tooker, had turned the tables by recalling Elizabeth's cure of a papist *in extremis*. J. Todd, 'Touching for the King's Evil', *The Modern Churchman* 32 (1942–3), pp. 301–2. See also Bloch, *Les Rois thaumaturges*, pp. 334–5, 421–2.

[15] Jacobo Valdesio auctore *De dignitate regum regnorumque Hispaniae, & honoriatori loco eis, seu eorum legatis a conciliis, ac Romana sede iure debito* (Granada, 1602). In what follows I use the identical text printed in his *Praerogativa Hispaniae, hoc est De dignitate et prae eminentia regum regnorum Hispaniae* (Frankfurt, 1626).

[16] 'De unctione hac omnibus Regibus debita, ac si peculiaris esset Regum Franciae, clamant Galli, solis illis ac Regibus Hierosolymitanis, & Siciliae debitam, & singulari quodam privilegio illis privatim concessam, cum oleo coelitus demisso ungantur Reges Galliae, & ideo ut uncti & consecrati epistolam celebrant, cum Pontifex summus missam agit, & Imperator Evangelium canit', Jacobo Valdes, *Praerogativa Hispaniae*, p. 273. The tradition reported by Martène, according to which, on entering Rome after his election, the emperor read the Gospel and the king of Sicily (or the king of France if present) read the Epistle, is described in Bloch, *Les Rois thaumaturges*, p. 203, n. 1, as 'une pure fantaisie' (cf. 1983 edn, below, n. 55), and nothing of the sort is authorised by the prescriptions in force in the 1430s. (Cf. B. Schimmelpfennig, *Die Zeremonienbücher der römischen Kurie im Mittelalter*, Bibliothek des Deutschen Historischen Instituts in Rom. Bd. 40 (Tübingen, 1973). However, the 14th-century *Ordines Romani* XV and XVI allowed the Emperor the privilege at matins at Christmas, and it was also exercised at Mass by Charles IV, Sigismund and (in 1468) Frederick III. See P. Browe, 'Zum Kommunionempfang des Mittelalters', *Jahrbuch für Liturgiewissenschaft* 12 (1934), p. 166; J. A. Jungmann, *Missarum sollemnia. Eine genetische Erklärung der romischen Messe*, i (Vienna, 1952), p. 567.

*The King's Touch and the Dean's Ministrations*

Valdés. The Gallic authors were in error. The kings of Spain did not owe their entitlement to anointing to a right acquired by an Aragonese *infante* in his capacity as king of Sicily in 1296, as 'some' had claimed allegedly on the strength of the irrefutable Zurita. *All* kings were entitled to be anointed, he insisted, citing Innocent III's decretal *De sacra unctione* in support: 'ius hoc generale est omnibus regibus Christianis'.[17] There was no denying that *ius iunctionis* appertained to all Christian kings, and to Spanish kings especially ('*praesertim Hispaniarum*').

For Valdés, Spanish custom confirmed what the Pope had conceded. From the anointing of Bamba in 672, *via* that of Alfonso VII 'by Calixtus II in the church of Compostela' in the twelfth century, to Alfonso XI's in 1332, there was a continuous tradition of Spanish unction.[18] And while on the subject, Valdés felt bound to make a point about Clovis and the oil which the Holy Ghost had supplied for his baptism. Having no desire to depreciate others and being exclusively concerned with the praise of his own, Valdés did not wish to comment on the alleged provenance of the oil with which the kings of France were anointed and on which all their pretensions was based.[19] That was not his point. His point was that Clovis's oil had been *baptismal* oil. And there was no connection between baptismal oil and the oil used for anointing kings.[20]

So the argument which the French had constructed from Clovis and his oil was in fact an argument against themselves. In the history of royal anointing, Clovis's baptism counted for nothing. What counted was the anointing of Bamba, an event marked by the miracle reported by Julian of Toledo of the column of vapour surmounted by a bee ascending from the king's head.[21]

---

[17] 'Primo autem dum Gallie istimant auctores, vel alii, ad Reges Galliae, Hierusalem & Siciliae tantum, vel Angliae etiam, ex quibusdam, & non ad alios pertinere ius unctionis, quamvis eorum opinio amplectenda foret, Regi Hispaniae, ut Regi Siciliae, & Hierusalem ius unctionis competit, quae illis Regibus familiaris & frequens fuit iuxta ritus, quibus scribit inunctum fuisse regem Federicum Siciliae Hieron. Zurita part. I, *annal. libr.* 5. c.17, & alii auctores id de regibus Siciliae affirmantes, sed necessum non est, ut deveniamus ad honorem a Sicilia hauriendum, cum toto coelo errent, qui existimant his solis Regibus ius ungendi competere, nam ius hoc generale est omnibus regibus Christianis, non solum ex DD. doctrina, sed *extext.* Innocentii III *in cap. 1 §1 de sacra unct.*', Valdes, *Praerogativa Hispaniae*, pp. 274–5.

[18] *Ibid.*, pp. 275–6.

[19] 'ne invidere potius alienae laudi, quam cumulum nostrae gloriae adferre videar', *ibid.*, p. 280.

[20] 'ab oleo baptismatis ad oleum, quo Reges inunguntur, argumentum deduci non potest', *ibid.*, p. 281.

[21] 'Vnde patet potius retorqueri argumentum in Gallos, & ex eo Hispaniam maiores acquirere vires, cum ipsi non possint certo affirmare, nec de baptismate Clodouaei

---

Despite all his exegesis of the histories of Clovis and Bamba, however, Valdés' case remained fatally flawed. It failed to carry conviction, and it failed to do so not only because his argument was defective as to detail – as, for example, regarding his reading of Innocent III's decretal, which far from being concerned to establish 'a general law for the anointing of Christian kings' had in fact been intent on restating the Gelasian distinction implicit in the differentiation that ought to exist between the head-anointing of bishops and the arm-smearing of those kings who were indeed oiled;[22] or his illusory citations of Zurita and Garibay;[23] or his reference to Alfonso VII's anointing at Compostela by Pope Calixtus II, which reveals that Valdés had fallen victim to the False Chroniclers of his day.[24] Serious though all of this was, altogether more damaging in 1602 was the fact that the anointing of Alfonso XI had happened such a very long time ago. Where was the evidence for the existence of the tradition that Spanish kings were anointed kings? The awkward fact was that there was none.

miraculum circa oleum, & in vnctione sit exploratum nullum accidisse, apud Hispanos vero & baptismate & in unctione regum sint omnino certa miracula', p. 293. Cf. Julian of Toledo, *Historia Wambae*, c. 4: *Opera*, i, ed. W. Levison, intro. J. N. Hillgarth, Corpus Christianorum: Series Latina 115 (1976), p. 220.

[22] 'Refert autem inter pontificis et principis unctionem, quia caput pontificis chrismate consecratur, brachium vero principis oleo delinitur, ut ostendatur, quanta sit differentia inter auctoritatem pontificis et principis potestatem:X 1. 15. de sacra unctione, c. un.'. E. Friedberg, ed., *Corpus iuris canonici*, ii (Leipzig, 1881), p. 133. (As is notorious, the kings of France and England ignored Innocent's directive: above, n. 10.)

[23] Above, n. 17: cf. J. Zurita, *Anales de Aragón*, 19 vols, ed. A. Canellas López (Zaragoza 1970), ii, p. 491. Zurita's alleged authority for the assertion that Spanish kings also enjoyed the right to read the epistle and gospel at mass (p. 277) is equally baseless: cf. *Anales de Aragón*, vii, pp. 28–9, x, p. 68, iii (1972), pp. 302 and 849–50; iv (1973), pp. 849–50. Valdés' observation in this connection that 'Reges Hispaniae' were canons of León and Burgos was presumably occasioned by the emperor's enjoyment of a canonry of St Peter's. Cf. M. Dykmans, *Le Cérémonial papal de la fin du Moyen Age à la Renaissance*, ii. *De Rome en Avignon ou Le Cérémonial de Jacques Stefaneschi* (Brussels and Rome, 1981), p. 438. As to his assertion 'idemque in Regibus Nauarrae vsus fuit, quod omnes vngerentur, vt meminit Garibai' (p. 277), again two of the passages cited (xxvi. 1, xxvii. 4) have nothing at all to say on the subject: E. de Garibay, *Compendio historial delas chronicas y universal historia de todos los Reyes de España, donde se escriven las vidas de los Reyes de Nauarra*, iii (Barcelona, 1628), pp. 223–6, 271–4; while the third, concerning Philip of Evreux's anointing at Pamplona in 1329 (xvii. 1: pp. 265–6), merely serves to draw attention to the inveterate opposition of the Navarrese to imported French ceremonial. See J. M. Lacarra, *El juramento de los reyes de Navarra (1234–1329)* (Madrid, 1972); Linehan, *History and the Historians*, pp. 391–2.

[24] See my 'The Toledo forgeries c.1150–c.1300': *Fälschungen im Mittelalter*, i, *Monumenta Germaniae Historica* Schriften 33/i (Hanover 1988) repr. *Past and Present in Medieval Spain* (Aldershot, 1992), pp. 672–4.

*The King's Touch and the Dean's Ministrations*

In the 1990s a solution to the problem posed by the absence of evidence of royal anointing has been sought in the concept of 'invisible anointing'.[25] Not even Valdés thought of that – though, true, his method of dealing with the problem was hardly less ingenious. Although the kings of Spain were fully entitled to be anointed, he stated, they had ceased to avail themselves of the privilege, because the exercise of it was otiose. Ceremonies for the purpose of demonstrating *fidelitas* were redundant amongst Spaniards, because Spaniards and *fidelitas* – his subjects' fidelity to their king, the king's to the Church – were synonymous anyway. Moreover, he added – introducing a distinction which Alfonso X had deployed in the 1250s in respect of the hereditary ruler's superiority over the elected emperor – it was *elected* kings who had themselves anointed. And the kings of Spain were, of course, kings by hereditary right.[26] Not that their voluntary abstention from anointing disqualified them from healing the sick, Valdés wished it to be understood. That God-given power of theirs was immortal, he stated – though, on inspection, his account of the curative powers enjoyed by Spain's anointable monarchs proves as unpersuasive as his disquisition on the institution of Spanish anointing itself.[27] Nor was

[25] 'Para la época Trastámara, la falta de un rito de unción regia no impidió el que existiera una creencia por la que se veía en los monarcas castellanos a reyes ungidos': J. M. Nieto Soria, *Ceremonias de la realeza. Propaganda y legitimación de la Castilla Trastámara* (Madrid 1993), p. 40; and *Iglesia y génesis del estado moderno en Castilla (1369–1480)* (Madrid 1993), p. 225, referring to the same author's *Fundamentos ideológicos del poder real en Castilla (siglos XIII–XVI)* (Madrid, 1988), pp. 62–5. Cf. Linehan, *History and the Historians*, pp. 428–30, 441–2.

[26] 'Cum igitur Reges Hispaniae iure inungi possint, & servatum aliquo tempore fuerit, postea non uti his ceremoniis, & ritibus Reges voluerunt, nam videntur adhiberi solemnitates, & ceremoniae istae, ut fidelitas illis, & observantia a subditis seruentur, & ipsi servent eam Ecclesiae, sed in Hispania, cum adeo omnes fideles sint, non eo funguntur ritu, ut ostendant subditi nulla solemnitate opus esse, ut illi fidelitatem praestent, ad quam nati videntur quadam propensa natura, nec etiam Reges indigere admonitione hac, ut Ecclesiae obediant, & in eius fide colenda, & augenda omnem operam praestant, cum proni, & omni tempore parati sint ad omnem pro Ecclesia curam, & defensionem suscipiendam. Item, & quia illi unctione utebantur, qui electi erant, sed Reges successione, et iure sanguinis, non electionis hodie succedunt in regno', Valdes, *Praerogativa Hispaniae*, p. 277. Cf. *Partida* 2.1.8: *Las Siete Partidas del Rey don Alfonso el Sabio*, ed. Real Academia de la Historia (Madrid, 1807) [repr. Madrid, 1972], ii. pp. 9–10; Linehan, *History and the Historians*, pp. 430–1.

[27] 'Hoc autem aegros sanandi immortale munus divinitus collatum est a Deo optimo maximo etiam Regibus Hispaniae, ilam [*sic*] Reges Aragoniae aegrotis morbo strummarum salutem contulisse auctor est Beuter libr. 2 c. 50' (p. 327). In fact, the authority cited refers to the curative powers of the kings of France, inherited from Louis IX, in respect of 'las porcillas' or 'las porcellanas': A. Beuter, *Segunda parte de la Coronica General de toda España, y especialmente del Reyno de Valencia* (Valencia, 1604) [the *editio princeps* was not available to me], p. 288. As to the claim, 'quod Reges Hispaniae signo

there much more to be said for his representation of the case when he returned to the charge in 1626. In fact, there was nothing to be said for it all. It was the very same case as before, to the letter.

So much for Valdés. Cotton, by contrast, had plenty to say about Spain's deficiencies in comparison with England. The alleged 'precedencie' of a land 'first tainted with the heresie of Priscilianism, then with *Gothish* Arianism, and after defaced with *Moorish* Mahumetism'[28] was soon disposed of. In pride of place on his list of evidences for the 'Subsequence of Spain', however, was the consideration that:

> The Kings of *Castile* are never anointed, neither hath the *Spanish* Throne that vertue to endow the King therein invested, with the power to heal the Kings evil: For into *France* do yearly come multitudes of *Spaniards* to be healed therof.[29]

There are two points about Cotton's observation to be noted. One is the confirmation it provides of something that Professor Barlow remarked upon in his refreshingly sane account of the subject: namely, the apparently high proportion of those who came to be cured of the 'royal disease' by Philip the Fair in 1307–8 who were *foreigners*.[30] The other is the fact that Cotton was already deploying those categories which, more or less unconsciously, modern students of sacral monarchy also assume: categories which those very historians who are most insistent in rejecting the notion of normative Anglo-French sacrality are particularly in the habit of invoking, mantra-like, as a sort of talisman against the crypto-positivists and other ideological backsliders.[31]

---

crucis expellerent Daemonia', the evidence of the two witnesses adduced ('notat Cassaneus in Cathologo gloriae mundi 5 part. consi. I versi. provisum etiam est a Deo, & Carolus Tapia in Rub. de constitutionibus Pontificum [*sic*] capit. 1 nu. 3') is as unspecific as that of Valdés himself – who almost certainly was totally unaware of the ultimate justification, such as it was, for his confident contention. Cf. C. Tapia, *Commentarius in rubricam, et legem finalem ff. de constitutionibus Principum* (Marburg 1598), pp. 9–10; below, n. 48.

28 'Breif abstract', pp. 77–8.
29 *Ibid.*, p. 85. In refutation of the claim that it was only by 'Gallic authors' that the right to coronation and anointing was confined to the kings of Jerusalem, France, England and Sicily (above, n. 16), the evidence of the *Liber Provincialis* was available, e.g. Cambridge, St John's College, MS.G.9, unfol. [fols 12va-b: 'Rex Castelle non, Rex Legionis non, Rex Portugalensis non, Rex Aragonie non, Rex Noruargie non, Rex Nauarre non [and 12 more]. Et sciatis quod hodie non sunt plures reges christianorum nisi de nouo crearentur'. Italian, saec. xiv: M. R. James, *A Descriptive Catalogue of the Manuscripts in the Library of St John's College, Cambridge* (Cambridge, 1913), no. 177.
30 F. Barlow, 'The King's Evil', *English Historical Review* 95 (1980), p. 23.
31 See Linehan, *History and the Historians*, pp. 427–9.

*The King's Touch and the Dean's Ministrations*

These reflections lead on to consideration of Jacques Le Goff's study of the French coronation *ordo* of 1250. The Bibliothèque Nationale manuscript in which that *ordo* is found, we are there told, 'has the unique quality of containing a description of a ceremony accompanied by a series of images'.[32] Unique in the year 1250, no doubt. But not so when the Escorial manuscript containing the *ordo* commissioned by Alfonso XI of Castile for his anointing and coronation in 1332 – Valdes's most recent historical instance in 1602 – is taken into account.

The *Escorial ordo* for the anointing and coronation of the king of Castile is also an illustrated *ordo* – and a work long overdue for full-scale facsimile treatment, one would have thought. Like the poem from twelfth-century France analysed by Professor Jordan,[33] its compilation was (at least in part) occasioned by knowledge of the dynasty's salvation, in this case knowledge of the long-awaited pregnancy of Alfonso XI's queen, María of Portugal. Like the French *ordo* of 1250 (presumably), it was compiled by a bishop – but not a Castilian one. The author of this Castilian *ordo* was the bishop of Coimbra, a Portuguese see. But again, the bishop of this Portuguese see was not Portuguese. He was French, a member of the Ebrard family which hailed from Quercy.[34]

In the prologue to his Castilian *ordo* the French bishop of the Portuguese see stated that he had scoured the papal *camera* for the best and most up-to-date examples of how such ceremonial should be conducted.[35] And in order to ensure that on the day no mistakes were made he was providing the king with an *ordo* for his *sagra* written in the vernacular and illustrated with pictures: 'scripta en romanço con sus ystorias pintadas'[36] – though when the time came, in August 1332, Alfonso XI rejected the bishop of

---

[32] 'A coronation program for the age of Saint Louis: the *ordo* of 1250', *Coronations: Medieval and Early Modern Monarchic Ritual*, ed. J. M. Bak (Berkeley, 1990), p. 46. One of the images is that of the archbishop anointing the king's forehead with an implement which J.-C. Bonne, in the same volume, describes as a 'golden nail': 'The Manuscript of the Ordo of 1250 and its Illuminations', *ibid.*, p. 66 and Fig. 4.1. But was this really a nail? Is the illustration not likelier to have been intended to represent one of the thorns from the crown of thorns which Louis IX had recently added to his relic collection? Other considerations apart, if the presiding archbishop had been wielding a nail would not his wrist have been cocked, darts-player fashion?

[33] See Jordan, above, pp. 171–86.

[34] P. David, 'Français du Midi dans les évêchés portugais (1279–1390)', *Bull. des Études Portugaises* 9 (1943), pp. 26ff.

[35] Although other such works are to be found in the lists of this period published by Fr. Ehrle, e.g. *Historia Bibliothecae Romanorum Pontificum tum Bonifatianae tum Avenionensis* (Rome, 1890), and A. Pelzer (*Addenda et emendanda ad Francisci Ehrle Historiae*, tom. i (Vatican Library, 1947), there is nothing of this description to be found.

[36] *Un ceremonial inédito de coronación de los reyes de Castilla*, ed. C. Sánchez-Albornoz (1943) repr. in *Estudios sobre las instituciones medievales españolas* (Mexico, 1965), p. 753.

Coimbra's carefully scripted *ordo* altogether. On the day, the king of Castile opted for something more distinctively Spanish, for an *ordo* in which churchmen were as little involved as possible and the king crowned himself, and crowned himself in a church in which – like the canons of Rheims who, as Jacques Le Goff has noted, appear so very much 'at home' in the illustrations of the 1250 *ordo*[37] – he was *really* at home: not in any of the cathedrals of his kingdom (and above all not in the cathedral of Toledo, to which, incidentally, Louis IX had presented *inter alia* one of the thorns from Christ's crown in 1248,[38] thereby equipping the primatial see to host a ceremony on a par with that described in the French *ordo* of 1250) but at home in his own dynastic pantheon, in the church of Las Huelgas at Burgos.

By August 1332 Alfonso XI had already made his ceremonial royal entry into Seville beneath a golden canopy. He had already had himself knighted by that extraordinary articulated statue of Santiago, that ingenious device capable of circumventing the hazard to hierarchical navigation which, in Alain Boureau's words, constituted such an 'obstacle to royal sacrality in the West'.[39]

The assistance of the articulated statue saved Alfonso XI from having his special Castilian sacrality compromised (or, at this short distance from the late Walter Ullmann's college, I suppose I should say *stunted*) by churchmen. In Castile in 1332 we encounter the same determination not to be compromised that is evident in the twelfth-century mosaics in the Martorana and at Monreale, with their depiction of the kings of Sicily receiving their crown not from an ecclesiastical minister but from Christ Himself,[40] or in the fourteenth-century Aragonese coronation *ordo*, with

---

[37] Le Goff, 'A Coronation Program', p. 49.

[38] 'Unam de spinis sacrosancte spinee corone eiusdem Domini', which, together with relics of the Cross, the tunic from Christ's passion and his shroud, as well as a ration of the Virgin's milk, the king of France had acquired 'de thesauro imperii Constantinopolitani'. Louis' letter, now preserved in the reliquary in Toledo cathedral in which these treasures are kept, is in *Viage de España*, ed. A. Ponz (Madrid, 1787), pp. 119–20. The 'ampolla de christal con so cobertero e con so pie de plata dorada en que esta el espina' is mentioned in the list of the contents of the Toledo treasury of c.1255: F. J. Hernández, *Los cartularios de Toledo. Catálogo documental*, Monvmenta Ecclesiae Toletanae Historica, I/1 (Madrid 1985), n. 532; Linehan, *History and the Historians*, p. 450.

[39] *Ibid.*, pp. 635–6 and 581–601; Linehan, 'Alfonso XI of Castile and the Arm of Santiago (with a Note on the Pope's Foot)', in *Miscellanea Domenico Maffei dicata. Historia – Ius – Studium*, ed. A. García y García and P. Weimar (Goldbach, 1995), iv, pp. 121–46; A. Boureau, 'Un obstacle à la sacralité royale en Occident. Le principe hiérarchique', *La Royauté sacrée*, 29ff.

[40] See Romuald of Salerno, *Chronicon*, ad. an. 1166, ed. C. A. Garufi, *Rerum Italicarum SS*, new edn, VII/i (Città di Castello, 1914–1935), p. 254; E. Kitzinger, 'The Gregorian Reform and the Visual Arts: A Problem of Method', *Transactions of the Royal Historical Society*, 5th ser. 22 (1972), pp. 87–102.

*The King's Touch and the Dean's Ministrations*

its prohibition of the hands-on ceremonial of the French *ordines*. In the *Corona de Aragón*, strict taboo prevented anyone other than the king himself from so much as touching the regalia.[41]

Now we are aware of the gulf between theory and practice in Castile in 1332. We are aware of the gulf because we possess a contemporary account of what actually happened in the church of Las Huelgas in the August of that year, an account which states that the king crowned himself. But for that account we might have mistaken prescription for description, and have committed the error of assuming that because the bishop of Coimbra's *ordo* existed in August 1332 it must also have been used then. It is an error all too easily committed, one which (even with the text of the Chronicle of Alfonso XI open on their desks) historians of the reign of Alfonso XI are making all the time.[42]

As Reinhard Elze's recent study of the so-called 'Ordo of Alcobaça' amply demonstrates, however, it is the sort of error which it is perfectly possible to avoid. Here again is a case of survival which does not imply use. The fact that the 'Ordo of Alcobaça', an *ordo* for the anointing and coronation of a king, survives in a thirteenth-century Portuguese manuscript does not mean that that was how Portugal's thirteenth-century kings entered into their inheritance. Its survival is no proof of its employment. Indeed, its very text indicates the opposite. The prayer that it contains for the prosperity of 'ecclesia *Francie* vel *Yspanie*' reveals its true nature. The 'Ordo of Alcobaça' was, in Elze's words, a 'kind of blueprint for any eventuality'.[43] It was a liturgiologist's collectors' item. In that sense closely analogous to the so-called 'Ceremonial of Cardeña' from twelfth-century Castile,[44] its prescriptions were as little illustrative of the austerely non-sacral realities of Portuguese kingmaking as (for example) the prescriptions of King John's charter to the English Church were of church–state relations in fourteenth-century Córdoba, where for some reason the text of that English charter at some time came to rest.[45]

The fact that the monastery of Alcobaça once possessed a copy of the

---

[41] A. Canellas López, ed., *Los cartularios de San Salvador de Zaragoza*, 4 vols (Zaragoza, 1989), no. 1600; B. Palacios Martín, *La coronación de los reyes de Aragón 1204–1410. Aportación al estudio de las estructuras medievales* (Valencia, 1975), pp. 201ff.

[42] Linehan, 'Alfonso XI of Castile and the Arm of Santiago', p. 138.

[43] 'Ein Krönungsordo aus Portugal', *Memoriam sanctorum venerantes. Miscellanea in onore di Mons. Victor Saxer, Studi di Antichità Cristiana*, 48 (Città del Vaticano, 1992), pp. 323–4: 'eine Art Angebot für alle Fälle', p. 327.

[44] Linehan, *History and the Historians*, pp. 241–4.

[45] *Ibid.*, p. 643.

twelfth-century *Liber Sancti Jacobi*[46] affords no argument either for regarding Alcobaça as a twelfth-century pilgrimage centre. Like the 'Ceremonial of Cardeña', the 'Ordo of Alcobaça' was an alien clone. Yet that is
not how historians have adjudged the 'Ceremonial of Cardeña'. They have
treated the alien clone as an indigenous growth. They have assumed that
because its text has survived in a Castilian library, the ceremonial itself
must have been enacted in a Castilian setting. And this they have done
partly because they have considered the text in isolation, and have failed to
allow for the realities of the society with which they have associated it and
for their knowledge from other sources of the nature of those realities.

Provided allowance is made for the realities of Castile in the 1330s,
Alfonso XI's rejection of the Escorial *ordo* will come as no surprise. Nor
will the story which the same Alfonso XI was told in the 1340s by the
Franciscan bishop Alvarus Pelagius – the story of which so much has been
made down the years, of Sancho IV's exorcism of a woman possessed by
the devil. As Alvarus recalled the event, with his foot on the woman's
throat, and with the woman cursing him as he did so, the king of Castile
had driven out the devil by reading words from a little book.[47]

Whether or not he was aware of it, this story was the basis for Valdés's
claim in 1602 that the kings of Spain were competent to cast out devils.[48]
Ever since Marc Bloch gave it fresh currency in 1924, however, its significance has been generally misunderstood – again, particularly by those
scholars who claim to be most rootedly opposed to the concept of normative sacrality. Bloch, of course, did not misread the story as a report of a
curing of the king's evil; the malignity which it describes is not physical
malignity. Even so, even Bloch was prepared to take Alvarus at his word:[49]
the same Alvarus who also reports that *felix Sancius* had ordered the
expulsion of no fewer than 5,000 prostitutes from his court on pain of
having their breasts cut off, 'quod multis factum fuit'.[50]

Like Bloch, later historians have also taken Alvarus at his word. But as
well as neglecting the implications of Bloch's reflection that 'la même
tradition se retrouve chez divers auteurs du XVIIe siècle',[51] they have also

---

[46] C. Hohler, 'A Note on *Jacobus*', *Journal of the Warburg and Courtauld Institutes* 35 (1972),
pp. 60–1.
[47] Alvarus Pelagius, *Speculum regum*, i, ed. M. Pinto de Meneses (Lisbon, 1955), p. 54.
[48] Above, n. 27.
[49] 'Alvarez relate un fait précis dont il a fort bien pu en effet être le spectateur. La même
tradition se retrouve chez divers auteurs du XVIIe siècle. On n'a pas le droit de la
révoquer en doute', Bloch, *Les Rois thaumaturges*, p. 152.
[50] *Speculum regum*, i, p. 368.
[51] The need for chronological caution in this regard is demonstrated by Nieto Soria's
*Fundamentos ideológicos*. See my review in *Speculum* 65 (1990), pp. 469–72.

*The King's Touch and the Dean's Ministrations*

overlooked something which Bloch had not failed to note, namely Alvarus's description as mere 'lies and dreams' (*apocrifum vel sompnium*) of
the 'gratia curationis' to which the kings of France and England laid claim.
And to this may be added further testimony from another of Alvarus's
works, one which was not yet in print when *Les Rois thaumaturges* was
being written, in which the claim of foreign kings to possess a *hereditary*
'virtus curativa' is condemned as no less heretical 'because such grace is
given by the Holy Spirit'. 'Non ab homine hereditatur', Alvarus insisted,
echoing the objection that William of Malmesbury had made more than
200 years before to the claim of the kings of France to have inherited such
powers.[52]

So what is happening here, in the friar-bishop's reminder to his king in
the 1340s of the demonstration of what we might call the sacral prowess of
that king's grandfather? Again, we have to make proper allowance for the
other things we think we know about the circumstances of the age to
which the story belongs.

Sancho IV had not inherited *virtus curativa* from his father, Alfonso X.
He had not inherited any *virtus* at all. What he had inherited from him was
the curse, the tremendous paternal curse which Alfonso had placed upon
the son who had risen in rebellion against him in 1282: the curse which
extended to Sancho's descendants in perpetuity ('por siempre jamas'). We
know that Alfonso X's curse haunted Sancho on his deathbed, and that it
continued to haunt his descendants, down to Alfonso XI and beyond. It
did so because it delegitimised Sancho's posterity. It blighted the dynasty.

As counterpart to inherited *virtus*, the function of the dynastic curse
deserves the sort of close attention that the monastic curse in an earlier
period has recently received.[53] In the case of the story of Sancho's act of
healing, it was not the king's inherited *virtus* that was at issue but his own
*virtus*, the intrinsic *virtus* of 'felix Sancius'. Whether real or imagined half
a century on, Sancho's *virtus* served a compensatory purpose, just as his
coronation in 1284 had done. Kings of Castile were not ordinarily
crowned.[54] Nor did they ordinarily perform miracles. Here as elsewhere,
the claim to possession of the power to do so was, as stated by Le Goff, 'un

---

[52] For which see Bloch, *Les Rois thaumaturges*, pp. 43–9. See also Linehan, *History and the
Historians*, pp. 503–4; Barlow, 'The King's Evil', pp. 17–18.
[53] Lester K. Little, *Benedictine Maledictions: Liturgical Cursing in Romanesque France* (Ith-
aca and London, 1993). See J. R. Craddock, 'Dynasty in Dispute: Alfonso X el Sabio and
the Succession to the Throne of Castile in History and Legend', *Viator* 17 (1986), pp.
197–219.
[54] Linehan, *History and the Historians*, pp. 446, 494.

instrument dynastique'.[55] Nothing more clearly indicates the atypical nature of the incident reported by Alvarus than the detail that it was necessary for the king of Castile in the 1340s to be informed that the *virtus* which his grandfather had demonstrated was one which he also possessed. This was unfamiliar territory for a king of Castile, just as anointing was an unfamiliar experience, necessitating the recruitment of a foreign bishop to provide an order of service. One is reminded of Barlow's observation apropos of Philip the Fair's deathbed instruction of his son, the future Louis X, in the technique of touching the sick. 'It is . . . a little odd that young Louis was not familiar with it. Where had he been those twenty-five or so years?'[56]

Alfonso XI was not familiar with all the paraphernalia of Anglo-French sacrality either. But in his case ignorance stemmed from inherited hostility to a set of beliefs which his great-grandfather had described as rubbish. When Alfonso X had been urged to cure a girl at Córdoba of what sounds suspiciously like scrofula, he had refused to comply. As always, it was the Virgin who did the necessary. That was the point of the story, which occurs in one of Alfonso's own *cantigas* in her honour. In passing, however, the king is made to say to those who had asked him to heal the girl himself, on the grounds that *all* Christian kings were competent to do so, 'When you tell me that I have this power you are talking rubbish.' It was a claim, he said, for which he would not give so much as 'a rotten fig'.

The story of the scrofulous girl of Córdoba – which unfortunately occurs in one of the unillustrated *cantigas* – has been told before.[57] Another, which so far as I am aware has not been mentioned in the present context, comes from Alfonso's secular *cantigas* and concerns not a single volume, as in the case of Alvarus's anecdote concerning Sancho IV's little book, but an entire library – the library of sex-manuals belonging to the dean of Cádiz.

This *cantiga* is not illustrated either (none of the secular *cantigas* are; it would have been a considerable undertaking). Nor is this the proper occasion to discuss this most pornographic specimen of Alfonso's poetic output; indeed, it is difficult to imagine the occasion at which it would be proper. Yet it does deserve mention, if only in order to draw attention to the fact that its description of the redoubtable dean's patent remedy for curing women of the king's evil, or 'St Marcoul's fire', is the king's own

---

[55] Intro. to Bloch, *Les Rois thaumaturges*, new edn (Paris, 1983), p. xvii.

[56] Barlow, 'The King's Evil', p. 24.

[57] T. F. Ruiz, 'Une royauté sans sacre: la monarchie castillane du bas Moyen Age', *Annales – É-S-C* 39 (1984), p. 444. See Linehan, *History and the Historians*, p. 504, n.151.

description, and to make the point that if the dean's touch really was the only therapy available in a land whose kings did not condescend to provide a service themselves, then it is hardly surprising that in the year 1600 Spaniards in search of a remedy were flooding into France in the numbers reported by Sir Robert Cotton.

What the king wrote –

> E, con tod esto, ayuda faz al
> con o[s] liuros que tem, per bõa fe:
> Se acha molher que aia mal
> deste fogo que de SSam Marèal [h]e,
> assy ual per foder encantar
> que fodendo lhi faz bem Semelhar
> que [h]e geada ou neue, non al –[58]

can be translated more or less, and more rather than less politely, as follows:

> And, this apart, the learned dean can do
> Things with his books to which you'd not aspire.
> If, let us say, he finds a lady who
> Is writhing ravaged by St Marcoul's fire,
> What with his manual, tool-kit and his know-how,
> He'll quickly turn her smould'ring ash to snow. How?
> By dousing with his bookish balm, of course, and easing
> with his literary screw.

In more ways than one, the tale of the dean of Cádiz shifts the focus of discussion of royal sacrality to hitherto unvisited areas, only one of which can detain us here. Twelfth-century exegesis of the story of David and Bathsheba had suggested that the seed of the anointed king had been capable of stopping his paramour's menstrual flow.[59] May the king of

---

[58] *Cantigas d'escarnho e de mal dizer dos cancioneiros medievais galego-portugueses*, ed. M. Rodrigues Lapa (Vigo, 1970), pp. 42–3. For speculation regarding the contents of the dean's shelves, but not the significance of that 'fogo que de Sam Marcal e', see F. Márques Villanueva, 'Las lecturas del deán de Cádiz en una *cantiga de mal dizer*', in *Studies on the 'Cantigas de Santa Maria': Art, Music and Poetry. Proceedings of the International Symposium on the 'Cantigas de Santa Maria' of Alfonso X, el Sabio (1221–1284) in Commemoration of its 700th Anniversary Year – 1981 (New York, November 19–21)*, ed. J. Katz and J. E. Keller (Madison, 1987), pp. 329–54. For his identity, see P. A. Solé, 'La iglesia gaditana en el siglo XIII', in *Cádiz en el siglo XIII. Actas de Las Jornadas Conmemorativas del VII Centenario de la muerte de Alfonso X el Sabio* (Cádiz, 1983), p. 44.
[59] 'Quae cum ingressa esset ad illum dormivit cum ea statimque sanctificata est ab inmunditia sua. Et reversa est domum suam concepto fetu', 2 Sam. 11: 4–5. See P. Buc, 'David's

Castile's *cantiga* have been intended as comment on his French cousin's alleged sacral prowess, therefore? Perhaps. At any event, the treatment of the incident in the Alfonsine *General Estoria* avoids all mention of the tradition reported by Petrus Comestor. Although, like its precursor Rodrigo of Toledo's *Breviarium historie catholice*, elsewhere the *General Estoria* depends largely on the *Historia scholastica*, here, in common with the *Breviarium*, it prefers a strictly physiological explanation of Bathsheba's delivery from her condition.[60]

If space permitted, at this point discussion might move on from nature's way to Scandinavia, and in particular to consideration of the parallels and resemblances between the image of the peninsular monarch projected in the second of Alfonso X's *Siete Partidas* and in his son Sancho's *Castigos e documentos* (a *Speculum regum* of the 1290s) on the one hand, and the mid-thirteenth-century Norwegian *Speculum* on the other, and thus contribute to that morphological exercise from which further study of royal sacrality stands to benefit.[61] For although the circumstances of the two regions were so very different, from all three works there emerges the figure of a vicar of God whose sacrality owed nothing either to unction or to miracle-working.[62]

I began with a seventeenth-century Englishman's animadversions regarding the virtues of Spanish kings, and will end with the animadversions of a thirteenth-century Castilian regarding the virtues of the most notable French ruler of the recent past. I use the word *animadversion* advisedly. It was the word which the archbishop of Toledo, D. Gonzalo Pérez, used at the beginning of the *consilium* on the subject of the sanctity of Louis IX which he submitted to Boniface VIII in 1297.[63]

Adultery with Bathsheba and the Healing Power of the Capetian Kings', *Viator* 24 (1993), pp. 101–20.

[60] *Ibid.*, p. 108. See also *Roderici Ximenii de Rada Breviarium Historie Catholice*, V. 8, ed. J. Fernández Valverde, Corpus Christianorum: Continuatio Medievalis 72A (1992), p. 273: 'dicitur quod paciebatur menstruum, et cum in primo concubitu concepisset, cessauit menstruus sanguinis, quem natura dicitur conseruari in alimoniam futuri fetus'; Alfonso el Sabio, *General Estoria* II/ii, ed. A. G. Solalinde *et al.* (Madrid, 1961), p. 363*b*: 'E dizen vnos que auia ella entonçes su camisa; e desque el rey a ella llego, que luego la dexo aquello. E desque vio commo fincaua linpia de aquella natura, sintio commo era prennada e enbiolo dezir a Dauid'. The *Cantigas de Santa María* record two miraculous cures of the 'fogo de San Marçal', nos. 84 and 91. Both were attributed to the Virgin. The latter was enacted 'en França'.

[61] See J. Ravel, 'La royauté sacrée. Eléments pour un débat', *La Royauté sacrée*, pp. 16–17.

[62] See Linehan, *History and the Historians*, pp. 431ff; S. Bagge, *The Political Thought of the King's Mirror* (Odense, 1987), pp. 43ff, 130ff; E. M. Jónsson, 'La situation du Speculum Regale dans la littérature occidentale', *Études germaniques* 42 (1987), pp. 391–408.

[63] P. Linehan and F. J. Hernández, ' "Animadverto": A Recently Discovered Consilium Concerning the Sanctity of King Louis IX', *Revue Mabillon*, n.s. 5, 66 (1994), pp. 83–105.

### The King's Touch and the Dean's Ministrations

'Animadverto', the archbishop's treatment of his theme commences, in the words of the Shunammite woman's greeting of Elisha in IV Kgs. 4: 9 ('Animadverto quod vir Dei sanctus est iste'), before proceeding to review the king's qualifications for canonisation, qualifications which are not sacral but exclusively saintly. For a number of reasons, Gonzalo Pérez's *consilium* is an extraordinary text; and in parts it is extraordinarily difficult to read: a draft, on paper, with many corrections, excisions and insertions, much of it in a very cursive hand. As is so often the case, the most interesting parts are the parts that have been most nearly deleted. From what it has proved possible to decipher, however – which is, in fact, almost all of it – there emerges a silhouette of the identikit holy king at the very end of the thirteenth century.

Interesting though it is for what it contains, the archbishop's *consilium* is even more interesting for what it does not. There is, for example, nothing here on the subject of Louis' inherited qualities: a subject on which Charles of Anjou was not short of ideas, and which certainly might have been expected to appeal to a Castilian archbishop considering the case of the son of a Castilian mother. Nothing, either, about cures performed by the king. Not that we would have expected anything of the sort, even from one who claimed to have witnessed the king in operation.[64] For, as Jacques Le Goff has already observed, so far as contemporaries were concerned it was the king's life and his *opera virtuosa* that counted, not his miracles.[65]

The archbishop's claim to eyewitness status is entirely credible. He had been in Paris in the 1250s.[66] Moreover, in 1297, Boniface VIII seems to have taken his testimony seriously. Though Gonzalo Pérez's tortuous attempt to make something of the king's miracles ultimately failed, nevertheless the phrases which the *consilium* has in common with one of Boniface's sermons on the occasion of the canonisation in August 1297 do seem to indicate that the pope paid careful attention to the archbishop of Toledo's memoir. This is especially so in its account of Louis' crusading exploits and the 'miseries of a captive dog' ('penas captivi canis') that he

---

[64] 'in operibus uirtuosis circa que qualiter se habuerit super aliqua tamen que audiui, aliquando uidi, possum testimonium perhibere': *ibid.*, p. 104, n. 25.

[65] Barlow, 'The King's Evil', p. 22. See J. Le Goff, 'Saint de l'Église et saint du peuple: les miracles officiels de saint Louis entre sa mort et sa canonisation (1270–1297)', *Histoire sociale, sensibilités collectives et mentalités. Mélanges Robert Mandrou* (Paris, 1985), p. 179: 'Plus largement si on scrute l'ensemble de l'oeuvre des biographes de saint Louis entre 1270 et le début du XIVe siècle on a bien l'impression que ce qui compte surtout à leurs yeux, c'est la vie plus que les miracles'.

[66] Dr Hernández and the present writer have a full-scale study of this remarkable and remarkably neglected churchman's career in preparation.

had endured for the cause. But this sounds defeatist. On the terrain that Jacques Le Goff has made so peculiarly his own, therefore, let it finally be noted that the biblical exemplar with whom the Castilian archbishop wished the French king to be associated was not the downbeat Josiah, the ruler after whose reign Judah was overwhelmed. It was Abraham.[67]

---

[67] 'Ita quod dici potest de eo quod de Abraham dicitur: Ibat profficiens adque sucrescens donec magnus veementer effectus est': Linehan and Hernández, p. 105. See also J. Le Goff, 'Royauté biblique et idéal monarchique médiéval: Saint Louis et Josias', in *Les Juifs au regard de l'histoire. Mélanges en l'honneur de B. Blumenkranz*, ed. G. Dahan (Paris, 1985), p. 166, where the common pattern of Josiah and Louis is discerned in the resemblance of the new leaf which the former turned in the eighteenth year of his reign (IV Kings 22: 3) to the latter's transformed demeanour after the crusade of 1248. See C. F. Fraker, 'Abraham in the "General Estoria"', in *Alfonso X of Castile, the Learned King (1221–1284): An International Symposium, Harvard University, 17 November 1984* (Cambridge, Mass., 1990), pp. 17–29.

# X

## 'QUEDAM DE QUIBUS DUBITANS':
## ON PREACHING THE CRUSADE IN ALFONSO X'S CASTILE [1]

In terms of dramatic content, Alfonso X's return to Castile from his meeting with Pope Gregory X at Beaucaire was altogether the equal of Henry IV of Germany's journey to Canossa almost two hundred years before. The effect, however, was wholly different. For whereas by appealing to the priest in Gregory VII the bare-footed German ruler's *démarche* may have called the other's bluff, in December 1275 there was no disguising the fact that the learned king returned home a broken man. On setting out for his encounter with the pontiff fourteen months earlier, he had been in his pomp. Now, seriously ill, possibly even cancerous, and with the imperial strategy by which for almost two decades all his endeavours had been influenced shot from under him, in little over a year as well as the possibility of an empire he had lost his son and heir and, in addition to other close relations to whom he was attached, his archbishop of Toledo also. It was at this point that the reign of Alfonso X began to unravel.

Immediately the old peninsular agenda resurfaced itself. The Marinid forces of Abu Yusuf which had already claimed the archbishop D. Sancho's scalp were still at the gate. When the king reached Valladolid in the last week of February 1276, therefore, measures to deal with that threat were the absolute priority. [2]

All this is familiar enough. What is not is the information contained in the following account of what ensued when the ancient call to arms was sounded again and Castile returned to the problem of its ancestral foe. Though not wholly unknown, the evidence on which it is chiefly based –the correspondence in the spring of 1276 between the archbishop of Seville, D. Remondo de Losaña, and the prior provincial of the Spanish Dominicans, to whom the former had entrusted the task of preaching the Spanish crusade on the strength of the crusade indulgences which had for some time been gathering dust somewhere in the Castilian chancery and which, until recently, Alfonso X in his euphoria had perhaps imagined might be left there for ever– has never previously been fully exploited. [3]

1. The research on which the present work is based was facilitated by the author's receipt of a British Academy Research Grant in 1997-8, principally for the purpose of enabling him to conduct a survey of papal materials in Portuguese archives for the period 1198-1417. He herewith expresses his gratitude to the Academy.

2. M. GONZÁLEZ JIMÉNEZ, ed., *Crónica de Alfonso X. Según el Ms. II/2777 de la Biblioteca del Palacio Real (Madrid)*, Murcia 1999, n. 283 *apud* cap. 67.

3. [Lisbon,] A[rquivos] N[acionais/]T[orre do] T[ombo], Corporações Religiosas, S. Domingos de Santarém, maço 1, docs. 5, 6, 6A: an instrument of some 3,000 words in 158 lines (Appendix I). Brief extracts of these items have been published by A. do ROSÁRIO, 'Rótulo de São Domingos de Santarém. Documentos inéditos sobre Cruzada a pregar pelos Dominicanos 1276. I – Carta de Fr. João Árias': *Actas*

# X

Though, as is the case with so many of the leading figures of Alfonso X's entourage, he still awaits a proper study, D. Remondo de Losaña can safely be described as one of the *rey Sabio*'s closest intimates.[4] *Hoc et preterea nihil*, however: that apart, there is little that can be said about this model (and therefore faceless) civil servant. It is heartening therefore to find him angry for once, as we find him in his exchanges with the Dominican prior provincial in the spring of 1276 –and not only angry but evidently very angry.

While the king had been visiting the pope, taking with him his other principal councillor, the notary for Castile,[5] it was to D. Remondo that the affairs of the kingdom had been entrusted and from Seville that he had administered them.[6] Likewise, it was to him that the preaching of the crusade had been assigned. From Valladolid on 28 February 1276 he remitted the task to the prior provincial. It was then that the trouble began.

When he sent him the summary of papal authorities on which he was to proceed [Appendix I, **II. a-q**], the archbishop doubtless expected that fr. Juan Arias would speed the matter forward by setting his brethren to work, preaching, exhorting and collecting throughout the kingdom. On receiving the archbishop's instructions at Palencia two or three days later, however, the prior was assailed by doubts, doubts regarding their basis in law: 'quedam de quibus dubitans', he therefore requested better particulars from D. Remondo. And on or soon after 8 March these were sent to him in the form of copies of the two letters of Clement IV (*Non sine misterio* [**II.r**] [7] and *De tue*

---

*das III Jornadas de História Medieval do Algarve e Andaluzia*, Loulé 1989, 55-69 [of 15 lines from **I.a**, **I.b**] and by M. GONZÁLEZ JIMÉNEZ, *Diplomatario andaluz de Alfonso X*, Seville 1991, xcvii [of 5 lines from **II.c**, **IV.b**].

4. A. BALLESTEROS, 'Don Remondo de Losana', *Correo Erudito* 1 (1940-41) 313-18, is a notably perfunctory piece. According to E. COSTA Y BELDA, from the content of *Non sine misterio* (below) 'parece deducirse que era miembro de la orden dominicana': 'Las constituciones de don Raimundo de Losaña para el cabildo de Sevilla', *HID* 5 (1978) 171. The author does not explain the basis of his deduction, which merely repeats a long descredited myth which Ballesteros had previously revived, describing it as 'no inverosímil', on the remarkable grounds that 'el apelativo *Maestro*' (attributed to D. Remondo in 1251) 'denota su condición de religioso dominico': *Alfonso X el Sabio*, Barcelona 1963, 320-22. The ancient canard is finally disposed of by the evidence considered here, and in particular by D. Remondo's woeful ignorance of the Order's peninsular organisation (I. **IV.a**).

5. Gonzalo Pérez (*alias* Gudiel), archdeacon of Toledo and notary for Castile, for whose role at this stage of the reign see the forthcoming monograph by Dr F. J. Hernández and the present writer, chap. 6.

6. From where it was that on 8 and 9 December 1274 he subdelegated papal directives regarding the Portuguese Order of Avis: ANTT, S. Bento de Avis, maço 2, cx. 2, nos 120, 114.

7. Dated 26 June 1265, this is an extended version of the registered version of 26 March 1265 (E. JORDAN, *Les Registres de Clément IV*, Paris 1893-1945, no.15/ S. DOMÍNGUEZ SÁNCHEZ, *Documentos de Clemente IV (1265-1268) referentes a España*, León 1995, no. 5) as printed from a copy of 1294 preserved in AC Burgos by F. J. PEREDA LLARENA, *Documentación de la Catedral de Burgos (1254-1293)*, Burgos n.d., no. 73. (Another copy is preserved in AC Toledo, O.4.L.1.10.). Otherwise, the only difference between the two versions consists in two cases of minor rearrangement of word-order to satisfy the requirements of the *cursus*.

*circumspectionis* [**II.s**])[8] on which those instructions claimed to be based: certified copies provided by a number of bishops about court [Appendix I, **II. r, s**].

Yet fr. Juan Arias remained uneasy and, having inspected the dossier, a fortnight later returned to the charge. And here is the principal interest of the matter. With the enemies of the Cross at the very gates of the kingdom, the mortals remains of the archbishop of Toledo whom they had dismembered only recently interred, and the succession question a burning issue, here was the prior provincial of the Dominicans engaging the archbishop of Seville in casuistical discussion, for all the world as if they were involved in scholastic debate within sheltered cloisters.[9] It appears extraordinary that the succession of questions rehearsed in Appendix I, **III** should have been asked in such circumstances, in the cannon's mouth as it were – and all the more so that with St Dominic's Castile in such dire straits it should have been the Castilian principal of St Dominic's own order who was asking them.

Meanwhile, in this very year, Fr. Rodrigo de Cerrato OP was penning his *Vitae sanctorum*, designed to reconcile impoverished clerics to their miserable circumstances by reminding them of how very much worse things had been for their holy predecessors.[10] What hope can there have been for Alfonso X's Castile in 1276, though, when Fr. Rodrigo's superior was raising the series of objections related in Appendix I, **III**? The confrontation of law and theology, envisaged as Manichaean principles locked in conflict for possession of the soul of the Western Church, as Marsiglio of Padua was to envisage them, could hardly have been more eloquently represented.[11] The effect of the 'letter that killeth' where it was least expected to be encountered can rarely have been proved more corrosive. When two years earlier the former Dominican Master General, Humbert de Romans, had enumerated the arguments and objections which were hampering the preaching of a successful crusade he had not thought to include quibbling on the part of illustrious members of his own Order.[12]

---

8. Dated 2 July 1265, incorporating text of Innocent III, *Ad liberandum* [14 Dec. 1215: A. POTTHAST, *Regesta Pontificum Romanorum inde ab a. post Christum natum MCXCVIII ad an. MCCCIV*, 5012]. Not recorded in any of the papal registers of Clement IV, nor noted by POTTHAST or DOMÍNGUEZ SÁNCHEZ.

9. It is to be noted that the Burgos cortes of May-July 1276, at which the succession question was high on the agenda and almost certainly settled in favour of the Infante Sancho, was followed in September by a meeting there of the provincial chapter of the Dominican Order: E. S. PROCTER, *Curia and Cortes in León and Castile 1072-1295*, Cambridge 1980, 139-40; C. DOUAIS, *Acta capitulorum provincialium Ordinis Fratrum Praedicatorum. Première province de Provence, province Romaine, province d'Espagne, 1239-1302*, Toulouse 1894, 624. Note also that at this stage fr. Juan Arias was on good terms with both Alfonso X and Queen Violante (**I.a, I.b**).

10. Peter LINEHAN, *History and the Historians of Medieval Spain*, Oxford 1993, 522.

11. Idem, *The Spanish Church and the Papacy in the Thirteenth Century*, Cambridge 1971, 86.

12. *Opus tripartitum*, ed. E BROWN, *Fasciculus rerum expetendarum et fugiendarum*, ii, London 1690, 191-7. Cf. E. T. BRETT, *Humbert of Romans. His life and views of thirteenth-century society*, Toronto 1984, 176-86.

For, with Castile *in extremis* in 1276, what was it that was gnawing at the prior provincial's conscientious vitals? What other than the archbishop's terminological confusion between 'procuratores' and 'vicarii' and between houses and convents, and the question whether members of the Order recruited to the task of preaching the Spanish crusade were to be recruited in person or *ex officio* [Appendix I, **III. a-e**]. Then there were the sanctions which the archbishop had specified for which the letters of Pope Clement IV adduced by him provided no authority. These represented a problem of substance. By what authority, he wanted to know – 'qua auctoritate' – were *they*, the archbishop's executors, to proceed regarding the exhumation of Christians who had provided aid and comfort to the enemy, deprivation and confiscation of their worldly goods, and the dispensation of clerics who had continued to enjoy the income of their benefices whilst excommunicated in return for the surrender of a proportion of that income [ibid., **III. f**]? [13]

When in 1280 D. Raimundo again recruited Dominicans to preach the cross on his behalf, he was at least able to provide some semblance of an answer to the question. [14] In March 1276, however, he plainly could not, and on being challenged had to concede that 'those things were indeed not contained in the letters of the lord Clement', claiming airily that they were however to be found 'in other letters of various popes sent to us'. And if the friars were not able to proceed on that assurance then let them do so on the strength of those evidences which *had* been provided. [15] March 1276 was no time for archival research. In March 1276 what was needed was action. And D. Raimundo was certainly active. On the reasonable assumption that the diplomatic bag took less than a day to pass between the archbishop in Valladolid and the prior provincial in Palencia, it is apparent that, whereas the latter spent some fifteen days in preparing his package of problems and demanding authorised copies of the papal letters, [16] his correspondent responded more or less by return, in not much more than four. In the circumstances, the archbishop's patience was almost heroic.

But it was not inexhaustible. And the captious friar's quiddities were calculated to test it to the limit. After raising those matters regarding which he had been instructed to act for which there appeared to be no papal authority, the prior provincial turned to those regarding which, although they were mentioned in the papal rescript, *per contra* he had received no instructions at all. Was the archbishop making alternative arrangements as to these, he inquired, or was it his expectation that the friars would implement the papal instructions despite the absence of any archiepiscopal directive so to do? [17] The question remained unanswered.

---

13. Cf. Appendix I, **II. h, i, o**.
14. Appendix II, **52, 51, 56** (though none of them is identifiable with any known papal letter).
15. Appendix I, **IV. f**.
16. Below, n. 37.
17. Appendix I, **III.g**. The particulars of these can be reconstructed from Clement IV's two letters and the inventory of 1280, as follows: Appendix II, **6-7, 11, 17, 20, 28, 31-32, 40, 50-54, 57-59**.

It was not the only one of the prior provincial's questions that remained unanswered. For as well as being reluctant to be drawn into such debate, the archbishop was plainly incapable of engaging in it. Witness his lame response to the objection that the 'privileges and immunity' enjoyed by preachers of the crusade did not extend to the *indulgentia peccatorum*. Though many thought it did, he claimed ('uisum est pluribus'), he was not prepared to become engaged in a metaphysical enquiry regarding the definition of these categories. He would stand by the papal text –whatever the papal text might mean (**III.h, IV.h**). Nor was he rising to the challenge to explain why the friars should put pressure on the dying to change their wills (**IV.i, j**)– an activity at which they were reputed to be particularly adept, at least in their own interest. [18]

Even less was he inclined to take issue with the prior provincial regarding the latter's conscientious objection to his earlier instruction to prevent the preaching of the cross for any other purpose than Castile's concerns (**II.n**). There could be no challenging the refusal of Fr. Juan Arias to comply with this instruction, since at the General Council of Lyons just two years before (the prior provincial recalled) not only had Pope Gregory X enjoined him and his friars to preach the Holy Land Crusade (as he remembered: 'prout mihi uidetur'), he had also excommunicated any who sought to damage that sacred enterprise (**III.k, IV.k**).[19] On the next point at issue there could be no compromise either. By far the most interesting item of the two churchmen's exchanges, it went to the very heart of the credibility of Castile's claim to be fighting Christendom's battle.

It was essential, said the friar, for men to be rallied to the joint defence of the faith and the fatherland. But how, pray, did the archbishop suppose that they would be so persuaded, even to the extent of laying down their lives for the cause? 'For if the trumpet give an uncertain sound, who shall prepare himself to the battle?', he asked, quoting St Paul. And wherein lay this uncertainty? Where, he answered, but in a call to arms which limited itself to repetition of the ancient mantra, 'Take the cross because Christians are at risk'? What sort of response was that to be expected to produce when no mention was made of the resources available, of the effort with which it was to be undertaken, or of the time-scale envisaged? (**III.l**).

It is a revealing outburst, is this, coming as it did just two years after Gregory X had sought the advice of all those experts as to why crusading morale was at such a low ebb, and Humbert de Romans had identified Christian slothfulness and lukewarmness

---

18. Witness Bishop Bruno of Olmütz's observation to Gregory X in 1274 ('Habent enim dicti fratres in civitatibus quasi omnium hominum sepulturas. Semen clericorum, quod in testamentis quandoque steterat, nunc a testamentis dinoscitur penitus occidisse'): C. HÖFLER, 'Analecten zur Geschichte Deutschlands und Italiens', *Abhandlungen der Historischen Classe der königlich bayerischen Akademie der Wissenschaften*, 4/3(B), Munich 1846, 24. Cf. Peter LINEHAN, 'A tale of two cities: capitular Burgos and mendicant Burgos in the thirteenth century', in D. Abulafia *et al.*, eds, *Church and City 1000-1500. Essays in honour of Christopher Brooke*, Cambridge 1992, 86-8.

19. A liberal description of the Council's sanctions against those hindering collection of the crusading tithe or trading in armaments with the enemy: G. ALBERIGO *et al.*, *Conciliorum Oecumenicorum Decreta*, 3rd edn, Bologna 1973 [=*COD*], i. 311.

X

*–segnities* and *tepiditas–* as an underlying cause.[20] Now the prior provincial confirmed that diagnosis. 'In mora *non segniter* est agendum' (**I.a**). 'Ad defensionem fidei et patrie homines sunt *non segniter* inducendi' (**III.l**). Humbert's criticism had referred to Christendom at large. According to his *confrère*, however, Castile's Christians were reluctant to rouse themselves too, and in defence not only of the faith but also of the fatherland.[21] Here was another example of the tendency to prefer private interests to those of the community which the bishop of Olmütz had identified as a besetting sin of the age.[22] And for this situation, responsibility lay with the archbishop of Seville, he implied, and his failure in the field of public relations. He had quoted I Corinthians 14.8. Did he have in mind also the following verse of that epistle: 'Ita et vos per linguam nisi manifestum sermonem dederitis quomodo scietur id quod dicitur. Eritis enim in aera loquentes.' 'Except ye utter by the tongue words easy to be understood, how shall it be known what is spoken? For ye shall speak into the air.'

But now the archbishop did rouse himself, throwing the friar's words back in his face in evident indignation. With what resources and what effort were the enemy to be confronted?, he had been asked. With *maximum* resources and *maximum* effort, he replied.[23] Likewise in respect of where and when (though actually the friar had not mentioned *places* at all), he proceeded to list those frontier strongholds whose strength was in fact very much in question, instancing Jerez de la Frontera, Morón, Marchena, Carmona, Écija and Puebla de Cazalla in particular. As to *time*, well time of course was of the essence. Time was needed for the collection of the harvest in those parts. But that could not be done without the protective presence of warriors. In a word, warriors were needed at *all* times. And while on the subject of time, let it be remembered that the time to be served by warriors seeking the indulgence was four months minimum (**IV.l**).

By comparison, the remainder of their exchange was of minor interest, largely concerning the practicalities of propaganda and collection. On one point fr. Juan Arias was adamant however: his friars were not to handle money (**III.p**). Come what may, they would be continuing in their vocation. And that vocation involved travelling. The *predicatores generales* whom the prior provincial was appointing to act might

---

20. *Opus tripartitum*, chaps 18-19 (ed. 198-9).
21. For this familiar pairing, see LINEHAN, *History and the Historians*, 294ff; Ariel GUIANCE, *Los discursos sobre la muerte en la Castilla medieval (siglos VII-XV)*, Valladolid 1998, 349. The prior-provincial also cites it at **I.a**.
22. 'Periculosa tempora jam venerunt, in quibus homines se ipsos amantes praeponunt commodo reipublicae rem privatam': HÖFLER, 'Analecten', 19-20. 'Haec pestis' the bishop called it, instancing divided elections as one of its manifestations, as exemplified by two recent cases: 'jam praeteritum et jam instans: praeteritum in electione Regis Hispaniae et comitis Richardi; et nunc Regis Hispaniae et comitis Rudolphi.'
23. The text here appears corrupt: 'Illud arbitrio uestro et illorum quibus uices commiseritis relinquatur, sed quidem uideritis secundum qualitatem personarum et quantitatem rerum illorum qui ire debuerint uel mittere bellatores' might be emended to 'Illud arbitrio uestro et illorum quibus uices commiseritis relinquatur *seu quorum* uideritis...'

134

well be moved on at any time. And then there might well be no one to act in wherever it was. The archbishop had better understand that. On that score, let there be no complaint thereafter that the prior provincial had been negligent (**III.m**).

If the truth were told, however, the prior provincial was taking an unduly high line, and the archbishop might well have responded with more asperity than in fact he did. For by 1276 the friars' anxiety to be here today and gone tomorrow was already a thing of the past. In fact, by then too many of them were settling down to an altogether more sedentary existence. Their increasing tendency to do so, and their penchant for living off the fat of the land, had indeed been both a matter of debate and a cause for criticism at the recent General Council. [24]

In copying this correspondence to his brethren, the superiors of the Compostela, Ribadavia and Tuy houses, the prior provincial stated that, because they were 'prudent men', by reading it carefully they would know how to proceed in the matter (**I.a**). This was perhaps said with tongue in cheek. For in fact nothing could have been less clear than how they were to do so. Had the archbishop waited just another month, he would have had *Exurgat Deus*, the privilege of the Dominican pope Innocent V, to use as his base text. [25] As it was, he and the royal chancery had evidently been taken by surprise and had had their confusion regarding the authorities on which they relied ruthlessly exposed. Combined with the laborious procedure stipulated for the copying of the 'multitude of letters' and their distribution across vast distances, that circumstance more or less ensured that, even if the provincial chapter of the Order may have served to hasten the process somewhat, [26] the enemy was likely to have reached the Pyrenees before the crusade was even preached. And, if as it passed from house to house it continued to accumulate errors of transcription to the extent exhibited by the time it reached Santarém, then by that stage the dossier would have been rendered almost totally incomprehensible anyway. [27]

As to the archbishop's performance meanwhile, there was more than a suggestion of that institutionalised arrogance which had characterised the Castilian rulers' dealings with successive pontiffs over the previous generation. As is notorious, Alfonso X, like his father before him, had continued to exact the *tercias* without papal licence. [28] The slipshod nature of D. Remondo's commission to the prior provincial indicates

---

24. Cf. (e.g.) the observations on the subject of the activities of the friars in general provided by the bishop of Olmütz on that occasion, by way of response to Gregory X's request for advice on the subject of what was to be done about the Holy Land: HÖFLER, 'Analecten', 23-4; Peter LINEHAN, *The Ladies of Zamora*, Manchester 1997 [Spanish translation, *Las Dueñas de Zamora*, Barcelona 2000], 28-9, 133ff.

25. Addressed 'uenerabili fratri archiepiscopo Ispalensi' and entrusting to him 'predicationem crucis in regnis et terris aliis dicti regis [*scil*. Castelle et Legionis illustris]', dated 'V non. aprilis [*sic!*] anno... primo' [1276] in the copy done at Burgos for Sancho IV's collectors (20 June 1290): AC Toledo, O.4.L.1.10. Cf. the variant text, also addressed to D. Remondo, publ. RAYNALDUS, *Annales ecclesiastici*, XXII, Bar-le-Duc 1870, 373, in which the archbishop's authority extends to the kingdom of Aragón (whence POTTHAST 21135 *sine nota chronologica*).

26. Above, n. 9.

27. Indeed the script of the ex-Santarém document looks rather later than 1276.

28. LINEHAN, *Spanish Church and the Papacy*, 111ff.

that this most loyal of the king's servants was imbued with the selfsame spirit of casualness.

By 1276, however, less and less were the king and his satellites able to act with impunity. Indeed, already in 1265 there had been signs of a hardening of papal attitudes, though in the perilous circumstances created by the current Mudéjar revolt Clement IV proved incapable of remaining resolute. Thus, just as the second issue of *Non sine misterio* in the June of that year extended the scope of the privileges granted to Alfonso in the previous March, so too in course of these very same months the pontiff's resolve to curb him faltered. Denouncing Alfonso initially as sunk 'in peccato notorio et mortali' on account of his retention of the *tercias*, and refusing him any grant of ecclesiastical revenues until he relinquished them, first Clement moderated his language and then agreed to settle for a written promise from the king to mend his ways. [29]

But by 1280 the Castilian climate had chilled further, and when in the March of that year the archbishop of Seville recruited another Dominican to preach the crusade for him, he did so in the immediate aftermath of Nicholas III's frontal attack on Alfonso X delivered through the agency of his nuncio Bishop Pietro of Rieti. [30]

It would be a work of supererogation (as well as testing the patience of readers of *Historia. Instituciones. Documentos* beyond endurance) to review the list of authorities which D. Remondo presented to fr. Gutierre OP item by item. Where they are identifiable, the information is supplied in the notes to Appendix II. Two features of his presentation do deserve notice however. One is that, by contrast with 1276, in 1280 his authorities *are* identified, including that for the surrender of illicitly sequestered tithes and the gargantuan task which that process presupposed. [31] Indeed, the contrast with 1276 could hardly have been sharper. His material is arranged under 23 headings, accounting for 46 items, with another 18 indulgences (II.**47-64**), unclassifiable under any of these *articuli* tagged on at the end: a rag-bag in short, though a rag-bag exhaling something of an air of desperateness (e.g. II.**57**). The

---

29. Ibid., 208. Cf. E. Pásztor regarding 'il tono… lievemente mitigato nei confronti del re' of the second version of the papal reproof [=*Reg. Clem. IV*, 890 /DOMÍNGUEZ SÁNCHEZ, no. 32]: 'Per la storia dei registri pontifici nel Duecento', *Archivum Historiae Pontificiae* 6 (1968) 85-6. Virtual capitulation soon followed: DOMÍNGUEZ SÁNCHEZ, no. 33.

30. LINEHAN, *Spanish Church and the Papacy*, 218-20; idem, 'The Spanish Church revisited: the episcopal *gravamina* of 1279': B. TIERNEY AND P. LINEHAN, eds., *Authority and Power. Studies on Medieval Law and Government presented to Walter Ullmann on his seventieth birthday*, Cambridge 1980, 127-47.

31. 'Cum nonnulli clerici et laici, non ratione ecclesiarum, pacifice et sine controuersia quasdam dicantur decimas possidere, quod tibi sit liberum de fructibus earumdem perceptis hactenus quartam recipere pro ipsius negoti subsidio portionem, dictique clerici et laici residuum fructuum eorumdem in predictum conuertere subsidium per se ipsos uel tibi, si maluerint, exhibere in idem subsidium conuertendum, ita quod ipsi ad restitutionem aliam minime teneantur sed inde remaneant penitus absoluti, dummodo decimas ipsas ecclesiis dimittant in posterum ad quas spectant, auctoritate concedimus supradicta': *Non sine misterio*. (Presumably the offer was open to the king of Castile as well as to others.)

X

drubbing the archbishop had received at the hands of the prior provincial four years before had left its mark.

On the other hand, it is observable that the process of rationalising the royal record had not advanced as far as might have been expected. The contents of Innocent V's *Exurgat Deus*, for example, seem hardly to have been exploited at all. Where that privilege seems to be referred to, the references are in the most general form (II.**4, 9, 13, 18, 25, 30, 55**), as a rule are only dubiously attributable to that Pope Innocent, [32] and are cited merely as appendages to the two privileges of Clement IV which had done service in 1276: *Non sine misterio* (in its June 1265 recension) and *De tue circumspectionis*, and to the first of them in particular. The royal case in 1280 rested squarely on those two superannuated evidences, the second of which in fact dated to the year 1215 and reiterated the provisions decreed at Innocent III's Fourth Lateran Council for the relief not of Spain but specifically for that of the Holy Land. To those of Gregory X's Lyons Council of 1274 there is no trace of an allusion. [33] One begins to understand why amidst the plethora of material in the Third *Partida* relating to chancery procedure and related matters there is not a single law on the subject of *filing*.

Less than a year before, the Castilian bishops had complained to Nicholas III on this very aspect of the king's activities:

> *Item impetratis ab apostolica sede privilegiis vel obtentis utitur etiam ultra concessionis tempus pro sue beneplacito voluntatis, non facta de ipsis originalibus copia illis ad quos privilegia dicta spectant...*

In 1279 the king's advisors had had no answer to the charge. [34] Late in the day though it was, by the following year they were perhaps at last beginning to learn the lesson. [35]

---

32. How were the recipients of these instructions in 1280 to know *which* Pope Innocent was being referred to – Innocent III, Innocent IV, or Innocent V? Were there texts attached? If so, the task of copying was on an even more heroic scale than in 1276.

33. For the continuing degree of D. Remondo's dependence on *Non sine misterio* at this date, see the notes to Appendix II. His case is based, clause by clause, on the papal letter of 1265.

34. Linehan, 'The Spanish Church revisited', 145-6. For a further example of Alfonsine sharp practice – the deployment in 1264 of a papal indulgence granted with an 'ad tempus congruum' shelf-life in 1246, see González Jiménez, *Diplomatario andaluz*, no. 286.

35. Appendix II, *ad fin.*: 'Comissio ista post annum non ualeat.'

# X

I Palencia, 5 April 1276

*Copy for the convent of Santarém OP of rotulus of correspondence between D. Remondo de Losaña, archbishop of Seville, and fr. Juan Arias, prior provincial of the Spanish province of the Order of Preachers, concerning the preaching of the Spanish Crusade.* [36]

II Valladolid, 28 February 1276

*D. Remondo de Losaña commits the preaching of the Crusade to members of the Order of Preachers to be nominated by fr. Juan Arias.*

III Palencia, 16 March 1276

*Fr. Juan Arias seeks clarification from D. Remondo de Losaña regarding particulars of his commission.*

IV Valladolid, 21 March 1276

*D. Remondo de Losaña responds to the queries raised by fr. Juan Arias.*

ANTT, Corporações Religiosas, S. Domingos de Santarém, maço 1, docs. 5, 6, 6A

[I.a] [C]larissimis in Christo patribus fratri Laurentio priori Compostellano et fratri Johanni priori Ripauiensi et fratri Petro preposito domus Tudensis, frater Johannes fratrum predicatorum in Ispania seruus indignus salutem in omnium saluatore. Nouis periculis noua sunt adhibenda remedia et ubi periculum est in mora non segniter est agendum. Cum igitur sarraceni de Affrica in multitudine graui et animo contumaci fines nostros inuaserint et intendant, ut timetur, nos in breui grauiter impugnare, nos oportet armis nostre milicie opportunis tanto periculo pro uiribus obuiare. Arma autem milicie nostre non carnalia sed potencia domini sunt, oratio assidua et deuota predicacio efficax et discreta. Hinc est igitur quod uobis direximus presentibus supplicandum et etiam iniungendum quod pro defensione fidei et patrie piis et assiduis orationibus apud dominum insistatis, hoc idem uestris fratribus iniungentes et eos super hoc frequencius exortantes et in predicationibus uestris et confessionibus et communibus locucionibus populos excitetis ut ad resistendum aduersariis fidei se non differant strenue properare. Ad hoc autem efficaciter faciendum uos mouere debet zelus fidei cuius predicatores estis, et pugiles esse debetis cum necessitas hoc requirit et amor patrie ac domini naturalis,

---

36. In accordance with the arrangements described in **I.b**, the text is copied from that issued by fr. Juan Arias. It abounds in scribal errors which combine with its sometimes agricultural Latin, the indistinguis hability of the letters *n* and *u*, and eccentric punctuation occasionally to obscure the sense (e.g. the transposition 'significaretis' < 'magnificemus' [**III.l, IV.l**]). Such errors are noted below only when they seem to be of substance. Both here and in Appendix II, original spelling is retained (e.g. with the letters *t* and *c* used interchangeably), and punctuation is provided as necessary. Word(s) or letter(s) supplied thus: [...].
Paper; no contemporary endorsements. Mistakenly archivised as three items.

*'Quedan de quibus dubitans'*: on preaching the crusade in Alfonso X's Castile

scilicet domini nostri regis, qui super hoc affectuosius me rogauit. Ad populos autem efficacius excitandos uisum fuit domino nostro regi quod deberemus crucem contra sarracenos de Affrica et de Yspania predicare secundum indulgentias que sibi super hoc a Romana curia sunt concesse. Et ideo dominus archiepiscopus Yspalensis, huius predicationis executor ab eadem Romana curia delegatus, de uoluntate ipsius domini regis uobis et predicatoribus generalibus, uni in quolibet conuentu uel domo quos ego nominauero uel quos uicarii uel priores quibus ego iniunxero nominabunt comisit dicte predicacionis crucis officium exequendum. Ego autem concedo uobis quod quilibet uestrum in conuentu uel domo sua nominet unum predicatorem generalem cum consilio discretorum qui huiusmodi officium exequatur. Ut autem caucius et securius ipsum officium exequi ualeatis mitto uobis in serie presentis rotuli translatum littere comissiue domini archiepiscopi Yspalensis et translata quarumdam litterarum papalium et translata quarumdam remissiuarum super quibusdam dubiis explanandis. Vos autem sicut homines prudentes attendatis diligenter tenorem dictarum omnium litterarum et ex illis plene colligere poteritis qualiter in ipso negocio procedere debeatis.

[II] Raymundus diuina miseracione sancte Yspalensis ecclesie archiepiscopus et crucis negocii executor religioso uiro, prouido ac discreto fratri Johanni Arie priori prouinciali fratrum predicatorum in Yspania salutem et mandatis apostolicis obedire. Quia ex transacta in nobis uita didicimus quid de subscripta conuersacione uestra et fratrum uestrorum presumere debeamus, confidentes tamquam de uobis ipsis de uestre consciencie puritate, uobis, prioribus conuentualibus, procuratoribus prouinciarum et predicatoribus generalibus, in quolibet conuentu uni quos uos magis aptos uideritis ad crucis negocium exequendum uices apostolicas nobis comissas super negocio crucis in tota Yspania, super quibusdam articulis inferius annotatis duximus committendas, exortantes in domino quatenus secundum quod urgens negocium postulat et requirit hoc presens negocium exequamini sollicite et instanter, scituri pro certo quod plena omnium peccaminum indulgencia a sede apostolica conceditur omnibus illis qui per annum huius officii predicationis fideliter exercuntur. Que autem uobis comittimus sunt hec:

[a] quod possitis proponere uerbum crucis et conuenientibus ad ipsam predicacionem centum dies de iniunctis eis penitenciis relaxare;

[b] et quod possitis absoluere illos qui in clericos manus iniecerint uiolentas, dummodo passis dampna uel iniurias satisfaciant competenter et non sit difficilis et enormis excessus qui sint merito ad sedem apostolicam remittendi;

[c] et quod possitis indulgere hiis qui assumpto crucis signaculo ad preliandum contra sarracenos Affrice ac Yspanie in personis propriis et expensis processerint et illis qui non in personis propriis illuc accesserint sed in suis expensis ydoneos bellatores destinauerint, et illis similiter qui licet in alienis expensis propriis tamen personis illuc accesserint et laborem assumpte peregrinacionis impleuerint plenam suorum ueniam peccatorum;

[d] et similiter indulgere hiis qui de bonis propriis iuxta quantitatem subsidii et deuocionis affectum ad subuencionem istius negocii congrue ministrabunt indulgentiam supradictam;

[e] et concedere crucesignatis eadem priuilegia et immunitates que habent crucesignati ad subsidium terre sancte, et si aliqui crucesignatorum medio tempore ipsis ad uotum exequendum

X

assignato decesserint quod habeant plene illas indulgencias et gratias que adeuntibus in terre sancte seruicio sunt concesse;

**[f]** et concedere omnibus fidelibus undecumque fuerint qui crucis assumpto signaculo in subsidium et domini regis crucis negocium prosequentis accesserint easdem indulgencias et gratias que a sede apostolica pro Yspanis specialiter sunt obtente;

**[g]** et quod possitis uota ieiuniorum, abstinencie, ultramarine atque cuiuslibet alterius peregrinacionis in huiusmodi subsidium commutare.

**[h]** Comittimus etiam quod denuncietis excommunicatos per Romanos pontifices omnes christianos qui sarracenis contra christianos opem, consilium uel auxilium occultum uel manifestum impenderint uel eis arma uel uictualia miserint in mercimoniis uel alio quoque modo, et quod tales ad ecclesiasticam sepulturam nullatenus admittantur, et si eos ibi sepelire contigerit exhumentur nisi signa penitencie probarentur forsitan processisse.

**[i]** Denuncietis etiam tales esse priuatos hereditatibus, prebendis, honoribus, iurisdiccionibus et ceteris bonis que tenent ab ecclesiis et bona sua temporalia esse per ipsos ad quos pertinent confiscanda.

**[j]** Item comittimus quod excommunicetis omnes illos qui secreta regis aut aliorum christianorum reuelare seu nunciare presumpserint sarracenis ut sibi cauere ualeant ab eisdam seu etiam resistere uel nocere; et

**[k]** quod possitis absoluere excommunicatos pro eo quod portauerint merces, arma siue alia prohibita sarracenis uel eo quod eis contra christianos auxilium, consilium impenderint uel fauorem.

**[l]** Comittimus etiam quod possitis concedere fratribus milicie Templi, Hospitalis Jherosolomitani, Sepulcri dominici, Sancti Jacobi et aliis cuiuscumque sint ordinis qui personaliter ipsum negocium prosequantur uel ad hoc bellatores ydoneos destinauerint uel subsidium dederint illam indulgenciam quam consideratis circunstanciis attendendis secundum dominum uideretis expedire;

**[m]** item quod indulgeatis .xx. dies de iniuncta penitencia omnibus diebus singulis quibus rogauerint Deum pro rege ac regina ac filiis eorum et exercitu eius et pro illis qui eidem in prosecucione huiusmodi impenderint consilium, auxilium et fauorem.

**[n]** Item comittimus quod interdicatis ex parte summi pontificis quibuslibet quibus pro terre sancte uel cuiuslibet alterius subsidio crucis predicacio est comissa ut in huiusmodi negocio in uestro prioratu aliquatenus non procedant, et si necesse fuerit eos per censuram ecclesiasticam compescatis, non obstante si est eis indultum quod non possint excommunicari, interdici uel suspendi;

**[o]** item quod possitis dispensare cum clericis de Yspania qui excommunicationis sententiis innodati beneficiorum suorum perceperint prouentus super retencione prouentuum huiusmodi dummodo certam prouentuum eorundem iuxta arbitrium uestrum exibeant porcionem.

'*Quedan de quibus dubitans*': on preaching the crusade in Alfonso X's Castile

**[p]** Iniungatis etiam uestris fratribus quod omnes predicent crucem et predicacionibus suis inducant homines ut in testamentis suis aliquid relinquant in redempcionem captiuorum uel in bellatores ydoneos in tante necessitatis articulo conuertendum, eisdem supradictam indulgenciam concedentes.

In huiusmodi indulgenciis concedendis discrecio uestra et aliorum taliter sit attenta quod arbitretur quantum quis iuxta quantitatem suam dare possit in presentis negocii subsidium uel quales mittere debeat bellatores. Et ne de ista comissione alicui dubitacionis scrupulum oriatur presentem cartam sigillo nostro fecimus sigillari. Dat. apud Vallemoleti .iii. kal. marcii, anno domini .M.CC.LXX.V.

**[q]** Comittimus etiam uobis quod possitis cum clericis qui manus uiolentas in personas ecclesiasticas iniecerint super irregularitatibus quos inde contraxerint dispensare.

**[r]** [C]lemens episcopus seruus seruorum Dei uenerabili fratri [nostro] archiepiscopo Yspalensi salutem et apostolicam benedictionem. *Non sine misterio...* Dat. Perusii, VI kal. julii pontificatus nostri anno primo [26 June 1265]. [37]

**[s]** [C]lemens episcopus seruus seruorum Dei uenerabili fratri [nostro] archiepiscopo Yspalensi salutem et apostolicam benedictionem. *De tue circumspectionis...* Dat. Perusii, VI non.. julii pontificatus nostri anno primo [2 July 1265]. [38]

**III** [R]euerendo in Christo patri ac domino R. dei gracia archiepiscopo Ispalensi frater Johannes fratrum predicatorum in Hispania seruus indignus obedienciam debitam et deuotam. Ad sancte predicationis crucis officium quondam per me et fratres alios quibus illud uestra duxit paternitas comittendum propono dare operam efficacem. Sunt tamen quedam de quibus dubitans duxi uestram discretam et expertam prouidenciam consulendam.

**[a]** Cum comiseritis mihi predicationis crucis officium. et procuratoribus prouinciarum et prioribus conuentualibus et uni predicatori generali de quo mihi uidebar in quolibet conuentu, nescio quid per procuratores prouinciarum intelligere debeamus, cum nos in tota Ispania non prouincias sed prouinciam, nec procuratores prouincie sed uicarios habeamus, et ideo uellem scire si per procuratores uicarios intelligere noluistis.

**[b]** Item cum contingat priores prouinciales et uicarios et priores conuentuales mori et interdum etiam amoueri, uellem scire si intenditis comittere illis tantum qui modo in dictis sunt officiis constituti uel eis et illis qui sibi sunt pro tempore successuri.

---

37. In *vidimus* by bishops John of Palencia and Stephen of Calahorra 'requisiti per uenerabilem patrem dominum Raymundum archiepiscopum Yspalensem', dated Valladolid, '.VIII. id. Marcii anno domini. M.CC.LXX.V.' (8 March 1276), that date indicating that fr. Juan Arias had requested the copies of **r** and **s** after receiving D. Remondo's commission. Not transcribed here, the two papal letters occupy 78 lines of the document.
38. In *vidimus* by bishops John of Palencia and Stephen of Calahorra 'requisiti per uenerabilem patrem dominum Raymundum archiepiscopum Yspalensem', Valladolid, 8 March 1276. Copy, with same date, in AC Toledo, O.4.L.1.10.

[c] Item cum contingat predicatores generales mori uel in priores eligi uel ad remotas partes mitti uel modo aliquo impediri, uellem scire si est uoluntas uestra quod quibusdam sic impeditis ego alios nominarem qui loco illorum auctoritate uestra dictum predicationis officium exequantur.

[d] Item cum habeamus in prouincia quasdam domos que non sunt conuentus, sicut est domus Tudensis, Bitoriensis, Xereciensis[39] et alie que loco priorum habeant prepositos qui presunt fratribus, uellem scire si est uoluntas uestra quod in his domibus preposito et unus predicator generalis in qualibet earum quem ego duxero mandandum dicte predicationis officium exequantur, sicut de conuentibus ordinastis.

[e] Item uellem ad cautelam si uobis placeret quod prior prouincialis aliquem uel aliquos de istis fratribus quibus dictum officium iniunxistis possem a dicto officio amouere et alium uel alios loco eius uel eorum sustituere cum sibi hoc faciendum ex causa legitima uideretur. Hoc autem ideo dico quia hoc posset in casu et ordini et negocio expedire.

[f] Item cum in littera comissionis nobis quosdam articulos comittatis qui in littera domini Clementis minime continentur, utpote
    [i] quod denunciemus exhumandos illos qui contra christianos sarracenis auxilium impendentes,
    [ii] item quod denunciemus eos priuatos hereditatibus etc.,
    [iii] item quod possimus dispensare cum clericis de Ispania qui excommunicati uel interdicti prouentus ecclesie perceperunt super retencione prouentuum huiusmodi etc., uellem scire qua auctoritate ista exequi debeamus.

[g] Item cum in littera domini Clementis quedam contineantur de quibus mentionem in comissionis littera non fecistis, utpote quod comissarii uestri possint exclusis excommunicatis et interdictis diuina celebrare uel facere celebrari in locis ecclesiastico suppositis interdicto, uellem scire si est intencio uestra aliquem uobis specialiter reseruare de illis que dominus Clemens uobis comisit uestris comissariis iniungenda, an simpliciter nobis comittere sicut in ipsa domini pape littera continetur.

[h] Item cum in eadem littera domini Clementis dicatur sicut 'Volumus preterea et concedimus ut illi qui in officio predicationis crucis pro presenti negocio per unius anni spacium duxerint laborandum illis priuilegio et immunitate gaudeant que personaliter in terre sancte subsidium transeuntibus in generali concilio noscuntur esse concessa',[40] non uidetur per illam litteram predicatoribus crucis concedi indulgenciam peccatorum que conceditur adeuntibus terram sanctam sed solum priuilegia et immunitates, cum priuilegia et immunitates ab ipsa indulgencia distinguantur, sicut patet ex tenore dictorum priuilegiorum et indulgenciarum et immunitatum a domino papa Clemente uobis transmisse in cuius principio sic dicitur.

---

39. Tuy, Vitoria, Jérez
40. Citing *Non sine misterio*

*'Quedan de quibus dubitans'*: on preaching the crusade in Alfonso X's Castile

[i] Verum quia in litteris ipsis habet mencio de priuilegiis et indulgenciis et immunitatibus uellem ergo scire quid super hec senciat uestra prouidencia circumspecta.

[j] Item scripsistis mihi in littera comissionis quod iniungerem fratribus quod inducerent homines ut in testamentis relinquerent etc., supradictam indulgenciam concedentes, cum tamen in littera domini pape dicatur quod talibus danda sit indulgencia secundum quantitatem subsidii et deuocionis affectum. Hoc autem ideo dico quia litteram comissionis oportebit me mittere fratribus et forte sic accipient sicut superficialiter [littera]<sup>41</sup> ipsa sonat.

[k] Item comissistis nobis quod interdiceremus ex parte summi pontificis omnem aliam predicationem crucis, quod ego facere non auderem cum dominus papa mandauerit mihi quod ego per me et fratres meos predicarem crucem in terram sanctam, et me presente in concilio generali etiam excommunicauerit prout mihi uidetur omnes qui impedirent negocium terre sancte. Et ideo, quicquid sit de aliis predicationibus, illam non auderem cum bona consciencia impedire.

[l] Ceterum quia necessitas imminet, sicut credo, ut ad defensionem fidei et patrie homines sunt non segniter inducendi, uellem si placeret paternitati uestre quod significaretis mihi aliquid certum per quod<sup>42</sup> eos excitare ad interritum<sup>43</sup> negocium ualeamus. Quis enim se parabit ad prelium si incertam uocem dederit tuba?<sup>44</sup> Quid autem incertius quantum ad presens negocium quam dicere<sup>45</sup> hominibus, 'Accipiatis crucem quia periculum imminet christianis', [cum] non dicatur ulterius quibus auxiliis, quo conatu, quo tempore aduersariis resistere intendamus?

[m] Item poterit contigere quod predicator generalis cui in uno conuentu comittetur officium dicte predicationis ad conuentum alium transferatur, et in uno conuentu nullus erit predicator generalis qui hoc officium predicandi crucem [exequetur] et in alio erunt plures. Hoc autem parum aut nil nocebit negocio sed ideo uobis significo quia si hoc ad uos perueniret et si casum forsitan nesciretis possetis credere quod ego ordinationem uestram obseruare minime faciebam.

[n] Item cum propter latitudinem prouincie Ispanie ego non habeam plenam noticiam de omnibus predicatoribus generalibus, forsitan expediret quod uos comitteretis quod non<sup>46</sup> solum illi quos ego nominarem sed etiam illi quos nominarent uicarii uel priores quibus ego super hoc scriberem dicte predicationis officium exequere[n]tur ita causam, quod ordinacio uestra seruaretur, scilicet quod non nominarentur plures quam uos in comissionis littera ordinastis.

[o] Ultimo sciat uestra paternitas quod ad exequendum sepedicte predicationis officium ita celeriter ut negocio expediret nos poterit retardare prolixitas et multitudo litterarum et latitudo prouincie et defectus etiam nunciorum. Oportebit enim me mittere fratribus et conuentibus de tota Ispania litteras comissionis et translata que uestra paternitas mihi misit quod absque mora et sine laboribus et impensis duci non poterit ad effectum?

---

41. Word largely erased
42. MS. quos quod
43. MS. exitare ad interium
44. I Cor. 14.8, misremembering 'bellum' as 'prelium'
45. MS. dare
46. MS. nullum

**[p]** Item si aliqui uoluerint aliquid dare pro indulgencia uel pro parte indulgencie impetranda, quero cui mandabimus pecuniam ipsam dari? Ego enim nollem quod per fratres nostros dicta pecunia colligatur. Et forsitan super hoc uobis priuilegium est concessum.

**[q]** Item si aliqui uoluerint redimere crucem, quero utrum eam oporteat ad uos personaliter accedere uel quod in hoc casu eis consulere debeamus?

Rogo autem paternitatem quod si placet super premissis michi rescribere non tardetis ut sicut quibus super hoc negocio sum scripturus qualiter in predicto negocio habeant procedere plenius instruantur. Valeat diu uestra paternitas et me et ordinem nostram habeat in sui gratia commendatos. Dat. Palencie, xvii kal. aprilis.

**IV** [R]aymundus diuina miseratione sancte Ispalensis ecclesie archiepiscopus et crucis negocii executor religioso uiro prouido ac discreto fratri Johanni priori prouinciali fratrum predicatorum in Ispania salutem in eo qui est omnium uera salus.

**[a]** Super illis nostre comissionis articulis de quibus uestra nos duxit discrecio consulendos taliter respondemus quod per procuratores prouinciarum intelligimus uicarios prouincie ac prepositos quos habetis in uestris conuentibus seu domibus licet procuratores prouinciarum in comissionis nostre litteris inserantur cum nobis esset incognitum usque modo uos non procuratores sed uicarios ac prepositos appellare, nec memores fuimus cum uobis direximus scripta nostra in tota Ispania prouinciam non prouincias uos habere. Per hoc autem querite consultationi noueritis esse responsum quod illarum domorum que non sunt conuentus prepositi et unus predicator generalis in qualibet earum quibus predicationis officium duxeritis comittendum libere possunt exequi officium antedictum.

**[b]** Ille autem questionis articulus quo quesiuistis cum contingat interdum priores prouinciales ac uicarios et priores conuentuales mori etiam interdum et amoueri ante dictum officium extendatur ad illos qui sunt eis pro tempore successuri, nil dubitationis continere uidetur cum non sub nominibus personarum sed officiorum petans [47] huiusmodi comissa.

**[c]** Super illo etiam de quo uestra religio per nos uoluit esse certa, quod si contingat predicatores generales mori uel eligi in priores uel ad remotas partes mitti uel alias impediri, respondemus quod possitis auctoritate nostra alios nominare ad huiusmodi officium exequendum. Ad respondentes dicimus quod prior prouincialis quem ad istud officium instituit poterit remouere et alium sustituere cum ex qua causa uiderit expedire.

**[f]** Preterea dubitastis cum in comissione nostra plures articuli quam in littera domini Clementis inserantur qua auctoritate illos exequi debeatis. Ad quod talem damus responsum quod etsi in litteris domini Clementis ea minime continentur, in aliis tamen litteris diuersorum paparum ad nos missis proculdubio inseruntur, quorum auctoritate uobis comittimus exequenda. Super quo uobis uel fratribus uestris quos ad hoc duxeritis deputando fide per apostolica scripta faciemus, nichilominus si interim uos dubitare contingat super non expressis in littera domini

---

47. *Sic.* Word(s) missing, e.g. 'fuerint mandata'?

*'Quedan de quibus dubitans'*: on preaching the crusade in Alfonso X's Castile

Clementis super expressis in eis libere procedatis. Ad illam questionem dicimus quod illa tamen comittere intelligimus que in comissionis nostre litteris continentur expressa, licet in rescripto domini Clementis plura alia sint inserta.

[h] Ad illum autem consultacionis articulum quo querere uoluistis predicatoribus crucis concedatur indulgencia peccatorum que conceditur adeuntibus terram sanctam cum littera domini Clementis sic dicatur 'Volumus preterea' etc., taliter respondemus quod per illa uerba scilicet 'priuilegiis et immunitate gaudeant' etc., uisum est pluribus concedi indulgenciam peccatorum. Nos autem per scripta nostra plus concedere ac comittere non intendimus quam ex rescripto apostolico colligatur. Illud etiam, nos nolumus ignorare comissionem nostram debere intelligi et exequi secundum quod ex rescripto apostolico manifestius edocetur.

[k] Super alio etiam diximus quod non curamus, et si non interdicatis aliam predicationem crucis in subsidium terre sancte, ex quo sicut scripsistis salua conscientia interdicere non audetis.

[l] Ad aliud insuper quod scripsistis quod magnificemus[48] uerbum certum quidem, scilicet 'quibus auxiliis, quo conatu, quo loco et tempore aduersariis resistere' debueramus, respondemus quod cum multiplici auxilio et conatu resistendum sit inimicis. Illud arbitrio uestro et illorum quibus uices commiseritis relinquatur, sed quidem uideritis secundum qualitatem personarum et quantitatem rerum illorum qui ire debuerint uel mittere be l latores. De locis uero qui multum indigent defensoribus, longum esset per singula enarrare, cum omnia loca frontarie, sed plus et minus, necesse habeant defensores. Verumptamen Xerecim[49] et illa castra que sunt in illo confinio plurium indigent auxilio et conatu, item Moron, Marchena, Carmona, Eçija, Caçralla et alia multa castra, quare eis, quia maiori auxilio indigent, est potissime succurrendum. Tempus etiam quo conatu et auxilio indiget illa terra iam imminet cum tempus colligendarum messium appropinquat que sine auxilio bellatorum colligi non ualebunt. Unde deceetero omni tempore sunt necessarii bellatores. De tempore etiam dicimus quod ad minus per quatuor menses euntes pro redimenda cruce et indulgencia obtinenda ibi debeant commorari.

[m] Item, etsi predicator generalis cui in uno conuentu comittitur officium predicandi ad locum alium transferatur, licet in eo nullus predicator generalis remaneat, uidetur nobis ut alteri fratri eiusdem conuentus si ydoneus inueniatur ibidem huiusmodi officium comittatur. Aliter discrecionis uestre arbitrio relinquimus ordinandum.

[n] Illud etiam uobis concedimus ut, cum propter latitudinem prouincie non habeatis noticiam predicatorum generalium, quod possitis per uos et uicarios uel priores nominare predicatores generales et eis hoc officium comittere exequendum.

[o] Ut autem hoc officium uobis ac ordini uestro non sit totaliter honerosum, expensas quas pro cartis scribendis et pro nunciis transportandis de collecta pecunia uel proximo colligenda secundum uestre fidelitatis arbitrium ordinauimus faciendas.

---

48. For 'significemus'? Cf. **III.l**.
49. MS. Xerecinam

[p] Ubi autem pecunia quam pro indulgencia obtinenda offerri contingerit debeat custodiri, et per quos debeant colligi, respondemus quod secundum quod ordinatum est in archa ad hoc specialiter deputata dicta pecunia reponatur sub trium testimonio custodienda sub tribus clauibus, quarum unam teneat unus frater uester quem uos uel prior uel uicarius deputabit. Et aliam persona aliqua uel canonicus ecclesie cathedralis ibi alteram deponi uolumus et seruari, et aliam teneat aliquis probus suus de ciuitate uel loco.[50] Si uero arca non fuerit ad hoc signata ubi est ecclesia cathedralis secundum predictum modum archa ponatur ibidem et pecunia custodiatur. Ubi ecclesia non fuerit cathedralis uel conuentualis in conuentu uel domo uestra ipsam archam poni uolumus et pecuniam conseruari sub modo superius anotato.[51]

[q] Ad ultimum respondemus quod redimentes crucem ad nos personaliter accedere non oportet cum per uos et fratres uestros quibus est comissum officium consuli eis possit. Dat. Valleoleti, xii kal. aprilis, anno domini .M.CC.LXX.V.

[I.b] Ut autem tenor dictarum litterarum ad uos possit cicius peruenire uolo et ordino quod prior Compostellanus uel tenens uices eius istum eundem rotulum, retento penes se translato eius, infra octo dies a receptione ipsius priori Ripauiensi mittere teneatur. Prior uero Ripauiensis, retento penes se translato eius, ipsum preposito Tudensi infra octo dies a receptione ipsius mittere non postponat. Noueritis insuper quod regina Castelle per se ipsam presencialiter me rogauit quod, preter ea que facta sunt pro domino Fernando in capitulo precedenti[52] et fieri debent in futuro capitulo pro ipso et pro domino Sancio quondam archiepiscopo Toletano, fratribus de Ispania pro animabus ipsorum orationes iniungere speciales. Ego autem, precibus eius non ualens nec uolens resistere, promisi ei quod de omnibus fratribus sacerdotibus de Ispania iniungerem pro animabus illorum missas singulas celebrandas. Unde rogo quod dictas missas celebretis et faciatis a uestris fratribus celebrari. Ut autem nulli in dubium ueniant omnia supradicta sigillum nostrum duxi presenti rotulo apponendum. Dat. Palencie, anno domini .M.CC.LXX.VI. in die sancto Pasche.

---

50. Confusion in text here.
51. Cf. The provisions for the collection of the crusading tenth decreed at II Lyons: *COD*, 311.
52. Cf. DOUAIS, *Acta capitulorum*, 622: 'Ista sunt suffragia defunctorum. Pro domino Fernando, filio domini regis Castellae. Quilibet sacerdos unam missam et quilibet conventus unam missam' (León 1275).

## APPENDIX II

Lisbon, 28 March 1280. Bishop Durandus Paes of Évora certifies the text of letters patent of *Archbishop Raimundo of Seville to fr. Gutierre OP* (Badajoz 28 February 1280).

ANTT, Corporações Religiosas, S. Domingos de Santarém, maço 1, doc. 8.Parchment. No endorsements. *Sigillum deperditum*. Conventions as in Appendix I.

Nouerint uniuersi presentes litteras inspecturi quod nos D. permissione diuina Elborensis episcopus uidimus et diligenter inspeximus patentes litteras reuerendi patris domini Raymundi archiepiscopi Ispalensis non rassas, non cancellatas, non abolitas nec uiciatas in aliqua parte sui, uero sigillo eiusdem domini archiepiscopi sigillatas, quarum tenor talis est:

Raymundus diuina miseratione sancte Ispalensis ecclesie archiepiscopus et crucis negocii exsecutor religioso uiro prouido et discreto fratri Guterrio de Ordine Predicatorum salutem et sinceram in domino karitatem. Noueritis summum pontificem Clementem quartum nobis super facto cruce signate salubres et uarias direxisse indulgencias quarum una[53] articulos continet subsequentes,

[1] quorum primus talis est, quod nos possimus predicare crucem in regnis Ispanie et Januensi et Pisana ciuitatibus et crucis predicatione comitere.[54] [2] Et dominus Alexander papa concessit uniuersis prelatis Ispanie quod possent predicare crucem contra sarracenos Affrice.

[3] Secundus articulus nobis comissus littere domini Clementis[55] est, ut illi qui in personis propriis et expensis processerint aduersus sarracenos Affrice ac Ispanie et illi qui non in personis propriis sed in suis tamen expensis uiros ydoneos destinauerint, illi etiam qui licet alienis expensis in propriis tamen personis iuerint, et illi similiter qui iuxta quantitatem subsidii et deuocionis affectum ad subuencionem ipsius negocii de bonis suis congrue ministrabunt, habeant plenam suorum ueniam peccatorum de quibus corde contriti et ore confessi fuerint. [4, 5] Istam eandem indulgenciam concesserunt dominus Innocentius[56] et Alexander[57] Ispanie transfretantibus, mittentibus uel subuenientibus contra Affrice sarracenos.

---

53. i.e. Clement IV, *Non sine misterio* in its extended version (above, n. 7) [hereinafter *Nsm*]
54. *Nsm*
55. *Nsm*
56. ?Innocent V, *Exurgat Deus* [hereinafter *ED*].
57. Alexander IV, *Circa exaltationem* (27 July 1259). Text, as reported in 1264: T. MINGUELLA Y ARNEDO, *Historia de Sigüenza y de sus obispos*, i, Madrid 1910, 601 (misdated 27 July 1258); GONZÁLEZ JIMÉNEZ, *Diplomatario andaluz*, no. 286 (misdated 27 August 1259).

[6] Tercius articulus domini Clementis[58] nobis comissus est, ut qui naues proprias exhibuerint uel eas studuerint fabricare contra sarracenos Affrice ac Ispanie habeant indulgenciam supradictam.

[7] Quartus articulus domini Clementis [59] nobis comissus est, quod recipiat cruce signatos et familias et bona eorum sub protectione sua et consistant sub diocesanorum suorum deffensione, et si contra hoc quis presumpserit per diocesanum loci ubi fuerint appellatione remota censura ecclesiastica compellatur. [8] Consimilem indulgentiam concessit dominus Urbanus proficiscentibus aduersus sarracenos Affrice ac Ispanie, [9, 10] et dominus Innocentius[60] et Alexander illis qui transffretarent aduersus Affrice sarracenos.

[11] Quintus articulus domini Clementis[61] nobis comissus est, quod si cruce signati aduersus sarracenos Ispanie ac Affrice fuerint astricti iuramento ad soluendas usuras, quod nos possimus compellere creditores censura ecclesiastica per nos uel per alios ad remittendum iuramentum et ut desistant ulterius ab usurarum exactione, et si forte aliquis creditorum debitores ad solucionem coegerit usurarum ad eas redendum simili districtione appellatione remota compellamus; quod iudei compellantur per secularem potestatem remittere usuras et donec remisserint ab omnibus christifidelibus tam in mercimoniis quam in aliis sub excommunicationis pena eis omnimode communio denegetur. Istam eandem indulgenciam concessit [12] Urbanus papa per nos fieri cruce signatis contra sarracenos Affrice ac Ispanie, et [13, 14] dominus Innocentius [62] et Alexander cruce signatis ad transffretandum contra Affrice sarracenos.

[15] Sextus articulus domini Clementis[63] nobis comissus est, quod cruce signati aduersus sarracenos Affrice ac Ispanie gaudeant illis priuilegiis et immunitatibus quibus gaudent cruce signati ad subsidium terre sancte. [16] Hoc idem concessit Alexander[64] cruce signatis profecturis in Affricam.

[17] Septimus articulus domini Clementis[65] nobis comissus est, quod non possint conueniri cruce signati extra suas dioceses per litteras sedis apostolice uel legatorum ipsius nisi de indulto huiusmodi plenam et expressam fecerint mencionem, dummodo parati existant coram suis iudicibus querelantibus respondere, et qui eos contra indultum huiusmodi presumpserint molestare per nos et nostros comissarios censura ecclesiastica compescantur. [18] Hanc eandem indulgenciam concessit dominus Innocentius [66] crucesignatis contra Affrice sarracenos.

---

58. *Nsm*
59. *Nsm*
60. *ED*
61. *Nsm*
62. Innocent IV, *Carissimus* (4 Oct. 1252): É. BERGER, *Les Registres d'Innocent IV,* 6030/A. QUINTANA PRIETO, *La documentación pontificia de Inocencio IV (1243-1254)*, Rome 1987, no. 808 (misdated 12 Oct. 1252); ?*ED*.
63. *Nsm*
64. Alexander IV, *Ad regimen* (13 May 1255): C. BOUREL DE LA RONCIÈRE *et al.*, *Les Registres d'Alexandre IV*, 483/I. RODRÍGUEZ DE LAMA, *La documentación pontificia de Alejandro IV (1254-1261)*, Rome 1976, no. 62.
65. *Nsm*
66. *ED*

'*Quedan de quibus dubitans*': on preaching the crusade in Alfonso X's Castile

[19] VIII articulus domini Clementis [67] est nobis comissus, quod nos et nostri comissarii possimus conuocare cleros et populos ad proponendum eis uerbum crucis et indulgere centum dies uere penitentibus et confessis, audientibus uerbum domini reuerenter.

[20] VIIII articulus domini Clementis est nobis comissus, quod nos et nostri comissarii possimus nobis et familiis nostris celebrare diuina et facere celebrari ac populis proponere uerbum dei in ecclesiis ecclesiastico interdicto suppositis, excommunicatis et interdictis exclusis et non pulsatis campanis, uoce submissa et januis clausis.

[21] X articulus domini Clementis nobis comissus est, quod possimus nos et nostri comissarii absoluere excommunicatos pro eo quod portauerint merces uel arma siue alia prohibita sarracenis.

[22] XI articulus domini Clementis nobis comissus est, quod nos et nostri comissarii possimus absoluere cruce signatos excommunicatos eo quod auxilium uel consilium contra christianos impenderint sarracenis.

[23] XII articulus domini Clementis nobis comissus est, quod nos et comissarii nostri possimus absoluere manuum iniectores in clericos seculares uirosque religiosos et incendiarios, dummodo excessus non fuerit dificilis et enormis, et satisfaciant lesis de dampnis et iniuriis. [24, 25] Hoc idem concessit Alexander papa [68] et Innocentius [69] cruce signatis aduersus Affrice sarracenos, [26] et dominus Innocentius concessit amplius quod possent absolui uiolatores ecclesiarumet locorum sociorum. [27] Item Urbanus [70] papa concessit quod possent absolui manuum iniectores.

[28] XIII articulus domini Clementis [71] nobis comissus est, quod nos et comissarii nostri possimus dispensare cum irregularibus clericis qui postquam incurrerunt sentenciam a canone uel ab homine se diuinis officiis inmiscuissent. [29] Hoc idem concessit nobis dominus Urbanus. [72] [30] Et dominus Innocentius [73] concessit similem dispensacionem clericis yrregularibus cruce signatis ad Affricam [*sic*].

[31] XIIII articulus domini Clementis [74] nobis comissus est, quod nos et comissarii nostri possimus dispensare cum irregularibus qui cum essent excommunicati receperunt ordines, absolucionis beneficio non obtento.

---

67. [**19-23**] *Nsm*
68. Alexander IV, *Cum tibi* (17 Oct. 1255): *Reg. Alex. IV*, 862/RODRÍGUEZ DE LAMA, no. 117.
69. *ED*
70. Urban IV, *Inter occupationes* (3 Oct. 1263): J. GUIRAUD AND S. CLÉMENCET, *Les Registres d'Urbain IV*, 468/ I. RODRÍGUEZ DE LAMA, *La documentación pontificia de Urbano IV (1261-1264)*, Rome 1981, no. 108.
71. *Nsm*
72. As n. 70.
73. *ED*
74. [**31-33**] *Nsm*

[32] XV articulus domini Clementis nobis comissus est, quod clerici uel layci qui detinent decimas non nomine ecclesie[75] pacifice et sine controuersia quod liberum sit nobis recipere quartam partem pro subsidio negocii crucis, et ipsi clerici et layci residuum fructuum eorundem in predictum conuertere subsidium ualeant per se ipsos uel nobis si maluerint exibere in idem subsidium conuertendum ita quod ipsi ad restitucionem aliam minime teneantur sed inde remaneant penitus absoluti, dummodo in posterum ipsas decimas dimittant ecclesiis ad quas spectant.

[33] XVI articulus domini Clementis nobis comissus est, quod crucesignati qui decesserint medio tempore assignato eisdem a nobis ad uotum exequendum illarum indulgenciarum et graciarum sint plene participes que obeuntibus[76] in terre sancte subsidium sunt concesse. [34] Et dominus Alexander concessit quod cruce signati qui decederent antequam trasfretarent aduersus sarracenos de Affrica haberent illam indulgentiam quam cruce signati in terre sancte subsidium [haberent] si antequam trasfretarent decederent.

[35] XVII articulus domini Clementis[77] nobis comissus est, quod nos possimus concedere fratribus milicie Templi, Hospitalis Ierosolimitani, Sepulcri Dominici, Sancti Jacobi et aliis cuiuscumque sint ordinis qui personaliter ipsum negocium prosequentur uel ad hoc bellatores ydoneos destinarint uel subsidium dederint illam indulgenciam quam consideratis circumstanciis attendendis secundum deum uiderimus expedire.

[36] XVIII articulus domini Clementis nobis comissus est, quod nos et nostri comissarii possimus commutare ab Ispanis uotum ieiuniorum et ultramarine adque cuiuslibet alterius peregrinacionis in subsidium negocii sepedicti. [37] Et dominus Alexander[78] concessit quod possent comutari uota abstinencie et peregrinacionis in uoto africano.

[38] XVIIII articulus domini Clementis[79] nobis comissus est, quod illi qui in officio predicacionis pro presenti negocio per unius anni spacium duxerint laborandum illis priuilegio et immunitate gaudeant que personaliter trasfretantibus in terre sancte subsidium in generali concilio sunt concessa.

[39] XX articulus domini Clementis nobis comissus est, quod possimus comittere premissa personis ydoneis, non obstante aliqua indulgencia per quam a susceptione huiusmodi ualeant aliquatenus excusari.

[40] XXI articulus domini Clementis nobis comissus est, quod possimus compellere per censuram ecclesiasticam crucesignatorum quoslibet, cuiuscumque dignitatis uel condicionis existant, ut infra certum terminum prefigendum a nobis uel uotum crucis redimant uel illud executuri ad locum destinatum accedant. [41] Idem concessit dominus Innocentius in concilio

---

75. Sic. Cf. *Nsm*: non ratione ecclesiarum
76. MS. abeuntibus (!)
77. **[35-36]** *Nsm*
78. As n. 68.
79. **[38-40]** *Nsm*

generali.[80] **[42]** Et dominus Alexander concessit quod dispensaretur cum inabilibus et legitimo impedimento detentis ut redimerent et haberent indulgenciam supradictam.

**[43]** XXII articulus domini Clementis[81] nobis comissus est, quod interdicatis ex parte summi pontificis quibuslibet quibus pro terre sancte uel cuiuslibet/[31] alterius subsidio crucis predicacio est comissa, ut in huiusmodi negocio sibi comisso in supradictis regnis aliquatenus non procedant sed eidem supersedeant eos si necesse fuerit per censuram ecclesiasticam compescendo, non obstante si eis sit indultum quod non possint excommunicari, interdici uel suspendi. **[44]** Et est alia indulgencia domini Clementis per se nobis comissa consimilis isti articulo in omnibus.

**[45]** XXIII articulus domini Clementis est quod indulget ^viginti dies de iniuncta penitencia omnibus uere penitentibus et confessis diebus singulis quibus rogauerint deum pro rege et regina ac filiis eorum et exercitum eius et pro illis qui eidem in prosecutione huiusmodi impenderint auxilium, consilium et fauorem.[82] **[46]** Est alia indulgencia domini Clementis per se nobis comissa consimilis isti.[83]

**[47]** Alia domini Clementis est per se nobis comissa quod omnes fideles undecumque fuerint qui crucis assumpto signaculo in subsidium domini regis crucis negocium prosequitis (*sic*) accesserint gaudeant eisdem indulgenciis et graciis que a sede apostolica pro ispanis specialiter sunt obtenta.

**[48]** Alia domini Clementis est per se nobis comissa quod qui secreta regis aut christianorum aliorum reuelare seu nunciare presumpserit sarracenis, ut sibi cauere ualeant ab eisdem seu eciam resistere uel nocere, excommunicentur per nos generali etiam excommunicacione et denuncientur usque ad satisfactionem condignam.

**[49]** Alia domini Innocentii est quod excommunicentur omnes christiani qui sarracenis de Affrica contra dominum regem impenderint consilium, auxilium uel fauorem et excommunicati publice nuncientur, et ipse excommunicat eos in concilio generali.[84]

**[50]** Alia domini Clementis est per se nobis comissa quod feramus generalem excommunicacionis sententiam in omnes illos qui receperint a sarracenis stipendia citra mare ut christianos inpugnent nisi, publice moniti in ecclesiis ut infra certum terminum peremtorie prefigendum a nobis, destituerint ab huiusmodi presumpcione detestabili et dampnosa et usque ad satisfactionem condignam faciamus uel expedire uiderimus solempniter publicari, contradictores per censuram ecclesiasticam appellatione postposita compescendo. Et si forte in eadem sententia prestiterint indurati bona eorum per ipsos ad quos pertinent confiscentur.

---

80. Innocent III, *Ad liberandum*; or Innocent IV, *Afflicti corde: COD*, i. 268, 298.
81. *Nsm*
82. *Nsm*
83. Clement IV, *Quod voluit* (23 March 1265): *Reg. Clem IV*, no. 17/DOMÍNGUEZ SÁNCHEZ, n°. 4.
84. As n. 80: *COD*, i. 270, 300.

[51] Alia domini Clementis est per se [nobis comissa] quod archiepiscopi et episcopi Ispanie excommunicent christianos stipendiarios qui se in partem Aggarenicam conuerterint et christianos et fidem eorum inpugnantes, si moniti infra certum terminum prefigendum a nobis archiepiscopo Ispalensi, habita regia securitate non destiterint, et faciamus denunciari excommunicatos, pulsatis campanis et candelis accensis diebus dominicis et festiuis, et quod denunciemus eos priuatos hereditati, in feudis, honoribus, iurisdicionibus et ceteris bonis ad ipsos spectantibus que tenent ab ecclesiis quibus dominus papa extunc priuat eos. Si uero clerici fuerint et infra certum terminum non destiterint, cuiusque gradus et condicionis fuerint, officiis et beneficiis ecclesiasticis que obtinent priuemus eosdem et inabiles esse statuamus ad alia beneficia obtinenda, quorum priuacionem et inabilitatem uult dominus papa per nos et alios archiepiscopos et episcopos publicari. Et si qui clerici uel layci tam nobiles quam innobiles trastulerint se decetero in auxilium sarracenorum Affrice uel Ispanie ut expugnent christianos et fidem eorum, ut superius est expressum, eo ipso penis subiaceant supradictis, et archiepiscopi ac episcopi tam illorum quam istorum carere faciamus ecclesiastica sepultura et exhumari eorum corpora si ea contigerit cimiteriis fidelium sepeliri, contradictores etc. non obstante etc.

[52] Alia domini Clementis est per se [nobis comissa] quod christiani qui presumpserint in auxilium sarracenorum se conferre et cum eis christianos alios impugnare eo ipso late sentencie canone sint astricti. Et si quis eorum decesserint sic ligati et corpora eorum tradita fuerint ecclesiastice sepulture, illa corpora, nisi in eis dum uiuebant signa penitencie apparuerint et super hoc possit fieri plena fides, exhumentur cimiterio fidelium caritura, contradictores etc.

[53] Alia domini Clementis est nobis per se comissa quod christiani Ispanie qui adinuicem guerras habent uel sunt inposterum durante huiusmodi negocio habituri, quod nos moneamus eos ut infra certum terminum ineant pacis federa uel treugas quamdiu tempestatis huiusmodi prelia durauerint duraturas, alioquin in eos qui parere neglexerint generalem excommunicationis sententiam proferamus et usque ad satisfactionem condignam faciamus sollempniter publicari.

[54] Alia domini Clementis nobis comissa est quod possimus usuras, rapinas et alia male acquisita recipere per nos uel per alium per triennium in regnis regis Castelle ab illis solummodo qui sponte ac uoluntarie absque coaccione aliqua uoluerint exibere dummodo quibus ipsorum restitutio fieri debeat inueniri et sciri omnino non possint edictis in locis competentibus propositis et ea duratura ualeamus in promocionem[85] negocii supradicti. Verumtamen si aliud ex istis dimiserimus uel restituerimus ac detentio illa a quibus ea receperimus hoc non possit eis ad liberacionem et quantum ad illud non habeantur absoluti.

[55] Ad hoc factum alia domini Innocentii[86] quod possint exigi et recipi usure et male acquisita ab illis qui dare uoluerint.

[56] Alia domini Clementis per se nobis comissa est quod possimus dispensare cum clericis de Ispania qui excommunicacionis sentenciis innodati beneficiorum suorum perceperunt prouentus, si alias beneficia ipsa canonice obtineant super retencionem prouentuum huiusmodi,

---

85. *MS*. impromocionem
86. *ED*.

dummodo certam prouentuum eorundem iuxta arbitrium nostrum uel comissariorum nostrorum exhibeant porcionem in subsidium dicti regis contra sarracenos Africe ac Ispanie.

[57] Alia est domini Clementis per se nobis comissa quod possimus absoluere per nos uel alium seu alios in ciuitatibus et diocesibus Januensi et Pisana singulares personas cruce signatas a sententia quam incurrerunt pro eo quod adeserunt Palealogo et Manfredo contra inhibicionem sedis apostolice, dummodo personaliter prosequatur negocium uel idoneos miserit bellatores aut de bonis suis iuxta arbitrium nostrum uel comissariorum nostrorum congruam miserint porcionem, recepto prius iuramento quod stent mandatis ecclesie, et recepta ab eis sufficienti et ydonea caucione quod eis ulterius non adherebunt contra ecclesiam uel fideles.

[58] Alia domini Clementis per se nobis comissa est quod possimus absoluere per nos uel alium iuxta traditam nobis formam Januenses et Pisanos tam ciuitatum quam diocesum a sententiis excommunicacionis et interdicti a sede apostolica generaliter promulgatis quas incurrerent pro eo quod adeserunt irreuerenter sarracenis seu Grecis scismaticis, dummodo ipsum negocium personaliter prosequatur, et quod denunciemus eis quod nisi a die quo iter arripuerint ad exequendum uotum crucis per annum continue in eodem subsidio personaliter moram traxerint eos uult dominus papa memoratas sentencias incurrere ipso facto.

[59] Alia domini Clementis est per se nobis comissa quod possimus exercere censuram ecclesiasticam per nos et nostros comissarios in contradictores et rebelles et resistentes nobis in huiusmodi predicacionis negocio, non obstante quod interdici, suspendi uel excommunicari non possint etc.

[60] Alia domini Innocentii[87] est quod clerici Ispanie qui trasfretauerint cum rege uel uicario eius habeant beneficia sua integre ac si personaliter residerent in ecclesiis per quinquennium ex quo iter arripuerint, contradictores etc. [61] Hoc idem concesserunt per triennium in concilio generali[88] quod possint per idem tempus beneficia obligare.

[62] Et Alexander papa concessit clericis Ispanie trasfretantibus in Africam uel illuc mittentibus in expensis propriis idoneos bellatores quod habeant beneficia integre a tempore passagii usque ad triennium et ea recipere per idem tempus ualeant seu ecclesia obligare.

[63] Item dominus Innocencius[89] concessit quod clerici excommunicati propter concubinatum per constitucionem domini Sabinensis[90] qui trasfretarent in Affricam uel mitterent ydoneos bellatores uel darent quantum expenderent uel circa, si trasfretarent cum rege uel eius uicario, concubinis prorsus abiectis et prestita caucione de ipsis non assumendis, uel aliis absoluerentur uel dispensaretur cum eis super iregularitatibus.

---

87. Innocent IV, *Signo uiuifice* (14 May 1254): *Reg. Inn. IV*/QUINTANA PRIETO, n°. 955.

88. As n. 80: *COD*, i. 267, 298.

89. Innocent IV, *Carissimus* (4 Oct. 1252): *Reg. Inn. IV*/QUINTANA PRIETO, no. 807 (misdated 12 Oct. 1252).

90. Jean d'Abbeville, cardinal bishop of Sabina, papal legate to the Spanish kingdoms 1228-9. See LINEHAN, *The Spanish Church and the Papacy*, chaps 2-3; idem, 'A papal legation and its aftermath: Cardinal John of Abbeville in Spain and Portugal, 1228-1229': *Studi Ennio Cortese* (forthcoming).

**[64]** Alia Alexandri[91] est quod executores crucis habeant liberam facultatem recipiendi ab executoribus testamentorum sponte ad id negocium dare uolentibus, indistinte personis aliquibus non expressis, legata seu relicta.

Igitur nos supradictus archiepiscopus et crucis negocii exsecutor uobis fratri Guterrio, de quo plene confidimus, omnia predicta plenarie in regno Portugalie in uirtute obediencie comittimus exequenda et uni ex fratribus uestri ordinis in singulis conuentibus predicti regni quos magis uideritis ad hoc aptos quibus eidem uices ducimus comittendas. Et ne de comisione huiusmodi alicui dubitacionis scrupulus oriatur presentem cartam sigillo nostro fecimus sigillari. Comissio ista post annum non ualeat. Dat. apud Pacam, tercio kal. martii anno domini M.CC.LXXnono.

Nos uero precibus supradicti fratris Guterrii inclinati in testimonium premissorum presentes litteras fecimus nostri sigilli munimine communiri. Dat. Ulixbone, V kal. aprilis, Era M.CCC.XVIII.

---

91. As n. 68.

# XI

# THE INVENTION OF TOLEDO

*In Memory of Leonard Boyle, O.P.,*
*sometime Prefect of the Vatican Library*
*(† 1999)*

I T NEVER WAS my intention to be thought fashionable. It was only after I had surrendered to Asmodeo's blandishments and suggested entitling this meditation «The Invention of Toledo», and was beginning to regret doing so, that I was asked to look at a Hollywood script for a programme on the ever-interesting subject of «Convivencia», one of the propositions of which I found to be that Europe was only «invented» some time after 1085, that is to say some three and a half centuries after Charles Martel's victory at Tours in 732, which the Mozarabic chronicler of 754 had not hesitated to describe as a victory of the *europenses* over the *arabes*[1].

This was disorientating and rather put me off the whole «invention» idea. We are being asked to envisage Europeans without a Europe for them to inhabit, just as in the 1860s Italians were being encouraged to invent a place called Italy for them to live in. This evening I shall not be attempting to conjure a Toledo out of pre-existing *toledanos*. Nor shall I be specu-lating on the Herculean or Babylonian or Hebrew origins of the imperial

---

1. *Cron. Muzarabica*, § 65, edited by Iohannes Gil, *Corpvs Scriptorvm Mvzarabicorvm*, I, Madrid: Consejo Superior de Investigaciones Científicas, 1973, p. 43.

city or on any of the other nineteen pre-Roman possibilities that so preoccupied Toledo's early modern historians[2], or on the interest in the place that the excavation of the Visigothic city has recently prompted. However, it *is* in the Visigothic period that I start. For whereas the Mozarabic chronicler of 754 reported the battle of Tours, but not the battle of Covadonga, with Toledo's first historian, Rodrigo Jiménez de Rada, it is the opposite. It is not Tours he remembers but Covadonga, because Covadonga was the symbolic link with the great days of Toledo and, in particular, with a Visigothic Spain governed by its Toledo councils[3]. Note how the chronicler's next chapter concerns the transfer of Toledo's sacred relics, Toledo's ark of the covenant, to the Asturias for safe keeping[4].

The Visigothic regime was the template to which every modern system of government had to conform and the model to which it needed to aspire. Such was D. Rodrigo's message at the Fourth Lateran Council in 1215, which he had dominated as he ridiculed belief in the mission of Santiago and dismissed the pretensions of Toledo's competitors for peninsular primacy –or at least as he dominated it in Toledo tradition and iconography, to the extent indeed that the illustration of that scene contained in the Toledo *Notule de primatu* manuscript of 1253 gives the impression that it was he rather than the pope who had presided over the occasion[5]. For here it is D. Rodrigo who orchestrates the whole event as its central and its largest figure, with the pontiff just another of a surrounding group of attendant metropolitans: an iconographical arrangement plainly intended

2. See Pedro de Alcocer, *Hystoria, o descripcion dela Imperial cibdad de Toledo*, Toledo: J. Ferrer, 1554 [repr. Madrid: Instituto Provincial de Investigaciones y Estudios Toledanos, 1973], fols. 5v-9r; Francisco de Pisa, *Descripcion de la imperial ciudad de Toledo e historia de sus antigüedades*, I, Toledo: Diego Rodríguez, 1617, fols. 11vb-14ra.

3. *Historia de rebus Hispanie* [henceforth *DrH*], IV.1-2, edited by J. Fernández Valverde, C[orpus] C[hristianorum] C[ollectio] M[ediaevalis], vol. LXXII. I, Tvrnholti: Brepols, 1987, pp. 114-117.

4. *DrH*, IV. 3 (ed. pp. 118-119). See Peter Linehan, *History and the Historians of Medieval Spain*, Oxford: Clarendon Press, 1993, chap. 12.

5. Patrick Henriet, «Political struggle and the legitimation of the Toledan primacy: the *Pars Concilii Laterani*», in *Building Legitimacy. Political discourses and forms of legitimacy in medieval societies*, edited by I. Alonso *et al.*, Leiden & Boston: Brill, 2004, pp. 293-316 (at pp. 299-300). For the date of the *Notule* MS. (Biblioteca Nacional, Madrid, Vitr. 15-5; *olim* Biblioteca del Cabildo, Toledo, MS. 15-22) and description, see H. Flórez, *España Sagrada*, Madrid: Antonio Marín, 1767, XXIII, pp. 360-361; Ramón Gonzálvez *apud* Francisco Javier Hernández, *Los cartularios de Toledo. Catálogo documental*, Madrid: Fundación Ramón Areces, 1985, pp. xviii-xix.

to echo that of the Visigothic councils in the same manuscript where arch-bishop and king preside co-equally over those assemblies[6]. So much for 1215, as remembered in 1253. Let me now turn to the inter-vening period, between 1217 and 1239, and to the treatment of them in the second chapter of the recent, splendid, enormous, often intricate and some-times questionable book of Diego Catalán and Enrique Jerez, wherein the reader is treated to a minute analysis of a bundle of facts («un haz de hechos») and their interconnectednesses[7]. Catalán and Jerez remind us of the vain attempt of the *sayyid* of Valencia, Abū-Zayd, to surrender his kingdom in 1229 to the ruler of Castile rather than to the ruler of Aragon; also of the archbishop of Toledo's invocation of Visigothic provincial arrangements ten years later in order to secure the ecclesiastical equivalent of this initiative.

Now the project of bringing the church of Valencia under Toledo's authority was a doomed venture if ever there was one, and for all his rummaging for precedents in Castile's ecclesiastical libraries and archives, the archbishop failed to carry the day (as would anyway have been the case even if he had managed to persuade the papal court, since then the king of Aragon would have intervened, in accordance with the familiar precept recorded in D. Rodrigo's own History: «Quo uolunt reges uadunt leges»)[8]. Such was the burden of Aragonese opinion as voiced by Vidal de Canellas, the Bologna-trained bishop of Huesca. Where had the archbishop of Toledo been during the siege of Valencia in the previous year?, he asked. With whose blood and money had the place been conquered in 1238? In the event of a Mudéjar uprising there, what could the archbishop of Toledo at eight days' distance do? Castilians would not come to the assistance of Catalans and Aragonese, even if the king of Castile allowed them to (which of course he wouldn't)[9]. Pragmatism ruled.

By juxtaposing these two developments, the secular and the ecclesias-tical, Catalán and Jerez treat them as somehow related, with the one the corollary of the other, and with the implication that king and archbishop were working in concert, ploughing the same furrow. This is questionable.

---

6. P. Linehan, *History and the Historians*, ills. II (a) and (b) (after p. 366).

7. *«Rodericus» romanzado en los reinos de Aragón, Castilla y Navarra*, Madrid: Fundación Ramón Menéndez Pidal: 2005, pp. 71, 78.

8. *DrH*, VI. 25 (ed. p. 208).

9. V. Castell Maiques, *Proceso sobre la ordenación de la Iglesia valentina entre los arzobispos de Toledo, Rodrigo Jiménez de Rada, y de Tarragona, Pedro de Albalat (1238-1246)*, Valencia: Corts Valencianes, 1996, I, p. 479.

It is questionable for a reason which these authors do not consider, namely that it was in precisely these years that the ways of king and archbishop may be said to have diverged, and to have diverged decisively. A clue to what that reason was is contained in the report they themselves provide of the archbishop's return from Rome at the beginning of 1218 endowed with the title of «legate of the apostolic see» and armed with a papal grant of primatial jurisdiction in the as yet unreconquered province of Seville. The archbishop will have felt «satisfecho», the writers surmise –and as in 1617 Francisco de Pisa had surmised[10].

But, if so, his rapture will have been modified, by a keen sense of loss. As recently as July 1206 Alfonso VIII had confirmed the archbishop of Toledo's possession of the *cancillería* of Castile in perpetuity –that is, in Roman law terms not only *ususfructus* of the office but also *dominium* of it, with the entitlement to concede it to another. During the brief reign of the boy king, Enrique, don Rodrigo was well placed to profit from that office. But the (perhaps accidental) death of the young Enrique in June 1217[11] had set in train a process which would soon invalidate that privilege, with the first stage of that process the appointment, later that year, of the abbot of Santander, Juan de Soria, as chancellor to Fernando III, and after the conjunction of the two kingdoms in 1230 in the person of Fernando its culmination in the replacement of the archbishop as *ex officio* chancellor of Castile[12]. So the primatial grant and the legation should be seen less as a cause for satisfaction to D. Rodrigo than as a token of consolation for his recent loss of both profit and prestige and for the initiation of a process which in the event was to prove irreversible. In short, at the very moment when the archbishop was contemplating the apotheosis of his church in both script and stone, he was deprived of his traditional role as the king's right hand man and the conduit of royal favour, and so were his successors[13].

10. D. Catalán & E. Jerez, «*Rodericus*» *romanzado*, p. 67; F. de Pisa, *Descripcion*, fol. 184ra («con otras muchas gracias que el pontifice le concedio, con las quales boluio muy alegre a España»).

11. *Cf.* Simon R. Doubleday, *The Lara Family. Crown and nobility in medieval Spain*, Cambridge, Mass.: Harvard University Press, 2001, pp. 55-56.

12. Julio González, *Reinado y diplomas de Fernando III*, Córdoba: Publicaciones del Monte de Piedad y Caja de Ahorros de Córdoba, 1980-86, II, num. 2; Peter Linehan, «Don Rodrigo and the government of the kingdom», *Cahiers de linguistique et de civilisation hispaniques médiévales*, 26 (2003), pp. 87-99.

13. P. Linehan, *History and the Historians*, pp. 338-345.

Previous writers, sustained perhaps by the unspoken conviction that the bishops of a canonised king could never have been in discord with one another, have gone so far as to suggest that in both 1217 and 1231 the transfer was made on the archbishop's own recommendation[14]. It has even been suggested that the pair were cousins. If so, blood was evidently thinner than water[15]. No, the case was probably otherwise[16]. And it was a case that did not go by default. In 1231-2, at the very moment at which the chancery was being conveyed to him, Juan de Soria found his promotion to the see of Osma delayed by a year and a half or more. And by whom if not by his Toledo metropolitan?[17] Juan de Soria was currently acknowledging that the chancery was the archbishop's by right («ad vos de iure spectantem») and promising to surrender the chancellorship of Castile to the archbishop when he died or if, before that, he were promoted to a see outside the province of Toledo. The king had already admitted that the transfer was being made at his instigation («ad preces meas») and undertaken to ensure that the office reverted eventually to the archbishop or his successor, and the archbishop had a royal privilege guaranteeing as much. Nevertheless, neither in 1240, when don Juan was translated from Osma to the exempt see of Burgos, nor on his death in 1246 was his promise honoured and the chancery restored to the archbishop. Almost a century later the issue still remained a live one. Because the original instrument containing the chancellor's promise «era meester de mostrar en muchos logares» and was therefore worn by constant use, as late as August 1329 the treasurer of the church of Toledo was concerned to secure an authenticated copy of it[18].

The salient point though, the point to be seized here, is the compensatory nature of the papal privileges of January 1218. Deprived of the secular ascendancy that possession of the *royal* chancery provided, the archbishop was seeking ghostly confirmation from the *papal* chancery of, firstly, his ecclesiastical primacy and, second, his entitlement to the church of Zuqueca,

---

14. Luciano Serrano, «El canciller de Fernando III de Castilla», *Hispania*, 1 (1941), pp. 3-40 (6); J. González, *Fernando III*, I, p. 506.

15. Thus Roger Wright, *Late Latin and Early Romance in Spain and Carolingian France*, Liverpool: Francis Cairns, 1982, p. 257.

16. P. Linehan, «Don Rodrigo».

17. *Idem*, «D. Juan de Soria: unas apostillas», in *Fernando III y su tiempo (1201-1252)*, VIII *Congreso de Estudios Medievales*, León: Fundación Sánchez-Albornoz, 2003, pp. 377-393 (381).

18. «la qual mostrada el dicho thesorero dixo quela dicha carta era me[n]ester de mostrar en muchos logares et por periglos que podrian acaesçer en terminos e en otros logares»: [Madrid,] A[rchivo] H[istorico] N[acional], Clero, carp. 3019/8.

which the archbishop had persuaded the pontiff was identical with the Visigothic see of Oreto[19]. (There was also a third privilege, to which I will come in a minute.) It was no coincidence that in 1231, in the very month of the transfer of the archbishop's *ex officio* chancellorship to D. Juan, D. Rodrigo had these privileges confirmed by Gregory IX[20]. The chancellor don Juan had replaced the archbishop as the intimate of infantes, with his will recalling the visits he had made with them to Paris and Murcia[21]. More than that, the history of Castile he was author of began with the counts of Castile and had nothing to say about the history of the Visigoths, which was what gave D. Rodrigo's History its teleology and purpose. Now here was a *fractura historiográfica* if ever there was one[22]. So the spectacle of the chancellor celebrating the first mass in the purified mosque of reconquered Córdoba in 1236 may well have seemed a threat to that primatial jurisdiction regarding which D. Rodrigo had recently been so exercised. At any rate, his description of the scene seems to be the only occasion in his chronicle on which he describes himself as primate[23]. Moreover, with the capture of Córdoba Fernando III appears to have liberated himself too –from the tutelage of his mother[24] and from what remained of the tutelage of D. Rodrigo. When, in April 1237, Gregory IX was concerned to encourage Fernando III to make peace with the king of Navarre, it was

19. Demetrio Mansilla, *La documentación pontificia de Honorio III (1216-1227)*, Rome: Instituto Español de Historia Eclesiástica, 1965, nums. 153, 144. For further implications of this exercise, see P. Linehan, *History and the Historians*, pp. 340-344.

20. A[rchivo de la] C[atedral de] Toledo, X.7.A.3.6, X.1.A.1.3a [«Zucheta»] (4, 8 Apr. 1231; printed Santiago Dóminguez Sánchez, *Documentos de Gregorio IX (1227-1241) referentes a España*, León: Universidad de León, Secretariado de Publicaciones, 2004, nums. 176, 179 [«Çucheta» in Archivio Segreto Vaticano, Reg. Vat. 15, fol. 77r]; Peter Linehan, «Juan de Soria: the chancellor as chronicler», *e-Spania*, 2 (2007), http://www.e-spania.paris-sorbonne.fr [net visited at 2007-03-30].

21. L. Serrano, «El canciller», pp. 39-40.

22. Francisco Bautista, «Escritura cronística e ideología histórica: la *Chronica latina regum Castellae*», *e-Spania*, 2 (2007), http://www.e-spania.paris-sorbonne.fr [net visited at 2007-06-30]; *Cf. idem*, «Hacia una nueva 'versión' de la *Estoria de España*: texto y forma de la *Versión de Sancho IV*», *Incipit*, 23 (2003), pp. 1-59 (at p. 48).

23. *DRH*, IX.17$_8$ (ed. p. 299).

24. Whom he informed from afar of his «firmum propositum» (to proceed to Córdoba) «quod nulla ratione poterat inmutari»: *Chronica latina regum Castellae*, c. 70, edited by Luis Charlo Brea, CCCM, vol. LXXIII (1997), 112$_{24-5}$. See Peter Linehan, «On further thought: Lucas of Tuy, Rodrigo of Toledo and the Alfonsine histories», *Anuario de Estudios Medievales*, 27:1 (1998) [repr. P. Linehan, *The Processes of Politics and the Rule of Law: Studies on the Iberian kingdoms and papal Rome in the Middle Ages*, Aldershot: Ashgate, 2002], p. 421.

not to the queen-mother and the archbishop that he wrote for support but to the queen-mother and the chancellor[25].

Now Fernando III's action in divesting himself of the services of his *ex officio* chancellors (the archbishop of Compostela was another casualty of the process) was in accordance with developments within other monarchies at this time (France and Portugal for example) and also reflected a domestic power struggle in which the queen-mother was involved[26]. But if, as Mr Donald Rumsfeld has acutely observed, «Stuff happens», it is also the case that «consequences follow». The consequences of the *coup* of 1217 were far-reaching. Until then, with a boy king on the throne, D. Rodrigo had held the reins of power. By March 1243, the date of the first redaction of his chronicle, he had care of the clerical education of two of Fernando III's younger sons at Toledo. But now the effect of the relationship was the opposite. Now, the Infantes Felipe and Sancho were being groomed to succeed to the government of the churches of Toledo and Seville: a novel manner of securing a state-dominated church in the post-Hildebrandine age[27].

I mentioned a third papal privilege of January 1218. This was the one appointing the archbishop of Toledo papal legate. But since 1218 D. Rodrigo had fallen from papal favour by colluding with a nefarious papal agent, and in January 1222 the papal registers describe him as papal legate for the last time[28]. In Roman circles his reputation seems never to have recovered. At any rate, on the death in 1246 of the chancellor D. Juan the canon law regarding broken oaths was not invoked against Fernando III[29]. Not that the king ran much of a risk of incurring a papal rebuke at this date, even if the archbishop of Toledo had not been in the shadows. With Fernando

---

25. Léon Cadier, «Bulles originales du XIII$^e$ siècle conservées dans les Archives de Navarre», *Mélanges d'Archéologie et d'Histoire*, 7 (1887), pp. 268-338 (nums. 23-24).

26. P. Linehan, «D. Rodrigo», p. 95; Georges Martin, «Régner sans régner. Bérengère de Castille (1214-1246) au miroir de l'historiographie de son temps», *e-Spania*, 1 (2006), http://www.e-spania.paris-sorbonne.fr [net visited at 2007-03-30].

27. See Francisco Javier Hernández & Peter Linehan, *The Mozarabic Cardinal. The life and times of Gonzalo Pérez Gudiel*, Florence: SISMEL & Edizioni del Galluzzo, 2004, pp. 30-32.

28. D. Mansilla, *Honorio III*, nums. 148, 390; Peter Linehan, *Spanish Church and the Papacy in the Thirteenth Century*, Cambridge: Cambridge University Press, 1971, pp. 8-9. Undeterred, he was still describing himself as such three years later: AHN, Órdenes Militares, Uclés, carp. 58, num. 23.

29. X 2.24 *de iureiurando*.

poised to attack Seville, the pontiff was prepared to grant him the resources of the Castilian Church for the purpose; and perhaps even more[30]. When D. Rodrigo died in 1247 the prospect of Seville's recovery, which had haunted him for at least thirty years, was imminent. With it were awakened Toledo's fears for the ecclesiastical primacy which the southern city had enjoyed when Leander and Isidore had been its bishops. There is no need here to recount the battle fought by the chroniclers over this rocky terrain. Suffice it to say that the recent publication of Dr Emma Falque's eagerly awaited edition of the *Chronicon Mundi* and the attentions of a new generation of codicologically literate scholars, notably Enrique Jerez, have left the reputation of Lucas of Tuy further enhanced[31]. Moreover, his versatility in other areas will soon be demonstrated when, in a paper still in press, he is revealed in a new guise, as the author of an eschatological work concerning SS. Francis and Dominic dated by its editor to 1234[32].

In his recent distinguished thesis on the subject of don Lucas, Dr Jerez has observed that «frente a tan brillante origen para la ciudad de Guadalquivir, la fundación de Toledo a cargo de dos cónsules romanos, tardía y desabrida, queda en inferioridad»[33]. He has in mind, on the one hand, Isidore of Seville's connexion of «Yspanus» and «Yspalis»: the first king of *Yspania* and the «famous city» he built (CM, $124_{16}$); on the other, the altogether more modest origins of Toledo (and of its name) in its foundation by the Roman consuls Tolemon and Brutus (CM, $73_{2-4}$)[34]. Don

30. As to more, see P. Linehan, *Spanish Church and the Papacy*, p. 123. Manuel González Jiménez states the sum in question (4000 marks sterling) to have been a loan connected with the conquest of Seville (*Fernando III el Santo*, Seville: Fundación José Manuel Lara, 2006, p. 230). It is more likely to have comprised payments of *census* withheld by the king. See *Les registres d'Urbain IV*, edited by Jean Guiraud, Paris: Thoron & Fils/Albert Fontemoing, 1899, I, cameral num. 478.

31. *Chronicon mundi* [henceforth *CM*], edited by Emma Falque, CCCM, vol. LXXIV (2003); P. Linehan, *History and the Historians*, pp. 357-379, with the additions provided by Enrique Jerez, «El Tudense en su siglo: transmisión y recepción del *Chronicon mundi* en el Doscientos», in *El relato historiográfico: textos y tradiciones en la España medieval*, edited by Francisco Bautista, P[apers of the] M[edieval] H[ispanic] R[esearch] S[eminar] 48, Department of Hispanic Studies, Queen Mary, University of London, 2006, pp. 19-57, esp. pp. 28-29, 32-35.

32. Robert Lerner, «The Vision of 'John, Hermit of the Asturias': Lucas of Tuy, apostolic religion, and eschatalogical expectation», *Traditio*, 61 (2006), pp. 195-225.

33. Enrique Jerez, «El *Chronicon mundi* de Lucas de Tuy (*c.* 1238): técnicas compositivas y motivaciones ideológicas», Ph.D. diss. [Tesis doctoral], Universidad Autónoma Madrid, Dpto. Filología Española (Fac. Filosofía y Letras), 2006, p. 143, num. 425.

34. The story seems to have originated with Pelayo of Oviedo: Cruz Montero Garrido, *La Historia, creación literaria. El ejemplo de Quatrocientos*, Madrid: Fundación Ramón Menéndez Pidal & Universidad Autónoma de Madrid, 1994-1995, pp. 217-218.

Rodrigo, following on, had suggested something less grand for Seville (with «Hispalis» derived from *pali*: the planks or pales on which the earliest habitations of the place rested; DrH, $16_{9\text{-}12}$), but, though false etymologies, even those derived from St Isidore[35], combined happily enough with creative antiquarianism, he was unable to propose anything more elevated for his own city: either that or he lacked the nerve to do so (DrH, $14_{46\text{-}50}$).

Toledo's riposte, when it came, was based on neither of these devices. Eventually it would rest on the practice of promoting Toledo's reputation and prestige by injecting alien material into the historiographical mainstream. The process was already underway in D. Rodrigo's History, in the author's account of his own role at Las Navas, his presence in the rearguard shoulder to shoulder with Alfonso VIII, and the king's conversations with him, and with him alone, both before and at the height of battle ($VIII.8_{13\text{-}14}$: «in ultima acie»; $VIII.10_{12\text{-}18, 21\text{-}25, 48\text{-}52}$). True or not –and, according to the Latin chronicler, only kings occupied the rearguard ($24_{17\text{-}18}$) while D. Lucas fails to mention the archbishop's presence at Las Navas at all (IV.91) –the tendency to conjoin archbishop and king in close association can thus be dated to the year 1243, a date at which, at least in theory, the archbishop's historic cancillerial proximity to the king might still have been salvaged.

Ten years later, after the death of D. Rodrigo and two brief pontificates, it was apparent, even to Toledo patriots (indeed, especially to Toledo patriots) that no such restoration was to happen. In granting Seville the *fuero* of Toledo, Fernando III had described the southern city as «mayor [...] et mas noble [...] de las otras ciudades de Espanna»[36]. In Toledo itself it seems to have been at this point that wishful thinking began to take hold. Thus, in the *Estoria de los godos*, the earliest romance version of D. Rodrigo's History, to which Catalán and Jerez have recently drawn attention, dating it to 1252/3, the role of D. Rodrigo before Las Navas is recorded in terms which improved on D. Rodrigo himself. Whereas the archbishop had reported how the danger to the city of Toledo that the muster of foreigners of so many discrepant 'nations, customs, *tongues* and cults' represented had been neutralised by the king's evacuation of them to the Huerta del Rey, now it was «por conseio del arçobispo» that the king was said to have

---

35. *Etymologiarum*, XV.1.71, edited by W. M. Lindsay, Oxonii: E typographeo Clarendoniano, 1911, whence also «G. Petri de Calciata Rithmi de Iulia Romula seu Ispalensi urbe», edited by R. Carande Herrero, *Chronica Hispana saeculi XIII*, CCCM, vol. LXXIII (1997), lin. 17-20.

36. J. González, *Fernando III*, III, num. 825.

done so[37]. And more. As Aengus Ward has observed, according to the *Estoria* in the battle itself the king was a broken reed. It was the bishops who showed the way –and especially the archbishop of Toledo[38].

What Catalán and Jerez do not mention is that 1253 is also the date of the *Notule de primatu* manuscript: that is, of the manuscript to which I referred earlier in which the archbishop of Toledo is shown lording it over the Visigothic councils and D. Rodrigo is reported to have addressed the Lateran Council in all manner of languages. And it is not only the recurrence of that linguistic theme that invites closer investigation. Although down the ages both the authenticity of the *Notule*'s account of 1215 and its ostensible date have been regularly rejected[39], there was plainly something astir in Toledo in May 1253 –or, as the manuscript calculates, 6629 years after Adam and 2640 after the foundation of the city, making Toledo more than six hundred years older than Rome. Here, along with the various papal licences allegedly authorising D. Rodrigo to disregard recent Lateran legislation, is the earliest claim that his legation was to continue for ten years[40].

I suspect that whether or not the contents of the *Notule* be credible[41], the date of them is, that 1253 was the year in which history and reality diverged and fiction intervened, and that this was a development not unconnected with the arrival on the Toledo scene in 1252 of the king's brother the Infante Sancho, as procurator and then archbishop. By April 1255 Sancho de Castilla was subscribing royal privileges as... «chanceller del rey» and in the safety of his church describing himself as «regie maiestatis

37. D. Catalán & E. Jerez, «*Rodericus*» *romanzado*, p. 54.

38. A. Ward, «Rodrigo Ximénez de Rada: auteur et acteur en Castille à la fin du XIIIe siècle», *Cahiers de linguistique et de civilisation hispaniques médiévales*, 26 (2003), pp. 283-294 (287-289). Ward favours a date nearer 1280 for the *Estoria*.

39. El Marqués de Mondéjar and P. Fita, both dismissing its content as spurious, proposed dates of 1432 and 1320 respectively: Fidel Fita, «Santiago de Galicia. Nuevas impugnaciones y nueva defensa», V-VI, *Razón y Fe*, 2 (1902), pp. 178-195 (180), 3 (1902), pp. 49-61 (61).

40. Although the legatine privilege (in any case granted not by Innocent III but by Honorius III) contained no such provision (ACT, I.4.N.1.20: D. Mansilla, *Honorio III*, num. 148), Toledo historiography succeeded in foisting the ten-year term onto posterity: F. de Pisa, *Descripcion*, fol. 184ra; P. Linehan, *Spanish Church*, p. 8 num. 4. The archbishop is reported to have been allowed to promote upto three hundred illegitimate clergy to ecclesiastical dignities and to dispense «excommunicati, sacrilegi, irregulares et concubinarii»: F. Fita, «Santiago de Galicia», 2 (1902), p. 184.

41. As P. Henriet appears to think: «Political struggle», pp. 295-296.

cancellarius»[42]. But this was honorific only, as was the resumption of the same title at the same time by the archbishop of Compostela[43]. The reality was that Alfonso X's chancery had been overhauled and that its operations were now in the hands of notaries[44].

A new component was provided between 1272 and 1275 when, as well as «chanceller de Castilla» (or «del rey») Archbishop Sancho de Aragón was listed as «capellán mayor del rey»[45]. Now, this *did* distinguish him from the archbishop of Compostela (who was anyway out of favour with the king)[46] as well as placing him in both the first and second offices of trust in the royal household and, according to the *Siete Partidas*, situating him between the Almighty and the king on the one hand and between the king and his subjects on the other[47].

All the elements of the rest of what I have to say to you this evening were now assembled. When an «official history» became available in the Alfonsine *Estoria de España* Toledo's friends were ready to adjust the historical record in Toledo's favour by breaking the Isidorian claim to a connexion between Seville and Spain and so bringing Seville down a peg or two (*EE* 9a$_{26}$)[48]. But because the *Estoria*'s account of Visigothic Toledo had taken final form in the lifetime of *el rey Sabio*, it was to the more recent past that the fabricators looked to make their mark, and to the figure of Alfonso VII in particular, whose remains were the cathedral's most substantial royal

42. *Diplomatario andaluz de Alfonso X*, edited by Manuel González Jiménez, Seville: El Monte. Caja de Huelva y Sevilla, 1991, num. 146; AC Toledo, E.8.D.1.18 (F. J. Hernández & P. Linehan, *Mozarabic Cardinal*, p. 76).

43. D. Sancho of Castile's use of the title continued until his death in October 1261, with D. Juan of Compostela similarly described after October 1255: M. González Jiménez, *Diplomatario andaluz*, nums. 162 ¥ 246.

44. F. J. Hernández & P. Linehan, *Mozarabic Cardinal*, pp. 70-71.

45. M. González Jiménez, *Diplomatario andaluz*, nums. 397, 399, 404-405, 412.

46. Because Gonzalo Gómez García had been imposed on Alfonso by Gregory X in preference for the king's candidate for the see: F. J. Hernández & P. Linehan, *Mozarabic Cardinal*, p. 150. By contrast with his predecessor, Archbishop Gonzalo Gómez is never accorded the title of chancellor: M. González Jiménez, *Diplomatario andaluz*, nums. 404 & 458 (July 1273-December 1279).

47. «Chanciller es el segundo oficial de casa del rey de aquellos que tienen oficios de poridat; ca bien asi como el capellan es medianero entre Dios et el rey espiritualmente en fecho de su alma, otrosi lo es el chanciller entre él et los homes quanto en las cosas temporales»: *Part.* 2.9.3-4 (*Las Siete Partidas del rey don Alfonso el Sabio*, edited by Real Academia de la Historia, Madrid 1807: La Imprenta Real [repr. Madrid: Ediciones Atlas, 1972], II, pp. 59-61.

48. Whereas the report of Toledo's origins in *EE*, 7a$_{53}$ repeats that of *De rebus Hispanie*.

trophy. The reburial of those remains during the reign of Sancho IV consti-tuted a red letter day for the imperial city and it is in what Francisco Bautista tells us we have again to call its «Versión amplificada»[49] that we find the history of the Emperor's reign being put to the service and the greater glory of Toledo's archbishops. *That* was the «Emperor Alfonso» he chose to be buried next to; not, as Dr Bizzarri unaccountably states, his father Alfonso X[50]. In the «Versión amplificada» two particularly egregious examples of the wishful thinking already referred to occur, both concerning the reign of Alfonso VII. The first is its treatment of the imperial coronation of 1135. Precisely what had happened at León that Pentecost, whether or not the king had crowned himself for example, the *Cronica Adefonsi Imperatoris* had failed to explain. Nor had it so much as mentioned the archbishop of Toledo[51]. But in the «Versión amplificada» it is Archbishop Raimundo who is the centre of attention. All the archbishops, bishops and abbots present, with «ell primas de Toledo» at their head, «bendixieron la corona, et bendixieron a el, et conssagraronlo todo; et tomaron [...] la corona, diziendo sus bendiciones, et pusierongela en la cabeça, et alli fue emperador coro-nado»[52]. Accordingly it comes as no surprise to learn that at the emperor's death-bed in 1157 «llego a el don Johan, arçobispo de Toledo et primas de las Espannas, que era y con ell et siempre con ell andaua, ca nunqua se partie dell nin en la frontera nin en la tierra». As chief mourner and the kingdom's spokesman, the archbishop launches into a lengthy speech of farewell to the moribund monarch running to twenty-nine lines in Menéndez Pidal's edition, before leaving him to die in peace[53]. Thus was confirmed the archbishop's special relationship with the king and his ascendancy over him, liturgical, political and spiritual. It will not have been forgotten that one of the main functions, or privileges, of the king's *capellán mayor* was to hear the king's confession[54].

Affecting stories such as these became part of Toledo's history, and for them Menéndez Pidal sought credible sources, «fuentes fidedignas». But he

49. «La Estoria de España en época de Sancho IV: sobre los reyes de Asturias», *PMHRS*, 50 (2006), pp. 8-9; *cf. idem*, «Hacia una nueva 'versión' de la *Estoria de España*».

50. Hugo O. Bizzarri, «'Castigos del rey D. Sancho IV': una reinterpretación», *PMHRS*, 37 (2004), p. 70.

51. P. Linehan, *History and the Historians*, pp. 235ff.

52. *Primera Crónica General de España*, edited by Ramón Menéndez Pidal, Madrid: Gredos, 1955, c. 974 (p. 654a$_{34-45}$); P. Linehan, *History and the Historians*, pp. 463ff.

53. *Primera Crónica General*, c. 982 (p. 662a$_8$-b$_{47}$).

54. *Part.* 2.9.3 («et quel sepa apercebir de las cosas de que se debe guardar: ca á él es tenudo de se confesar mas que á otri»: ed. cit., II, 59).

sought in vain[55]. Their origins have rather to be looked for in the author's wistful, semi-autobiographical description of Archbishop Juan in 1157: «siempre con ell andaua, ca nunqua se partie dell nin en la frontera nin en la tierra», reminiscent as it is of D. Rodrigo's account of his inseparable relationship with the king at Las Navas. And who *was* the author? One possibility would be someone who enjoyed a similar intimate relationship with his own king, namely Sancho IV's real-life archbishop of Toledo, or otherwise someone close to him. As a mitred manifestation of his king, Archbishop Gonzalo Pérez of Toledo (the mis-named Gudiel) played Aaron to Sancho's Moses, which was how the *Castigos* attributed to Sancho characterized the ecclesiastical and the secular powers, as twin vicars of God, with each bearing his symbol of office, the crozier and the sceptre respectively, and each having its own independent sphere but also a capacity for bringing its resources to the assistance of the other[56].

As a product of the royal chancery himself, he was so acutely aware of the importance, both real and symbolic, of control of that department that, when appointed to the see of Toledo in May 1280, he had adopted the belt-and-braces policy of describing himself as *both* chancellor of Castile *and* royal notary[57]. Accordingly, amongst the jottings long known as *Anales Toledanos Terceros*, we find a description of negotiations with the French at Bayona in 1290 and, at the head of the Castilian delegation... don Gonzalo Pérez: «Et los que tractauan esta paç por el rei de [Ca]stiella era el arcobispo don Goncaluo de Toledo» etc. –as became the effective head of the king's chancery[58]. For more than a century these *anales* have been associated with Jofré de Loaisa[59], and Jofré de Loaisa, as well as being the

55.  F. de Pisa, *Descripcion*, fols. 167rb-va, 170ra; P. Linehan, *History and the Historians*, p. 463n.

56.  *Castigos del rey don Sancho IV*, edited by Hugo O. Bizzarri, Frankfurt am Main: Vervuert & Madrid: Iberoamericana, 2001, p. 172. *Cf.* the strikingly different exegesis of the contemporary Augustinus Triumphus, cit. Michael J. Wilks, *The Problem of Sovereignty in the Later Middle Ages. The papal monarchy with Augustinus Triumphus and the publicists*, Cambridge: Cambridge University Press, 1964, p. 395: «Moyses repraesentabat Christum cuius vicem papa gerit in terris [...] Similiter Aaron Christum repraesentabat [...] Aliter tamen Moyses et aliter Aaron Christum significabant, quia Moyses significabat Christum ut legislator, Aaron vero ut summus sacerdos».

57.  F. J. Hernández & P. Linehan, *Mozarabic Cardinal*, pp. 185-186.

58.  Enrique Jerez, «El *oficio* historiográfico: los Anales Toledanos Terceros en su entorno», *La Corónica*, 32.3 (2004), pp. 109-161 (150-153): D. Catalán & E. Jerez, *«Rodericus» romanzado*, pp. 597-598.

59.  A relationship first noticed by Antonio Paz y Mélia in his review of Alfred Morel-Fatio's edition of Jofré's chronicle: *Revista de Archivos, Bibliotecas y Museos*, 3 (1899), p. 729.

author of a continuation of D. Rodrigo's History, was a member of Gonzalo Pérez's circle[60]. By that year the royal chancery was styling the former protégé of Archbishop Sancho of Castile as «chanceller mayor en los regnos de Castiella e de Leon e de Andalucia» and by 1294 as «chanceller mayor en todos nuestros regnos»[61]. True, for a man who was the product of Alfonso's chancery, at one level the prostitution of his historiographical activity, and the recourse to fiction, would have represented a sad decline from the scrupulous standards of Alfonso's glory days –especially if, as Dr Hernández and I have suggested, it was he who, as archdeacon of Toledo and notary for Castile in the early 1270s, was responsible for the collection of the documentary material which seventy years later was to find its way into the *Crónica de Alfonso X*[62]. But, in that capacity he would have been familiar with and would have had free access to the historical materials assembled by Alfonso X.

I have said more than enough elsewhere about «Gudiel» and about the tantalising but never quite conclusive indications of his responsibility for the elaborations of Toledo's past in the «Versión amplificada». Here suffice it to remark that, for him as well as don Rodrigo, cathedral building and the creation of historical fiction were complementary activities. Though one looked forward and the other back, the same ethos informed both, and consonant with that ethos were Sancho IV's privilege, as alleged by Jofré, promising that all future kings of Castile would be crowned in Toledo cathedral, and the adaptation of a coronation *ordo* from a German imperial model for that purpose[63]. The illustration to the privilege in which Sancho promises to be buried in Toledo cathedral shows king and archbishop seated in exact horizontal equivalence, exactly as in the representations of kings and archbishops presiding over Visigothic councils in the

60. Francisco Javier Hernández, «Noticias sobre Jofré de Loaisa y Ferrán Martínez», *Revista Canadiense de Estudios Hispánicos*, 4 (1980), pp. 281-309.

61. F. J. Hernández & P. Linehan, *Mozarabic Cardinal*, p. 266, *q. v.* for criticism of this interpretation.

62. *Idem*, pp. 129-131. For reasons not stated, Manuel González Jiménez contends that this section of the *Crónica* was compiled in the years 1282-1284: *Crónica de Alfonso X según el MS. 2777 de la Biblioteca del Palacio Real (Madrid)*, Murcia: Real Academia Alfonso X el Sabio, 2000, p. xxxii.

63. Peter Linehan, «The Toledo forgeries *c.* 1150 - *c.* 1300», *Falschungen im Mittelalter. Internationaler Kongre? der Monumenta Germaniae Historica, München, 16-19. September 1986*, I, MGH Schriften 33.1; Hannover: Hahnsche Buchhandlung, 1988 [repr. P. Linehan, *Past and Present in Medieval Spain*, Aldershot: Variorum, 1992], pp. 643-674 (666-667).

*Notule de primatu* manuscript[64]. How appropriate therefore is Dr Bautista's conjecture that the completion of this version of the Alfonsine History was timed to coincide with Sancho IV's accomplishment of the royal pantheon within the cathedral[65]. This is not to suggest that Jofré de Loaisa and a Toledo lobby, or mafia, were responsible for all the amplifications of the «Versión amplificada». For example, although on the awkward matter of Seville's ancient primacy the subversive D. Lucas had been muted[66], it would be difficult to ascribe to a Toledan sympathiser the passage celebrating the miracles and preaching of Santiago[67] –unless its inclusion is to be regarded as an oversight attributable to the scramble to meet that 1289 deadline[68]. Be that as it may, the practice of inferring authorship from apparent motivation may be thought a questionable procedure anyway, as also may be the tendency to regard a writer's apparent failure to quote from or even acknowledge the existence of another work as automatically disqualifying him from the authorship of it. Is it not a fallacy, one perhaps based on modern experience, to assume that historians are incapable of original thought and of original ways of expressing it and that anything they may say must have been adapted from someone else? We have already seen how that assumption underestimates

---

64. *Idem, History and the Historians*, pp. 482-485. *Cf.* Fernando Gutiérrez Baños, *Las empresas artísticas de Sancho IV el Bravo*, Valladolid: Junta de Castilla y León, Consejería de Educación y Cultura, 1997, pp. 186-190.

65. F. Bautista, *La Estoria de España*, pp. 51-54.

66. But not altogether silenced. According to Lucas's fifteenth-century translator, Fernando III incorporated Seville to León and made it subject to the Fuero juzgo: *Crónica de España por Lucas, obispo de Túy*, edited by Julio Puyol, Madrid: Rev. de Archivos, Bibliotecas y Museos, 1926, p. 445. Seville had been granted the *fuero* of Toledo in 1251: F. J. Hernández & P. Linehan, *Mozarabic Cardinal*, p. 68. At one level therefore the Leonese mafia remained alive and well. But the influence is not unidirectional. Despite its promotion of St. Isidore, the extended Lucas omits the notice of the *Estoria de España* that Fernando III entered Seville «dia [...] de la traslaçion de sant Esidro de Leon [22 December], arçobispo que fue de Seuilla» in favour of that of S. Clemente: the day prearranged for the surrender of the *alcázar* [23 November: a Monday in 1248], misreporting it as a Sunday: Puyol, pp. 443-4. *Cf. Primera Crónica General*, cc. 1123, 1125 (p. 767a$_{20}$,b$_{10}$).

67. F. Bautista, *La Estoria de España*, pp. 26, 83-84, 97-98. *Cf.* the downbeat D. Rodrigo at Las Navas, as described in the *Sumario Analístico de la Historia Gothica*, edited by Aengus Ward, PMHRS, 56 (2007), pp. 26, 97-98.

68. Was this the reason why, in the words of J. B. Crespo Arce, «el texto que presenta E$_2$ está plagado de imperfecciones, tanto estructurales como puntuales», failing even to verify the year of the reconquest of Toledo?: «La complejidad textual de la historiografía alfonsí», *Actas del XIV Congreso de la Asociación Internacional de Hispanistas, New York, 16-21 de Julio de 2001*, Newark, Del.: Juan de la Cuesta, 2004, I, pp. 55-65 (56).

practitioners of the calibre of Bishop Pelayo of Oviedo[69]. For the affecting account in the «Versión amplificada» of the death of Alfonso VII Menéndez Pidal cited «[una] fuente desconocida, quizá poetica»[70]. But why not «una invención, quizá insólita»? Why should *inventio* not be counted amongst the historiographer's resources, along with *auctoritas* and *memoria*?[71] –always provided we do not expect the *Cui bono?* test mechanistically applied to identify the author. In the present case, for example, to treat the «toledanisation» of the historical record as an expression of Sancho IV's political philosophy *tout court* and king and archbishop as in intimate collaboration would appear highly questionable[72]. The fit is not that exact. The absence from Toledo cathedral's title deeds of Sancho's coronation privilege described by Master Jofré's speaks for itself.

Many loose ends remain. In the masterly analysis of Catalán and Jerez I find no mention of the item listed amongst the contents of Archbishop Sancho of Aragón's chapel, the «quaderno de fechos de Toledo que comienza 'En guarda del arçidiagno de Toledo'»[73]. Yet here is an item –«un quaderno de fechos de Toledo»– which sounds as if it might deserve discussion in relation to the *Anales Toledanos Terceros* (the bifolio enclosing

69. Above, n. 34.

70. *Primera Crónica General*, II, p. cxciv.

71. *Cf.* Inés Fernández-Ordóñez, «La composición por etapas de la *Chronica latina regum Castellae* (1223-1237) de Juan de Osma», *e-Spania*, 2 (2007), pp. 1-35 (32-35), http://www.e-spania.paris-sorbonne.fr [net visited at 2007-06-30].

72. *Cf.* Georges Martin, «L'escarboucle de Saint-Denis, le roi de France et l'empereur des Espagnes», in *Saint-Denis et la royauté. Études offertes à Bernard Guenée*, edited by F. Autrand, C. Gauvard & J.-M. Moeglin, Paris: Publications de la Sorbonne, 1999, pp. 439-462 (458). C. L. Chamberlin regards the king as the manipulator-in-chief («undoubtedly with the intimate collaboration of Archbishop Gonzalo»): «'Unless the Pen Writes as it Should': the proto-cult of Saint Fernando III in Seville in the thirteenth and fourteenth centuries», in *Sevilla 1248. Congreso Internacional conmemorativo del 750 aniversario de la conquista de la ciudad de Sevilla por Fernando III, rey de Castilla y León. Sevilla, Real Alcázar, 23-27 de noviembre de 1998*, edited by M. González Jiménez, Madrid: Ayuntamiento de Sevilla & Fundación Ramón Areces, 2000, pp. 389-417 (406), while F. Gutiérrez Baños, *Empresas artísticas*, p. 189, speaks of «una confluencia de intereses». Regarding the *Lucidario*, F. Gómez-Redondo discerns «una orientación religiosa, impulsada en la corte de Sancho posiblemente por clérigos cercanos al cardenal Gudiel»: *Historia de la prosa medieval castellana, I, La creación del discurso prosístico: el entramado cortesano*, Madrid: Cátedra, 1998, p. 912. As to the differing nuances observable in historical compilations of the period, A. Ward observes: «it is hard to imagine separate teams beavering away in the 1280s at differentiated histories of Iberia in the cathedral without knowledge of each other»: *Sumario Analístico*, p. 29. Hard yes, but also intriguing.

73. F. J. Hernández & P. Linehan, *Mozarabic Cardinal*, p. 142, n. 149.

what used to be called the *Anales Toledanos Quartos*: now the *Sumario analístico de la Historia Gothica*), the work penned, according to Catalán and Jerez, by Archdeacon Jofré of Toledo in the spring of 1280[74]. If there is a connexion, though, there is also a problem. For in the spring of 1280 this *quaderno* was nowhere near the archdeacon. It was in the possession of Archbishop Sancho's creditors, and was not released by them until 1284[75]. That is not the only problem. Another concerns Archdeacon Jofré of Toledo himself and in particular the question whether in 1280 Jofré de Loaisa was an archdeacon at all. Of course, Catalán and Jerez insist that he was, stating that the dispute regarding succession to that office had been decided in Jofré's favour by Pope Nicholas III in 1278. But this is wrong. It is wrong because it was Pope Nicholas IV who decided in Jofré's favour, and not until after 1288 that he did so[76]. Only after that date was Jofré de Loaisa *de iure* archdeacon of Toledo.

True, he may have been *de facto* archdeacon before that, and may not have let the difference worry him unduly. And, if so, as an accomplice of his archbishop that would have been wholly appropriate. For Gudiel was one of nature's survivors. The story of his political resurrection after King Sancho's succession is a remarkable one. But Catalán and Jerez are also wrong in claiming that he returned to the old king's side in the last months of Alfonso's reign[77]. So too is Dr Bizzarri in reporting that it was he who

---

74. D. Catalán & E. Jerez, «*Rodericus*» *romanzado*, pp. 566-594.

75. New York, Hispanic Society of America, MS. B190 (printed F. J. Hernández & P. Linehan, *Mozarabic Cardinal*, p. 499).

76. D. Catalán & E. Jerez, «*Rodericus*» *romanzado*, p. 571. The error derives ultimately from Ramón Gonzálvez's attribution to the pontificate of Nicholas III (1277-1280) of a papal letter copied in ACT O.3.C.1.3 («El arcediano Jofre de Loaysa y el 'fecho de coronados'», in *Estudios en homenaje a D. Claudio Sánchez Albornoz en sus 90 años*, III, Buenos Aires: Instituto de Historia de España, 1985, pp. 241-262 (244). However, the date of this («Laterani non. martii pontificatus nostri anno primo») can only refer to that of Nicholas IV (1288-1292), as references in the text to letters on the subject issued by the pontiff's immediate predecessor, Honorius IV, confirm. The reader of Gonzálvez's article is likely to have been misled by what purports to be a quotation from the papal text referring to the abbot of Covarrubias «qui se gerit pro electo toletano» (p. 244), and therefore to a date before 1280. In fact, the letter's description of the abbot is of one «qui se tunc pro electo Toletano gerebat». See F. J. Hernández & P. Linehan, *Mozarabic Cardinal*, p. 171. It is to be noted that on diplomatic grounds the copy can be shown to have been made not from the papal register but from the original.

77. D. Catalán & E. Jerez, «*Rodericus*» *romanzado*, p. 594, in accordance with the further misdating by R. Gonzálvez Ruiz, *Hombres y libros de Toledo (1086-1300)*, Madrid: Fundación Ramón Areces, 1997, pp. 359-360. *Cf.* F. J. Hernández & P. Linehan, *Mozarabic Cardinal*, p. 240.

crowned Sancho in Toledo cathedral[78]. It was precisely the fact that like Archbishop Gonzalo of Compostela he had *not* been the king's man for Toledo in the first place, that he had *not* returned while the old king was still alive, and that he had *not* been at Toledo at the start of the new reign that made the development of his relationship with the new king so notable. By a curious irony, most modern scholars have been deluded by purveyors of historical fiction into believing that no such special relationship can have existed because the archbishop was driven into exile by *ira regia* in 1286[79]. This too is wrong. Gonzalo Pérez stayed, and develop the relationship did –though it did not survive the death of that king.

With the death of Sancho IV in 1295 the special relationship waned. The moment had passed. In 1311 Sancho's son would describe Gonzalo Pérez's successor but one as his «fechura». That was the word that, when writing to Alfonso X from Rome[80] at the time of his appointment in May 1280, Gonzalo Pérez had used to describe himself. The same word, but with very different connotations in the two places[81]. A sentence in another letter from the earlier date, and destined for the then Infante, shows what had been lost. It had been addressed «a uos, que siempre nos amastes e nos onrrastes de que erades moço pequenno a aca»[82].

But in a sense the failure of that relationship hardly mattered since by then sufficient of the historical past had been toledanized for the archbishop to rest in peace. The placebo to which a Toledo deprived of

78. H. O. Bizzarri, «*Castigos del rey D. Sancho IV*», p. 17.

79. Misinformation originating with the anonymous author of certain «Vidas de los arzobispos de Toledo» written after 1588. Amongst those recently misled have been Manuel Alonso, «Bibliotecas medievales de los arzobispos de Toledo», *Razón y Fe*, 123 (1941), pp. 295-309 (at p. 302); *Johannis Aegidii Zamorensis. 'Historia Naturalis'*, edited by Avelino Domínguez García & Luis García Ballester, [Valladolid]: Junta de Castilla y León, Consejería de Cultura y Turismo, 1994, I, pp. 30-31; Germán Orduna, «La elite intelectual de la escuela catedralicia de Toledo y la literatura en época de Sancho IV», in *La literatura en la época de Sancho IV (Actas del Congreso Internacional «La literatura en la época de Sancho IV», Alcalá de Henares, 21-24 de febrero de 1994)*, edited by Carlos Alvar & Juan Manuel Lucía Megías, Alcalá de Henares: Servicio de Publicaciones, Universidad de Alcalá, 1996, pp. 53-62; G. Martin, «L'escarboucle de Saint-Denis», p. 460; and F. Gómez-Redondo, *Historia de la prosa*, I, p. 861. *Cf.* F. J. Hernández & P. Linehan, *Mozarabic Cardinal*, p. 423 n. 73.

80. And it was from Rome that he did so and not, as D. Catalán & E. Jerez variously contend, from Viterbo or Orvieto: «*Rodericus*» *romanzado*, pp. 549, 570, 602.

81. F. J. Hernández & P. Linehan, *Mozarabic Cardinal*, p. 442; Antonio Benavides, *Memorias de D. Fernando IV de Castilla*, Madrid: J. Rodríguez, 1860, II, num. 550 (cit. F. J. Hernández & P. Linehan, p. 405).

82. *Idem, Mozarabic Cardinal*, p. 446.

nourishment had turned was found to have therapeutic virtues of its own. To return to my point of departure, the process ensured that in death, as never in life, D. Rodrigo came to be identified with his king and, because his king was a saint, to be treated as immune from the criticism of historians[83]. In the 1590s another member of the Loaisa clan, Archbishop García de Loaisa, attempted to improve on the record of 1253, and in 1902 Padre Fita brandishing a sword for Santiago denounced him and sought to tar D. García and everything back to 1253 with the brush of the False Chroniclers[84]. Padre Fita was right about many things. He was probably wrong about that.

---

83. See the judgement of E. Estella, sometime archivist of Toledo cathedral, cit. P. Linehan, «D. Rodrigo», p. 87, n. 1.

84. F. Fita, «Santiago de Galicia», *Razón y Fe*, 4, 2 (1902), pp. 35-45 (36-38, 45).

# XII

## El cuatro de mayo de 1282

Hoy a hablarles sobre Alfonso X y su relación con la Iglesia Hispánica. O, más bien, sobre una pequeña parcela de tan amplia materia. Fundamentalmente sobre un día concreto del mes de mayo de 1282 y sobre lo que un único documento puede revelarnos sobre la ruptura de relaciones entre Alfonso y sus eclesiásticos. Por lo tanto, éste será un ejercicio histórico a la antigua usanza, cuyo título, expresado en términos más *à la mode* podría ser algo así como: 'Hacia una aproximación a la historia del día 4 de mayo de 1282: un ensayo positivista de historia eclesiástica'.[1]

Pero antes de entrar en materia debo reseñarles brevemente el devenir de esas relaciones durante la década anterior, es decir, desde las portentosas cortes de Burgos de 1272. Tal y como nos informa la *Crónica* del reino, en aquella ocasión –víspera de la rebelión acaudillada por el infante don Felipe–, los prelados trataron de complicar la vida al monarca con premeditación y alevosía:

> "Los perlados del regno que eran alli con el rey en aquellas Cortes trabajáronse de poner departimiento entre el rey e aquellos ricos omnes et plazíales que non ouiese y asosiego".

No obstante, la *Crónica,* esta *Crónica* tan discutible, dice que un escollo considerable impedía a Alfonso desterrar a tales obispos de su reino ('Quisiéralos

---

[1] Agradezco la ayuda que me han prestado con la traducción de este trabajo Javier Rodríguez Molina y, una vez más, Francisco Hernández, principal enderezador de mi torcido castellano.

echar del regno'[2]). Este escollo no era otro que la necesidad de contentar al pontífice, de quien en última instancia dependían en 1272 las aspiraciones del monarca para acceder al trono imperial. De esa misma fecha procede una carta enviada al recientemente elegido Gregorio X, que se ha conservado en un borrador y que probablemente fue enteramente compuesto por el notario de Castilla, Gonzalo Pérez, el mal llamado 'Gudiel'. En dicha carta el rey resalta todos los servicios que sus antecesores habían llevado a cabo a favor de 'la Iglesia':

> "A lo que nos conseiades que siempre amemos la Eglesia, este conseio tenemos por bueno e por sancto e gradeçemosuoslo mucho e fazemoslo assi quanto nos podemos e deuemoslo fazer, por dos razones: la una por la bondat e securidat del regno, e la otra porque lo fizieron todos aquellos onde nos venimos".[3]

En este momento tan delicado de su reinado, Alfonso deja bien claro cuál es su actitud respecto a 'la Iglesia', pero guarda silencio respecto a los obispos. Quizá prudentemente.

La *Crónica* también calla y nos deja a oscuras sobre la identidad de los obispos confabulados de 1272 y sobre la naturaleza de sus reivindicaciones. Respecto a los obispos, Ballesteros ha sugerido que probablemente fueran los titulares de las sedes gallegas y leonesas;[4] aspecto que conviene tener en cuenta cuando lleguemos a los sucesos de 1282. En cuanto a sus reivindicaciones, podemos pensar que no serían muy diferentes de aquellas *gravamina* que los *universi prelati Hispanie* habían dirigido al colegio cardenalicio en 1262-63, protestando contra el impuesto decretado por Urbano IV a la Iglesia Castellana para sufragar a los exiliados del reino de Apulia y del Imperio Latino de Constantinopla.[5] También podemos suponer que esto no era sino un anticipo de nuevas demandas papales en beneficio del moribundo reino latino de Jerusalén porque, a lo largo de todo su pontificado, la Cruzada de Oriente fue, en palabras de Runciman, una ardiente aspiración ('burning desire') de Gregorio X.[6]

---

[2] C[rónica de] A[lfonso] X [según el Ms. II/2777 de la Biblioteca del Palacio Real] (Madrid), ed. M. GONZÁLEZ JIMÉNEZ, Murcia, 1999, c. 26.
[3] AC Toledo, dsn, publ. F. J. HERNÁNDEZ Y P. LINEHAN, The Mozarabic Cardinal. The life and times of Gonzalo Pérez Gudiel, Florencia, 2004, 439.
[4] Alfonso X, Barcelona, 1963, p. 584.
[5] E. BENITO RUANO, "La iglesia española ante la caída del Imperio Latino de Constantinopla", Hispania Sacra, 11 (1958), esp. p. 17; P. LINEHAN, "The Gravamina of the Castilian Church in 1262-3", English Historical Review, 85 (1970), 730-754 [reimpr. LINEHAN, Spanish Church and Society, 1150-1300, London, 1983].
[6] The Sicilian Vespers, Harmondswoth, 1960, 167.

Pero en 1272 esta no era la única preocupación económica de los prelados, que debían enfrentarse con otro problema que pesaba sobre ellos como una losa. Este problema lo encarnaba el propio rey, cuya apropiación indebida de las 'terciae decimarum' había denunciado Clemente IV en 1265 como 'rapinam vilissimam tam dampnabilem quam dampnosam'.[7] La subvención de la décima parte de las rentas eclesiásticas que Alfonso solicitó para sufragar los gastos militares durante la revuelta de los mudéjares le fue otorgada a condición de que el rey renunciara públicamente a la contribución forzosa otorgada a su padre por Inocencio IV exclusivamente para la campaña de la reconquista de Sevilla.[8] El arzobispo de Sevilla, Raimundo de Losana, leal servidor del rey, fue la persona elegida para recordar a Alfonso, *simpliciter et secreto,* que mientras continuara beneficiándose de las *tercias* estaría en pecado mortal: una situación ciertamente poco propicia para un candidato al trono del Sacro Imperio Romano.[9] Tampoco era una tarea fácil para el arzobispo, quien, como era previsible, dejó de cumplirla. Dos años después, el pontífice tuvo que volver a escribirle de nuevo sobre el mismo asunto. El hecho de que lo hiciera dos *días* después de escribir a Alfonso en relación con su pretensión de acceder al trono imperial no sería ninguna coincidencia[10]. Roma no olvidaba tales cosas.

Todo esto sucedía en junio de 1265. Y así continuaron las cosas. Toda la atención recaía ahora sobre el monarca. En marzo de 1267 los prelados de Castilla se reunieron en Brihuega bajo la presidencia de Sancho de Aragón, arzobispo electo de Toledo. Lamentablemente, el documento palentino que recoge estas intervenciones resulta ilegible en su mayor parte, por lo que ignoramos cuáles fueron los defectos sobre la administración del Rey Sabio denunciados por los prelados castellanos. Pero lo que sí sabemos es que en aquella ocasión estuvieron presentes al menos seis de los ocho sufragáneos de la provincia toledana, obispos a quienes desagradaba sobremanera la excesiva confianza con que Alfonso trataba a sus 'blasfemos consejeros judíos', como ellos les llamaban. '*Nephas est'*, dice el documento, nefasto es preferirles a los cristianos.[11] En este contexto resulta chocante que entre los firmantes de las actas de esta asamblea exclusivamente episcopal, se encontraran Pedro Lorenzo de Cuenca y Agustín de Osma, personajes ambos que pertenecían a aquella corte alfonsina tan dominada por los judíos.

---

[7] *Les Registres de Clément IV,* ed. E. JORDAN, París, 1893-1945, n. 890 (=S. DOMÍNGUEZ SÁNCHEZ, *Documentos de Clemente IV (1265-1268) referentes a España,* León, 1996. n. 32).

[8] P. LINEHAN, *The Spanish Church and the Papacy in the Thirteenth Century,* Cambridge 1971, 111-12.

[9] *Les Registres de Clément IV,* ut. cit.

[10] Ibid., nos. 1205, 1206 (=DOMÍNGUEZ SÁNCHEZ, *Documentos de Clemente IV,* nos. 131, 132).

[11] "...quia nephas est ut blasphemantibus Christi iudeis maior habeatur fides quam Christi fidelibus christianios": AC Palencia, 4/1/3.

150

Después de 1272, cuando Fernando de la Cerda, 'por mandado del rey', se entrevistó con los prelados en Peñafiel mientras Alfonso se dirigía a Beaucaire (1275), también acudieron *ricos omes*, pero no hubo quejas específicas contra el rey. En Peñafiel, las quejas se redujeron a cuestiones jurídicas relativas a la intromisión de algunos jueces seculares en materias de competencia eclesiástica y al fracaso de las autoridades seculares a la hora de validar y ejecutar sentencias eclesiásticas.[12] Sólo después de Beaucaire comenzaron los eclesiásticos a manifestar abiertamente su malestar contra Alfonso y su manipulación de los textos de las cartas papales – hasta tal punto que en 1276, con los moros a las puertas, el mismísimo prior provincial de los dominicos declaró que no estaba dispuesto a predicar la Cruzada.[13] Así fue como ocurrió finalmente el encotronazo con el monarca en 1279.

En 1269, el consejo del rey Jaime de Aragón a su yerno, Alfonso de Castilla, había sido

"Que si se veía incapaz de mantener el amor y el afecto de todos sus vasallos, que mantuviera al menos el afecto de la Iglesia, del pueblo y de las ciudades … porque Dios ama a estas gentes más que a los caballeros, porque los caballeros se alzan más fácilmente contra su señor que los otros".[14]

Pero en 1279, Alfonso había perdido todos esos apoyos: la Iglesia, el pueblo y las ciudades, los caballeros. Tras conocer la decisión de Beaucaire, nada de lo que anteriormente le había disuadido de expulsar a los obispos tenía ya fuerza alguna. Así que, al igual que el rey Juan de Inglaterra durante el entredicho de su reinado a principios de siglo, Alfonso se sintió libre para apropiarse hasta del plomo de los tejados de las iglesias. En consecuencia, durante este año el conflicto entre Alfonso X y sus obispos se desbordó y provocó una catarata de denuncias ante el Papa Nicolás III, cuyo eco no tardó en llegar a Castilla a través de la legación del obispo de Rieti. Esta vez, estaba bien claro quién era el responsable de todos sus problemas. El responsable de todos sus problemas no era otro que el rey.

El rey tuvo que responder a quince reivindicaciones. En 1980, cuando publiqué sus réplicas, señalé cómo actuaron Alfonso y el infante don Sancho. En verdad, no se tomaron mucho interés en el asunto. Más de la mitad de sus réplicas no ofrece justificación alguna. Nada dijeron, por ejemplo, sobre el problema

---

12 Ibid., 1/1/2; R. Menéndez Pidal (ed.), *Docs. lingüísticos de España*, Madrid, 1919, n. 229.

13 P. Linehan, "'*Quedam de quibus dubitans*'. On preaching the crusade in Alfonso X's Castile", *HID*, 27 (2000), 103-128

14 *Llibre dels Fets del rei En Jaume*, ed. J. Bruguera, Barcelona 1991, c. 498.

recurrente de sus consejeros judíos. Pero no quiero perder más tiempo relatándoles todas y cada una de las réplicas que dirigieron a los que les pedían explicaciones, como por ejemplo la exorbitante exigencia de que el rey fuera beneficiario vitalicio de las *tercias* y de los ingresos procedentes de las iglesias vacantes. Tampoco tengo intención de volver a indagar en la idea de que fue Gudiel quien orquestó la protesta episcopal.[15] Pero sí me detendré, apenas un instante, en las razones que Alfonso dio sobre el exilio forzoso del obispo de León, dada la importancia que el informe del nuncio concede tanto a este hecho como al maltrato del arzobispo de Compostela, y dado que en la traducción gallega de la *Crónica de Castilla* podemos leer que el informe negativo de estos dos obispos sobre las acciones de Alfonso fue lo que provocó la decisión papal de negar el imperio al rey, si bien esta afirmación resulta cronológicamente inadmisible.[16]

El exilio forzoso había sido un instrumento de control de la política alfonsina durante mucho más tiempo del que los historiadores de su reinado se han preocupado de reconocer. Nada menos que en 1263 –mucho antes de los 'desnaturamientos' voluntarios de 1276 y de los años siguientes– el Papa Urbano IV había intercedido ante Alfonso a favor de cuatro miembros de la Orden de Calatrava –Alfonso Garcés y tres más– quienes, en opinión del pontífice, habían sido falsamente acusados de haberse coaligado con los enemigos del rey, y que por esa razón habían sido desterrados ('forbanniri'). El papa solicitó al rey que anulara dicha sentencia ('rebanniri').[17] Ambos términos pertenecen al lenguaje jurídico, y son poco usuales en una carta papal. Seguramente Alfonso

---

15 HERNÁNDEZ & LINEHAN, *The Mozarabic Cardinal*, 180-1.

16 AC Toledo, X.1.B.1.4; P. LINEHAN, "The Spanish Church revisited: the episcopal *gravamina* of 1279", en B. TIERNEY y P. LINEHAN (eds.), *Authority and Power. Studies on medieval law and government presented to Walter Ullmann on his Seventieth birthday*, Cambridge, 1980, 127-47 [reimpr. *Spanish Church and Society*]; IDEM, *History and the Historians of Medieval Spain*, Oxford 1993, 509. Véase también C. de AYALA MARTÍNEZ, "Las relaciones de Alfonso X con la Santa Sede durante el pontificado de Nicolás III (1277-1280)", en J. C. MIGUEL RODRÍGUEZ et al. (eds.), Madrid, 1989, 137-51.

17 "Sane ex petitione dilectorum filiorum Alfonsi Garsie, Gomecii Gundisalvi, Martini Lupi et Raynerii, fratrum ordinis Calatraviensis, nobis innotuit quod olim falso excellentie regali suggesto quod iidem fratres contra eam [*scil*. regiam maiestatem] adversariis tuis prestiterant et prestabant auxilium, consilium et favorem eos occasione huiusmodi ab eorum domo in tuo regno consistente fecisti eici et de regno ipso nichilominus forbanniri, qui hac de causa extra idem regnum coguntur non sine approbrio dicti ordinis exulare. Quia igitur in hiis si vera sunt evidenter anime tue saluti detrahitur serenitatem regiam rogamus et hortamur attente quatinus dictos fratres pro nostra et apostolice sedis reverentia facias rebanniri ac in domo et regno predictis libere commorari permictas": *Salutem tuam plenis*, 18 Jan. 1263: Madrid, AHN, OO. MM., Calatrava, carp. 444, n. 57. Cf. BALLESTEROS, *Alfonso X*, 350, quien, citando a J. ORTEGA Y COTES, *Bullarium Ordinis Militiæ de Calatrava*, Madrid, 1761, 121, cree que el documento lo encabezan seis individuos y no cuatro, por haber leído mal 'Gomecio' como 'Genecio' y 'Lupi' como 'Luys', asombrándose

Garcés y sus compañeros, que conocían bien las definiciones jurídicas con las que operaba el rey, sugirieron al papa la inclusión de estos términos en su carta. No está muy claro de qué manera había ofendido al rey Alfonso Garcés –el comendador de Martos que tan funestamente aconsejó al arzobispo Sancho de Aragón en 1275[18]. Sin embargo, conocemos de sobra la ofensa que llevó al exilio al obispo de León, Martín Fernández, antes notario del rey en León. Su ofensa consistía en ser el padrino de Fernando de la Cerda. Por lo tanto, es perfectamente comprensible que hubiese sido un firme defensor de la causa de los hijos del Infante. Canónicamente era obligatorio.[19] Por esta razón, tal y como el nuncio recoge en su informe de 1279, "manifiesta cosa es que el fuyendo la persecucion del Rey que mendiga y anda desterrado en tierras estrannas"[20].

Lo que resulta un tanto incomprensible es la rapidez con que el obispo y su iglesia se alían en 1282 con el enemigo declarado de la causa de la Cerda, es decir con el infante don Sancho.

Contra la acusación de que se había impedido a los obispos reunirse para discutir sus reivindicaciones, en 1279 el rey y su hijo dieron la callada por respuesta[21]. La razón de tal prohibición era, por supuesto, que reuniones de ese tipo podrían resultar subversivas. Circunstancia que se había verificado en la reunión de Brihuega de 1267, y que se verificaría de nuevo en Valladolid en mayo de 1282.

Pero antes de centrar mi atención en este último suceso, déjenme que les cuente algo sobre una obra comenzada en 1281 por un judío castellano que vivía en Egipto, Isaac ibn Sahula, titulada *Meshal Haqadmoni*, de la cual contamos desde hace poco con una excelente traducción inglesa a cargo del Prof. Raphael Loewe. Una de las fábulas protagonizada por animales que contiene esta aguda sátira de la sociedad castellana en tiempos de Alfonso X, cuenta que los animales convocaron una asamblea para debatir cómo debían proceder ante

---

a continuación de que el documento "nos revela un hecho del cual no poseemos antecedente ningun.". ORTEGA Y COTES había contado cinco.

[18] *CAX*, c. 63.

[19] En 1270 Fernando de la Cerda había recibido a los vasallos del obispo y sus posesiones bajo su protección "como si fueran míos": J. M. RUIZ ASENCIO y J. A. MARTÍN FUERTES, *Colección documental del Archivo de la Catedral de Leon, IX (1269-1300)*, León, 1994, n. 2294. Durante los primeros años del reinado alfonsí, Martín Fernández había sido un leal servidor de la monarquía, y por lo menos hasta mayo de 1254 ocupó el cargo de notario de León (el infante don Fernando había nacido en octubre de 1255: M. GONZÁLEZ JIMÉNEZ, (ed.), *Diplomatario andaluz de Alfonso X*, Sevilla, 1991, n. 136; G. DAUMET, *Mémoire sur les relations de la France et de la Castille de 1255 à 1320*, París, 1913, 11, y en 1269 había sido testigo de los esponsales del infante con su prometida francesa: *ibid.*, 156, donde se le describe (p. 15) como "canciller del Infante".

[20] LINEHAN, "Spanish Church revisited", 142.

[21] Ibid., 146.

los incesantes estragos que su rey, el León, les infligía. A través de esta alegoría, el autor describe cómo el buey incitó a todos los animales que tenían cuernos a acorralar a su torturador y luchar con él hasta matarlo. Pero el asno silvestre aconsejó obrar con precaución. Porque

"Repression on himself he needs must bring
Who insurrection moves against his king.
Was ever there a subject raised his arm
Against the Lord's anointed, without harm?"

["Quien se alza en rebelión y al rey quiere suplantar
Bien merece la pena que viene de traicionar.
Nadie puede amenazar al ungido del Señor
Si no quiere terminar castigado y sin perdón"].

En lugar de lo que proponía el buey, el asno les recomendó partir hacia 'tierras lejanas' y, a su debido tiempo, hacer lo que se proponían, ya que allí descubrirían 'una tierra fértil, generosa y llena de paz'.[22] Evidentemente, Ibn Sahula, que era originario de Guadalajara, estaba pensando al escribir esto en la situación de Castilla en los exiliados en Francia y Roma –Lope Díaz de Haro y los prelados de León y Compostela– y en Alfonso, a quien claramente veía reflejado en la figura del León. Cierto es (creo yo) que Alfonso jamás había sido ungido.[23] Pero no debemos olvidar lo reacios que se mostraban los hombres del siglo XIII a la hora de atacar directamente al rey, incluso si éste no había sido ungido.

Esto fue exactamente lo que sucedió en Valladolid cuando el infante don Sancho llamó a los exiliados a su lado y el modo de acción propuesto por el buey fue el que prevaleció.

1282 fue un año decisivo para la Historia de España, y el encuentro planeado en Valladolid en Pascua pudo haber sido su apogeo. El Infante don Sancho había invitado al rey de Aragón con el objeto de que éste tuviera representación en aquel encuentro el domingo, 29 de marzo, circunstancia que don Pedro mencionó a Alfonso dos días después de la reunión.[24] Pero mientras infantes y procuradores se reunían en Valladolid, en Palermo un soldado francés que se

---

[22] R. Loewe (ed. y trad.), *Isaac Ibn Sahula. Meshal Haqadmoni. Fables from the Distant Past*, Oxford/Portland, OR., 2004, 60-66.

[23] P. Linehan, "The accession of Alfonso X (1252) and the origins of the War of the Spanish Succession", en D. W. Lomax y D. MacKenzie (eds.), *God and Man in Medieval Spain. Essays in honour of J. R. L. Highfield*, Warminster, 1989 [reimpr. *Past and Present in Medieval Spain*, Aldershot, 1992], 59-79.

[24] *M[emorial] H[istórico] E[spañol]*, II, Madrid 1851, n. 197.

había emborrachado intentó violar a la mujer de un siciliano; en cuestión de horas la guarnición angevina fue pasada a cuchillo, se iniciaron las operaciones para expulsar a los franceses de Italia, y el reino fue ofrecido a los aragoneses. De este modo, la Pascua de 1282 se convirtió en una fecha triunfal para Aragón, y los sucesos de estos días terminaron con las ambiciones castellanas en Europa durante los siguientes doscientos años, por lo menos.

Por este motivo, la Pascua de 1282 pasó a ser conocida con el nombre de 'Vísperas Sicilianas'. Entretanto, la reunión de Valladolid que, por pura coincidencia, había sido convocada para el mismo día, fue aplazada. Para que se lograra hubo que recurrir a otro tipo de argumentos, tales como amenazas e intimidaciones. Así es como se trató a los dirigentes de la Iglesia. Una cosa era la adhesión a la causa rebelde de la reina y los infantes, pero otra muy distinta era llevar este apoyo a sus últimas consecuencias. Como en la fábula de Isaac ibn Sahula, los castellanos no estaban habituados a derrocar a sus reyes. Los allí presentes no sabían muy bien qué hacer. ¿No se había dado una situación similar anteriormente, en tiempos de Alfonso III?, tal vez se preguntaría alguno. Pero aquello había sucedido cuatrocientos años atrás. ¿Qué pensaban los obispos, quienes, al menos ellos, podrían haber entendido la relevancia del caso de otro 'rey inútil', Sancho II de Portugal, un precedente que parece haber ocupado algunas mentes desde la vuelta real de Beaucaire.[25] Durante años, los obispos se habían quejado del trato que el rey les había dispensado. Pero en abril de 1282, al menos al principio, dudaron sobre la conveniencia de romper sus relaciones con la corona y aliarse con los rebeldes.

Tales dudas se ven reflejadas claramente en la protesta elevada por los obispos de Burgos y Palencia, quienes, en vista de las bien conocidas simpatías hacia Alfonso del arzobispo de Sevilla, Remondo de Losana, y debido a las ausencias de los arzobispos de Toledo y Compostela, eran los prelados de mayor rango e importancia residentes en el reino, y no solo por ese motivo, sino también debido a la influencia internacional de la orden franciscana, a la que pertenecía el miembro el primero, y por razón del importantísimo peso político del segundo, que era a la vez primo del infante don Sancho y hermano de la mujer a la que éste se uniría en una relación absolutamente probida por todas las reglas del derecho canónico.

Así, cuando el día 22 de abril los infantes Pedro y Juan, hermanos del rey, irrumpieron en sus aposentos de forma "violenta e inesperada" y les conminaron a ponerse de lado de Sancho para que apoyaran la idea de que el rey

---

25 R. P. KINKADE, "Alfonso X, *Cantiga* 235, and the events of 1269-1278", *Speculum*, 67 (1992), 312, 321. Cf. HERNÁNDEZ & LINEHAN, *The Mozarabic Cardinal*, 234.

don Alfonso debía ser privado de su autoridad para gobernar, ellos se negaron a hacer tal cosa. Pensaban que esta decisión era (según decían) "en extremo difícil de tomar, y que requería una reflexión más cuidadosa antes de llevarse a cabo." Especialmente desagradable les resultaba el espectáculo de "tantos abades de nuestras diócesis que confraternizan y se conjuran con los laicos, en perjuicio de la libertad eclesiástica" y –esperen a oír esto– "y en contra de los estatutos del Señor de Sabina". Esta última apelación a su conciencia es especialmente jugosa, porque este 'Señor de Sabina' no era otro que Juan de Abbeville, el legado pontificio cuyas prescripciones sobre la reforma de la iglesia castellana, especialmente las que exigían convocar concilios y sínodos periódicamente, habían sido alegremente olvidadas por clérigos y obispos durante … más de cincuenta años.

No obstante, cuando se les amenazó con la muerte si no obedecían, ambos asistieron a la lectura de la sentencia contra el rey –"si sentencia puede llamarse", como dijeron–, aunque no estuvieron presentes a su publicación durante la lectura. Declararon que si habían añadido sus sellos al documento, lo habían hecho por miedo, y así trataron de desvincularse de un instrumento que privaba al padre del poder regio y designaba a su hijo para sustituirle.[26]

Este hecho muestra que en una fecha tan tardía como el 22 de abril, don Sancho no tenía todavía todos los votos. Pero durante el fin de semana del 2 al 4 de mayo el curso de los acontecimientos cambió radicalmente. El sábado (día 2), cuarenta abades cluniacenses, cistercienses y premonstratenses de los monasterios de Castilla y León seguían mencionando al viejo monarca como reinante sobre la lista usual de reinos con que era siempre citado, sin proponer cosa más subversiva que la idea de rezar unos por otros. Ocho o nueve eran leoneses[27]. Esto fue el sábado.

Llegado el lunes, día 4, las cosas habían cambiado. Algo había sucedido el domingo. Puede que la voluntad de los obispos y abades se viera influenciada por todos los privilegios que el Infante generosamente les estaba otorgando.[28] O tal vez –tal vez– al comenzar aquella semana de ruegos, el Espíritu Santo había respondido a sus súplicas en busca de consejo.

---

[26] F. J. Pereda Llarena, *Documentación de la catedral de Burgos (1254-1293)*, Burgos, 1984, 237-41. En la legislación del Concilio de Valladolid de 1229(?) no encontramos tales *statuta domini Sabinensis*: *Colección documental del Archivo de la Catedral de Leon*, VI *(1188-1230)*, León, 1991, n. 1955. Cf. P. Linehan, "A papal legation and its aftermath: Cardinal John of Abbeville in Spain and Portugal, 1228-1229", en I. Birocchi *et al.*, *A Ennio Cortese*, Roma, 2001, II. 236-56.

[27] *MHE*, II, 67-8, mal fechado el 3 de mayo; y seguido por L. Fernández Martín, "La participación de los monasterios en la 'hermandad' de los reinos de Castilla, León y Galicia (1282-1284)", *Hispania Sacra*, 25 (1972), 9. Véase Apéndice.

[28] M. González Jiménez, "Sancho IV, Infante", *HID*, 28 (2001), 194-9.

Porque llegado lunes la delegación leonesa se había constituido como grupo de presión formado por siete de los abades que habían participado en los actos del sábado y veinte paisanos más: cinco obispos y los representantes de otras cuatro sedes leonesas. Todos ellos constituyeron una hermandad eclesiástica en apoyo del Infante. A la primera oportunidad de sedición nacional, los eclesiásticos de los reinos de Castilla y León parecían volver a la situación anterior a la reunión de los reinos de 1230. La línea de fractura entre los reinos seguía abierta. Las tensiones que posteriormente estallarían durante la minoría de edad de Fernando IV, con el espectro de una nueva partición de los reinos[29], empezaron a hacerse patentes en el Valladolid de 1282.

Los castellanos parecen no haberse involucrado en esta conjura. No hay constancia de que existiera una *hermandad* equivalente integrada por los eclesiásticos de Castilla. Los historiadores del reinado de Alfonso X no parecen haber reparado en este hecho, ni tampoco parecen haberse preguntado hasta qué punto el máximo dirigente de la iglesia castellana, don Gonzalo Pérez, pudo haber sido el responsable de mantener a sus obispos y abades durante los dos años siguientes en el mismo estado de indefinición en que él se mantuvo, frente a las presiones de ambos bandos, con el único objetivo de preservar su propio estatus.[30]

Fue entonces cuando los obispos y abades leoneses suscribieron una declaración conjunta que calificaba al rey únicamente como 'el muy ilustre señor don Alfonso' (nada quedaba de los títulos desplegados dos días antes, nada de aquel 'illustrissimus rex Castelle, Legionis, Toleti, Galleciae, Hispalis, Cordubae, Murcia etc.' del sábado).[31] Debemos insistir en que estos juegos verbales con las formas de tratamiento para referirse al rey resultan altamente reveladores, pues nos indican hacia dónde se inclinaba la lealtad de cada uno. Así, cuando en 1285 el obispo Suero Pérez modificó su testamento, negó el título de rey a don Sancho, que le había exiliado de su sede, y se lo devolvió a su padre, que ya había fallecido.[32]

---

[29] P. LINEHAN, "Castile, Navarre and Portugal", en M. JONES (ed.), *The New Cambridge Medieval History*, VI, *c. 1300-c. 1415*, Cambridge, 2000, 623.

[30] HERNÁNDEZ & LINEHAN, *The Mozarabic Cardinal*, 213-43. Tal vez resulte significativo el hecho de que, en su relación de estos acontecimientos, el analista de Silos mencione expresamente a los obispos de Palencia y Burgos, junto con su colega zamorano: D. W. LOMAX, "Una crónica inédita de Silos", en *Homenaje a Fray Justo Pérez de Urbel*, Silos, 1976, I, 333. La ausencia de declaraciones similares por parte del episcopado castellano no puede atribuirse a las vacantes que hubiera por estas fechas en las sedes castellanas: M. GONZÁLEZ JIMÉNEZ, *Diplomatario Andaluz*, n. 501.

[31] *MHE*, II. p. 67.

[32] P. LINEHAN, "Don Suero Pérez" en LINEHAN & J. C. de LERA MAÍLLO, *Las postrimerías de un obispo alfonsín. D. Suero Pérez, el de Zamora*, Zamora, 2003, 49, 123.

Aquel lunes todos los presentes acordaron primero reunirse cada dos
años, como medida para garantizar sus inmunidades y libertades. Eso fue todo.
Pero hubo algo más. De hecho, la medida no llegaba a la altura de lo prescrito
por Juan de Abbeville, pero sobrepasaba lo que Alfonso había permitido hacer
a los obispos durante todo su reinado. Una de las quejas que más eco tuvo en
1279 había sido que "los prelados y los cabildos de la tierra no tenían libertad
para reunirse y discutir las injusticias cometidas sobre los eclesiásticos".[33] En el
año 1279 ese había sido el límite de las ambiciones episcopales. Y así era al principio del cuarto día. Pero durante este cuarto día, surgieron nuevas ambiciones.
Como en julio de 1936, al principio de la Guerra Civil, el paso del tiempo
favoreció el triunfo de ideas más radicales; entre ellas, la convicción de que era
urgente y necesario que la hermandad eclesiástica se vinculara a la hermandad
concejil de los reinos de León y de Galicia, castigando con severas penas a los
eclesiásticos que se ausentaran de sus reuniones.[34] A medida que avanzaba el día,
los recién llegados se sumaban a la causa, indicando su adhesión con las rúbricas
y los sellos que fueron adhiriendo a los pergaminos con las actas de aquel día,
convencidos de que eran la última tabla de salvación a que podían agarrarse.

Ese mismo día, en un intento tan prudente como inútil de asegurarse el
apoyo de la influyente orden dominicana después de que su máximo dirigente se
hubiese coligado con los dos obispos renuentes, la reina doña Violante conven-
ció a su hijo, el infante rebelde, de que tomase a la orden bajo su protección.[35]

Diez días antes, de acuerdo con el Conde de Barcelos, al alcalde mayor de
Toledo, Diego Alfonso, le había parecido apropiado –*lhe pareçia cousa onesta*– que
Sancho no fuera llamado rey mientras su padre viviera.[36] Y el infante tuvo a bien
esta disposición, y de hecho parece que se abstuvo celosamente de intitularse con
otros tratamientos que no fueran el de "hijo mayor y heredero del muy noble don
Alfonso por la gracia de Dios rey de Castilla, etc.", mientras, según el testimonio
de la *Crónica*, concedía a los demandantes "todo aquello que le solicitaban".[37]

---

33 "Item prelatis et capitulis terre sue non est liberum convenire ut tractarent de premissis et aliis
gravaminibus quae ipsis et aliis personis ecclesiasticis pro tempore inferuntur." Ni el rey ni su hijo
ofrecieron respuesta alguna a esta queja (resumida como "en razon delos prelados que no se osan
ayuntar"): LINEHAN, "Spanish Church revisited", 146.
34 *MHE*, II, p. 70.
35 Madrid, AHN, Clero, carp. 3501/1; PEREDA LLARENA, *Documentación. de la catedral de Burgos*, 238.
Los obispos dominicos permanecieron fieles al rey hasta el final: M. GONZÁLEZ JIMÉNEZ, *Diplomatario andaluz*, n. 520; HERNÁNDEZ & LINEHAN, *The Mozarabic Cardinal*, 240, nota 103.
36 L. F. LINDLEY CINTRA (ed.), *Crónica Geral de Espanha de 1344*, IV, Lisboa, 1990, 512-13.
37 *CAX*, c. 76. La carta del 20 de mayo 1282 dirigida al *concejo* de Orihuela en la que se intitula rey es
una copia tardía; al igual que la dirigida desde Treviño el 7 de agosto de 1282, que se conserva en una
confirmación de la chancillería de Alfonso XI de 1318 (aunque es cierto que el Infante se encontraba

Por supuesto, este comportamiento era una ficción destinada a guardar el decoro regio. La realidad era muy distinta, puesto que a lo largo del fin de semana la clase dirigente de León, incluyendo al estamento eclesiástico, había abandonado al viejo rey. El obispo de León no se encontraba allí personalmente. Probablemente, estaba todavía en la curia papal (aunque hacia mediados de octubre había llegado a Oporto; es de suponer que muy prudentemente había decidido regresar a la Península por mar, mejor que por tierra firme).[38] Tal y como nos revela en uno de sus pliegos uno de los documentos sobre los cuales hablaré a continuación, en la reunión del 4 de mayo el obispo había estado representado por su notario, el arcediano Martinus Johannis[39]. Tampoco había ninguna representación del arzobispo de Compostela, por la sencilla razón de que había muerto.[40] Por lo demás, todas las sedes del reino de León estaban representadas y todas apoyaron la causa de don Sancho el 4 de mayo. O, más exactamente, *casi* todas. No les voy a aburrir con detalles de quiénes permanecieron fieles al rey. Los dejo al pie de la página.[41]

---

en Treviño aquel día): J. M. del Estal, *Documentos inéditos de Alfonso X y del Infante su hijo Don Sancho,* Alicante 1984, 119; C. de Ayala Martínez, "La monarquía y las ordenes militares durante el reinado de Alfonso X", *Hispania,* 51 (1991), 460, nota 160; M. González Jiménez, "Sancho IV, Infante", n. 211.

[38] Hernández & Linehan, *The Mozarabic Cardinal,* 215.

[39] Martinus Johannis aparece como arcediano de Cea (León) en agosto de 1282: Ruiz Asencio & Martín Fuertes, *Colección documental del Archivo de la Catedral de Leon,* IX, n. 2419.

[40] Debido seguramente a la "saña" con que el rey le había tratado, según la opinión del infante, quien el día anterior había revocado todos los malos usos de su padre contra la iglesia de Santiago desde la muerte del arzobispo Juan Arias quince años atrás: A. López Ferreiro, *Historia de la Santa Iglesia de Santiago de Compostela,* V, Santiago de Compostela, 1902, 241-4; App. XLII.

[41] La cabeza visible de los leales al rey era el obispo dominico de Ávila, fray Ademar, que sufriría el exilio por su lealtad: Hernández & Linehan, *The Mozarabic Cardinal,* 243, nota. Pero ¿dónde se encontraba en 1282 el obispo de Ciudad Rodrigo, D. Pedro, que ocupó su sede entre diciembre de 1279 y julio de 1284? (M. González Jiménez, *Diplomatario andaluz,* n. 458, M. Gaibrois de Ballesteros, *Historia del reinado de Sancho IV de Castilla,* III, Madrid, 1928, n. 12). ¿Tal vez, imitando a Gudiel, escondiéndose en su caso en Portugal? (El obispo Melendo de Ciudad Rodrigo que registra González Jiménez en diciembre de 1281 [n. 487] debe tratarse de un error de una de las fuentes del autor. P. B. Gams hace referencia a *alteram [seriem episcoporum], quam mihi dedit D. Vicente de la Fuente, quum essem Matriti, [et quam] casu adverso perdidi: Series episcopum ecclesiae catholicae,* Ratisbona, 1873, 66]) Por lo tanto, ¿qué otros obispos leoneses se encontraban con Alfonso? Sin tener en cuenta al renegado Alfonso de Coria, en mayo de 1281 y en julio de 1282 un tal don Simón aparece registrado como obispo electo de esa localidad (González Jiménez, nos. 481-2, 501). En cuanto a la sede de Badajoz, considerando que D. Gil de Badajoz se encontraba en Valladolid en mayo de 1282, su supuesta presencia con el rey Alfonso dos meses después (González Jiménez, n. 501) indica otra vez la inutilidad de las listas de "confirmantes" en privilegios reales de la época, como queda también demostrado por una carta del 21 de julio de 1282 que restringe el derecho a acogerse a sagrado, una medida que según consta en la carta fue adoptada por el rey tras haberla consultado con sus "hermanos e hijos...y con los Maestres y otros hombres buenos de las Órdenes que ý eran" (i.e. en Sevilla); aunque resulta imposible que tal reunión con sus "herma-

Prefiero terminar con una breve consideración sobre tres comunicados que han sobrevivido hasta hoy.

El ansia del estamento eclesiástico por aliarse con el infante fue más bien obscena, como revela la premura con que se llevó a cabo, una premura de la que queda constancia gráfica en las abigarradas adiciones de las firmas de los obispos y abades en los cuatro márgenes del ejemplar zamorano de la hermandad, fechado el día 4.[42] La importancia de este aspecto gráfico del documento se hace aún más patente si comparamos la lista de los confirmantes con los nombres que aparecen en otros dos ejemplares del mismo instrumento, redactados ambos el mismo día y dirigidos al monasterio de San Pedro de Montes y a la iglesia de Coria y tenidos en cuenta más abajo, en el Apéndice.[43]

La comparación de estos tres documentos y las distintas proporciones del número, siempre en aumento, de obispos y abades que se unieron al infante nos informa del orden en el que la cancillería del Infante emitió estas copias durante aquel ajetreado lunes: primero, la de San Pedro de Montes, después la de Zamora y en último lugar la de Coria. Podemos estar seguros de que el orden de estos tres ejemplares es el propuesto, porque en la copia de Zamora el obispo Alfonso de Coria aparece en el margen superior del documento, mientras que en la copia de Coria, que es la que sigue el texto publicado en el *Memorial Histórico Español*,[44] el nombre del obispo aparece listado dentro del cuerpo del texto.

Si no cuento mal, el ejemplar de Zamora tiene 31 agujeros para sellos, y 37 el ejemplar de Coria (del que tengo una fotocopia no muy buena). Con los más o menos cuarenta engrosamientos emitidos, aquellos eran muchos sellos, mucha cera, y mucho trabajo para una cancillería incipiente. Los expertos en paleografía y diplomática presentes seguramente advertirán otras características importantes. Creo que tengo tiempo para reseñar solamente algunas de ellas:

1) en **B** el nombre del abad de S. María de Melón consta tanto en el cuerpo del texto como en el margen superior: esto es una muestra de la frenética actividad de los clérigos de la cancillería;

---

nos e hijos" hubiera tenido lugar durante los cuatro meses anteriores: J. Rodríguez Molina (ed.), *Colección documental del Archivo Municipal de Úbeda*, Granada 1990, n. 42.

[42] AC Zamora, leg. 13, n. 23. Estoy muy agradecido al archivero de la catedral de Zamora, José Carlos de Lera Maíllo por haberme generosamente facilitado las imágenes que han servido de base a este trabajo. El documento citado es el n. 946 de la imprescindible guía del Sr. Lera, *Catálogo de los documentos medievales de la catedral de Zamora*, Zamora 1999.

[43] A. Quintana Prieto, *Tumbo Viejo de San Pedro de Montes*, León 1971, 481-2; J. L. Martín Martín, *Documentación medieval de la iglesia catedral de Coria*, Salamanca 1989, 55-7.

[44] *MHE*, II, pp. 68-70.

2) en **A** la llegada con retraso del arcediano de León, Martinus Johannis, está registrada como un 'post scriptum' ('Post hec...'); en **C** todavía está esperando. Queda marginado tanto documental como socialmente. ¿Porqué?

3) el nombre de Fernandus, prior de Sta. Cristina de Ribas de Sil registrado en **A** no se encuentra en **B**, ni en **C**, ni en **D**;

4) en **C** encontramos que el cabildo de Orense, con sede vacante en 1282, había enviado *dos* procuradores, con lo que se plantea la posibilidad de que fueran representantes de facciones enfrentadas dentro del cabildo.

5) también en **C** encontramos que un procurador afirma estar allí en representación del obispo y del cabildo de Mondoñedo. Pero de acuerdo con **B** el obispo de Mondoñedo se encontraba allí en persona.

6) ¿por qué estaba la iglesia de Lugo representada por un procurador del cabildo cuando había un obispo, don Alfonso, que podía haber realizado esta función?[45]

Tan solo dos observaciones más. La primera es que únicamente en **D** encontramos los 'estatutos' de las así llamadas 'cortes de Valladolid', a sea los estatutos que, desde su publicación en el *Memorial Histórico Español* de 1851 se han considerado como normativos.[46] Esta circunstancia arroja alguna luz sobre el desarrollo de esas 'ideas radicales' a que he aludido arriba y que todavía no se habían manifestado cuando A y B eran escritos pocas horas antes.

Mi segunda observación se refiere a la ausencia en **D** de los procuradores que se mencionan en **A** y en **C** como representantes de los cabildos de las sedes vacantes o ausentes de Salamanca, León, Orense y Lugo. Esto me parece intrigante, porque según el derecho canónico los procuradores nombrados correctamente poseían toda la autoridad de aquellos a quienes representaban. De hecho, cuando en 1279 Alfonso y su hijo fueron acusados de 'sacar pedidos y ayudas' de los prelados y eclesiásticos, respondieron a esta acusación con muy poca franqueza y con el argumento de que ni los prelados ni los eclesiásticos tenían potestad para efectuar estos pagos sin el permiso del papa, porque "los prelados non son sennores para poder esto otorgar "mas solament procuradores".[47] En otras palabras, el obispo es tan solo el guardián de su iglesia. No tiene el derecho de disponer a discreción de los bienes de la misma. Y sobre esta cuestión,

[45] M. GONZÁLEZ JIMÉNEZ, *Diplomatario andaluz*, nos. 487, 501 (febrero, julio de 1282). Alfonso Yáñez había desaparecido en marzo de 1283 (ibid., 508), fecha a partir de la cual la sede aparece citada como vacante. Cf. M. RISCO, *España Sagrada*, 41, Madrid 1794, 77-80.
[46] *MHE*, II, pp. 69-70.
[47] "...Ca esto es cosa que aun los prelados fuessen requeridos e quisiessen consentir non lo pueden fazer menos de licencia dela eglesia de Roma. Ca los prelados non son sennores para poder esto otorgar mas solament procuradores": LINEHAN, "Spanish Church revisited", 143-4.

tenían toda la razón. Lo que esta cita recoge es un principio básico que, desde la recopilación de Graciano, todo decretista conocía perfectamente. En realidad Alfonso citaba textualmente el escrito de Hostiensis, la principal autoridad en materia de derecho canónico de su tiempo. *Episcopus dominus non est sed procurator.*[48] Pero, con la confusión que se vivió aquel lunes, todos estos supuestos legales se olvidaron y se marginó a los procuradores capitulares.

Les dejo que mediten sobre estas curiosidades.

Antes de acabar, quisiera exponerles una última observación. He mencionado la existencia de tres únicas copias del acta del 4 de mayo de 1282. Pero tuvieron que emitirse unas cuarenta más. Era importante. Recuérdense. La posesión de una de estas copias constituiría sin duda una prueba de lealtad hacia el Infante y serviría como garantía de supervivencia, tanto política como física. Recuerden la situación en que se encontraban los dos obispos castellanos solo diez días antes, amenazados en sus cuerpos y en sus parientes por el sanguinario Infante, tal como le ocurrirá a Gudiel diez y ocho meses después.[49] A la vez que emitían este torrente de copias, los clérigos de la cancillería del infante don Sancho aprendían a tener en cuenta la ampliación de los conversos al bando rebelde, y por eso dejaron espacio en blanco para incluir nuevos nombres. Por eso el expectante escriba del ejemplar de Coria dejó también un espacio en blanco en la mitad del texto de los citados estatutos,[50] y, al copiarlo más tarde al tumbo de su casa, el ingenuo copista monacal del ejemplar de San Pedro de Montes no entendió la intención de su predecesor y volvió a dejar un inútil espacio en blanco.[51]

Y ya para terminar, déjenme que les recuerde una vez más la existencia de las varias docenas de copias de la hermandad del 4 de mayo de 1282 que he mencionado. No ganaremos nada si nos limitamos a repetir cómodamente lo que nuestros predecesores aprendieron de los suyos. El futuro de nuestra comprensión del pasado, y no menos de nuestra comprensión de la complejidad que las relaciones humanas alcanzaron en los últimos años del reinado de Alfonso X, se cifra en la vuelta a los archivos:[52] a la ida al archivo, que es lo más.

---

[48] *Summa Aurea super titulis Decretalium*, Coloniae, 1612, col. 337 ("De procuratoribus"). Cf. B. TIERNEY, *Foundations of the Conciliar Theory*, Cambridge, 1955, 119: "It was this idea of the prelate as proctor of his corporation that Hostiensis was to emphasize as an integral part of his theory of corporation structure."

[49] HERNÁNDEZ & LINEHAN, *The Mozarabic Cardinal*, 235, 454-5.

[50] MARTÍN, *Documentación de Coria*, 57.

[51] QUINTANA PRIETO, *Tumbo Viejo de San Pedro de Montes*, 482.

[52] Ver el estudio de M. C. USON FINKENZELLER, "El documento de hermandad de los concejos castellanos de 27 de mayo de 1282, del Archivo Municipal de Nájera: estudio crítico", en *Actas del Primer Coloquio de Sigilografía, Madrid, 2 al 4 de abril de 1987*, Madrid 1990, 193-231, quien se interesa principalmente en las características físicas del instrumento.,

| A. S. Pedro de Montes, *Tumbo Viejo*, fo. 148 | B. AC Zamora, leg. 13, no. 23 | C. AC Zamora, leg. 13, no. 23, marginalia | D. AC Coria, leg. 14, no. 1 |
|---|---|---|---|
| **OBISPOS** | | | |
| Melendus Astoricensis | / | | / |
| Sugerius Zamorensis | / | | / |
| | Munio Mindoniensis | | / |
| | Fernandus Tudensis | | / |
| Egidius Pacensis | / | | / |
| | | Alfonsus Coriensis | / |
| **ABADES/PRIORES** | | | |
| *Martinus S. Facundi (Sahagún) | / | | / |
| *Johannes Celenove (S. Salvador de Calanova) | / | | / |
| Johannes S. Martini [S. Martín Pinario] civ. Compostellane | / | | / |
| Arias de Spinareto [*unidentified:* ?=S. Martín de Sperautano] | / | | / |
| Fernandus [S. Juan Bautista] de Corias | / | | / |
| Pelagius de [S. María de] Obona | Hoc Bona | | Hecbona |
| Petrus de (S. Pedro de) Antealtares | | | / |
| *Johannes S. Petri de Montibus | / | | / |
| Johannes prior S. Petri de *?Rocins* (S. Pedro de Rocas) | de Rochis | | / |
| Fernandus Villenove de Laurenciana | / | | / |

| A. S. Pedro de Montes, *Tumbo Viejo*, fo. 148 | B. AC Zamora, leg. 13, no. 23 | C. AC Zamora, leg. 13, no. 23, marginalia | D. AC Coria, leg. 14, no. 1 |
|---|---|---|---|
| *Petrus Martini S. Petri Elisoncie, OSB (Eslonza) | X | Petrus S. Petri de Allonza [*sic*] | Petrus S. Petri de Aldonça |
|  |  | Antonius Pontis de Dios, OSB (?dioc. Braga) | / |
| *Martinus de Moreruela | / |  | / |
| *Dominicus Vallis Paradisi (Valparaíso) | / |  | / |
| *Dominicus Saltus Novalis (Sandoval) | / |  | / |
| Petrus de Melone (Melón) | / | / | / |
| Henricus de *Onya* Oya | / |  | / |
| Dominicus de Sobrado | / |  | / |
| Arias de *Osoria*, Cist. Ord. (Osera) | X | abbas Ursarie (Osera) | Fernandus de Usaria |
|  |  | Martinus abb. de Nucariis (Nogales), Cist. Ord. |  |
| Dominicus de Villoria (de Orbijo) | / |  | / |
| ?*Dominicus S. Leonardi de Alva | / |  | / |
| *Petrus S. Michaelis de Monte | / |  | / |
| Fernandus S. Saturnini Metinensis (Medina del Campo), O. Praem. | / |  | / |
| fr. Petrus, Ord. Sepulcri Dominici in Yspania |  | 'Gerardus prior Sepulcri Dominici in Yspania' | fr. Petrus prior Ord. Sepulcri Dominici in Yspania |

| A. S. Pedro de Montes *Tumbo Viejo*, fo. 148 | B. AC Zamora, leg. 13, no. 23 | C. AC Zamora, leg. 13, no. 23, marginalia | D. AC Coria, leg. 14, no. 1 |
|---|---|---|---|
| | | POST HEC... | |
| Martinus Johannis Legionensis archidiaconus et domini principis [sic] capellanus... Legionensis cap. procurator | | 'Martinus Johannis archidiaconus Legionensis et domini pape capellanus et notarius ep. Legionensis cuius sum procurator' | |
| Fernandus prior S. Cristine de Ripa Silis (Biba de Sil) | | | |
| ...et pro mon. S. Stephani de Ripa Silis | | | |
| ...et pro mon. de Juncaria de Spadanedo (Junquera) | | 'J. Petri can. de Juncaria procurator prioris et conventus eiusdem...' | |
| Rodericus archidiaconus procurator cap. Salmantine | | | |
| Johannes Petri procurator S. Ysidori Legionensis | | | |
| | | Johannes Petri procurator cap. Auriensis | |
| | | P. Velasci procurator cap. Auriensis | |
| | | Alfonsus Fernandi procurator cap. Lucensis | |
| * monasterios leoneses así indicados se habían asociado con los monasterios castellanos día 2 de mayo | | (...) Pelagii procurator ep. et cap. Mindoniensis | |

Carta de hermandad de los abades de monasterios del reino de León.
Archivo Catedral de Zamora

# XIII

## A MISATTRIBUTED TOMB AND ITS IMPLICATIONS: CARDINAL ORDOÑO ÁLVAREZ AND HIS FRIENDS AND RELATIONS[1]

If questions are never asked regarding the whereabouts of the mortal remains of Ordoño Álvarez, the supposedly Portuguese cardinal bishop of Tusculum (†1285), that is because they are believed to have been answered already, and to have been answered by competent authorities to the effect that Cardinal Ordoño Álvarez is interred beneath a slab tomb in the Roman basilica of SS. Quattro Coronati. The purpose of this Note is threefold: to establish that the body in the Roman tomb is in fact not that of the supposedly Portuguese cardinal; to demonstrate that the supposedly Portuguese cardinal was not Portuguese at all; and to offer some suggestions as to the real identity of the tenant of that Roman tomb and the reasons for his being there.

To begin with what is regarded as certain, as reported by the Austrian Academy's 1981 survey of Roman funerary monuments. There the damaged inscription of the SS. Quattro Coronati tomb is rendered thus:

[ / ]ONI · ORDONII · ARCHIEP(ISCOP)I BRACAREN(SIS) · ET · FILI(VS) · NOBILIS · VI|RI · D(OMI)NI · PETRI · MAURIQVE | BARONIS · DE · CASTELLA · CVI(VS) ANIMA · REQUIE[SCAT · IN · PACE · AME[N]

and the tomb is identified as that of the Portuguese cardinal bishop of Tusculum[2].

Yet if the remains contained within that tomb really were those of Cardinal Ordoño Álvarez, why did its inscription describe the cardinal as archbishop of Braga, the see from which he had been translated ten years before his death? And that is not the only

[1] The authors are indebted to Professor John Crook (St John's College, Cambridge) and Professor Julian Gardner (University of Warwick) for their perceptive comments on earlier versions of what follows, and to Dr Alberto Torra (Archivo de la Corona de Aragón, Barcelona) for his assistance in establishing the text of the letter published *infra*, n. 34.
    [2] *Die mittelalterlichen Grabmäler in Rom und Latium vom 13. bis zum 15. Jahrhundert, I. Die Grabplatten und Tafeln*, ed. J. GARMS, R. JUFFINGER and B. WARD-PERKINS, Rom 1981, p. 271, with photograph opposite, the symbol | indicating the two corners of the monument and the square brackets the editors'conjectural reading of obliterated details. From personal inspection of the tomb and study of the editors'photograph, the latter's account of it appears to the present authors correct, other than for the following: for ONI read D(OMI)NI; for ARCHIEP(ISCOP)I BRACAREN(SIS) read ARCHIEP(ISCOP)I · BRACAREN(SIS); and for MAURIQVE read MANRIQVE. Perhaps because it is undated, the tomb passed unreported by V. FORCELLA, *Iscrizioni delle chiese e di altri edificii di Roma dal secolo XI fino ai giorni nostri, raccolte e pubblicate*, 14 vols, Roma 1869-1884, VII, p. 285-296.

difficulty presented by the universally accepted identification of its inhabitant. For all that the entire short side of the slab with the beginning of its inscription as well as part of its continuation is missing, what remains intact – and in particular the genitive and nominative construction "Ordonii… *et filius*" – constitutes another. In short, the SS. Quattro Coronati tomb is plainly not the cardinal's tomb at all. It is what it states it is, that of a son of D. Pedro Manrique, *baro* of Castile, a person the precise nature of whose association with D. Ordoño was doubtless specified on the missing part of the inscription – but regarding whose identity all that can be deduced from the evidence provided by the monument is that he died while D. Ordoño was still archbishop, namely sometime between 23 May 1275, when Gregory X put D. Ordoño into Portugal's primatial see[3], and 12 March 1278, when Nicholas III awarded him the red hat[4].

As to the cardinal's present whereabouts, there is sufficient reason to believe that he lies buried beneath the rubble to which the cloister of the old cathedral of Salamanca was reduced in and after 1785, in accordance with what had been reported by Thomas ab Incarnatione shortly before that date[5]. For although the surviving

---

[3] J. GUIRAUD, *Les Registres de Grégoire X (1271-1276)*, Paris 1892-1906, nr. 607; printed S. DOMÍNGUEZ SÁNCHEZ, *Documentos de Gregorio X (1272-1276) referentes a España*, León 1997, nr. 177, with his patronymic rendered as «Alurz»in accordance with the authoritative C. EUBEL, *Hierarchia Catholica medii et recentioris aevi*, I, Monasterii 1913, p. 144. Wherever it was that Eubel got «Alurz» from (and it was not from Reg. Vat. 37, fol. 228v-9, as stated by him), the misreading of «Álvarez» is now firmly established in the literature. Thus *Diplomatic Documents preserved in the Public Record Office*, ed. P. CHAPLAIS, I, *1101-1272*, London 1964, index (giving the marginally more credible «Alurtz»).

[4] EUBEL, *Hierarchia*, I, p.10.

[5] «Ordonius Lusitanus ex nobilibus parentibus Alvaro Dias & Tarasia Petri, primum Abbas Fonsellensis [*sic*] in ecclesia Palentina […] die 17 Junii anno 1285 Romae e vivis excessit, ejus corpus ad Salamantinam Ecclesiam fuit translatum ubi jacet»: *Historia Ecclesiae Lusitanae per singula saecula ab Evangelio promulgato*, 4 vols, Coimbra 1759-1763), IV, p. 280, relying apparently on J. CARDOSO, *Agiologio Lusitano dos sanctos, e varoens illustres em virtude do reino de Portugal, e suas conquistas*, 4 vols, Lisboa 1652-1744, III, p. 730, who records the text on the Salamanca tomb («junto á capella de N. Senhora da Estrella») as follows: «Quinto kal. julii obiit famulus Dei Ordonius, Archiepiscopus Bracarensis, pater pauperum. Anno 1250», with the explanation as to its last part that as bishop of Salamanca «alguns annos» he had surrendered to the poor «o principal de suas rendas & bens patrimoniaes», thereby earning for himself the title «Pae de Pobres & Necessitados» (p. 717). While there is no reason to question Cardoso's report that D. Ordoño «ordenou em seu testamento, que trouxessem a ella [Salamanca] seu corpo, onde jaz sepultado em tumulo de pedra, con Misa dotada splendidamente pelo descanço perpetuo de sua alma» (p. 717), the date as reported bears no relation to the cardinal's obit (he was still alive in September 1285 but dead by the end of that year: L. WADDING ET AL., *Annales Minorum*, 25 vols, Romae etc. 1731-1933), V, p. 490-492; EUBEL, *Hierarchia*, I, p. 11), or indeed to that of any other archbishop of Braga, as Cardoso conceded («parece que foi esculpido alguns annos depois. […] O numero dos annos julgamos estar viciado», p. 730), failing however to notice the curious omission of any reference to D. Ordoño's status as cardinal. *Via* R. da Cunha (*Historia Ecclesiastica dos Arcebispos de Braga, e dos Santos e Varões Illustres que florecerão neste Arcebispado*, 2 vols, Braga 1634-1635, II, p. 162-163), Cardoso was in turn quoting a letter of December 1634 from Gil González Davila (*coronista real* to Felipe IV of Spain) to the archbishop of Braga, Agostinho de Castro, in which mention was made of an instrument in the Salamanca archive bearing D. Ordoño's seal and establishing an anniversary there («pareceme que por el mes de Agosto») as well as of «un libro becerro, que aquella Iglesia tiene escrito en su Sacristia o Contaduria mayor» in which the same anniversary was recorded. It seems that none of these records has survived. For the destruction of the cloister of the old cathedral see M. GÓMEZ MORENO, *Catálogo monumental de España. Provincia de Salamanca. Texto*, Madrid 1967, p. 108-109.

documentation provides no evidence of a connexion with the church of Salamanca during his lifetime[6], in March 1295 and July 1298 anniversaries for the repose of the cardinal's soul were established in the cathedral there[7], with the dates of their establishment and the funding of them possibly from properties in the local *judería* perhaps indicating both the recent repatriation of his body (or part thereof)[8] some ten years after his death in Rome and the existence of a particular association with that particular *barrio* dating from his student days[9]. What the Portuguese affiliation of the two benefactors – Gonçalo Gomez canon of Coimbra and Bishop João of Lisbon – cannot to be construed as, however, is corroboration of the venerable tradition that D. Ordoño Álvarez was himself of Portuguese origin. For – painful though it may prove for those to whom, in common with Thomas ab Incarnatione and his attachment to "Ordonius Lusitanus", the national origins of cardinals matter – in fact D. Ordoño was of Leonese stock.

The family to which he belonged had long played a prominent part in the affairs of Church and State in the kingdom of Castile, by which the kingdom of León had been overshadowed since the year 1230. As the grandson of Fernando III's first *alcalde* of reconquered Jaén in 1246 (Ordoño Álvarez de Asturias, *señor* of Noreña, a stronghold situated some twelve kilometres from Oviedo) and the son of the mighty Alvar Díaz de Asturias («one of the most powerful lords in the kingdom of León», as he has been

---

[6] *Pace* the assertion of M. CAETANO DE SOUSA, *Catalogo historico dos summos pontifices, cardeaes, arcebispos e bispos portuguezes*, Lisboa 1725 (Collecçãm dos documentos e memorias da Academia Real da Historia Portugueza, XXXIII), p. 11-12, that he was bishop of Salamanca in 1272, he was not so described on the occasion of his promotion to the see of Braga in 1275 (*supra*, n. 3) but rather, as was observed by J. A. FERREIRA, *Fastos episcopaes da igreja primacial de Braga*, 2 vols, Famalicão 1928-1930, II, p. 71, as abbot of Husillos. By reason both of slapdash use of the work of González Davila and his dating of D. Ordoño's *death* to June 1278, the argument adduced by J. Veríssimo Serrão in favour of the Salamanca pontificate has to be rejected: *Portugueses no estudo de Salamanca*, Lisboa 1962, p. 25-26. In similar vein, R. da Cunha, as well as being unaware that D. Ordoño had been raised to the purple, was of opinion that he expired at Salamanca in 1279: *Historia Ecclesiastica*, p. 164. (Nor is there documentary support for Sousa's further allegation that his body was brought there «por disposição sua»: a claim repeated by F. de Almeida, whose entry in *Dictionnaire d'histoire et géographie ecclésiastiques*, II, [1914], col. 867, is based on only a fragment of Cardoso's account of the matter.)

[7] J. L. MARTÍN MARTÍN ET AL., *Documentos de los archivos catedralicio y diocesano de Salamanca (siglos XII-XIII)*, Salamanca 1977, nr. 433 («por el anima del ondrado padre don Ordono, cardenal que fue en Roma» on the first Saturday after the feast of the Assumption); nr. 452 («por el anima del ondrado padre don Ordonno, cardenal que fue de Tusculana en Roma» four days after the same feastday). Each benefactor also reserved benefits for himself and, respectively, members of his own family and Fernando Eanes, sometime dean of Braga. Again, the mid-August dates specified, though they coincide with that of the anniversary established by the cardinal according to González Davila (*supra*, n. 5), bear no relation to the season of his death – which in the cathedral of Cuenca was commemorated on 18 March: J. TRENCHS ODENA, *El necrologio-obituario de la cathedral de Cuenca. Noticias históricas y crónica de la vida ciudadana*, «Anuario de Estudios Medievales» 12 (1982), p. 365.

[8] Partition of the corpse was still canonically allowable in 1298. It would not be so for much longer. See E. A. R. BROWN, *Death and the Human Body in the Later Middle Ages: the Legislation of Boniface VIII on the Division of the Corpse*, «Viator» 12 (1981), p. 221-270.

[9] Cf. Cardoso's report of his anniversary at Salamanca, «o qual se consumou de sorte nas letras humanas, & diuinas, na famosa Vniuersidad daquella cidade cathedral» on 17 June (the date of his death, according to Thomas ab Incarnatione): *Agiologio*, III, p. 717. Cardoso was unaware of the fact that in the years during which Ordoño might have been a student there «divine letters» were not yet part of the Salamanca curriculum.

described), the cardinal was, in the words of his contemporary, the Franciscan polymath Gil de Zamora, «distinguished by nobility of blood»[10]. Moreover, he was also very well-connected by reason of his relationship to certain other great Castilian clans, in particular through Teresa García de Braganza, the sister of his paternal grandmother, to the trans-Pyrenean branch of the Lara family, Teresa having married Rodrigo Pérez Manrique, son of Pedro Manrique de Lara, *señor de Molina* and *vicomte* of Narbonne († 1202). Indeed it was, we suggest, the son of Teresa García and Rodrigo Pérez Manrique, Pedro Rodríguez Manrique, who is the "nobilis vir dominus Petrus Manrique baro de Castella" referred to in the inscription of the Roman tomb, and a son of the latter whose mortal remains are those interred beneath it[11]. If we are correct about this – and the tomb's heraldic decoration, the two escutcheons marshalled with the distinctive Lara *calderas* (on a shield with leather guiges, a bend within a bordure semy of cauldrons) supports the hypothesis[12] – then the missing part of its inscription may be conjectured to have read more or less as follows:

AN(N)O · D(OMI)NI · MCCCLXXV[//]· HIC · IACET · [/// · ?CON|SANGUINEUS] D(OMI)NI · ORDONII · ARCHIEP(ISCOP)I BRACAREN(SIS) · ET · FILI(VS) · NOBILIS ·VI|RI · D(OMI)NI · PETRI · MANRIQVE · | BARONIS · DE · CASTELLA · CVI(VS) ANIMA ·REQUIE[SCAT · IN · PACE · AMEN][13].

[10] A. BALLESTEROS Y BERETTA, *Alfonso X el Sabio*, Barcelona 1963, p. 519; P. LINEHAN, *The Ladies of Zamora*, Manchester 1997, p. 71, n. 45. For the family, see J. M. TRELLES VILLADEMOROS, *Asturias ilustrada, origen de la nobleza de España, su antiguedad, y diferencias*, 2 vols, Madrid 1736-1739, II, p. 397-398; *Livros Velhos de Linhagens*, eds. J. PIEL and J. MATTOSO, Lisboa 1980 (Portugaliæ Monumenta Historica, n.s., 1), p. 288-289; also J. I. RUIZ DE LA PEÑA SOLAR, *Historia de Asturias. Baja Edad Media*, Vitoria 1977, p. 13-15; A. FERNÁNDEZ SUÁREZ, *Orígenes y ascensión de un linaje nobiliario asturiano: los Álvarez de Noreña*, «Asturiensia Medievalia» 8 (1995-1996), p. 256 (although the cardinal's membership of the family is strangely neglected by both authors); *Fray Juan Gil de Zamora, O.F.M., De preconiis Hispanie. Estudio preliminar y edición crítica*, ed. M. DE CASTRO Y CASTRO, Madrid 1955, p. 152: «Dominus Ordonius, Episcopus Tusculanus, qui tam elegantia corporis quam modestia sermonis et operis, nobilitate sanguinis adhuc pollet» (*post* 1278).

[11] L. SALAZAR Y CASTRO, *Historia genealógica de la Casa de Lara*, Madrid 1696; (facsimile edn, 5 vols, Bilbao, 1988), I, p. 290-307. For a hard-pruned genealogical tree of the Lara family, see S. R. DOUBLEDAY, *The Lara Family. Crown and Nobility in Medieval Spain*, Cambridge, Mass. 2001, p. 189.

[12] Or in the terminology of Spanish heraldry (wherein the bar sinister signifies not a bastard but a cadet descent): «en el campo una banda, en bordura ocho calderas». The same heraldic elements, disposed alternately rather than being conflated (cauldrons and, on shields, a bend), occur as a frieze on the tomb of Alvar Fernández de Lara (son of Pedro Manrique's paternal cousin, †1239 *vel paulum post*) in the monastery of San Zoilo de Carrión (Palencia): C. J. ARA GIL, *Un grupo de sepulcros palentinos del siglo XIII. Los primeros talleres de Carrión de los Condes, Pedro Pintor y Roi Martínez de Burueva*, in *Seminario Alfonso VIII y su época. II Curso de Cultura Medieval (Aguilar de Campóo, 1-6 octubre 1990)*, Madrid 1992, p. 26, 44. (As to D. Ordoño's own arms as cardinal, the sketch in A. CIACONIUS, *Vitae et res gestae pontificum Romanorum et Sanctae Ecclesiae Romanae cardinalium ab initio nascentis Ecclesiae, usque ad Urbanum VIII pontificem maximum*, Romae 1630, col. 761, is of dubious value).

[13] For alternative formulations in use at this time («Hic requiescit [*or* iacet] nobilis vir N.N [*or* corpus nobilis viri N.N.] qui obiit A.D...»), see I. KAJANTO, *Classical and Christian Studies in the Latin Epitaphs of Medieval and Renaissance Rome*, Helsinki 1980 (Annales Academiæ Scientiarum Fennicæ, ser. B., tom. 203), p. 17.

But as to the name of the deceased we remain in ignorance, since the only son of "dominus Petrus Manrique baro de Castella" known to historians of his house, García Fernández Manrique, remained active on the Castilian scene until well into the fourteenth century[14]. García Fernández's sibling therefore remains anonymous – though for reasons to be explained in what follows it is suggested that he might deserve the sobriquet "the Castilian malcontent".

Those reasons have to do with the cardinal's more immediate family and its role during the middle years of the reign of Alfonso X. Prior to 1275 Ordoño Álvarez had risen without trace, altogether in accordance with Gil de Zamora's thumbnail sketch of him as a smooth operator. And although the belief that he had been connected with the church of Burgos derives from Cardoso's egregious attribution of the secular abbey of Husillos to Burgos rather than to the church of Palencia[15], his occupancy of the abbacy of Husillos is itself significant, appointment to benefices there having for many years been reserved for fast-track ecclesiastical bureaucrats. In the 1240s the Castilian cardinal Gil Torres seems to have exercised a measure of control over promotions to the place. And perhaps Ordoño was indebted to that arch-fixer, as were so many of his contemporaries, for a helping-hand not only onto the bottom rung of the ladder of ecclesiastical preferment but also for assistance further up the scale[16]. After Cardinal Gil's death in 1254, however (when Ordoño would just have been beginning to be an interesting proposition), admission to this *École normale supérieure* of its time and place seems to have been more or less in the gift of the Castilian king. In view of the services that his father and grandfather had rendered the crown, it would be little to be wondered at, therefore, if sometime before 1272 Alfonso X had ushered D. Ordoño into the headship of that institution[17].

---

[14] SALAZAR Y CASTRO, *Historia*, I, p. 303-304; M. GAIBROIS DE BALLESTEROS, *Historia del reinado de Sancho IV de Castilla*, 3 vols, Madrid 1922-1928, I, p. lxvi, lxxi; II, p. 89, 131; F. J. HERNÁNDEZ, *Las rentas del rey. Sociedad y fisco en el reino castellano del siglo XIII*, 2 vols, Madrid 1993, I, p. 33, 130, 151, 152, 166.

[15] «Fonsellense na Igreja maior de Burgos»: *Agiologio*, III, p. 717. We have found no mention of Ordoño Álvarez either in the Burgos documentation or in the Vatican Registers of the period. The most recent entry in the Burgos *obituario*, *El obispado de Burgos y Castilla primitiva desde el siglo V al XIII*, ed. L. SERRANO, 3 vols, Madrid 1935-1936, III, p. 373-392, is of the year 1274 (p. 386).

[16] It may be no more than a matter of coincidence that in and after 1254 the Orsini cardinal who, as Pope Nicholas III, was to award D. Ordoño the red hat in 1278, was active as executor of the will of Gil Torres: *Collectionis Bullarum Sacrosanctae Basilicae Vaticanae*, ed. PH. DIONYSII ET AL., 3 vols, Romae, 1747-52, I, p. 137; P. EGIDI, *L'abbazia di S. Martino al Cimino secondo documenti inediti*, «Rivista Storica Benedettina» 2 (1907), p. 191-195. The function of Husillos in the history of the development of ecclesiastical bureaucracy in the thirteenth century deserves attention (see meanwhile P. LINEHAN, *The Spanish Church and the Papacy in the Thirteenth Century*, Cambridge 1971, p. 294-295). Members of its chapter regularly feature in documentation of the period (*e.g.*, ID., *The Economics of Episcopal Politics: the Cautionary Tale of Bishop Suero Pérez of Zamora*, in ID., *The Processes of Politics and the Rule of Law*, Aldershot 2002, item V, p. 14). For one, Juan Álvarez (sometime abbot of Husillos, bishop of Osma [†1296], and possibly yet another, unacknowledged, blood relation of D. Ordoño) and his will with its various bequests to the place as well as of properties in Asturias, see Madrid, Biblioteca Nacional, MS 704, fols. 255v-264r; F. J. HERNÁNDEZ & P. LINEHAN, *The Mozarabic Cardinal. The Life and Times of Gonzalo Pérez Gudiel*, Firenze 2003, chap. 10.

[17] Albeit in the scant documentation of the *abadía* (now preserved at the church of Ampudia, dioc. Palencia), for sight of copies of which we are obliged to Dr Francisco Hernández, there is no evidence of his physical presence at Husillos during these years.

«Sometime before 1272», because in that year there occurred the rebellion of a large part of the Castilian nobility in which the future cardinal's father, Alvar Díaz de Asturias, was deeply implicated[18], with the result that for Alfonso X, whose commitment to conspiracy theory was absolute, D. Ordoño was thereafter politically suspect[19]. Indeed, it may well be that it was at this point and for this reason that D. Ordoño opted to absent himself from Castile altogether and to seek advancement instead at the court of the recently elected Pope Gregory X.

We would give much to know something of the activities of this upwardly mobile ecclesiastic between then and 1275, when he was preferred to Braga, the primatial see of Portugal, in accordance with what appears to have been a policy of the papal curia of seeking to penetrate the closed ecclesiastical establishments of Castile and Portugal by exchanging churchmen across the political frontier in both directions: a policy which, although continued until well into the following century, was to have but little effect. Anyway, for all the good that he could do in Portugal, D. Ordoño might as usefully have been preferred to the see of Pekin, since in 1275 most members of the Portuguese episcopate were in awe of Afonso III, and were either maintaining a low profile at home or languishing in Italian exile. It was for this reason that within five months of D. Ordoño's archiepiscopal appointment Gregory X had ordered the king to mend his ways, threatening him with extreme measures if he failed to comply[20].

So D. Ordoño was at Rome and Viterbo, or wherever else the curia took him, with Petrus Hispanus, cardinal-bishop of Tusculum (his predecessor at Braga and Pope John XXI from September 1276) presumably interesting himself in his welfare, but in so far as his Portuguese responsibilities were concerned with virtually nothing for him to do. Yet he did not need to remain entirely idle.

For the malcontents whose activities had disrupted Castile in 1272-1273 had not been placated. With the succession issue occasioned by the death of the heir to the

---

[18] *Crónica de Alfonso X, según el MS. II/2777 de la Biblioteca del Palacio Real (Madrid)*, ed. M. GONZÁLEZ JIMÉNEZ, Murcia 2000, chaps. 20, 23, 35, 40, 43 (p. 66, 76, 110, 115, 124).

[19] Fernández Suárez's assumption that the presence of Pedro Álvarez, D. Ordoño's brother, at the discussions with Alfonso X at Almagro in 1273 meant that their father's involvement in the recent rising «tampoco parece que... haya tenido mayores consecuencias a nivel político» («Orígenes y ascensión», 255), fails to allow for the fact that the discussions at Almagro were peace talks between a beleaguered monarch and a rebellious aristocracy. See J. O'CALLAGHAN, *The Learned King. The Reign of Alfonso X of Castile*, Philadelphia 1993, p. 225-229.

[20] GUIRAUD, *Les Registres de Grégoire X*, nr. 628. FERREIRA, *Fastos*, II, p. 70, infers Ordoño's presence in Portugal from the inclusion of his name amongst those who confirmed Afonso's grant of the *foral* of Castro Marim (Lisbon, July 1277), omitting to notice the presence in the same «witness list» of such celebrated personalities as «ecclesia Colimbriensis vacat conf.» and «ecclesia Visensis vacat conf.»: *Portugaliæ Monumenta Historica. Leges et Constitutiones*, I, Lisboa 1856, p. 734-736. Since April 1277 Afonso had been declared excommunicate throughout the kingdom by fr. Nicholas OFM, the papal nuncio who had been attended at Braga not by the archbishop but by his vicar: A. de Herculano, whose account of the state of Portugal in the later 1270s (*História de Portugal desde o começo da monarquia até o fim do reinado de Afonso III*, Lisboa 1846-1853) remains the best treatment of the subject: ed. J. MATTOSO. (4 vols, Lisboa 1981-1989), III, p. 183-185. See also M. A. F. MARQUES, *O papado e Portugal no tempo de D. Afonso III (1245-1279)*, diss. Faculdade de Letras, Universidade de Coimbra 1990, p. 164, 566-569.

# XIII

throne, Fernando de la Cerda, in 1275 dividing the political establishment between the supporters of Alfonso X's grandson, Alfonso de la Cerda, and his second son the Infante Sancho, they had merely moved abroad. And at the centre of that establishment a particularly solemn moral responsibility had devolved upon Juan Núñez de Lara, since it was to him, the head of the Lara clan, that Fernando de la Cerda on his deathbed had entrusted not only the custody of his two young sons but also the prosecution of the rights of succession to the throne of the elder of them, the young Alfonso, as the heir of the king's eldest son[21].

As the senior Spanish churchman at the papal curia, the archbishop of Braga in exile can scarcely have remained aloof from these developments or uninfluenced by the politicking that continued after the furore of 1272-1273 had ostensibly subsided. In particular, the extension of the Castilian power-struggle into the county of Narbonne in 1275-1276, and the manoeuverings orchestrated by Alfonso X in order to destabilise the region and subvert the authority of the king of France in those parts, are unlikely to have escaped his attention, not least because his connexions with the Lara clan made the *vicomtes* of Narbonne his relations too[22] – just as indeed they may also have been the relations of Alfonso X after a fashion[23]. D. Ordoño's Roman household may therefore well have provided a refuge for those members of the Lara affinity who by definition were not party to that particular piece of mischief, an intrigue part of the purpose of which was to frustrate the alliance of Juan Núñez de Lara and the king of France, Philip III, in the de la Cerda interest[24]. As to the latter, the winter of 1277-1278 proved crucial, for in the course of it Alfonso X acknowl-

---

[21] JOFRÉ DE LOAYSA, *Crónica de los reyes de Castilla*, cap. 12, ed. A. GARCÍA MARTÍNEZ, Murcia 1982, p. 90; *Crónica de Alfonso X*, cap. 64 (ed. cit., p. 184): «Et don Juan Núnnez prometió que lo cumpliría segunt que don Ferrando gelo mandó».

[22] Paris, Archives Nationales, J.1033, n. 7, discussed HERNÁNDEZ - LINEHAN, *The Mozarabic Cardinal*, chap. 6. See also A. M[olinier], n. 29 to C. DEVIC - J. VAISSETE, *Histoire générale de Languedoc*, 12 vols, Toulouse, 1876-1892, X, p. 409-424, whence G. DAUMET, *Mémoire sur les relations de la France et de la Castille de 1255 à 1320*, Paris 1913, p. 37-40. As late as 1281 Alfonso would resume his Narbonne offensive by marrying his son the Infante Pedro to Marguerite, sister of the current *vicomte*: *Crónica de Alfonso X*, cap. 75, ed. cit., p. 212.

[23] This relationship is altogether less certain however. Alfonso's half-brother the Infante Fernando had married Laura de Montfort, *señora* of Espernon (A. DUCHESNE, *Histoire généalogique de la maison de Bethune*, Paris 1639, p. 276) and, according to R. DEL ARCO, *Sepulcros de la casa real de Castilla*, Madrid 1954, p. 228, Laura de Montfort was the daughter of Aymeri V of Narbonne. But del Arco cites no evidence, and there is the further problem that when Aymeri V acquired the county of Narbonne in 1270 (DEVIC - VAISSETE, *Histoire*, VI, p. 923), the Infante Fernando had already been dead for a year. The entire issue is obscured by the lack of consensus amongst historians regarding the numbering of the counts of Narbonne (with, for example, the Aymeri who succeeded in 1270 being recorded by Devic and Vaissete [IX, p. 1202] as both Aymeri V and Aymeri IV, and by SALAZAR Y CASTRO, *Historia*, I, p. 170, as «Aymerico VI». Further confusion is introduced by DOUBLEDAY, *Lara Family*, p. 189. Cf. M. TORRES SEVILLA - QUIÑONES DE LEÓN, *Linajes nobiliarios en León y Castilla (siglos IX-XIIII)*, Valladolid 1999, p. 226.

[24] DOUBLEDAY, *Lara Family*, p. 80-85; DAUMET, *Mémoire*, p. 30-33, 157-62 (though Daumet's account, following Salazar y Castro's, complicates the issue by dividing Juan Núñez de Lara [†1294] into two, Juan Núñez de Lara I and Juan Núñez de Lara II. For a measure of clarification see S. DE MOXÓ, *De la nobleza vieja a la nobleza nueva. La transformación nobiliaria castellana en la baja Edad Media*, «Cuadernos de Historia» 3 [1969], p. 32).

edged the Infante Sancho as his heir[25], whereupon the de la Cerda sympathisers followed Juan Núñez de Lara into opposition, and in some cases into exile. Prominent amongst those who disappeared from the Castilian scene at this time was Pedro Rodríguez Manrique. In noting his absence after December 1279, Salazar de Castro assumed that he had gone to France on family business. But he may have had other reasons for distancing himself from Castile, and also an alternative destination[26]. He may, for example, have gone to Rome, where sometime between May 1275 and March 1278 his son, "the Castilian malcontent", had died and been interred in the basilica of SS. Quattro Coronati[27].

Although there is nothing to suggest that D. Ordoño himself was in any way associated with the church wherein his name is recorded only on account of his relationship to the occupant of the tomb which has hitherto been assumed to be his, it was none the less that same basilica that that other enemy of Alfonso X, his own brother the turbulent Infante Enrique, had adopted as his headquarters when he was Senator of the City in 1267-1268[28]. True, earlier senators had also made the place their stronghold, and in 1257 the formidable Cardinal Ottaviano degli Ubaldini had resided there[29]. Even so, the possibility remains that the lavishly decorated church on the Celian Hill, strategically placed as it was between the Lateran and the Capitol, was somehow associated with opposition to the Castilian *status quo* in the later 1270s[30].

As for D. Ordoño, whether or not he had the father of the deceased malcontent as his Roman house guest between 1280 and 1284, he remained true to Gil de Zamora's characterization of him as modesty in word and deed incarnate. He maintained a low profile. Even allowing for Alfonso X's practice during these years of causing episcopal sees to remain vacant more or less as a matter of course, thereby

---

[25] O'CALLAGHAN, *The Learned King*, p. 239.

[26] SALAZAR Y CASTRO, *Historia*, I, p. 301, remarking that he remained absent from Castile until after Alfonso X's death in 1284. Through the Traba/Lara nexus Pedro Rodríguez Manrique was connected to Simón Ruiz, *señor* de los Cameros, done to death by Alfonso X in April or May 1277, together with Alfonso's brother the Infante Fadrique, in circumstances that remain obscure: *ibidem*, I, p. 300; R. P. KINKADE, *Alfonso X, "Cantiga 235", and the Events of 1269-1278*, «Speculum» 67 (1992), p. 313-317.

[27] *Supra*, n. 3. In this connexion it is to be noted that whereas the Castilian *senoríos* of Pedro Rodríguez Manrique passed to his son García Fernández, those of Montpézat (west of Nîmes) and Lacq (north-west of Pau) did not: SALAZAR Y CASTRO, *Historia*, I, p. 299-300. May it be that they had been bequeathed to García Fernández's sibling, «the Castilian malcontent»?

[28] G. DEL GIUDICE, *Don Arrigo Infante di Castiglia. Narrazione istorica*, Napoli 1875, p. 43, n. 1.

[29] For the will (August 1257) of Emmanuele Maggi, senator, «in palacio Sanctorum quattuor de urbe domini Octaviani [Ubaldini] cardinalis curante», see P. GUERRINI, *Parentele viscontee a Brescia*, «Archivio Storico Lombardo» 56 (1929), p. 109; and for the custody of the place under Cardinal Stefano Conti (*vicarius urbis*, 1244-1246): A. SOHN, *Bilder als Zeichen der Herrschaft. Die Silversterkapelle in SS. Quattro Coronati (Rom)*, «Archivum Historiae Pontificiae» 35 (1997), p. 12-14, 39-44.

[30] *Ibidem*. The recently discovered thirteenth-century frescoes in the adjacent convent further attest to the importance of the place at this period. See A. DRAGHI, *Il ciclo di affreschi rinvenuto nel Convento dei SS. Quattro Coronati a Roma: un capitolo inedito della pittura romana del Duecento*, «Rivista dell'Istituto Nazionale d'Archeologia e Storia dell'Arte» 54 (1999), p. 115-159, esp. p. 119-120: «Nei documenti dell'epoca il complesso dei SS. Quattro Coronati appare avere una funzione non chiaramente definita, o meglio una pluralità di funzioni».

denying all cardinals the opportunity of engaging in ecclesiastical jobbery within the kingdom of Castile, his restraint in the matter was nevertheless of almost heroic proportions, standing in the sharpest possible contrast to the manner in which Cardinal Gil Torres had operated thirty years before[31]. Though, of course, it is probably always as well to allow for the possibility of fresh discoveries in some hitherto incompletely explored Spanish archive, the fact remains that so far as Castile was concerned Cardinal Ordoño's only intervention in Castilian affairs in these years appears to have been his participation in the granting of a collective indulgence in favour of the in every sense marginal cathedral of Santo Domingo de la Calzada[32]. Certainly, when the beleagured prioress of Las Dueñas de Zamora, tears streaming from her eyes, appealed to him to intervene in order to rid her convent of the attention of the altogether too attentive friars up the road, she appealed to him in vain[33].

Yet, for all this, behind the scenes he was far from inactive, prevailing upon Pere III of Aragón to intercede with Alfonso X and the Infante Sancho on his brother's behalf (in return for which, as an unedited letter of the king quite brazenly reveals, Pere counted upon him to support his candidate for the see of Zaragoza)[34], and

---

[31] The papal registers for the period between March 1278 and September 1285 record just one case of peninsular involvement, as co-judge of a disputed election to the Portuguese see of Lamego: M. PROU, *Les Registres d'Honorius IV*, Paris 1886-1888, nr. 528. For Cardinal Gil's ceaseless interventions in the affairs of the Castilian Church and the extent of his patronage system, see LINEHAN, *Spanish Church and the Papacy*, p. 276-295. D. Ordoño, by comparison, may be credited with a single chaplain prepared to own himself as such in Castile in the late 1270s: *Colección documental del Archivo de la Catedral de León*, ed. J. M. RUIZ ASENCIO - J. A. MARTÍN FUERTES, IX. 1269-1300, León 1994, nr. 2381. For further particulars see HERNÁNDEZ - LINEHAN, *The Mozarabic Cardinal*, chaps. 7, 10.

[32] C. LÓPEZ DE SILANES - E. SÁINZ RIPA, *Colección diplomática Calceatense. Archivo catedral (años 1125-1397)*, Logroño 1985, nr. 51 (Oct. 1283).

[33] LINEHAN, *Ladies of Zamora*, p. 57-58.

[34] «Domino Ordonio episcopo Tusculano et sancte Romane ecclesie cardinali ex parte regis. Ex parte paternitatis vestre dilectus consiliarius noster H. de Mataplana venerabilis Cesaraugustanus electus nos affectuose rogav[it] ut cum illustri rege Castelle ac dompno Sancio nepote nostro carissimo daremus operam efficacem ut nobilem virum Alvarum Didaci fratrem vestrum ad suam gratiam restituerent tam honorabiliter quam decenter. Rogavit nos etiam idem electus ex parte vestra ut Martino Petri de Oscha domicello vestro qui diu vobis servivit assignaremus aliquid in redditibus omni anno. Nos autem propter sollempnem fame vestre preconium, et quia pro certo tenemus vos esse nostrum specialem amicum, sumus semper parati libenter vestre obtemperare in omnibus voluntati. Et ecce, apud illustrem regem Castelle ac dompnum Sancium efficaciter intendimus per specialem nuncium quem ad ipsos destinandum duximus ut prefatum nobilem cum honore ad suam restituant gratiam et nostris precibus ipsum promoveant et honorent. Martino autem Petri domicello vestro quia vobis servivit fideliter benefaciemus gratanter et ad presens .xx. libras jaccenses eidem in redditibus assignamus. Ceterum, paternitatis vestre credimus non latere ~~presumimus~~ notitiam [*sic*] affeccionem quam habeamus ad promocionem Massiliensis prepositi ad Cesaraugustanam ecclesiam, ad quam electus extitit sicud nostis. Nos etiam ex relatione fideli pro certo didiscimus [*sic*] quod ipsius prepositi Massiliensis promocio ad prefatam Cesaraugustanam ecclesiam totaliter est in vobis cum eius adversarius nollet nec auderet a vestris beneplacitis in aliquo discrepare. Paternitatem igitur vestram de qua fiduciam plenissimam gerimus quantum possumus deprecamur quatinus sicut nos ad promocionem vestrorum sumus semper parati ad vestri gratiam tam liberaliter quam gratanter sic et vos vice mutua ad promocionem nostrorum et signanter istius velitis si placuerit dare operam efficacem ut ex mutuis obsequiis mutua inter nos crescat dilectio omni die» (Pere III to D. Ordoño, Alcira, 6 Dec. 1281: Barcelona, Archivo de la Corona de Aragón, Reg. 47, fol. 113r). Regarding the divided election to the see of Zaragoza in 1280, the candidature of the provost of Marseilles, Hugo de Mataplana, and Martin IV's appointment of Cardinal Ordoño

conspiring to frustrate Alfonso's own attempt to intrude his candidate into the see of Toledo[35]. The cosy understanding upon which the king of Aragón felt able to presume when writing to his "special friend" in December 1281, and his expectation that by means of favours mutually proferred their mutual affection might be further strengthened, strongly suggest that when the Infante Sancho rose in rebellion against Alfonso X four months later, and Pere III took the Infante's side, the Leonese cardinal's sympathies would have lain in the same direction, in common with those members both of his immediate family and its wider ramifications who had made themselves conspicuous within the political opposition throughout the previous decade[36] – as well perhaps as with the occupant of the tomb in SS. Quattro Coronati. Though deprived of that tomb therefore, D. Ordoño Álvarez, whose remains came home sometime after 1285, whereas those of its anonymous inhabitant did not, deserves closer attention than he has previously received from students of those troubled years of the history of Castile about which he knew so much more than it will ever be possible to bring fully to light.

PETER LINEHAN
MARGARITA TORRES SEVILLA

---

as auditor of the case, see E. LANGLOIS, *Les Registres de Nicolas IV (1288-1292)*, [Paris 1887-1893], nr. 873; LAMBERTO DE ZARAGOZA, *Teatro histórico de las iglesias del reyno de Aragón*, [9 vols, Pamplona-Zaragoza, 1780-1807], II, p. 251-252. Doubtless the cardinal had also been instrumental in securing the papal dispensation of the uncanonical marriage of the same Alvar Díaz (de Noreña) and María Juánez in February 1279: J. GAY - S. VITTE-CLÉMENCET, *Les Registres de Nicolas III*, Paris 1898-1938, nr. 441 (printed S. DOMÍNGUEZ SÁNCHEZ, *Documentos de Nicolás III (1277-1280) referentes a España*, León 1999, nr. 104). See also PIEL - MATTOSO, *Livros Velhos de Linhagens*, p. 289. On the outbreak of the Infante Sancho's rebellion in 1282, his other brother, Pedro Álvarez, the conspirator of 1271-72, who, according to the Marqués de Mondéjar (Gaspar Ibáñez de Segovia), *Memorias históricas del Rey D. Alonso el Sabio i observaciones a su chrónica*, ed. F. CERDÁ Y RICO; Madrid 1777, p. 344, had also been implicated in the conspiracy preceding the deaths of the Infante Fadrique and Simón Ruiz de los Cameros in 1277 (*supra*, n. 26), would be appointed his *mayordomo mayor*.

[35] L. SALAZAR DE MENDOZA, *Cronología histórica de los Arzobispos de Toledo*, Madrid, Real Academia de la Historia, MS 9/1128, fol. 299v. This was in May 1280. For further particulars see HERNÁNDEZ - LINEHAN, *The Mozarabic Cardinal*, chap. 6.

[36] It is to be noted that although at Agreda in March 1281 Pere III (with Hugo de Mataplana *inter alios* in attendance) had acknowledged Alfonso X's rights to the castle of Albarracín (the stronghold on the Castilian-Aragonese frontier from which Juan Núñez de Lara had been operating on behalf of Alfonso de la Cerda), on the same occasion he had also indicated (i) that it was with the Infante Sancho that he meant to do business in future, (ii) that the Infantes de la Cerda were in his keeping, and (iii) that by the time of his writing to the cardinal he would have received accounts of proceedings at the Cortes of Sevilla (Nov. 1281), whereafter all of which there could be no disguising the extent of Castilian disaffection: C. DE AYALA MARTÍNEZ, *Paces castellano-aragonesas de Campillo-Agreda (1281)*, in *En la España Medieval*, V, 1986 (Estudios en memoria del prof. D. Claudio Sánchez-Albornoz, 1), p. 158-163; DOUBLEDAY, *Lara Family*, p. 82-6; O'CALLAGHAN, *The Learned King*, p. 253-258.

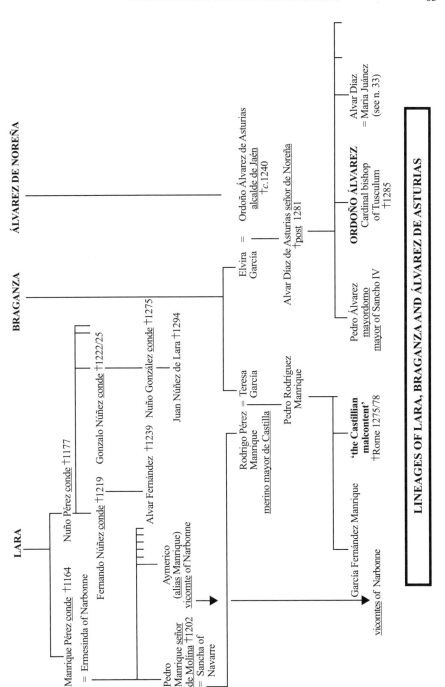

LINEAGES OF LARA, BRAGANZA AND ÁLVAREZ DE ASTURIAS

# XIV

## The English Mission of Cardinal Petrus Hispanus, the Chronicle of Walter of Guisborough, and news from Castile at Carlisle (1307)

In the absence of significant documentary discoveries, it is unlikely that there will ever be much new to be said on the subject of Boniface VIII's arbitration of the conflicting claims to Gascony of Edward I of England and Philip IV of France in June 1298. Frequently remarked upon by students of diplomatic because it was delivered by the pope in his personal capacity, not as pontiff but as Benedictus Gaitanus, the arbitration and award (or *pronuntiatio*) have been regularly pored over down the ages.[1] No account has previously been taken of the contemporary text of that award preserved in the archive of Toledo cathedral, however, of its reason for being there, or of the incidental interest it possesses for students of English history.[2] On the face of it, it appears to have nothing to do with the history of Castile.

What it does have to do with Dr Pierre Chaplais spotted when I sought the benefit of his advice on its diplomatic features and his opinion regarding its date. These were, respectively, that he was 'reasonably sure (. . .) that the scribe is not French' ('I see no reason why he could not be English, judging by the letter-forms or abbreviations'), and that 'the date of the writing is probably *c*. 1300, although it could be a decade or two later.'[3] These observations would scarcely justify a note on the subject, however. What perhaps does is the striking resemblance observed by Dr Chaplais between it and the text of the Bonifacian award preserved in the chronicle of Walter of Guisborough – a characteristically genial aperçu of that doyen of palaeographers and prince of diplomatists to whom the following pages, for what they are worth, are dedicated in gratitude and admiration.

Walter of Guisborough seems to have completed his chronicle in or soon after the first decade of the fourteenth century. A canon of the Augustinian house in Cleveland by whose name he is known, he is perhaps less highly rated by English historians now than in the mid-nineteenth century when his editor praised him as 'remarkable for a judicious taste, a moderation of mind, and great clearness of

1. G. Digard, *Philippe le Bel et le Saint-Siège de 1285 à 1304* (2 vols, Paris, 1936), i. 345–53, 358–69; J. R. Strayer, *The Reign of Philip the Fair* (Princeton, N.J., 1980), pp. 319–22. I am much obliged to Pierre Chaplais and Magnus Ryan for their critical comments on an earlier version of this Note.

2. T[oledo], A[rchivo de la] C[atedral] de T[oledo], A.7.G.1.30 (parchment, a single membrane, width 190 mm narrowing to 166 mm; length 916 mm).

3. Personal letter to the author, 11 Sept. 1998.

perception'.[4] For all that his northern vantage point might be thought to lend a measure of authority to his account of events in those parts during the last twenty years of the reign of Edward I, what in fact Walter did not copy from others he was largely content to compile from such gossip as came his way, his horror stories from Scotland, of elderly religious pushed off bridges (for example), being provided by refugee confrères unburdening themselves at Guisborough.[5] It seems to have been by an analogous process that he acquired the text of the papal award of 1298 under consideration, reference to which here will chiefly be made by way of the most recent edition of his chronicle, that of the late Professor Harry Rothwell.[6]

Comparison of the Toledo text of the award (T) with Guisborough's (G) is complicated, however, not only by the evident corruption of Guisborough's text between the time when it left his pen and the copying of Rothwell's putative MS. β, the lost source of its entire surviving progeny,[7] but also by the deficiencies of Rothwell's edition.[8] Without a re-examination of the entire complex of manuscripts, therefore, the precise extent of the relationship between T and G cannot be gauged with entire certainty. Nor of course even then could any conclusion be more than approximate. Nor indeed would the results of such an exercise justify the labour involved. With the occasional assistance of Hamilton's earlier edition, however, sufficient indication of the nature of that relationship is provided by comparing their texts of the award with that of the engrossed original preserved in the English public records (R) and the registered copy in the Vatican archive.[9]

Between T and G there are as many as 110 textual variants identifiable, which on the face of it might seem rather to dispose of than to corroborate the hypothesis of their relationship. However, of these

4. *Chronicon domini Walteri de Hemingburgh*, ed. H. C. Hamilton (English Historical Society, 2 vols, London, 1848–9), i. p. xi.

5. A. Gransden, *Historical Writing in England c.550–c.1307* (London, 1974), pp. 470–76 at p. 473.

6. *The Chronicle of Walter of Guisborough previously edited as the Chronicle of Walter of Hemingford or Heminburgh* (Camden Third Series vol. LXXXIX; London, 1957). (References to G in this edition, as well as to T and R (*infra*, n. 9.) are given by page and/or line number.)

7. Ibid., p. xx.

8. For example, a check of Trinity College Cambridge, MS. R.9.7 (Rothwell's MS. A3), fos 106ᵛ–107ʳ, reveals the following unnoticed variants to the text of the passage under consideration in what follows: 317.22 Francie<Francorum; 317.25 ac<ab; 317.28 difinitorem<diffinitorem; 318.3 cupimus vigere<vigere cupimus; 318.8 eis<eisque; 318.12 et omni<ut omni; 318.16 trewge<treuge; 318.19 *om.* inite; 318.20 atque<atque atque; 318.22 ad ducere<ac ducere; 318.22 quindecim<.xv.; 318.27 tertium decimum<.xiii.; 318.29 Idque<Illudque.

9. T. Rymer, *Foedera, Conventiones, Litterae* . . . , vol. I.ii (London, 1816), pp. 894–5 [R]; G. Digard et al., *Les Registres de Boniface VIII (1294–1303)* (Paris, 1884–1939), no. 2826. For the French and English originals see, respectively, B. Barbiche, *Les Actes pontificaux originaux des Archives Nationales de Paris* (3 vols, Vatican City, 1975–82), ii. no. 2090; J. Sayers, *Original Papal Documents in England and Wales from the Accession of Pope Innocent III to the Death of Pope Benedict XI (1198–1304)* (Oxford, 1999), no. 999.

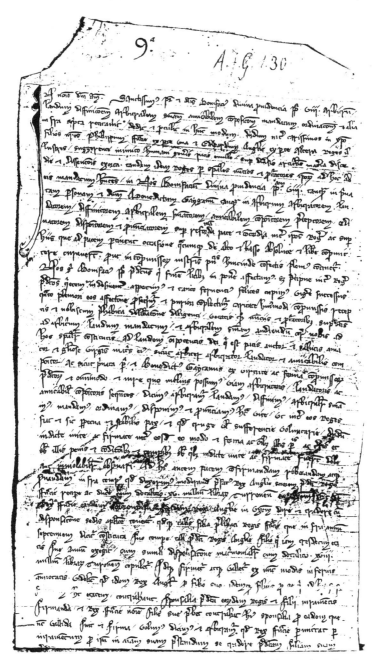

Fig. 1. The opening lines of the draft of the Anglo-French 'pronuntiatio' by Benedictus Gaitanus (Pope Boniface VIII) in Archivo de la Catedral de Toledo, A. 7. G. 1. 30.

XIV

variants almost a quarter (24) can reasonably be discounted as scribal lapses, mis-spellings and the like, while regarding the remainder, although with respect to R, T's text is closer in 52 cases and G's in 29, again almost all are differences of minor significance – that is to say are matters of spelling (e.g. 'diffinimus' for 'difinimus': T65; G 320.18) or reversal of word order (e.g. 'cupimus vigere' T14; 'vigere cupimus' *apud* Trinity Coll. Cambridge MS cit., fo. 106ᵛ [cf. G 318.3]). Less therefore turns upon the differences between the two texts than upon what they have in common.

Or rather, upon what they *lack* in common. What they lack in common when compared with R (that is to say, the agreed text of the award as it was presented to the agents of the Kings of England and France at Rome on 30 June 1298) are five passages – the *same* five passages. It is these lacunae, four of them substantial in extent, that permit the status of the texts of the award presented by T and G to be established.

Complex and far-reaching though the opposing arguments presented to the pope had been,[10] the terms of that award were wholly straightforward. The warring parties were to commit themselves to a 'perpetual and stable peace', they were to return to the *status quo ante*, and were to guarantee the future by use of that sovereign remedy against rancour and the revival of hostilities, holy matrimony. Edward I was to marry Philip IV's sister Margaret, and Edward's son and heir Philip's daughter Isabella.

Now, the success of an agreement as broad-brush as this was plainly bound to depend upon the settlement of detailed arrangements by the civil servants of the two sides. If there was to be any chance of its influencing affairs then a common understanding would first need to have been established regarding at least (i) the scope of the settlement, (ii) the fulfilment of the matrimonial undertakings of the King of England and his heir, and (iii) provision for enforcement of the agreements. It is precisely in respect of these three matters that the texts in T and G are identically defective.[11]

From this it must follow that T and G both derive from drafts, related albeit different drafts, of the award, and that both date from sometime in the days or weeks during which forms of words acceptable to both parties were being sought, and the desperate representatives of the count of Flanders were striving to save the English alliance, that is from shortly

10. H. Rothwell, 'Edward I's case against Philip the Fair over Gascony in 1298', *ante*, xlii (1927), 572–82; P. Chaplais, *English Medieval Diplomatic Practice, Part I* (2 vols, London, 1982), ii. 422–30. Cf. G. Barraclough, 'Edward I and Adolf of Nassau. A chapter of mediaeval diplomatic history', *Cambridge Historical Journal*, vi (1938–40), 252–4.

11. The clauses and phrases omitted are those printed in R. 894b.62–5, 895a.59 (i: scope of agreement; restitution of ships etc. seized by the English and the Gascons to include those 'ante guerram occupat[i]'); 895a.8–10, 18–21 (ii: procedure for provision of pledges by Edward I regarding fulfilment of marriage alliances); 895a.343–5 (iii: security clause). The omission of these passages is systematically noted by Hamilton, ii. 162–6, and partially by Rothwell, pp. 317–20.

before 27 June 1298 when Benedict Caetani, acting as a 'private person' at the instance of the French, published the award which three days later he ratified in his capacity as pontiff.[12] In view of the lacunae in T and G regarding the particulars of the proposed Anglo-French matrimonial alliances, it perhaps deserves to be remarked not only that as late as the very day of the publication of the award the Flemish ambassadors were still seeking to save their count's alliance with England but also that for them it was the long-mooted match of Edward of Caernarfon and the daughter of Gui de Dampierre that was the linchpin of their doomed grand strategy – a match 'based on agreements between the parents and confirmed by oath', as they insisted, and therefore, as it was not necessary for them to explain, one which enjoyed the protection of canon law.[13]

The preliminary nature of T and G would also account for the fact that, whereas, as was proper, in the engrossments of the award sent to the royal combatants the principals were referred to by name, in both T and G Edward I, his heir and their future consorts appear either as 'so and so' (as *talis* or variants thereof) or simply as 'the sister of the king of France'.[14] Moreover, it may be that it was the first of these peculiarities in the text that he was copying (the letter 'n', for 'nominata' perhaps, where the name of Edward II's queen ought to have been)[15] that caused the scribe of Rothwell's MS. A3 then to substitute 'E.' when he found Edward II described as *tali* predicti regis Anglie filio', and three lines later to break off his transcription altogether, thereby bringing Guisborough's chronicle in Rothwell's γ family of manuscripts to an abrupt (and hitherto unexplained) end in mid-sentence.

12. Digard, *Philippe le Bel*, ii. 304–8; F. Funck-Brentano, *Philippe le Bel en Flandre* (Paris, 1897), pp. 288–91. For the Flemish attempt (14/24 June 1298) to persuade Boniface to proceed 'en lieu de Dieu en terre, et souverains [sic] dou roy de France, en espirituel et en temporel' and the pope's reply that, although possessed of such authority, he chose not to exercise it on this occasion, see J. B. M. C. Kervyn de Lettenhove, *Études sur l'histoire du XIIIème siècle. Recherches sur la part que l'Ordre de Cîteaux et le comte de Flandre prirent à la lutte de Boniface VIII et de Philippe le Bel* (Mémoires de l'Académie Royale de Belgique, 28; Brussels, 1854), p. 43.

13. 'Ex convenientibus inter parentes habitis et jurejurando vallatis': ibid., p. 35. 'Vous savés' – the Flemish ambassadors reminded their English opposite numbers at Rome on 30 June – 'les aloiances et les convenances qui sont entre le roy and mons' de Flandres. Nuls descors n'en a estet, ne mise faite, et là n'appartient nuls dis. Nous créons certainement et avons bien fiance que li roys les tenra por se loaiuté et por se honneur, et ce li priera et requerra adiés mesires' (ibid., p. 49). Cf. M. Prestwich, *Edward I* (London, 1988), p. 388.

14. G. 318.19–29 *apud* MS. Trinity Coll. Cambridge: 'Ad huiusmodi autem pacem confirmandum (. . .) prefato regi Anglie sororem [thus T; R. 895a.7: Margaretam sororem] dicti regis Francie recipere ac ducere (. . .) tenea[n]tur. (. . .) Quodque n. [T. talis; R. 895a.14: Isabellis] filia prelibati regis Francie (. . .) suo tempore E. [T. tali; R. 895a.15: Edvardo] predicti regis Anglie filio (. . .) copuletur'.

15. For the various attempts of the copyists to make sense of 'n.' see Rothwell, *Chronicle*, 318 note g, with the resolution 'i.e. enim' and the comment: 'If the reading of β was not simply N (or other convention) it must have been *Isabella* in an extremely corrupt form'(!). Cf. Hamilton, *Chronicon*, ii. 164 n. 3.

The resemblance between **T** and **G** having been established (though not the priority of one over the other securely determined),[16] the question remaining to be considered is how it was that Guisborough acquired his half-baked text of the papal award.

To this question, on this occasion we should not expect an answer from Toledo. Even were the texts of **T** and **G** identical, which they are not, there would be no point in seeking an explanation of Guisborough's text across the Pyrenees. Across the Pennines is a different matter, however. For in the spring of 1307 the papal envoy Cardinal Peter of Sabina was there, at the Carlisle parliament, charged with the task of implementing that part of the 1298 award which related to the marriage of the future Edward II of England and Isabelle of France – 'ut predictum est', as Guisborough himself reported, referring back to his account of nine years before.[17] And, as Guisborough also reports, the cardinal remained there for two months, detained by the dying Edward I, and was 'greatly honoured'.[18]

And if that was so, if the cardinal really was in Carlisle for as much as two months – and Guisborough 'has a fair amount of information about Carlisle where there was a house of Augustinian canons'[19] – then members of his *familia* there will have had time on their hands and ample leisure to devote themselves to what another English chronicler, in best St Albans tradition, reported to be the secondary purpose of the cardinal's coming, namely that of fleecing the natives.[20] A report circulating at the time, and preserved in a newsletter out of Carlisle,

---

16. As the following six examples indicate:

| T. Philippum Francie | G. Philippum regem Francorum | R. Philippum Francorum; |
|---|---|---|
| audiendum coram nobis | audiendum eisque coram nobis | audiendum eisque coram nobis; |
| per quam negocio istud | per quam negotium istud | per quam poenam negotium istud; |
| successores eius valeant | successores eius valeant | successores ipsius valeant; |
| iuribus que | viribus suis que | viribus, quae; |
| satisfieri faciat | satisfieri faciat competenter | faciat satisfieri. |

It is furthermore to be noted that neither **T** nor **G** begins or ends with a date and that both conclude without the names of witnesses and notarial attestations printed in **R**. The former begins 'In nomine domini Amen. Sanctissimus pater', and the latter 'Dudum inter karissimos', and both end at 'dante domino valeamus' (cf. **R**, 894a.71–4, 78; 895b.48).

17. 'Venitque ibi cum magno apparatu cardinalis Hispanie missus a domino papa pro maritagio filii regis cum filia regis Francie adimplendo secundum ordinacionem bone memorie quondam pape Bonifacii qui super hoc secundum quod predictum est certum ordinauerat': loc. cit., p. 370. Having left Bordeaux on 27 November 1306, and, although expected to have arrived by Christmas, the cardinal reached London on 11 February (according to the *Annales Londonienses*) and Carlisle sometime in March: *Registrum Roberti Winchelsey Cantuariensis archiepiscopi*, ed. R. Graham (2 vols, Canterbury & York Soc.; Oxford, 1952, 1956), ii. 1330; *Foedera*, I.ii.1005; *Chronicles of the Reigns of Edward I. and Edward II*, ed. W. Stubbs (Rolls Ser., 2 vols, London, 1882–3), i. 150. Cf. W. E. Lunt, *Financial Relations of the Papacy with England to 1327* (Cambridge, Mass., 1939), p. 165 n. 5; H. Johnstone, *Edward of Carnarvon 1284–1307* (Manchester, 1946), pp. 118–19. Clement V's letters announcing his appointment had reached Lanercost from Bordeaux within twelve days (*Foedera*, loc. cit.). But cardinals moved more slowly than the post.

18. Rothwell, *Chronicle*, p. 371.

19. Gransden, *Historical Writing*, p. 474.

20. 'ad perficiendum ordinatum matrimonium inter progenitum regis Angliae Edwardum et filiam regis Franciae Isabellam; et ad Anglicanas ecclesias depilandum': *Flores Historiarum*, III, *AD 1265 to AD 1326*, ed. H. R. Luard (Rolls Ser.; London, 1890), p. 136 (s.a. 1306).

states that the English and Welsh procurations being demanded by the cardinal amounted to the outrageous ('outraiouse') sum of £400,000 (*and* sixty-five shillings!):[21] an estimate perhaps rather on the high side, although as well as awarding the Spaniard an annual pension of fifty marks the old King did indeed allow him to exact all the procurations specified by the pontiff.[22] Even so, not much of this royal largesse (or the promise thereof) in favour of his 'very dear friend', as the King described the cardinal in advance of his arrival,[23] will have percolated down to members of the cardinal's *familia*, and in the late spring of 1307 whether or not they were condemned to remain in Carlisle for two whole months while news was awaited regarding Philip of France's willingness to satisfy the condition set by Edward I for assenting to the marriage of his son (namely the surrender of the castle of Mauléon),[24] as they eked out the interminable days and windy weeks, remote from the apricots ripening in Apulia, one or other of them with access to the detritus of the nuncio's chancery may well have been willing to engage in some private business of his own on the side.

Thus perhaps it was, by private treaty one fine day (or late one fine evening) in Carlisle in 1307, that someone secured what he was led to believe was an authorized copy of the authentic text of the award of nine years before ('secundum quod predictum est'),[25] the in fact addled

---

21. H. G. Richardson and G. O. Sayles, 'The Parliament of Carlisle, 1307 – some new documents', *ante*, liii (1938), 437. Likewise, the St Albans continuator reported the royal council's instruction that the nuncio's exorbitant demands be halved, to the level of what the legate Ottobono had been allowed (in 1265–8): *Flores Historiarum*, III, loc. cit.

22. A licence which, in view of the heated debates at Carlisle on the subject of papal taxation, casts doubt on the correctness of the suggestion that although 'ostensibly' he had been sent 'to treat for peace between France and England, (. . .) actually [he had come] to deal with the ecclesiastical questions that were to be raised' there: I. S. Leadam and J. F. Baldwin, *Select Cases before the King's Council 1243–1482* (Selden Society, vol. XXXV; Cambridge Mass., 1918), p. 18 n. 6; *Foedera*, I.ii. 1015, 1017. Cf. W. E. Lunt, 'William Testa and the Parliament of Carlisle', *ante*, xli (1926), 338–44. In fact, when the cardinal left England in November 1307, having presided at the old King's funeral, all that Edward II permitted him to take with him was one thousand marks 'in pecunia numerata pro expensis suis': *Foedera*, II.i (1818), p. 15; *Willelmi Rishanger quondam monachi S. Albani et quorundam anonymorum Chronica et Annales*, ed. H. T. Riley (Rolls Ser.; London, 1865), p. 423.

23. *Foedera*, I.ii.1005, 1006 (Dec. 1306).

24. Rothwell, *Chronicle*, p. 371. According to the *Chronicon de Lanercost*, however (and it was at Lanercost priory, a short distance from Carlisle, that Edward I resided in advance of the Parliament of Carlisle: J. R. H. Moorman, 'Edward I at Lanercost Priory', *ante*, lxvii (1952), 161–74), it was just five days after the arrival of the King and the cardinal in Carlisle (a week later than the cardinal had been expected: *Foedera*, I.ii.1009), namely on 24 March (Good Friday), that 'peace between the two kings was proclaimed there' and that the archbishop of York, William Greenfield, announced 'quod filius regis Angliae filiam regis Franciae duceret in uxorem, sicut prius etiam per dominum papam Bonifacium extiterat ordinatum': ed. J. Stevenson (Maitland Club; Edinburgh, 1839), p. 206.

25. Cf. the Lanercost chronicler's description (loc. cit.) of the nuncio's account of the purpose of his legation, delivered in Carlisle cathedral 'coram maximo populo et clero' on 22 March: 'Et ostendit eis formam bonam in quam dominus papa et dominus rex Franciae consenserant, si domino regi Angliae complaceret, scilicet, quod filius regis Angliae et haeres, dominus Edwardus, Isabellam filiam regis Franciae duceret in uxorem.' The 'forma bona' cannot have been other than the relevant extract of the text of the award of 1298. Presumably it was read out in Latin with a Spanish accent. No wonder if over the following days there was a market in Carlisle for the text itself.

version of the award which then found its way into Guisborough's chronicle. Thus perhaps it was that William of Guisborough's supplier of information, in acquiring his text from a dealer in 'commercial productions' scarcely distinguishable from the pedlar of the aforementioned newsletter,[26] was sold a pup.[27] *Perhaps* it was. But was it? Although **T** and **G** were demonstrably in some sense related, the chronicler might even so have acquired his text of the award otherwise and elsewhere. However, there is good reason for suspecting that it was indeed at Carlisle in 1307 that he did so.

That reason is the nuncio whom the chronicler set eyes on in that year, the cardinal bishop of Sabina, Pedro Rodríguez. Better known as Petrus Hispanus, in 1298 Pedro Rodríguez had been one of the most influential figures in the papal curia. As Boniface VIII's referendary, the official without whose acquiescence no petition reached the pope's attention, he would have been much visited by all parties with any interest in the drafting of the Anglo-French settlement.[28] An operator on the grand scale, he was almost everyone's friend, not just Edward I's, enjoying and servicing an enormous clientele which included Archbishop Winchelsey

---

26. Richardson and Sayles, 'The Parliament of Carlisle', 430.

27. And perhaps not only Guisborough, for the very same characteristics (failure to identify the marriage partners by name and omission of clauses regarding pledges; *supra*, notes, 14, 11 [ii]) are also observable in the condensed and abbreviated extract of the text of the award contained in the Worcester Annals, ed. H. R. Luard, *Annales monastici*, (Rolls Ser., 5 vols, London, 1864–9), iv. 538. From its location, inserted into his account of events of 28 July 1298, the day when the sun ran red and (as he believed, mistakenly) the battle of Göllheim was fought, it is evident that the Worcester annalist's text was spliced into his report at a later date. The editor's marginal description of it as 'apparently abridged carelessly from the document in the Foedera, i. pp. 894, 895' reveals that Luard shared Rothwell's assumptions regarding the provenance of the information conveyed by his chronicler (*supra*, n. 15).

28. The first holder of the office of referendary, and the only one of Boniface VIII's cardinals to remain with him to the bitter end ('for he, like Boniface, was great of heart'), Petrus Hispanus is first encountered on the Roman scene in 1292, as the future pontiff's chaplain: P. Santini, *De referendariorum ac signaturae historico-iuridico Evolutione* (Rome, 1945), p. 11; T. S. R. Boase, *Boniface VIII* (London, 1933), p. 379; G. F. Nüske, 'Untersuchungen über das Personal der päpstlichen Kanzlei, 1254–1304, Erster Teil', *Archiv für Diplomatik*, xx (1974), 143. Although regularly described as a former papal notary, no reference to him in either that or any other cancillerial capacity is recorded by Nüske. He awaits serious study. See meanwhile D. Mansilla, 'El cardenal "Petrus Hispanus" obispo de Burgos (1300–1303)', *Hispania Sacra*, ix (1956), 243–80; T. Schmidt, *Der Bonifaz-Prozess. Verfahren der Papstanklage in der Zeit Bonifaz' VIII. und Clemens' V.* (Cologne–Vienna, 1989), p. 150. As Nüske rightly observes (p. 144, n. 15), 'Mit keinem der gleichnamigen Kanonisten des 13. Jh. ist der Kardinal Petrus Hispanus identisch.' However, no notice has hitherto been taken of the 'repertorio de derechos (. . .) intitulado "Memoriale Petri Hispani episcopi Sabiniensis [*sic*] cardinalis." Comienca: "A proposito", e acaba: "en el § an spoliatus et cetera" ', a copy of which was in the chapter library of Palencia cathedral in 1481: see J. M. Ruiz Asencio, 'Documentos sobre manuscritos medievales de la catedral de Palencia': *Actas del II Congreso de Historia de Palencia. 27, 28 y 29 de abril de 1989*, vol. II (Palencia, 1990), pp. 30, 35, nos 17a, 17b. (Can this 'Memoriale' have been identical with the 'Epistolare' which in his will of Nov. 1311 Cardinal Leonardo da Guarcino ordered to be restored to the late Spanish cardinal's executors? Cf. A. Paravicini Bagliani, *I testamenti dei cardinali del Duecento* (Rome, 1980), p. 395.)

of Canterbury[29] – though because he was Castilian by birth, as matters stood between Castile and Aragón in the later 1290s he drew the line at the Aragonese.[30] Aragonese apart, however, he was at the service of all Spaniards at the papal curia. Thus Ferrán Martínez, archdeacon of Madrid, in the prologue to the earliest of the Spanish novels of chivalry, the *Libro del Caballero Zifar*, a prologue in which the tale is told of its author's recovery from Rome (against all the odds and only by virtue of the referendary's overcoming Pope Boniface's objections) of the body of his former patron, Gonzalo Pérez 'Gudiel'.[31]

Archbishop of Toledo from 1280 until 1298, Gonzalo Pérez 'Gudiel' had died as cardinal bishop of Albano in November 1299. In June 1298, however, he had been in Rome angling for the red hat, his securing of which in the December of that year was to no small degree due to the aforesaid referendary.[32] Meanwhile he was at a loose end in Rome, having come there under something of a cloud, and had been doing what he could to make himself agreeable to the pope, for example by offering him gratuitous advice on the currently interesting subject of the claims of Louis IX of France to the title of sanctity.[33]

So in the summer of 1298 'Gudiel' was constantly in and out of the referendary's apartments.[34] Earlier in his career he had been in the

29. Despite his son's earlier courting of the cardinal with rich gifts, not too much should be made of the King's own expressions of cordiality in 1306 (*supra*, n. 23), however. In Feb. 1303 it was not only to the Spaniard's *amicitia* that Edward had appealed but also to that of all other members of the college of cardinals: Johnstone, *Edward of Carnarvon*, p. 118, n. 4; *Foedera*, I.ii.948. Moreover, in 1294 Petrus Hispanus had been the 'friend' of the commune of Bruges, which the King of England was far from being: M. Kervyn de Lettenhove, *Histoire de Flandre* (6 vols, Brussels, 1847–50), ii. 594. For Winchelsey's gratitude (July 1299) on account of the referendary's curial vigilance on his and his church's behalf, see *Reg. Winchelsey*, ii. 559, and for the archbishop's reliance on him thereafter, notably in his differences with the community of St Augustine's Canterbury, ibid. (index).

30. 'Your enemy and persecutor' was how Berengar de Pavo, the Aragonese proctor at Rome, described him to King Jaume II in October 1299: H. Finke, *Acta Aragonensia* (3 vols, Berlin 1908–22), i. 71–2.

31. *El Libro del Caballero Zifar*, ed. C. P. Wagner (Ann Arbor, Mich., 1929), pp. 1–8; F. J. Hernández, 'Ferrán Martínez, escrivano del rey, canónigo de Toledo, y autor del *Libro del Cavallero Zifar*', *Revista de Archivos, Bibliotecas y Museos*, lxxxi (1978), pp. 289–325; Peter Linehan, *History and the Historians of Medieval Spain* (Oxford, 1993), pp. 535–48.

32. In March 1299 Gudiel thanked the Queen Mother of Castile, María de Molina, for 'vestras ad magistrum Petrum domini pape referendarium deprecatorias litteras' in support of his campaign to have his nephew, Gonzalo Palomeque, succeed him as archbishop of Toledo, while in July 1302 it was a sense of reverence for the man to whom he was so indebted 'por quanta ayuda el recibiera del en la Corte de Roma' that, when traversing the diocese of Burgos, of which the referendary had once been bishop, that nephew made the supreme sacrifice for an archbishop of Toledo, of refraining from having his primatial cross raised aloft: ACT, A.7.G.1.13; X.8.B.1.1.

33. Peter Linehan and F. J. Hernández, '"Animadverto": a recently discovered consilium concerning the sanctity of King Louis IX', *Revue Mabillon*, n.s. v [lxvi] (1994), 83–105; Peter Linehan, *The Ladies of Zamora* (Manchester, 1997), pp. 119–28.

34. In this connexion it is to be noted that both parties to the 1298 award employed the same proctor, Nicholas de Vico (Barbiche, Sayers, *supra*, n. 9), which, given the ultimately uncontentious nature of the settlement, was in itself unremarkable, but which nevertheless deserves mention because at various dates in 1301 and 1302 the proctor and the referendary were to be found in close association: Barbiche, nos. 2167, 2197; Sayers, no. 1024.

service of successive kings of Castile, first as Alfonso X's notary for Castile and then, during the reign of Sancho IV, as chancellor of the kingdom. In this capacity, as well as acquiring considerable expertise in matters diplomatic, he had developed the habit of accumulating interesting examples of discarded drafts and minutes of diplomatic instruments. It is these squirrel-like instincts of an obsessive hoarder of drafts and minutes of his own letters that make it possible on occasion to follow the intricate process of his changes of mind as he sought for the right form of words to extricate himself from the series of tight corners into which his political ventures periodically led him.[35] Nor was this interest of his confined to evidences relating to his own affairs. To the contents of other people's desks and waste paper baskets he seems to have been magnetically attracted. On earlier visits to the papal curia he had acquired discarded drafts of part of *Nephandum scelus*, Gregory X's tremendous condemnation of Guy de Montfort for the murder of the English prince Henry of Almain in 1271, and of Nicholas III's constitution of 1278 regarding the government of the city of Rome.[36] As he wandered in and out of the referendary's department in the summer of 1298, therefore, nothing was more natural than that, with or without leave to do so, the acquisitive Castilian should have gathered up the copy of an early draft of the Anglo-French settlement as a trophy to be added to those which, although they have nothing to do with the place, are preserved in the Toledo archive to this day – just as it had nothing to do with Carlisle in particular that that draft's close relation came to rest in northern England some nine years later.

But is that as much as this enquiry amounts to, a conjectural reconstruction of deals done behind windy walls in Carlisle and pilfering off desks in the vicinity of the papal chamber? Bearing in mind the transformation in European affairs that occurred between 1298 and 1307, and the troubled affairs of the kingdom of Castile in particular, perhaps not.

Perhaps what is evidenced here may also be read as providing a commentary of a sort on the history of that turbulent decade. Perhaps the failure of the English chroniclers to record the full details of the award of 1298 was not wholly fortuitous. Guisborough and the Worcester annalist apart, those of them who mentioned the matter at all (including the usually well-informed St Albans and Bury writers) did so only in the most cursory manner and made no reference to its

35. See F. J. Hernández and Peter Linehan, *The Mozarabic Cardinal: the life and times of Gonzalo Pérez Gudiel* (in press), chs 6–12.
36. Peter Linehan, 'A papal constitution in the making: "Fundamenta militantis ecclesie" (18 July 1278)': idem, ed., *Life, Law and Letters: Historical Studies in honour of Antonio García y García*: *Studia Gratiana*, xxix (Rome, 1998), pp. 575–91.

terms.[37] After all, for Edward I that award was nothing less than a humiliation,[38] yet another disaster on top of the events of the previous year. Why therefore should he have wanted to have its details publicized? 'Both Edward I and his opponents in 1297 clearly recognized the importance of propaganda', it has been observed,[39] and in 1298, as well as being humiliated in Gascony, the King had cravenly abandoned his Flemish allies.[40] The war against France had been his 'most unsuccessful venture'. 'An immense sum of money' having been spent, 'Edward had very little to show for such an investment. It is hardly surprising that his principal subjects were bitterly resentful, and that these were not merely years of extreme difficulty abroad, but also of intense political controversy at home.'[41]

But by 1303 'Edward had won.'[42] No matter that the lower levels of society were crushed into the ground,[43] at court morale was high. By the summer of 1303 the situation in Gascony had been transformed. And by 1307, as the King lay on his deathbed, sustained by 'part of the sponge from which Christ received the wine while on the cross' and easy access to concoctions of oil of bayberries and gum laudanum,[44] the lesser powers were beating a path to his door again. If the newsletter in circulation at the time of the parliament is to be believed, as well as the items on his formal agenda the Spanish cardinal brought with him an indenture to which the 'counts and barons of the land of Spain' were party to the effect that in the event of Fernando IV of Castile dying

37. Rishanger, *Chronica*, p. 184; *The Chronicle of Bury St. Edmunds 1212–1301*, ed. A. Gransden (London, 1964), p. 143. See also *Annales Londonienses*, p. 104 (noting that at the time of writing the pope's peace 'adhuc non fuerat totaliter solidata'). Cf. Gransden, *Historical Writing*, p. 451, for indications that elsewhere the Worcester annalist too had his information from sources close to the English court.

38. 'Si favorable que fût déjà au roi de France la teneur de cette sentence, puisqu'elle ne semblait prévoir qu'une restitution partielle des territoires confisqués sur Edouard et qu'elle maintenait le principe de la soumission féodale, les actes qui l'accompagnaient témoignaient d'une complaisance encore plus entière aux intentions de Philippe le Bel': Digard, *Philippe le Bel*, i. 365–6.

39. M. Prestwich, *Documents illustrating the Crisis of 1297–98 in England* (Camden Fourth Series, vol. 24; London, 1980), p. 25.

40. The King of France hated them and was powerful whereas they lacked both men and money, occupied a low place on the King of England's agenda, and had never cared for the English themselves: of all this the archbishop of Dublin and his colleagues informed the Flemish agents at Rome as time ran out – but, adopting the same device as the pope, so informed them not as Edward's ambassadors but as private individuals ('chascuns à par lui comme amis'): Kervyn de Lettenhove, *Études*, pp. 42–3.

41. Prestwich, *Edward I*, pp. 398, 400.

42. D. A. Carpenter in *The New Cambridge Medieval History*, V, *c.1198–c.1300*, ed. D. Abulafia (Cambridge, 1999), p. 350. Cf. Malcolm Vale, *The Origins of the Hundred Years War. The Angevin Legacy 1250–1340* (2nd edn, Oxford, 1996), pp. 219–24.

43. J. R. Maddicott, *The English Peasantry and the Demands of the Crown 1294–1341* (Past and Present Supplement 1; 1975).

44. Moorman, 'Edward I' , pp. 169, 173.

childless then as his mother's son the next king of Castile should be Prince Edward of England.[45]

On the face of it, this proposal appears altogether as 'fantastic' as Professor Johnstone described it in 1946.[46] Its substance apart, moreover, there is also the form in which it was presented to be explained. For by any reckoning an indenture implies an agreement involving at least two parties. So with whom did the Spanish counts and barons believe themselves to have entered into some form of agreement in 1307? Who, on the strength of a text 'careless, corrupt, and difficult to translate',[47] was or were to be construed as the other party or parties to that agreement? Was it the King of England (a possibility to which what may have been Edward I's own tentative testing of the diplomatic waters lends a certain degree of credibility)?[48] Or may it have been the Spanish cardinal himself?[49] But in that case, by what warrant (as Edward I was accustomed to enquire) might a Spanish cardinal have been fishing in such waters? Indeed, by what warrant might *any* cardinal have been doing so?

Questions such as these neither were nor are unanswerable, however. For, although he had been out of Spain for twenty years or more, the Spanish cardinal nevertheless remained sufficiently influential there for the King of France to urge him to intervene with Fernando IV on behalf of the Infante Fernando de la Cerda.[50] The report circulating at Carlisle may not have been entirely without foundation therefore, not least because in the spring of 1307, despite their five years of marriage there was still no sign of the twenty-one-year-old Fernando IV and his seventeen-year-old queen, Constanza of Portugal, producing an heir,[51] the kingdom of Castile was in a state of anarchy, with the Infante D. Juan (the king's uncle) and Diego López de Haro furiously contesting the inheritance of the lordship of Vizcaya, the Spanish jurists deadlocked on the question, and D. Diego's referral of the matter to papal arbitration

---

45. 'Dautre part, le Cardenal ad endenture ensemblement oue countes e barouns de la terre Despaigne au prince Dengleterre de la seignurie Despaigne, pur taunt com le roi Despaigne morist saunz heir de son corps e le prince Dangleterre est plus procheyn de saunk de part sa mere, par quey le senuyre de la terre luy est grante': Richardson and Sayles, 'The Parliament of Carlisle', 436 [text as corrected in H. G. Richardson and G. O. Sayles, *The English Parliament in the Middle Ages* (London, 1981), XII, p. 437].

46. *Edward of Carnarvon*, p. 120.

47. Ibid., pp. 117 n. 7.

48. *Infra*, n. 62. Perhaps no particular significance is to be attached to the king's courtesy in sending his son to greet the nuncio at Dover: Johnstone, *Edward of Carnarvon*, p. 118.

49. As suggested by Johnstone, p. 120.

50. G. Daumet, *Mémoire sur les relations de la France et de la Castille de 1255 à 1320* (Paris, 1913), pp. 134, 230, where the undated letter is assigned to the year 1309 and its addressee ('P. episcopo Sabinensi') is unaccountably identified as Guillaume de Pierre Godin (the cardinal of the same title who was legate to Castile in 1321–2). Judging both by its contents and by what is known of the course of the relationship of the king and the Infante Fernando de la Cerda at this time, the letter is more likely to belong to the year 1304. Cf. C. González Mínguez, *Fernando IV de Castilla (1295–1312). La guerra civil y el predominio de la nobleza* (Vitoria, 1976), pp. 175–7, 196.

51. The earliest mention of their first-born, the Infanta Leonor, is of mid December 1307: ibid., p. 250.

on the grounds that his opponent was perjured occasioning further controversy, controversy in which no doubt the Spanish cardinal was also involved.[52] In the spring of 1307, moreover, not only was the question of the succession to Fernando IV in doubt. So also was that of Fernando's own legitimacy. Six years earlier his situation as the child of a marriage extravagantly uncanonical by any reckoning had been regularized by means of a papal dispensation which, but for the exertions of Petrus Hispanus, must surely have cost even more than the ten thousand marks of silver charged for it by Boniface VIII.[53] Since then, however, the question had arisen whether that exorbitant sum had not been money wasted. For, as the archbishop of Toledo's man reported from Perugia in April 1305, nine months into the conclave which was to result in the election of Clement V, and in the context of the dead pontiff's continuing persecution by the French King and the Colonna cardinals, it was now urged that 'everything that Boniface had done had to be revoked and annulled as the acts of one who had not been pope.'[54] True, as a result of the discreet rendezvous in the conclave lavatory between Petrus Hispanus and the leader of the pro-French cardinals, and the consequent election in June 1305 of a pontiff acceptable to the King of France, at the time of the Carlisle Parliament that outcome had been realized.[55] But with the dead pontiff's tormentor-in-chief Guillaume de Nogaret still set upon having Boniface VIII's pontificate declared a nullity,[56] it nevertheless remained a real possibility, providing the Castilian establishment with sufficient cause for concern regarding the King's legitimacy and therewith the royal succession in general. For if Fernando IV was a bastard then so were his surviving siblings, the infantes D. Pedro and D. Felipe and the infanta Doña Beatriz (who suffered the further disadvantage of being betrothed to Afonso IV of

52. Ibid., pp. 211–37. Against the proposal to involve Clement V it was objected that, regardless of D. Juan's alleged perjury, the pope was incompetent to intervene because 'the king and his kingdoms of Castile and León were exempt from the church of Rome', an exemption which Fernando's predecessors had always defended ('guardaron siempre'), albeit at a later stage the pope did in fact intervene: *Crónica del rey don Fernando Cuarto: Crónicas de los Reyes de Castilla*, ed. C. Rosell (Biblioteca de Autores Españoles, vol. LXVI.1; Madrid, 1875), pp. 139b (cf. p. 149b). Regrettably, no account has survived of the particulars of the arguments advanced by D. Juan's jurists involving issues so close in substance to those soon to be debated in the course of the far more celebrated exchanges regarding the sovereign status of the kingdom of Sicily. Cf. J. L. Bermejo, 'El proceso sobre Vizcaya a través de la Crónica de Fernando IV', *Estudios Vizcáinos*, iii (1971), pp. 7–14; P. Gachon, *Étude sur le manuscrit G 1036 des Archives Départmentales de la Lozère. Pièces relatives au débat du Pape Clément V avec l'Empereur Henri VII* (Montpellier, 1894).
53. *Crónica*, p. 119a; H. Finke, *Aus den Tagen Bonifaz VIII.* (Münster, 1902), p. xxvii; Linehan, *History and the Historians*, pp. 540–41.
54. M. Gaibrois de Ballestros and H. Finke, 'Roma despues de la muerte de Bonifacio VIII. Un informe de 1305', *Boletín de la Real Academia de la Historia*, lxxxiv (1924), 353; M. Gaibrois de Ballesteros, 'Comentarios a un documento de 1305, desde el punto de vista castellano', ibid., 438.
55. Finke, *Acta Aragonensia*, i. 191–2.
56. J. Coste, *Boniface VIII en procès. Articles d'accusation et dépositions des témoins (1303–1311)* (Rome, 1995), pp. 357–61. Cf. J. Rivière, *Le Problème de l'Église et de l'État au temps de Philippe le Bel. Étude de théologie positive* (Paris, 1926), pp. 109–15; Boase, *Boniface VIII*, pp. 344–9.

Portugal).[57] Nor could that remnant of the dynastic struggles of thirty years before, the Infante Alfonso de la Cerda, be regarded as a viable candidate since, although ultimately designated Alfonso X's heir, in which capacity he had styled himself King Alfonso XI, in 1304 the Infante had undertaken to renounce his regal pretensions, albeit on conditions. And even if three years later those conditions remained less than fully satisfied, as the altogether too willing cypher of Jaume II of Aragón he was universally regarded as damaged goods.[58] With the throne occupied by the arguably illegitimate, and certainly childless, son of a father who had died in his thirty-seventh year, it was therefore entirely understandable both that those 'counts and barons of Spain' should have looked further afield for a solution and also that they should have searched three generations back from the present reign, beyond the genealogical thickets in which the kings of Castile had been entangled over the previous thirty years, and have found what they were looking for not in a descendant of Alfonso X but rather in the son of Alfonso X's half-sister, Leonor, Edward I of England's Queen Eleanor.[59] 'Fantastic' though it may have appeared in 1946 therefore, in 1307 here was a solution not without precedent in Castile's recent history.[60] It was to 'gossip which started as a baseless *canard*', gossip fed by knowledge of that history, that Hilda Johnstone was inclined to attribute the rumour of the future Edward II's Castilian prospects.[61] But the cosy parenthesis of Edward I's letter to the pope while the cardinal was en route for England – that Petrus Hispanus 'should have a special affection for our dear son Edward, since he [Edward] is of Spanish descent, and from that land the cardinal also originated' – suggests that there was more to it than that and that the copy of Archbishop Rodrigo of Toledo's *De rebus Hispanie* which was in the English Exchequer in 1320 was not there by accident.[62]

In fact, nothing came of course of the proposal brought to Carlisle in the spring of 1307, for in the July of that same year Edward I died at Burgh-by-Sands not far distant, and in August 1311 the Queen of Castile at last bore a son, the future Alfonso XI. The outcome might so easily have been otherwise, however. For the sentence of disinheritance which Alfonso X had pronounced against Sancho IV had also applied 'por

57. R. del Arco, *Sepulcros de la casa real de Castilla* (Madrid, 1954), pp. 271–2.

58. González Mínguez, *Fernando IV*, pp. 179–91, 275.

59. The genealogical table provided by Johnstone (*Edward of Carnarvon*, p. 120) confuses the issue by failing to record the two marriages of Fernando III and representing Eleanor of Castile as senior to Alfonso X. See next page for figure.

60. In 1284 Alfonso X had determined that were his De la Cerda grandsons to die without issue his kingdom should pass to Philip III of France, the grandson of Blanche of Castile 'porque viene derechamente de linea derecha onde nos venimos': A. G. Solalinde, *Antología de Alfonso X el Sabio* (6th edn, Madrid, 1977), p. 232.

61. Johnstone, *Edward of Carnavon*, p. 121.

62. *Foedera*, I.ii.1007. For the copy of the archbishop's History, and the suggestion that it may have belonged to Edward I, see M. T. Clanchy, *From Memory to Written Record. England 1066–1307* (London, 1979), p. 132.

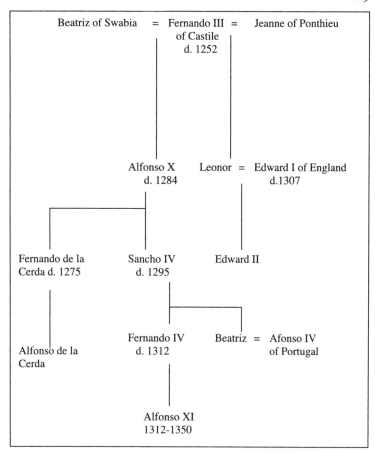

Beatriz of Swabia  =  Fernando III  =  Jeanne of Ponthieu
                       of Castile
                       d. 1252

Alfonso X        Leonor  =  Edward I of England
d. 1284                     d.1307

Fernando de la    Sancho IV      Edward II
Cerda d. 1275     d. 1295

Fernando IV    Beatriz  =  Afonso IV
Alfonso de la      d. 1312                  of Portugal
Cerda

Alfonso XI
1312-1350

siempre jamás' to Sancho's posterity, and the sensible effects of that stigma did not fade with time.[63] Moreover, whether or not the torpid Fernando was indeed the father of the energetic Alfonso,[64] only by little over a year did he survive the child's birth.

In 1307 meanwhile, there was another, and specifically English, reason for regarding the *démarche* of the 'counts and barons of the land of Spain' as altogether less outlandish than has been suggested. This was Vizcaya's proximity to Gascony. Developments in that area were always of pressing concern to Edward I. In the course of the previous month indeed he had written to Fernando IV, ventilating yet again the grievances raised by his subjects there, the merchants of Bayonne, in particular the plundering of

63. Solalinde, *Antología*, p. 227. Cf. J. R. Craddock, 'Dynasty in dispute: Alfonso X el Sabio and the succession to the throne of Castile and Leon in history and legend', *Viator*, xvii (1986), 197–219.

64. Cf. Linehan, *History and the Historians*, p. 614.

their shipping by Spanish pirates.[65] *Si vieillesse pouvoit* . . . If only he had been a younger man, if only the Scots had not still been demanding his attention again, perhaps Edward might have been tempted towards a new initiative and a fresh departure in grand strategy at the expense of the King of France. After all, 'the possibility of the first English prince of Wales becoming also the first English king of Spain' – a grim prospect for a land with troubles enough of its own at the time, be it observed, as well as a possibility of which Spanish historians seem to have remained blissfully unaware – 'is more startling to modern ears than it would seem to the cosmopolitan world of the early fourteenth century. There was nothing, for example, violently disturbing to contemporary thought when thirty-three years later, in January 1340, Edward of Carnarvon's son and successor began not only his fourteenth regnal year as king of England, but also his first as king of France.'[66]

In other words, if only a very few pieces on the European diplomatic chessboard had been differently distributed in 1307 the Hundred Years' War might well have begun sooner rather than later, then rather than in 1340.[67] As the English King reminded his Castilian opposite number, the question of Spanish piracy in Gascon waters had remained unsettled since the reign of Sancho IV.[68] It had been a live issue in the weeks during which the terms of the Anglo-French award were being hammered out in the summer of 1298, three years after Sancho's death, and Gonzalo Pérez 'Gudiel', archbishop of Toledo and King Sancho's sometime chancellor, had been in and out of the referendary's office. (It might be supposed therefore that it was not just an inveterate collector's itchy fingers that caused the archbishop to bear T off to his lodgings – though in fact, by the summer of 1298 Gudiel seems no longer to have regarded himself as a Castilian functionary. With the kingdom of Castile in an even worse state than it was to be when reports of the other Spanish cardinal's interest in its future circulated at Carlisle nine years later, there is reason to believe that by then Gudiel had entirely severed his links with his native land.)[69]

Such speculations apart, however, the relationship of T and G proposed here, and the connexions between the papal curia, Toledo, Guisborough and Carlisle which have been suggested, at the very least raise the possibility of implications more far-reaching than might have been expected to have emerged from the perusal of a limited number of

65. *Foedera*, I.ii.1010 (27 Feb. 1307).
66. Johnstone, *Edward of Carnarvon*, p. 121.
67. Cf. Vale, *Origins*, pp. 227 & sqq.
68. *Foedera*, I.ii.789–90, 805; M. Gaibrois de Ballesteros, *Historia del reinado de Sancho IV de Castilla*, (3 vols, Madrid, 1922–8), ii. 215–16, 324; Digard, *Philippe le Bel*, i. 345.
69. Even to the extent of being prepared in the following year to seek to ingratiate himself with Castile's Aragonese enemy: Barcelona, Archivo de la Corona de Aragón, Cartas reales diplomáticas, Jaume II, no. 593 (summarized Finke, *Acta Aragonensia*, i. 59–60; printed Hernández and Linehan, *The Mozarabic Cardinal*, app. XVIII). Cf. M. Gaibrois de Ballesteros, *María de Molina. Tres veces reina* (2nd edn, Madrid, 1967), pp. 110–13; González Mínguez, *Fernando IV*, pp. 74–82.

textual variants in a printed edition and the inspection of a manuscript in a library just across the wall from the place in which this Note has been written.

# XV

PATRONAGE AND INDEBTEDNESS:
PORTUGAL, CASTILE AND THE PAPAL
COURT AROUND THE YEAR 1300*

In the standard biographies of Boniface VIII consideration of Portuguese affairs has been largely ignored, with Boase for example, in his still valuable study,
limiting himself to the observation that negotiation of the 40 articles of the Portuguese Church ('a piece of work that raised problems and formed opinions', and
one in which the then Cardinal Benedetto Caetani was involved) 'must be given
no small place in the genesis of *Clericis laicos* and *Unam sanctam*'.[1] Such is the
context, but not the content, of the present note.

At the time of Nicholas IV's election in February 1288, for thirteen long
years the king and kingdom of Portugal had been suffering the consequences of
excommunication and interdict, as specified in 'De regno Portugalie', Gregory X's
'constitution, ordinance and provision' of September 1275.[2] The gravity of these
consequences was described by the pope in various communications to King
Dinis, on the one hand the cumulative effects of deprivation of the sacraments,[3] on
the other the abuses reportedly inflicted upon ecclesiastics by laymen who, under
cover of custom ('which it were better to call corruption'), were claiming that their
patronal rights entitled them and their families to force themselves upon churches
and monasteries, demanding hospitality, flooding the cloisters with dubious company, and robbing the men of religion not only of the contents of their larders but
also of the solace of their beds.[4]

* I am grateful to Maria João Branco, André Vitória, and members of the LZR Seminar (University of Cambridge) for the benefit of their precious assistance.

1. T. S. R. Boase, *Boniface VIII* (London, 1933), 18. Likewise, A. Paravicini Bagliani, *Bonifacio
VIII* (Turin, 2003), 27n.

2. *Reg. Greg. X*, 628; summarized in A. Herculano, *Hist. de Portugal*, III. 173-6.

3. 'Hec est forma', 16 March 1289: *Reg. Nich. IV*, 718; A. D. de Sousa Costa, 'Concilio provincial de Compostela realizado em 1292, com a participação de bispos portugueses, e a data do efectuado
no tempo do Arcebispo D. João Arias. (No ambiente das Concordatas de el-Rei D. Dinis)', *Itinerarium*,
32 (1987), 393-470, at p. 410.

4. '… pretendentes ex abusu consuetudinem que dicenda est potius corruptela, ad monasteria et
ecclesias predicta causa exigendi et accipiendi violenter hospitia pro sue voluntatis libito cum comitiva

Since the death of the Portuguese pope, John XXI, in May 1277 and in February 1279 that of Afonso III, reconciled to Rome just as the grim reaper reached out for him, the sometime archbishop of Braga, Cardinal Ordoño Álvarez (albeit not himself Portuguese, as traditionally claimed) had been on hand to oversee Portuguese interests. And both before and after the cardinal's death in the last months of 1285 there had been abortive attempts at negotiation:[5] the beginnings of approximation towards a settlement of papal-Portuguese differences, the Portuguese consequences of which were to prove more far-reaching even than Boase suggested, preceded 1288.[6] Nevertheless, it was not until the June of that year that D. Dinis gave the process firm direction by appointing two of the most notable of his up-and-coming clerics, Martinho Pires cantor of Évora and João Martins de Soalhães, canon of Coimbra, to act as his proctors at the papal court.[7]

Although a case might be made for revisiting the ensuing diplomatic exchanges and the complexities of the Eleven and then the Forty Articles,[8] that is not my purpose here. Instead, I wish to focus on that pair of upwardly mobile clerics,[9] in 1288 both of them already royal clerks, and on one in particular of the influential friends they acquired at the papal curia.

If the indexes to the French School's calendars of the papal registers for the years since Nicholas III created him cardinal-deacon of S. Maria in Via Lata in 1278 are anything to go by,[10] Giacomo Colonna had hitherto had no particular connexion with Portuguese affairs. But by the end of 1289 João Martins was his

---

militum, armigerorum et peditum accedentes, victualia frequenter a personis monasteriorum et ecclesiarum predictarum sibi postulant exhiberi et frequenter celariorum panis, vini et annone aliorumque victualium claves per violentiam rapientes victualia ipsa non solum suis usibus necessaria capiunt sed ea dissipant enormiter et consumunt ac, mulieres inhonestas plerumque introducentes, dormitoria fratrum intrare ac lectos et pannos ipsorum fratrum violenter accipere non verentur tam per se ipsos quam suos famulos servientes dictorum fratrum quietem clamoribus et loquelis inhonestis ac tumultuosis incessibus perturbantes': 'Hii sunt articuli', 3 Sept. 1289: (A[rquivo] D[istrital,] B[raga], Cx. Bulas 1, no. 21=Archivio Segreto Vaticano, Reg. Vat. 44, c. 458, fo. 208v [Reg. Nich. IV, 1353]).

5. P. LINEHAN, The Ladies of Zamora (Manchester, 1996), 100; idem & Margarita TORRES SEVILLA, 'A misattributed tomb and its implications: Cardinal Ordoño Álvarez and his friends and relations', Rivista di Storia della Chiesa in Italia, 57 (2003), 53-63.

6. Nicholas IV,'Occurrit', epitomizing the history of relations between Portuguese crown and Portuguese episcopate since the pontificate of Clement IV and the course of negotiations leading to the 40 Articles, hereby confirmed subject to ratification by the political nation, and specifying the course of disciplinary action to be followed in the event of non-compliance by the king or his successors (7 March 1289): Reg. Nich. IV, 717; A. MERCATI, Raccolta di Concordati su materie ecclesiastiche tra la Santa Sede e le autorità civili, I. 1098-1914 (Vatican City 1954), 107-11.

7. Ibid., 105-6.

8. COSTA, 'Concilio provincial de Compostela', 406-14; idem, 'D. Frei Tello, arcebispo-primaz, e as concordatas de D. Dinis', in IX Centenário da dedicação da Sé de Braga. Congresso Internacional. Actas, II/i (Braga 1990), 283-316, at 300-5; F. F. LOPES, 'A propósito do conflito entre a Igreja e Portugal no tempo de D. Dinis' [1964], in LOPES, Colectânea de Estudos de História e Literatura, III (Lisbon, 1997), 185-94.

9. For Martinho PIRES, see H. V. VILAR, As dimensões de um poder. A diocese de Évora na Idade Média, Lisbon 1999, 74-9; for João Martins, J. A. FERREIRA, Fastos episcopães da Igreja primacial de Braga (sec. III-sec. XX), II (Famalicão, 1930), 113-25.

10. Which they may not be, those to the Registers of Martin IV being plainly defective.

chaplain, and it was on the cardinal's recommendation as well as out of consideration for the king that he was dispensed to enjoy a substantial portfolio of ecclesiastical benefices in plurality.[11] Earlier still, Cardinal Giacomo had been busying himself with Portuguese affairs, in the previous March enabling Vasco Peres, one of his Portuguese chaplains, to secure an indulgence for the bishop of Viseu,[12] and, as is indicated by certain notarial annotations on the top-left corner of the recto of the instrument, making himself responsible for the acquisition of additional engrossments of the bull absolving D. Dinis.[13] It was through his agency that in March 1290 the pontiff instructed the new archbishop of Braga, D. Tello, to consecrate the Roman church of S. Lucia 'quatuor portarum'.[14] And in the following May he was again active, this time in connexion with the issue of the papal privilege authorising the division along national lines of the Order of Santiago.[15]

Nicholas IV's bull of foundation of the University of Lisbon (9 August 1290) affords a further example of the historical value of such diplomatic minutiae. The letter, 'De statu regni', has been frequently published.[16] But hitherto no attention has been paid to the information on the right of the fold where the scribe identified himself.[17] The evidence there that Portugal's principal friend at the papal court at the time of the foundation of its first university was none other than the same Cardinal Giacomo Colonna may go some way to explain why, in the years immediately following, that institution's progress was so erratic. It was not only the hostility of the Lisbon locals specified by D. Dinis in February 1308 that caused the migration of the Portuguese *studium* to Coimbra.[18] It was also the *studium*'s lack over the previous decade of an influential champion at the papal court.

For although Giacomo Colonna was one of the members of the college of cardinals to whom the election as archbishop of Braga of Martinho Pires, the cantor of Évora and the earlier of the king's proctors to gain promotion, was referred

---

11. The church of S. Miguel de Avoo, dioc. Coimbra (with care of souls), canonries and prebends in the churches of Lisbon, Coimbra and Lamego, 'et quedam prestimonia sine cura in diversis ecclesiis', in addition to which he was now permitted to enjoy 'unum aliud beneficium, cum cura vel sine': *Reg. Nich. IV*, 1727 (1 Dec. 1289); printed COSTA, 'Concílio provincial', 417-18.

12. IAN/TT, Sé de Viseu, mç. 11 (Pontificios), no. 4, dorse: 'Mag[iste]r Velascus Petri capellanus d[omi]ni Iac[obi] diac[oni] card[inalis] hanc impet[rat] | indulgenciam pro d[omi]no Visen. ep[iscop] o': 'Licet malorum incentor' (23 March 1289) = *Reg. Nich. IV*, 796.

13. IAN/TT, Cx. Bulas, mç. 8, no. 5: 'fiant iiij. de mandato d[omi]ni Iac[obi]' (meaning 'make four engrossments of this on the instruction of Cardinal Giacomo'): 'Fili carissime' (23 March 1289) = *Reg. Nich. IV*, 795. (There was no other Cardinal Giacomo in the curia at this time.)

14. *Reg. Nich. IV*, 2399 (13 Mar. 1290).

15. IAN/TT, C. E. (Bulas), cx. 4, no. 17 (*Reg. Nich.* IV, 7555): 'Pastoralis officii', the scribe's signature reading 'Io. Gall. de mandato d[omi]ni Ia. card'. Io. Gall. – Iohannes de Gallicano – was a member of Cardinal Giacomo's *familia*: G. F. NÜSKE, 'Untersuchungen über das Personal der päpstlichen Kanzlei 1254-1304 [II]', *Archiv für Diplomatik*, 21 (1975), 249-431, at 277-8.

16. Most recently by A. MOREIRA DE SÁ, *Chartularium Universitatis Portucalensis*, I *(1288-1377)*, (Lisbon, 1966), 12-14. It appears in the papal register as *Reg. Nich. IV*, 3102.

17. 'Io. Gal. de man[dato] | .I. de Col[um]pna': IAN/TT, Cx. Bulas, mç. 12, no. 2.

18. *Reg. Clem. V*, 2666; MOREIRA DE SÁ, *Chartularium Universitatis Portucalensis*, I. 39-40.

for examination seven months into Boniface VIII's pontificate,[19] the Colonna cardinals' subsequent quarrel with the pontiff and their deposition from the college of cardinals in 1297 fatally damaged any cause with which they were associated. Thus, while the Montpellier *studium*, also favoured by Nicholas IV, continued to prosper, the Lisbon *studium* languished.[20] Evidence of the pope's unremitting vendetta against the Colonna and their associates is found throughout Europe. In Portugal, because Laurentius de Fuscis de Berta, canon and archdeacon of Braga, was the chaplain and chamberlain of Cardinal Pietro, he was deprived of his benefices and replaced by another Italian absentee, this one unqualified for appointment by both age and orders.[21] For the same reason *inter alia*, in Castile a similar fate overtook Bishop Velasco of Ciudad Rodrigo.[22]

Exempt from this persecution, evidently because they enjoyed the favour of King Dinis, were João Martins de Soalhães and Geraldo Domingues, dean of Braga, chaplain of Cardinal Giacomo[23] and in October 1297 Roman proctor of João Martins.[24] By then João Martins himself was bishop of Lisbon, his refusal to accept election to the see of Braga in 1292 having resulted in the appointment of Martinho Pires.[25] Now, at the request of King Dinis, and doubtless because the king had need of him at home, he was dispensed from making the 'ad limina' visit to the papal court.[26] Equally, though, business of his own demanded his presence at Rome, notably an enquiry initiated in November 1298 into the complaint of the bishop of Coimbra, Pedro Collaço, that his church had suffered enormous loss on account of the transfer of properties to João Martins 'not as bishop but as a private person' by Pedro's predecessor Aimerico.[27] In March 1299 the case was being argued at the

---

19. *Reg. Bon. VIII*, 344 (printed S. DOMÍNGUEZ SÁNCHEZ, *Documentos de Bonifacio VIII (1294-1303) referentes a España* [León, 2006], no. 120).

20. G. ROMESTAN, 'Nicolas IV et la fondation de l'Université de Montpellier', in E. MENESTÒ, *Niccolò IV: un pontificato tra Oriente ed Occidente* (Spoleto, 1991), 39-52.

21. *Reg. Bon. VIII*, 2164 (DOMÍNGUEZ SÁNCHEZ, no. 476).

22. *Reg. Bon. VIII*, 2031 (DOMÍNGUEZ SÁNCHEZ, no. 447).

23. As such, in January 1292 he was dispensed to enjoy benefices in plurality, including canonries at Braga, Lisbon, Coimbra and Lamego. One of the executors of this provision was the cantor of Évora, MARTINHO PIRES: *Reg. Nich. IV*, 6504-5. See A. M. S. A. RODRIGUES *et al.*, *Os capitulares Bracarenses (1245-1374): notícias biográficas* (Lisbon, 2005), 59.

24. 'In nostra proposuisti', 10 Oct. 1297, granting permission to borrow up to 400 marks of silver: ADB, Gav. das Notícias Várias, no. 22. A loan for that sum from the members of the Ammanati Company was raised later that month: ADB, Gav. das Notícias Várias, no. 23.

25. Above, n. 19. According to this account, 'cum eum ex certa causa de iure non possint eligere, postularunt', but João renounced the postulation. H. V. VILAR and M. C. BRANCO, 'Servir, gouverner et leguer: l'évêque Geraldo Domingues (1285-1321)', *A Igreja e o Clero Português no Contexto Europeu* (Lisbon, 2005), 95-116, at 100, suggest that illegitimacy was the problem. If so, it did not stand in the way of his election to Lisbon in March 1294, a carefully orchestrated affair in which mistakes were avoided by vesting all powers of election in a single canon, Petrus Remigii: ADB, Gav. dos Privilegios, 5. When translating him (and his archive, whence this note) to Braga in 1313 Clement V abrogated 'omnem defectum seu impedimentum quodlibet': ADB, Gav. dos Arcebispos, 45.

26. 'Celsitudinis tue litteris', 4 Oct. 1297: ADB, Gav. das Notícias Várias, no. 21.

27. '... non tamen sicut episcopo set tanquam private persone per ipsum et heredes ipsius in perpetuum possidenda concessit, receptis ab eo propter hoc quibusdam aliis casalibus que tunc ad ipsum

Lateran before the acting 'auditor litterarum contradictarum', Huguccio de Vercellis, canon of Bruges.[28] And at Anagni on 6 September 1301 both João Martins and Geraldo Domingues (since the previous year bishop of Porto)[29] were there in person because it was in the papal presence that on that day each of them sought leave to borrow three thousand gold florins on the security of themselves and their sees.[30]

Loans such as these, earmarked for provision of 'necessities' and advancement of their churches' affairs, were of course routinely raised by prelates at the curia. What is interesting about these two though is that it was on that same day, 6 September 1301, that the long-desired, and hugely expensive, papal bull legitimising Fernando IV of Castile and his siblings was at last secured by the agents of Fernando's mother, María de Molina.[31]

In the triumphal account of that achievement, one that had been worked for by fair means and foul for a decade or more, the Castilian chronicle of Fernando's reign made much of María de Molina's success in scrimping and saving the ten thousand silver marks demanded by the pope. And it was common knowledge how much the success of the negotiation owed to the exertions of the papal referendary, the Castilian Petrus Hispanus.[32]

Although the nature of the relationship between the three thousand Portuguese gold florins and the ten thousand Castilian silver marks is uncertain,[33] certain remarks contained in three letters home from the king of Aragon's men at Rome sheds some light on the question. The first, from Godofrè de Foix and dated 25 August, told of the arrival three days earlier of the bishops of Coimbra and Porto and of two of Fernando IV's knights (Fernando being described, in accordance with Aragonese ideology, as the son not of *King* Sancho but of the '*late lord* Sancho of Castile'). They had come for three reasons: two dispensations and a legitimization. Their principal interest was in Fernando IV's union with Dinis's daughter, Constança (Jaume II of Aragón's niece) and that of Dinis's son Afonso (the future Afonso IV) with Fernando's sister Beatriz. The legitimization issue came last.[34] The

---

Iohannem episcopum sue dumtaxat ratione persone et non ratione Ulixbonen. ecclesie pertinebant': ADB, Gav. dos Coutos, no. 88.

28. Ibid.

29. VILAR & BRANCO, 'Servir, gouverner', 103

30. *Reg. Bon. VIII*, 4121 (DOMÍNGUEZ SÁNCHEZ, no. 816-17).

31. *Reg. Bon. VIII*, 4403 (DOMÍNGUEZ SÁNCHEZ, no. 818).

32. A. MARCOS POUS, 'Los dos matrimonios de Sancho IV de Castilla', *Escuela Española de Arqueología e Historia en Roma: Cuadernos de Trabajo*, 8 (1956), 7-108; *Crónica de Fernando IV*, c. 8 (p. 119a); P. LINEHAN, *History and the Historians of Medieval Spain* (Oxford, 1993), 540.

33. F. BAETHGEN, 'Quellen und Untersuchungen zur Geschichte des päpstlichen Hof- und Finanzverwaltung unter Bonifaz VIII', *Quellen und Forschungen aus Italienischen Archiven und Bibliotheken*, 20 (1928-9), 114-237, at 234 (Oct. 1301, 3 *marche=5 floreni auri*). Cf. W. E. LUNT, *Financial Relations of the Papacy with England to 1327* (Cambridge, Mass., 1939), 467, quoting an exchange rate of five florins to the mark.

34. 'Episcopi Colimberiensis [sic] et Portugalensis nuncii regis Portugalie et duo milites Ferrandi filii quondam domini Sancii de Castella intraverunt Anagniam die martis ante festum beati Bartholomei et fuerunt obtime excepti [*leg*. recepti] et aiunt eis commissa tria. Primo est concessa dispensacio, quod dictus Ferrandus possit contrahere matrimonium cum filia (regis) Portugalensis (?) nepte vestra,

author of the other, Guerau d'Albalat, writing on 14 September, reported that he had been in conversation with 'the bishop' (subsequently identified as the bishop of Lisbon), who stated that the referendary (Petrus Hispanus) led them to believe that the matter was a foregone conclusion. But the pope was causing complications. For while he was prepared to make free with dispensations, on the legitimization question his one object was to screw as much as he could out of 'them',[35] 'they' appearing to be the Castilian and Portuguese contingents collectively. Such was the pope's way with everyone he wanted money from.[36]

But by any account there was dissension, the Aragonese agent continued, because the pope wanted more gold than they had brought, and they were unwilling to make up for the shortfall in silver.[37] What the Aragonese perhaps did not know was that some of that gold had been used to fund not Fernando's legitimization but rather the dispensation for him to marry the king of Portugal's daughter; in other words, not for acquiescence in the consequences of the king of Castile's parents' incest but for permission for him to commit incest of his own.[38] So in fact, and doubtless on account of the efforts of French diplomacy to raise the stakes beyond breaking point, Boniface's policy of milking petitioners extended to petitioners for dispensations, with the result that at a critical moment of the history of Castile its ruler was reduced to turning to a couple of Portuguese bishops in order to fulfil obligations entered into (at the treaty of Alcañices four years earlier), to honour his side of a dynastic deal, and so beget a 'fijo de bendicion' and lawful heir.[39]

---

secundo quod filius regis Portugalie possit contrahere cum filia predicti domini Sancii, tercio quod dominus papa legitimabit et habilitabit predictum Ferrandum et fratres suos ad successionem omnem, que eis poterit (?) obvenire': H. Finke, *Aus den Tagen Bonifaz VIII.* (Münster-in-W., 1902), xxiii. Godofrè was evidently misinformed about the identity of the first Portuguese prelate. Cf. the report of another Aragonese agent, Guerau d'Albalat, and his knowledge of the bishop of Lisbon: '...quod octava die assumptionis beate Marie [22 August] [veneru]nt Anagniam episcopus Lixbonensis et episcopus Portugalensis cum quibusdam militibus Castellanis et quodam fratre Uclesii, qui consuevit esse in Lorcha, et fuerunt per papam et referendarium mirabiliter bene recepti et illa die cum referendario comederunt. Pecierunt autem a papa, ut dispensaret, quod inter filios domini Sancii et regis Portugalie possint contrahi matrimonia. Item et quod legitimaret filios dicti Sancii et eos redderet habiles ad regni successionem et quod per suam dispensationem et declaracionem: hiis intellectis secrete *ab episcopo Lixbonensi, cuius notitiam magnam et familiaritatem habui, cum vos, serenissime domine, ad regem Portugalie me misistis*' [my emphasis]: idem, *Acta Aragonensia*, I (Berlin, 1908), 102-3. For Albalat's presence in Portugal in 1294, referred to here: ibid, 106.

35. In letters dated ten days after issue of the bull of legitimization, the pope was at pains to emphasise the enormity of what he had granted: an act of grace that abolished the infamy of the king's parents and cleansed the blackened reputation of the royal house, for which there was no precedent ('auctoritas') in his predecessors' acts, he insisted: *Reg. Bon. VIII*, 4404 (DÓMINGUEZ SÁNCHEZ, no. 819).

36. '...quod refferendarius fecerat eos venire, quasi super re certa. Set modo papa intricabat negocia. Nam super matrimoniis contrahendis inter predictos volebat dispensare libenter. Set super legitimacione non ita cito. (...) Papa tamen non propter aliud ab initio exageravit negocium, nisi ut maiorem peccuniam posset extorquere ab eis. Talem enim modum servat in omnibus, a quibus peccuniam sperat habere. (...)': FINKE, *Aus den Tagen.*, xxvii-xxviii.

37. 'Nunc autem est dissensio inter eos, quia papa petit aurum et plus quam aportaverint, ipsi nolunt dare marchas argenti ad valorem auri': ibid., xxviii.

38. Constança was the great grand-daughter of Alfonso X, Fernando the grandson.

39. Cf. LINEHAN, *History and the Historians*, 539-40. For Castile's fractured economy and society at this time, see *Crón. Fernando IV*, c. 3 (p. 110a), and the report of the Aragonese agent Bernat de Sarría

As Fernando IV freely acknowledged almost four years later, three thousand of the six thousand florins they had borrowed between them had gone towards the cost of that dispensation: 'Sepades que don Johan, obispo de Lixbona, et don Giraldo, obispo del Porto, me prestaron en corte de Roma, pora la mi despensaçion, tres mill florines d'oro,' and that he had undertaken to repay them over three years from the rents of the city of Seville: 'Et yo tove por bien de gelos poner en las rentas de y, de Seuilla, quelos ayan d'aqui a tres años, cada año mill florines' -- though he might as well have done so from the revenues of the Castilian Church, which, after rebuking him and his predecessors for having helped themselves to for more than sixty years, the pope had licensed him to continue to do for a further three.[40]

In September 1301 it had been altogether to the advantage of D. Dinis to have Fernando IV's successional qualifications attended to, for he was just four months away from marrying his daughter to him.[41] In the spring of 1304 he allowed himself to be persuaded by his wife, Isabel of Aragón, to subsidize his son-in-law to the tune of a million *maravedíes*.[42] Moreover, he was also seeking to advance the prospects of his bastard son Afonso Sanches, and to secure for him a dispensation to marry a lady to whom he was related in the very same degree as Fernando IV's parents had been. In October 1302 the pontiff referred the matter to the dependable judgment of Bishops Fernando Martins of Évora and ... João Martins of Lisbon.[43]

As to the reasons for the bishops' anxiety about repayment almost four years later, the death of Boniface VIII in October 1303 and the earliest stages of the process reversing the anti-Colonna measures of 1297 provide the beginnings of an answer. During the vacancy following Benedict XI's brief pontificate, the publication, in Paris in early September 1304, of Guillaume de Nogaret's *protestationes*, with their description of Boniface as 'not true pope' but as a 'thief and robber', heretic, idolater, sodomite etc. was followed by rumours of the rehabilitation of the Colonna. Again, news of this was promptly conveyed home by the Aragonese royal agents at Rome.[44] And in April 1305, with the papal vacancy continuing, so did the church of Toledo's man at Perugia in a letter full of gossip, rumour and fact, a vivid letter concerning the 'bad state' of the city of Rome and the armed bands of Colonna and Orsini fighting to control it – though for our purposes what is of particular interest is the strength of support it reported for the view that 'everything that Boniface did has to be revoked and annulled, being the work of one who was not pope': precisely as Boniface himself had revoked and annulled everything that his predecessor Celestine V had done, regarding the

on 20 June 1301, 'la terra de Castela es en fort anol estament e y a gran carestia': A. GIMÉNEZ SOLER, *Don Juan Manuel. Biografía y estudio crítico* (Zaragoza, 1932), 251.

40. Appendix II, lin. 25-27; *Reg. Bon. VIII*, 4407 (DOMÍNGUEZ SÁNCHEZ, no. 820).

41. C. GONZÁLEZ MÍNGUEZ, *Fernando IV de Castilla (1295-1312). La guerra civil y el predominio de la nobleza* (Vitoria, 1976), 128.

42. Ibid., 153. Cf. FINKE, *Aus den Tagen*, xxviii: 'Preterea, inclite domine, dixit michi episcopus Lixbonensis, quod se reputat clericum vestrum' (G. de Albalat to Jaume II of Aragón).

43. *Reg. Bon. VIII*, 4937 (DOMÍNGUEZ SÁNCHEZ, no. 936); VILAR, *As dimensões*, 69-74.

44. J. COSTE, *Boniface VIII en procès. Articles d'accusation et dépositions des témoins (1303-1311)* (Rome, 1995), 218-19, 241-4; FINKE, *Acta Aragonensia*, I. 185.

Order of Santiago for example.[45] For, even worse than Boniface's Celestine, it was now being said that Boniface himself had not only not been pope; he had not even been Christian; he had been the enemy of Christ, a Patarene and 'omne sin ley':[46] charges plainly based on Nogaret's accusations. To the archbishop of Toledo as he read this its implication would have been alarmingly clear.

In brief, if all the late pope's acts were annulled, the royal dispensation of 1301 would be worthless, and the king of Castile would revert to being a bastard without right of succession. If Boniface had not been pope, the king of Castile's dispensation was no dispensation, and if his dispensation was no dispensation, many consequences followed, of which the likelihood that the king would feel no pressing anxiety to repay those who had helped him acquire a now worthless document was arguably the least important – except of course for the bishops of Lisbon and Porto. Such no doubt was the conclusion that occurred to Fernando IV's Portuguese creditors, one of whom, Geraldo Domingues of Porto, was in Castile between January and April 1305 representing D. Dinis at the ratification of the Arbitration of Torrellas which marked the end of ten-years of warfare between Castile and Aragón: the conclusion of a diplomatic process based on the assumption that Fernando's title was good.[47] Now, as the parties assembled at the Cistercian monastery of Huerta on the Castilian-Aragonese border, that assumption was thrown into doubt.

The death in mid-April of Fernando's Jewish *almoxarife*, Samuel de Vilforado, the only man even remotely capable of reducing the royal finances to order,[48] constituted a further reverse for the king's creditors. But Fernando had pledged his Seville revenues as security, so after their appointment at Lisbon on 2 June thither the bishops' agents betook themselves.[49] They had already secured from the king letters patent and a mandate addressed to the *recabdadores* of his rents at Seville, ordering repayment of the debt over a period of three years, with the former specifying impressive sanctions in the event of non-compliance.[50] Just how empty those threats were was now revealed when the debt-collectors reached Seville and presented their documentation to Samuel Abenxuxem, the king's *almoxarife*, at his house in the *judería* there. Frustratingly, at this point of the narrative the document

45. A. Bartolomei Romagnoli, 'Le bolle di Celestino V cassate da Bonifacio VIII', *Archivum Historiae Pontificiae*, 37 (1999), 61-83. For the effect of the revocation on the peninsular status of the Order of Santiago, see D. W. Lomax, 'El rey Don Diniz de Portugal y la Orden de Santiago', *Hidalguía*, 30 (1982), 477-87, at 481-3; P. A. Linehan and P. N. R. Zutshi, '*Fiat A*. The earliest known roll of petitions signed by the pope (1307)', *English Historical Review*, 122 (2007), 998-1015, at 1004-5.

46. M. Gaibrois de Ballesteros, 'Roma despues de la muerte de Bonifacio VIII', *Boletín de la Real Academia de la Historia*, 84 (1924), 351-6, at 353.

47. González Mínguez, *Fernando* IV, 177, 196-7.

48. Ibid., 140, 204.

49. Appendix I.

50. Atienza, 8, 10 March 1305: 'Et non fagan ende al por ninguna manera, si non, a los cuerpos τ a quanto ouiesen, me tornaria por ello' (Appendix II, lin. 17). Payment was stipulated in the period between 1 December and '[el] dia de la çinquesma' (Quinquagesima, which in the year 1304-5 had fallen on 28 February). On 2 June the term had been stated to be Pentecost, i.e. four days later: Appendix I.

published below is badly damaged. But enough of it is legible to demonstrate the precarious state of the royal finances.

The *almoxarife* declined to make payments from the income of 'la Frontera' because the king had committed it to 'Johan Nunez -- Juan Núñez de Lara – *adelantado de la frontera*, one of Fernando's principal tormentors and a long-term adherent of the La Cerda claimant to the Castilian throne.[51] Neither the king nor Juan Núñez had authorised him to make disbursements. And even if he had he could not have done so since, what with hoarding of wheat by the municipalities, the Military Orders, the *terceros* and the grain-warehouses, the supplying of Alfonso Pérez de Guzmán's requirements at Tarifa, the problems of defence throughout the region, and what was owed to those who had to have money 'en la nomina del Rey' there was a deficit in the accounts of some 800,000 *maravedíes* and nothing to be had.[52]

So far had royal authority slipped by 1292 that Sancho IV had found himself obliged to countersign his own mandates.[53] By July 1305 it had slipped further: Fernando IV had his cheques refused. Civil order had not been restored by the ending of civil war. The king of Castile was outside his own fiscal loop while the independence enjoyed by his Jewish *almoxarife* at Seville demonstrated his own impotence and the futility of the legislation decreed at the recent cortes of Medina del Campo, not least the prohibition of the likes of D. Samuel from holding public office.[54] While the careers of his two Portuguese creditors lay before them, with primacy in the one case and butchery in the other,[55] for Castile and its ruler in the summer of 1305 the only immediate prospect was bankruptcy.

---

51. González Mínguez, *Fernando IV, passim*; S. R. Doubleday, *The Lara Family. Crown and nobility in medieval Spain* (Cambridge, Mass., 2001), 92-5.

52. Cf. the 'Nómina de la Frontera' for 1290, printed F. J. Hernández, *Las rentas del rey. Sociedad y fisco en los reinos castellano-leoneses del siglo XIII* (Madrid, 1993), I.391-418.

53. F. J. Hernández & P. Linehan, *The Mozarabic Cardinal. The life and times of Gonzalo Pérez Gudiel* (Florence, 2004), 352.

54. *Cortes de los antiguos reinos de León y de Castilla*, ed. Real Academia de la Historia, I (Madrid 1861), 172-9 (§9: 'Otrosi a lo que nos pidieron que los judios non fuesen cogedores nin sobre cogedores nin arrendadores, tenemos por bien que lo non sean').

55. Geraldo Domingues was translated to the see of Palencia in 1307 (borrowing a further 6,000 florins at Avignon to assist the process). There he was able to attend on D. Constança, one of those whose marriages he had helped facilitate in 1301. As bishop of Évora, he was done to death in 1321 by another beneficiary of Pope Boniface's acquiescent attitude in such matters, the bastard pretender to the Portuguese throne Afonso Sanches (above, p. 217): IAN/TT, C. E. (Bulas), cx. 4, no. 39; Vilar and Branco, 'Servir, gouverner', 95ff.

## APPENDIX

### I

1305, 2, June. Lisbon

A. Braga, Arquivo Distrital, Colecção Cronológica, pasta 5, no. 220. Parchment. To left, attachment for missing seal; to right, double ogival seal depicting the Virgin and Child, inscription illegible.

Sepam quantos esta presente procuraçom virem que Nos, Johanne et Giraldo, pela merçee de deus bispos de Lixbona et do Porto, fazemos et ordinhamos et stabeleçemos nossos procuradores liidimos et abastosos don Affonso Perez de Gozmam e don Roy Perez d'Alcala, cada huum deles per si, pera reçeber mill floriis d'ouro por nos et en nosso nome de qual quer ou de quaes quer que aiam de recadar et reçeber rendas et dereytos por el Rey don Fernando en Seuilla, os quaes mil floriis lhys manda o dito Rey don Fernando per sa carta que den a nos ou a quem nos mandarmos, por este Penticoste, dos tres mil floriis que lhy nos enprestamos na Corte de Roma pera sa despensaçom. E damos lhys poder a anbhos et a cada huum delos per si pera dar carta ou cartas, estormento ou estormentos de quitaçom ou de quitaçoens daqueles floriis que reçeberem, et aa qual ou aa quales de quantos reçeberem. En testemoynho da qual coussa mandamus ende fazer esta procuraçom et seelar dos nossos seelos. Feyta foy a procuraçom en Lixbona, dous dias andados do mes de juynho, Era de mill et trezentos et Quareenta et tres annos.

### II

1305 July, 1. Seville

A. Braga, Arquivo Distrital, Colecção Cronológica, pasta 5, no. 223.- Parchment instrument of 44 lines; damage to lin. 7-15 and 39-44. Word(s) supplied from sense are shown within square brackets; -------- indicates lost text.

Jueves primero dia del mes de julio era de mill τ trezientos τ quarenta τ tres años. Yo Pero Ferrandez escriuano publico de Scuilla, con los otros escriuanos que aqui|₂ pusieron sus nombres en testimonio, fuemos a la juderia, a casa de don Samuel Abenxuxem, almoxarife de Seuilla, con Domingos Peres clerigo del obispo de Lixbona|₃ por mandado de Ruy Peres de Alcala, alcalle mayor por el Rey en Seuilla, en que enbio mandar por vna su aluala que fuesemos con este Domingos Peres|₄ a dar le testimonio de dos cartas que el auie a amostrar al dicho almoxarife por mandado del obispo de Lixbona, et del obispo del Puerto de|₅ Portogal. Et estando presente el dicho Domingos Peres ante este almoxarife, leymos le estas dos cartas, que dize la vna en esta manera:

"Sabham quantos|₆ esta stromento uirem τ leer ouirem que ena era ·Mª. trezientos τ quarenta τ tres annos, conuem asaber, dez dias del mes de juno ena çidade de Lixboa|₇ en preseça de min, Loureço Eanes, poblico tabalion da dita çidade, e dos otros que a deante son escriptos, os onrados padres τ sennores don J[ohan] τ Giraldo|₈ por la graca de deus bispos de Lixboa τ do Porto, mostraron τ fazer leer τ publicar vna carta aberta τ seelada do verdadey ---- ente do|₉ muyto alto τ muy noble sennor don Ferrando, por la graçia de dios Rey de Castela, dante os onrados τ sages Fernam Verm ---------- Johan Ferrens|₁₀ aluazil da dita çidade de Lixbona, da qual carta o teor de ueruo a ueruo tal he:

'Sepan quantos esta carta uieren commo yo [don Ferrando, por] la gracia de|₁₁ dios Rey de Castiella, de Toledo, de Leon, de Gallizia, de Seuilla, de Cordoua, de Murçia, de Jahen, del Alg[arbe, τ señor] de Molina otorgo|₁₂ e connosco que, por los tres mill florines d'oro que uos don Johan, obispo de Lixbona, et don Guiraldo, obispo do Porto, ------------la corte de Roma|₁₃ pora la mi despensaçion que yo que uolo mande d[ar] -------------- cadanno mill florines, et sennaladament --------- Seuilla. Et mando|₁₄ a qual⁵⁶ quier o a quales quier que ouieren de re[cabdar por mi las rentas de la] villa de Seuilla, quier en renta o en [fialdat o en] otra manera qual quier, que|₁₅ uos den a uos, los dichos don Johan τ don G[uiraldo] ---------dezir por uuestra carta con el traslado desta [traslada]do de escriuano publico, |₁₆ los mill florines deste primero año, daqui al dia de çinquesma, esta primera que uiene. Et los otros, otrossi, cada año por las cinquesmas, segund dicho es. Et non|₁₇ fagan ende al por ninguna manera, si non, a los cuerpos τ a quanto ouiesen, me tornaria por ello. Et tomen el traslado desta mi carta signado de escriuano publico et|₁₈ la suya de pagamiento. Et yo mandar gelos he reçebir en cuenta. Et por que esta sea firme τ estable mande uos dar esta mi carta seellada con mio siello de|₁₉ çera colgado. Dada en Atiença, ocho dias de março, era de mill e trezientos τ quarenta τ tres años. Yo Johan Sanchez la fiz escriuir por mandado del Rey.'

La qual|₂₀ carta perleuda τ publicada, os ditos obispos pediron a os ditos alcaydes [sic] τ aluazil que dese a mim, sobredito taballiom, sua outoridade ordinhayra de tornar a dita carta⁵⁷ en|₂₁ publica forma τ lhys dar en huum poblico estromento, escripto con mia maao τ asinado de meu sinal.

Et eu sobridito taballiom, d'outoridade dos ditos alcayde τ aluazil, adita|₂₂ carta en publica forma torney τ ena este estrumento τ mia maao proprua [sic] screuy con mia maao⁵⁸ enel pugi en testimonio de uerdade que tal he. Testes: Petro Meendes, Steuam Phy-|₂₃lippe, Alfonso Eanes, mercadores de Lixbona, Alfonso Paaez maestrescola de Lixbona τ otros muytos.

Et la otra carta dezia en esta manera:

'Don Ferrando, por la carta [sic] de dios|₂₄ Rey de Castiella, de Toledo, de Leon, de Gallizia, de Seuilla, de Cordoua, de Murçia, de Jahen, del Algarbe, et señor de Molina, a qual quier o aquales quier que ayan|₂₅ de recabdar las rentas de Seuilla en renta o en fialdat o en otra manera qual quier,⁵⁹ salut τ gracia. Sepades que don Johan, obispo de Lixbona, et don Giraldo, obispo|₂₆ del Porto, me prestaron en corte de Roma, pora la mi despensaçion, tres mill florines d'oro. Et yo tove por bien de gelos poner en las rentas de y de Seuilla|₂₇ quelos ayan d'aqui a tres años, cada año mill florines. Et desto les di mi carta seellada con mio seello de çera colgado, en commo los ayan cadaño desdel primero|₂₈ dia del año fasta el dia de çinquesma. Por que uos mando que, delos maravedis que uos por mi recabdades delas rentas de Seuilla que dedes ende a los dichos|₂₉ obispos, o a quien ellos uos enbiaren dezir por sus cartas, los mill florines d'oro que an de auer deste año⁶⁰ começo primero

---

56. MS: aqual.
57. 'carta' repeated, marked for deletion
58. dittography
59. que deleted
60. add. que

158

dia de dezienbre que agora paso, que|[30] fue en la era de mill τ trezientos τ quarenta τ dos
años, τ se acabara postrimero dia de nouienbre dela era desta carta. Et dadgelos por esta
çinques|[31]ma primera que viene desta misma era, et eso mismo cada año los otros florines
que fincan, fasta que sean pagados dellos. Et non fagades ende al por ninguna|[32] manera. Et
yo mandar uos los he reçebir en cuenta. Et, quando fueren pagados destos tres mill florines,
tomad dellos la carta del seello colgado que ellos tienen de|[33] mi en este razon.

Dada en Atiença, diez dias de março, era de mill τ trezientos τ quarenta τ tres años. Yo
Johan Martinez la fiz escriuir por mandado del Rey. Pedro Gomez.'

Et el dicho don Samuel Abenxuxem oyo las cartas τ, luego que fueron leydas, res-
pondio τ dixo que el que tenie por don Johan Nuñez las rentas de|[35] la Frontera, que las
arrendo de nuestro señor el Rey, et que non veye carta del Rey en que mandase a don Johan
Nunez que gelos diese, nin carta de don Johan|[36] pora este almoxarife en que mandase que
gelo cumpliese; et quando tales cartas troxiesse non les podria auer, por que ay mengua
de vnas ochoçientos vezes mill maravedis|[37] por los descuentos que el Rey a de reçebir en
cuenta a don Iohan por las sacas del pan quel uedaron los conçejos τ por las otras cosas
quel tomaron|[38] delos derechos del Rey, et por las sacas del pan, que tomaron las ordenes
en sus lugares, et por las sacas de todos los otros señorios de la frontera [τ] |[39] por las ter-
cias del pan que menguan τ por la alfondiga dela farina, et por otros muchos maravedis que
el Rey puso en esta almoxarifadgo, mas de que...|[40] en manera que de lo que y puede auer
non se puede complir lo que a de auer don Alfonso Perez pora Tarifa, nin la su soldada nin
bas[tecimiento?]...... |[41] delos castiellos que .......... por la tenençia, nin a los otros que an de
auer dineros en la nomina del Rey, que por este......... |[42] por ...... auer m[engua?] destos dineros ..........
florines ca de buena ment cumplirse mandamiento de nuestro ...........................|[43] de que
.......... puso .............. [Pero] Ferrandez escriuano sobredicho quel d[ .........] |[44] firmado de
mi τ delos otros escriuanos................... digelo que fue folgo ca .......... |[45] Johan Gomes la
escriui. Et yo, Johan Garçia, escriuano .......... Gutierrez, escriuano de Seui[lla] et yo Pero
Ferrandez, escriuano publico sobredicho ----- escrivir----- en el mi sig[61]

---

61. *Signum* in form of four-pointed star

# Fiat A: *the Earliest Known Roll of Petitions Signed by the Pope (1307)**

THE vast majority of papal letters in the Middle Ages were issued not on the initiative of the pope or his government but in response to petitions, or supplications, addressed to him from all over Latin Christendom. In response to petitions, the papacy issued letters bestowing favours on religious orders and churches, and spiritual benefits on individuals, making provisions to ecclesiastical benefices, appointing judges delegate and so forth. These letters were popular with petitioners; otherwise, they would not have gone to the trouble and expense of impetrating them. The system of petitioning the pope helps to explain how the papacy, with limited material resources at its direct disposal, was able to exert its authority over a vast geographical area, far wider than that controlled by any secular ruler. This system was indeed an essential element of papal government.

The petitions themselves are of value as indications of the desires and aspirations of those who submitted them. They are not extant in significant numbers prior to the pontificate of Clement VI (1342–52), when a series of registers (the *Registra Supplicationum* in the Vatican Archives) containing copies of petitions granted by the pope begins.[1] The poor rate of survival of petitions outside the *Registra Supplicationum* is understandable. If the pope granted a petition and a letter was issued in response, it was the letter that possessed legal validity, not the petition.[2] Accordingly, the petitioner may well have felt that there was little reason to preserve the petition. If the pope rejected the petition, there was doubtless even less reason to do so. Yet it is clear that the petitioners or their proctors, at least on some occasions, were given the opportunity to retrieve the petitions and did so, hence their sporadic survival in the petitioners' archives.[3]

Petitions were submitted either individually or in groups. In the case of the latter, there might be a sufficient number of petitions to form a roll; hence, such groups of petitions were called *rotuli*. Under Clement

* We are particularly indebted to Dr Barbara Bombi (University of Kent at Canterbury), Mme Anne Goulet (Archives Départementales des Basses-Pyrénées, Pau), Professor Francisco Hernández (Carleton University, Ottawa), Dr Enrique Jerez (Universidad Autónoma, Madrid) and Dr Alberto Torra (Archivo de la Corona de Aragón, Barcelona) for their generous assistance in the preparation of this article.

1. See P. Zutshi, 'The Origins of the Registration of Petitions in the Papal Chancery in the First Half of the Fourteenth Century', in H. Millet, ed., *Suppliques et requêtes: le gouvernement par la grâce en Occident* (Collection de l'École française de Rome, 310; Rome, 2003), 177–91.

2. The pope as a special concession might grant that his signature on the petition should suffice and that the petitioner did not need to have a letter produced; but there is no known case of this before the fifteenth century: see H. Bresslau, *Handbuch der Urkundenlehre für Deutschland und Italien* (2nd edn, Leipzig and Berlin, 1912–31), ii, 24.

3. Cf. G. Battelli, 'Supplice al papa di Giacomo II, re di Maiorca e di Giacomo II, re di Aragona', *Anuario de Estudios Medievales*, xxxi, no. I (2001), 3–24 at 7, 8.

VII of Avignon, it was stated that a *rotulus* should contain at least six petitions.[4] Powerful individuals submitted *rotuli* on behalf of their protégés, while the longest *rotuli* were those submitted by universities requesting benefices for their members.[5]

It is necessary to distinguish between the various ways in which petitions have come down to us. A number of original petitions of the fourteenth century, written on strips of parchment or paper or in the form of rolls, survive. Such petitions are of particular interest, since they show the precise format and phraseology of the petition and enable one to distinguish the different hands that are present. The pope's response (in the form *Fiat* followed by an initial) is in another hand from that of the text and is almost certainly autograph.[6] The original petition usually contains a dating clause, which does not derive from the petitioner but was added after the petition had been approved by an officer later called the *datator*.[7] After they had been approved and dated, the petitions were passed to *abbreviatores*, who were responsible for preparing drafts, or minutes, of the letters in response to the petitions. This process of 'distribution' is normally recorded on original petitions in the form *R(ecipe) M. N.*, where 'M.' is the name of the *abbreviator* being addressed and 'N.' that of the vice chancellor.[8]

---

4. *Regulae cancellariae apostolicae: die päpstlichen Kanzleiregeln von Johannes XXII. bis Nikolaus V.* (Innsbruck, 1888), 112, §96; Battelli, 'Suppliche', 6.

5. On which see E. F. Jacob, 'English University Clerks in the Later Middle Ages, 2: Petitions for Benefices During the Great Schism', in his *Essays in the Conciliar Epoch* (3rd edn, Manchester, 1963), 223–39; D. E. R. Watt, 'University Clerks and Rolls of Petitions for Benefices', *Speculum*, xxiv (1959), 213–19; W. J. Courtenay, ed., Rotuli Parisienses: *Supplications to the Pope from the University of Paris*, (Leiden, Boston and Cologne, 2002), i, *1316–49*.

6. This is the implication of the passage in the chancery rules of John XXII, referring to petitions for provisions, in J. Teige, 'Beiträge zum päpstlichen Kanzleiwesen des XIII. und XIV. Jahrhunderts', *Mittheilungen des Instituts für Österreichische Geschichtsforschung*, xvii (1896), 408–40 at 429, §47, and of a passage quoted by G. Tellenbach, *Repertorium Germanicum*, Neue Folge II, *Urban VI., Bonifaz IX., Innocenz VII. und Gregor XII* (Berlin, 1933–61), ii, 46\*. There is unambiguous evidence of autograph signature with special concessions made by the pope: see, e.g. Ottenthal, *Regulae*, 2, §5; 4, §12; 57, §8, and the further references in W. von Hofmann, *Forschungen zur Geschichte der kurialen Behörden vom Schisma bis zur Reformation* (Bibliothek des Deutschen Historischen Instituts in Rom, 12, 13; Rome, 1914), i, 72, n. 1. The material published by U. Berlière, 'Épaves d'archives pontificales du XIVe siècle', *Revue Bénédictine*, xxiv (1907), 456–78, xxv (1908), 19–47 at 33, supports the view that the pope's signature is autograph. See also the references from the registers of Clement VII and earlier collected by E. Göller, *Repertorium Germanicum*, Neue Folge I, *Clemens VII. von Avignon* (Berlin, 1916), 75\* and n. 3, where arguments are advanced against the scepticism of Hofmann and Kehr as to whether the pope's reply was autograph. Certain types of petitions were approved not by the pope but by the vicechancellor, who signed with *Concessum*.

7. Bresslau, op. cit., ii, 110–12.

8. Numerous examples occur in Berlière, 'Épaves', though Berlière incorrectly extends the 'R.' of *Recipe*. See also P. Acht, 'Der Recipe-Vermerk auf den Urkunden Papst Bonifaz' VIII.', *Zeitschrift für bayerische Landesgeschichte*, xviii (1955), 243–55.

In addition to original petitions, there are copies which derive from the originals. These are scattered in various libraries and archives,[9] but by far the largest concentration of them is represented by the registers of petitions in the Vatican Archives. These include the precise wording of the pope's response and the date but not normally the *Recipe* mark, although this mark does appear from time to time in the sole surviving register of petitions of Boniface IX.[10]

More problematic than original petitions or copies deriving from them are petitions which have the format and general appearance of originals but which bear no indication that they were ever handed in or approved. There are some examples preserved in the register of Andrea Sapiti, proctor of the king of England at the papal curia in the early fourteenth century,[11] and elsewhere. There are four possible interpretations of such petitions. (1) They were submitted and approved, but they were not signed by the pope or the vicechancellor, they did not receive any chancery marks, nor were they dated.[12] (2) The petitioners, having had them drawn up, for some reason refrained from presenting them. (3) They are versions (whether drafts or *copies figurées*) kept by the petitioners of petitions which were submitted. (4) They were submitted but rejected.[13] The applicability of these different interpretations varies according to the date of the petition.

9. For example, Gonville and Caius College, Cambridge, MS 253 (497), fo. ii[v], has a copy of a petition from Thomas de Lisle, bishop of Ely, granted on 9 Sept. 1349, which includes the papal *Fiat*, the date and the *Recipe* mark. Although it appears that neither the *Fiat* clause nor the *Recipe* mark was copied in full, the copy almost certainly derives from the original petition. For a description of the manuscript, mentioning the petition, see M. R. James, *A Descriptive Catalogue of the Manuscripts in the Library of Gonville and Caius College* (Cambridge, 1907), i, 307–9. See also *Calendar of Entries in the Papal Registers Relating to Great Britain and Ireland: Petitions to the Pope* (London, 1896), i, 175.

10. Vatican Archives, Reg. Suppl. 104A (formerly in the Royal Library at Eichstätt): G. Erler, 'Ein Band des Supplikenregisters Bonifatius' IX. in der königlichen Bibliothek zu Eichstätt', *Historisches Jahrbuch*, viii (1887), 487–95, where the names of the *abbreviatores* are listed on p. 492 (except 'P. de Estulo', who appears on fo. 100v).

11. Vatican Library, Barb. lat. 2126, e.g. a petition from Nicholas Cantilupe sewn in between fos 31 and 32 (143 and 145 of the modern foliation). On Sapiti and his register, see J. P. Kirsch, 'Andreas Sapiti, englischer Prokurator an der Kurie im 14. Jahrhundert', *Historisches Jahrbuch*, xiv (1898), 582–603; P. N. R. Zutshi, 'Proctors Acting for English Petitioners in the Chancery of the Avignon Popes (1305–1378)', *Journal of Ecclesiastical History*, xxxv (1984), 15–29 at 24–7; B. Bombi, 'Andrea Sapiti, un procuratore trecentesco, fra la curia avignonese, Firenze e l'Inghilterra', *Mélanges de l'École Française de Rome—Moyen Age*, cxv (2003), 897–929. Barbara Bombi has prepared an edition of the register, which is now in press.

12. F. Bartoloni regarded many of the petitions that he published in 'Suppliche pontificie dei secoli XIII e XIV', *Bullettino dell'Istituto Storico Italiano per il Medio Evo e Archivio Muratoriano*, lxvii (1955), 1–187, as falling into this category. G. Tessier, 'Du nouveau sur les suppliques', *Bibliothèque de l'École des Chartes*, cxiv (1956), 186–92, rightly doubts whether some of these petitions were actually submitted. See also n. 14 and 15.

13. P. Gasnault regards a group of such petitions published in his article 'Quatre suppliques inédites adressées à Jean XXII', *Bullettino dell'Archivio Paleografico Italiano*, ii, iii, part I (1956–57), 317–23, as falling within this fourth category, but it is at least as likely that they fall within the second or third. The third interpretation was favoured by Angelo Mercati, who published two of the petitions in 'Documenti dall'Archivio Segreto Vaticano', *Lateranum*, ns, xv (1949), 1–37 at 7 (=Gasnault, 320, 321, no. 2) and 9, 10 (=Gasnault, 322, 323, no. 4). Mercati called a petition of this type an original, by which he wished to imply that it preceded the version actually handed in. The latter he called 'copia d'ufficio'. However, we follow the usual terminology in calling the petition that was handed in the original.

While it is clear that a particular interest attaches to petitions approved by the pope which survive in the original, they are unfortunately not common, especially before the mid-fourteenth century. Moreover, the status of many of the earlier petitions is ambiguous because they bear no evidence that they were submitted or approved. As we have seen, such petitions can be interpreted in different ways. The earliest extant petition which may actually have been approved was addressed to Alexander IV and dates from 1261. It survives in two versions, which bear no indication of approval and no dating clause, but one of them displays a *Recipe* mark, recording its distribution to an *abbreviator* for the preparation of the draft: 'R(ecipe) Ricc(arde)'.[14] It is therefore possible that the petition was approved but that at this date it was not the practice, or at least not the invariable practice, of the pope or the vicechancellor to sign the petitions that he had approved. A comparable case is a petition of 1279–80 addressed to Nicholas III.[15] This petition likewise has no sign of approval and no dating clause, but a draft of a letter in response to it was written on the same piece of parchment, which might lead one to suppose that this is the exemplar of the petition which was actually approved. From the thirteenth century the only petitions known at present which contain explicit marks of approval are those requesting the appointment of judges to hear cases in the curia. The pope or the vicechancellor (it is often uncertain which) signed the petitions with *Audiat* followed by the name of the judge.[16] Such petitions, once approved, were sufficient for the appointment of the judges. They did not result in the issue of papal letters and they are therefore different in character from the petitions that form the subject of the present article.

The earliest original petitions granted with the pope's *Fiat* date from the pontificate of Clement V. They make up a roll of eight petitions submitted by Jaume II, king of Aragon, which Heinrich Finke dated 7–17 October 1305 and published in his *Acta Aragonensia* from the manuscript in the Archivo de la Corona de Aragón, Barcelona.[17] Five petitions were signed *Fiat*, in one case with detailed additional stipulations. One of these received a temporising response, and two no response at all. The absence

14. Bartoloni, 'Suppliche', 43–6 and pl. 5.

15. G. Battelli, 'Una supplica e una minuta di Nicolò III', *Quellen und Forschungen aus italienischen Archiven und Bibliotheken*, xxxiii (1942), 33–50.

16. See M. Tangl, ed., *Die päpstlichen Kanzleiordnungen von 1200–1500* (Innsbruck, 1894), 45; F. E. Schneider, *Die Römische Rota* (Paderborn, 1914), i, 31, n. 2; Bresslau, *Urkundenlehre*, ii, 20–2; Bartoloni, 'Suppliche', 64, 65, 77, 78, 92, 94 (these are not original petitions but notarial copies in which the notary public carefully recorded the *Audiat* mark); Tessier, 'Du nouveau sur les suppliques', 190–2.

17. H. Finke, ed., *Acta Aragonensia* (Berlin, 1908–22), iii, pp. xxvii, xxviii. They were printed again in R. Fawtier's introduction to *Les registres de Boniface VIII (1294–1303)* (Paris, 1884–1939), iv, pp. xxxix, xl, and by G. Battelli, 'Suppliche al papa', 10–14 and pls 2, 3. There is also a description and a facsimile in W. Foerster, *Urkundenlehre in Abbildungen* (Bern, 1951), no. 30. Finke initially assigned these petitions to the pontificate of Boniface VIII, an attribution followed by Bresslau, *Urkundenlehre*, ii, 11 (before the appearance of *Acta Aragonensia*), and by Bartoloni, 'Suppliche', 8.

of a response normally means rejection, but one of these two petitions was too general for an appropriate response.[18] At the foot of the parchment is the note of distribution: *R(ecipe) Ban. G. R.*[19] The first name, *Ban.*, is that of the *abbreviator* who was commissioned to prepare the draft, Bandinus de Senis.[20] The second name, *G.R.*, is that of the officer who distributed the petitions to the *abbreviatores*. Later in the century, this was normally the vicechancellor, but *G.R.* cannot represent the vicechancellor, who at this time was Petrus Arnaldi de Bearnio.[21] Rather he is almost certainly the *referendarius*, Guillelmus Ruffati.[22] The office of referendary first appears at the turn of the thirteenth and fourteenth centuries. Its occupant was a curialist of high rank, who enjoyed the personal confidence of the pope. His main function seems to have been to present petitions to the pope and to advise him about them.[23]

There are three different types of additions made in the papal curia to the text of the roll in Barcelona: *Fiat*, the lengthier comments on the granting of the petitions, and the *Recipe* mark. It is not easy to decide who was responsible for writing these annotations. In the case of *Fiat*, it would be natural to assume that it was the pope. This is most unlikely, however, for the hand of *Fiat* is different from that of *Fiat A* found in the Madrid *rotulus* published in the Appendix, which will be shown to be the autograph signature of Clement V.[24] It is possible that all three types of addition to the Madrid roll are in the same hand. This would mean that they were written by the *referendarius*, if indeed he it was who wrote the *Recipe* mark. It also implies that the pope dictated to the *referendarius* his *Fiat* and the two lengthier comments.[25]

A similar *Recipe* mark occurs on a separate individual petition from Jaume II to the pope: *R(ecipe) Ban. G.R. card.*[26] The only difference is

18. Battelli, 'Suppliche', 14: 'Item supplicat, quod uos dignemini admittere aliquas peticiones, quas pro subditis suis offeret.'
19. See also n 26 and 75.
20. Battelli, 'Suppliche', 12.
21. P. M. Baumgarten, *Von der apostolischen Kanzlei: Untersuchungen über die päpstlichen Tabellionen und die Vizekanzler der Heiligen Römischen Kirche im XIII., XIV. und XV. Jahrhundert* (Cologne, 1908), 90, 91; Bresslau, *Urkundenlehre*, i, 255, 256; P. M. Baumgarten, 'Über einige päpstliche Kanzleibeamte des 13. und 14. Jahrhunderts', *Römische Quartalschrift*, Supplementheft xx (1913), 37–102 at 94.
22. Finke, ed., *Acta Aragonensia*, iii, p. xxix.
23. See P. N. R. Zutshi, 'The Office of Notary in the Papal Chancery in the Mid-Fourteenth Century', in K. Borchardt and E. Bünz, eds., *Forschungen zur Reichs-, Papst- und Landesgeschichte Peter Herde zum 65. Geburtstag von Freunden, Schülern und Kollegen dargebracht* (Stuttgart, 1998), ii, 665–83 at 668 (with further references).
24. See n 68.
25. Cf. P. Herde, *Beiträge zum päpstlichen Kanzlei- und Urkundenwesen im 13. Jahrhundert* (2nd edn, Kallmünz Opf., 1967), 156. Battelli, 'Suppliche', 12, suggests that *Fiat* was written by the pope and the longer comments by the vicechancellor.
26. Archivo de la Corona de Aragón, Cancellería, Pergaminos de Jaime II, extrainventario núm. 62 (b) (formerly extrainventario núm. 3312); printed in Finke, ed., *Acta Aragonensia*, iii, p. xxviii, but not in Battelli, 'Suppliche'. Our particular thanks are due to Dr Alberto Torra for information on the question of reclassification in the Barcelona archive and for the provision of photographs.

# XVI

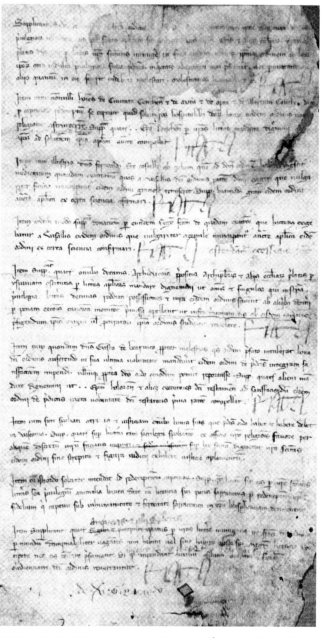

Fig. 1 Madrid, Archivo Histórico Nacional, Sección de Órdenes Militares, Uclés, carp. 99/ii no. 32. Reproduced by kind permission of Ministerio de Cultura, Archivo Histórico Nacional.

that Guillelmus Ruffati is now designated a cardinal. He was elevated to the cardinalate on 15 December 1305, and he died on 24 February 1311.[27] The petition must therefore date from this period. It is most likely to date from 1305 to 1307, for it was granted with the word *Fiat* alone and, as we shall see, the form of the *Fiat* mark appears to have changed by late 1307. The *Recipe* mark suggests that Guillelmus Ruffati continued to act as *referendarius* after his promotion.

Dating from two years after the roll of 1305 is a roll of petitions in the Archivo Histórico Nacional, Madrid, a small part of which has been previously published but with questions other than these in mind.[28] It survives among the archives of the convent of Uclés, which was the headquarters of the Order of Santiago, and contains nine petitions submitted by the Order to Pope Clement V.[29]

In 1307 the Order of Santiago was embroiled in one of the many crises of its fortunes, on this occasion consequent upon two circumstances in particular. One of these was the continued striving of the Order's Portuguese houses for the restoration of Nicholas IV's ordinance of 1290 granting virtual independence. Although this had initially been confirmed by Celestine V, it was then revoked and on a single day both reconfirmed (*ex certa scientia!*)[30] and re-revoked by him before being abrogated by Boniface VIII in July 1295, though only temporarily as it turned out.[31] The other was the anarchic state of the kingdom of Castile at the time, a deserted land wherein, during the seven-year minority of Fernando IV which commenced at the Cortes of Valladolid of that same year (1295), there were, as the chronicler lamented, more hares to be seen than flocks.[32] And this situation, which continued more or less unchanged throughout the reign, with neither truth nor firmness to be found on one side or the other,[33] was further aggravated by the

27. C. Eubel, *Hierarchia Catholica Medii Aevi* (2nd edn, Münster, 1913), 14.

28. E. Benito Ruano, 'La Orden de Santiago en Francia', *Hispania*, xxxvii (1977), 5–56 at 44, 45, no. 19. This edition is in certain respects defective.

29. Madrid, Archivo Histórico Nacional, Órdenes Militares (henceforth AHN, OO. MM.), Uclés, carp. 99/ii, no. 32; printed in the Appendix.

30. For the meaning of this term see n 49.

31. A. Caetano de Sousa, *Provas da historia genealogica da Casa Real Portugueza* (Lisbon, 1739), i, 93–5; D. W. Lomax, 'El rey Don Diniz de Portugal y la Orden de Santiago', *Hidalguía*, xxx (1982), 477–87 at 481–3. Charges of neglect by successive Castilian masters were reiterated in the Portuguese *rotulus* of petitions (1318–19) requesting renewal of Nicholas IV's ordinance, printed, together with the consequent papal letters, in A. D. de Sousa Costa, ed., *Monumenta Portugaliae Vaticana*, ii. *Súplicas dos pontificados dos papas de Avinhão Clemente VII e Bento XIII e do papa de Roma Bonifácio IX* (Braga, 1970), pp. lvi–lxxxix.

32. J. de Loaysa, *Crónica de los reyes de Castilla*, ed. A. García Martínez (Murcia, n.d.), 176; F. J. Hernández and P. Linehan, *The Mozarabic Cardinal. The life and times of Gonzalo Pérez Gudiel* (Florence, 2004), 349–63.

33. As the king of Aragon's agent reported in 1311: A. Giménez Soler, *D. Juan Manuel. Biografía y estudio crítico* (Zaragoza, 1932), 392. Cf. C. González Mínguez, *Fernando IV de Castilla (1295–1312). La guerra civil y el predominio de la nobleza* (Vitoria, 1976); P. Linehan, 'Castile, Navarre and Portugal', in M. Jones, ed., *The New Cambridge Medieval History* vi (Cambridge, 2000), 620–6.

authoritarian character of Juan Osórez, Master General of the Order and the king's former *mayordomo mayor*.[34] For although on account of his services to Fernando, the Order profited in ways to which two of the petitions of 1307 (nos 3 and 4) refer, some eight years before they were submitted the *comendadores* of various frontier fortresses had threatened to surrender those places to the enemy unless they were guaranteed their *encomiendas* for life, and at the Mérida chapter three years later, amidst charges of economic mismanagement, Juan Osórez was to be forced into retirement.[35] Such was the context of the Order's petitions in December 1307, which moreover were submitted at a time when the performance and very *raison d'être* of military orders everywhere were both under scrutiny. Only two months had passed since Philip IV's notorious dawn raid on the French Templars.

Of the nine petitions submitted in 1307, some referred to long-standing grievances, others to issues which had surfaced only recently. Numbers 1 and 5 called for the sort of blanket protection against nameless prelates and their depredations that religious orders always asked for when approaching the Apostolic See (and it must be remembered that the Order of Santiago was a protected species),[36] no. 9 addressed the question of fugitives from the Order,[37] while no. 2 was concerned with the specific matter of the alleged failure of the *concejos* of Cuenca and of the towns of Moya, Huete and Alarcón, all places within the diocese of Cuenca in which the convent of Uclés was situated, to honour the undertaking, entered into more than a century before, to provide for the hospitals of the Order in those locations dedicated to the welfare of the prisoners redeemed from captivity by the Muslim foe.[38] This was pretty routine business.

---

34. González Mínguez, *Fernando IV*, 128.

35. C. de Ayala Martínez, *Las Órdenes militares hispánicas en la Edad Media (siglos XII-XV)* (Madrid, 2003), 213, 214, 217—despite the fact that over the previous two years he had continued to be regarded as a political heavyweight: González Mínguez, *Fernando IV*, 249, 284, 293. A letter of Boniface VIII (5 Jan. 1300) concerns the rebellion of the *comendadores* (printed in *Les registres de Boniface VIII*, ed. G. Digard, M. Faucon, A. Thomas and R. Fawtier, ii, cols 542, 543, no. 3334). Above the text of the original letter and on another of the same day (AHN, OO. MM., Uclés, carp. 4/ii, no. 20; carp. 328, no. 22) is written 'P. Is.', perhaps a reference to the referendary Petrus Hispanus, for whose career and for whose services to Castilian petitioners, see D. Mansilla, 'El cardenal "Petrus Hispanus" obispo de Burgos (1300–1303)', *Hispania Sacra*, ix (1956), 243–80; Hernández and Linehan, *The Mozarabic Cardinal*, 382–91. Had the Spanish cardinal been with the curia in 1307, rather than in England, the Order's petitions might have fared better: P. Linehan, 'The English Mission of Cardinal Petrus Hispanus, the Chronicle of Walter of Guisborough, and News from Castile at Carlisle (1307)', *ante*, cxvi (2002), 605–21 at 610, 611.

36. For the Order's immediate subjection to the Roman Church, dating from 1175, see D. W. Lomax, *La Orden de Santiago (1170–1275)* (Madrid, 1965), 17–19.

37. In Apr. 1307 the abbot of Morimond had requested Fernando IV to adopt similar measures against fugitives from the Order of Calatrava: I. J. de Ortega y Cotes, J.F. Álvarez de Baquedano and P. de Ortega Zuñiga y Aranda, *Bullarium Ordinis Militiæ de Calatrava* (henceforth *Bull. Calatrava*) (Madrid, 1761; repr., 1981), 160.

38. For the Order's hospital at Huete, and the commitment undertaken by the local *concejo* in 1198 to provide it with annual support in the shape of wheat, sheep, lambs and money, see AHN, OO. MM., Uclés, carp. 100/i, nos 1 and 5; J. Díaz Ibáñez, *El clero y la vida religiosa en Huete durante la Edad Media* (Cuenca, 1996), 47.

The implications of those petitions relating to recent royal grants to the Order (nos 3–4) were, by contrast, substantial. These asked for papal confirmation of Fernando IV's remission to the Master of half of the exactions (*servicia*) due to the king from the Order's vassals—though curiously not of the other half that the king had remitted (had there been an earlier application to Rome on that account, of which we know nothing?).[39]

Also substantial were the Order's interests in Gascony, to which the following petitions referred. Here (no. 6) the pope was asked to bring to book the bishop of Oloron and other executors of the late Gaston (VII) de Montcada, *vicomte* of Béarn, represented in the Order's deposition as a tearaway persecutor of its interests who had seen the light as the light failed him. In fact, the *vicomte's* last will, a huge document dated 22 April 1290, contains no mention of the Order of Santiago. It may therefore be conjectured that the papal chancery had not taken the precaution of verifying the Order's claim (as it was to do, for example, in the case of the alleged royal grant which was the subject of petition no. 4) by requiring sight of the will. And that hypothesis finds support in the otherwise inexplicable circumstance that it was to Bishop Raimund of Lescar, one of the *vicomte's* executors, that the mandate occasioned by petition no. 6 requiring the executors' compliance with the *vicomte's* supposed dying wishes was addressed. It is further corroborated by the fact that the bishop of Oloron, Gaillard de Leduix, and his co-executors failed to comply with the pontiff's instructions.[40] Number 7 asked for the

---

39. This earlier grant had been made in Nov. 1301: *Bullarium equestris ordinis S. Iacobi de Spatha* (henceforth *Bull. Santiago*), ed. A. F. Aguado de Cordova, A. A. Aleman y Rosales and J. Lopez Agurleta (Madrid, 1719), 247. In Nov. 1302, Fernando IV had granted Juan Osórez 'la meitad de los servicios e pechos que nos ovieren a dar los vuestros vasallos de todos los logares que vos e vuestra orden avedes en nuestros reynos', adding: 'Esto vos demos demas de la otra meitad que vos diemos por nuestro privilegio para siempre jamas, segun se contiene en el nuestro privilegio que vos mandamos dar en esta razon, e la otra meytad para vos en vuestra vida, e asi avedes de aver daqui adelante todos los pechos, servicios e pedidos de vuestros logares'; this on account of his loyal service 'e sennaladamente en nuestra criança': *Bull. Santiago*, 247, 248—although, as Ayala Martínez observes, the Master's support for the boy king in 1295 had been less unequivocal than was later claimed: *Las Órdenes militares*, 512. Similar grants of one half of the payments due from their vassals were made to the Orders of Alcántara and Calatrava in Nov. 1306 and Feb. 1309, respectively: I. J. Ortega y Cotes, *Bullarium Ordinis Militiæ de Alcantara, olim S. Juliani de Pereiro* (Madrid, 1759), 137, 138; *Bull. Calatrava*, 160–3.

40. 'Post hec autem executores huius testamenti mei facio, constituo et relinquo venerabiles in Christo patres episcopos Lascurren. et Oloren., abbatem Luccen. qui vel se vel qui pro tempore sint futuri': Pau, Archives Départementales des Basses-Pyrénées, E 293, fo. 7r (fifteenth-century copy; contents summarised by P. Raymond, *Inventaire-sommaire des Archives Départementales antérieures à 1790. Basses-Pyrénées* (Paris, 1867), iv, 73, and, tendentiously, by P. de Marca, *Histoire de Bearn* (Paris, 1640), 673–8; cf. P. Tucoo-Chala, *La vicomté de Béarn et le problème de sa souveraineté* (Bordeaux, 1961), 68, 69). On 10 Feb. 1308, Clement wrote again to the bishop of Lescar, this time instructing him to proceed against certain nameless 'sons of iniquity' who had appropriated tithes, lands, etc. of the Order: AHN, OO. MM., Uclés, carp. 4/ii, no. 25 (Benito Ruano, ed., 'La Orden de Santiago en Francia', 46). See further P. Josserand, 'L'Ordre de Santiago en France au Moyen Âge', in A. Rucquoi, ed., *Saint Jacques et la France. Actes du Colloque des 18 et 19 janvier 2001 à la Fondation Singer-Polignac* (Paris, 2003), 451–68.

institution of a more widespread investigation outwith the constraints of ordinary canonical procedure into the 'sacrilegious spoliation' committed in that region.[41]

Such letters as were issued in response to the petitions are all dated 21 December 1307, and this may well be the date on which the petitions were approved. Three of them (nos 1, 5 and 6) received the response *Fiat A* with no further stipulations on the part of the pope. All these seem to have resulted in the issue of letters which can be traced in the Archivo Histórico Nacional, in the *Bullarium* of the Order and in the papal registers:

| | AHN, OO. MM., Uclés | *Bull. Santiago* | *Regestum Clementis V*[42] |
|---|---|---|---|
| 1 | carp. 4/ii, no. 26 | p. 252, no. i | no. 2590 |
| 5 | cf. carp. 4/ii, no. 24 | cf. p. 252, no. ii | cf. no. 2591[43] |
| 6 | carp. 124/ii, no. 20 | pp. 252–53, no. iii | no. 2588[44] |

Three petitions (nos 2, 4 and 9) were likewise marked *Fiat A* but their responses contain additional stipulations. The latter are written in a different hand or hands from that of the petitions, but in *whose* hand or hands is unclear.[45] These petitions require treatment in somewhat greater detail. In no. 2 three words have been added above 'ipsos ad

---

41. For the summary procedure *sine strepitu et figura iudicii*, which dated from at the latest 1234, and which the Council of Vienne was soon to extend to entire categories of litigation, see C. Lefebvre, 'Les origines romaines de la procédure sommaire aux XIIe et XIIIe siècles', *Ephemerides Iuris Canonici*, xii (1956), 149–97; L. Auvray, S. Vitte-Clémencet and L. Carolus-Barré, eds., *Les registres de Grégoire IX* (4 vols., Paris, 1890–1955), no. 2106 (S. Domínguez Sánchez, ed., *Documentos de Gregorio IX [1227–1241] referentes a España* (León, 2004), no. 402).

42. *Regestum Clementis Papae V* (8 vols, Rome, 1885–92, with tables by Y. Lanhers *et al.*, 2 vols, Paris, 1948–57).

43. Addressed to the archbishop of Toledo (who was Gonzalo Díaz Palomeque).

44. Addressed to the bishop of Lescar, Raimund Ogerius; also printed in Benito Ruano, 'La orden de Santiago in Francia', 45, 46, no. 20. Information subsequently received revealed that this was the wrong response and the late *vicomte's* actions were belatedly vindicated. A papal letter dated 17 June 1308 records that ownership of the castles and places of Moncaup and Momy (dioc. Tarbes and Lescar, respectively), which the *vicomte* and his ancestors had granted to the Order 'pia liberalitate', had been challenged by the archbishop of Auch, leading Gaston to resume control and to entrust them to his son, the cleric Jean, until the dispute was resolved: an arrangement now approved by the pontiff for the remainder of Jean's lifetime: Vatican Archives, Reg. Vat. 55, fo. 171v (*Regestum Clementis V*, ii, no. 3220). The date of the confiscation referred to is not stated, though, as recorded by the provincial council summoned by the long-lived Amanieu II d'Armagnac (archbishop of Auch from 1261 until 1318), at the time of Gaston's death the bishop of Lescar had been similarly deprived of control of his episcopal city by Gaston's son-in-law and heir Count Roger-Bernard III of Foix and the count's wife Marguerite of Béarn: P. Olhagaray, *Histoire des comtes de Foix, Bearn, et Navarre, diligemment recueillie* … (Paris, 1629), 224; J. Duffour, ed., *Livre Rouge du chapitre metropolitain de Ste Marie d'Auch* (Archives Historiques de la Gascogne, 2nd ser., fasc. 11; Paris-Auch, 1907), 41. By 1322 both places had been returned to the Order: Benito Ruano, 17–19, 47.

45. See the Appendix.

solucionem ipsius apostolica auctoritate compellat'. They are difficult to decipher but they appear to read 'prout iustum fuerit'. These words do not occur in the letter issued in response to the petition, although it does contain the proviso 'si est ita'.[46] Number 9 contains both a replacement and an addition. While the Order had requested papal letters addressed to 'regibus et principibus christianis', these words were deleted and replaced by 'archiepiscopis et aliis prelatis'. The corresponding letter in fact carried the standard address 'universis archiepiscopis et episcopis ad quos presentes littere pervenerint'.[47] And above 'sed quod impendant auxilium, consilium, operam et fauorem' has been written: 'inuocato ad hoc si opus fuerit auxilium brachii secularis'. This phrase was taken up in the letter.[48]

Numbers 3 and 4 request papal confirmation *ex certa scientia* of grants allegedly made to the Order by Fernando IV. This would mean that the confirmations followed from the pope's 'certain knowledge' of the circumstances and their validity was not dependent on the accuracy of statements in the petitions. The advantages to the petitioner of such a concession, which was granted rather rarely, are obvious.[49] The pope signed each petition with *Fiat A*, but in the case of the second petition it was followed by the words 'ostendantur concessionis littere', a requirement which doubtless applied to both petitions. It was a prudent precaution inasmuch as the king's grant of 8 November 1302 had specified exemption from payment of *acémilas* from the Order's vassals in the dioceses of Toledo and Cuenca,[50] whereas the petition contains no such territorial limitation.[51] Thus, the papal chancery, before issuing confirmations from the pope's certain knowledge, wished to inspect

---

46. Vatican Archives, Reg. Vat. 55, fo. 51v: '… fraternitati tue [*scil.* episcopo Conchensi] per apostolica scripta mandamus quatinus si est ita dictos homines ad solutionem huius pecunie iuxta formam huius [*sic*] votorum emissorum ab ipsis dictis hospitalibus faciendam monitione premissa per censuram ecclesiasticam appellatione remota preuia ratione compellas'. Cf. *Regestum Clementis V*, ii, no. 2587.

47. Reg. Vat. 55, fo. 51v. Cf. *Regestum Clementis V*, ii, no. 2589.

48. Reg. Vat. 55, fo. 51v.

49. Cf. O. Hageneder, *Probleme des päpstlichen Kirchenregiments im hohen Mittelalter (Ex certa scientia, non obstante, Registerführung)* (Lectiones eruditorum extraneorum in Facultate Philosophica Universitatis Carolinae Pragensis factae, iv; Prague, 1995); idem., 'Die Rechtskraft spätmittelalterlicher Papst- und Herrscherurkunden: *ex certa scientia, non obstantibus* und *propter importunitatem petentium*', in P. Herde and H. Jakobs, eds., *Papsturkunde und europäisches Urkundenwesen (Archiv für Diplomatik*, Beiheft VII, 1999), 401–29; idem., 'Kanonisches Recht, Papsturkunde und Herrscherurkunde: Überlegungen zu einer vergleichenden Diplomatik am Beispiel der Urkunden Friedrichs III.', *Archiv für Diplomatik*, xlii (1996), 419–43 at 425–7; idem., 'Päpstliche Reskripttechnik: Kanonistische Lehre und kuriale Praxis', in Martin Bertram, ed., *Stagnation oder Fortbildung: Aspekte des allgemeinen Kirchenrechts im 14. und 15. Jahrhundert* (Bibliothek des Deutschen Historischen Instituts in Rom, 108; Tübingen, 2005), 181–96 at 183–92.

50. Cf. *Bull. Santiago*, 248. For *acémilas* (a tax in lieu of the obligation to provide the royal host with mules), see M. A. Ladero Quesada, *Fiscalidad y poder real en Castilla (1252–1369)* (Madrid, 1993), 46, 47.

51. The same applies to the engrossment, on which see n. 53.

the royal grants referred to by the Order. The register of the proctor Andrea Sapiti contains other examples of requests for the confirmation *ex certa scientia* of existing documents; in each case the document needed to be inspected by the vice chancellor.[52]

How did the Order react to this qualified approval on the part of the pope and his chancery? A fortunate survival is of assistance in answering this question. It is a letter engrossed, but not issued, in response to the second of the petitions relating to the alleged royal grants (no. 4).[53] This shows that the Order's proctor proceeded to have a draft composed on the basis of the petition and then a fair copy prepared on the basis of the draft. Like the petition, the engrossment refers to the confirmation being made *ex certa scientia*. The recto of the letters displays an 'R' in the top right corner which doubtless stands for *Registranda* or *Registrande* and shows that it was to be registered.[54] In the top left corner is an 'l', probably standing for *lecta* or *lecte* and written by the head of the chancery (the vicechancellor or the *regens cancellariam*) to show that the final checking and approval of the letter had taken place, prior to the letter's issue.[55] The presence of this 'l' is all the more remarkable because the letter was not actually issued. It was never sealed, for only the right-hand set of holes through which the silk threads for attaching the *bulla* to the parchment would have passed is present, not the left-hand set. The evidence suggests that, with the *bullator* about to commit the Church to a certain course of action, there was a change of plan.

On the dorse is the name of the proctor who was seeking to impetrate the letter on behalf of the Order, 'Alfonsus L[...]'. This must be Alfonsus Lucensis, with 'Lucensis' referring to Lugo in Galicia rather than to Lucca in Tuscany. Alfonsus was the Order's proctor in 1307–8.[56] He succeeded Petrus Zamorensis (of Zamora), who acted in 1306,[57] and one of the 'big cats' of the curia, Andreas de Setia, who between 1266

---

52. See B. Bombi, 'Der Geschäftsgang der Suppliken im ersten Viertel des 14. Jahrhunderts, einige Beispiele, anhand des Registers des Kurienprokurators Andrea Sapiti', *Archiv für Diplomatik*, li (2005), 253–83.

53. AHN, OO. MM., Uclés, carp. 5/ii, no. 13.

54. P. N. R. Zutshi, *Original papal letters in England, 1305–1415* (Index Actorum Romanorum Pontificum ab Innocentio III ad Martinum V electum, v; Vatican City, 1990), p. lxxxiii.

55. Cf. ibid., pp. lxxiv, lxxv.

56. His name appears on two letters issued in response to the *rotulus*: AHN, OO. MM., Uclés, carp. 4/ii no. 26 and carp. 124/ii, no. 20, both of 21 Dec. 1307. We have also noticed it on the following letters: AHN, OO. MM., Uclés, carp. 5/ii, no. 14 (10 Feb. 1308), carp. 4/ii, no. 25, and carp. 5/ii, no. 9, both of 20 Feb. 1308. Between 1296 and 1302 another native of Lugo, Martinus, had also been active as proctor: P. Linehan, 'Proctors Representing Spanish Interests at the Papal Court, 1216–1303', *Archivum Historiae Pontificiae*, xvii (1979), 69–123 at 117.

57. AHN, OO. MM., Uclés, carp. 311, no. 21 (13 June 1306).

and 1300 is regularly to be found endorsing letters for the Order,[58] and who was followed by Iacobus de Aquamundula,[59] Leonardus de Jullano and Bernardus de Gotrico.[60] There is no registration mark on the dorse (which would take the form of a large 'R') to show that the letter had been registered, and the letter does not appear in the papal registers. Above the text is an inconspicuous note reading 'videantur littere regis'. This doubtless served as a warning to the chancery personnel that the letter was not to be issued until the royal letters could be inspected. It echoed the words 'ostendantur concessionis littere' written on the petition.

Another striking feature of the letter is that the dating clause is incomplete: 'Dat. Pictavis _ pontificatus nostri anno _ '. Gaps have been left for the day and the month and for the pontifical year. Only the place is given, Poitiers, where Clement V resided from 16 October 1307 to 29 March 1308.[61] The omission in the dating clause is understandable because, unlike most of the petitions granted by Clement V's successors,[62] the roll of petitions was not dated. The same applies to the Barcelona rolls of petitions approved by him in 1305 and c 1309.[63] The draft composed in response to our petition no. 4 was doubtless also undated. Accordingly, when the scribe came to engross the letter, he did not know what date to write and left the blank spaces. They would of course have been filled in if the letter had actually been issued. The scribe was sufficiently confident to give the place, because Clement resided at Poitiers for several months. On the other hand, the dorse contains the

---

58. AHN, OO. MM., Uclés, carp. 4/i, nos 7, 8, 10 (9 Nov. 1266), carp. 4/ii, no. 23 (2 Mar. 1300). For the description of him (1292–94) as one of 'tres leones magnos' with whom the proctor of the dean and chapter of Tudela had had to deal, see P. Linehan, 'Spanish Litigants and their Agents at the Thirteenth-Century Papal Curia', in S. Kuttner and K. Pennington, eds, *Proceedings of the Fifth International Congress of Medieval Canon Law, Salamanca, 21–25 September 1976* (Vatican City, 1980), 487–501 at 500–1. In 1273 the Masters of the Orders of Calatrava, Alcántara and Avis appointed him their proctor: *Colección diplomática medieval de la Orden de Alcántara (1157?–1494)*, B. Palacios Martín, ed., i (Madrid, 2000), 213, no. 336, where he appears as 'Andreas de Serra'. His other clients included Llywelyn, Prince of Wales. He is last encountered, acting for the archbishop of Toledo, in Nov. 1302. See also Linehan, 'Proctors Representing Spanish Interests', 113; Hernández and Linehan, *The Mozarabic Cardinal*, 323.

59. Iacobus endorsed the following original letters: AHN, OO. MM., Uclés, carp. 99/ii, nos 33, 34 (8 Jan. 1306), carp. 4/ii, no. 27 (17 Dec. 1311), carp. 4/ii, nos 28–30 (18 Dec. 1311), carp. 94, no. 57 (5 Jan. 1312), carp. 222, no. 3 (9 Jan. 1312), carp. 99/ii, no. 35, and carp. 100/i, no. 4 (13 Feb. 1312), carp. 74, no. 8 (15 Feb. 1312).

60. AHN, OO. MM., Uclés, carps. 2/ii, no. 27 (15 Mar. 1312) and 98, no. 18 (5 Apr. 1312), respectively.

61. *Regestum Clementis V: Tables (Table chronologique, Table des incipit)*, 35–7.

62. See E.-A. Van Moé, 'Suppliques originales adressées à Jean XXII, Clément VI et Innocent VI', *Bibliothèque de l'École des Chartes*, xcii (1931), 253–76; M.-H. Laurent, 'Trois nouveaux rôles de suppliques per *fiat* présentés à des papes du XIVe siècle', *Mélanges d'Archéologie et d'Histoire*, lxvi (1954), 219–39. By contrast, the petition published by T. Gasparrini Leporace, 'Una supplica originale per *fiat* del papa Giovanni XXII', *Bullettino dell'Istituto Storico Italiano per il Medio Evo e Archivio Muratoriano*, lxxv (1963), 247–57, was not dated. See also Bresslau, *Urkundenlehre*, ii, 110, n. 1.

63. Battelli, 'Suppliche', 10–14, 20–4.

note of a date which must have been added after the scribe had engrossed the letter. Written in an inconspicuous curial hand, it reads: 'Dat. Pictauis xxii die ianuarii'. It presumably represents the date that would have been assigned to the letter if had been issued (although it would have appeared in the form 'xi kal. februarii'). The date is just over a month later than the date of the three letters issued in response to the *rotulus.* There is evidence of a comparable process in writing the dating clause of numerous papal letters which *were* issued. In these, the whole dating clause or part of it is in different ink (and much more rarely in a different hand) from that of the rest of the text and was evidently added later.[64] Indeed, in the case of at least one letter issued in response to the *rotulus,* the words 'xii kal. ianuarii' are a later addition.[65]

The most likely explanation of the failure of the papal chancery to issue Uclés, carp. 5/ii, no. 13 is that the Order of Santiago was unable to produce the royal letters referred to in the petition or that it did produce them but they were defective.[66] It is possible that petition no. 3 suffered a fate similar to no. 4, with a letter being engrossed which proved to be abortive; but in this case direct evidence is lacking.

The response to two petitions, nos 7 and 8, remains to be mentioned. The *rotulus* contains no indication that they were approved, nor have we been able to trace any papal letters according the requests. It is almost certain that the absence of the papal signature means that they were rejected. Indeed, no. 8, which sought permission to redeem Christian captives from the Saracens by trading them for 'brute animals', was contrary to both canon law and papal policy, though in its dealings with the Order papal practice had not always coincided with that policy.[67]

There can be no doubt that it was Pope Clement V who wrote the words *Fiat A* on the Madrid *rotulus.* In the fourteenth century, only the pope and the cardinal penitentiary signed petitions with *Fiat,* and the subject matter of the Madrid petitions is such that they cannot have come within the competence of the cardinal penitentiary.[68] The initial 'A' deserves close attention. It is the earliest case of the pope's use of an initial in this context. No initial appears on petitions from the thirteenth century,[69] and we can say with some confidence that the initial was an innovation of Clement V's time. In 1305 Clement signed a roll of eight

64. See Zutshi, *Original Papal Letters,* pp. lxiii, lxiv.

65. AHN, OO. MM., Uclés, carp. 4/ii, no. 24. This may also apply to carp. 124/ii, no. 20. On the other hand, there is no difference in the ink in carp. 4/ii, no. 26.

66. See n. 39.

67. *Liber Extra,* 5.6.6, 11, 17, *apud* E. Friedberg, ed., *Corpus iuris canonici* (2 vols, Leipzig, 1879–81), ii, cols 773–7. Cf. *Reg. Greg. IX,* nos 2063, 4723 (Domínguez Sánchez, ed., *Documentos de Gregorio IX,* nos 385, 823).

68. On which see E. Göller, *Die päpstliche Pönitentiarie von ihrem Ursprung bis zu ihrer Umgestaltung unter Pius V.,* I, i, ii (Bibliothek des Kgl. Preuss. Historischen Instituts in Rom, iii, iv; Rome, 1907).

69. See n 14 and 15.

petitions now in Barcelona with *Fiat* alone.[70] It is likely therefore that the 'A' was introduced between 1305 and 1307. But, one cannot exclude the possibility that the change occurred more haphazardly and that there was a period when the practice was not consistent.

The Madrid roll enables one to reinterpret another group of petitions in Barcelona, dating from *c.* 1309.[71] The five petitions are followed by comments—in two instances quite lengthy ones—evidently deriving from a curialist of high rank, perhaps the vicechancellor or the referendary. The comments concerning the first and second petitions are in turn followed by a large and rather carelessly written letter 'A'. The editor of these petitions, the late Giulio Battelli, noted the presence of the 'A' but was unable to offer a satisfactory explanation for it.[72] It is only by comparison with the Madrid roll that one can interpret it correctly. It is in the same hand as the 'A' of the Madrid roll, and it is the autograph signature of Clement V, indicating his approval of these two petitions. The absence of the 'A' from the remaining three petitions shows that they were not approved. This is not surprising since the comments made in the curia about these petitions were restrictive or equivocal. The presence of the pope's signature by two of the petitions shows that we have here a group of original petitions.[73]

The question arises of what Clement's 'A' stands for. Later in the fourteenth century, the initial was that of the baptismal, family or other name of the pope prior to his elevation to the papacy. During the Great Schism, in both the Roman and conciliar obediences, and after the re-establishment of unity, it was regularly the initial of his baptismal name.[74] Clement V before he became pope was Bertrand de Got, archbishop of Bordeaux, so that the 'A' does not represent his baptismal name, family name or office. Did Clement choose 'A' simply because it is the first letter of the alphabet and he was the first pope to use an initial? While this is no more than a hypothesis, it receives some support from the practice under Clement V's immediate successor, John XXII. John chose 'B' as his initial, even though his name before becoming pope was Jacques Duèse. Yet, unfortunately for this explanation, the next pope, Benedict XII, did not use 'C', but rather 'B'. Prior to his election his name was Jacques Fournier, and why he chose 'B' is unclear. 'B' is of course the initial of Benedict, but if he used it for this reason he is the only pope to have selected the initial of his papal name.

70. Battelli, 'Suppliche', 10–14 and pls 2, 3.

71. Ibid., 20–4 and pls 6, 7 (not pl. 8, as stated ibid., 20).

72. Ibid., 22.

73. Battelli, loc. cit., suggests that it is a copy.

74. The classic accounts (e.g. Bresslau, *Urkundenlehre*, ii, 105–6; B. Katterbach, *Specimina Supplicationum ex Registris Vaticanis* (2 vols, Rome, 1927), i, p. ix), state that this practice began with Boniface IX (el. 1389), but Urban VI (el. 1378), whose name before becoming pope was Bartolomeo Prignano, signed with 'B' (Bartoloni, 'Suppliche', 186 and pl. 7).

Benedict's successor, Clement VI (Pierre Roger), chose the letter 'R' and was thus the first pope to use the initial of his family name.

At the foot of the Madrid roll is an annotation which concerns the production of drafts of letters in response to the petitions. It appears to read 'de v. G.R. card'. *G.R. card.*, the author of this instruction, is Cardinal Guillelmus Ruffati, who signed a petition in Barcelona in identical terms.[75] More problematic is the beginning of the note. It does not contain 'R.' (for *Recipe*) or the name of the *abbreviator* who was to produce the drafts, which is what one normally finds in this position. Perhaps 'v.' was meant to indicate the number five and refers to producing drafts for the five petitions in the roll that the pope had granted without qualification.

The dorse of the *rotulus* does not contain any annotations deriving from the papal curia. In particular, there is no registration mark, nor does this mark appear on the other original petitions addressed to Clement V discussed above, which tends to confirm the view that during his pontificate it was not yet the practice to enregister petitions. The first clear evidence of this comes under John XXII.[76]

The *rotulus* published below, together with other extant *rotuli* and individual petitions, enables students of the subject to attempt to sketch how the treatment of petitions developed in the thirteenth and fourteenth centuries. The very limited evidence from the thirteenth century implies that petitions for papal letters did not then receive any mark to show that they had been approved. By 1305 this had changed and such petitions were approved with the word *Fiat* dictated, it seems, by the pope to the *referendarius*. Yet within another two years or so, the practice had again changed. It was now the pope himself who signed with *Fiat* and an initial, a method of approving petitions that was to endure for centuries.

*St John's College, Cambridge*          P.A. LINEHAN
*Corpus Christi College, Cambridge*          P.N.R. ZUTSHI

# Appendix

AHN, OO. MM., Uclés, carp. 99/ii, no. 32

A single sheet of parchment measuring 330 × 178–183 mm. The sheet is damp-stained, and in places the text is faint and difficult to read. There are a few small holes, but they do not involve any loss of text.

Between three and five hands are distinguishable, all contemporary: (i) The hand which wrote the text of the *rotulus*. (ii) The hand which wrote

75. See n 26.
76. See Zutshi, 'The Beginnings of the Registration of Petitions', *passim*.

the response 'Fiat A' seven times in large, bold letters. (iii) The hand which wrote 'ostendantur concessionis littere' after 'Fiat A' in no. 4. This is quite different from hand (ii). (iv) The hand which made additions to nos 2 and 9. Possibly this hand is the same as hand (iii), but the additions that hands (iii) and (iv) made are too brief and faint to allow any secure conclusion. (v) The hand of the final annotation 'de v. G.R. card.', possibly identical to hands (iii) or (iv) or both, but the annotation is too brief to provide sufficient material for comparison.

Hand (i) seems to be Spanish and suggests that the petition was written in Spain or by a Spaniard at the curia. The remaining hands appear to be curial. Hand (ii) is that of Pope Clement V. Hand (iii) is unlikely to be that of the pope. It may be the hand of the referendary Guillelmus Ruffati (hand v) or that of an official of the papal chancery. Hand (iv) likewise is either that of Guillelmus Ruffati or that of a chancery official. Hand (v) is that of Cardinal Guillelmus Ruffati, presumably acting as referendary.

The edition follows the spelling of the manuscript, but punctuation, capitalisation and the numbering of the petitions are editorial.

[1] Supplicant sanctitati uestre magister et fratres ordinis [milicie] Sancti Iacobi quatinus, cum ipsorum ordo auctoritate/priuilegiorum indultorum eis per sedem apostolicam sit exemptus, archiepiscopis, episcopis et aliis ecclesiarum Yspanie/prelatis dignemini per litteras uestre sanctitatis iniungere ut fratres eiusdem ordinis ipsumque ordinem ac loca/ipsorum contra indulta priuilegiorum suorum predictorum inquietare aliquatenus non presumant nec permittant ab/aliis quantum in eis fuerit indebite molestari, molestatores huiusmodi, etc.[77] Fiat A

[2] Item cum nonnulli homines de ciuitate Conchensi et de Moya et de Opta et de Alarcum Conchensis diocesis/pro captiuorum redemptione se certum quid soluturos hospitalibus dictorum locorum eiusdem ordinis vot[o seu?][78]/religione astrinxerint, supplicant quatinus .. episcopo Conchensi per uestras litteras mandare dignemini quod/ipsos ad solucionem ipsius[79] apostolica auctoritate compellat. Fiat A

[3] Item cum illustris dominus Fernandus rex Castelle ob zelum quem ad dictam ordinem habere dignoscitur/medietatem quarundam exactionum quas a uasallis dicti ordinis ratione dominii exigit que uulga-/riter seruicia nuncupantur eidem ordini graciose remiserit, supplicant huiusmodi gratiam eidem ordini/auctoritate apostolica ex certa sciencia confirmari. Fiat A

[4] Item eodem modo supplicant donacionem per eundem regem factam de quadam exactione que hactenus exige-/batur a vasallis eiusdem ordinis que uulgariter azemile nuncupantur auctoritate apostolica eidem ordini/ex certa sciencia confirmari. Fiat A ostendantur concessionis littere.

---

77. 'molestatores huiusmodi per censuram ecclesiasticam appellatione postposita compescendo' in Reg. Vat. 55, fo. 52r.
78. Word illegible beneath stain.
79. In hand (iv) above 'ipsius': 'prout iustum fuerit'.

# XVI

[5] Item supplicant quatinus omnibus decanis, archidiaconis, prepositis, archipresbiteris et aliis ecclesiarum prelatis per/Yspaniam constitutis per litteras apostolicas mandare dignemini ut omnes et singulos qui instrumenta,/priuilegia, litteras, decimas, redditus, possessiones et iura eiusdem ordinis sciuerint ab aliquibus detineri/per penam excommunicationis canonica monitione premissa compellant ut infra terminum eis ab eisdem canonice/prefigendum ipsis magistro uel procuratori ipsius ordinis studeant reuelare. Fiat A

[6] Item cum quondam dominus Gasto de Bearnico propter molestias quas ordini prefato intulerat, bona/dicti ordinis auferendo, in sua ultima uoluntate mandauerit eidem ordini de predictis integram sa-/tisfactionem impendi nullumque propterea dictus ordo commodum potuerit reportasse, supplicant quatinus alicui man-/dare dignemini ut .. episcopum Holorensem et alios executores dicti testamenti ad satisfaciendum eidem/ ordini de predictis iuxta uoluntatem dicti testatoris preuia ratione compellat. Fiat A

[7] Item cum sint spoliati contra ius et iusticiam omnibus bonis suis que predictus ordo habet et habere debet/in Vasconia, supplicant quatinus super huiusmodi tam sacrilega spoliatione ex officio uestro religionis fauore per/ aliquem discretum uirum faciatis inquiri et secundum inquisitionem super hoc factam dignetur uestra sanctitas/eidem ordini sine strepitu et figura iudicii exhibere iusticie complementum.

[8] Item cum iste ordo solerter intendat ad redemptionem captiuorum, supplicant quatinus licitum sit eis per uestre sanctitatis/litteras seu priuilegium animalia bruta dare cum licencia sui prioris sarracenis pro redemptione Christi-/fidelium qui captiui sub inhumanitate et ferocitate sarracenica in Christi blasphemiam detinentur.

[9] Item supplicant quatinus regibus et principibus christianis[80] per uestras litteras iniungatis ut fratres dicti ordinis/per mundum dampnabiliter uagantes cum habitu uel sine habitu absque sui magistri licencia re-/cipere nec eis comunicare presumant, sed quod impendant auxilium, consilium, operam et fauorem[81] [ut] ad/obedienciam dicti ordinis reuertantur. Fiat A

*Below text:* de v. G.R. card.

---

80. 'regibus et principibus christianis' deleted and 'archiepiscopis et aliis prelatis' substituted in hand (iv).
81. Above 'quod ... fauorem': in hand (iv), 'inuocato ad hoc si opus fuerit auxilium [*sic*] brachii secularis'.

# INDEX